DEVIANCE

THE INTERACTIONIST PERSPECTIVE

Text and readings in the sociology of deviance

EARL RUBINGTON
Northeastern University

MARTIN S. WEINBERG
Indiana University

Deviance

FIFTH
EDITION

THE INTERACTIONIST PERSPECTIVE

Macmillan Publishing Company
New York

Macmillan Publishing Company
866 Third Avenue, New York, New York 10022

Collier Macmillan Canada, Inc.

Library of Congress Cataloging-in-Publication Data

Deviance, the interactionist perspective.

  1. Deviant behavior.   2. Social interaction.
I. Rubington, Earl.   II. Weinberg, Martin S.
HM291.D4836   1987   302.5′42   86-2917
ISBN 0-02-404390-7

Printing: 1 2 3 4 5 6 7   Year: 7 8 9 0 1 2 3

ISBN 0-02-404390-7

To
Sara and Alex,
Barbara, Ellana, and Minkie

PREFACE

The purpose of this book has been to present students with recent and important work in the sociology of deviance. We have, however, limited ourselves to one particular approach to this study. We call this approach the interactionist perspective.

The interactionist approach to the study of deviance is by no means new. But until the appearance of the first edition of *Deviance: The Interactionist Perspective,* students had to search for statements of the approach as well as for studies that exemplified it. The purpose of the first edition, then, was to present the interactionist approach to the study of deviance and to make readily available the excellent studies that set forth or illustrate it. In the succeeding editions, we have updated the readings and made special efforts to make our own text more readable.

We see this book as having two major uses. As a statement on the interactionist perspective on deviance and a collection of readings employing that approach, the book can be used in deviance courses that are taught from the interactionist point of view. The second use is that of adjunct to deviance courses that are organized around other points of view. Most of the papers presented in this book can very easily stand on their own merits, and even if the book does nothing more than familiarize readers with these works, it will have served its purpose.

In this edition, because of the spate of fine interactionist work that has appeared since the fourth edition, we have incorporated nineteen new readings. To make room for them, we have removed some of the "classics" from the readings and now discuss them in our own text. In this way, we have tried to continue to update *Deviance: The Interactionist Perspective.*

E. R.
M. S. W.

CONTENTS

GENERAL INTRODUCTION

This book examines deviance as a social phenomenon. Central to this approach is the notion that deviance is, above all, a matter of social definition. That is, an alleged behavior or condition is "deviant" if people say it is. The social aspect of deviance becomes clear when someone perceives another person as departing from accepted norms, interprets the person to be some kind of deviant, and influences others also to regard the person as deviant and to act on the basis of that interpretation. As a *social* phenomenon, then, deviance consists of a set of interpretations and social reactions.

When people are interpreted as being deviant, they are usually regarded as being a particular *type* of deviant. These types may be general (e.g., ex-convict, mentally ill, sexually "loose," retarded), or they may be more specific (e.g., car thief, paranoid schizophrenic, call girl, Mongoloid). Whether these labels are general or specific, they usually suggest what one can expect of the so-called deviant and how one should act toward the deviant (e.g., with suspicion, avoidance, vigilance, vengeance). And in coming to terms with such labeling the "deviants" may revise their self-concepts and their actions in accordance with the way they have been labeled. For example, a child who has been typed by school authorities as having a speech problem may become self-conscious and shy, with a concomitant loss of self-esteem, because s/he has been told s/he doesn't talk properly.

At the same time, social typing does allow people to relate to one another in an organized manner. Imagine how much more complicated it would be for policemen, for example, to do their jobs if they did not have a set of categories in which to place people ("she's a hooker"; "he's a junkie"; "he looks like he might be casing that store"; "she's a teenaged runaway"; "he's a derelict with no place to go").

The interactionist perspective focuses on just such issues as these—how people typify one another; how they relate to one another on the basis of these typifications; and the consequences of these social processes. As such, the interactionist perspective helps immensely in our understanding not only of the sociology of deviance but also of social process in general.

The Plan of the Book

The selections that follow spell out the interactionist perspective in greater detail. The first half of the book, which consists of Parts I and II, deals with how people define some persons as deviant and act on the basis of these definitions. Part I shows how deviance is dealt with in primary groups and informal relations and how a person is singled out and assigned a deviant status by intimates such as family members. Part II deals with these processes in the formal regulation of deviance. For example, it considers how agents of social control, such as the police, define persons as deviants, how they act on these definitions, and what some of the consequences of formal sanctions are.

The second half of the book (Parts III and IV) discusses the deviants themselves: how they respond to being typed by others, how they type themselves, and how they form deviant groups. Part III examines how deviants develop and sustain their own subcultures and how people become involved in them. Part IV shows how persons may take on deviant identities through self-typing, how they manage deviant identities, and how they may eventually regain "respectability."

This book, then, focuses not on people's motivations for doing things that are regarded as deviant but rather on the *sociology* of deviance—the processes that divide society into different types of people and the social effects of these processes.

Part I THE SOCIAL DEVIANT

Sociology is the study of social relations. Sociologists study how people arrive at common definitions of their situation; how they form groups based on such definitions; how they go on to set down rules of conduct, assign social roles to each other, and enforce their rules. Sociologists examine these questions as part of the larger question: How is social order produced and sustained?

Deviance refers to an alleged breach of social order. By looking at deviance we can come to a better understanding of the dominant social order. At the same time, the study of deviance also sheds light on the way "deviant" patterns and lifestyles are themselves organized.

There are at least two ways of studying deviance as a social phenomenon. The first is to approach deviance as objectively given; the second, as subjectively problematic.

Deviance as objectively given. Sociologists who treat deviance as objectively given delineate the norms and values of the society under study and regard any deviation from these norms and values as "deviant." These sociologists generally make three assumptions. First, they assume that there is widespread consensus in the society in the realm of norms and values; this widespread agreement, they believe, makes it relatively easy to identify deviance. Second, they assume that deviance typically evokes negative sanctions such as gossip or legal action. Third, they assume that the punishment meted out to the deviant reaffirms for the group that it is bound by a set of common values and norms. The major questions raised by this approach are the following: What sociocultural conditions are most likely to produce deviance? Why do people continue to deviate despite the negative sanctions that are brought to bear on them? and How can deviance best be minimized or controlled?

From these assumptions and questions, certain procedures have evolved for studying deviants. First list the "do's" and "don'ts" of the society or group. Then study the official records kept on persons who violate these rules. Interview persons appearing in these records and consult agents of social control such as police and judges. Try to discover the ways in which deviants differ from nondeviants (e.g., are deviants more likely than nondeviants to come from broken homes?) in order to discern the kinds of social and cultural conditions that seem to make deviant behavior more likely. Try to derive a theory to "explain" deviance, and then apply the theory for the correction and prevention of deviance.

The strength of this approach is the sharpness and simplicity with which it phrases questions. The weak points of this approach follow from its key assumptions. In the United States there are so many different groups and ways of thinking that people often do not agree on values and norms. Because of this lack of agreement, and also because of the fact that some people get caught whereas others avoid discovery, it is often very difficult and complex to identify who is deviant and who is not. Also, most social control agencies operate with selective enforcement, so that certain categories of people are more likely than others to be punished for their deviance. Thus the nature, causes, and consequences of deviance are neither simple nor uniform.

Deviance as subjectively problematic. Sociologists who focus on the social differentiation of deviants generally make another set of assumptions. First, they assume that when people and groups interact they communicate with one another by means of shared symbols (verbal and body language, style of dress, etc.). Through such symbolic communication, it is assumed, people are able to type one another and formulate their actions accordingly. Second, they assume that deviance can best be understood in terms of this process, that deviant labels are symbols that differentiate and stigmatize the people to whom they are applied. Finally, sociologists using this approach assume that people act on the basis of such definitions. Thus people treat the alleged deviant differently from other people. The alleged deviant, in turn, may also react to this definition. On the basis of these assumptions, sociologists using this perspective focus on social definitions and on how these influence social interaction. On the one hand, they focus on the perspective and actions of those who define a person as being deviant. They look at the circumstances under which a person is most likely to get set apart as deviant, how a person is cast into a deviant role, what actions others take on the basis of that definition of a person, and the consequences of these actions. On the other hand, these sociologists also focus on the perspective and reactions of the person adjudged to be deviant. They consider how a person reacts to being so adjudged, how a person adopts a deviant role, what changes in group memberships result, and what changes occur in the alleged deviant's self-concept.

Whereas the objectively given approach focuses primarily on the characteristics of the deviant or the conditions that give rise to deviant acts, the subjectively problematic approach focuses on the definitions and actions both of the deviants themselves and of the people who label them deviant, and on the social interaction between the two. Thus we call the latter approach the interactionist perspective.

This book adopts the interactionist perspective, approaching deviance as subjectively problematic rather than as objectively given. In this book, then, deviants are considered simply as people who are socially typed in a certain way. Such typing usually involves an attempt to make sense of seemingly aberrant acts. As people seek to make sense of such acts, they generally employ stereotypical interpretations that define the actor as a particular kind of person (a kook, a drunk, a psychopath, etc.), that include a judgment about the moral quality of the deviant or his or her motives, and that suggest how a person should act toward the deviant. The social definitions of deviance, then, consist of a *description,* an *evaluation,* and a *prescription.* For example, a "kook" is a person who is mildly eccentric (description). The term connotes that "kooks" are odd but not particularly evil or dangerous (evaluation). Thus one may display dislike or friendly disrespect toward them (prescription). A person who comes to be defined as a "psychopath," on the other hand, is considered to be both odd and severely unpredictable (description). The psychopath is often regarded as self-centered, evil, and dangerous (evaluation). And the psychopath is to be taken seriously at all times; a person who shows dislike or disrespect toward a "psychopath" does so at great personal risk (prescription). Thus the definition of a person as a particular type of deviant organizes people's responses to that person. And the more people who share the definition that a person is a particular type of deviant, the greater the consequences.

Taking the subjective approach to deviance, Part I of this book examines such phenomena more specifically. The topics treated in this part of the book include how people type, or label, others as deviants; the accommodations people make to the so-called deviance; the cultural context of typing; and how people may collaborate to exclude deviants from their midst.

The Process of Social Typing

Sociologically, deviance is approached here in terms of social differentiation. This differentiation arises from the perception that something is amiss. If a potential typer, or labeler, ignores or excuses the alleged aberrant quality of a person or event, it goes unlabeled as deviant. For instance, a person who works hard is expected sometimes to be tired and cranky, and in such situations people may not attach any particular importance to this behavior. Once an act or a person is typed as "deviant," however, a variety of social phenomena may come into play. These phenomena include who types whom, on what grounds, in what ways, before or after what acts (real or imputed), in front of what audience, and with what effects.

Let us for a moment consider the conditions that seem to make typing more effective. First, typing generally has the most effect when the typer, the person typed as deviant, and other people all share and understand the deviant definition in their social relationships. The typer and others act toward the "deviant" in accord with their shared understanding of the situation. Aware of having been so typed, the deviant, in turn, takes that shared understanding into account in relating to people. Thus, willingly or otherwise, all parties may subscribe to the definition. When this happens, the definition of the person as a particular type of deviant is most socially effective, or confirmed. As an example, Frank Tannenbaum, one of the fathers of the interactionist perspective on deviance, has said: "The process of making the criminal . . . is a process of tagging, defining, identifying, segregating, describing, emphasizing, and evoking the very traits that are complained of. . . . The person becomes the thing he is described as being." Tannenbaum says that "the community cannot deal with people whom it cannot define" and that "the young delinquent becomes bad because he is defined as bad and because he is not believed if he is good."[1]

Second, social types are generally more apt to be accepted by other people if a high-ranking person does the typing. Effective social typing usually flows down rather than

[1] Frank Tannenbaum, *Crime and the Community*, New York: Columbia University Press, 1938; pp. 19–20.

up the social structure. For example, an honor bestowed by the President of the United States is more likely to be consequential than an honor bestowed by a low-ranking official. Conversely, a denunciation by a very high-ranking person such as the president of a company will usually carry more weight, and be confirmed by more people, than a denunciation by a low-ranking person such as one of the company's janitors.

Third, deviant typing is also more apt to be effective if there is a sense that the alleged deviant is violating important norms and that the violations are extreme. For instance, if factory workers are tacitly expected to turn out only a limited amount of work, a worker who produces much more than the norm may be singled out and ostracized as a "rate-buster." On the other hand, a person who jaywalks is unlikely to be typed and treated as a deviant.

Fourth, it also seems that negative social typing is more readily accepted than positive typing. For one thing, "misery loves company"; people find comfort in learning about the frailties of others. In addition, norms seem to be highlighted more by infraction than by conformity. Also, negative typing is seen as a valuable safeguard if the type indicates an aberrant pattern that will probably continue and that has major consequences. Some police officers, for instance, expect upper-class adolescents to misbehave in their youth but later to become influential and respected citizens, while they expect slum adolescents who are vandals, troublemakers, or delinquents to become hardened criminals in adulthood; thus such police officers are more likely to negatively type slum youths than upper-class youths who break the same laws.

Fifth, typing will be accepted more readily if the audience stands to gain from the labeling. Endorsing attention to another person's deviant behavior, for example, may divert attention from one's own. It may also sustain a status difference between oneself and the so-called deviant.

When social typing is effective, there are three kinds of consequences that most often follow: self-fulfilling prophecy, typecasting, and recasting. In the self-fulfilling prophecy, typing is based on false beliefs about the alleged deviant, but the actions other people take on the basis of these false beliefs eventually make them become a reality. For example, both black and white police officers believe that it is more difficult to arrest blacks than whites. As a result, they tend to use more force in arresting blacks, and in turn they experience more resistance from blacks. In typecasting, the deviant stereotype is so widely accepted that confirmation of the typing proceeds rapidly, and typer, audience, and the person typed relate to each other in an automatic manner. For instance, if one person types another as a thief, any audience can generally predict and understand the typer's attitudes and actions. In recasting, the most complex of the three consequences, the deviant is expected to behave conventionally and is encouraged to disprove the deviant typing (e.g., to reform). Probation officers, for example, may encourage conventionality by restricting the opportunities of their probationers to continue their deviant ways. In the first two consequences of typing, the typer and audience restrict the deviant's opportunities to disprove the deviant typing. In recasting, the typer and the audience restrict the deviant's opportunities to confirm the deviant typing.

Accommodation to Deviance

As noted previously, sociologically, deviants are persons who have been effectively labeled as deviant, and *effectively* means simply that the label does in fact affect social relations. The person who has been typed as a deviant, for example, acquires a special status that carries a set of new rights and duties or changes in old ones, and a new set of expectations about future conduct. Thus when people type a certain person as deviant, they imply, "We now expect you to engage in deviant actions." In some cases, this expectation amounts to a license to deviate, as when a group may not only tolerate but actually shelter a deviant in its midst. More often, however, the expectation of deviant conduct gives other people license to treat the deviant in a demeaning way.

The pace of events in the labeling process is one of the critical factors in this entire process. If aberrant conduct occurs only gradually and irregularly within a small, intimate group, deviant typing may not take place at all. Even if the events place some immediate strain on relationships, members of the group may adjust to the strain without perceiving the person any differently. Eventually, though, some critical point may be reached at which the group becomes aware that things are not what they used to be. Sometimes the members of the group have long entertained suspicions of deviance, and their accommodation represents an acknowledgment that the deviation is here to stay. In other instances, though, even as they type the person as deviant, group members may be optimistic that the deviance is only temporary. In any case, the group's accommodation to the so-called deviance has usually been going on for some time before labeling actually occurs.

The Cultural Context

The process of social typing occurs within a cultural context. Each culture, for example, has its own assortment and corresponding vocabulary of types. Thus in our own culture we no longer talk about "witches"; consequently, no one is so typed. Similarly, if we had no word for or concept of "psychopath," no one would be so typed. The culture's repertoire of deviant types and stereotypes is ordinarily created, defined, sustained, and controlled by highly valued realms of the culture (e.g., psychiatry, law, religion). In addition, it should also be noted, different categories are used in different subcultures. "Sinners," for example, are typed only in the religious sector.

Because different groups and cultures have different ideas about deviance, however, typing often has an ethnocentric bias. People in one culture or subculture may be quick to type an outsider as deviant, for instance, simply because the outsider's lifestyle is so different from their own. Among persons within the same culture or subculture, on the other hand, the risks of being typed deviant are usually smaller.

Once a person has been labeled, the question of how to relate to the deviant is more easily resolved when cultural prescriptions exist. These include the prescriptions, for example, that sick people should be treated and evil people punished. In sum, typing is easier to act on when cultural guidelines exist.

The Role of Third Parties

As already noted, in intimate, primary groups, people are usually slower to type one of their members as deviant than are outsiders. Such in-group labeling does happen at times, however, particularly if the deviant's aberrant behavior has begun to cause considerable strain for the rest of the group. When this happens, the typing of the person as deviant is often facilitated or precipitated by some outsider or outside agency—in short, by some third party.

In some cases the third party may act without solicitation. A wife, for example, may fail to recognize that her husband is involved with another woman until the community gossip (the third party) so informs her; she may then type her husband as a "son of a bitch" and may, through separation or divorce, exclude him from the family.

In other cases a member of the primary group may seek out the third party in order to validate such typing or to exclude the deviant from the group. If a man's wife is emotionally disturbed, for example, he may turn to third parties outside the family (a psychiatrist, the courts, the sheriff, etc.) in order to remove his wife from the home, officially labeling her as mentally disturbed and seeking treatment for her.

Thus we have seen some of the ways in which the social definition of deviants proceeds. A real or imputed violation of norms can activate the process of social typing, and a variety of social factors affect its success. The nature and likelihood of this typing are influenced by the cultural context. People may at first attempt to accommodate these alleged violations. Over the course of time, however, the deviant may no longer be protected. Third parties may intervene, and at that point exclusion of the deviant may take place.

1 THE PROCESS OF SOCIAL TYPING

Alleged deviance implies that some norm has been violated. Yet not all such violations are noticed and labeled as deviant. Also, different groups are quicker to label certain types of violations as deviant, and the same group may be quicker to label at one time than another.

In the first reading Becker describes a number of conditions that are involved when a person is labeled deviant; he also discusses the consequences of such labeling. In the next selection Kitsuse uses homosexuality to illustrate how people type a person as deviant and how they then act on this social definition. In the final selection Erikson discusses the basis on which communities single out certain types of conduct to be defined as deviant.

Outsiders   HOWARD S. BECKER

Deviance and the Responses of Others

[One sociological view] . . . defines deviance as the infraction of some agreed-upon rule. It then goes on to ask who breaks rules, and to search for the factors in their personalities and life situations that might account for the infractions. This assumes that those who have broken a rule constitute a homogeneous category, because they have committed the same deviant act.

Such an assumption seems to me to ignore the central fact about deviance: it is created by society. I do not mean this in the way it is ordinarily understood, in which the causes of deviance are located in the social situation of the deviant or in "social factors" which prompt his action. I mean, rather, that *social groups create deviance by making the rules whose infraction constitutes deviance,* and by applying those rules to particular people and labeling them as outsiders. From this point of view, deviance is *not* a quality of the act the person commits, but rather a consequence of the application by others of rules and sanctions to an "offender." The deviant is one to whom that label has successfully been applied; deviant behavior is behavior that people so label.[1]

Since deviance is, among other things, a consequence of the responses of others to a person's act, students of deviance cannot assume that they are dealing with a homogeneous category when they study people who have been labeled deviant. That is, they cannot assume that those people have actually committed a deviant act or broken some rule, because the process of labeling may not be infallible; some people may be labeled deviant who in fact have not broken a rule. Furthermore, they cannot assume that the category of those labeled deviant will contain all those who actually have broken a rule, for many offenders may escape apprehension and thus fail to be included in the population of "deviants" they study. Insofar as the category lacks homogeneity and fails to include all the cases that belong in it, one cannot reasonably expect to find common factors of personality or life situation that will account for the supposed deviance.

What, then, do people who have been labeled deviant have in common? At the least, they share the label and the experience of being labeled as outsiders. I will begin my analysis with this basic similarity and view deviance as the product of a transaction that takes place between some social group and one who is viewed by that group as a rule-breaker. I will be less concerned with the personal and social characteristics of deviants than with the process by which they come to be thought of as outsiders and their reactions to that judgment. . . .

The point is that the response of other people has to be regarded as problematic. Just because one has committed an infraction of a rule does not mean that others will respond as though this had happened. (Conversely, just because one has not violated a rule does not mean that he may not be treated, in some circumstances, as though he had.)

The degree to which other people will respond to a given act as deviant varies greatly. Several kinds of variation seem worth noting. First of all, there is variation over time. A person believed to have committed a given "deviant" act may at one time be responded to much more leniently than he would be at some other time. The occurrence of "drives" against various kinds of deviance illustrates this clearly. At various times, enforcement officials may decide to make an all-out attack on some particular kind of deviance, such as gambling, drug addiction, or homosexuality. It is obviously much more dangerous to engage in one of these activities when a drive is on than at any other time. (In a very interesting study of crime news in Colorado newspapers, Davis found that the amount of crime reported in Colorado newspapers showed very little association with actual changes in the

[1] The most important earlier statements of this view can be found in Frank Tannenbaum, *Crime and the Community* (New York: Columbia University Press, 1938), and E. M. Lemert, *Social Pathology* (New York: McGraw-Hill Book Co., Inc., 1951). A recent article stating a position very similar to mine is John Kitsuse, "Societal Reaction to Deviance: Problems of Theory and Method," *Social Problems*, 9 (Winter, 1962), 247–256.

amount of crime taking place in Colorado. And, further, that people's estimate of how much increase there had been in crime in Colorado was associated with the increase in the amount of crime news but not with any increase in the amount of crime.)[2]

The degree to which an act will be treated as deviant depends also on who commits the act and who feels he has been harmed by it. Rules tend to be applied more to some persons than others. Studies of juvenile delinquency make the point clearly. Boys from middle-class areas do not get as far in the legal process when they are apprehended as do boys from slum areas. The middle-class boy is less likely, when picked up by the police, to be taken to the station; less likely when taken to the station to be booked; and it is extremely unlikely that he will be convicted and sentenced.[3] This variation occurs even though the original infraction of the rule is the same in the two cases. Similarly, the law is differentially applied to Negroes and whites. It is well known that a Negro believed to have attacked a white woman is much more likely to be punished than a white man who commits the same offense; it is only slightly less well known that a Negro who murders another Negro is much less likely to be punished than a white man who commits murder.[4] This, of course, is one of the main points of Sutherland's analysis of white-collar crime: crimes committed by corporations are almost always prosecuted as civil cases, but the same crime committed by an individual is ordinarily treated as a criminal offense.[5]

Some rules are enforced only when they result in certain consequences. The unmarried mother furnishes a clear example. Vincent[6] points out that illicit sexual relations seldom result in severe punishment or social censure for the offenders. If, however, a girl becomes pregnant as a result of such activities the reaction of others is likely to be severe. (The illicit pregnancy is also an interesting example of the differential enforcement of rules on different categories of people. Vincent notes that unmarried fathers escape the severe censure visited on the mother.)

Why repeat these commonplace observations? Because, taken together, they support the proposition that deviance is not a simple quality, present in some kinds of behavior and absent in others. Rather, it is the product of a process which involves responses of other people to the behavior. The same behavior may be an infraction of the rules at one time and not at another; may be an infraction when committed by one person, but not when committed by another; some rules are broken with impunity, others are not. In short, whether a given act is deviant or not depends in part on the nature of the act (that is, whether or not it violates some rule) and in part on what other people do about it.

Some people may object that this is merely a terminological quibble, that one can, after all, define terms any way he wants to and that if some people want to speak of rule-breaking behavior as deviant without reference to the reactions of others they are free to do so. This, of course, is true. Yet it might be worthwhile to refer to such behavior as *rule-breaking behavior* and reserve the term *deviant* for those labeled as deviant by some segment of society. I do not insist that this usage be followed. But it should be clear that insofar as a scientist uses "deviant" to refer to any rule-breaking behavior and takes as his subject of study only those who have been *labeled* deviant, he will be hampered by the disparities between the two categories.

If we take as the object of our attention behavior which comes to be labeled as deviant, we must recognize that we cannot know whether a given act will be categorized as deviant until the response of others has occurred. Deviance is not a quality that lies in behavior itself, but in the interaction between the person who commits an act and those who respond to it. . . .

In any case, being branded as deviant has important consequences for one's further social participation and self-image. The most important consequence is a drastic change in the individual's public identity. Committing the improper act and being publicly caught at it place him in a new status. He has been revealed as a

[2] F. James Davis, "Crime News in Colorado Newspapers," *American Journal of Sociology,* LVII (January, 1952), 325–330.

[3] See Albert K. Cohen and James F. Short, Jr., "Juvenile Delinquency," in Robert K. Merton and Robert A. Nisbet, eds., *Contemporary Social Problems* (New York: Harcourt, Brace, and World, 1961), p. 87.

[4] See Harold Garfinkel, "Research Notes on Inter- and Intra-Racial Homicides," *Social Forces,* 27 (May, 1949), 369–381.

[5] Edwin H. Sutherland, "White Collar Criminality," *American Sociological Review,* V (February, 1940), 1–12.

[6] Clark Vincent, *Unmarried Mothers* (New York: The Free Press of Glencoe, 1961), pp. 3–5.

different kind of person from the kind he was supposed to be. He is labeled a "fairy," "dope fiend," "nut" or "lunatic," and treated accordingly.

In analyzing the consequences of assuming a deviant identity let us make use of Hughes' distinction between master and auxiliary status traits.[7] Hughes notes that most statuses have one key trait which serves to distinguish those who belong from those who do not. Thus the doctor, whatever else he may be, is a person who has a certificate stating that he has fulfilled certain requirements and is licensed to practice medicine; this is the master trait. As Hughes points out, in our society a doctor is also informally expected to have a number of auxiliary traits: most people expect him to be upper middle class, white, male, and Protestant. When he is not there is a sense that he has in some way failed to fill the bill. Similarly, though skin color is the master status trait determining who is Negro and who is white, Negroes are informally expected to have certain status traits and not to have others; people are surprised and find it anomalous if a Negro turns out to be a doctor or a college professor. People often have the master status trait but lack some of the auxiliary, informally expected characteristics; for example, one may be a doctor but be female or Negro.

Hughes deals with this phenomenon in regard to statuses that are well thought of, desired and desirable (noting that one may have the formal qualifications for entry into a status but be denied full entry because of lack of the proper auxiliary traits), but the same process occurs in the case of deviant statuses. Possession of one deviant trait may have a generalized symbolic value, so that people automatically assume that its bearer possesses other undesirable traits allegedly associated with it.

To be labeled a criminal one need only commit a single criminal offense, and this is all the term formally refers to. Yet the word carries a number of connotations specifying auxiliary traits characteristic of anyone bearing the label. A man who has been convicted of housebreaking and thereby labeled criminal is presumed to be a person likely to break into other houses; the police, in rounding up known offenders for investigation after a crime has been committed, operate on this premise. Further, he is considered likely to commit other kinds of crimes as well, because he has shown himself to be a person without "respect for the law." Thus, apprehension for one deviant act exposes a person to the likelihood that he will be regarded as deviant or undesirable in other respects.

There is one other element in Hughes' analysis we can borrow with profit: the distinction between master and subordinate statuses.[8] Some statuses, in our society as in others, override all other statuses and have a certain priority. Race is one of these. Membership in the Negro race, as socially defined, will override most other status considerations in most other situations; the fact that one is a physician or middle-class or female will not protect one from being treated as a Negro first and any of these other things second. The status of deviant (depending on the kind of deviance) is this kind of master status. One receives the status as a result of breaking a rule, and the identification proves to be more important than most others. One will be identified as a deviant first, before other identifications are made. . . .

[7] Everett C. Hughes, "Dilemmas and Contradictions of Status," *American Journal of Sociology*, L (March, 1945), 353–359.

[8] *Ibid*.

Societal Reaction to Deviant Behavior

JOHN I. KITSUSE

Sociological theory and research in the area traditionally known as "social pathology" have been concerned primarily with the classification and analysis of *deviant forms of behavior* and relatively little attention has been given to societal reactions to deviance.[1] In a recent paper, Merton has noted this lack of a "systematic *classification* of the responses of the conventional or conforming members of a group to deviant behavior."[2] Similarly, Cohen has observed that "a sociology of deviant behavior-conformity will have to devise ways of conceptualizing responses to deviant behavior from the standpoint of their relevance to the production or extinction of deviant behavior."[3] In this paper, I shall discuss some of the theoretical and methodological issues posed by the problem of societal reactions to deviant behavior and report on a preliminary attempt to formulate a research design which specifically takes them into account.

I propose to shift the focus of theory and research from the forms of deviant behavior to the *processes by which persons come to be defined as deviant by others*. Such a shift requires that the sociologist view as problematic what he generally assumes as given—namely, that certain forms of behavior are *per se* deviant and are so defined by the "conventional or conforming members of a group." This assumption is frequently called into question on empirical grounds when the societal reaction to behaviors defined as deviant by the sociologist is non-existent, indifferent, or at most mildly disapproving. For example, in his discussion of "ritualism" as a form of deviant behavior, Merton states that it is not that such behavior is treated by others as deviant which identifies it as deviant "since the overt behavior is institutionally permitted, though not culturally prescribed."[4] Rather, the behavior is deviant because it "clearly represents a departure from the cultural model in which men are obliged to move onward and upward in the social hierarchy."[5] The discrepancy between the theoretically hypothesized and empirically observable societal reaction is also noted by Lemert: "It is fairly easy to think of situations in which serious offenses against laws commanding public respect have only mild penalty or have gone entirely unpunished. Conversely, cases are easily discovered in which a somewhat minor violation of legal rules has provoked surprisingly stringent penalties."[6]

Clearly, the forms of behavior *per se* do not activate the processes of societal reaction which sociologically differentiate deviants from non-deviants. Thus, a central problem for theory and research in the sociology of deviance may be stated as follows: What are the behaviors which are defined by members of the group, community, or society as deviant, and how do those definitions organize and activate the societal reactions by which persons come to be differentiated and treated as deviants? In formulating the problem in this way, the point of view of those who interpret and define behavior as deviant must explicitly be incorporated into a sociological definition of deviance. Accordingly, deviance may be conceived as a process by which the members of a group, community, or society (1) interpret behavior as deviant, (2) define persons who so behave as a certain kind of deviant, and (3) accord them the treatment considered appropriate to such deviants. In the following pages, this conception of deviance and societal reaction will be applied to the processes by which persons come to be defined and treated as homosexuals.

Reprinted from "Societal Reaction to Deviant Behavior: Problems of Theory and Method," *Social Problems*, Vol. 9, No. 3 (Winter 1962), pp. 247–256, by permission of the Society for the Study of Social Problems and the author.

[1] A notable exception is the work of Edwin M. Lemert who systematically incorporates the concept of societal reaction in his theory of sociopathic behavior. See *Social Pathology*, McGraw-Hill: New York, 1951.

[2] Robert K. Merton, "Social Conformity, Deviation, and Opportunity-Structures: A Comment on the Contributions of Dubin and Cloward," *American Sociological Review*, 24 (1959), pp. 177–189.

[3] Albert K. Cohen, "The Study of Social Disorganization and Deviant Behavior," in *Sociology Today*, R. Merton, L. Broom, and L. Cottrell, eds., Basic Books: New York, 1959, pp. 465–466.

[4] Robert K. Merton, *Social Theory and Social Structure*, revised, Free Press: New York, 1957, p. 150.

[5] *Ibid.*, p. 150.

[6] *Op. cit.*, p. 55.

Societal Reactions to "Homosexual Behavior"

As a form of deviant behavior, homosexuality presents a strategically important theoretical and empirical problem for the study of deviance. In the sociological and anthropological literature[7] homosexual behavior and the societal reactions to it are conceptualized within the framework of ascribed sex statuses and the socialization of individuals to those statuses. The ascription of sex statuses is presumed to provide a complex of culturally prescribed roles and behaviors which individuals are expected to learn and perform. Homosexual roles and behaviors are conceived to be "inappropriate" to the individual's ascribed sex status, and thus theoretically they are defined as deviant.

With reference to American society, Allison Davis states: "Sex-typing of behavior and privileges is even more rigid and lasting in our society than is age-typing. Indeed, sexual status and color-caste status are the only life-long forms of rank. In our society, one can escape them in approved fashion only by death. Whereas sexual mobility is somewhat less rare today than formerly, sex-inappropriate behavior, social or physical, is still one of the most severely punished infractions of our social code."[8] In Lemert's terminology, norms concerning sex-appropriate behavior have a high degree of "compulsiveness" and social disapproval of violations is stringent and effective.[9] Homosexuals themselves appear to share this conception of the societal reaction to their behavior, activities, and subculture.[10]

Such a view of homosexuality would lead one to hypothesize that "sex-appropriate" (and conversely "sex-inappropriate") behaviors are unambiguously prescribed, deviations from those prescriptions are invariably interpreted as immoral, and the reactions of the conventional and conforming members of the society to such deviations are uniformly severe and effective. The evidence which apparently supports this hypothesis is not difficult to find, particularly with reference to the definition and treatment of male homosexuals. Individuals who are publicly identified as homosexuals are frequently denied the social, economic, and legal rights of "normal" males. Socially they may be treated as objects of amusement, ridicule, scorn, and often fear; economically they may be summarily dismissed from employment; legally they are frequently subject to interrogation and harassment by police.

In citing such evidence, however, it is important to note that the societal reaction to and the differentiation of homosexuals from the "normal" population is a consequence of the fact that the former are "known" to be homosexuals by some individuals, groups or agencies. Thus, within the framework of the present formulation of homosexuality as a form of deviant behavior, the processes by which individuals come to be "known" and treated as sexually deviant will be viewed as problematic and a problem for empirical investigation. I shall not be concerned here with the so-called "latent homosexual" unless he is so defined by others and differentially treated as a consequence of that definition. Nor will I be concerned with the variety of "internal" conflicts which may form the "clinical" picture of the homosexual except insofar as such conflicts are manifested in behavior leading others to conceive of him as a homosexual. In short, I shall proceed on the principle that it is only when individuals are defined and identified by others as homosexuals and accorded the treatment considered "appropriate" for individuals so defined that a homosexual "population" is produced for sociological investigation.[11] With reference to homosexuality, then, the empirical questions are: What forms of behavior do per-

---

[7] For examples, see Talcott Parsons and Robert F. Bales, *Family Socialization and Interaction Process,* Free Press: New York, 1955, pp. 103–105; Ruth Benedict, "Continuities and Discontinuities in Cultural Conditioning," *Psychiatry,* 1 (1938), pp. 161–167; Abram Kardiner and Associates, *Psychological Frontiers of Society,* Columbia University Press: New York, 1945, pp. 57, 88, etc.; Clifford Kirkpatrick, *The Family,* Ronald Press: New York, 1955, pp. 57–58; Margaret Mead, *Sex and Temperament,* William Morrow: New York, 1955.

[8] Allison Davis, "American Status Systems and the Socialization of the Child," *American Sociological Review,* 6 (1941), p. 350.

[9] *Op. cit.,* Chapter 4.

[10] Evelyn Hooker, "Sequences in Homosexual Identification," read at the meetings of the American Sociological Association, 1960; Donald Webster Cory, *The Homosexual in America,* Greenburg: New York, 1951, esp. Part I.

[11] This principle has been suggested by Harold Garfinkel. See "Some Sociological Concepts and Methods for Psychiatrists," *Psychiatric Research Reports,* 6 (1956), pp. 181–195.

sons in the social system consider to be "sex-inappropriate," how do they interpret such behaviors, and what are the consequences of those interpretations for their reactions to individuals who are perceived to manifest such behaviors?

In a preliminary attempt to investigate these questions, an interview schedule was constructed[12] and administered to approximately seven hundred individuals, most of whom were college undergraduates. The sample was neither random nor representative of any specified population, and the generalizability of the interview materials is limited except insofar as they are relevant to the previously noted hypothesis that homosexual behavior is uniformly defined, interpreted, and negatively sanctioned. The interview materials will therefore be used for the purpose of illustrating the theory and method of the present conception of deviance and societal reaction.

The objectives of the interview were threefold: It attempted to document (1) the behavior forms which are interpreted as deviant, (2) the processes by which persons who manifest such behaviors are defined and (3) treated as deviant. Thus, in the construction of the interview schedule, what the interviewees considered to be "deviant" behavior, the interpretations of such behavior, and the actions of subjects toward those perceived as deviant were addressed as empirical questions. Labels such as alcoholic, illiterate, illegitimate child, and ex-convict were assumed to be categories employed by persons in everyday life to classify deviants, but the behavior forms by which they identify individuals as deviants were treated as problematic. "Sexual deviant" was one of ten categories of deviants about which subjects were questioned in the interview. Among the more than seven hundred subjects interviewed, seventy-five stated they had "known" a homosexual and responded to questions concerning their experiences with such individuals. The data presented below are drawn from the protocols of interviews with this group of subjects.

The interview proceeded as follows:

The subject was asked "Have you ever known anyone who was a sexual deviant?" If he questioned the meaning of "deviant," the subject was asked to consider the question using his own meaning of "sexual deviant."

When the subject stated he had known a sexual deviant—a homosexual in this case—as he defined the term, he was asked to think about the most recent incident involving him in an encounter with such a person. He was then asked "When was the first time you noticed (found out) that this person was a homosexual?" followed by "What was the situation? What did you notice about him? How did he behave?" This line of questioning was focused on the interaction between the subject and the alleged deviant to obtain a detailed description of the situation which led the subject to define the person as homosexual. The subject's description of the person's behavior was systematically probed to clarify the terms of his description, particularly those which were interpretive rather than descriptive.

Evidence of Homosexuality

Responses to the question "When was the first time you noticed (found out) that this person was homosexual?" and the related probes suggest that an individual's sexual "normality" may be called into question with reference to two broad categories of evidence. (a) *Indirect evidence* in the form of a rumor, an acquaintance's experience with the individual in question subsequently communicated to the subject, or general reputational information concerning the individual's behavior, associates, and sexual predilections may be the occasion for suspecting him to be "different." Many subjects reported that they first "found out" or "knew" that the individuals in question were homosexuals through the reports of others or by "reputation." Such information was generally accepted by the subjects without independent verification. Indeed, the information provided a new perspective for their retrospective as well as prospective observations and interpretations of the individuals' behaviors. An example of how hearsay organizes observation and interpretation is the following statement by a 35-year-old male (a draftsman):

I: Then this lieutenant was a homosexual?
S: Yes.
I: How did you find out about it?
S: The guy he approached told me. After that, I watched him. Our company was small and

---

[12]The interview schedule and methods were conceived and constructed in consultation with Aaron V. Cicourel.

we had a bar for both enlisted men and officers. He would come in and try to be friendly with one or two of the guys.

I: Weren't the other officers friendly?

S: Sure, they would come in for an occasional drink; some of them had been with the company for three years and they would sometimes slap you on the back, but he tried to get over friendly.

I: What do you mean "over friendly"?

S: He had only been there a week. He would try to push himself on a couple of guys—he spent more time with the enlisted personnel than is expected from an officer.

(b) *Direct observation* by the subject of the individual's behavior may be the basis for calling the latter's sexual "normality" into question. The descriptions of behavior which subjects took to be indicative of homosexuality varied widely and were often vague. Most frequently the behaviors cited were those *"which everyone knows"* are indications of homosexuality. For example, a 20-year-old male subject reports an encounter with a stranger at a bar:

I: What happened during your conversation?

S: He asked me if I went to college and I said I did. Then he asked me what I was studying. When I told him psychology he appeared very interested.

I: What do you mean "interested"?

S: Well, you know queers really go for this psychology stuff.

I: Then what happened?

S: Ah, let's see. I'm not exactly sure, but somehow we got into an argument about psychology and to prove my point I told him to pick an area of study. Well, he appeared to be very pensive and after a great thought he said, "Okay, let's take homosexuality."

I: What did you make of that?

S: Well, by now I figured the guy was queer so I got the hell outta there.

The responses of other subjects suggest that an individual is particularly suspect when he is observed to behave in a manner which deviates from the *behaviors-held-in-common* among members of the group to which he belongs. For example, a behavior which is presumed to be held-in-common among sailors in the U.S. Navy is intense and active sexual activity. When a sailor does not affirm, at least verbally, his interest in such activity, his competence as a "male" may be called into question. A 22-year-old engineer, recently discharged from the Navy, responds to the "how did you first know" question as follows:

All of a sudden you just get suspicious of something. I began to wonder about him. He didn't go in for leave activities that most sailors go for. You know, girls and high times. He just never was interested and when you have been out at sea for a month or two you're interested. That just wasn't Navy, and he was a career man.

Although the responses of our subjects indicate there are many behavioral gestures which "everyone knows" are indicators of homosexuality in males, there are relatively few such gestures that lead persons to suspect females of homosexuality. Following is an excerpt from a 21-year-old college co-ed whose remarks illustrate this lack of definite indicators *prior* to her labeling of an acquaintance as a homosexual:

I: When was the first time you noticed she was a deviant?

S: I didn't notice it. I thought she had a masculine appearance when I first saw her anyway.

I: What do you mean?

S: Oh, her haircut, her heavy eyebrows. She had a rather husky build.

I: Exactly when did you think she had a masculine appearance?

S: It was long after [the first meeting] that I found out that she was "one."

I: How do you define it?

S: Well, a lesbian. I don't know too much about them. It was _____ who told me about her.

I: Did you notice anything else about her [at the first meeting]?

S: No, because you really don't know unless you're looking for those things.

Unlike "effeminate" appearance and gestures in males, "masculine" appearance in females is apparently less likely to be immediately linked to the suspicion or imputation of homosexuality. The statements of the subject quoted above indicate that although "masculine appearance" is an important element in her conception of a lesbian, its significance did not become apparent to her until a third person told her the girl was a homosexual. The remarks of other subjects in our sample who state they have "known" female homosexuals reveal a similar ambiguity in their interpretations of what they describe as indicators of sexual deviance.

A third form of evidence by direct observation is behaviors which the subjects interpreted to be *overt sexual propositions*. Descriptions of such propositions ranged from what the subjects considered to be unmistakable evidence of the person's sexual deviance to ambiguous gestures which they did not attempt to question in the situation. The following is an excerpt from an interview with a 24-year-old male school teacher who recounts an experience in a Korean Army barrack:

I: What questions did he [the alleged homosexual] ask?

S: "How long have you been in Korea?" I told him. "What do you think of these Korean girls?" which I answered, "Not too much because they are dirty." I thought he was probably homesick and wanted someone to talk to. I do not remember what he said then until he said, "How much do you have?" I answered him by saying, "I don't know, about average I guess." Then he said, "Can I feel it just once?" To this I responded with, "Get the hell out of here," and I gave him a shove when he reached for me as he asked the question.

In a number of interviews, the subjects' statements indicate that they interpreted the sequence of the alleged deviants' behavior as progressively inappropriate or peculiar in the course of their interaction with them. The link between such behavior and their judgment that a sexual proposition was being made was frequently established by the subjects' growing realization of its deviant character. A 21-year-old male subject recalls the following experience involving his high school tennis coach who had invited him to dinner:

S: Anyway, when I get there he served dinner, and as I think back on it—I didn't notice it at the time—but I remember that he did act sort of effeminate. Finally he got up to change a record and picked up some of my English

themes. Then he brought them over and sat down beside me. He began to explain some of my mistakes in my themes, and in the meantime he slipped his arms around me.

I: Would you say that this was done in a friendly manner or with an intent of hugging you or something?

S: Well, no, it was just a friendly gesture of putting his arm around my shoulder. At that time, I didn't think anything of it, but as he continued to explain my mistakes, he started to rub my back. Then he asked me if I wanted a back rub. So I said, "No! I don't need one." At this time, I began thinking something was funny anyway. So I said that I had to go. . . .

The Imputation of Homosexuality

When a detailed description of the subject's evidence concerning the alleged homosexual was obtained, he was asked, "What did you make of that?" to elicit information about how he interpreted the persons observed or reported behavior. This line of questioning yielded data on the inferential process by which the subject linked his information about the individual to the deviant category "homosexual."

A general pattern revealed by the subjects' responses to this section of the interview schedule is that when an individual's sexual "normality" is called into question, by whatever form of evidence, the imputation of homosexuality is documented by *retrospective interpretations* of the deviant's behavior, a process by which the subject re-interprets the individual's past behavior in the light of the new information concerning his sexual deviance. This process is particularly evident in cases where the prior relationship between the subject and the alleged homosexual was more than a chance encounter or casual acquaintanceship. The subjects indicate that they reviewed their past interactions with the individuals in question, searching for subtle cues and nuances of behavior which might give further evidence of the alleged deviance. This retrospective reading generally provided the subjects with just such evidence to support the conclusion that "this is what was going on all the time."

Some of the subjects who were interviewed were themselves aware of their retrospective interpretations in defining individuals as sexually deviant. For example, a 23-year-old female graduate student states:

I: Will you tell me more about the situation?
S: Well, their relationship was a continuous one, although I think that it is a friendship now as I don't see them together as I used to; I don't think it is still homosexual. When I see them together, they don't seem to be displaying the affection openly as they did when I first realized the situation.
I: How do you mean "openly"?
S: Well, they would hold each other's hand in public places.
I: And what did you make of this?
S: Well, I really don't know, because I like to hold people's hands, too! I guess I actually didn't see this as directly connected with the situation. What I mean is that, if I hadn't seen the other incident [she had observed the two girls in bed together] I probably wouldn't have thought of it [i.e., hand-holding] very much. . . . Well, actually, there were a few things that I questioned later on that I hadn't thought really very much about. . . . I can remember her being quite affectionate towards me several times when we were in our room together, like putting her arm around my shoulder. Or I remember one time specifically when she asked me for a kiss. I was shocked at the time, but I laughed it off jokingly.

The Interactional Contexts of Societal Reactions

When the description of the alleged deviant's behavior and the subject's interpretations of that behavior were recorded, the subject was asked "What did you do then?" This question was directed toward documenting societal reactions to deviant behavior. Forms of behavior *per se* do not differentiate deviants from non-deviants; it is the responses of the conventional and conforming members of the society who identify and interpret behavior as deviant which sociologically transform persons into deviants. Thus, in the formulation of deviance proposed here, if the subject observes an individual's behavior and defines it as deviant but does not accord him differential treatment as a consequence of that definition, the individual is not sociologically deviant.

The reactions of the subjects to individuals they defined as homosexuals ranged from immediate withdrawal from the scene of interaction and avoidance of further encounters with the alleged deviants to the maintenance of the prior relationship virtually unaltered by the imputation of deviance. The following responses to the question "What did you do then?" illustrate the variation in sanctions directed toward persons defined as homosexuals.

Explicit disapproval and immediate withdrawal: The most negatively toned and clearly articulated reaction reported by our subjects is that of the previously quoted Korean War veteran. It is interesting to note that extreme physical punishment as a reaction to persons defined as homosexuals, a reaction which is commonly verbalized by "normal" males as proper treatment of "queers," is not reported by any of the subjects. When physical force is used, it is invariably in response to the deviant's direct physical overtures, and even then it is relatively mild, e.g., "I gave him a shove when he reached for me."

Explicit disapproval and subsequent withdrawal: In the following excerpt, a 20-year-old male college student describes an encounter with a man whom he met in a coffee shop. In the course of their conversation, the man admitted his homosexuality to the subject. The two left the coffee shop and walked together to the subway station.

I: What happened then?
S: We got to the subway whereupon he suggested that he hail a cab and take me up to Times Square—a distance of almost 40 blocks.
I: Did you agree, and what did you think?
S: Yes, I thought he was just being very nice and I had no qualms about getting in a cab with a homosexual since I was quite sure I could protect myself against any advances in a cab.
I: What happened then?
S: When we had ridden a little distance, he put his hand on my knee, and I promptly removed it saying that it just wasn't right and that I wanted nothing of it. However, after a while, he put his hand back. This time I didn't take it away for a while because I was interested in what he would do. It was the funniest thing—he rubbed and caressed my knee the same way in which I would have

done this to a girl. This time I took his hand and hit him across the chest with it, telling him to "cut it out." Finally, we got to Times Square, and I got out.

This example and that provided by the Korean War veteran's reaction to behavior interpreted as overt sexual propositions suggest the possibility that responses to persons suspected of homosexuality or defined as homosexuals on the basis of more indirect evidence of appearance, "confessions," hearsay, reputation, or association will vary within an even wider range of applied sanctions. Indeed, the statements of subjects concerning their responses to persons alleged to be deviant on such evidence indicate that the modal reaction is disapproval, implicitly rather than explicitly communicated, and a restriction of interaction through partial withdrawal and avoidance. It should be noted further that although the subject's silent withdrawal from an established relationship with an alleged deviant may represent a stronger disapproval than an explicitly communicated, physically enforced sanction against a stranger, moral indignation or revulsion is not necessarily communicated to the deviant. The subject's prior relationship with the alleged deviant and the demands of propriety in subsequent interactions with him qualify the form and intensity of the sanctions which are applied. Thus, when the organization of the subject's day-to-day activities "forces" him into interaction with the deviant, expressions of disapproval are frequently constrained and diffused by the rules of deference and demeanor.[13] The following excerpts provide illustrations:

Implicit disapproval and partial withdrawal: A 20-year-old co-ed's reaction to a girl she concluded was a homosexual was expressed as follows:

Well, I didn't want to be alone with X [the homosexual] because the four of us had two connecting rooms and I was in the room with X. As much as I liked the girl and felt sorry for her, I knew she could really wring me through the wringer. So the rest decided that I should tell her that if she and Y wanted to be homos, to do it somewhere else and not in the room.

No disapproval and relationship sustained: The "live and let live" response to homosexu-

als, which is implied in the preceding reaction, was not uncommon among the subjects. Some subjects not only affirmed the right of the homosexual to "live his own life" but also reported that their knowledge of the deviance has had little or no effect upon their subsequent relationships with the deviants. In this regard, the mildest reaction, so mild that it might be considered no reaction at all, was that of a 19-year-old male college student:

I: What was your reaction to him?
S: My reactions to him have always been friendly because he seems like a very friendly person. Uh, and he has a very nice sense of humor and I've never been repelled by anything he's said. For one thing, I think he's tremendously interesting because he seems to have such a wide range for background. . . .
I: When was the last time you saw this person?
S: Last night. . . . I was sitting in a restaurant and he walked in with some friends. . . . He just stopped in and said hello, and was his usual friendly self.
I: What in particular happened after that?
S: Actually, nothing. He sat down with his friends, and we exchanged a few words about the records that were playing on the juke box. But nothing, actually. . . .

The theoretical significance of these data for the conception of deviance and societal reaction presented here is not that the subjects' information is of dubious accuracy or questionable relevance as evidence of homosexuality. Nor is it that the subjects' interpretations of them are unreasonable, unjustifiable, or spurious. They suggest rather that the conceptions of persons in everyday life concerning "sex-appropriate" or "sex-inappropriate" behavior may lead them to interpret a variety of behavioral forms as indications of the same deviation, and the "same" behavioral forms as indications of a variety of deviant as well as "normal" behavior. An individual's sexual "normality" may be made problematic by his interpretations and reinterpretations of his behavior by others, and the interpretive process may be activated by a wide range of situational behaviors which lend new significance to the individual's past and present

[13] Erving Goffman, "The Nature of Deference and Demeanor," *American Anthropologist,* 58 (1956), pp. 473–502.

behavior. His behavior with respect to speech, interests, dress, dating, or relations with other males are not *per se* significant in the deviant-defining process. The data suggest that the critical feature of the deviant-defining process is not the behavior of individuals who are defined as deviant, but rather the interpretations others make of their behaviors, whatever those behaviors may be.

With specific reference to homosexuality as a form of deviant behavior, the interview materials suggest that while reactions toward persons defined as homosexuals tend to be negatively toned, they are far from homogeneous as to the forms or intensity of the sanctions invoked and applied. Indeed, reactions which may appear to the sociological observer or to the deviant himself as negative sanctions, such as withdrawal or avoidance, may be expressions of embarrassment, a reluctance to share the burden of the deviant's problems, fear of the deviant, etc., as well as moral indignation or revulsion. In none of the interviews does the subject react with extreme violence, explicitly define or directly accuse the deviant of being a "queer," "fairy," or other terms of opprobrium, nor did any of them initiate legal actions against the deviant. In view of the extreme negative sanctions against homosexuality which are posited on theoretical grounds, the generally mild reactions of our subjects are striking.

The relative absence of extreme and overtly expressed negative sanctions against homosexuals among our subjects may, of course, reflect the higher than average educational level of the sample. A sample of subjects less biased toward the highly educated, middle-class segment of the population than was interviewed in this preliminary study may be expected to reflect a more definite pattern with reference to such negative reactions. We must, therefore, be cautious in generalizing the range of reactions among our subjects to the general population. It is equally important to note, however, that these data do indicate that reactions to homosexuals in American society are not *societal* in the sense of being uniform within a narrow range; rather, they are significantly conditioned by sub-cultural as well as situational factors. Thus, not only are the processes by which persons come to be defined as homosexuals contingent upon the interpretations of their behavior by others, but also the sanctions imposed and the treatment they are accorded as a consequence of that definition vary widely among conventional members of various sub-cultural groups.

The larger implications of these data are that a sociological theory of deviance must explicitly take into account the variety and range of conceptions held by persons, groups, and agencies within the society concerning any form of behavior. The increasing differentiation of groups, institutions, and sub-cultures in modern society generates a continually changing range of alternatives and tolerance for the expression of sexual as well as other forms of behavior. Consequently, it is difficult if not impossible to theoretically derive a set of *specific behavioral prescriptions* which will in fact be normatively supported, uniformly practiced, and socially enforced by more than a segment of the total population. Under such conditions, it is not the fact that individuals engage in behaviors which diverge from some theoretically posited "institutionalized expectations" or even that such behaviors are defined as deviant by the conventional and conforming members of the society which is of primary significance for the study of deviance. A sociological theory of deviance must focus specifically upon the interactions which not only define behaviors as deviant but also organize and activate the application of sanctions by individuals, groups, or agencies. For in modern society, the socially significant differentiation of deviants from the non-deviant population is increasingly contingent upon circumstances of situation, place, social and personal biography, and the bureaucratically organized activities of agencies of control.[14]

---

[14] For a discussion of such contingencies, see Edwin M. Lemert, *op. cit.*, Chapter 4, and Erving Goffman, "The Moral Career of the Mental Patient," *Psychiatry,* 22 (1959), pp. 123–142.

Notes on the Sociology of Deviance

KAI T. ERIKSON

From a sociological standpoint, deviance can be defined as conduct which is generally thought to require the attention of social control agencies—that is, conduct about which "something should be done." Deviance is not a property *inherent in* certain forms of behavior; it is a property *conferred upon* these forms by the audiences which directly or indirectly witness them. The critical variable in the study of deviance, then, is the social audience rather than the individual actor, since it is the audience which eventually determines whether or not any episode of behavior or any class of episodes is labeled deviant.

This definition may seem a little indirect, but it has the advantage of bringing a neglected sociological issue into proper focus. When a community acts to control the behavior of one of its members, it is engaged in a very intricate process of selection. After all, even the worst miscreant in society conforms most of the time, if only in the sense that he uses the correct spoon at mealtime, takes good care of his mother, or in a thousand other ways respects the ordinary conventions of his group; and if the community elects to bring sanctions against him for the occasions when he does misbehave, it is responding to a few deviant details set within a vast array of entirely acceptable conduct. Thus it happens that a moment of deviation may become the measure of a person's position in society. He may be jailed or hospitalized, certified as a full-time deviant, despite the fact that only a fraction of his behavior was in any way unusual or dangerous. The community has taken note of a few scattered particles of behavior and has decided that they reflect what kind of person he "really" is.

The screening device which sifts these telling details out of the person's over-all performance, then, is a very important instrument of social control. We know very little about the properties of this screen, but we do know that it takes many factors into account which are not directly related to the deviant act itself: it is sensitive to the suspect's social class, his past record as an offender, the amount of remorse he manages to convey, and many similar concerns which take hold in the shifting moods of the community. This may not be so obvious when the screen is dealing with extreme forms of deviance like serious crimes, but in the day-by-day filtering processes which take place through the community this feature is easily observable. Some men who drink too much are called alcoholics and others are not, some men who act oddly are committed to hospitals and others are not, some men who have no visible means of support are hauled into court and others are not—and the difference between those who earn a deviant label and those who go their own way in peace depends almost entirely on the way in which the community sifts out and codes the many details of behavior to which it is a witness. In this respect, the community screen may be a more relevant subject for sociological research than the actual behavior which is filtered through it.

Once the problem is phrased in this way we can ask: How does a community decide what forms of conduct should be singled out for this kind of attention? The conventional answer to this question, of course, is that society sets up the machinery of control in order to protect itself against the "harmful" effects of deviation, in much the same way that an organism mobilizes its resources to combat an invasion of germs. Yet this simple view of the matter has not always proven to be a very productive one. In the first place, as Durkheim and Mead pointed out some years ago, it is by no means clear that all acts considered deviant in a culture are in fact (or even in principle) harmful to group life.[1] In the second place, it is gradually becoming more evident to sociologists engaged in this area of research that deviant behavior can play an important part in keeping the social order intact.

This raises a number of interesting questions for sociology.

In recent years, sociological theory has become more and more concerned with the concept "social system"—an organization of so-

This is a slightly revised version of a paper that appeared in *Social Problems*, Vol. 9, No. 4 (Spring 1962), pp. 307–314; reprinted by permission of the Society for the Study of Social Problems and the author.

[1] Emile Durkheim, *The Division of Labor in Society* (translated by George Simpson), New York: The Free Press of Glencoe, 1952; and George Herbert Mead, "The Psychology of Punitive Justice," *American Journal of Sociology,* 23 (1918), 577–602.

ciety's component parts into a form which sustains internal equilibrium, resists change, and is boundary maintaining. In its most abstract form, the "system" concept describes a highly complex network of relations, but the scheme is generally used by sociologists to draw attention to those forces in the social order which promote a high level of uniformity among human actors and a high degree of symmetry within human institutions. The main organizational drift of a system, then, is seen as centripetal: it acts to draw the behavior of actors toward those centers in social space where the core values of the group are figuratively located, bringing them within range of basic norms. Any conduct which is neither attracted toward this nerve center by the rewards of conformity nor compelled toward it by other social pressures is considered "out of control," which is to say, deviant.

This basic model has provided the theme for most contemporary thinking about deviation, and as a result little attention has been given to the notion that systems operate to maintain boundaries. To say that a system maintains boundaries is to say that it controls the fluctuation of its constituent parts so that the whole retains a defined range of activity, a unique pattern of constancy and stability, within the larger environment.[2] Because the range of human behavior is potentially so wide, social groups maintain boundaries in the sense that they try to limit the flow of behavior within their domain so that it circulates within a defined cultural territory. Boundaries, then, are an important point of reference for persons participating in any system. A people may define its boundaries by referring to a geographical location, a set of honored traditions, a particular religious or political viewpoint, an occupational specialty, a common language, or just some local way of doing things; but in any case, members of the group have some idea about the contours of the niche they occupy in social space. They know where the group begins and ends as a special entity; they know what kinds of experience "belong" within these precincts and what kinds do not.

For all its apparent abstractness, a social system is organized around the movements of persons joined together in regular social relations. The only material found in a system for marking boundaries, then, is the behavior of its participants; and the kinds of behavior which best per-

form this function are often deviant, since they represent the most extreme variety of conduct to be found within the experience of the group. In this sense, transactions taking place between deviant persons on the one side and agencies of control on the other are boundary maintaining mechanisms. They mark the outside limits of the area within which the norm has jurisdiction, and in this way assert how much diversity and variability can be contained within the system before it begins to lose its distinct structure, its cultural integrity.

A social norm is rarely expressed as a firm rule or official code. It is an abstract synthesis of the many separate times a community has stated its sentiments on a given kind of issue. Thus the norm has a history much like that of an article of common law: it is an accumulation of decisions made by the community over a long period of time which gradually gathers enough moral eminence to serve as a precedent for future decisions. And like an article of common law, the norm retains its validity only if it is regularly used as a basis for judgment. Each time the group censures some act of deviation, then, it sharpens the authority of the violated norm and declares again where the boundaries of the group are located.

It is important to notice that these transactions between deviant persons and agents of control have always attracted a good deal of attention in this and other cultures. In our own past, both the trial and punishment of deviant offenders took place in the public market and gave the crowd a chance to participate in a direct, active way. Today we no longer parade deviants in the town square or expose them to the carnival atmosphere of Tyburn, but it is interesting to note that the "reform" which brought about this change in penal policy coincided almost precisely with the development of newspapers as media of public information. Perhaps this is no more than an accident of history, but it is nevertheless true that newspapers (and now radio and television) offer their readers the same kind of entertainment once supplied by public hangings or the use of stocks and pillories. An enormous amount of modern "news" is devoted to reports about deviant behavior and its punishment: indeed the largest circulation newspaper in the United States prints very little else. Yet how do we explain what makes these

---

[2]Cf. Talcott Parsons, *The Social System, op. cit.*

items "newsworthy" or why they command the great attention they do? Perhaps they satisfy a number of psychological perversities among the mass audience, as commentators sometimes point out, but at the same time they constitute our main source of information about the normative contours of society. In a figurative sense, at least, morality and immorality meet at the public scaffold, and it is during this meeting that the community declares where the line between them should be drawn.

People who gather together into communities need to be able to describe and anticipate those areas of experience which lie outside the immediate compass of the group—the unseen dangers which in any culture and in any age seem to threaten its security. Traditional folklore depicting demons, devils, witches and evil spirits, may be one way to give form to these otherwise formless dangers, but the visible deviant is another kind of reminder. As a trespasser against the group norms, he represents those forces which lie outside the group's boundaries: he informs us, as it were, what evil looks like, what shapes the devil can assume. And in doing so, he shows us the difference between the inside of the group and the outside. It may well be that without this ongoing drama at the outer edges of group space, the community would have no inner sense of identity and cohesion, no sense of the contrasts which set it off as a special place in the larger world.

Thus deviance cannot be dismissed simply as behavior which *disrupts* stability in society, but may itself be, in controlled quantities, an important condition for *preserving* stability. . . .

2 ACCOMMODATION TO DEVIANCE

When an alleged violation of norms has occurred, people may respond in a variety of ways. At first they may fail to notice the alleged deviation. When they do notice it, they may respond in several different ways: they may optimize, neutralize, normalize, or pessimize. To optimize is simply to see the assumed deviance as only temporary. To neutralize is to disregard it as not really significant. To normalize is to regard it as but a variation of normal behavior. To pessimize is to regard the deviance as permanent. These can be considered accommodations when they enable people to live with the deviance.

In the first reading in this chapter Marian Yarrow, Charlotte Schwartz, Harriet Murphy, and Leila Deasy describe the ways in which wives manage, for a time, to normalize their husbands' mental illness. Michael Lynch then shows how family members and close associates accommodate persons who are a source of trouble for others. In the final reading Joan Jackson describes the various stages wives go through in trying to deal with their husbands' alcoholism.

The Psychological Meaning of Mental Illness in the Family

MARIAN RADKE YARROW, CHARLOTTE GREEN SCHWARTZ, HARRIET S. MURPHY, and LEILA CALHOUN DEASY

The manifestations of mental illness are almost as varied as the spectrum of human behavior. Moreover, they are expressed not only in disturbance and functional impairment for the sick person but also in disruptive interactions with others. The mentally ill person is often, in his illness, a markedly deviant person, though certainly less so than the popular stereotype of the "insane." One wonders what were the initial phases of the impact of mental illness upon those within the ill person's social environment. How were the disorders of illness interpreted and tolerated? What did the patients, prior to hospitalization, communicate of their needs, and how did others—those closest to the ill persons—attempt, psychologically and behaviorally, to cope with the behavior? How did these persons come to be recognized by other family members as needing psychiatric help?

This paper presents an analysis of cognitive and emotional problems encountered by the wife in coping with the mental illness of the husband. It is concerned with the factors which lead to the reorganization of the wife's perceptions of her husband from a *well* man to a man who is mentally sick or in need of hospitalization in a mental hospital. The process whereby the wife attempts to understand and interpret her husband's manifestations of mental illness is best communicated by considering first the concrete details of a single wife's experiences. The findings and interpretations based on the total sample are presented following the case analysis.

Illustrative Case

Robert F., a 35-year-old cab driver, was admitted to Saint Elizabeth's Hospital with a diagnosis of schizophrenia. How did Mr. F. get to the mental hospital? Here is a very condensed version of what his wife told an interviewer a few weeks later.

Mrs. F. related certain events, swift and dramatic, which led directly to the hospitalization. The day before admission, Mr. F. went shopping with his wife, which he had never done before, and expressed worry lest he lose her. This was in her words, "rather strange." (*His behavior is not in keeping with her expectations for him.*) Later that day, Mr. F. thought a TV program was about him and that the set was "after him." "Then I was getting worried." (*She recognizes the bizarre nature of his reactions. She becomes concerned.*)

That night, Mr. F. kept talking. He reproached himself for not working enough to give his wife surprises. Suddenly, he exclaimed he did have a surprise for her—he was going to kill her. "I was petrified and said to him, 'What do you mean?' Then, he began to cry and told me not to let him hurt me and to do for him what I would want him to do for me. I asked him what was wrong. He said he had cancer. . . . He began talking about his grandfather's mustache and said there was a worm growing out of it." She remembered his watching little worms in the fish bowl and thought his idea came from that. Mr. F. said he had killed his grandfather. He asked Mrs. F. to forgive him and wondered if she were his mother or God. She denied this. He vowed he was being punished for killing people during the war. "I thought maybe . . . worrying about the war so much . . . had gotten the best of him. (*She tries to understand his behavior. She stretches the range of normality to include it.*) I thought he should see a psychiatrist . . . I don't know how to explain it. He was shaking. I knew it was beyond what I could do . . . I was afraid of him . . . I thought he was losing his normal mental attitude and mentality, but I wouldn't say that he was insane or crazy, because he had always bossed me around before . . . ." (*She shifts back and forth in thinking his problem is psychiatric and in feeling it is normal behavior that could be accounted for in terms of their own experience.*) Mr. F. talked on through the night. Sometime in the morning, he "seemed to straighten out" and drove his wife to work. (*This behavior tends to balance out the preceding disturbed activities. She quickly returns to a normal referent.*)

Reprinted from the *Journal of Social Issues*, Vol. 11, No. 4 (1955), pp. 12–24.

At noon, Mr. F. walked into a store where his wife worked as a clerk. "I couldn't make any sense of what he was saying. He kept getting angry because I wouldn't talk to him. . . . Finally, the boss's wife told me to go home." En route, Mr. F. said his male organs were blown up and little seeds covered him. Mrs. F. denied seeing them and announced she planned to call his mother. "He began crying and I had to promise not to. I said, . . . 'Don't you think you should go to a psychiatrist?' and he said, 'No, there is nothing wrong with me.' . . . Then we came home, and I went to pay a bill . . ." (*Again she considers, but is not fully committed to, the idea that psychiatric help is needed.*)

Back at their apartment, Mr. F. talked of repairing his cab while Mrs. F. thought of returning to work and getting someone to call a doctor. Suddenly, he started chasing her around the apartment and growling like a lion. Mrs. F. screamed, Mr. F. ran out of the apartment, and Mrs. F. slammed and locked the door. "When he started roaring and growling, then I thought he was crazy. That wasn't a human sound. You couldn't say a thing to him . . ." Later, Mrs. F. learned that her husband went to a nearby church, created a scene, and was taken to the hospital by the police. (*Thoroughly threatened, she defines problem as psychiatric.*)

What occurred before these events which precipitated the hospitalization? Going back to their early married life, approximately three years before hospitalization, Mrs. F. told of her husband's irregular work habits and long-standing complaints of severe headaches. "When we were first married, he didn't work much and I didn't worry as long as we could pay the bills." Mrs. F. figured they were just married and wanted to be together a lot. (*Personal norms and expectations are built up.*)

At Thanksgiving, six months after marriage, Mr. F. "got sick and stopped working." During the war he contracted malaria, he explained, which always recurred at that time of year. "He wouldn't get out of bed or eat. . . . He thought he was constipated and he had nightmares. . . . What I noticed most was his perspiring so much. He was crabby. You couldn't get him to go to a doctor. . . . I noticed he was nervous. He's always been a nervous person. . . . Any little thing that would go wrong would upset him—if I didn't get a drawer closed right. . . . His friends are nervous, too. . . . I came to the conclusion that maybe I was happy-go-lucky and everyone else was a bundle of nerves. . . . For a cab driver, he worked hard—most cab drivers loaf. When he felt good, he worked hard. He didn't work so hard when he didn't." (*She adapts to his behavior. The atypical is normalized as his type of personality and appropriate to his subculture.*)

As the months and years went by, Mrs. F. changed jobs frequently, but she worked more regularly than did her husband. He continued to work sporadically, get sick intermittently, appear "nervous and tense" and refrain from seeking medical care. Mrs. F. "couldn't say what was wrong." She had first one idea, then another, about his behavior. "I knew it wasn't right for him to be acting sick like he did." Then, "I was beginning to think he was getting lazy because there wasn't anything I could see." During one period, Mrs. F. surmised he was carrying on with another woman. "I was right on the verge of going, until he explained it wasn't anyone else." (*There is a building up of deviant behavior to a point near her tolerance limits. Her interpretations shift repeatedly.*)

About two and a half years before admission, Mrs. F. began talking to friends about her husband's actions and her lack of success in getting him to a doctor. "I got disgusted and said if he didn't go to a doctor, I would leave him. I got Bill (the owner of Mr. F.'s cab) to talk to him. . . . I begged, threatened, fussed . . ." After that, Mr. F. went to a VA doctor for one visit, overslept for his second appointment and never returned. He said the doctor told him nothing was wrong.

When Mr. F. was well and working, Mrs. F. "never stopped to think about it." "You live from day to day . . . When something isn't nice, I don't think about it. If you stop to think about things, you can worry yourself sick . . . He said he wished he could live in my world. He'd never seem to be able to put his thinking off the way I do . . ." (*Her mode of operating permits her to tolerate his behavior.*)

Concurrently, other situations confronted Mrs. F. Off and on, Mr. F. talked of a coming revolution as a result of which Negroes and Jews would take over the world. If Mrs. F. argued that she didn't believe it, Mr. F. called her "dumb" and "stupid." "The best thing to do was to change the subject." Eighteen months before admission, Mr. F. began awakening his wife to tell of nightmares about wartime experiences, but she "didn't think about it." Three months later, he decided he wanted to do something besides drive a cab. He worked on an invention but discovered it was patented. Then, he began to write a book about his wartime experiences and science. "If you saw what he wrote, you couldn't see anything wrong with it. . . . He just wasn't making any money." Mrs. F. did think it was "silly" when Mr. F. went to talk to Einstein about his ideas and couldn't understand why he didn't talk to someone in town. Nevertheless, she accompanied him on the trip. (*With the further accumulation of deviant behavior, she becomes less and less able to tolerate it. The perceived seriousness of his condition is attenuated so long as she is able to find something acceptable or understandable in his behavior.*)

Three days before admission, Mr. F. stopped taking baths and changing clothes. Two nights before admission, he awakened his wife to tell her he had just figured out that the book he was writing had nothing to do with science or the world, only with himself. "He said he had been worrying about things for ten years and that writing a book solved what had been worrying him for ten years." Mrs. F. told him to burn his writings if they had nothing to do with science. It was the following morning that Mrs. F. first noticed her husband's behavior as "rather strange."

In the long prelude to Mr. F.'s hospitalization, one can see many of the difficulties which arise for the wife as the husband's behavior no longer conforms and as it strains the limits of the wife's expectations for him. At some stage the wife defines the situation as one requiring help, eventually psychiatric help. Our analysis is concerned primarily with the process of the wife's getting to this stage in interpreting and responding to the husband's behavior. In the preceding case are many reactions which appear as general trends in the data group. These trends can be systematized in terms of the following focal aspects of the process:

1. The wife's threshold for initially discerning a problem depends on the accumulation of various kinds of behavior which are not readily understandable or acceptable to her.
2. This accumulation forces upon the wife the necessity for examining and adjusting expectations for herself and her husband which permit her to account for his behavior.
3. The wife is in an "overlapping" situation, of problem—not problem or of normal—not normal. Her interpretations shift back and forth.
4. Adaptations to the atypical behavior of the husband occur. There is testing and waiting for additional cues in coming to any given interpretation, as in most problem solving. The wife mobilizes strong defenses against the husband's deviant behavior. These defenses take form in such reactions as denying, attenuating, balancing and normalizing the husband's problems.
5. Eventually there is a threshold point at which the perception breaks, when the wife comes to the relatively stable conclusion that the problem is a psychiatric one and/or that she cannot alone cope with the husband's behavior.

These processes are elaborated in the following analysis of the wives' responses.

Method of Data Collection

Ideally, to study this problem one might like to interview the wives as they struggled with the developing illness. This is precluded, however, by the fact that the problem is not "visible" until psychiatric help is sought. The data, therefore, are the wives' reconstructions of their earlier experiences and accounts of their current reactions during the husband's hospitalization.

It is recognized that recollections of the prehospital period may well include systematic biases, such as distortions, omissions and increased organization and clarity. As a reliability check, a number of wives, just before the husband's discharge from the hospital, were asked again to describe the events and feelings of the prehospital period. In general, the two reports are markedly similar; often details are added and others are elaborated, but events tend to be substantially the same. While this check attests to the consistency of the wives' reporting, it has, of course, the contamination of overlearning which comes from many retellings of these events.

The Beginnings of the Wife's Concern

In the early interviews, the wife was asked to describe the beginnings of the problem which led

TABLE 1.   Reported Problem Behavior at Time of the Wife's Initial Concern and at Time of the Husband's Admission to Hospital

Problem Behavior	Initially		At Hospital Admission	
	Psychotics N	Psycho-neurotics N	Psychotics N	Psycho-neurotics N
Physical problems, complaints, worries	12	5	7	5
Deviations from routines of behavior	17	9	13	9
Expression of inadequacy or hopelessness	4	1	5	2
Nervous, irritable, worried	19	10	18	9
Withdrawal (verbal, physical)	5	1	6	1
Changes or accentuations in personality "traits" (slovenly, deceptive, forgetful)	5	6	7	6
Aggressive or assaultive and suicidal behavior	6	3	10	6
Strange or bizarre thoughts, delusions, hallucinations and strange behavior	11	1	15	2
Excessive drinking	4	7	3	4
Violation of codes of "decency"	3	1	3	2
Number of Respondents	23	10	23	10

to her husband's hospitalization. ("Could you tell me when you first noticed that your husband was different?") This question was intended to provide an orientation for the wife to reconstruct the sequence and details of events and feelings which characterized the period preceding hospitalization. The interviewer provided a minimum of structuring in order that the wife's emphases and organization could be obtained.

In retrospect, the wives usually cannot pinpoint the time the husband's problem emerged. Neither can they clearly carve it out from the contexts of the husband's personality and family expectations. The subjective beginnings are seldom localized in a single strange or disturbing reaction on the husband's part but rather in the piling up of behavior and feelings. We have seen this process for Mrs. F. There is a similar accumulation for the majority of wives, although the time periods and kinds of reported behavior vary. Thus, Mrs. Q. verbalizes the impact of a concentration of changes which occur within a period of a few weeks. Her explicit recognition of a problem comes when she adds up this array: her husband stays out late, doesn't eat or sleep, has obscene thoughts, argues with her, hits her, talks continuously, "cannot appreciate the beautiful scene" and "cannot appreciate me or the baby."

The problem behaviors reported by the wives are given in Table 1. They are ordered roughly; the behaviors listed first occurred primarily, but not exclusively, within the family; those later occurred in the more public domain. Whether the behavior is public or private does not seem to be a very significant factor in determining the wife's threshold for perceiving a problem.

There are many indications that these behaviors, now organized as a problem, have occurred many times before. This is especially true where alcoholism, physical complaints or personality "weaknesses" enter the picture. The wives indicate how, earlier, they had assimilated these characteristics into their own expectations in a variety of ways: the characteristics were congruent with their image of their husbands, they fitted their differential standards for men and women (men being less able to stand up to troubles), they had social or environmental justifications, etc.

When and how behavior becomes defined as problematic appears to be a highly individual matter. In some instances, it is when the wife can no longer manage her husband (he will no longer respond to her usual prods); in others, when his behavior destroys the status quo (when her goals and living routines are disorganized); and, in still others, when she cannot explain his

TABLE 2. Initial Interpretations of the Husband's Behavior

Interpretation	Psychotics N	Psychoneurotics N
Nothing really wrong	3	0
"Character" weakness and "controllable" behavior (lazy, mean, etc.)	6	3
Physical problem	6	0
Normal response to crisis	3	1
Mildly emotionally disturbed	1	2
"Something" seriously wrong	2	2
Serious emotional or mental problem	2	2
Number of Respondents	23	10

behavior. One can speculate that her level of tolerance for his behavior is a function of her specific personality needs and vulnerabilities, her personal and family value systems and the social supports and prohibitions regarding the husbands' symptomatic behavior.

Initial Interpretations of Husband's Problem

Once the behavior is organized as a problem, it tends also to be interpreted as some particular kind of problem. More often than not, however, the husband's difficulties are not seen initially as manifestations of mental illness or even as emotional problems (Table 2).

Early interpretations often tend to be organized around physical difficulties (18% of cases) or "character" problems (27%). To a very marked degree, these orientations grow out of the wives' long-standing appraisals of their husbands as weak and ineffective or physically sick men. These wives describe their husbands as spoiled, lacking will-power, exaggerating little complaints and acting like babies. This is especially marked where alcoholism complicates the husband's symptomatology. For example, Mrs. Y., whose husband was chronically alcoholic, aggressive and threatening to her, "raving," and who "chewed his nails until they almost bled," interprets his difficulty thus: "He was just spoiled rotten. He never outgrew it. He told me when he was a child he could get his own way if he insisted, and he is still that way." This quotation is the prototype of many of its kind.

Some wives, on the other hand, locate the problem in the environment. They expect the husband to change as the environmental crisis subsides. Several wives, while enumerating difficulties and concluding that there is a problem, in the same breath say it is really nothing to be concerned about.

Where the wives interpret the husband's difficulty as emotional in nature, they tend to be inconsistently "judgmental" and "understanding." The psychoneurotics are more often perceived initially by their wives as having emotional problems or as being mentally ill than are the psychotics. This is true even though many more clinical signs (bizarre, confused, delusional, aggressive and disoriented behavior) are reported by the wives of the psychotics than of the psychoneurotics.

Initial interpretations, whatever their content, are seldom held with great confidence by the wives. Many recall their early reactions to their husbands' behaviors as full of puzzling confusion and uncertainty. Something is wrong, they know, but, in general, they stop short of a firm explanation. Thus, Mrs. M. reports, "He was kind of worried. He was kind of worried before, not exactly worried . . ." She thought of his many physical complaints; she "racked" her "brain" and told her husband, "Of course, he didn't feel good." Finally, he stayed home from work with "no special complaints, just blah," and she "began to realize it was more deeply seated."

Changing Perceptions of the Husband's Problem

The fog and uneasiness in the wife's early attempts to understand and cope with the husband's difficulties are followed, typically, by painful psychological struggles to resolve the uncertainties and to change the current situation. Usually, the wife's perceptions of the husband's problems undergo a series of changes before hospitalization is sought or effected, irrespective of the length of time elapsing between the beginnings of concern and hospitalization.

Viewing these changes macroscopically, three relatively distinct patterns of successive redefinitions of the husband's problems are apparent. One sequence (slightly less than half the cases) is characterized by a progressive intensification; interpretations are altered in a definite direction—toward seeing the problem as mental illness. Mrs. O. illustrates this progression. Initially, she thought her husband was "unsure of himself." "He was worried, too, about getting old." These ideas moved to: "He'd drink to forget. . . . He just didn't have the confidence. . . . He'd forget little things. . . . He'd wear a suit weeks on end if I didn't take it away from him. . . . He'd say nasty things." Then, when Mr. O. seemed "so confused," "to forget all kinds of things . . . where he'd come from . . . to go to work," and made "nasty, cutting remarks all the time," she began to think in terms of a serious personality disturbance. "I did think he knew that something was wrong . . . that he was sick. He was never any different this last while and I couldn't stand it any more. . . . You don't know what a relief it was . . ." (when he was hospitalized). The husband's drinking, his failure to be tidy, his nastiness, etc., lose significance in their own right. They move from emphasis to relief and are recast as signs of "something deeper," something that brought "it" on.

Some wives whose interpretations move in the direction of seeing their husbands as mentally ill hold conceptions of mental illness and of personality that do not permit assigning the husband all aspects of the sick role. Frequently, they use the interpretation of mental illness as an angry epithet or as a threatening prediction for the husband. This is exemplified in such references as: "I told him he should have his head examined," "I called him a half-wit," "I told him if he's not careful, he'll be a mental case." To many of these wives, the hospital is regarded as the "end of the road."

Other wives showing this pattern of change hold conceptions of emotional disturbance which more easily permit them to assign to their husbands the role of patient as the signs of illness become more apparent. They do not as often regard hospitalization in a mental hospital as

the "last step." Nevertheless, their feelings toward their husbands may contain components equally as angry and rejecting as those of the wives with the less sophisticated ideas regarding mental illness.

A somewhat different pattern of sequential changes in interpreting the husband's difficulties (about one-fifth of the cases) is to be found among wives who appear to cast around for situationally and momentarily adequate explanations. As the situation changes or as the husband's behavior changes, these wives find reasons or excuses but lack an underlying or synthesizing theory. Successive interpretations tend to bear little relation to one another. Situational factors tend to lead them to seeing their husbands as mentally ill. Immediate, serious and direct physical threats or the influence of others may be the deciding factor. For example, a friend or employer may insist that the husband see a psychiatrist, and the wife goes along with the decision.

A third pattern of successive redefinitions (slightly less than one-third of the cases) revolves around an orientation outside the framework of emotional problems or mental illness. In these cases, the wife's specific explanations change but pivot around a denial that the husband is mentally ill.

A few wives seem not to change their interpretations about their husband's difficulties. They maintain the same explanation throughout the development of his illness, some within the psychiatric framework, others rigidly outside that framework.

Despite the characteristic shiftings in interpretations, in the group as a whole, there tend to be persisting underlying themes in the individual wife's perceptions that remain essentially unaltered. These themes are a function of her systems of thinking about normality and abnormality and about valued and devalued behavior.

The Process of Recognizing the Husband's Problem as Mental Illness

In the total situation confronting the wife, there are a number of factors, apparent in our data, which make it difficult for the wife to recognize and accept the husband's behavior in a mental-emotional-psychiatric framework. Many cross-currents seem to influence the process.

The husband's behavior itself is a fluctuating

stimulus. He is not worried and complaining all of the time. His delusions and hallucinations may not persist. His hostility toward the wife may be followed by warm attentiveness. She has, then, the problem of deciding whether his "strange" behavior is significant. The greater saliency of one or the other of his responses at any moment of time depends in some degree upon the behavior sequence which has occurred most recently.

The relationship between husband and wife also supplies a variety of images and contexts which can justify varied conclusions about the husband's current behavior. The wife is likely to adapt to behavior which occurs in their day to day relationships. Therefore, symptomatic reactions which are intensifications of long-standing response patterns become part of the fabric of life and are not easily disentangled as "symptomatic."

Communications between husband and wife regarding the husband's difficulties act sometimes to impede and sometimes to further the process of seeing the difficulties within a psychiatric framework. We have seen both kinds of influences in our data. Mr. and Mrs. F. were quite unable to communicate effectively about Mr. F.'s problems. On the one hand, he counters his wife's urging that he see a doctor with denials that anything is wrong. On the other hand, in his own way through his symptoms, he tries to communicate his problems, but she responds only to his verbalized statements, taking them at face value.

Mr. and Mrs. K. participate together quite differently, examining Mr. K.'s fears that he is being followed by the F.B.I., that their house has been wired and that he is going to be fired. His wife tentatively shares his suspicions. At the same time, they discuss the possibility of paranoid reactions.

The larger social context contributes, too, in the wife's perceptual tug of war. Others with whom she can compare her husband provide contrasts to his deviance, but others (Mr. F.'s nervous friends) also provide parallels to his problems. The "outsiders," seeing less of her husband, often discount the wife's alarm when she presses them for opinions. In other instances, the friend or employer, less adapted to or defended against the husband's symptoms, helps her to define his problem as psychiatric.

This task before the wife, of defining her husband's difficulties, can be conceptualized as an "overlapping" situation (in Lewin's terms), in which the relative potencies of the several effective influences fluctuate. The wife is responding to the various sets of forces simultaneously. Thus, several conclusions or interpretations of the problem are simultaneously "suspended in balance," and they shift back and forth in emphasis and relief. Seldom, however, does she seem to be balancing off clear-cut alternatives, such as physical versus mental. Her complex perceptions (even those of Mrs. F. who is extreme in misperceiving cues) are more "sophisticated" than the casual questioner might be led to conclude.

Thus far, we have ignored the personally threatening aspects of recognizing mental illness in one's spouse, and the defenses which are mobilized to meet this threat. It is assumed that it is threatening to the wife not only to realize that the husband is mentally ill but further to consider her own possible role in the development of the disorder, to give up modes of relating to her husband that may have had satisfactions for her and to see a future as the wife of a mental patient. Our data provide systematic information only on the first aspect of this problem, on the forms of defense against the recognition of the illness. One or more of the following defenses are manifested in three-fourths of our cases.

The most obvious form of defense in the wife's response is the tendency to *normalize* the husband's neurotic and psychotic symptoms. His behavior is explained, justified or made acceptable by seeing it also in herself or by assuring herself that the particular behavior occurs again and again among persons who are not ill. Illustrative of this reaction is the wife who reports her husband's hallucinations and assures herself that this is normal because she herself heard voices when she was in the menopause. Another wife responds to her husband's physical complaints, fears, worries, nightmares, and delusions with "A lot of normal people think there's something wrong when there isn't. I think men are that way; his father is that way."

When behavior cannot be normalized, it can be made to seem less severe or less important in a total picture than an outsider might see it. By finding some grounds for the behavior or something explainable about it, the wife achieves at least momentary *attenuation* of the seriousness of it. Thus, Mrs. F. is able to discount partly the strangeness of her husband's descriptions of the worms growing out of his grandfather's mustache when she recalls his watching the worms in the fish bowl. There may be attenuation, too, by seeing the behavior as "momentary." ("You could talk him out of his ideas.") or by rethinking the problem and seeing it in a different light.

By *balancing* acceptable with unacceptable behavior or "strange" with "normal" behavior, some wives can conclude that the husband is not seriously disturbed. Thus, it is very important to Mrs. R. that her husband kissed her goodbye before he left for the hospital. This response cancels out his hostile feelings toward her and the possibility that he is mentally ill. Similarly, Mrs. V. reasons that her husband cannot be "out of his mind" for he had reminded her of things she must not forget to do when he went to the hospital.

Defense sometimes amounts to a thoroughgoing *denial*. This takes the form of denying that the behavior perceived can be interpreted in an emotional or psychiatric framework. In some instances, the wife reports vividly on such behavior as repeated thoughts of suicide, efforts to harm her and the like and sums it up with "I thought it was just a whim." Other wives bend their efforts toward proving the implausibility of mental illness.

After the husband is hospitalized, it might be expected that these denials would decrease to a negligible level. This is not wholly the case, however. A breakdown of the wives' interpretations just following the husband's admission to the hospital shows that roughly a fifth still interpret their husband's behavior in another framework than that of a serious emotional problem or mental illness. Another fifth ambivalently and sporadically interpret the behavior as an emotional or mental problem. The remainder hold relatively stable interpretations within this framework.

After the husband has been hospitalized for some time, many wives reflect on their earlier tendencies to avoid a definition of mental illness. Such reactions are almost identically described by these wives: "I put it out of my mind—I didn't want to face it—anything but a mental illness." "Maybe I was aware of it. But you know you push things away from you and keep hoping." "Now you think maybe you should have known about it. Maybe you should have done more than you did and that worries me."

Discussion

The findings on the perceptions of mental illness by the wives of patients are in line with general findings in studies of perception. Behavior which is unfamiliar and incongruent and unlikely in terms of current expectations and needs will not be readily recognized, and stressful or threatening stimuli will tend to be misperceived or perceived with difficulty or delay.

We have attempted to describe the factors which help the wife maintain a picture of her husband as normal and those which push her in the direction of accepting a psychiatric definition of his problem. The kind and intensity of the symptomatic behavior, its persistence over time, the husband's interpretation of his problem, interpretations and defining actions of others, including professionals, all play a role. In addition, the wives come to this experience with different concepts of psychological processes and of the nature of emotional illness, itself, as well as with different tolerances for emotional disturbance. As we have seen, there are also many supports in society for maintaining a picture of normality concerning the husband's behavior. Social pressures and expectations not only keep *behavior* in line but to a great extent *perceptions* of behavior as well. . . .

Accommodation to Madness   MICHAEL LYNCH

People are committed to mental hospitals after informal efforts to accommodate them in society fail. Studies report that spouses of prospective mental patients (Cumming and Cumming, 1957; Mayo et al., 1971; Sampson et al., 1962; Spitzer et al., 1971; Yarrow et al., 1955), co-workers (Lemert, 1962), and police officers (Bittner, 1967) claim that they contact psychiatric authorities only as a last resort, when informal methods of "care" are unavailable or are overwhelmed by the extremity of the person's disorder. There is widespread reluctance, especially in lower-class families (Hollingshead and Redlich, 1958:172–79; Myers and Roberts, 1959:213–20), to take a perspective on relational disorders which supports professional intervention and hospitalization. As a result, the population of potential mental patients is said to vastly outnumber the population of professionally treated patients (Srole et al., 1962). Accommodating families can hide potential patients from official scrutiny by placing few demands upon them and allowing them to "exist as if in a one-person chronic ward, insulated from all but those in a highly tolerant household" (Freeman and Simmons, 1958:148).

Such observations suggest that a massive program of community care exists independently of formally established programs of inpatient and outpatient treatment. Countless numbers of undiagnosed, but troublesome, individuals, as well as an increasing number of diagnosed outpatients, are consigned by default to the informal care of family and community. Although the social characteristics of professionally administered mental health care institutions have been exhaustively analyzed, the practices that make up ordinary lay-operated "institutions" of care remain largely unexamined. In this study I call attention to such accommodation practices,

elaborate upon previous descriptions of the practices, and present some conjectures on the social construction of the individual.

Accommodation practices are interactional techniques that people use to manage persons they view as persistent sources of trouble. Accommodation implies attempts to "live with" persistent and ineradicable troubles.[1] Previous studies mention a number of accommodation practices. Lemert (1962) describes how people exclude distrusted individuals from their organization's covert activities by employing methods of "spurious interaction." Such forms of interaction are:

. . . distinguished by patronizing, evasion, "humoring," guiding conversation onto selected topics, underreaction, and silence, all calculated either to prevent intense interaction or to protect individual and group values by restricting access to them. When the interaction is between two or more persons in the individual's presence it is cued by a whole repertoire of subtle expressive signs which are meaningful only to them (1962:8).

Other methods for managing perceived "troublemakers" include: isolation and avoidance (Lemert, 1962; Sampson et al., 1962), relieving an individual of ordinary responsibilities associated with their roles (Sampson et al., 1962); hiding liquor bottles from a heavily drinking spouse (Jackson, 1954); and "babying" (Jackson, 1954).

Some studies (Yarrow et al., 1955) treat accommodation practices as sources of delay in the recognition and treatment of mental illness; others (Goffman, 1961, 1969; Lemert, 1962) portray them as primary constituents of "illness." Whether the studies assume a realist or a societal reaction perspective on the nature of mental illness, they attempt to explain how per-

"Accommodation Practices: Vernacular Treatments of Madness," *Social Problems*, Vol. 31, No. 2 (December, 1983), pp. 152–164, by permission of the Society for the Study of Social Problems and the author.

The author thanks Renee Anspach, David Davis, Robert Emerson, Harold Garfinkel, Richard Hilbert, James Holstein, Melvin Pollner, and Steven Vandewater for their comments. The exercise on accommodation practices which I used in this research was adapted from a similar exercise used by Robert Emerson and Melvin Pollner in their courses on the Sociology of Mental Illness at the University of California, Los Angeles. During part of this research I was supported by a fellowship from the National Institute's of Mental Health Postdoctoral Training Program in Mental Health Evaluation Research, (# MH 14583). Correspondence to: School of Social Sciences, University of California, Irvine, CA.

[1] The equally interesting topic of how patients accommodate to their own disorders (Critchley, 1971:290; O. Sacks, 1974:227) is not included in this discussion of interactional practices.

sons become mental patients by reconstructing the social backgrounds of hospitalized patients. As Emerson and Messinger (1977:131) point out, retrospective analyses of the "careers" of diagnosed mental patients presuppose a specific pathological outcome to the "prepatient's" biography. To avoid this problem, social scientists need to abandon retrospective methods and analyze contemporary situations where troublesome individuals are accommodated. Such people are not yet patients, and may never attain that status. Therefore, institutional records cannot be used to locate cases for study. An appropriate way to find them is to use vernacular accounts of madness or mental illness, and to document the patterns of accommodation that others use to control such troublesome people.

The Study

This study is an analysis of the results of an assignment which I gave to students in classes on the sociology of mental illness in 1981 and 1982. I instructed students to locate someone in a familiar social environment who was identified by others (and perhaps by themselves) as "crazy"; the subject need not appear "mentally ill," but need only be a *personal* and *persistent* source of trouble for others. The vast majority of the students had little trouble finding such subjects. I instructed them to interview persons who consistently dealt with the troublemaker in a living or work situation. The interviews were to focus on the practices used by others to "live with" the troublemaker from day to day. Students who were personally acquainted with the troublemaker were encouraged to refer to their own recollections and observations in addition to their interviews. They were instructed not to interview or otherwise disturb the troublemakers. Each student wrote a 5–7 page paper on accommodation practices with an appendix of notes from their interviews.

The Subjects

The persons the students interviewed described subjects who had already developed to an intermediate stage in the "natural history of trouble" (Emerson and Messinger, 1977). Few troublemakers carried formal designations of mental illness, but each was associated with recurrent organizational troubles. The troubles were defined non-relationally (Goffman, 1969);

they were attributed to the personal agency of a troublemaker, and any possible mitigating factors were no longer considered pertinent. Although the students and their interviewees claimed a consensus on the fact that *something* was wrong with the troublemaker, just what was wrong was often a matter of speculation. Troublemakers' friends and acquaintances sometimes resorted to amateur psychologizing to account for the subjects' "problem," but often they expressed moral exasperation and disgust, without any mention of a possible "illness."

Students and those they interviewed used a rich variety of vernacular epithets for personal character types to identify their subjects. These included common insults, "crazy" terms used as insults, and a few straightforward "illness" designators. The following expressions illustrate different shadings in the ambiguity of the troublemakers' statuses as moral offenders and/or "sick" persons:

1. Commonplace vernacular terms for faults and faulted persons, without reference to insanity: "bullshitter," "bird" (as in "turkey"), "off the wall," "spiteful, nasty girl," "rude and argumentative," "an obnoxious pest," "catty," "space cadet," "chronic complainer," "frivolous and ridiculous," and nicknames such as "Ozone" and "The Deviant."
2. Vernacular cognates of madness which do not necessarily compel the serious connotation of illness: "crazy," "nuts," "bananas," "weird," "strange," "unpredictable," "highly emotional," "attention seeking and manipulative," "explosive, angry," and "sick."
3. Amateur uses of accounts associated with the helping professions: "paranoid," "developmentally disabled," "chemically imbalanced in the brain," "low self-esteem," "obsessed with food," and "alcoholic."

Except in a few cases when students reported a specific medical diagnosis, their accounts did not provide unique labels corresponding to stable categories of disorder. They did, however, point to a history of incidents supporting the conclusion that *something* was wrong with the person in question.

Some accounts emphasized that it was impossible to describe just what was wrong with the person. There was far more to the trouble than could be described by a few episodes: "disgusting eating habits," "he smells terrible," "he stands too close to people," "she asks you to repeat things over and over again," "she is so promiscuous that one of the fraternities has a song about fucking her!" Not all accounts were wholly negative or rejecting. At least some acquaintances whom students interviewed expressed some affection or attachment to troublemakers, or an obligation to maintain a minimal level of civility toward the person.

In the few cases where the troublemaker had a history of mental or neurological disorder, students reported that their informants used the illness to excuse incidents believed to be symptomatic of the disorder. Such special understandings did not entirely replace more hostile reactions, for many of the "symptoms" were also personal offenses:

Margaret explained that she always attempts to start off calm when dealing with Joan and thinking of her as being a "lonely and sick woman," but that Joan "gets you so angry that it is difficult to stay level-headed and then I start screaming and have to leave." (Student report of an interview concerning a "senile" woman.)

The students investigated a number of different organizational environments. Fraternities and sororities were most popular, followed by families (both nuclear and extended), dormitory residents, work groups, friendship cliques, athletic teams, and residents of apartment suites and local neighborhoods. One case dealt with a board and care home; another described a group of students on a retreat. Among the work groups observed were employees of a book store, a clothing store, a pharmacy, and a fast food restaurant. One noteworthy case involved a rock and roll band and its crew on a national tour. In each of these cases, membership in the group or organization provided the local basis of the troublemaker's existence. Membership furnished the context for day-to-day interactions with the troublemaker, and for accumulating an oral history of the troublemaker's antics. In the following discussion, I will use the term *members* to refer to all those who knew or related to the troublesome person through common membership in some organized group, network of relationship, acquaintance, or friendship.[2]

Because of the highly sensitive nature of the interactional circumstances which the students were investigating, I repeatedly asked them to respect the privacy of their subjects. They proved to be highly skilled at doing so, perhaps because they relied upon their own skills at performing accommodation practices to hide their inquiries from the troublemaker's attention.

I did not initially design the assignment in order to gather data for my own analysis. However, after reading the students' reports on their observations and interviews I found that despite their variability in descriptive and analytic quality and their obvious shortcomings as data, they described a diversity of accommodation practices, and suggested recurrent features of those practices which were not comprehensively treated in the literature. The information seemed worth reporting and students gave me permission to quote from their papers. I analyzed material from 32 of the student reports, each of which discussed a different case. In the remainder of this paper, all quotes not attributed to sources come from the students' papers.

I have organized accommodation practices under three thematic headings: (1) practices which *isolate* the troublemaker within the group; (2) practices which *manipulate* the troublemaker's behavior, perception, and understanding; and (3) practices which members use to influence how others react to the troublemaker. The first set of practices defines and limits the troublemaker's chances for interaction, expression, and feedback within the group. The second set directs the details of the troublemaker's actions and establishes the discrepant meanings of those actions for "self" and "other." The third set includes attempts to make the troublemaker's public identity into a covert communal project.

Minimizing Contact with the Troublemaker

Avoiding and *ignoring* were the two accommodation practices mentioned most often by students. Both were methods for minimizing contact with the troublemaker, and had the effect of isolating the troublemaker within the organizational network. While both were negative methods of behavior control, attenuating the troublemaker's actual and possible occasions

---

[2] Here the term *member* does not bear the more radical implication of "a mastery of natural language," defined in Garfinkel and Sacks (1970:350).

of interaction, they worked quite differently. Avoiding limited the gross *possibility* of interaction, while ignoring worked *within* ongoing occasions of interaction to limit the interactional *reality* of the encounter. Where avoiding created an absence of encounter, ignoring created a dim semblance to ordinary interaction.

Avoiding

In virtually every student's account, one or more of the members they interviewed mentioned that they actively avoided the troublemaker. Avoidance created an interactional vacuum around the troublemaker. Members managed to stay out of the way of the troublemaker without actually requesting or commanding the troublemaker to stay away from them. Methods of avoidance included individual and joint tactics such as "ducking into restrooms," "keeping a lookout for her at all times," and "hiding behind a newspaper or book."

Some members were better placed than others within the structure of the organization to avoid the troublemaker. In larger organizations like fraternities and sororities, persons could stake out positions which minimized contact with the troublemaker. In more intimate circles avoidance ran more of a risk of calling attention to the *absence* of usual interactional involvement. Avoidance *did* occur in such intimate groups as families (Sampson *et al.,* 1962), but only at the cost of threatening the very integrity of the group.

Ignoring/Not Taking Seriously

Ignoring differed from avoiding because it entailed at least some interaction, though of an attenuated and inauthentic kind. One account described conversations with the troublemaker as being "reduced to superficial 'hellos,' most of which are directed at her feet; there is an obvious lack of eye contact." Many accounts mentioned the superficiality of interactions with troublemakers. In some cases this was accomplished by what one student called "rehearsed and phony responses" to limit the openness of their conversations to a few stock sequences.[3]

Although ignoring entailed interaction, it was like avoidance in that it circumscribed the troublemaker's interactional possibilities. Where avoidance operated to limit, in a gross way, the intersection of pathways between troublemaker and other members, ignoring operated intensively to trivialize the troublemaker's apparent involvements in group activities.[4] Bids for positive notice were ignored, and had little effect on the troublemaker's position within the group.

Directly Managing the Troublemaker's Actions

Members used a number of more direct interventions to control and limit the troublemaker's behavior, including humoring, screening, taking over, orienting to local prospects of normality, and practical jokes and retaliations. While such methods had little hope of permanently modifying the behavior, they were used to curtail episodic disruptions by the troublemaker.

Humoring

Members often used the term humoring to describe attempts to manage the troublemaker by maintaining a veneer of agreement and geniality in the face of actions which would ordinarily evoke protest or disgust. For example, in the case of "an obnoxiously argumentative person," members offered superficial tokens of agreement in response to even the most outlandish pronouncements for the sake of avoiding more extreme disruptions.

Humoring was often made possible through insight into recurrent features of the troublemaker's behavior. Members recognized recurrent situations in ordinary interactions which triggered peculiar reactions by the troublemaker. They developed a heightened awareness of ordinary and seemingly innocuous details of interaction which could touch off an explosive reaction. One student described how her parents managed a "crazy aunt," who she said was prone to sudden and violent verbal assaults:

My parents avoided discussing specific topics and persons that they knew distressed her. Whenever she be-

---

[3] A topic needing further study is how members use greetings and other conversational "adjacency pairs" (Sacks *et al.,* 1974) to foreclose conversation with troublemakers at the earliest convenient point, but in such a way as not to call attention to their action as a snub.

[4] See Wulbert (n.d.) for a poignant discussion of trivializing practices.

gan talking about an arousable [sic] event or person, my parents and her husband attempted to change the subject.[5]

Although members rationalized humoring as a way "to make it easy for everybody," they did not always find it easy to withhold their reactions to interactional offenses. A student wrote about her efforts to prepare her fiance for a first encounter with her grandmother, said to be suffering from senile dementia, Alzheimer type;

I attempted to explain to him that he should not say anything controversial, agree with whatever she says, and generally stay quiet as much as possible. [He assured her that everything would be okay, but when he was confronted with the actual grandmother, the assurance proved quite fragile.] That encounter proved to be quite an experience for Charles—we left Grandma's house with Charles screaming back at her for his self-worth.

Other accounts mentioned the strain and difficulty of trying to humor troublemakers. They described an exceedingly fragile interactional situation which was prone to break down at any moment:

You don't want to set him off, so you're very careful about what you do and say. You become tense trying to keep everything calm, and then something happens to screw it up anyway: The car won't start, or a light bulb blows. It's all my fault because I'm a rotten wife and mother.

Humoring often entailed obedience or deference to what members claimed (when not within earshot of the troublemaker) were outrageous or absurd demands:

Everyone did what she asked in order to please her and not cause any bad scenes.

In some cases, members exerted special efforts or underwent severe inconvenience for the sake of a person they secretly despised. Not surprisingly, such efforts often, though not always, were exerted by persons over whom the troublemaker had formal authority. In one case the members of a crew traveling with a rock and roll band would set up the troublesome member's equipment before that of the others and set up

daily meetings with him to discuss his "technical needs," while at the same time they believed it was foolish of him to demand such special attention. They described the special meetings and favors as a "bogus accommodation." In every case, whether correlated with formal divisions of authority or not, humoring contributed to the troublemaker's sense of interactional power over others.

Humoring always included a degree of duplicity in which members "kept a straight face" when interacting with the troublemaker or acted in complicity with the troublemaker's premises—premises which members otherwise discounted as delusional or absurd:

We played along with her fantasy of a boyfriend, "John." We never said what a complete fool she was for waiting for him.

Commonly, members practiced *serial* duplicity by waiting until the troublemaker was out of earshot to display for one another's appreciation the "real" understanding they had previously suppressed:

They pretend to know what she is talking about, they act as if they are interested . . . they make remarks when she is gone.

At other times they practiced *simultaneous* duplicity by showing interest and serious engagement to the troublemaker's face while expressing detachment and sarcasm to one another through furtive glances, gestures, and double entendres (Lemert, 1962:8).

Those employees who she is not facing will make distorted faces and roll their eyes around to reaffirm the fact that she is a little slow. All the time this occurs Susan is totally oblivious to it, or at least she pretends to be.

In one fraternity, members devised a specific hand gesture (described as "wing flapping") which they displayed for one another when interacting with a troublemaker they called "the bird."

Members occasionally rationalized their duplicity by describing the troublemaker as a self-absorbed and "dense" person, whose lack of

---

[5] Jefferson and Lee (1980) characterize some of the detailed ways in which participants in ordinary conversations head off "troubles talk" and transform it to "business as usual." Such procedures are much more varied and intricate than can adequately be described by such phrases as "changing the subject."

orientation to others provided ample opportunity for their play:

> People speak sarcastically to him, and Joe, so wrapped up in himself, believes what they are saying and hears only what he wants to hear.

Screening

Jackson (1954:572) reported that alcoholics' wives attempted to manage their husbands' heavy drinking by hiding or emptying liquor bottles in the house and curtailing their husbands' funds. One student described a similar practice used by friends of a person who they feared had suicidal tendencies. They systematically removed from the person's environment any objects that could be used to commit suicide.

Screening and monitoring of troublemakers' surroundings also occurred in the interactional realm. A few accounts mentioned attempts to monitor the moods of a troublemaker, and to screen the person's potential interactions on the basis of attributed mood. When one sorority's troublemaker was perceived to be especially volatile, members acted as her covert receptionists by turning away her visitors, explaining that she was not in or was ill. In this case members were concerned not only to control the potential actions of the individual, but also to conceal those actions from others, and by doing so to protect the collective "image" of their sorority from contamination.

Taking Over

A number of accounts mentioned efforts by members to do activities which ordinarily would be done by someone in the troublemaker's social position. Like published accounts of cases in which husbands or mothers take over the household duties of a wife (Sampson *et al.*, 1962), the apartment mates of a troublemaker washed dishes and paid bills for her "as if she wasn't there." A circle of friends insisted on driving the automobile of a man they considered dangerously impulsive. Fraternity members gradually and unofficially took over the duties of their social chairman in fear of the consequences of his erratic actions and inappropriate attire. Taking over sometimes included such intimate personal functions as grooming and dressing, as when the spouse of a drunk diligently prepared her husband for necessary public appearances.

Orienting to Local Prospects of Normality

Yarrow *et al.* (1955) mention that wives of mental patients sustained efforts to live with their husbands by treating interludes between episodes as the beginnings of "recovery" rather than as periods of calm before the inevitable storms. By keeping tabs on the latest developments in the troublemaker's behavior, members were often able to determine when it was "safe" to treat the troublemaker as a "normal" person. This method was not always as unrealistic as one would be led to believe from Yarrow *et al.* (1955). Since most troublemakers were viewed as persons whose difficulties, though inherent, were intermittent, living with them required knowing what to expect in the immediate interactional future:

> I have observed the occasion when a friend at the fraternity house entered the television room and remained in the rear of the room, totally quiet, watching Danny, waiting for a signal telling him how to act. When Danny turned and spoke to him in a friendly, jovial manner, the young man enthusiastically pulled his chair up to sit next to Danny and began speaking freely.

Members described many troublemakers as persons with likeable and even admirable qualities, whose friendship was valued during their "good times." When a member anticipated an encounter with a troublemaker, he or she wanted most of all to avoid touching off a "bad scene." The local culture of gossip surrounding a troublemaker tended to facilitate such an aim by providing a running file on the current state of his or her moods. By using the latest news members could decide when to avoid encounters and when they could approach the troublemaker without undue wariness.

Practical Jokes and Retaliations

Although direct expressions of hostility toward troublemakers were rarely mentioned, it is possible that they occurred more frequently than was admitted. Practical jokes and other forms of retaliation were designed not to reveal their authors. The troublemaker would be "clued in" that *somebody* despised him or was otherwise "out to get" him, but he would be left to imagine just who it was. Some jokes were particularly cruel, and were aimed at the troublemaker's particular vulnerabilities. A member of a touring rock and roll band was known to have difficulty forming relationships with women:

They would get girls to call his room and make dates they would never keep. Apparently, the spotlight operator was the author of a series of hot love letters of a mythical girl who was following Moog [a pseudonym for the troublemaker] from town to town and would soon appear in his bedroom. The crew must have been laughing their heads off for days. Moog was reading the letters out loud in the dressing room.

Influencing the Reaction to the Troublemaker

A group of practices, instead of focusing solely on the troublemaker's interactional behavior, attempted to control others' *reactions to* and *interpretations of* that behavior. These accommodations recognized that there could be serious consequences in the reactions of outsiders—non-members—to the troublemaker. Such practices included efforts by members to control the reactions of persons outside the group; and to control assessments not only of the individual troublemaker, but of the group as well. The responsibilities for, and social consequences of, the individual's behavior were thus adopted by members as a collective project.

Turning the Troublemaker into a Notorious Character

In stories to outsiders as well as others in the group, members were sometimes able to turn the troublemaker into a fascinating and almost admirable character. A classic case was the fraternity "animal." Although litanies of crude, offensive, and assaultive actions were recounted, the character's antics were also portrayed with evident delight. Such descriptions incorporated elements of heroism, the prowess of the brawler, or the fearlessness and outrageousness of a prankster. In one case a student reported that the fraternity troublemaker, nicknamed "the deviant," was supported and encouraged by a minority faction who claimed to an outsider that he was merely "a little wild," and that nothing was wrong with him. This faction seemed unembarrassed by, and perhaps a bit proud of, the troublemaker's "animal" qualities that others might ascribe to the fraternity as well. The

quasi-heroic or comical repute of the troublemaker did not overshadow many members' distaste for the disruptions, but it did constitute a supportive moral counterpoint.

Shadowing

In one instance a group of students living in a dorm arranged covertly to escort their troublemaker on his frequent trips to local bars. He had a reputation for drinking more than his capacity and then challenging all comers to fights. To inhibit such adventures members of the group volunteered to accompany him under various pretexts, and to quell any disputes he precipitated during the drinking sessions. In the case of the member of the rock and roll band, other members chaperoned him during interviews with media critics. When he said something potentially offensive, his chaperon attempted to turn his statement into a joke. Another account described efforts by a group to spy on a member who they believed was likely to do something rash or violent.

Advance Notices

As Lemert (1962) points out, members often build a legacy of apocryphal stories about their troublemaker. Stories told by one member to another about the troublemaker's latest antics provided a common source of entertainment, and perhaps solidarity. Some members admitted that they could not imagine what they would talk about with one another if not the troublemaker's behavior:

The highlight of the day is hearing the latest story about Joanie.

Such gleeful renditions helped to prepare non-members for first encounters with the troublemaker.

A few students mentioned that the troublemakers they studied appeared normal or even charming during initial encounters, but that members soon warned them to be careful about getting involved with the person. Subsequent experience confirmed the warnings, although it was difficult to discern whether this was a result of their accuracy or of the wariness they engendered.

Members of a group that included a persistently troublesome character "apologized for him beforehand'' to persons who shortly would be doing business with him. They also warned women he approached that he was "a jerk." In addition to preparing such persons for upcoming encounters, the apologies and warnings carried the tacit claim that "we're not like him." This mitigated any potential contamination of the group's moral reputation.

Hiding and Diluting the Troublemaker

Some fraternities and sororities institutionalized a "station" for hiding troublemakers during parties and teas where new members were recruited. Troublemakers were assigned out-of-the-way positions in social gatherings and, in some cases, were accompanied at all times by other members whose job it was to cut off the troublemaker's interaction with prospective members.

The methods used for hiding and diluting were especially artful when they included pretexts to conceal from the troublemakers that their role had been diminished. The troublemaker in the rock and roll band was said to embarrass other members with "distasteful ego tripping" on stage during public concerts. Such "ego trips" were characterized by loud and "awful" playing on his instrument and extravagant posturing in attempts to draw the audience's attention to himself. These displays were countered by the sound and light men in the crew.

On those nights the sound man would turn up the monitors on stage so Moog sounded loud to himself and would turn down Moog in the [concert] hall and on the radio.

Simultaneously, the lighting director would "bathe him in darkness" by dimming the spotlights on him. These practices, in effect, technically created a delusional experience for the troublemaker. They produced a systematic distortion of his perception of the world and simultaneously diminished his public place in that world.

Covering for/Covering up

Friends and intimates sometimes went to great lengths to smooth over the damages and insults done to others by the troublemaker. The husband of a "crazy woman" monitored his wife's offenses during her "episodes" and followed in the wake of the destruction with

apologies and sometimes monetary reparations to offended neighbors. Similar efforts at restoring normality also occurred in immediate interactional contexts:

Before she will even tell you her name, she is telling you how one day she was hitchhiking and was gang raped by the five men who picked her up. This caused so many problems for her that she ended up in a mental hospital and is now a lesbian. The look on people's faces is complete shock. . . . Those hearing this story for the first time will sit in shock as if in a catatonic stupor, with wide eyes and their mouths dropped open, absolutely speechless. Someone who has already heard this story will break the silence by continuing with the previous conversation, . . . putting it on extinction by ignoring it as if she never said anything.

Members sometimes conspired, ostensibly on behalf of the troublemaker, to prevent the relevant authorities from detecting the existence and extent of the troubles. One group of girls in a freshman dorm deliberately lied to hide the fact that one of their members was having great difficulty and, in their estimation, was potentially suicidal. When her parents asked how she was doing the students responded that she was doing "fine." Members tried to contain her problems and to create a "blockade" around any appearances of her problems that might attract the attentions of university authorities. Once underway, such coverups gained momentum, since the prospect of exposure increasingly threatened to make members culpable for not bringing the matter to the attention of remedial agents.

Discussion

A prevailing theme in the students' accounts of accommodation practices was the avoidance of confrontation. They described confrontation as potentially "unpleasant," to be avoided even when considerable damage and hardship had been suffered:

When students' money began disappearing from their rooms, we had a group meeting to discuss our mode of intervention. Although we all believed Chris was responsible, we did not confront her. Instead, we simply decided to make sure we locked our bedroom doors when not in our rooms.

In general, a number of reasons for avoiding confrontation were given, including the anticipation of denial by the troublemaker, fear that the troublemaker would create a "bad scene," and the belief that confrontation would make no difference in the long run.

Less direct methods were used to communicate the group's opinions to the troublemaker. Instead of telling the troublemaker in so many words, members employed a peculiar sort of gamesmanship. Systematic "leaks" were used to *barely* and *ambiguously* expose the duplicity and conspiracy, so that the troublemaker would realize something was going on, but would be unable or unwilling to accuse specific offenders. Duplicitous gestures or comments which operated *just* on the fringes of the troublemaker's awareness produced maximum impact.

The successful operation of these practices relied, in part, on the troublemaker's complicity in the conspiracy of silence.

Once I was in the room next door to her and the girls were imitating her. Two minutes later she walked in asking [us] to be quiet because she was trying to sleep. I thought I was going to die. Obviously Tammy realized what was going on as the walls are extremely thin; however, Tammy seems to be conspiring on the side of her "friends" to prevent any confrontation of the actual situation.

Hostilities were therefore expressed, and retaliations achieved, often with rather specific reference to the particular offenses and their presumed source. At the same time, they remained "submerged" in a peculiar way. They were not submerged in a psychological "unconscious," since both members and troublemakers were aware of what was going on. Instead, both members and troublemakers made every effort to assure that the trouble did not disturb the overtly normal interaction. "Business as usual" was preserved at the cost of keeping secret deep hostilities within the organization.

A few accounts did mention instances of explicit confrontation. However, members claimed that such confrontations did not alter troublemakers' subsequent behaviors; instead they resulted in misunderstandings or were received by troublemakers in a defensive or unresponsive way.

Efforts to remove troublemakers from organi-zations were rarely described, though members of the rock band eventually expelled their troublemaker after he hired a lawyer to redress his grievances against the group. In another case a fraternity "de-pledged" a new recruit who had not yet been fully initiated. In no other case was an established member removed, although numerous dramatic offenses were recounted and widespread dislike for troublemakers was commonly reported.

Taken as a whole, accommodation practices reveal *the organizational construction of the normal individual*. The individual is relied upon both in commonsense reasoning and social theory as a source of compliance with the standards of the larger society. The normal individual successfully adapts to the constraints imposed by social structure. Troublemakers were viewed as persons who, for various reasons, could not be given full *responsibility* for maintaining normality. Instead, the burden of maintaining the individual's normal behavior and appearance was taken up by others. Troublemakers were not overtly sanctioned; instead, they were shaped and guided through the superficial performances of ordinary action. Their integration into society was not a cumulative mastery learned "from inside"; it was a constant project executed by others from the "outside."

Accommodation practices allow us to glimpse the project of the self as a practical struggle. A semblance of normal individuality for troublemakers was a carefully constructed artifact produced by members. When the responsibility for normality is assumed as an individual birthright, it appears inevitable that conformity or defiance proceeds "from inside" the individual, just as it appears in commonsense that gender is a natural inheritance. In the latter instance, a transsexual's unusual experience indicates the extent to which the ordinary behavior and appearance of being female is detachable from the individual's birthright, and can be explicated as a practical accomplishment (Garfinkel, 1967). Similarly, for the organizational colleagues of a troublemaker, the elements of normal individuality cannot be relied upon, but must be achieved through deliberate practice. Members together performed the work of minding the troublemaker's business, of guiding the troublemaker through normal interactional pathways, and of filling the responsibilities and appearances associated with the troublemaker's presence for others.[6]

Of course, such projects were less than successful; members complained of the undue burden, disruptions occurred despite their efforts, and the troublemaker was provided with a diminished self and a distorted reality. Perhaps all would have been better off had they "left the self inside where it belongs." Nevertheless, accommodation practices enable us to see the extent to which the division between self and other is permeable, and subject to negotiation and manipulation. We can see that individual responsibility for the conduct of affairs is separable from the actual performance of those affairs. Troublemakers were manipulated into a tenuous conformity by members who relied upon the fact that such conformity would be attributed to the individual's responsibility. The individual was thus reduced to the subject of an informal code of responsibility, separable from any substantive source of action (Goffman, 1969:357).

Implications

Previous research on accommodation practices in the societal reaction tradition has suggested that the individual symptoms of disorder can be explained in reference to social organization (Goffman, 1969; Lemert, 1962). I have not been concerned with how individual *disorder* is generated by social reaction. My interest instead has been to investigate how individual *normality* is socially constructed. This issue has both practical and theoretical consequences.

On a practical level, given the current institutional emphasis on the "community care" of mental disorders, it should be useful to know as much as possible about ordinary "institutions" of accommodation. The descriptive inventory provided in this study goes a small distance in that direction. Based on this study, it appears that accommodation practices are analogous, on a social level, to individual "defense mechanisms" (Henry, 1972:49). What remains to be

determined is whether some of the practices are more effective than others; whether, like Freudian defense mechanisms, some can be viewed as pathological whereas others are relatively effective. It also remains to be seen whether accommodation practices can be improved by instruction, and operated in a humane and insightful fashion.

On a theoretical level, the analysis of accommodation practices enables us to consider the self as a social and normative construct as much as an internal province of operations. This is more than to say that the self is an *attribution* by others, since accommodation includes concrete actions to manipulate and maintain a semblance of normal selfhood on behalf of a troublemaker. In psychology and social-psychology, an inscrutable ego is normally required as a locus of operations for directing behavior and impression management (the latter by reacting to the reactions of others). Here we see both behavior and impression management being directed by overt and covert operations external to the individual. By implication, the individual's domain of action and responsibility is only provisionally established if it can be taken over by others.

Accommodation practices integrate the troublemaker into society, while requiring minimal initiative from the troublemaker. At the extreme, the troublemaker can be turned into a puppet whose behavior (especially in its more public consequences) is divorced from internal control. The individual is never altogether out of the picture, since at every turn individual responsibility is attributed. The puppet is given life (a life not of its making) through the conventional appearance of its overt actions. Instead of an ego projecting significant symbols outward, we find the surface of an individual being managed and shaped by communal activity, with or without the individual's knowledge and compliance. Whether this applies more generally than to the pathological circumstances described here remains to be established, but my research suggests that the individual self is a moral and attributional construct not to be confused with the theoretical requirements of social action.

---

[6]My discussion of the social production of the individual is heavily indebted to Pollner and Wikler's (1981) treatment of that theme. Pollner and Wikler (1981) discuss a family's efforts to construct the appearance of normality for their (officially diagnosed) profoundly retarded daughter. Not only does *normality* become a communal project in these cases, *abnormality* becomes shared as well. One student in my research described an alcoholic's family as "three characters revolving around a central theme—alcoholism." The preoccupation with alcohol was shared along with the *denial* that the man's drinking was an official problem.

REFERENCES

Bittner, Egon. 1967. "Police Discretion in Emergency Apprehension of Mentally Ill Persons." *Social Problems,* 14(3):278–292.

Critchley, MacDonald. 1971. *The Parietal Lobes.* New York: Hafner Publishing Co.

Cumming, Elaine and John Cumming. 1957. *Closed Ranks.* Cambridge, MA: Harvard University Press.

Emerson, Robert and Sheldon Messinger. 1977. "The Micro-politics of Trouble." *Social Problems,* 25(2):121–134.

Freeman, Howard and Ozzie Simmons. 1958. "Mental Patients in the Community: Family Settings and Performance Levels." *American Sociological Review,* 23(2):147–154.

Garfinkel, Harold. 1967. *Studies in Ethnomethodology.* Englewood Cliffs, NJ: Prentice-Hall.

Garfinkel, Harold and Harvey Sacks. 1970. "Formal Structures of Practical Actions." In John McKinney and Edward Tiryakian (eds.), Theoretical Sociology: Perspectives and Development. New York: Appleton-Century Crofts, pp. 337–366.

Goffman, Erving. 1961. *Asylums.* Garden City, NY: Doubleday.

———. 1969. "The Insanity of Place." *Psychiatry,* 32(4):352–388.

Henry, Jules. 1972. *Pathways to Madness.* New York: Random House.

Hollingshead, August and Frederick Redlich. 1958. *Social Class and Mental Illness.* New York: Wiley.

Jackson, Joan. 1954. "The Adjustment of the Family to the Crisis of Alcoholism." *Quarterly Journal of Studies on Alcohol,* 15(4):562–586.

Jefferson, Gail and John Lee. 1980. "The Analysis of Conversations in Which Anxieties and Troubles Are Expressed." Unpublished report for the Social Science Research Counsel, University of Manchester, England.

Lemert, Edwin. 1962. "Paranoia and the Dynamics of Exclusion." *Sociometry,* 25(1):2–20.

Mayo, Clara, Ronald Havelock, and Diane Lear Simpson. 1971. "Attitudes Towards Mental Illness among Psychiatric Patients and Their Wives." *Journal of Clinical Psychology,* 27(1):128–132.

Myers, Jerome and Bertram Roberts. 1959. *Family and Class Dynamics.* New York: Wiley.

Pollner, Melvin and Lynn Wikler. 1981. "The Social Construction of Unreality: A Case Study of the Practices of Family Sham and Delusion." Unpublished paper, Department of Sociology, University of California, Los Angeles.

Sacks, Harvey, Emanuel Schegloff, and Gail Jefferson. 1974. "A Simplest Systematics for the Organization of Turn Taking in Conversation." *Language,* 50(4):696–735.

Sacks, Oliver. 1974. *Awakenings.* New York: Doubleday.

Sampson, Harold, Sheldon Messinger, and Robert Towne. 1962. "Family Processes and Becoming a Mental Patient." *American Journal of Sociology,* 68(1):88–98.

Spitzer, Stephan, Patricia Morgan, and Robert Swanson. 1971. "Determinants of the Psychiatric Patient Career: Family Reaction Patterns and Social Work Intervention." *Social Service Review,* 45(1):74–85.

Srole, Leo, Thomas Langer, Stanley Michael, Marvin Opler, and Thomas Rennie. 1962. *Mental Health in the Metropolis: The Midtown Manhattan Study.* New York: McGraw-Hill.

Wulbert, Roland. n.d. "Second Thoughts about Commonplaces." Unpublished paper, Department of Sociology, Columbia University (circa, 1974).

Yarrow, Marian, Charlotte Schwartz, Harriet Murphy, and Leila Deasy. 1955. "The Psychological Meaning of Mental Illness in the Family." *Journal of Social Issues,* 11(4):12–24.

The Adjustment of the Family to the Crisis of Alcoholism   JOAN K. JACKSON

. . . Over a 3-year period, the present investigator has been an active participant in the Alcoholics Anonymous Auxiliary in Seattle. This group is composed partly of women whose husbands are or were members of Alcoholics Anonymous, and partly of women whose husbands are excessive drinkers but have never contacted Alcoholics Anonymous. At a typical meeting one fifth would be the wives of Alcoholics Anonymous members who have been sober for some time; the husbands of another fifth would have recently joined the fellowship; the remainder would be equally divided between those whose husbands were "on and off" the Alcoholics Anonymous program and those whose husbands had as yet not had any contact with Alcoholics Anonymous.

At least an hour and a half of each formal meeting of this group is taken up with a frank discussion of the current family problems of the members. As in other meetings of Alcoholics Anonymous the questions are posed by describing the situation which gives rise to the problem and the answers are a narration of the personal experiences of other wives who have had a similar problem, rather than direct advice. Verbatim shorthand notes have been taken of all discussions, at the request of the group, who also make use of the notes for the group's purposes. Informal contact has been maintained with past and present members. In the past three years 50 women have been members of this group.

The families represented by these women are at present in many different stages of adjustment and have passed through several stages during the past few years. The continuous contact over a prolonged period permits generalizations about processes and changes in family adjustments.

In addition, in connection with research on hospitalized alcoholics, many of their wives have been interviewed. The interviews with the hospitalized alcoholics, as with male members of Alcoholics Anonymous, have also provided information on family interactions. Further information has been derived from another group

of wives, not connected with Alcoholics Anonymous, and from probation officers, social workers and court officials.

The following presentation is limited insofar as it deals only with families seeking help for the alcoholism of the husband. Other families are known to have solved the problem through divorce, often without having attempted to help the alcoholic member first. Others never seek help and never separate. There were no marked differences between the two groups seeking help, one through the hospital and one through the A.A. Auxiliary. The wives of hospitalized alcoholics gave a history of the family crisis similar to that given by women in the Auxiliary.

A second limitation is that only the families of male alcoholics are dealt with. It is recognized that the findings cannot be generalized to the families of alcoholic women without further research. Due to differences between men and women in their roles in the family as well as in the pattern of drinking, it would be expected that male and female alcoholics would in some ways have a different effect on family structure and function.

A third limitation is imposed for the sake of clarity and brevity: only the accounts of the wives of their attempts to stabilize their family adjustments will be dealt with. For any complete picture, the view of the alcoholic husband would also have to be included.

It must be emphasized that this paper deals with the definitions of the family situations by the wives, rather than with the actual situation. It has been noted that frequently wife and husband do not agree on what has occurred. The degree to which the definition of the situation by the wife or husband correlates with actual behavior is a question which must be left for further research.

The families represented in this study are from the middle and lower classes. The occupations of the husbands prior to excessive drinking include small business owners, salesmen, business executives, skilled and semiskilled workers. Prior to marriage the wives have been nurses,

Reprinted from *Quarterly Journal of Studies on Alcohol,* Vol. 15 (December, 1954), pp. 564–586.

From the Department of Psychiatry, University of Washington School of Medicine, Seattle, Washington. This report is part of an alcoholism project at the University of Washington which has been supported by the State of Washington Research Fund under Initiative 171.

secretaries, teachers, saleswomen, cooks or waitresses. The economic status of the childhood families of these husbands and wives ranged from very wealthy to very poor.

Method

From the records of discussions of the Alcoholics Anonymous Auxiliary, the statements of each wife were extracted and arranged in a time sequence. Notes on informal contacts were added at the point in the sequence where they occurred. The interviews with the wives of hospitalized alcoholics were similarly treated. These working records on individual families were then examined for uniformities of behavior and for regularities in changes over time.

The similarities in the process of adjustment to an alcoholic family member are presented here as stages of variable duration. It should be stressed that only the similarities are dealt with. Although the wives have shared the patterns dealt with here, there have been marked differences in the length of time between stages, in the number of stages passed through up to the present time, and in the relative importance to the family constellation of any one type of behavior. For example, all admitted nagging but the amount of nagging was variable.

When the report of this analysis was completed it was read before a meeting of the Auxiliary with a request for correction of any errors in fact or interpretation. Corrections could be presented either anonymously or publicly from the floor. Only one correction was suggested and has been incorporated. The investigator is convinced that her relationship with the group is such that there would be no reticence about offering corrections. Throughout her contact with this group her role has been that of one who is being taught, very similar to the role of the new member. The over-all response of the group to the presentation indicated that the members individually felt that they had been portrayed accurately.

The sense of having similar problems and similar experiences is indicated also in the reactions of new members to the Auxiliary's summarization of the notes of their discussions. Copies of these summaries are given to new members, who commonly state that they find it a relief to see that their problems are far from unique and that there are methods which successfully overcome them.

Statement of the Problem

For purposes of this presentation, the family is seen as involved in a cumulative crisis. All family members behave in a manner which they hope will resolve the crisis and permit a return to stability. Each member's action is influenced by his previous personality structure, by his previous role and status in the family group, and by the history of the crisis and its effects on his personality, roles and status up to that point. Action is also influenced by the past effectiveness of that particular action as a means of social control before and during the crisis. The behavior of family members in each phase of the crisis contributes to the form which the crisis takes in the following stages and sets limits on possible behavior in subsequent stages.

Family members are influenced, in addition, by the cultural definitions of alcoholism as evidence of weakness, inadequacy or sinfulness; by the cultural prescriptions for the roles of family members; and by the cultural values of family solidarity, sanctity and self-sufficiency. Alcoholism in the family poses a situation defined by the culture as shameful but for the handling of which there are no prescriptions which are effective or which permit direct action not in conflict with other cultural prescriptions. While in crises such as illness or death the family members can draw on cultural definitions of appropriate behavior for procedures which will terminate the crisis, this is not the case with alcoholism in the family. The cultural view has been that alcoholism is shameful and should not occur. Only recently has any information been offered to guide families in their behavior toward their alcoholic member and, as yet, this information resides more in technical journals than in the media of mass communication. Thus, in facing alcoholism, the family is in an unstructured situation and must find the techniques for handling it through trial and error.

Stages in Family Adjustment to an Alcoholic Member

The Beginning of the Marriage. At the time marriage was considered, the drinking of most of the men was within socially acceptable limits. In a few cases the men were already alcoholics but managed to hide this from their fiancées. They drank only moderately or not at all when on dates and often avoided friends and relatives who might expose their excessive drinking. The relatives and friends who were introduced to the fiancée were those who had hopes that "marriage would straighten him out" and thus said nothing about the drinking. In a small number of cases the men spoke with their fiancées of their alcoholism. The women had no conception of what alcoholism meant, other than that it involved more than the usual frequency of drinking, and they entered the marriage with little more preparation than if they had known nothing about it.

Stage 1. Incidents of excessive drinking begin and, although they are sporadic, place strains on the husband–wife interaction. In attempts to minimize drinking, problems in marital adjustment not related to the drinking are avoided.

Stage 2. Social isolation of the family begins as incidents of excessive drinking multiply. The increasing isolation magnifies the importance of family interactions and events. Behavior and thought become drinking-centered. Husband–wife adjustment deteriorates and tension rises. The wife begins to feel self-pity and to lose her self-confidence as her behavior fails to stabilize her husband's drinking. There is an attempt still to maintain the original family structure, which is disrupted anew with each episode of drinking, and as a result the children begin to show emotional disturbance.

Stage 3. The family gives up attempts to control the drinking and begins to behave in a manner geared to relieve tension rather than achieve long-term ends. The disturbance of the children becomes more marked. There is no longer an attempt to support the alcoholic in his roles as husband and father. The wife begins to worry about her own sanity and about her inability to make decisions or act to change the situation.

Stage 4. The wife takes over control of the family and the husband is seen as a recalcitrant child. Pity and strong protective feelings largely replace the earlier resentment and hostility. The family becomes more stable and organized in a manner to minimize the disruptive behavior of the husband. The self-confidence of the wife begins to be rebuilt.

Stage 5. The wife separates from her husband if she can resolve the problems and conflicts surrounding this action.

Stage 6. The wife and children reorganize as a family without the husband.

Stage 7. The husband achieves sobriety and the family, which had become organized around an alcoholic husband, reorganizes to include a sober father and experiences problems in reinstating him in his former roles.

Stage 1. Attempts to Deny the Problem

Usually the first experience with drinking as a problem arises in a social situation. The husband drinks in a manner which is inappropriate to the social setting and the expectations of others present. The wife feels embarrassed on the first occasion and humiliated as it occurs more frequently. After several such incidents she and her husband talk over his behavior. The husband either formulates an explanation for the episode and assures her that such behavior will not occur again; or he refuses to discuss it at all. For a time afterward he drinks appropriately and drinking seems to be a problem no longer. The wife looks back on the incidents and feels that she has exaggerated them, feels ashamed of herself for her disloyalty and for her behavior. The husband, in evaluating the incident, feels shame also and vows such episodes will not recur. As a result, both husband and wife attempt to make it up to the other and, for a time, try to play their conceptions of the ideal husband and wife roles, minimizing or avoiding other difficulties which arise in the marriage. They thus create the illusion of a "perfect" marriage.

Eventually another inappropriate drinking episode occurs and the pattern is repeated. The wife worries but takes action only in the situations in which inappropriate drinking occurs, as each long intervening period of acceptable drinking behavior convinces her that a recurrence is unlikely. As time goes on, in attempting to cope with individual episodes, she runs the gamut of possible trial and error behaviors, learning that none is permanently effective.

If she speaks to other people about her husband's drinking, she is usually assured that there is no need for concern, that her husband can control his drinking and that her fears are exaggerated. Some friends possibly admit that his drinking is too heavy and give advice on how they handled similar situations with their husbands. These friends convince her that her problem will be solved as soon as she hits upon the right formula for dealing with her husband's drinking.

During this stage the husband–wife interaction is in no way "abnormal." In a society in which a large proportion of the men drink, most wives have at some time had occasion to be concerned, even though only briefly, with an episode of drinking which they considered inappropriate (1). In a society in which the status of the family depends on that of the husband, the wife feels threatened by any behavior on his part which might lower it. Inappropriate drinking is regarded by her as a threat to the family's reputation and standing in the community. The wife attempts to exert control and often finds herself blocked by the sacredness of drinking behavior to men in America. Drinking is a private matter and not any business of the wife's. On the whole, a man reacts to his wife's suggestion that he has not adequately controlled his drinking with resentment, rebelliousness and a display of emotion which makes rational discussion difficult. The type of husband–wife interaction outlined in this stage has occurred in many American families in which the husband never became an excessive drinker.

Stage 2. Attempts to Eliminate the Problem

Stage 2 begins when the family experiences social isolation because of the husband's drinking. Invitations to the homes of friends become less frequent. When the couple does visit friends, drinks are not served or are limited, thus emphasizing the reason for exclusion from other social activities of the friendship group. Discussions of drinking begin to be side-stepped awkwardly by friends, the wife and the husband.

By this time the periods of socially acceptable drinking are becoming shorter. The wife, fearing that the full extent of her husband's drinking will become known, begins to withdraw from social participation, hoping to reduce the visibility of his behavior, and thus the threat to family status.

Isolation is further intensified because the family usually acts in accordance with the cultural dictate that it should be self-sufficient and manage to resolve its own problems without recourse to outside aid. Any experiences which they have had with well-meaning outsiders, usually relatives, have tended to strengthen this conviction. The husband has defined such relatives as interfering and the situation has deteriorated rather than improved.

With increasing isolation, the family members begin to lose perspective on their interaction and on their problems. Thrown into closer contact with one another as outside contacts diminish,

the behavior of each member assumes exaggerated importance. The drinking behavior becomes the focus of anxiety. Gradually all family difficulties become attributed to it. (For example, the mother who is cross with her children will feel that, if her husband had not been drinking, she would not have been so tense and would not have been angry.) The fear that the full extent of drinking may be discovered mounts steadily; the conceptualization of the consequences of such a discovery becomes increasingly vague and, as a result, more anxiety-provoking. The family feels different from others and alone with its shameful secret.

Attempts to cover up increase. The employer who calls to inquire about the husband's absence from work is given excuses. The wife is afraid to face the consequences of loss of the husband's pay check in addition to her other concerns. Questions from the children are evaded or they are told that their father is ill. The wife lives in terror of the day when the children will be told by others of the nature of the "illness." She is also afraid that the children may describe their father's symptoms to teachers or neighbors. Still feeling that the family must solve its own problems, she keeps her troubles to herself and hesitates to seek outside help. If her husband beats her, she will bear it rather than call in the police. (Indeed, often she has no idea that this is even a possibility.) Her increased isolation has left her without the advice of others as to sources of help in the community. If she knows of them, an agency contact means to her an admission of the complete failure of her family as an independent unit. For the middle-class woman particularly, recourse to social agencies and law-enforcement agencies means a terrifying admission of loss of status.

During this stage, husband and wife are drawing further apart. Each feels resentful of the behavior of the other. When this resentment is expressed, further drinking occurs. When it is not, tension mounts and the next drinking episode is that much more destructive of family relationships. The reasons for drinking are explored frantically. Both husband and wife feel that if only they could discover the reason, all members of the family could gear their behavior to making drinking unnecessary. The discussions become increasingly unproductive, as it is the husband's growing conviction that his wife does not and cannot understand him.

On her part, the wife begins to feel that she is

a failure, that she has been unable to fulfill the major cultural obligations of a wife to meet her husband's needs. With her increasing isolation, her sense of worth derives almost entirely from her roles as wife and mother. Each failure to help her husband gnaws away at her sense of adequacy as a person.

Periods of sobriety or socially acceptable drinking still occur. These periods keep the wife from making a permanent or stable adjustment. During them her husband, in his guilt, treats her like a queen. His behavior renews her hope and rekindles positive feelings toward him. Her sense of worth is bolstered temporarily and she grasps desperately at her husband's reassurance that she is really a fine person and not a failure and an unlovable shrew. The periods of sobriety also keep her family from facing the inability of the husband to control his drinking. The inaccuracies of the cultural stereotype of the alcoholic—particularly that he is in a constant state of inebriation—also contribute to the family's rejection of the idea of alcoholism, as the husband seems to demonstrate from time to time that he can control his drinking.

Family efforts to control the husband become desperate. There are no culturally prescribed behavior patterns for handling such a situation and the family is forced to evolve its own techniques. Many different types of behavior are tried but none brings consistent results; there seems to be no way of predicting the consequences of any action that may be taken. All attempts to stabilize or structure the situation to permit consistent behavior fail. Threats of leaving, hiding his liquor away, emptying the bottles down the drain, curtailing his money, are tried in rapid succession, but none is effective. Less punitive methods, as discussing the situation when he is sober, babying him during hangovers, and trying to drink with him to keep him in the home, are attempted and fail. All behavior becomes oriented around the drinking, and the thought of family members becomes obsessive on this subject. As no action seems to be successful in achieving its goal, the wife persists in trial-and-error behavior with mounting frustration. Long-term goals recede into the background and become secondary to just keeping the husband from drinking today.

There is still an attempt to maintain the illusion of husband–wife–children roles. When father is sober, the children are expected to give him respect and obedience. The wife also defers to him in his role as head of the household. Each drinking event thus disrupts family functioning anew. The children begin to show emotional disturbances as a result of the inconsistencies of parental behavior. During periods when the husband is drinking the wife tries to shield them from the knowledge and effects of his behavior, at the same time drawing them closer to herself and deriving emotional support from them. In sober periods, the father tries to regain their favor. Due to experiencing directly only pleasant interactions with their father, considerable affection is often felt for him by the children. This affection becomes increasingly difficult for the isolated wife to tolerate, and an additional source of conflict. She feels that she needs and deserves the love and support of her children and, at the same time, she feels it important to maintain the children's picture of their father. She counts on the husband's affection for the children to motivate a cessation of drinking as he comes to realize the effects of his behavior on them.

In this stage, self-pity begins to be felt by the wife, if it has not entered previously. It continues in various degrees throughout the succeeding stages. In an attempt to handle her deepening sense of inadequacy, the wife often tries to convince herself that she is right and her husband wrong, and this also continues through the following stages. At this point the wife often resembles what Whalen (2) describes as "The Sufferer."

Stage 3. Disorganization

The wife begins to adopt a "What's the use?" attitude and to accept her husband's drinking as a problem likely to be permanent. Attempts to understand one another become less frequent. Sober periods still engender hope, but hope qualified by skepticism; they bring about a lessening of anxiety and this is defined as happiness.

By this time some customary patterns of husband–wife–children interaction have evolved. Techniques which have had some effectiveness in controlling the husband in the past or in relieving pent-up frustration are used by the wife. She nags, berates or retreats into silence. Husband and wife are both on the alert, the wife watching for increasing irritability and restlessness which mean a recurrence of drinking, and the husband for veiled aspersions on his behavior or character.

The children are increasingly torn in their loyalties as they become tools in the struggle between mother and father. If the children are at an age of comprehension, they have usually learned the true nature of their family situation, either from outsiders or from their mother, who has given up attempts to bolster her husband's position as father. The children are often bewildered, but questioning their parents brings no satisfactory answers as the parents themselves do not understand what is happening. Some children become terrified; some have increasing behavior problems within and outside the home; others seem on the surface to accept the situation calmly.[1]

During periods of the husband's drinking, the hostility, resentment and frustrations felt by the couple are allowed expression. Both may resort to violence—the wife in self-defense or because she can find no other outlet for her feelings. In those cases in which the wife retaliates to violence in kind, she feels a mixture of relief and intense shame at having deviated so far from what she conceives to be "the behavior of a normal woman."

When the wife looks at her present behavior, she worries about her "normality." In comparing the person she was in the early years of her marriage with the person she has become, she is frightened. She finds herself nagging and unable to control herself. She resolves to stand up to her husband when he is belligerent but instead finds herself cringing in terror and then despises herself for her lack of courage. If she retaliates with violence, she is filled with self-loathing at behaving in an "unwomanly" manner. She finds herself compulsively searching for bottles, knowing full well that finding them will change nothing, and is worried because she engages in such senseless behavior. She worries about her inability to take constructive action of any kind. She is confused about where her loyalty lies, whether with her husband or her children. She feels she is a failure as a wife, mother and person. She believes she should be strong in the face of adversity and instead feels herself weak.

The wife begins to find herself avoiding sexual contact with her husband when he has been drinking. Sex under these circumstances, she feels, is sex for its own sake rather than an indication of affection for her. Her husband's lack of consideration of her needs to be satisfied leaves her feeling frustrated. The lack of sexual responsiveness reflects her emotional withdrawal from him in other areas of family life. Her husband, on his part, feels frustrated and rejected; he accuses her of frigidity and this adds to her concern about her adequacy as a woman.[2]

By this time the opening wedge has been inserted into the self-sufficiency of the family. The husband has often been in difficulty with the police and the wife has learned that police protection is available. An emergency has occurred in which the seeking of outside help was the only possible action to take; subsequent calls for aid from outsiders do not require the same degree of urgency before they can be undertaken. However, guilt and a lessening of self-respect and self-confidence accompany this method of resolving emergencies. The husband intensifies these feelings by speaking of the interference of outsiders, or of his night in jail.

In Stage 3 all is chaos. Few problems are met constructively. The husband and wife both feel trapped in an intolerable, unstructured situation which offers no way out. The wife's self-assurance is almost completely gone. She is afraid to take action and afraid to let things remain as they are. Fear is one of the major characteristics of this stage: fear of violence, fear of personality damage to the children, fear for her own sanity, fear that relatives will interfere, and fear that they will not help in an emergency. Added to this, the family feels alone in the world and helpless. The problems, and the behavior of family members in attempting to cope with them, seem so shameful that help from others is unthinkable. They feel that attempts to get help would meet only with rebuff, and that communication of the situation will engender disgust.

At this point the clinical picture which the wife presents is very similar to what Whalen (2) has described as "The Waverer."

---

[1] Some effects of alcoholism of the father on children have been discussed by Newell (3).

[2] It is of interest here that marriage counselors and students of marital adjustment are of the opinion that unhappy marriage results in poor sexual adjustment more often than poor sexual adjustment leads to unhappy marriage. If this proves to be true, it would be expected that most wives of alcoholics would find sex distasteful while their husbands are drinking. The wives of the inactive alcoholics report that their sexual adjustments with their husbands are currently satisfactory; many of those whose husbands are still drinking state that they enjoyed sexual relationships before the alcoholism was established.

Stage 4. Attempts to Reorganize in Spite of the Problem

Stage 4 begins when a crisis occurs which necessitates that action be taken. There may be no money or food in the house; the husband may have been violent to the children; or life on the level of Stage 3 may have become intolerable. At this point some wives leave, thus entering directly into Stage 5.

The wife who passes through Stage 4 usually begins to ease her husband out of his family roles. She assumes husband and father roles. This involves strengthening her role as mother and putting aside her role as wife. She becomes the manager of the home, the discipliner of the children, the decision-maker; she becomes somewhat like Whalen's (2) "Controller." She either ignores her husband as much as possible or treats him as her most recalcitrant child. Techniques are worked out for getting control of his pay check, if there still is one, and money is doled out to her husband on the condition of his good behavior. When he drinks, she threatens to leave him, locks him out of the house, refuses to pay his taxi bills, leaves him in jail overnight rather than pay his bail. Where her obligations to her husband conflict with those to her children, she decides in favor of the latter. As she views her husband increasingly as a child, pity and a sense of being desperately needed by him enter. Her inconsistent behavior toward him deriving from the lack of predictability inherent in the situation up to now, becomes reinforced by her mixed feelings toward him.

In this stage the husband often tries to set his will against hers in decisions about the children. If the children have been permitted to stay with a friend overnight, he may threaten to create a scene unless they return immediately. He may make almost desperate efforts to gain their affection and respect, his behavior ranging from getting them up in the middle of the night to fondle them, to giving them stiff lectures on children's obligations to fathers. Sometimes he will attempt to align the males of the family with him against the females. He may openly express resentment of the children and become belligerent toward them physically or verbally.

Much of the husband's behavior can be conceptualized as resulting from an increasing awareness of his isolation from the other members of the family and their steady withdrawal of respect and affection. It seems to be a desperate effort to regain what he has lost, but without any clear idea of how this can be accomplished—an effort to change a situation in which everyone is seen as against him; and, in reality, this is becoming more and more true. As the wife has taken over control of the family with some degree of success, he feels, and becomes, less and less necessary to the ongoing activity of the family. There are fewer and fewer roles left for him to play. He becomes aware that members of the family enjoy each other's company without him. When he is home he tries to enter this circle of warmth or to smash it. Either way he isolates himself further. He finds that the children discuss with the mother how to manage him and he sees the children acting on the basis of their mother's idea of him. The children refuse to pay attention to his demands: they talk back to him in the same way that they talk back to one another, adding pressure on him to assume the role of just another child. All this leaves him frustrated and, as a result, often aggressive or increasingly absent from home.

The children, on the whole, become more settled in their behavior as the wife takes over the family responsibilities. Decisions are made by her and upheld in the face of their father's attempts to interfere. Participation in activities outside the home is encouraged. Their patterns of interaction with their father are supported by the mother. Whereas in earlier stages the children often felt that there were causal connections between their actions and their father's drinking, they now accept his unpredictability. "Well," says a 6-year-old, "I'll just have to get used to it. I have a drunken father."

The family is more stabilized in one way but in other ways insecurities are multiplied. Pay checks are received less and less regularly. The violence or withdrawal of the father increases. When he is away the wife worries about automobile accidents or injury in fights, which become more and more probable as time passes. The husband may begin to be seriously ill from time to time; his behavior may become quite bizarre. Both of these signs of increasing illness arouse anxiety in the family.

During this stage hopes may rise high for father's "reform" when he begins to verbalize wishes to stop drinking, admits off and on his inability to stop, and sounds desperate for doing something about his drinking. Now may begin the trek to sanitariums for the middle-class alcoholic, to doctors, or to Alcoholics Anonymous. Where just the promise to stop drinking has failed to revive hope, sobriety through outside agencies has the ability to rekindle it brightly. There is the feeling that at last he is "taking really constructive action." In failure the discouragement is deeper. Here another wedge has been inserted into the self-sufficiency of the family.

By this time the wedges are many. The wife, finding she has managed to bring some semblance of order and stability to her family, while not exactly becoming a self-assured person, has regained some sense of worth which grows a little with each crisis she meets successfully. In addition, the very fact of taking action to stabilize the situation brings relief. On some occasion she may be able to approach social agencies for financial help, often during a period when the husband has temporarily deserted or is incarcerated. She may have gone to the family court; she may have consulted a lawyer about getting a restraining order when the husband was in a particularly belligerent state. She has begun to learn her way around among the many agencies which offer help.

Often she has had a talk with an Alcoholics Anonymous member and has begun to look into what is known about alcoholism. If she has attended a few Alcoholics Anonymous meetings, her sense of shame has been greatly alleviated as she finds so many others in the same boat. Her hopes rise as she meets alcoholics who have stopped drinking, and she feels relieved at being able to discuss her problems openly for the first time with an audience which understands fully. She begins to gain perspective on her problem and learns that she herself is involved in what happens to her husband, and that she must change. She exchanges techniques of management with other wives and receives their support in her decisions.

She learns that her husband is ill rather than merely "ornery," and this often serves to quell for the time being thoughts about leaving him which have begun to germinate as she has gained more self-confidence. She learns that help is available but also that her efforts to push him into help are unavailing. She is not only supported in her recently evolved behavior of thinking first of her family, but now this course also emerges from the realm of the unconceptualized and is set in an accepted rationale. She feels more secure in having a reason and a certainty that the group accepts her as "doing the right thing." When she reports deviations from what the group thinks is the "right way," her reasons are understood; she receives solid support but there is also pressure on her to alter her behavior again toward the acceptable. Blaming and self-pity are actively discouraged. In group discussions she still admits to such feelings but learns to recognize them as they arise and to go beyond them to more productive thinking.

How much her altered behavior changes the family situation is uncertain, but it helps her and gives her security from which to venture forth to further actions of a consistent and constructive type, constructive at least from the point of view of keeping her family on as even a keel as possible in the face of the disruptive influence of the husband. With new friends whom she can use as a sounding board for plans, and with her growing acquaintance with the alternatives and possible patterns of behavior, her thinking ceases to be circular and unproductive. Her anxiety about her own sanity is alleviated as she is reassured by others that they have experienced the same concern and that the remedy is to get her own life and her family under better control. As she accomplishes this, the difference in her feelings about herself convinces her that this is so.

Whether or not she has had a contact with wives of Alcoholics Anonymous members or other wives who have been through a similar experience and have emerged successfully, the very fact of taking hold of her situation and gradually making it more manageable adds to her self-confidence. As her husband is less and less able to care for himself or his family, she begins to feel that he needs her and that without her he would be destroyed. Such a feeling makes it difficult for her to think of leaving him. His almost complete social isolation at this point and his cries for help reinforce this conviction of being needed.

The drinking behavior is no longer hidden. Others obviously know about it, and this becomes accepted by the wife and children. Already isolated and insulated against possible rejection, the wife is often surprised to find that she has exaggerated her fears of what would happen were the situation known. However, the unpredictability of her husband's behavior makes her reluctant to form social relationships which could be violently disrupted or to involve others in the possible consequences of his behavior.

Stage 5. Efforts to Escape the Problem

Stage 5 may be the terminal one for the marriage. In this stage the wife separates from her husband. Sometimes the marriage is reestablished after a period of sobriety, when it appears certain that the husband will not drink again. If he does revert to drinking, the marriage is sometimes finally terminated but with less emotional stress than the first time. If the husband deserts, being no longer able to tolerate his lack of status in his family, Stage 6 may be entered abruptly.

The events precipitating the decision to terminate the marriage may be near-catastrophic, as when there is an attempt by the husband to kill the wife or children, or they may appear trivial to outsiders, being only the last straw to an accumulation of years.

The problems in coming to the decision to terminate the marriage cannot be underestimated. Some of these problems derive from emotional conflicts; some are related to very practical circumstances in the situation; some are precipitated by the conflicting advice of outsiders. With several children dependent on her, the wife must decide whether the present situation is more detrimental to them than future situations she can see arising if she should leave her husband. The question of where the money to live on will come from must be thought out. If she can get a job, will there be enough to provide for child care also while she is away from home? Should the children, who have already experienced such an unsettled life, be separated from her to be cared for by others? If the family still owns its own home, how can she retain control of it? If she leaves, where can she go? What can be done to tide the family over until her first earnings come in? How can she ensure her husband's continued absence from the home and thus be certain of the safety of individuals and property in her absence? These are only a small sample of the practical issues that must be dealt with in trying to think her way through to a decision to terminate the marriage.

Other pressures act on her to impede the decision-making process. "If he would only stay drunk till I carry out what I intend to do," is a frequent statement. When the husband realizes that his wife really means to leave, he frequently sobers up, watches his behavior in the home, plays on her latent and sometimes conscious feelings of her responsibility for the situation, stresses his need for her and that without her he is lost, tears away at any confidence she has that she will be able to manage by herself, and threatens her and the children with injury or with his own suicide if she carries out her intention.

The children, in the meantime, are pulling and pushing on her emotions. They think she is "spineless" to stay but unfair to father's chances for ultimate recovery if she leaves. Relatives, who were earlier alienated in her attempts to shield her family but now know of the situation, do not believe in its full ramifications. They often feel she is exaggerating and persuade her to stay with him. Especially is this true in the case of a "solitary drinker." His drinking has been so well concealed that the relatives have no way of knowing the true nature of the situation. Other relatives, afraid that they will be called on for support, exert pressure to keep the marriage intact and the husband thereby responsible for debts. Relatives who feel she should leave him overplay their hands by berating the husband in such a manner as to evoke her defense of him. This makes conscious the positive aspects of her relationship with him, causing her to waver in her decision. If she consults organized agencies, she often gets conflicting advice. The agencies concerned with the well-being of the family may counsel leaving; those concerned with rehabilitating the husband may press her to stay. In addition, help from public organizations almost always involves delay and is frequently not forthcoming at the point where she needs it most.

The wife must come to terms with her own mixed feelings about her husband, her marriage and herself before she can decide on such a step as breaking up the marriage. She must give up hope that she can be of any help to her husband. She must command enough self-confidence, after years of having it eroded, to be able to face an unknown future and leave the security of an unpalatable but familiar past and present. She must accept that she has failed in her marriage, not an easy thing to do after having devoted years to stopping up the cracks in the family structure as they appeared. Breaking up the marriage involves a complete alteration in the life goals toward which all her behavior has been oriented. It is hard for her to rid herself of the feeling that she married him and he is her responsibility. Having thought and planned for so long on a day-to-day basis, it is difficult to plan for a long-term future.

Her taking over of the family raises her self-confidence, but failure to carry through on decisions undermines the new gains that she has made. Vacillation in her decisions tends to exasperate the agencies trying to help her, and she begins to feel that help from them may not be forthcoming if she finally decides to leave.

Some events, however, help her to arrive at a decision. During the absences of her husband she has seen how manageable life can be and how smoothly her family can run. She finds that life goes on without him. The wife who is working comes to feel that "my husband is a luxury I can no longer afford." After a few short-term separations in which she tries out her wings successfully, leaving comes to look more possible. Another step on the path to leaving is the acceptance of the idea that, although she cannot help her husband, she can help her family. She often reaches a state of such emotional isolation from her husband that his behavior no longer disturbs her emotionally but is only something annoying which upsets daily routines and plans.

Stage 6. Reorganization of Part of the Family

The wife is without her husband and must reorganize her family on this basis. Substantially the process is similar to that in other divorced families, but with some additions. The divorce rarely cuts her relationship to her husband. Unless she and her family disappear, her husband may make attempts to come back. When drunk, he may endanger her job by calls at her place of work. He may attempt violence against members of the family, or he may contact the children and work to gain their loyalty so that pressure is put on the mother to accept him again. Looking back on her marriage, she forgets the full impact of the problem situation on her and on the children and feels more warmly toward her husband, and these feelings can still be manipulated by him. The wide circulation of information on alcoholism as an illness engenders guilt about having deserted a sick man. Gradually, however, the family becomes reorganized.

Stage 7. Recovery and Reorganization of the Whole Family

Stage 7 is entered if the husband achieves sobriety, whether or not separation has preceded. It was pointed out that in earlier stages most of the problems in the marriage were attributed to the alcoholism of the husband, and thus problems in adjustment not related directly to the drinking were unrecognized and unmet. Also, the "sober personality" of the husband was thought of as the "real" personality, with a resulting lack of recognition of other factors involved in his sober behavior, such as remorse and guilt over his actions, leading him to act to the best of his ability like "the ideal husband" when sober. Irritation or other signs of growing tension were viewed as indicators of further drinking, and hence the problems giving rise to them were walked around gingerly rather than faced and resolved. Lack of conflict and lack of drinking were defined as indicating a perfect adjustment. For the wife and husband facing a sober marriage after many years of an alcoholic marriage, the expectations of what marriage without alcoholism will be are unrealistically idealistic, and the reality of marriage almost inevitably brings disillusionments. The expectation that all would go well and that all problems be resolved with the cessation of the husband's drinking cannot be met and this threatens the marriage from time to time.

The beginning of sobriety for the husband does not bring too great hope to the family at first. They have been through this before but are willing to help him along and stand by him in the new attempt. As the length of sobriety increases, so do the hopes for its permanence and efforts to be of help. The wife at first finds it difficult to think more than in terms of today, waking each morning with fear of what the day will bring and sighing with relief at the end of each sober day.

With the continuation of sobriety, many problems begin to crop up. Mother has for years managed the family, and now father again wishes to be reinstated in his former roles. Usually the first role reestablished is that of breadwinner, and the economic problems of the family begin to be alleviated as debts are gradually paid and there is enough left over for current needs. With the resumption of this role, the husband feels that the family should also accept him at least as a partner in the management of the family. Even if the wife is willing to hand over some of the control of the children, for example, the children often are not able to accept this change easily. Their mother has been both parents for so long that it takes time to get used to the idea of consulting their father on problems and asking for his decisions. Often the father tries too hard to manage this change overnight, and the very pressure put on the children toward this end defeats him. In addition, he is unable to meet many of the demands the children make on him because he has never really become acquainted with them or learned to understand them and is lacking in much necessary background knowledge of their lives.

The wife, who finds it difficult to conceive of her husband as permanently sober, feels an unwillingness to let control slip from her hands. At the same time she realizes that reinstatement of her husband in his family roles is necessary to his sobriety. She also realizes that the closer his involvement in the family the greater the probability of his remaining sober. Yet she remembers events in the past in which his failure to handle his responsibilities was catastrophic to the family. Used to avoiding anything which might upset him, the wife often hesitates to discuss problems openly. At times, if she is successful in helping him to regain his roles as father, she feels resentful of his intrusion into territory she has come to regard as hers. If he makes errors in judgment which affect the family adversely, her former feelings of being his superior may come to the fore and affect her interaction with him. If the children begin to turn to him, she may feel a resurgence of self-pity at being left out and find herself attempting to swing the children back toward herself. Above all, however, she finds herself feeling resentful that some other agency achieved what she and the children could not.

Often the husband makes demands for obedience, for consideration and for pampering which members of the family feel unable to meet. He may become rather euphoric as his sobriety continues and feel superior for a time.

Gradually, however, the drinking problem sinks into the past and marital adjustment at some level is achieved. Even when this has occurred, the drinking problem crops up occasionally, as when the time comes for a decision about whether the children should be permitted to drink. The mother at such times becomes anxious, sees in the child traits which remind her of her husband, worries whether these are the traits which mean future alcoholism. At parties, at first, she is watchful and concerned about whether her husband will take a drink or not. Relatives and friends may, in a party mood, make the husband the center of attention by emphasizing his nondrinking. They may unwit-

tingly cast aspersions on his character by trying to convince him that he can now "drink like a man." Some relatives and friends have gone so far as secretly to "spike" a non-alcoholic drink and then cry "bottoms up!" without realizing the risk of reactivating patterns from the past.

If sobriety has come through Alcoholics Anonymous, the husband frequently throws himself so wholeheartedly into A.A. activities that his wife sees little of him and feels neglected. As she worries less about his drinking, she may press him to cut down on these activities. That this is dangerous, since A.A. activity is correlated with success in Alcoholics Anonymous, has been shown by Lahey (4). Also, the wife discovers that, though she has a sober husband, she is by no means free of alcoholics. In his Twelfth Step work, he may keep the house filled with men he is helping. In the past her husband has avoided self-searching; and now he may become excessively introspective, and it may be difficult for her to deal with this.

If the husband becomes sober through Alcoholics Anonymous and the wife participates actively in groups open to her, the thoughts of what is happening to her, to her husband and to her family will be verbalized and interpreted within the framework of the Alcoholics Anonymous philosophy and the situation will probably be more tolerable and more easily worked out. . . .

Summary

The onset of alcoholism in a family member has been viewed as precipitating a cumulative crisis for the family. Seven critical stages have been delineated. Each stage affects the form which the following one will take. The family finds itself in an unstructured situation which is undefined by the culture. Thus it is forced to evolve techniques of adjustment by trial and error. The unpredictability of the situation, added to its lack of structure, engenders anxiety in family members which gives rise to personality difficulties. Factors in the culture, in the environment and within the family situation prolong the crisis and deter the working out of permanent adjustment patterns. With the arrest of the alcoholism, the crisis enters its final stage. The family attempts to reorganize to include the ex-alcoholic and makes adjustments to the changes which have occurred in him.

It has been suggested that the clinical picture presented by the wife to helping agencies is not only indicative of a type of basic personality structure but also of the stage in family adjustment to an alcoholic. That the wives of alcoholics represent a rather limited number of personality types can be interpreted in two ways, which are not mutually exclusive.

(*a*) That women with certain personality attributes tend to select alcoholics or potential alcoholics as husbands in order to satisfy unconscious personality needs;

(*b*) That women undergoing similar experiences of stress, within similarly unstructured situations, defined by the culture and reacted to by members of the society in such a manner as to place limits on the range of possible behavior, will emerge from this experience showing many similar neurotic personality traits. As the situation evolves some of these personality traits will also change. Changes have been observed in the women studied which correlate with altered family interaction patterns. This hypothesis is supported also by observations on the behavior of individuals in other unstructured situations, in situations in which they were isolated from supporting group interaction. It is congruent also with the theory of reactions to increased and decreased stress.

REFERENCES

1. Club and Educational Bureaus of Newsweek. 1950. "Is Alcoholism Everyone's Problem?" Platform, N.Y., p. 3 (January).

2. Whalen, T. 1953. "Wives of Alcoholics: Four Types Observed in a Family Service Agency." *Quarterly Journal of Studies on Alcohol,* 14:632–641.

3. Newell, N. 1950. "Alcoholism and the Father-image." *Quarterly Journal of Studies on Alcohol,* 11:92–96.

4. Lahey, W. W. 1950. *A Comparison of Social and Personal Factors Identified with Selected Members of Alcoholics Anonymous.* Master's Thesis: University of Southern California.

③ THE CULTURAL CONTEXT

Cultures include ideas about different types of people. While most of these ideas deal with conventional types, many deal with deviant types. In analyzing these ideas about deviance, a number of questions can be posed. What categories of deviance are found in a particular culture? Who formulates these categories? Who has the right to apply these labels, and what norms affect the application and consequence of these labels? Finally, whose interests are served by these definitions of deviance?

In the first selection Edwin Schur describes how in American culture, concerns about appearance norms pervade women's lives. Peter Conrad discusses the medicalization of deviance and the implications of the creation of the ''hyperkinetic syndrome'' label by doctors. Finally, Jane Mercer claims that because higher-class people have a clearer definition of mental retardation than do lower-class people, higher-class parents are more likely to label one of their children retarded and to institutionalize the child.

Women and Appearance Norms

EDWIN M. SCHUR

Norms governing women's physical appearance, and perceived violations of them, deserve special attention . . . Such norms constitute a central element in the objectification and devaluation of females. They crucially influence the life goals and routine practices to which girls and young women are socialized. Concern about meeting these norms continues to pervade women's lives. Under prevailing criteria of personal worth, negative evaluations of physical appearance are likely to have a powerful impact on women's self-conceptions. Male socialization and ongoing male perceptions and behaviors are also heavily affected by the dominant prescriptions for female beauty. The preoccupation—of both men and women—with female appearance is, furthermore, a key ingredient in the "commoditization" of women's sexuality. . . .

Visual Objectification

Woman as object is not just a figure of speech. Females are not merely thought of as objects, they are *literally seen* as objects. The art critic John Berger (1977, p. 47) has commented that "*men act* and *women appear*. Men look at women. Women watch themselves being looked at. This determines not only most relations between men and women but also the relation of women to themselves. The surveyor of woman in herself is male. the surveyed, female. Thus she turns herself into an object—and most particularly an object of vision: a sight." Actually, one might better stress that she has "been turned" into an object, for women have not had much real choice in this matter. Even today few women feel free to ignore the dominant beauty prescriptions. On the contrary almost all must to some extent recognize that "becoming an attractive object is a role obligation" (Laws, 1979, p. 181). . . .

The persistence of beauty contests is, perhaps, the least important type of evidence that the visual objectifying of women is endemic to contemporary American culture. Among the many other more significant indicators are the following: female beauty imagery as the central device in much contemporary advertising; the amount of women's time, energy, and thinking that is devoted to self-beautification efforts (and the associated fact that weight, hair styles, clothing, and cosmetics continue to be staples of "women's talk"); the fact that female beautification supports several major industries—fashion, cosmetics, advertising (in large measure), and a substantial "diet industry"; and, most notably, the everyday behavior of men in our society—the aforementioned perpetual staring at women's bodies, the acceptability in the male subculture of supposedly "appreciative" references to a passing woman's body parts, such as "what an ass," "what a pair of tits," etc. The normative implication of all this for women is succinctly captured in the term "vital statistics"—a basis for evaluating female physical appearance of which there is no male counterpart. . . . Sociological and feminist critiques of the "cult of female beauty" have especially emphasized the following points: physical appearance is much more central to evaluations of women than it is to evaluations of men; this emphasis implicitly devalues women's other qualities and accomplishments; women's "looks" thereby become a commodity and a key determinant of their "success" or "failure"; the beauty norms used in evaluating women are excessively narrow and quite unrealistic; cultural reinforcement of such norms conveys to the ordinary woman a sense of her perpetual "deficiency."

The last two points are particularly significant in affecting perceptions of female deviance. As Una Stannard has stated, "the modern cult of women's beauty has nothing to do with what women naturally look like" (Stannard, 1972, p. 194; see also Densmore, 1972). Nonetheless, from girlhood on females are continuously exposed, especially through advertising and the mass media, to highly unrealistic "role models." The "ideal beauties" in the media, Stannard goes on to observe, "are always there to keep women permanently insecure about their looks, and that includes the great beauties as well. Indeed, the more beautiful a woman, the more she dreads time and younger beauties; for generally the beautiful woman's opinion of herself has depended almost solely on her looks" (Stannard, 1972, p. 196).

The ever-present danger of being deemed physically unattractive has, in fact, been a quite explicit theme—perhaps even the single most dominant one—in much advertising aimed at women. Commenting on the use of cosmetics, Germaine Greer has noted that "when they are used for adornment in a conscious and creative way, they are not emblems of inauthenticity: it is when they are presented as the real thing, covering unsightly blemishes, disguising a repulsive thing so that it is acceptable to the world that their function is deeply suspect" (Greer, 1972, p. 346). Sociological researchers often conclude that the media and advertising do not "create" behavior patterns or value priorities, they only "reinforce" them—in effect, merely giving people "what they want." But usually these conclusions have been based on limited studies aimed at testing only short-term and direct media effects.

In the case of female beauty norms, and women's related perceptions of themselves as likely norm-violators, the "mere reinforcement" claim is not entirely convincing. Sheila Rowbotham's (1973, p. 109) statement indicates why:

The cosmetics industry has mushroomed and created needs as well as products. The female who is the cosmetic ideal is more or less unattainable, no sooner captured she appears in another form. Playing on insecurity and anxiety the advertisers market goods which actually create new fears. Vaginal deodorants make people anxious about sexual odour. Acting on the assumption that women regard themselves through men's eyes as objects of pleasure, advertising and the media project a haunting and unreal image of womanhood. The persistent sense of dislocation between the unrealized female self and the projected female stereotypes has contributed to a sense of failure.

We shall return shortly to the question of whether recent changes in advertising have significantly altered its contribution to the visual objectification of women. . . .

A related aspect of the cult of female beauty deserves mention here—its effects on men. Critics have frequently deplored the unrealistic and limited role models provided for women. They less often have noted that "ideal beauty" imagery at the same time provides what might be called "object models" for men. Widespread imagery of this sort encourages and in a sense "trains" men to visually objectify women. It also provides physical criteria of assessment, according to which men are likely to find real women deficient. . . .

Negative Body-Consciousness

Under these circumstances, that part of a woman's self-conceptions which has to do with her physical appearance—her general attractiveness and, perhaps especially, her body shape—is routinely under siege. An array of associated behavior patterns emerges, and several related "disturbances" are formally diagnosed. Both the acknowledged disturbances and the more general behavior patterns strongly reflect "negative body-consciousness"—women not "feeling good about" their physical attributes.

Overweight and Stigma

Various studies have made clear that persons perceived to be significantly overweight are responded to negatively (see, for example, Allon, 1982). In early experiments young children were shown drawings of children with various physical disabilities, and asked to rank them ("tell me which boy—or girl—you like best," "next best," etc.). The drawing of an obese child received a lower (more negative) ranking overall than those of children having a facial disfigurement, sitting in a wheelchair, having a hand missing, or having crutches and a leg brace (Richardson, Goodman, Hastorf, and Dornbusch, 1961). In a related study, five samples of adult respondents were given the same type of test. They, too, "with few exceptions, ranked the overweight child as least likable" (Maddox, Back, and Liederman, 1968). The researchers concluded that their data (from these and other tests) "overwhelmingly support the [existence of an] essentially negative evaluation of overweight hypothesized to be characteristic in our society" (ibid., p. 10; see also discussion in Clinard and Meier, 1979, pp. 536–538).

Sociological analyses of group weight control programs have similarly recognized the stigma associated with being perceived as overweight. Natalie Allon discusses as latent functions of such groups the provision of opportunities for tension release, group support, and an atmosphere in which members can discuss various topics of concern which could not be so "easily discussed with the non-stigmatized'' (Allon, 1975, p. 60). Although Barbara Laslett and Carol Warren (1975) conclude that diet groups can use the stigma on overweight to advantage—in effect, branding the members as being "essentially fat" in order to reinforce their efforts to keep thin—this technique itself rests on the strength of the stigma members confront in the outside world.

Marcia Millman (1980), who has done extensive interview and observational research in organizations for the overweight, discusses fatness explicitly in deviance terms. Dismissing the claim that we are concerned about overweight because it is unhealthy, she notes, "Many other things we do to ourselves are unhealthy, yet they do not incite the same kind of shame, hostility, and disapproval. Furthermore, many people have strong reactions to weight even when a person is not fat enough for health to be affected'' (Millman, 1980, x). Fatness, Millman emphasizes, carries powerful symbolic meaning in our culture. As a result, being perceived as overweight deeply affects a person's overall identity. Fat persons are reacted to in (devaluing) categorical terms, and their self-conceptions may be shaped accordingly. There is a tendency, furthermore, to hold fat persons responsible for their condition—at least implicitly. Fatness is not viewed simply as a physical state, but also as evidence of some basic character defect. The overweight person, "especially if she is a woman, probably suffers more from the social and psychological stigma attached to obesity than she does from the actual physical condition. In a wide variety of ways she is negatively defined by her weight and excluded from full participation in the ranks of the normal'' (ibid., xi).

Case studies Millman presents illustrate the strong devaluation fat women regularly experience. For example, a young woman who was about twenty-five to fifty pounds overweight during college and in her twenties wrote in an autobiographical account:

I always felt that the first thing anyone would notice is that I was fat. And not only that I was fat, but that they would know *why* I was fat. They would know I was neurotic, that I was unsatisfied, that I was a pig, that I had problems. They could tell immediately that I was out of control. I always looked around to see if there was anyone as fat as me. I always wondered when I saw a fat woman, "Do I look like *that?*" (Millman, 1980, p. 80)

The stigma-imposing "master status" aspect of fatness is underscored when we consider the contrasting assessments of thin people. Except in extreme cases (such as anorexia nervosa, . . .) we infrequently identify and categorize people as "thin." This fact indicates too that these responses do not follow directly from biological condition alone. They vary because of differences in sociocultural meaning and emphasis. There is much reason to believe, furthermore, that the stigma-laden meanings attached to overweight have greater impact overall in our society on women than on men. It is true that many of the findings cited thus far imply stigma regardless of sex. And there is little doubt that males who are extremely fat will incur devaluation. Nonetheless our gender system's greater emphasis on female appearance does make a difference.

Women more than men present weight-related "disturbances," exhibit significant concern about their weight, and involve themselves in frequent weight control efforts. It is revealing that several evaluatively neutral terms used to describe fat men—"stocky," "heavy-set," "portly"—are not matched by counterpart terms for fat women. As Goffman notes in his study of advertising's "gender display," the fact that male figures in the ads are bigger than female figures reflects our society's tendency to define male physical weight positively—as a symbol of the "social weight" (power, authority, prestige, etc.) accorded to men (Goffman, 1979, p. 28).

Fear of Visual Deviance

It must be emphasized that . . . formally diagnosed disturbances [such as anorexia nervosa] represent only the most extreme cases of "negative body-consciousness." Such cases do show us where the conflicts and pressures generated by restrictive appearance norms potentially can lead. More significant, however, is the extent to which virtually *all* women in our society feel compelled to make continuous efforts not to "violate" these norms. Commercial exploitation of the theme of never-ending female "deficiencies" virtually guarantees that those efforts will never be fully successful. The very size of the "market" for appearance aids suggests the pervasiveness of female concern and conformity-seeking effort. According to a recent discussion of the cosmetics industry (*The New York Times*, Nov. 16, 1980, p. 22E), estimated consumer expenditures on cosmetics and personal hygiene products (in 1979) included the following: cosmetics—$2,656,800,000; women's hair products—$1,913,400,000; women's fragrances—$1,828,300,000; skin preparations—$1,552,400,000; feminine hygiene—$770,100,000; diet aids—$388,800,000.

As well as being the chief consumers of cosmetics and other self-presentation aids, women probably are the main purchasers of mass-marketed "beauty tip" books and the primary obtainers of purely "cosmetic" plastic surgery. These patterns too reflect the impact on women of the constantly reiterated female deficiency theme, and their consequent susceptibility to diverse offers of (usually male) expert advice and assistance (Ehrenreich and English, 1979). We do not have systematic data regarding recourse to cosmetic plastic surgery, but the extent to which such services now are advertised in daily newspapers implies a substantial population of potential "patients." According to one writer, there has been a recent "explosion in the field of cosmetic surgery." And he goes on to note, "Today, good plastic surgery can rejuvenate flaccid breasts, sagging buttocks, jelly stomachs, bags beneath the eyes, droopy lids, wrinkled foreheads, feathered lips, crow's-feet, and much else that was once thought to be an inevitable part of the aging process" (Hoge, 1980, p. 52; see also Al-Issa, 1980, pp. 291–295).

This last statement suggests a further point of importance concerning appearance norms. The extreme cultural emphasis on female physical appearance is a key element in the heightened devaluation of females as they get older. Youthfulness in either sex is likely to be prized in our "narcissistic" society (Lasch, 1979, Ch. IX). But because of the cult of female beauty it has been without question a more crucial asset for females than for males. If a woman's looks are treated as her major resource, she simply cannot "afford" to lose them. The natural aging process, therefore, necessarily has evoked among women a great deal of appearance-related anxiety. Advertising at the very least strongly reinforces such anxiety. . . .

Trends and Prospects

In this brief section on appearance norms, it has not been possible to provide in-depth discussion of such topics as fashion, the use of cosmetics, or the role of advertising. Opinions differ strongly regarding the extent to which such phenomena help to "cause" the objectification of women and the oppressiveness of appearance norms. Presentation of self, including appearance, will always be a significant factor in interpersonal relations (Stone, 1962; also Goffman, 1959). There is little doubt too that physical appearance will invariably be an element in sexual attraction. The sociological and feminist critiques do not necessarily deny this. They assert only that the emphasis in our society on (a narrowly defined version of) female beauty represents a gross and harmful distortion of what is natural, and that mass marketing helps to perpetuate that emphasis.

It may be asked whether there have been recent changes (in beauty norms and images, and in the marketing of them) which imply a more natural depiction of females. Today's advertising without question reflects an awareness of the women's liberation movement. In particular, women in the ads no longer are depicted exclusively as housewives and mothers. Yet if current ads show women in diverse work situations and more generally describe them as actively pursuing their own chosen goals, there is no corresponding evidence to suggest that the "woman as sex object" element in advertising has been significantly displaced. On the contrary, a standard technique is simply to place the old imagery in a new context, thereby exploiting two types of sales appeal. Thus, one sociologist who has studied advertising aimed at the "new woman" (Kasinitz, 1981, p. 27) notes that "the 'Cosmo girl' is not the romantic housewife or sexy secretary; she is the sexy executive vice president." And, he goes on to comment more generally, "The 'new woman' is presented as a dichotomy: totally 'feminine' (in the traditional sense), sexy and submissive, when *she* wants to be, yet tough, assertive, successful and fulfilled, when *she* wants to be" (ibid., p. 28; see also Cagan, 1978; Ehrenreich and English, 1979, pp. 285–297; and Gordon, 1983).

We know that, in actual fact, women are not by and large free to choose whether they do or do not wish to be "feminine" and "sexy"—unless they are prepared to face the negative responses they will elicit if they violate the norm. Most women today, no matter how successful, still "are not free to stop playing the beauty game'' (Stannard, 1972, p. 192). It is possible that some beauty norms are becoming a bit less restrictive. For example, clothing manufacturers recently have shown increased interest in producing fashionable clothes for ''large-size'' women (*The New York Times*, March 22, 1980, p. 18). This development, however, appears to reflect recognition of the existence of a large consumer ''market'' more than it does any inclination to relax appearance norms. The segregative implications of marketing such clothes as a special ''line'' and of displaying and selling them in a separate ''department'' within a clothing store suggest that the stigma on largeness even here continues to maintain considerable force.

Other recent trends that might have provided a basis for reducing the coercive power of appearance norms also have proven ineffective in this regard, again partly because the marketers were quick to anticipate and exploit them commercially. Thus our culture's recent preoccupation with self-awareness and body-awareness (see Schur, 1976; Lasch, 1979), health and physical fitness, might have fostered a more wholesome and nonjudgmental approach to physical appearance. Yet there is little evidence this has occurred. If anything, the overall effect seems to have been to make the achievement of ''perfection'' (e.g., in body shape) even more obligatory than before. And as regards the adoption of a more relaxed and ''natural'' appearance, commercial interests have promptly responded by creating and promoting a ''natural look'' in cosmetics and attire.

Finally, the somewhat increased attention recently to men's physical appearance, clothing, and ''beautification'' does not seem to imply any relaxing of the pressure on women to conform visually. Viewed in combination with the recent emphasis on female sexual assertiveness (see Schur, 1976; Ehrenreich and English, 1979, pp. 297–311), this trend seems at most to suggest the possibility that in the future there might be ''equal objectification'' of heterosexual males. If women increasingly were to ''see'' and respond to men as men have traditionally seen and responded to them, the change—while it might represent a kind of equalization—would not be a very satisfactory one. Males would then have to share the burden of coercion imposed by appearance norms. But it is by no means clear that the similar burden on women would thereby have been removed or even reduced.

REFERENCES

Al-Issa, Ihsan. 1980. *The Psychopathology of Women.* Englewood Cliffs, N.J.: Prentice-Hall.

Allon, Natalie. 1982. ''The Stigma of Overweight in Everyday Life.'' In Benjamin B. Wolman (ed.), *Psychological Aspects of Obesity.* New York: Van Nostrand Reinhold.

Berger, John. 1977. *Ways of Seeing.* New York: Penguin Books.

Cagan, Elizabeth. 1978. ''The Selling of the Women's Movement.'' *Social Policy* (May–June): 4–12.

Clinard, Marshall B. and Robert F. Meier. 1979. *Sociology of Deviant Behavior.* 5th ed. New York: Holt, Rinehart and Winston.

Ehrenreich, Barbara and Deirdre English. 1979. *For Her Own Good: 150 Years of the Experts' Advice to Women.* Garden City, N.Y.: Doubleday Anchor Books.

Goffman, Erving. 1959. *The Presentation of Self in Everyday Life.* Garden City, N.Y.: Doubleday Anchor Books.

———— 1979. *Gender Advertisements.* New York: Harper Colophon Books.

Gordon, Suzanne. 1983. ''Dressed for Success: The New Corporate Feminism.'' *The Nation,* 129 (February): 143–147.

Greer, Germaine. 1972. *The Female Eunuch.* New York: Bantam Books.

Hoge, Warren. 1980. ''Doctor Vanity: The Jet Set's Man in Rio.'' *The New York Times.* June 8, 44–70.

Kasinitz, Philip. 1981. ''The Image of the 'New Woman' in Advertising.'' Unpublished paper, New York University, Department of Sociology.

Lasch, Christopher. 1979. *The Culture of Narcissism.* New York: Warner Books.

Laslett, Barbara and Carol A. B. Warren. 1975. ''Losing Weight: The Organizational Promotion of Behavior Change.'' *Social Problems,* 23 (October): 69–80.

Laws, Judith Long. 1979 *The Second X: Sex Role and Social Role.* New York: Elsevier.

Maddox, George L., Kurt W. Back, and Veronica R. Liederman. 1968. ''Overweight as Social Deviance and Disability.'' *Journal Health and Social Behavior,* 9 (December): 287–298.

Millman, Marcia. 1980. *Such a Pretty Face: Being Fat in America.* New York: W. W. Norton.

Richardson, Stephen A., et al. 1961. ''Cultural Uniformity in Reaction to Physical Disabilities.'' *American Sociological Review,* 26 (April): 241–247.

Rowbotham, Sheila. 1973. *Woman's Consciousness, Man's World.* Baltimore: Penguin Books.

Schur, Edwin M. 1976. *The Awareness Trap.* New York: Quadrangle/The New York Times Book Co.

Stannard, Una. 1972. ''The Mask of Beauty.'' In Vivian Gornick and Barbara K. Moran (eds.), *Woman in Sexist Society.* New York: Signet Books.

Stone, Gregory P. 1962. ''Appearance and the Self.'' In Arnold M. Rose (ed.), *Human Behavior and Social Processes.* Boston: Houghton Mifflin.

The Medicalization of Deviance in American Culture PETER CONRAD

Introduction

The increasing medicalization of deviant behavior and the medical institution's role as an agent of social control has gained considerable notice (Freidson, 1970; Pitts, 1971; Kittrie, 1971; Zola, 1972). By medicalization we mean defining behavior as a medical problem or illness and mandating or licensing the medical profession to provide some type of treatment for it. Examples include alcoholism, drug addiction and treating violence as a genetic or brain disorder. This redefinition is not a new function of the medical institution: psychiatry and public health have always been concerned with social behavior and have traditionally functioned as agents of social control (Foucault, 1965; Szasz, 1970; Rosen, 1972). . . .

This paper describes how certain forms of behavior in children have become defined as a medical problem and how medicine has become a major agent for their social control since the discovery of hyperkinesis. By discovery we mean both origin of the diagnosis and treatment for this disorder; and discovery of children who exhibit this behavior. The first section analyzes the discovery of hyperkinesis and why it suddenly became popular in the 1960's. The second section will discuss the medicalization of deviant behavior and its ramifications.

The Medical Diagnosis of Hyperkinesis

Hyperkinesis is a relatively recent phenomenon as a medical diagnostic category. Only in the past two decades has it been available as a recognized diagnostic category and only in the last decade has it received widespread notice and medical popularity. However, the roots of the diagnosis and treatment of this clinical entity are found earlier.

Hyperkinesis is also known as Minimal Brain Dysfunction, Hyperactive Syndrome, Hyperkinetic Disorder of Childhood, and by several other diagnostic categories. Although the symptoms and the presumed etiology vary, in general the behaviors are quite similar and greatly overlap.[1] Typical symptom patterns for diagnosing the disorder include: extreme excess of motor activity (hyperactivity); very short attention span (the child flits from activity to activity); restlessness; fidgetiness; often wildly oscillating mood swings (he's fine one day, a terror the next); clumsiness; aggressive-like behavior; impulsivity; in school he cannot sit still, cannot comply with rules, has low frustration level; frequently there may be sleeping problems and acquisition of speech may be delayed (Stewart, 1966, 1970; Wender, 1971). Most of the symptoms for the disorder are deviant behaviors.[2] It is six times as prevalent among boys as among girls. We use the term hyperkinesis to represent all the diagnostic categories of this disorder.

The Discovery of Hyperkinesis

It is useful to divide the analysis into what might be considered *clinical factors* directly related to the diagnosis and treatment of hyperkinesis and *social factors* that set the context for the emergence of the new diagnostic category.

Clinical Factors
Bradley (1937) observed that amphetamine drugs had a spectacular effect in altering the behavior of school children who exhibited behavior disorders or learning disabilities. Fifteen of the thirty children he treated actually became more subdued in their behavior. Bradley termed

Reprinted from "The Discovery of Hyperkinesis: Notes on the Medicalization of Deviant Behavior," *Social Problems*, Vol. 23, No. 1 (October 1975), pp. 12–21, by permission of the Society for the Study of Social Problems and the author.

[1] The U.S.P.H.S. report (Clements, 1966) included 38 terms that were used to describe or distinguish the conditions that it labeled Minimal Brain Dysfunction. Although the literature attempts to differentiate M.B.D., hyperkinesis, hyperactive syndrome, and several other diagnostic labels, it is our belief that in practice they are almost interchangeable.

[2] For a fuller discussion of the construction of the diagnosis of hyperkinesis, see Conrad (1976), especially Chapter 6.

the effect of this medication paradoxical, since he expected that amphetamines would stimulate children as they stimulated adults. After the medication was discontinued the children's behavior returned to premedication level.

A scattering of reports in the medical literature on the utility of stimulant medications for "childhood behavior disorders" appeared in the next two decades. The next significant contribution was the work of Strauss and his associates (Strauss and Lehtinen, 1947) who found certain behavior (including hyperkinesis behaviors) in postencephaletic children suffering from what they called minimal brain injury (damage). This was the first time these behaviors were attributed to the new organic distinction of minimal brain damage.

This disorder still remained unnamed or else it was called a variety of names (usually just "childhood behavior disorder"). It did not appear as a specific diagnostic category until Laufer, et al. (1957) described it as the "hyperkinetic impulse disorder" in 1957. Upon finding "the salient characteristics of the behavior pattern . . . are strikingly similar to those with clear cut organic causation" these researchers described a disorder with no clear-cut history or evidence for organicity (Laufer, et al., 1957).

In 1966 a task force sponsored by the U.S. Public Health Service and the National Association for Crippled Children and Adults attempted to clarify the ambiguity and confusion in terminology and symptomology in diagnosing children's behavior and learning disorders. From over three dozen diagnoses, they agreed on the term "minimal brain dysfunction" as an overriding diagnosis that would include hyperkinesis and other disorders (Clements, 1966). Since this time M.B.D. has been the primary formal diagnosis or label.

In the middle 1950's a new drug, Ritalin, was synthesized, that has many qualities of amphetamines without some of their more undesirable side effects. In 1961 this drug was approved by the F.D.A. for use with children. Since this time there has been much research published on the use of Ritalin in the treatment of childhood behavior disorders. This medication became the "treatment of choice" for treating children with hyperkinesis.

Since the early sixties, more research appeared on the etiology, diagnosis and treatment of hyperkinesis (cf. DeLong, 1972; Grinspoon and Singer, 1973; Cole, 1975)—as much as three-quarters concerned with drug treatment of the disorder. There had been increasing publicity of the disorder in the mass media as well. The *Reader's Guide to Periodical Literature* had no articles on hyperkinesis before 1967, one each in 1968 and 1969 and a total of forty for 1970 through 1974 (a mean of eight per year).

Now hyperkinesis has become the most common child psychiatric problem (Gross and Wilson, 1974: 142); special pediatric clinics have been established to treat hyperkinetic children, and substantial federal funds have been invested in etiological and treatment research. Outside the medical profession, teachers have developed a working clinical knowledge of hyperkinesis' symptoms and treatment (cf. Robin and Bosco, 1973); articles appear regularly in mass circulation magazines and newspapers so that parents often come to clinics with knowledge of this diagnosis. Hyperkinesis is no longer the relatively esoteric diagnostic category it may have been twenty years ago, it is now a well-known clinical disorder.

Social Factors

The social factors affecting the discovery of hyperkinesis can be divided into two areas: (1) The Pharmaceutical Revolution; (2) Government Action.

(1) *The Pharmaceutical Revolution.* Since the 1930's the pharmaceutical industry has been synthesizing and manufacturing a large number of psychoactive drugs, contributing to a virtual revolution in drug making and drug taking in America (Silverman and Lee, 1974).

Psychoactive drugs are agents that affect the central nervous system. Benzedrine, Ritalin, and Dexedrine are all synthesized psychoactive stimulants which were indicated for narcolepsy, appetite control (as "diet pills"), mild depression, fatigue, and more recently hyperkinetic children.

Until the early sixties there was little or no promotion and advertisement of any of these medications for use with childhood disorders.[3]

[3] The American Medical Association's change in policy in accepting more pharmaceutical advertising in the late fifties may have been important. Probably the F.D.A. approval of the use of Ritalin for children in 1961 was more significant. Until 1970, Ritalin was advertised for treatment of "functional behavior problems in children." Since then, because of an F.D.A. order, it has only been promoted for treatment of M.B.D.

Then two major pharmaceutical firms (Smith, Kline and French, manufacturer of Dexedrine and CIBA, manufacturer of Ritalin) began to advertise in medical journals and through direct mailing and efforts of the "detail men." Most of this advertising of the pharmaceutical treatment of hyperkinesis was directed to the medical sphere; but some of the promotion was targeted for the educational sector also (Hentoff, 1972). This promotion was probably significant in disseminating information concerning the diagnosis and treatment of this newly discovered disorder.[4] Since 1955 the use of psychoactive medications (especially phenothiazines) for the treatment of persons who are mentally ill, along with the concurrent dramatic decline in inpatient populations, has made psychopharmacology an integral part of treatment for mental disorders. It has also undoubtedly increased the confidence in the medical profession for the pharmaceutical approach to mental and behavioral problems.

(2) *Government Action.* Since the publication of the U.S.P.H.S. report on M.B.D. there have been at least two significant governmental reports on treating school children with stimulant medications for behavior disorders. Both of these came as a response to the national publicity created by the *Washington Post* report (1970) that five to ten percent of the 62,000 grammar school children in Omaha, Nebraska were being treated with "behavior modification drugs to improve deportment and increase learning potential" (quoted in Grinspoon and Singer, 1973). Although the figures were later found to be a little exaggerated, it nevertheless spurred a Congressional investigation (U.S. Government Printing Office, 1970) and a conference sponsored by the Office of Child Development (1971) on the use of stimulant drugs in the treatment of behaviorally disturbed school children.

The Congressional Subcommittee on Privacy chaired by Congressman Cornelius E. Gallagher held hearings on the issue of prescribing drugs for hyperactive school children. In general, the committee showed great concern over the facility in which the medication was prescribed; more specifically that some children at least were receiving drugs from general practitioners whose primary diagnosis was based on teachers' and parents' reports that the child was doing poorly in school. There was also a concern with the absence of follow-up studies on the long-term effects of treatment.

The H.E.W. committee was a rather hastily convened group of professionals (a majority were M.D.'s) many of whom already had commitments to drug treatment for children's behavior problems. They recommended that only M.D.'s make the diagnosis and prescribe treatment, that the pharmaceutical companies promote the treatment of the disorder only through medical channels, that parents should not be coerced to accept any particular treatment and that long-term follow-up research should be done. This report served as blue ribbon approval for treating hyperkinesis with psychoactive medications.

Discussion

We will focus discussion on three issues: How children's deviant behavior became conceptualized as a medical problem; why this occurred when it did; and what are some of the implications of the medicalization of deviant behavior.

How does deviant behavior become conceptualized as a medical problem? We assume that before the discovery of hyperkinesis this type of deviance was seen as disruptive, disobedient, rebellious, anti-social or deviant behavior. Perhaps the label "emotionally disturbed" was sometimes used, when it was in vogue in the early sixties, and the child was usually managed in the context of the family or the school or in extreme cases, the child guidance clinic. How then did this constellation of deviant behaviors become a medical disorder?

The treatment was available long before the disorder treated was clearly conceptualized. It was twenty years after Bradley's discovery of the "paradoxical effect" of stimulants on certain deviant children that Laufer named the disorder and described its characteristic symptoms. Only in the late fifties were both the diagnostic label and the pharmaceutical treatment available. The pharmaceutical revolution in mental health and the increased interest in child psychiatry provided a favorable background for the dissemination of knowledge about this new disorder. The

---

[4]The drug industry spends fully 25 percent of its budget on promotion and advertising. See Coleman et al. (1966) for the role of the detail men and how physicians rely upon them for information.

latter probably made the medical profession more likely to consider behavior problems in children as within their clinical jurisdiction.

There were agents outside the medical profession itself that were significant in "promoting" hyperkinesis as a disorder within the medical framework. These agents might be conceptualized in Becker's terms as "moral entrepreneurs," those who crusade for creation and enforcement of the rules (Becker, 1963).[5] In this case the moral entrepreneurs were the pharmaceutical companies and the Association for Children with Learning Disabilities.

The pharmaceutical companies spent considerable time and money promoting stimulant medications for this new disorder. From the middle 1960's on, medical journals and the free "throwaway" magazines contained elaborate advertising for Ritalin and Dexedrine. These ads explained the utility of treating hyperkinesis and urged the physician to diagnose and treat hyperkinetic children. The ads run from one to six pages. For example, a two-page ad in 1971 stated:

MBD . . . MEDICAL MYTH OR DIAGNOSABLE DISEASE ENTITY What medical practitioner has not, at one time or another, been called upon to examine an impulsive, excitable hyperkinetic child? A child with difficulty in concentrating. Easily frustrated. Unusually aggressive. A classroom rebel. In the absence of any organic pathology, the conduct of such children was, until a few short years ago, usually dismissed as . . . spunkiness, or evidence of youthful vitality. But it is now evident that in many of these children the hyperkinetic syndrome exists as a distinct medical entity. This syndrome is readily diagnosed through patient histories, neurologic signs, and psychometric testing—has been classified by an expert panel convened by the United States Department of Health, Education and Welfare as Minimal Brain Dysfunction, MBD.

The pharmaceutical firms also supplied sophisticated packets of "diagnostic and treatment" information on hyperkinesis to physicians, paid for professional conferences on the subject, and supported research in the identification and treatment of the disorder. Clearly these corporations had a vested interest in the labeling and treatment of hyperkinesis; CIBA had $13 million profit from Ritalin alone in 1971, which was 15 percent of the total gross profits (Charles, 1971; Hentoff, 1972).

The other moral entrepreneur, less powerful than the pharmaceutical companies, but nevertheless influential, is the Association for Children with Learning Disabilities. Although their focus is not specifically on hyperkinetic children, they do include it in their conception of Learning Disabilities along with aphasia, reading problems like dyslexia and perceptual motor problems. Founded in the early 1950's by parents and professionals, it has functioned much as the National Association for Mental Health does for mental illness: promoting conferences, sponsoring legislation, providing social support. One of the main functions has been to disseminate information concerning this relatively new area in education, Learning Disabilities. While the organization does have a more educational than medical perspective, most of the literature indicates that for hyperkinesis members have adopted the medical model and the medical approach to the problem. They have sensitized teachers and schools to the conception of hyperkinesis as a medical problem.

The medical model of hyperactive behavior has become very well accepted in our society. Physicians find treatment relatively simple and the results sometimes spectacular. Hyperkinesis minimizes parents' guilt by emphasizing "it's not their fault, it's an organic problem" and allows for nonpunitive management or control of deviance. Medication often makes a child less disruptive in the classroom and sometimes aids a child in learning. Children often like their "magic pills" which make their behavior more socially acceptable and they probably benefit from a reduced stigma also.

The Medicalization of Deviant Behavior

Pitts has commented that "medicalization is one of the most effective means of social control and that it is destined to become the main mode of *formal* social control" (1971:391). Kittrie

---

[5] Freidson also notes the medical professional role as moral entrepreneur in this process also:

The profession does treat the illnesses laymen take to it, but it also seeks to discover illness of which the laymen may not even be aware. One of the greatest ambitions of the physician is to discover and describe a "new" disease or syndrome . . . (1970: 252).

(1971) has termed it "the coming of the therapeutic state."

Medicalization of mental illness dates at least from the seventeenth century (Foucault, 1965; Szasz, 1970). Even slaves who ran away were once considered to be suffering from the disease *drapedomania* (Chorover, 1973). In recent years alcoholism, violence, and drug addiction as well as hyperactive behavior in children have all become defined as medical problems, both in etiology or explanation of the behavior and the means of social control or treatment.

There are many reasons why this medicalization has occurred. Much scientific research, especially in pharmacology and genetics, has become technologically more sophisticated, and found more subtle correlates with human behavior. Sometimes these findings (as in the case of XYY chromosomes and violence) become etiological explanations for deviance. Pharmacological technology that makes new discoveries affecting behavior (e.g., antabuse, methadone and stimulants) are used as treatment for deviance. In part this application is encouraged by the prestige of the medical profession and its attachment to science. As Freidson notes, the medical profession has first claim to jurisdiction over anything that deals with the functioning of the body and especially anything that can be labeled illness (1970:251). Advances in genetics, pharmacology and "psychosurgery" also may advance medicine's jurisdiction over deviant behavior.

Second, the application of pharmacological technology is related to the humanitarian trend in the conception and control of deviant behavior. Alcoholism is no longer sin or even moral weakness, it is now a disease. Alcoholics are no longer arrested in many places for "public drunkenness," they are now somehow "treated," even if it is only to be dried out. Hyperactive children are now considered to have an illness rather than to be disruptive, disobedient, overactive problem children. They are not as likely to be the "bad boy" of the classroom; they are children with a medical disorder. Clearly there are some real humanitarian benefits to be gained by such a medical conceptualization of deviant behavior. There is less condemnation of the deviants (they have an illness, it is not their fault) and perhaps less social stigma. In some cases, even the medical treatment itself is more humanitarian social control than the criminal justice system.

There is, however, another side to the medicalization of deviant behavior. The four aspects of this side of the issue include (1) the problem of expert control; (2) medical social control; (3) the individualization of social problems; and (4) the "depoliticization" of deviant behavior.

1. *The problem of expert control.* The medical profession is a profession of experts; they have a monopoly on anything that can be conceptualized as illness. Because of the way the medical profession is organized and the mandate it has from society, decisions related to medical diagnoses and treatment are virtually controlled by medical professionals.

Some conditions that enter the medical domain are not *ipso facto* medical problems, especially deviant behavior, whether alcoholism, hyperactivity or drug addiction. By defining a problem as medical it is removed from the public realm where there can be discussion by ordinary people and put on a plane where only medical people can discuss it. As Reynolds states,

The increasing acceptance, especially among the more educated segments of our populace, of technical solutions—solutions administered by disinterested politically and morally neutral experts—results in the withdrawal of more and more areas of human experience from the realm of public discussion. For when drunkenness, juvenile delinquency, sub par performance and extreme political beliefs are seen as symptoms of an underlying illness or biological defect the merits and drawbacks of such behavior or beliefs need not be evaluated (1973:200–221).

The public may have their own conceptions of deviant behavior but that of the experts is usually dominant.

2. *Medical social control.* Defining deviant behavior as a medical problem allows certain things to be done that could not otherwise be considered; for example, the body may be cut open or psychoactive medications may be given. This treatment can be a form of social control.

In regard to drug treatment Lennard points out: "Psychoactive drugs, especially those legally prescribed, tend to restrain individuals from behavior and experience that are not complementary to the requirements of the dominant value system" (1971:57). These forms of medical social control presume a prior definition of deviance as a medical problem. Psychosurgery on an individual prone to violent outbursts requires a diagnosis that there was something wrong with his brain or nervous system. Similarly, prescribing drugs to restless, overactive and disruptive school children requires a diagnosis of hyperkinesis. These forms of social control, what Chorover (1973) has called "psychotechnology," are very powerful and often very efficient means of controlling deviance. These relatively new and increasingly popular forms of social control could not be utilized without the medicalization of deviant behavior. As is suggested from the discovery of hyperkinesis, if a mechanism of medical social control seems useful, then the deviant behavior it modifies will develop a medical label or diagnosis. No overt malevolence on the part of the medical profession is implied: rather it is part of a complex process, of which the medical profession is only a part. The larger process might be called the individualization of social problems.

3. *The individualization of social problems.* The medicalization of deviant behavior is part of a larger phenomenon that is prevalent in our society, the individualization of social problems. We tend to look for causes and solutions to complex social problems in the individual rather than in the social system. This view resembles Ryan's (1971) notion of "blaming the victim"; seeing the causes of the problem in individuals rather than in the society where they live. We then seek to change the "victim" rather than the society. The medical perspective of diagnosing an illness in an individual lends itself to the individualization of social problems. Rather than seeing certain deviant behaviors as symptomatic of problems in the social system, the medical perspective focuses on the individual diagnosing and treating the illness, generally ignoring the social situation.

Hyperkinesis serves as a good example. Both the school and the parents are concerned with the child's behavior; the child is very difficult at home and disruptive in school. No punishments or rewards seem consistently to work in modifying the behavior; and both parents and school are at their wits' end. A medical evaluation is suggested. The diagnoses of hyperkinetic behavior leads to prescribing stimulant medications. The child's behavior seems to become more socially acceptable, reducing problems in school and at home.

But there is an alternate perspective. By focusing on the symptoms and defining them as hyperkinesis we ignore the possibility that behavior is not an illness but an adaptation to a social situation. It diverts our attention from the family or school and from seriously entertaining the idea that the "problem" could be in the structure of the social system. And by giving medications we are essentially supporting the existing systems and do not allow this behavior to be a factor of change in the system.

4. *The depoliticization of deviant behavior.* Depoliticization of deviant behavior is a result of both the process of medicalization and individualization of social problems. To our western world, probably one of the clearest examples of such a depoliticization of deviant behavior occurred when political dissenters in the Soviet Union were declared mentally ill and confined in mental hospitals (cf. Conrad, 1972). This strategy served to neutralize the meaning of political protest and dissent, rendering it the ravings of mad persons.

The medicalization of deviant behavior depoliticizes deviance in the same manner. By defining the overactive, restless and disruptive child as hyperkinetic we ignore the meaning of behavior in the context of the social system. If we focused our analysis on the school system we might see the child's behavior as symptomatic of some "disorder" in the school or classroom situation, rather than symptomatic of an individual neurological disorder.

Conclusion

I have discussed the social ramifications of the medicalization of deviant behavior, using hyperkinesis as the example. A number of consequences of this medicalization have been outlined, including the depoliticization of deviant behavior, decision-making power of experts, and the role of medicine as an agent of social control. In the last analysis medical social control may be the central issue, as in this role medicine becomes a *de facto* agent of the *status quo*. The medical profession may not have entirely sought this role, but its members have been, in general, disturbingly unconcerned and unquestioning in their acceptance of it. With the increasing medical knowledge and technology it is likely that more deviant behavior will be medicalized and medicine's social control function will expand.

REFERENCES

Becker, Howard S. 1963. *Outsiders: Studies in the Sociology of Deviance.* New York: Free Press.
Bradley, Charles. 1937. "The Behavior of Children

Receiving Benzedrine." *American Journal of Psychiatry,* 94 (March): 577–585.

Charles, Alan. 1971. "The Case of Ritalin." *New Republic,* 23 (October): 17–19.

Chorover, Stephen L. 1973. "Big Brother and Psychotechnology." *Psychology Today* (October): 43–54.

Clements, Samuel D. 1966. "Task Force I: Minimal Brain Dysfunction in Children." National Institute of Neurological Diseases and Blindness, Monograph no. 3. Washington, D.C.: U.S. Department of Health, Education, and Welfare.

Cole, Sherwood. 1975. "Hyperactive Children: The Use of Stimulant Drugs Evaluated." *American Journal of Orthopsychiatry,* 45 (January): 28–37.

Coleman, James, Elihu Katz, and Herbert Menzel. 1966. *Medical Innovation.* Indianapolis: Bobbs-Merrill.

Conrad, Peter. 1972. "Ideological Deviance: An Analysis of the Soviet Use of Mental Hospitals for Political Dissenters." Unpublished manuscript.

Conrad, Peter. 1976. *Identifying Hyperactive Children: A Study in the Medicalization of Deviant Behavior.* Lexington, Mass.: D. C. Heath and Co.

DeLong, Arthur R. (1972). "What Have We Learned from Psychoactive Drugs Research with Hyperactives?" *American Journal of Diseases in Children,* 123 (February): 177–180.

Foucault, Michel. 1965. *Madness and Civilization.* New York: Pantheon.

Freidson, Eliot. 1970. *Profession of Medicine: A Study of the Sociology of Applied Knowledge.* New York: Dodd, Mead.

Grinspoon, Lester and Susan Singer. 1973. "Amphetamines in the Treatment of Hyperactive Children." *Harvard Educational Review,* 43 (November): 515–555.

Gross, Mortimer B. and William E. Wilson. 1974. *Minimal Brain Dysfunction.* New York: Brunner Mazel.

Hentoff, Nat (1972). "Drug Pushing in the Schools: The Professionals." *The Village Voice,* 22 (May): 21–23.

Kittrie, Nicholas. 1971. *The Right to Be Different.* Baltimore: Johns Hopkins Press.

Laufer, M. W., Denhoff, E., and Solomons, G. 1975. "Hyperkinetic Impulse Disorder in Children's Behavior Problems." *Psychosomatic Medicine,* 19 (January): 38–49.

Lennard, Henry L. and Associates. 1971. *Mystification and Drug Misuse.* New York: Harper and Row.

Office of Child Development. 1971. "Report of the Conference on the Use of Stimulant Drugs in Treatment of Behaviorally Disturbed Children." Washington, D.C.: Office of Child Development, Department of Health, Education and Welfare, January 11–12.

Pitts, Jesse. 1968. "Social Control: The Concept." In David Sills (ed.), *International Encyclopedia of the Social Sciences.* Vol. 14. New York: Macmillan.

Reynolds, Janice M. 1973. "The Medical Institution." In Larry T. Reynolds and James M. Henslin, *American Society: A Critical Analysis.* New York: David McKay.

Robin, Stanley S. and James J. Bosco. 1973. "Ritalin for School Children: The Teacher's Perspective." *Journal of School Health,* 47 (December): 624–628.

Rosen, George. 1972. "The Evolution of Social Medicine." In Howard E. Freeman, Sol Levine, and Leo Reeder, *Handbook of Medical Sociology.* Englewood Cliffs, N.J.: Prentice-Hall.

Ryan, William. 1970. *Blaming the Victim.* New York: Vintage.

Silverman, Milton and Philip R. Lee. 1974. *Pills, Profits and Politics.* Berkeley: University of California Press.

Sroufe, L. Alan and Mark Stewart. 1973. "Treating Problem Children with Stimulant Drugs." *New England Journal of Medicine* 289 (August 23): 407–421.

Stewart, Mark A. 1970. "Hyperactive Children." *Scientific American,* 222 (April): 794–798.

Stewart, Mark A., A. Ferris, N. P. Pitts, and A. G. Craig. 1966. "The Hyperactive Child Syndrome." *American Journal of Orthopsychiatry,* 36 (October): 861–867.

Strauss, A. A. and L. E. Lehtinen. 1947. *Psychopathology and Education of the Brain-Injured Child.* Vol. 1. New York: Grune and Stratton.

U.S. Government Printing Office. 1970. "Federal Involvement in the Use of Behavior Modification Drugs on Grammar School Children of the Right to Privacy Inquiry: Hearing Before a Subcommittee of the Committee on Government Operations." Washington, D.C.: 91st Congress, 2nd session (September 29).

Wender, Paul. 1971. *Minimal Brain Dysfunction in Children.* New York: John Wiley and Sons.

Zola, Irving. 1972. "Medicine as an Institution of Social Control." *Sociological Review,* 20 (November): 487–504.

Labelling the Mentally Retarded   JANE R. MERCER

The clinical perspective is the frame of reference most commonly adopted in studies of mental deficiency, mental illness, drug addiction, and other areas which the students of deviance choose to investigate.[1,2] This viewpoint is readily identified by several distinguishing characteristics.

First, the investigator accepts as the focus for study those individuals who have been labelled deviant. In so doing, he adopts the values of whatever social system has defined the person as deviant and assumes that its judgments are the valid measure of deviance. . . . Groups in the social structure sharing the values of the core culture tend to accept the labels attached as a consequence of the application of these values without serious questioning. . . .

A second distinguishing characteristic of the clinical perspective is the tendency to perceive deviance as an attribute of the person, as a meaning inherent in his behavior, appearance, or performance. Mental retardation, for example, is viewed as a characteristic of the person, a lack to be explained. This viewpoint results in a quest for etiology. Thus, the clinical perspective is essentially a medical frame of reference, for it sees deviance as individual pathology requiring diagnostic classification and etiological analysis for the purpose of determining proper treatment procedures and probable prognosis.

Three additional characteristics of the clinical perspective are the development of a diagnostic nomenclature, the creation of diagnostic instruments, and the professionalization of the diagnostic function.

When the investigator begins his research with the diagnostic designations assigned by official defining agents, he tends to assume that all individuals placed in a given category are essentially equivalent in respect to their deviance. . . . Individuals assigned to different categories of deviance are compared with each other or with a "normal" population consisting of persons who, for whatever reason, have escaped being labelled. The focus is on the individual.

Another characteristic of the clinical perspective is its assumption that the official definition is somehow the "right" definition. . . .

Finally, when deviance is perceived as individual pathology, social action tends to center upon changing the individual or, that failing, removing him from participation in society. Prevention and cure become the primary social goals. . . .

The social system perspective, on the other hand, attempts to see the definition of an individual's behavior as a function of the values of the social system within which he is being evaluated. The professional definers are studied as one of the most important of the evaluating social systems but within the context of other social systems which may or may not concur with official definitions.

Defining an individual as mentally ill, delinquent, or mentally retarded is viewed as an interpersonal process in which the definer makes a value judgment about the behavior of the persons being defined. . . . Deviation is not seen as a characteristic of the individual or as a meaning inherent in his behavior, but as a socially derived label which may be attached to his behavior by some social systems and not by others.[3]

. . . Thus, it follows that a person may be mentally retarded in one system and not men-

Reprinted from "Social System Perspective and Clinical Perspective: Frames of Reference for Understanding Career Patterns of People Labelled as Mentally Retarded," *Social Problems,* Vol. 13, No. 1 (Summer 1965), pp. 21–30, 33–34, by permission of the Society for the Study of Social Problems and the author.

Supported in part by the National Institute of Mental Health, Grant No. 3M-9130: Population Movement of Mental Defectives and Related Physical, Behavioral, Social, and Cultural Factors; and Grant No. MH-5687: Mental Retardation in a Community, Pacific State Hospital, Pomona, California. Appreciation for assistance is expressed to the Western Data Processing Center, Division of the Graduate School of Business Administration, University of California, Los Angeles.

[1] August B. Hollingshead and Frederick C. Redlich, *Social Class and Mental Illness,* New York: John Wiley and Sons, 1958, Chapter 11.

[2] H. E. Freeman and O. G. Simmons, "Social Class and Posthospital Performance Levels," *American Sociological Review,* 2 (June, 1959), p. 348.

[3] Howard S. Becker, editor, *The Other Side: Perspectives on Deviance,* New York: The Free Press, 1964.

tally retarded in another. He may change his label by changing his social group. This viewpoint frees us from the necessity of seeing the person as permanently stigmatized by a deviant label and makes it possible to understand otherwise obscure patterns in the life careers of individuals. . . . The research reported in this paper attempts to answer these questions about a group of persons who shared the common experience of having been labelled retarded by official defining agencies and placed in a public institution for the retarded. . . .

The specific question which this study seeks to investigate within the above framework is: "Why do the families of some individuals take them back home after a period of institutionalization in a hospital for the retarded while other families do not, when, according to official evaluations, these individuals show similar degrees of deviance, that is, have comparable intelligence test scores, and are of equivalent age, sex, ethnic status, and length of hospitalization?" . . .

Method

Two groups of labelled retardates were studied. One group consisted of patients who had been released to their families from a state hospital for the retarded and the other group consisted of a matched group of patients still resident in the hospital at the time of the study.[4]

Specifically, the released group was made up of all patients released to their families during a three year period (1957–59), who had not been readmitted to another institution for the retarded at the time of the study, and who were reported to be living within a one hundred mile radius of the hospital. Only those cases in which the family had assumed responsibility for the patient were included. Of the 76 patients who met these qualifications, it was possible to complete interviews with 63 of the families. Six families refused to be interviewed and seven could not be located.

The resident group was selected to match the released group in intelligence quotient, age, sex, ethnic status, and year of admission, other stud-

ies having demonstrated that these factors are related to the probability of release.[5]

The matched group of resident patients was selected in the following manner: all patients on the hospital rolls were sorted into two groups by sex, two groups by age, three groups by ethnic status, three groups by intelligence quotient, and two groups by year of admission. All released patients were likewise assigned to the proper category. Resident patients were then chosen at random from within each cell in sufficient numbers to correspond to the number of discharged patients also falling in that cell. Each resident case was required to have a family living within a one hundred mile radius of the hospital. If a case did not meet this requirement, another case was drawn randomly from the appropriate cell until there were an equal number of discharged and resident cases in each cell. Sex distribution in each group was 53 males and 23 females, ethnic distribution, 47 Caucasians, 20 Mexicans, and 9 Negroes.

. . . Table 1 presents the distribution of intelligence quotients, birth years, and years of admission for the interviewed cases. Of the 76 resident cases selected to match the released cases, interviews were completed with 70 families. Two refused to be interviewed and four families could not be located. Using a Kolmogorov–Smirnov Test of two independent samples, we found that all differences between the interviewed groups could be accounted for by chance.

When the 19 non-interviewed cases were compared with the 133 interviewed cases, no significant differences were found in the sex, age, I.Q., or ethnic status of the patients, or the socioeconomic level of the families. . . .

The hospital file for each patient selected for study was searched for relevant data and an interview was held with a family member. In 75 per cent of the cases the mother was interviewed; in 8 per cent the father was interviewed; and in the remaining cases some other relative served as informant. . . .

To clarify the circumstances under which the released group returned to their families, the respondent was asked two questions: "Who was the most important person in getting you to take _____ out of the hospital?" and "What were

[4]Pacific State Hospital, Pomona, California, is a state supported hospital for the mentally retarded with a population of approximately 3,000 patients.

[5]G. Tarjan, S. W. Wright, M. Kramer, P. H. Person, Jr., and R. Morgan, "The Natural History of Mental Deficiency in a State Hospital. I: Probabilities of Release and Death by Age, Intelligence Quotients, and Diagnosis," *AMA J. Dis. Childr.*, 96 (1958), pp. 64–70.

TABLE 1. Comparison of Interviewed Cases by Birth Year, Intelligence Quotient, and Year of Admission

Matched Variable	Released (63)	Resident (70)	Significance Level
Birth Year			
Before 1920	4	5	
1921–1930	13	12	
1931–1940	33	34	> .05 [1]
1941–1950	12	17	
1951–1960	1	2	
Intelligence Quotient			
0–9	2	4	
10–19	2	1	
20–29	4	3	
30–39	6	4	> .05 [1]
40–49	13	15	
50–59	14	18	
60–69	19	19	
70+	3	6	
Year of Admission			
Before 1945	5	9	
1945–1950	20	14	
1951–1956	33	31	> .05 [1]
1957 and later	5	16	

1. The Kolmogorov–Smirnov Test of two independent samples was used.

the main reasons you decided to have _____ discharged from the hospital?''

In 12 cases the parents reported that someone in the hospital, i.e., a social worker, family care mother, or a ward technician, had first suggested that the patient could be released to the family. In the 51 remaining cases the families were the active agents in release. Reasons given by the family for seeking a discharge are described in Table 2.

It is clear from this table that most of the patients who returned to their families returned because the family made an effort to secure their release. . . .

Findings

Social Status of Released Patients

Several indices were used to measure the socioeconomic level of the family of each retardate. A socioeconomic index score based on the occupation and education of the head of the household, weighted according in Hollingshead's system, was used as the basic measure. In addition, the interviewer rated the economic status of the street on which the patient's home was located, rated the physical condition of the housing unit, and completed a checklist of equipment present in the household. As can be seen in Table 3, the families of the released patients rated significantly lower than the families of the resident patients on every measure. The heads of the households in the families of released patients had less education and lower level jobs, the family residence was located among less affluent dwellings, the housing unit was in a poorer state of repair, and the dwelling was less elaborately furnished and equipped. Contrary to the pattern found in studies of those placed as mentally ill,[6] it is the "retardate" from lower socioeconomic background who is most likely to be released to his family while higher status "retardates" are more likely to remain in the hospital.

From the clinical perspective, several explanations may be proposed for these differences. It has been found in hospital populations that patients with an I.Q. below 50 are more likely to come from families which represent a cross-section of social levels, while those with an I.Q. between 50 and 70 are more likely to come from

[6] August B. Hollingshead and Frederick C. Redlich, 1958, *op. cit.*, Chapter 11.

TABLE 2.   The Release Process as Reported by the Families of Released Patients

	f	%
Hospital Initiated Releases	12	19
Family Initiated Releases		
Family opposed to placement from beginning	9	14
Parents lonely without patient or need him for some practical reason, e.g., to help with younger children, earn money, etc.	8	13
Patient was unhappy in the hospital. Hospital Failure: Mistreated patient, made him work too hard, etc.	6	9
Hospital Success: Patient improved enough to come home	9	14
Home conditions changed to permit return, e.g., found patient a job, mother's health better, etc.	10	16

TABLE 3.   Socioeconomic Differences Between Patients Released to Their Families and Those Still Resident in the State Hospital

Socioeconomic Measure		Released Living at Home (63) %	Resident in State Hospital (70) %	Significance Level
Socioeconomic Index Score of Head of Household	Above Median	36.5	61.4	
	Below Median	61.9	38.6	< .01 [3]
	Unknown	1.6	0.0	
Economic Status of Street [1]	Housing Value $10,000 and Above	29.0	55.1	
	Housing Value Less Than $10,000	71.0	44.9	< .05 [3]
Condition of Housing Unit [1]	Run Down	48.4	23.2	
	Average	46.8	57.2	< .05 [3]
	Above Average	4.8	18.8	
Household Equipment Scale [1]	0–2	19.0	11.9	
	3–5	27.6	20.9	< .05 [2]
	6–8	43.1	41.8	
	9–11	10.3	25.4	

1. Some cases are not included because data were not available.
2. Test of significance of difference between unrelated means was used.
3. Chi Square test was used.

low status families.[7] Since persons with higher I.Q.'s have a higher probability of release, this could account for higher rates of release for low status persons. However, in the present study, the tested level of intelligence was equal for both groups, and this hypothesis cannot be used as an explanation.

A second possible explanation from a clinical perspective might be based on the fact that persons who have more physical handicaps tend to be institutionalized for longer periods of time than persons with few handicaps.[8] Should it be found that high status patients have more physical handicaps than low status patients, then this could account for the latter's shorter hospitalization. Data from the present sample were ana-

[7]Georges Sabagh, Harvey F. Dingman, George Tarjan, and Stanley W. Wright, "Social Class and Ethnic Status of Patients Admitted to a State Hospital for the Retarded," *Pacific Sociological Review,* 2 (Fall, 1959), pp. 76–80.
[8]G. Tarjan, S. W. Wright, M. Kramer, R. H. Person, Jr., and R. Morgan, 96, 1958, *op. cit.,* pp. 64–70.

lyzed to determine whether there was a significant relationship between physical handicap and social status. Although released patients tended to have fewer physical handicaps than resident patients, this was irrespective of social status. When high status patients were compared with low status patients, 50% of the high status and 56% of the low status patients had no physical handicaps. A chi square of 1.9 indicates these differences could be accounted for by chance variation.

A third explanation from the clinical perspective may hinge on differences in the diagnostic categories to which retardates of different social status were assigned. . . . A diagnostic label of "familial" or "undifferentiated" ordinarily indicates that the individual has few or no physical stigmata and is essentially normal in body structure. All other categories ordinarily indicate that he has some type of physical symptomatology. Although released patients were more likely to be diagnosed as familial or undifferentiated than resident patients ($x^2 = 7.08$, $p < .01$), this, like physical handicap, was irrespective of social status. Fifty-seven per cent of the high status retardates, and 69% of the low status retardates were classified as either undifferentiated or familial, a difference which could be accounted for by chance. . . .

Divergent Definitions

In analyzing social status, four types of situations were identified. The modal category for resident patients was high social status with a smaller number of resident patients coming from low status families. The modal category for released patients was low status with a smaller number of released patients coming from higher status families. If we are correct in our hypothesis (that higher release rates for low status patients are related to the fact that the family social system is structurally more distant from the core culture and that its style of life, values, and definitions of the patient are more divergent from official definitions than that of high status families), we would expect the largest differences to occur when high status resident families are compared to low status released families. The two non-modal categories would be expected to fall at some intermediate point. For this reason, the analysis of all subsequent variables has retained these four basic classifications.

Table 4 presents the responses made to three questions asked to determine the extent to which the family concurred in the official label of "retardation," the extent to which they believed the patient's condition amenable to change, and the extent to which they anticipated that the individual could live outside the hospital and, perhaps, fill adult roles. The patterns of the divergent definitions of the situation which emerged for each group are illuminating.

When asked whether *he* believed the patient to be retarded, the high status parent more frequently concurred with the definitions of the official defining agencies while the low status parent was more prone to disagree outright or to be uncertain. This tendency is especially marked when the two modal categories are compared. While 33.3% of the parents of the low status released patients stated that they did not think the patient was retarded and 25.6% were uncertain whether he was retarded, only 4.6% of the parents of high status resident patients felt he was not retarded and 20.9% were uncertain.

When parents were asked whether they believed anything could change the patient's condition, the differences between all groups were significant at the .02 level or beyond. The high status parent was most likely to believe that nothing could change his child's condition, and this was significantly more characteristic of parents whose children were still in the hospital than those who had taken their child from the hospital on both status levels.

When asked what they saw in the future for their child, all groups again differed significantly in the expected direction. The modal, high status group was least optimistic and the modal, low status group, most optimistic about the future. Fully 46% of the parents of the latter group expressed the expectation that their child would get a job, marry, and fulfill the usual adult roles while only 6.9% of the modal, high status group responded in this fashion. High status parents, as a group, more frequently see their child playing dependent roles. It is interesting to note that, although a large percentage of parents of released patients believe the patient will be dependent, they demonstrate their willingness to accept responsibility for the retarded child themselves by their responding that they foresee him having a future in which he is dependent at home. Only 9.3% of the high status and 22.2% of the low status parents of the resident patients see this as a future prospect. Release to the family clearly appears to be contingent upon the

TABLE 4. Patterns of Deviant Definitions

Question	Response Categories	High Status Resident (43) %	High Status Released (23) %	Low Status Resident (27) %	Low Status Released (39) %	Significance Levels High Status Low Status	High Status Resident Low Status Released	High Status Resident High Status Released	Low Status Resident Low Status Released
1. We know that many people have told you _____ is retarded but we want to know what you think. Do you think he/she is retarded?	Yes	74.4	47.8	66.6	41.0				
	Uncertain	20.9	39.1	14.8	25.6	< .02 [1]	< .02 [1]	NS [1]	NS [1]
	No	4.6	13.0	18.5	33.3				
2. Do you believe anything can change _____'s condition?	Nothing	74.3	39.0	66.6	33.3				
	Uncertain	2.3	17.2	11.1	38.4	< .02 [2]	< .001 [2]	< .01 [2]	< .01 [2]
	Training, Medical Care, etc.	23.2	43.4	22.2	28.2				
3. What do you see in the future for _____ ?	Dependent in Institution	83.7	13.0	74.0	2.5				
	Dependent at Home	9.3	60.8	22.2	48.7	< .02 [2]	< .001 [2]	< .001 [2]	< .001 [2]
	Normal Adult Roles	6.9	26.0	3.7	46.1				

1. The Kolmogorov–Smirnov Test of two independent samples was used.

2. The Log-Likelihood Ratio Test was used. (Barnett, Wolf, "The Log-Likelihood Ratio Test [The G-Test]: Methods and Tables for a Test of Heterogeneity in Contingency Tables," *Annals of Human Genetics*, Vol. 21, Part 4, June 1957, pp. 397–409.)

willingness of the family to accept the patient's dependency, if they do not foresee him assuming independent adult roles.

Factors in the Labelling Process

From the social system perspective, retardation is viewed as a label placed upon an individual after someone has evaluated his behavior within a specific set of norms. Retardation is not a meaning necessarily inherent in the behavior of the individual. We have seen that the parents of low status, released patients tend to reject the label of retardation and to be optimistic about the future. We surmised that this divergent definition could well be related to factors in the process by which the child was first categorized as subnormal, such as his age at the time, the type of behavior which was used as a basis for making the evaluation, and the persons doing the labelling. Consequently, parents were asked specifically about these factors. Table 5 records their responses.

Children from lower status families were labelled as mentally subnormal at a significantly later age than children from high status families. Seventy-nine per cent of the patients in the high status, modal group were classified as retarded by the age of six while only 36.1% of those in the low status, modal group were identified at such an early age. The largest percentage of low status retardates were first classified after they reached public school age. This indicates that relatives and friends, who are the individuals most likely to observe and evaluate the behavior of young children, seldom saw anything deviant in the early development of lower status children later labelled retarded, but that the primary groups of higher status children did perceive early deviation.

This is related to the responses made when parents were asked what first prompted someone to believe the patient retarded. The modal, high status group reported slow development in 48.8% of the cases and various types of physical symptoms in an additional 20.9%, while only 14.7% and 11.8% of the modal, low status parents gave these responses. On the other hand, 55.9% of the modal, low status group were first labelled because they had problems learning in school, while this was true of only 9.3% of the modal high status group.

When parents were asked who was the most important person influencing them in placing the child in the hospital, a parallel pattern emerged. Medical persons are the most important single group for the modal high status persons while the police and welfare agencies loom very significant in 64.1% of the cases in the modal, low status group. These findings are similar to those of Hollingshead and Redlich in their study of paths to the hospital for the mentally ill.[9] Of additional interest is the fact that the person important in placement differentiates the low status released from the low status resident patient at the .01 level. The resident low status patient's path to the hospital is similar to that of the high status patient and markedly different from released low status persons. When authoritative figures such as police and welfare are primary forces in placement, the patient is more likely to return home.

We interpret these findings to mean that when the family—or persons whose advice is solicited by the family, i.e., medical persons—is "most important" in placing a person in a hospital for the retarded, the primary groups have themselves first defined the individual as a deviant and sought professional counsel. When their own suspicions are supported by official definitions, they are more likely to leave the patient in an institution.

Conversely, when a person is labelled retarded by an authoritative, governmental agency whose advice is not solicited and who, in the case of the police, may be perceived as a punishing agent, the family frequently rejects the official definition of the child as retarded and withdraws him from the institution at the first opportunity. This attitude was clearly exemplified by one mother who, when asked why the family had taken the child from the hospital, replied, "Why not? He had served his time."

The influence of the police as a factor in labelling the low status person as retarded may actually be greater than that shown in Table 5. Fifty per cent of the low status retardates had some type of police record while only 23% of the high status subnormals were known to the police, a difference significant beyond the .01 level. . . .

---

[9] August B. Hollingshead and Frederick C. Redlich, 1958, *op. cit.*, Chapter 11.

TABLE 5. Factors in the Labelling Process

Question	Response Categories	High Status Resident (43) %	High Status Released (23) %	Low Status Resident (27) %	Low Status Released (39) %	Significance Levels High Status Low Status	Resident High Released Low	Resident High Released High	Resident Low Released Low
1. How old was ___ when someone first said he was retarded?	1–2 years	44.1	18.1	23.2	16.7				
	3–6 years	34.8	50.0	30.2	19.4	<.001 [1]	<.02 [1]	NS [1]	NS [1]
	7–10 years	9.3	22.7	11.5	30.5				
	11–14 years	4.6	0.0	11.5	16.7				
	15 or over	6.9	9.1	23.2	16.7				
2. What was there about ___ that made you/them think he/she might be retarded?	Slow Development	48.8	30.4	19.2	14.7				
	Physical Symptoms	20.9	17.3	26.9	11.8				
	Behavioral Problems	20.9	21.7	15.4	17.6	<.005 [2]	<.001 [2]	NS [2]	NS [2]
	Couldn't Learn in School	9.3	30.4	38.5	55.9				
3. Who was the most important person in getting you to place ___ in the hospital?	Family	27.9	43.4	48.1	25.6				
	Medical or Psychological Person	37.2	30.4	11.1	2.5				
	Police or Welfare	13.9	17.3	18.5	64.1	<.01 [2]	<.001 [2]	NS [2]	<.01 [2]
	Schools or Other	20.9	8.6	22.2	7.6				

1. The Kolmogorov–Smirnov Test of two independent samples were used.
2. The Log-Likelihood Ratio Test was used. (Barnett, Wolf, "The Log-Likelihood Ratio Test [The G-Test]: Methods and Tables for a Test of Heterogeneity in Contingency Tables," *Annals of Human Genetics*, Vol. 21, Part 4, June 1957, pp. 397–409.)

Discussion and Conclusions

The life space of the individual may be viewed as a vast network of interlocking social systems through which the person moves during the course of his lifetime. Those systems which exist close to one another in the social structure tend, because of overlapping memberships and frequent communication, to evolve similar patterns of norms. Most individuals are born and live out their lives in a relatively limited segment of this social network and tend to contact mainly social systems which share common norms. When an individual's contacts are restricted to a circumscribed segment of the structure, this gives some stability to the evaluations which are made of his behavior and to the labels which are attached to him.

However, when the person's life career takes him into segments of the social network which are located at a distance from his point of origin, as when a Mexican-American child enters the public school or a Negro child gets picked up by the police, he is then judged by a new and different set of norms. Behavior which was perfectly acceptable in his primary social systems may now be judged as evidence of "mental retardation." At this point, he is caught up in the web of official definitions. However, because he has primary social systems which may not agree with these official labels, he may be able to return to that segment of the social structure which does not label him as deviant after he has fulfilled the minimal requirements of the official system. That is, he can drop out of school or he can "serve his time" in the state hospital and then go home. By changing his location in social space, he can change his label from "retarded" to "not much different from the rest of us." For example, the mother of a Mexican-American, male, adult patient who had been released from the hospital after being committed following an incident in which he allegedly made sexual advances to a young girl, told the author, "There is nothing wrong with Benny. He just can't read or write." Since the mother spoke only broken English, had no formal schooling, and could not read or write, Benny did not appear deviant to her. From her perspective, he didn't have anything wrong with him.

The child from a high status family has no such recourse. His primary social systems lie structurally close to the official social systems and tend to concur on what is acceptable. Definitions of his subnormality appear early in his life and are more universal in all his social groups. He cannot escape the retarded label because all his associates agree that he is a deviant.[10]

In conclusion, tentative answers may be given to the three questions raised earlier in this discussion. "Who sees whom as retarded?" Within the social system perspective, it becomes clear that persons who are clinically similar may be defined quite differently by their primary social systems. The person from lower status social systems is less likely to be perceived as mentally subnormal.

"What impact does this differential definition have on the life career of the person?" Apparently, these differential definitions do make a difference because the group which diverges most widely from official definitions is the group in which the most individuals are released from the institution to their families.

Finally, "What are the characteristics of the social systems which diverge most widely from official definitions?" These social systems seem to be characterized by low educational achievement, high levels of dependency, and high concentrations of ethnic minorities.

A social system perspective adds a useful dimension to the label "mental retardation" by its focus on the varied definitions which may be applied to behavior by different groups in society. For those interested in the care and treatment of persons officially labelled as mentally subnormal, it may be beneficial in some cases to seek systematically to relocate such individuals in the social structure in groups which will not define them as deviant. Rather than insisting that a family adopt official definitions of abnormality, we may frequently find it advisable to permit them to continue to view the patient within their own frame of reference and thus make it easier for them to accept him.

---

[10] Lewis Anthony Dexter, "On the Politics and Sociology of Stupidity in Our Society" in *The Other Side: Perspectives on Deviance,* edited by Howard S. Becker, New York: The Free Press, 1964, pp. 37–49.

4 THE ROLE OF THIRD PARTIES

As we noted in Chapter 1, deviance reflects a process of social definition. Such definition is often affected or facilitated by third parties. Family members, for example, may enlist an outside defining agent to help them define deviance. How successful the labeling will be depends on how much consensus the defining agent can muster, and consensus is much easier to attain when significant outsiders cooperate in the labeling. When an important person in the community, for example, speaks for the community in labeling someone as deviant, they generally succeed in altering that person's "total identity"; in doing so, they accomplish what Harold Garfinkel has aptly titled a "status degradation ceremony." *

In the first reading Erving Goffman points out how family members and outside defining agents collaborate in a process that culminates in a person's being committed to a mental hospital. Next, Edwin Lemert shows how people actually do conspire to exclude so-called paranoids. And, in the final reading, Jorge Bustamante describes the wetbacks' labor situation and how the failure of the Border Patrol to enforce immigration laws is related to the economic interests of powerful farmers; thus, in this case, the farmers, as third parties, are "antilaw entrepreneurs," defining wetbacks as deviants and initiating a status degradation ceremony only when they want to dispose of a complaining or unwanted wetback.

---

* Harold Garfinkel, "Conditions of Successful Degradation Ceremonies," *American Journal of Sociology* (March, 1956) 61:421.

The Moral Career of the Mental Patient

ERVING GOFFMAN

Traditionally the term *career* has been reserved for those who expect to enjoy the rises laid out within a respectable profession. The term is coming to be used, however, in a broadened sense to refer to any social strand of any person's course through life. The perspective of natural history is taken: unique outcomes are neglected in favor of such changes over time as are basic and common to the members of a social category, although occurring independently to each of them. Such a career is not a thing that can be brilliant or disappointing; it can no more be a success than a failure. In this light, I want to consider the mental patient, drawing mainly upon data collected during a year's participant observation of patient social life in a public mental hospital,[1] wherein an attempt was made to take the patient's point of view.

One value of the concept of career is its two-sidedness. One side is linked to internal matters held dearly and closely, such as image of self and felt identity; the other side concerns official position, jural relations, and style of life, and is part of a publicly accessible institutional complex. The concept of career, then, allows one to move back and forth between the personal and the public, between the self and its significant society, without having overly to rely for data upon what the person says he thinks he imagines himself to be.

This paper, then, is an exercise in the institutional approach to the study of self. The main concern will be with the *moral* aspects of career—that is, the regular sequence of changes that career entails in the person's self and in his framework of imagery for judging himself and others.[2]

The category "mental patient" itself will be understood in one strictly sociological sense. In this perspective, the psychiatric view of a person becomes significant only in so far as this view itself alters his social fate—an alteration which seems to become fundamental in our society when, and only when, the person is put through the process of hospitalization.[3] I therefore exclude certain neighboring categories: the undiscovered candidates who would be judged "sick" by psychiatric standards but who never come to be viewed as such by themselves or others, although they may cause everyone a great deal of trouble;[4] the office patient whom a

Reprinted by special permission of the author and The William Alanson White Psychiatric Foundation, Inc., from *Psychiatry: Journal for the Study of Interpersonal Processes*, Vol. 22 (May 1959), pp. 123–135. Copyright © 1959 by The William Alanson White Psychiatric Foundation, Inc.

[1] The study was conducted during 1955–56 under the auspices of the Laboratory of Socio-environmental Studies of the National Institute of Mental Health. I am grateful to the Laboratory Chief, John A. Clausen, and to Dr. Winfred Overholser, Superintendent, and the late Dr. Jay Hoffman, then First Assistant Physician of Saint Elizabeth's Hospital, Washington, D.C., for the ideal cooperation they freely provided. A preliminary report is contained in Goffman, "Interpersonal Persuasion," pp. 117–193; in *Group Processes: Transactions of the Third Conference,* edited by Bertram Schaffner; New York, Josiah Macy, Jr. Foundation, 1957. A shorter version of this paper was presented at the Annual Meeting of the American Sociological Society, Washington, D.C., August, 1957.

[2] Material on moral career can be found in early social anthropological work on ceremonies of status transition, and in classic social psychological descriptions of those spectacular changes in one's view of self that can accompany participation in social movements and sects. Recently new kinds of relevant data have been suggested by psychiatric interest in the problem of "identity" and sociological studies of work careers and "adult socialization."

[3] This point has recently been made by Elaine and John Cumming, *Closed Ranks;* Cambridge, Commonwealth Fund, Harvard Univ. Press, 1957; pp. 101–102. "Clinical experience supports the impression that many people define mental illness as 'That condition for which a person is treated in a mental hospital.' . . . Mental illness, it seems, is a condition which afflicts people who must go to a mental institution, but until they do almost anything they do is normal." Leila Deasy has pointed out to me the correspondence here with the situation in white collar crime. Of those who are detected in this activity, only the ones who do not manage to avoid going to prison find themselves accorded the social role of the criminal.

[4] Case records in mental hospitals are just now coming to be exploited to show the incredible amount of trouble a person may cause for himself and others before anyone begins to think about him psychiatrically, let alone take psychiatric action against him. See John A. Clausen and Marian Radke Yarrow, "Paths to the Mental Hospital," *J. Social Issues* (1955) 11:25–32; August B. Hollingshead and Frederick C. Redlich, *Social Class and Mental Illness;* New York, Wiley, 1958; pp. 173–174.

psychiatrist feels he can handle with drugs or shock on the outside; the mental client who engages in psychotherapeutic relationships. And I include anyone, however robust in temperament, who somehow gets caught up in the heavy machinery of mental hospital servicing. In this way the effects of being treated as a mental patient can be kept quite distinct from the effects upon a person's life of traits a clinician would view as psychopathological.[5] Persons who become mental hospital patients vary widely in the kind and degree of illness that a psychiatrist would impute to them, and in the attributes by which laymen would describe them. But once started on the way, they are confronted by some importantly similar circumstances and respond to these in some importantly similar ways. Since these similarities do not come from mental illness, they would seem to occur in spite of it. It is thus a tribute to the power of social forces that the uniform status of mental patient cannot only assure an aggregate of persons a common fate and eventually, because of this, a common character, but that this social reworking can be done upon what is perhaps the most obstinate diversity of human materials that can be brought together by society. . . .[6]

The career of the mental patient falls popularly and naturalistically into three main phases: the period prior to entering the hospital, which I shall call the *prepatient phase;* the period in the hospital, the *inpatient phase;* the period after discharge from the hospital, should this occur, namely, the *ex-patient phase.*[7] This paper will deal only with the first . . . [phase].

The Prepatient Phase

A relatively small group of prepatients come into the mental hospital willingly, because of their own idea of what will be good for them, or because of wholehearted agreement with the relevant members of their family. Presumably these recruits have found themselves acting in a way which is evidence to them that they are losing their minds or losing control of themselves. This view of oneself would seem to be one of the most pervasively threatening things that can happen to the self in our society, especially since it is likely to occur at a time when the person is in any case sufficiently troubled to exhibit the kind of symptom which he himself can see. As Sullivan described it,

What we discover in the self-system of a person undergoing schizophrenic changes or schizophrenic processes, is then, in its simplest form, an extremely fear-marked puzzlement, consisting of the use of rather generalized and anything but exquisitely refined referential processes in an attempt to cope with what is essentially a failure at being human—a failure at being anything that one could respect as worth being.[8]

Coupled with the person's disintegrative reevaluation of himself will be the new, almost equally pervasive circumstance of attempting to conceal from others what he takes to be the new fundamental facts about himself, and attempting to discover whether others too have discovered them.[9] Here I want to stress that perception of losing one's mind is based on culturally derived and socially engrained stereotypes as to the

---

[5] An illustration of how this perspective may be taken to all forms of deviancy may be found in Edwin Lemert, *Social Pathology;* New York, McGraw-Hill, 1951; see especially pp. 74–76. A specific application to mental defectives may be found in Stewart E. Perry, "Some Theoretic Problems of Mental Deficiency and Their Action Implications," *Psychiatry* (1954) 17:45–73; see especially p. 68.

[6] [Goffman developed this point more fully as follows.]

Whatever . . . the various patient's psychiatric diagnoses, and whatever the special ways in which social life on the "inside" is unique, the researcher can find that he is participating in a community not significantly different from any other he has studied. Conscientious objectors who voluntarily went to jail sometimes arrived at the same conclusion regarding criminal inmates. See, for example, Alfred Hassler, *Diary of a Self-made Convict;* Chicago, Regnery, 1954; p. 74.

[7] This simple picture is complicated by the somewhat special experience of roughly a third of ex-patients—namely, readmission to the hospital, this being the recidivist or "repatient" phase.

[8] Harry Stack Sullivan, *Clinical Studies in Psychiatry,* edited by Helen Swick Perry, Mary Ladd Gavel, and Martha Gibbon: New York, Norton, 1956; pp. 184–185.

[9] This moral experience can be contrasted with that of a person learning to become a marihuana . . . [user], whose discovery that he can be "high" and still "op" effectively without being detected apparently leads to a new level of use. See Howard S. Becker, "Marihuana Use and Social Control," *Social Problems* (1955) 3:35–44; see especially pp. 40–41.

significance of symptoms such as hearing voices, losing temporal and spatial orientation, and sensing that one is being followed, and that many of the most spectacular and convincing of these symptoms in some instances psychiatrically signify merely a temporary emotional upset in a stressful situation, however terrifying to the person at the time. Similarly, the anxiety consequent upon this perception of oneself, and the strategies devised to reduce this anxiety, are not a product of abnormal psychology, but would be exhibited by any person socialized into our culture who came to conceive of himself as someone losing his mind. Interestingly, subcultures in American society apparently differ in the amount of ready imagery and encouragement they supply for such self-views, leading to differential rates of *self*-referral; the capacity to take this disintegrative view of oneself without psychiatric prompting seems to be one of the questionable cultural privileges of the upper classes.[10]

For the person who has come to see himself—with whatever justification—as mentally unbalanced, entrance to the mental hospital can sometimes bring relief, perhaps in part because of the sudden transformation in the structure of his basic social situations; instead of being to himself a questionable person trying to maintain a role as a full one, he can become an officially questioned person known to himself to be not so questionable as that. In other cases, hospitalization can make matters worse for the willing patient, confirming by the objective situation what has theretofore been a matter of the private experience of self.

Once the willing prepatient enters the hospital, he may go through the same routine of experiences as do those who enter unwillingly. In any case, it is the latter that I mainly want to consider, since in America at present these are by far the more numerous kind.[11] Their approach to the institution takes one of three classic forms: they come because they have been implored by their family or threatened with the abrogation of family ties unless they go "willingly"; they come by force under police escort; they come under misapprehension purposely induced by others, this last restricted mainly to youthful prepatients.

The prepatient's career may be seen in terms of an extrusory model; he starts out with relationships and rights, and ends up, at the beginning of his hospital stay, with hardly any of either. The moral aspects of this career, then, typically begin with the experience of abandonment, disloyalty, and embitterment. This is the case even though to others it may be obvious that he was in need of treatment, and even though in the hospital he may soon come to agree.

The case histories of most mental patients document offense against some arrangement for face-to-face living—a domestic establishment, a work place, a semipublic organization such as a church or store, a public region such as a street or park. Often there is also a record of some *complainant,* some figure who takes that action against the offender which eventually leads to his hospitalization. This may not be the person who makes the first move, but it is the person who makes what turns out to be the first effective move. Here is the *social* beginning of the patient's career, regardless of where one might locate the psychological beginning of his mental illness.

The kinds of offenses which lead to hospitalization are felt to differ in nature from those which lead to other extrusory consequences—to imprisonment, divorce, loss of job, disownment, regional exile, noninstitutional psychiatric treatment, and so forth. But little seems known about these differentiating factors; and when one studies actual commitments, alternate outcomes frequently appear to have been possible. It seems true, moreover, that for every offense that leads to an effective complaint, there are many psychiatrically similar ones that never do. No action is taken; or action is taken which leads to other extrusory outcomes; or ineffective action is taken, leading to the mere pacifying or putting off of the person who complains. Thus, as Clausen and Yarrow have nicely shown, even offenders who are eventually hospitalized are

---

[10] See Hollingshead and Redlich, *op. cit.,* p. 187, Table 6, where relative frequency is given of self-referral by social class grouping.

[11] The distinction employed here between willing and unwilling patients cuts across the legal one, of voluntary and committed, since some persons who are glad to come to the mental hospital may be legally committed, and of those who come only because of strong familial pressure, some may sign themselves in as voluntary patients.

likely to have had a long series of ineffective actions taken against them.[12]

Separating those offenses which could have been used as grounds for hospitalizing the offender from those that are so used, one finds a vast number of what students of occupation call career contingencies.[13] Some of these contingencies in the mental patient's career have been suggested, if not explored, such as socioeconomic status, visibility of the offense, proximity to a mental hospital, amount of treatment facilities available, community regard for the type of treatment given in available hospitals, and so on.[14] For information about other contingencies one must rely on atrocity tales: a psychotic man is tolerated by his wife until she finds herself a boyfriend, or by his adult children until they move from a house to an apartment; an alcoholic is sent to a mental hospital because the jail is full, and a drug addict because he declines to avail himself of psychiatric treatment on the outside; a rebellious adolescent daughter can no longer be managed at home because she now threatens to have an open affair with an unsuitable companion; and so on. Correspondingly there is an equally important set of contingencies causing the person to by-pass this fate. And should the person enter the hospital, still another set of contingencies will help determine when he is to obtain a discharge—such as the desire of his family for his return, the availability of a "manageable" job, and so on. The society's official view is that inmates of mental hospitals are there primarily because they are suffering from mental illness. However, in the degree that the "mentally ill" outside hospitals numerically approach or surpass those inside hospitals, one could say that mental patients *distinctively* suffer not from mental illness, but from contingencies.

Career contingencies occur in conjunction with a second feature of the prepatient's career—the *circuit of agents*—and agencies—that participate fatefully in his passage from civilian to patient status.[15] Here is an instance of that increasingly important class of social system whose elements are agents and agencies, which are brought into systemic connection through having to take up and send on the same persons. Some of these agent-roles will be cited now, with the understanding that in any concrete circuit a role may be filled more than once, and a single person may fill more than one of them.

First is the *next-of-relation*—the person whom the prepatient sees as the most available of those upon whom he should be able to most depend in times of trouble; in this instance the last to doubt his sanity and the first to have done everything to save him from the fate which, it transpires, he has been approaching. The patient's next-of-relation is usually his next of kin; the special term is introduced because he need not be. Second is the *complainant,* the person who retrospectively appears to have started the person on his way to the hospital. Third are the *mediators*—the sequence of agents and agencies to which the prepatient is referred and through which he is relayed and processed on his way to the hospital. Here are included police, clergy, general medical practitioners, office psychiatrists, personnel in public clinics, lawyers, social service workers, school teachers, and so on. One of these agents will have the legal mandate to sanction commitment and will exercise it, and so those agents who precede him in the process will be involved in something whose outcome is not yet settled. When the mediators retire from the scene, the prepatient has become an inpatient, and the significant agent has become the hospital administrator.

While the complainant usually takes action in a lay capacity as a citizen, an employer, a neighbor, or a kinsman, mediators tend to be specialists and differ from those they serve in significant ways. They have experience in handling trouble, and some professional distance from what they handle. Except in the case of policemen, and perhaps some clergy, they tend to be

---

[12] Clausen and Yarrow, *op. cit.*

[13] An explicit application of this notion to the field of mental health may be found in Edwin M. Lemert, "Legal Commitment and Social Control," *Sociology and Social Research* (1946) 30:370–378.

[14] For example, Jerome K. Meyers and Leslie Schaffer, "Social Stratification and Psychiatric Practice: A Study of an Outpatient Clinic," *Amer. Sociological Rev.* (1954) 19:307–310. Lemert, see footnote 5; pp. 402–403. *Patients in Mental Institutions, 1941;* Washington, D.C., Department of Commerce, Bureau of the Census, 1941; p. 2.

[15] For one circuit of agents and its bearing on career contingencies, see Oswald Hall, "The Stages of a Medical Career," *Amer. J. Sociology* (1948) 53:327–336.

more psychiatrically oriented than the lay public, and will see the need for treatment at times when the public docs not.[16]

An interesting feature of these roles is the functional effects of their interdigitation. For example, the feelings of the patient will be influenced by whether or not the person who fills the role of complainant also has the role of next-of-relation—an embarrassing combination more prevalent, apparently, in the higher classes than in the lower.[17] Some of these emergent effects will be considered now.[18]

In the prepatient's progress from home to the hospital he may participate as a third person in what he may come to experience as a kind of *alienative coalition*. His next-of-relation presses him into coming to "talk things over" with a medical practitioner, an office psychiatrist, or some other counselor. Disinclination on his part may be met by threatening him with desertion, disownment, or other legal action, or by stressing the joint and explorative nature of the interview. But typically the next-of-relation will have set the interview up, in the sense of selecting the professional, arranging for time, telling the professional something about the case, and so on. This move effectively tends to establish the next-of-relation as the responsible person to whom pertinent findings can be divulged, while effectively establishing the other as the patient. The prepatient often goes to the interview with the understanding that he is going as an equal of someone who is so bound together with him that a third person could not come between them in fundamental matters; this after all, is one way in which close relationships are defined in our society. Upon arrival at the office the prepatient suddenly finds that he and his next-of-relation have not been accorded the same roles, and apparently that a prior understanding between the professional and the next-of-relation has been put in operation against him. In the extreme but common case the professional first sees the prepatient alone, in the role of advisor, while carefully avoiding talking things over seriously with them both together.[19] And even in those nonconsultative cases where public officials must forcibly extract a person from a family that wants to tolerate him, the next-of-relation is likely to be induced to "go along" with the official action, so that even here the prepatient may feel that an alienative coalition has been formed against him.

The moral experience of being third man in such a coalition is likely to embitter the prepatient, especially since his troubles have already probably led to some estrangement from his next-of-relation. After he enters the hospital, continued visits by his next-of-relation can give the patient the "insight" that his own best interests were being served. But the initial visits may temporarily strengthen his feeling of abandonment; he is likely to beg his visitor to get him out or at least to get him more privileges and to sympathize with the monstrousness of his plight—to which the visitor ordinarily can respond only by trying to maintain a hopeful note, by not "hearing" the requests, or by assuring the patient that the medical authorities know about these things and are doing what is medically best. The visitor then nonchalantly goes back into a world that the patient has learned is incredibly thick with freedom and privileges, causing the patient to feel that his next-of-relation is merely adding a pious gloss to a clear case of traitorous desertion.

The depth to which the patient may feel betrayed by his next-of-relation seems to be increased by the fact that another witnesses his betrayal—a factor which is apparently significant in many three-party situations. An offended person may well act forbearantly and accommodatively toward an offender when the two are alone, choosing peace ahead of justice. The presence of a witness, however, seems to add something to the implications of the offense. For then it is beyond the power of the offended and offender to forget about, erase, or suppress what has happened; the offense has become a public

---

[16] See Cumming and Cumming, *op. cit.;* p. 92.

[17] Hollingshead and Redlich, *op. cit.;* p. 187.

[18] For an analysis of some of these circuit implications for the inpatient, see Leila C. Deasy and Olive W. Quinn, "The Wife of the Mental Patient and the Hospital Psychiatrist," *J. Social Issues* (1955) 11:49–60. An interesting illustration of this kind of analysis may also be found in Alan G. Gowman, "Blindness and the Role of Companion," *Social Problems* (1956) 4:68–75. A general statement may be found in Robert Merton, "The Role Set: Problems in Sociological Theory," *British J. Sociology* (1957) 8:106–120.

[19] I have one case record of a man who claims he thought *he* was taking his wife to see the psychiatrist, not realizing until too late that his wife had made the arrangements.

social fact.[20] When the witness is a mental health commission as is sometimes the case, the witnessed betrayal can verge on a "degradation ceremony."[21] In such circumstances, the offended patient may feel that some kind of extensive reparative action is required before witnesses, if his honor and social weight are to be restored.

Two other aspects of sensed betrayal should be mentioned. First, those who suggest the possibility of another's entering a mental hospital are not likely to provide a realistic picture of how in fact it may strike him when he arrives. Often he is told that he will get required medical treatment and a rest, and may well be out in a few months or so. In some cases they may thus be concealing what they know, but I think, in general, they will be telling what they see as the truth. For here there is a quite relevant difference between patients and mediating professionals; mediators, more so than the public at large, may conceive of mental hospitals as short-term medical establishments where required rest and attention can be voluntarily obtained, and not as places of coerced exile. When the prepatient finally arrives he is likely to learn quite quickly, quite differently. He then finds that the information given him about life in the hospital has had the effect of his having put up less resistance to entering than he now sees he would have put up had he known the facts. Whatever the intentions of those who participated in his transition from person to patient, he may sense they have in effect "conned" him into his present predicament.

I am suggesting that the prepatient starts out with at least a portion of the rights, liberties, and satisfactions of the civilian and ends up on a psychiatric ward stripped of almost everything. The question here is *how* this stripping is managed. This is the second aspect of betrayal I want to consider.

As the prepatient may see it, the circuit of significant figures can function as a kind of *betrayal funnel*. Passage from person to patient may be effected through a series of linked stages, each managed by a different agent. While each stage tends to bring a sharp decrease in adult free status, each agent may try to maintain the fiction that no further decrease will occur. He may even manage to turn the prepatient over to the next agent while sustaining this note. Further, through words, cues, and gestures, the prepatient is implicitly asked by the current agent to join with him in sustaining a running line of polite small talk that tactfully avoids the administrative facts of the situation, becoming, with each stage, progressively more at odds with these facts. The spouse would rather not have to cry to get the prepatient to visit a psychiatrist; psychiatrists would rather not have a scene when the prepatient learns that he and his spouse are being seen separately and in different ways; the police infrequently bring a prepatient to the hospital in a strait jacket, finding it much easier all around to give him a cigarette, some kindly words, and freedom to relax in the back seat of the patrol car; and finally, the admitting psychiatrist finds he can do his work better in the relative quiet and luxury of the "admission suite" where, as an incidental consequence, the notion can survive that a mental hospital is indeed a comforting place. If the prepatient heeds all of these implied requests and is reasonably decent about the whole thing, he can travel the whole circuit from home to hospital without forcing anyone to look directly at what is happening or to deal with the raw emotion that his situation might well cause him to express. His showing consideration for those who are moving him toward the hospital allows them to show consideration for him, with the joint result that these interactions can be sustained with some of the protective harmony characteristic of ordinary face-to-face dealings. But should the new patient cast his mind back over the sequence of steps leading to hospitalization, he may feel that everyone's *current* comfort was being busily sustained while his long-range welfare was being undermined. This realization may constitute a moral experience that further separates him for the time from the people on the outside.[22]

---

[20] A paraphrase from Kurt Riezler, "The Social Psychology of Shame," *Amer. J. Sociology* (1943) 48:458.

[21] See Harold Garfinkel, "Conditions of Successful Degradation Ceremonies," *Amer. J. Sociology* (1956) 61:420–424.

[22] Concentration camp practices provide a good example of the function of the betrayal funnel in inducing cooperation and reducing struggle and fuss, although here the mediators could not be said to be acting in the best interests of the inmates. Police picking up persons from their homes would sometimes joke good-naturedly and offer to wait while coffee was being served. Gas chambers were fitted out like delousing rooms, and victims taking off their

I would now like to look at the circuit of career agents from the point of view of the agents themselves. Mediators in the person's transition from civil to patient status—as well as his keepers, once he is in the hospital—have an interest in establishing a responsible next-of-relation as the patient's deputy or *guardian;* should there be no obvious candidate for the role, someone may be sought out and pressed into it. Thus while a person is gradually being transformed into a patient, a next-of-relation is gradually being transformed into a guardian. With a guardian on the scene, the whole transition process can be kept tidy. He is likely to be familiar with the prepatient's civil involvements and business, and can tie up loose ends that might otherwise be left to entangle the hospital. Some of the prepatient's abrogated civil rights can be transferred to him, thus helping to sustain the legal fiction that while the prepatient does not actually have his rights he somehow actually has not lost them.

Inpatients commonly sense, at least for a time, that hospitalization is a massive unjust deprivation, and sometimes succeed in convincing a few persons on the outside that this is the case. It often turns out to be useful, then, for those identified with inflicting these deprivations, however justifiably, to be able to point to the cooperation and agreement of someone whose relationship to the patient places him above suspicion, firmly defining him as the person most likely to have the patient's personal interest at heart. If the guardian is satisfied with what is happening to the new inpatient, the world ought to be.[23]

Now it would seem that the greater the legitimate personal stake one party has in another, the better he can take the role of guardian to the other. But the structural arrangements in society which lead to the acknowledged merging of two persons' interests lead to additional consequences. For the person to whom the patient turns for help—for protection against such threats as involuntary commitment—is just the person to whom the mediators and hospital administrators logically turn for authorization. It is understandable, then, that some patients will come to sense, at least for a time, that the closeness of a relationship tells nothing of its trustworthiness.

There are still other functional effects emerging from this complement of roles. If and when the next-of-relation appeals to mediators for help in the trouble he is having with the prepatient, hospitalization may not, in fact, be in his mind. He may not even perceive the prepatient as mentally sick, or, if he does, he may not consistently hold to this view.[24] It is the circuit of mediators, with their great psychiatric sophistication and their belief in the medical character of mental hospitals, that will often define the situation for the next-of-relation, assuring him that hospitalization is a possible solution and a good one, that it involves no betrayal, but is rather a medical action taken in the best interests of the prepatient. Here the next-of-relation may learn that doing his duty to the prepatient may cause the prepatient to distrust and even hate him for the time. But the fact that this course of action may have had to be pointed out and prescribed by professionals, and be defined by them as a moral duty, relieves the next-of-relation of some of the guilt he may feel.[25] It is a poignant fact that an adult son or daughter may be pressed into the role of mediator, so that the hostility

---

clothes were told to note where they were leaving them. The sick, aged, weak, or insane who were selected for extermination were sometimes driven away in Red Cross ambulances to camps referred to by terms such as "observation hospital." See David Boder, *I Did Not Interview the Dead;* Urbana, Univ. of Illinois Press, 1949; p. 81; and Elie A. Cohen, *Human Behavior in the Concentration Camp;* London, Cape, 1954; pp. 32, 37, 107.

[23] Interviews collected by the Clausen group at NIMH suggest that when a wife comes to be a guardian the responsibility may disrupt previous distance from in-laws, leading either to a new supportive coalition with them or to a marked withdrawal from them.

[24] For an analysis of these nonpsychiatric kinds of perception, see Marian Radke Yarrow, Charlotte Green Schwartz, Harriet S. Murphy, and Leila Calhoun Deasy, "The Psychological Meaning of Mental Illness in the Family," *J. Social Issues* (1955) 11:12–24; Charlotte Green Schwartz, "Perspectives on Deviance—Wives' Definitions of Their Husbands' Mental Illness," *Psychiatry* (1957) 20:275–291.

[25] This guilt-carrying function is found, of course, in other role-complexes. Thus, when a middle-class couple engages in the process of legal separation or divorce, each of their lawyers usually takes the position that his job is to acquaint his client with all of the potential claims and rights, pressing his client into demanding these, in spite of any nicety of feelings about the rights and honorableness of the ex-partner. The client, in all good faith, can then say to self and to the ex-partner that the demands are being made only because the lawyer insists it is best to do so.

that might otherwise be directed against the spouse is passed on to the child.[26]

Once the prepatient is in the hospital, the same guilt-carrying function may become a significant part of the staff's job in regard to the next-of-relation.[27] These reasons for feeling that he himself has not betrayed the patient, even though the patient may then think so, can later provide the next-of-relation with a defensible line to take when visiting the patient in the hospital and a basis for hoping that the relationship can be re-established after its hospital moratorium. And of course this position, when sensed by the patient, can provide him with excuses for the next-of-relation, when and if he comes to look for them.[28]

Thus while the next-of-relation can perform important functions for the mediators and hospital administrators, they in turn can perform important functions for him. One finds, then, an emergent unintended exchange or reciprocation of functions, these functions themselves being often unintended.

The final point I want to consider about the prepatient's moral career is its peculiarly *retroactive* character. Until a person actually arrives at the hospital there usually seems no way of knowing for sure that he is destined to do so, given the determinative role of career contingencies. And until the point of hospitalization is reached, he or others may not conceive of him as a person who is becoming a mental patient. However, since he will be held against his will in the hospital, his next-of-relation and the hospital staff will be in great need of a rationale for the hardships they are sponsoring. The medical elements of the staff will also need evidence that they are still in the trade they were trained for. These problems are eased, no doubt unintentionally, by the case-history construction that is placed on the patient's past life, this having the effect of demonstrating that all along he had been becoming sick, that he finally became very sick, and that if he had not been hospitalized much worse things would have happened to him—all of which, of course, may be true. Incidentally, if the patient wants to make sense out of his stay in the hospital, and, as already suggested, keep alive the possibility of once again conceiving of his next-of-relation as a decent, well-meaning person, then he too will have reason to believe some of this psychiatric workup of his past.

Here is a very ticklish point for the sociology of careers. An important aspect of every career is the view the person constructs when he looks backward over his progress; in a sense, however, the whole of the prepatient career derives from this reconstruction. The fact of having had a prepatient career, starting with an effective complaint, becomes an important part of the mental patient's orientation, but this part can begin to be played only after hospitalization proves that what he had been having, but no longer has, is a career as a prepatient. . . .

[26] Recorded in the Clausen data.

[27] This point is made by Cumming, see *op. cit.;* p. 129.

[28] There is an interesting contrast here with the moral career of the tuberculosis patient. I am told by Julius Roth that tuberculous patients are likely to come to the hospital willingly, agreeing with their next-of-relation about treatment. Later in their hospital career, when they learn how long they yet have to stay and how depriving and irrational some of the hospital rulings are, they may seek to leave, be advised against this by the staff and by relatives, and only then begin to feel betrayed.

Paranoia and the Dynamics of Exclusion
EDWIN M. LEMERT

The paranoid process begins with persistent interpersonal difficulties between the individual and his family, or his work associates and superiors, or neighbors, or other persons in the community. These frequently or even typically arise out of bona fide or recognizable issues centering upon some actual or threatened loss of status for the individual. This is related to such things as the death of relatives, loss of a position, loss of professional certification, failure to be promoted, age and physiological life cycle changes, mutilations, and changes in family and marital relationships. The status changes are distinguished by the fact that they leave no alternative acceptable to the individual, from whence comes their "intolerable" or "unendurable" quality. For example: the man trained to be a teacher who loses his certificate, which means he can never teach; or the man of 50 years of age who is faced with loss of promotion which is a regular order of upward mobility in an organization, who knows that he can't "start over"; or the wife undergoing hysterectomy, which mutilates her image as a woman.

In cases where no dramatic status loss can be discovered, a series of failures often is present, failures which may have been accepted or adjusted to, but with progressive tension as each new status situation is entered. The unendurability of the current status loss, which may appear unimportant to others, is a function of an intensified commitment, in some cases born of an awareness that there is a quota placed on failures in our society. Under some such circumstances, failures have followed the person, and his reputation as a "difficult person" has preceded him. This means that he often has the status of a stranger on trial in each new group he enters, and that the groups or organizations willing to take a chance on him are marginal from the standpoint of their probable tolerance for his actions.

The behavior of the individual—arrogance, insults, presumption of privilege and exploitation of weaknesses in others—initially has a seg-mental or checkered pattern in that it is confined to status-committing interactions. Outside of these, the person's behavior may be quite acceptable—courteous, considerate, kind, even indulgent. Likewise, other persons and members of groups vary considerably in their tolerance for the relevant behavior, depending on the extent to which it threatens individual and organizational values, impedes functions, or sets in motion embarrassing sequences of social actions. In the early generic period, tolerance by others for the individual's aggressive behavior generally speaking is broad, and it is very likely to be interpreted as a variation of normal behavior, particularly in the absence of biographical knowledge of the person. At most, people observe that "there is something odd about him," or "he must be upset," or "he is just ornery," or "I don't quite understand him" [1].

At some point in the chain of interactions, a new configuration takes place in perceptions others have of the individual, with shifts in figure-ground relations. The individual, as we have already indicated, is an ambiguous figure, comparable to textbook figures of stairs or outlined cubes which reverse themselves when studied intently. From a normal variant the person becomes "unreliable," "untrustworthy," "dangerous," or someone with whom others "do not wish to be involved." An illustration nicely apropos of this came out in the reaction of the head of a music department in a university when he granted an interview to a man who had worked for years on a theory to compose music mathematically:

When he asked to be placed on the staff so that he could use the electronic computers of the University *I shifted my ground* . . . when I offered an objection to his theory, he became disturbed, so I changed my reaction to "yes and no."

As is clear from this, once the perceptual reorientation takes place, either as the outcome of continuous interaction or through the receipt

Reprinted from *Sociometry,* Vol. 25, No. 1 (March 1962), pp. 7–15, by permission of the author and the American Sociological Association.

The research for this paper was in part supported by a grant from the California State Department of Mental Hygiene, arranged with the assistance of Dr. W. A. Oliver, Associate Superintendent of Napa State Hospital, who also helped as a critical consultant and made the facilities of the hospital available.

of biographical information, interaction changes qualitatively. In our words it becomes *spurious,* distinguished by patronizing, evasion, "humoring," guiding conversation onto selected topics, underreaction, and silence, all calculated either to prevent intense interaction or to protect individual and group values by restricting access to them. When the interaction is between two or more persons it is cued by a whole repertoire of subtle expressive signs which are meaningful only to them.

The net effects of spurious interaction are to:

1. stop the flow of information to ego;
2. create a discrepancy between expressed ideas and affect among those with whom he interacts;
3. make the situation or the group image an ambiguous one for ego, much as he is for others.

Needless to say this kind of spurious interaction is one of the most difficult for an adult in our society to cope with, because it complicates or makes decisions impossible for him and also because it is morally invidious.[1]

The process from inclusion to exclusion is by no means an even one. Both individuals and members of groups change their perceptions and reactions, and vacillation is common, depending upon the interplay of values, anxieties and guilt on both sides. Members of an excluding group may decide they have been unfair and seek to bring the individual back into their confidence. This overture may be rejected or used by ego as a means of further attack. We have also found that ego may capitulate, sometimes abjectly, to others and seek group reentry, only to be rejected. In some cases compromises are struck and a partial reintegration of ego into informal social relations is achieved. The direction which informal exclusion takes depends upon ego's reactions, the degree of communication between his interactors, the composition and structure of the informal groups, and the perceptions of "key others" at points of interaction which directly affect ego's status.

Organizational Crisis and Formal Exclusion

Thus far we have discussed exclusion as an informal process. Informal exclusion may take place but leave ego's formal status in an organization intact. So long as this status is preserved and rewards are sufficient to validate it on his terms, an uneasy peace between him and others may prevail. Yet ego's social isolation and his strong commitments make him an unpredictable factor; furthermore the rate of change and internal power struggles, especially in large and complex organizations, means that preconditions of stability may be short lived.

Organizational crises involving a paranoid relationship arise in several ways. The individual may act in ways which arouse intolerable anxieties in others, who demand that "something be done." Again, by going to higher authority or making appeals outside the organization, he may set in motion procedures which leave those in power no other choice than to take action. In some situations ego remains relatively quiescent and does not openly attack the organization. Action against him is set off by growing anxieties or calculated motives of associates—in some cases his immediate superiors. Finally, regular organizational procedures incidental to promotion, retirement or reassignment may precipitate the crisis.

Assuming a critical situation in which the conflict between the individual and members of the organization leads to action to formally exclude him, several possibilities exist. One is the transfer of ego from one department, branch or division of the organization to another, a device frequently resorted to in the armed services or in large corporations. This requires that the individual be persuaded to make the change and that some department will accept him. While this may be accomplished in different ways, not infrequently artifice, withholding information, bribery, or thinly disguised threats figure conspicuously among the means by which the transfer is brought about. Needless to say, there is a limit to which transfers can be employed as a solution to the problem, contingent upon the size of the organization and the previous diffusion of knowledge about the transferee.

Solution number two we call encapsulation, which, in brief, is a reorganization and redefinition of ego's status. This has the effect of isolating him from the organization and making him directly responsible to one or two superiors who act as his intermediaries. The change is often made palatable to ego by enhancing some of the

---

[1] The interaction in some ways is similar to that used with children, particularly the *"enfant terrible."* The function of language in such interactions was studied by Sapir [2] years ago.

material rewards of his status. He may be nominally promoted or "kicked upstairs," given a larger office, or a separate secretary, or relieved of onerous duties. Sometimes a special status is created for him.

This type of solution often works because it is a kind of formal recognition by the organization of ego's intense commitment to his status and in part a victory for him over his enemies. It bypasses them and puts him into direct communication with higher authority who may communicate with him in a more direct manner. It also relieves his associates of further need to connive against him. This solution is sometimes used to dispose of troublesome corporation executives, high-ranking military officers, and academic *personae non gratae* in universities.

A third variety of solutions to the problem of paranoia in an organization is outright discharge, forced resignation or non-renewal of appointment. Finally, there may be an organized move to have the individual in the paranoid relationship placed on sick leave, or to compel him to take psychiatric treatment. The extreme expression of this is pressure (as on the family) or direct action to have the person committed to a mental hospital.

The order of the enumerated solutions to the paranoid problem in a rough way reflects the amount of risk associated with the alternatives, both as to the probabilities of failure and of damaging repercussions to the organization. Generally, organizations seem to show a good deal of resistance to making or carrying out decisions which require expulsion of the individual or forcing hospitalization, regardless of his mental condition. One reason for this is that the person may have power within the organization, based upon his position, or monopolized skills and information,[2] and unless there is a strong coalition against him the general conservatism of administrative judgments will run in his favor. Herman Wouk's novel of *The Caine Mutiny* dramatizes some of the difficulties of cashiering a person from a position of power in an essentially conservative military organization. An extreme of this conservatism is illustrated by one case in which we found a department head retained in his position in an organization even though he was actively hallucinating as well as expressing paranoid delusions.[3] Another factor

working on the individual's side is that discharge of a person in a position of power reflects unfavorably upon those who placed him there. Ingroup solidarity of administrators may be involved, and the methods of the opposition may create sympathy for ego at higher levels.

Even when the person is almost totally excluded and informally isolated within an organization, he may have power outside. This weighs heavily when the external power can be invoked in some way, or when it automatically leads to raising questions as to the internal workings of the organization. This touches upon the more salient reason for reluctance to eject an uncooperative and retaliatory person, even when he is relatively unimportant to the organization. We refer to a kind of negative power derived from the vulnerability of organizations to unfavorable publicity and exposure of their private lives that are likely if the crisis proceeds to formal hearings, case review or litigation. This is an imminent possibility where paranoia exists. If hospital commitment is attempted, there is a possibility that a jury trial will be demanded, which will force leaders of the organization to defend their actions. If the crisis turns into a legal contest of this sort, it is not easy to prove insanity, and there may be damage suits. Even if the facts heavily support the petitioners, such contests can only throw unfavorable light upon the organization.

The Conspiratorial Nature of Exclusion

A conclusion from the foregoing is that organizational vulnerability as well as anticipations of retaliations from the paranoid person lay a functional basis for conspiracy among those seeking to contain or oust him. Probabilities are strong that a coalition will appear within the organization, integrated by a common commitment to oppose the paranoid person. This, the exclusionist group, demands loyalty, solidarity and secrecy from its members; it acts in accord with a common scheme and in varying degrees utilizes techniques of manipulation and misrepresentation.

Conspiracy in rudimentary form can be detected in informal exclusion apart from an or-

---

[2] For a systematic analysis of the organizational difficulties in removing an "unpromotable" person from a position see [3].

[3] One of the cases in the first study.

ganizational crisis. This was illustrated in an office research team in which staff members huddled around a water cooler to discuss the unwanted associate. They also used office telephones to arrange coffee breaks without him and employed symbolic cues in his presence, such as humming the Dragnet theme song when he approached the group. An office rule against extraneous conversation was introduced with the collusion of supervisors, ostensibly for everyone, actually to restrict the behavior of the isolated worker. In another case an interview schedule designed by a researcher was changed at a conference arranged without him. When he sought an explanation at a subsequent conference, his associates pretended to have no knowledge of the changes.

Conspiratorial behavior comes into sharpest focus during organizational crises in which the exclusionists who initiate action become an embattled group. There is a concerted effort to gain consensus for this view, to solidify the group and to halt close interaction with those unwilling to completely join the coalition. Efforts are also made to neutralize those who remain uncommitted but who can't be kept ignorant of the plans afoot. Thus an external appearance of unanimity is given even if it doesn't exist.

Much of the behavior of the group at this time is strategic in nature, with determined calculations as to "what we will do if he does this or that." In one of our cases, a member on a board of trustees spoke of the "game being played" with the person in controversy with them. Planned action may be carried to the length of agreeing upon the exact words to be used when confronted or challenged by the paranoid individual. Above all there is continuous, precise communication among exclusionists, exemplified in one case by mutual exchanging of copies of all letters sent and received from ego.

Concern about secrecy in such groups is revealed by such things as carefully closing doors and lowering of voices when ego is brought under discussion. Meeting places and times may be varied from normal procedures; documents may be filed in unusual places and certain telephones may not be used during a paranoid crisis.

The visibility of the individual's behavior is greatly magnified during this period; often he is the main topic of conversation among the exclusionists, while rumors of the difficulties spread to other groups, which in some cases may be drawn into the controversy. At a certain juncture steps are taken to keep the members of the ingroup continually informed of the individual's movements and, if possible, of his plans. In effect, if not in form, this amounts to spying. Members of one embattled group, for example, hired an outside person unknown to their accuser to take notes on a speech he delivered to enlist a community organization on his side. In another case, a person having an office opening onto that of a department head was persuaded to act as an informant for the nucleus of persons working to depose the head from his position of authority. This group also seriously debated placing an all-night watch in front of their perceived malefactor's house.

Concomitant with the magnified visibility of the paranoid individual, come distortions of his image, most pronounced in the inner coterie of exclusionists. His size, physical strength, cunning, and anecdotes of his outrages are exaggerated, with a central thematic emphasis on the fact that he is dangerous. Some individuals give cause for such beliefs in that previously they have engaged in violence or threats, others do not. One encounters characteristic contradictions in interviews on this point, such as: "No, he has never struck anyone around here—just fought with the policemen at the State Capitol," or "No, I am not afraid of him, but one of these days he will explode."

It can be said parenthetically that the alleged dangerousness of paranoid persons storied in fiction and drama has never been systematically demonstrated. As a matter of fact, the only substantial data on this, from a study of delayed admissions, largely paranoid, to a mental hospital in Norway, disclosed that "neither the paranoiacs nor paranoids have been dangerous, and most not particularly troublesome" [4]. Our interpretation of this, as suggested earlier, is that the imputed dangerousness of the paranoid individual does not come from physical fear but from the organizational threat he presents and the need to justify collective action against him.[4]

However, this is not entirely tactical behavior—as is demonstrated by anxieties and tensions which mount among those in the coalition during the more critical phases of their interaction. Participants may develop fears quite analogous to those of classic conspirators. One leader

---

[4] *Supra*, p. 3.

in such a group spoke of the period of the paranoid crisis as a "week of terror," during which he was wracked with insomnia and "had to take his stomach pills." Projection was revealed by a trustee who, during a school crisis occasioned by discharge of an aggressive teacher, stated that he "watched his shadows," and "wondered if all would be well when he returned home at night." Such tensional states, working along with a kind of closure of communication within the group, are both a cause and an effect of amplified group interaction which distorts or symbolically rearranges the image of the person against whom they act.

Once the battle is won by the exclusionists, their version of the individual as dangerous becomes a crystallized rationale for official action. At this point misrepresentation becomes part of a more deliberate manipulation of ego. Gross misstatements, most frequently called "pretexts," become justifiable ways of getting his cooperation, for example, to get him to submit to psychiatric examination or detention preliminary to hospital commitment. This aspect of the process has been effectively detailed by Goffman, with his concept of a "betrayal funnel" through which a patient enters a hospital [5]. We need not elaborate on this, other than to confirm its occurrence in the exclusion process, complicated in our cases by legal strictures and the ubiquitous risk of litigation.

The Growth of Delusion

The general idea that the paranoid person symbolically fabricates the conspiracy against him is in our estimation incorrect or incomplete. Nor can we agree that he lacks insight, as is so frequently claimed. To the contrary, many paranoid persons properly realize that they are being isolated and excluded by concerted interaction, or that they are being manipulated. However, they are at a loss to estimate accurately or realistically the dimensions and form of the coalition arrayed against them.

As channels of communication are closed to the paranoid person, he has no means of getting feedback on consequences of his behavior, which is essential for correcting his interpretations of the social relationships and organization which he must rely on to define his status and give him identity. He can only read overt behavior without the informal context. Although he may properly infer that people are organized

against him, he can only use confrontation or formal inquisitorial procedures to try to prove this. The paranoid person must provoke strong feelings in order to receive any kind of meaningful communication from others—hence his accusations, his bluntness, his insults. Ordinarily this is non-deliberate; nevertheless, in one complex case we found the person consciously provoking discussions to get readings from others on his behavior. This man said of himself: "Some people would describe me as very perceptive, others would describe me as very imperceptive."

The need for communication and the identity which goes with it does a good deal to explain the preference of paranoid persons for formal, legalistic, written communications, and the care with which many of them preserve records of their contracts with others. In some ways the resort to litigation is best interpreted as the effort of the individual to compel selected others to interact directly with him as equals, to engineer a situation in which evasion is impossible. The fact that the person is seldom satisfied with the outcome of his letters, his petitions, complaints and writs testifies to their function as devices for establishing contact and interaction with others, as well as "setting the record straight." The wide professional tolerance of lawyers for aggressive behavior in court and the nature of Anglo-Saxon legal institutions, which grew out of a revolt against conspiratorial or star-chamber justice, mean that the individual will be heard. Furthermore his charges must be answered; otherwise he wins by default. Sometimes he wins small victories, even if he loses the big ones. He may earn grudging respect as an adversary, and sometimes shares a kind of legal camaraderie with others in the courts. He gains an identity through notoriety. . . .

REFERENCES

1. Cumming, E. and J. Cumming. 1957. *Closed Ranks*. Cambridge, Mass.: Harvard Press, Ch. 6.

2. Sapir, E. 1915. "Abnormal Types of Speech in Nootka." *Canada Department of Mines, Memoir 62* (5).

3. Levenson, B. 1961. "Bureaucratic Succession." In A. Etzioni (ed.), *Complex Organizations*. New York: Holt, Rinehart and Winston, pp. 362–395.

4. Ödegard, Ö. 1958. "A Clinical Study of Delayed Admissions to a Mental Hospital." *Mental Hygiene,* 42:66–67.

5. Goffman, E. 1959. "The Moral Career of the Mental Patient." *Psychiatry,* 22:127 ff.

The "Wetback" as Deviant   JORGE A. BUSTAMANTE

Introduction

Those who illegally stream across the Mexico-U.S. border are called "wetbacks" because they cross the Rio Grande without the benefit of a bridge. All other illegal migrants from Mexico are referred to by the same term. Thus, wetback characterizes anyone who enters illegally from Mexico. The term, then, carries an unavoidable connotation—one who has broken the law. This paper will deal with some of the questions that arise from that connotation. In the first part, we describe the historical emergence of the wetback, discussing the roles of the persons involved in the violation of the immigration law and some of the socioeconomic consequences of the wetback as a deviant. In the second part, we examine the wetback as a case of deviance through labeling theory. In this approach the deviant character of the wetback is analyzed as a process of interaction. Each role in this process will be discussed in terms of its interests, power, and consequences with respect to those of the roles of the other participants. Finally, the concept of "antilaw entrepreneur" is introduced, and its explanatory potential is indicated.

Historical Background

In 1882, during President Arthur's administration, the first immigration law was passed following a strong nativist movement. The same year the first "Chinese exclusion act" established significant limits to what was considered an "invasion of Orientals" who had been a preferred source of cheap labor for West Coast employers (Wittke 1949, p. 13). The search for cheap labor turned to Japanese and Filipino immigrants, who then became the target of "exclusionists." Campaigns like the "swat the Jap" campaign in Los Angeles and those inspired by the writings of Madison Grant and Lothrop Stoddard led to further restrictions of immigration from the Orient. The "Asian barred zone" provisions excluded immigration from Oriental countries as a source for cheap labor (Daniels and Kitano 1970, p. 53).

In the first decade of the century, eastern and southern European immigration became the focus of nativist and exclusionist crusades. Pressure generated by those movements crystallized in the appointment of a commission by the U.S. Congress to study immigration; the result of that study is known as the Dillingham Commission Report (1907–10). Throughout this voluminous report a long-debated distinction between the "old" and "new" immigration was made. It was argued that the values and occupations of the "old immigrants" (Anglo-Saxons and Nordics) were threatened by the "newer immigrants," southern and eastern Europeans and Asians (Hourwich 1912, p. 19). The distinction between new and old immigration created a dichotomy about which many pages of "scientific" reports were written in support of the undesirability of the new immigration.

Campaigns demanding restriction of the new immigration finally crystallized in the immigration laws of 1921 and 1924, which established quotas restricting immigration from all countries except those in the western hemisphere.

In the meantime, social scientists conducted research on the immigration phenomenon; they found empirical evidence showing that immigration to the United States has consistently supplied cheap labor (Eckler and Zoltnick 1949, p. 16; Hourwich 1912, pp. 167–72).

All countries which provided cheap labor for the United States were affected by the quota system established by the Immigration Act of 1921. Thus, the search for cheap labor turned to the western hemisphere, to which the quota system did not apply (Marden and Meyer 1968, p. 104); Mexican immigrants were found to be the most suitable replacement (Samora and Bustamante 1971). The suitability of Mexican labor rested on (1) geographical proximity; (2) the uninterrupted tradition of immigration, which was internal when most of the southwestern United States was still part of Mexico (McWilliams 1968, pp. 162–69); and (3) unemployment and unrest in Mexico, created by several years of revolution (Bustamante, in press).

A tremendous increase in Mexican immigration during the first quarter of the century (Grebler 1966, p. 20) corresponded to the increased demand for unskilled labor in the economic expansion of the Southwest. Mexicans crossed 1,870 miles of an almost completely open border (Gamio 1930, p. 10) to reach the steel industry in East Chicago (Samora and Lamanna 1970), railroad construction, and, most significantly, agricultural expansion in the Southwest (Samora 1971).

In this period the Mexican who wanted to legally cross the border had to go through a complicated procedure to be admitted into the United States. Those procedures included, in particular, a literacy test, "a condition which many immigrants cannot fulfill" (Gamio 1930, p. 11). Therefore, many took advantage of the "open" border policy toward Mexican laborers.

Moreover, the illegal immigrant could stay in the United States untroubled as long as he avoided the authorities who might disclose his status. Since no specific authorities were entrusted with apprehending illegal immigrants, the dangers of being caught were further minimized (Jones 1965, p. 13). Thus, the illegal immigrant's status was not visibly distinct from the legal immigrant's. The illegal entrant was able to maintain his violation in a state of "primary deviance" (Lemert 1951, pp. 70–78).

The appearance of the Border Patrol in 1924 altered the primary deviance of the illegal entrant by crystallizing a new social reaction to the violation of immigration laws. The new police force was to reveal those primary deviants, violators of immigration laws. In this process, the term "wetback," previously purely descriptive, acquired a new meaning. It became the "label" or "stigma" by which the illegal immigrant was made visible. At the same time, the label "wetback" also became the symbol by which the illegal immigrant was able to identify a new "me" for himself (Mead 1918, pp. 577–602), and a new role which better equipped him to meet the social reaction to his behavior (illegal entrance) (Lemert 1967, pp. 42–51).

The establishment of the Border Patrol in 1924 not only made the wetback more visible as a law breaker; it also brought changes in the patterns of behavior of the illegal immigrants. The freedom of interaction the illegal immigrant had had before 1924 was considerably reduced. He now had to walk, to speak, and to bear any treatment with the fear of being caught by or "turned in" to the Border Patrol.

The interaction most significantly changed was between illegal migrant worker and employer. Before 1924 labor conditions resulted from differential access to mechanisms of power and from the interplay of labor-force supply and demand. The organization of the Border Patrol brought a new factor: the illegal migrant could always be caught and sent back to Mexico. To be "turned in" became a threat always present in the migrant's mind that interfered with his social contacts. Social contacts, except for those with an employer or prospective employer, could be avoided for self-protection. The explicit or implicit threat of being denounced by the employer became a new significant element in the settlement of work contracts. It could be used to impose oppressive salaries and working conditions. In his search for a job he could no longer freely accept or reject a given offer; he always had to consider the alternative of being denounced to the Border Patrol.[1]

The importance of the "wetback problem" gains further emphasis in its numerical proportions. Although no reliable statistics exist on the actual number of wetbacks who have entered the United States, an approximate idea can be inferred from the records of expatriated wetbacks. Records for the period 1930–69 indicate that 7,486,470 apprehensions of wetbacks were made by the U.S. Immigration Authority (U.S. Immigration and Naturalization Service 1966, 1967–68). The highest rates were concentrated in the decades 1941–60, during which 5,953,210 expulsions of wetbacks were made. The size of the population involved clearly defines the importance of the problem.

When we look at the sociocultural characteristics of the persons involved, we see that the problem is much larger. Most are poor peasants

---

[1] Data from 493 interviews that I conducted with wetbacks in 1969 show that 8% of the interviewees were "turned in" by their employers without being paid for their work. A year later, similar situations were encountered by the author during a participant observation as a "wetback" conceived to validate previous findings (a report of these experiences and the larger research project appears in Samora 1971). Further evidence of these and other kinds of exploitation of the "wetback" are reported by Saunders and Leonard 1951, p. 72; Hadley 1956, p. 352; and Jones 1965, pp. 14–20.

from central and northern states in Mexico who come to the United States only to find work to survive (Samora 1971, p. 102). They are willing to accept anything—good or bad treatment, illness, starvation, low wages, poor living conditions; all are taken philosophically and accepted without struggle. Their struggle is concentrated on pure survival (Saunders and Leonard 1951, p. 6).

The Network of Social Relations of Wetbacks

Various groups of people come in contact with the wetback in the United States. In this section we will review four major groups: (1) the employer who benefits from a cheap labor pool, (2) the southwestern Mexican-American farm worker who suffers from the competition of these low-paid workers, (3) the lawmaker who is in the ambiguous position of defender of the law and protector of the "illegal" interests of farm entrepreneurs, and (4) the law enforcer who is directly responsible for enforcing the laws.

The Employer. In all economic enterprises, and in particular agricultural enterprises, labor constitutes a major segment of production costs. Rational manipulation of all instruments of production in pure economic terms requires the minimization of costs in all areas to achieve the highest possible economic return. Workers willing to accept labor contracts below going wages clearly become a positive asset in that they assure higher returns for the entrepreneur. Moreover, other economic advantages besides low wages accrue from the employment of wetback labor. First, in some kinds of employment no strict accounting of working hours is kept, since work contracts based on daily labor may involve as many as twelve hours (Hadley 1956, p. 347). Second, little or no responsibility for disability occurs, since the wetback must assume responsibility for his own injuries and accidents. Third, the employer is under no obligation, legal or otherwise, to provide health and medical services, sanitary facilities, or even decent housing (American G.I. Forum of Texas and Texas State Federation of Labor 1953, pp. 17–27). As a result, what the wetback receives as wages and other standard "fringe benefits" is determined only by the employer's conscience and the current standards of neighbors and friends (Hadley

1956, p. 347). Even in pure economic terms, then, the position of the rural entrepreneur vis-à-vis the wetback is highly advantageous; by using wetbacks as workers, farmers can maximize possible economic gains in labor costs (Samora 1971, pp. 98–103).

The Mexican-American Farm Worker. Whereas the rural entrepreneur gains by the presence of wetbacks, the Mexican-American rural workers lose in competition for jobs. They feel that wetbacks push work contract conditions to the lowest possible level, a "charity" level out of step with living requirements in the United States. Their personal suffering from such competition is unjust, since, while being penalized by this competition, they have to pay the costs of citizenship (e.g., income and other taxes) and receive little or no benefit from such required contributions. Further, wetbacks break the possible cohesion of the rural labor force, and so they lose bargaining power with rural entrepreneurs. Finally, the manipulation of the mass media and urban lobbying groups by the rural entrepreneur creates an artificial shortage of labor which serves to ensure the permanence of wetbacks. At the same time, Mexican-American workers are prevented from speaking in the mass media to unmask the artificial labor shortage (Hadley 1956, p. 345).

The Lawmaker. The lawmaker should be the one to bridge the gap between the conflicting demands of the entrepreneur and the Mexican-American. Nevertheless, the most general pattern followed by lawmakers is to consider the wetback problem and the working situation on the border as something unavoidable or expected. Legal attempts to effectively prevent the wetback from crossing the border are stricken from proposed codes by the lawmakers on the rationale that the farmer along the border wants wetback labor (U.S. Congress, Senate 1953, p. 10). The "realistic" attitude of these lawmakers seems to be either that it is convenient to conform or worthless to struggle against the situation. Thus, the U.S. immigration law is broken in order to maintain a supply of wetbacks. For many southern, and in particular Texas, legislators, there is no evil in maintaining the influx of wetbacks.

Protection of the interests of wetback employers by lawmakers is best illustrated by a law (U.S. Congress, 8 U.S.C., section 1324, 1952) which makes it a felony to be a wetback but not to hire one.[2] This is a paradoxical situation which legitimizes the hiring of wetbacks in spite of the general recognition that it is the possibility of being hired that attracts Mexican workers to cross illegally to the United States. This situation was pointed out by Ruben Salazar (recently killed in the Chicago Moratorium in Los Angeles) in an article published in the *Los Angeles Times* (April 27, 1970): "There is no law against hiring wetbacks. There is only a law against being a wetback" (Samora 1971, p. 139).

The Law Enforcer. The Border Patrol is directly responsible for the prevention of wetback crossings and for the apprehension of wetbacks already in the United States. Theoretically, such a role would place the patrol in direct confrontation with the rural entrepreneurs using wetback labor, inasmuch as they enforce laws made in the interests of the total society. Their activities would, in part, protect the immediate interests of the legal rural workers.

Nevertheless, evidence suggests that such relationships of reciprocity are not realized (Saunders and Leonard 1951, p. 68); instead, the conflict between the Border Patrol and entrepreneurs is somehow transformed into covert cooperation through a "pattern of evasion" of the law (see Williams 1951). This transformation involves the following: first, the entrepreneurs offer little resistance to the apprehension of wetbacks, in exchange for the patrol's overlooking the wetbacks when work needs to be done. Second, wetbacks openly at work may informally legitimate their status as workers and thus remain unharassed. Third, complete enforcement of the law by state and national authorities, and with minimum cooperation from local people, is theoretically possible (Saunders and Leonard 1951, p. 68).

The Labeling Approach to Deviant Behavior

Theories which view deviance as a quality of the deviant act or the actor cannot help us understand the wetback as deviant. "Wetback" became the label for a deviant after the appearance of the Border Patrol, and various social groups came to *react* differently to the presence of wetbacks. It is singularly characteristic of this deviant type that it occurs in a cross-cultural context; as a Mexican, the wetback breaks an American law and receives negative legal sanction while, at the same time, he positively fulfills the needs of specific American groups. This context of deviance fits well into the framework of labeling theory. According to Becker (1963, p. 91), deviance cannot be viewed as homogeneous because it results from interaction and consists of particular responses by various social groups to a particular behavior of the prospective deviant or outsider.

In this context, we must analyze the wetback in interaction, singling out the responses of the various groups making up the network which labels his behavior as deviant. The deviant character of the wetback, then, lies not in him nor in his behavior but in the superimposition of the deviant label on him.

Becker's use of labeling theory in deviance is of particular interest to us because of his stress on the political dimensions of the labeling processes. He emphasizes the fact that the legal norms and the behavior classified as deviant must be viewed as part of a political process in which group A, *in conflict* with group B, defines the rules for group B. The degree of group A's success in imposing such rules and in enforcing them depends primarily upon the political and economic power of group A. Furthermore, the will of group A is often an expression of a class interest rather than solely of individual members of group A. In such a case, enforcement of the rules becomes applicable to all members of that class, excluding members of group B whose class interests are the same as group A's.

Becker further indicates that labeling always begins with the initiative of a "moral entrepreneur" (Becker 1963, pp. 147–63), a leader (individual or group) who crusades for new rules to stop something that he views as wrong. Moral

---

[2] That law provides that "any person who willfully or knowingly conceals, harbors, or shields from detection, in any place including any building or by any means of transportation, or who encourages or induces, or attempts to encourage or induce, either directly or indirectly, the entry into the United States of any alien shall be guilty of a felony. Upon conviction he shall be punished by a fine not exceeding $2,000 or by imprisonment for a term not exceeding five years, or both, for each alien in respect to whom the violation occurs. *Provided, however, that for the purposes of this section, employment, including the usual and normal practices incident to employment, shall not be deemed to constitute harboring*" (italics added; Samora 1971, p. 139).

entrepreneurs are interested in the content of rules and are very often involved in what they view as humanitarian or moral reformism. In their crusades, they typically say they want to help those beneath them to achieve a better status, and in the process "they add to the power they derive from the legitimacy of their moral position the power they derive from their superior position in society" (Becker 1963, p. 149). The outcome of a successful moral crusade is the establishment of a new set of rules (i.e., the immigration laws of 1921 and 1924) and corresponding enforcement agencies and officials (i.e., the U.S. Border Patrol). The new law enforcers justify their existence by attempting to fulfill the new activities, and, in their performance, they try to win the respect of prominent persons.

Once a law and its enforcers come into existence the process of labeling becomes independent of the moral entrepreneur. The enforcer becomes the most important actor, and while enforcing the law he stigmatizes or labels certain individuals as deviants. Thus, there is a process of interaction in which some actors will enforce rules "in the service of their own interest," whereas others, also "in the service of their own interest," commit acts labeled as deviant (Becker 1963, p. 162).

The Wetback Labeling Process

The labeling process started with a moral crusade under the leadership of moral entrepreneurs representing the moral spirit of the American legal system. The results of the crusade were new legal codes (the immigration laws of 1921 and 1924) and the establishment of organizations and specialized personnel (e.g., the Border Patrol) to implement the new codes. The moral component of the legitimization of the new codes rest on the righteousness of the law, inasmuch as it protects the interests of nationals who otherwise would be defenseless against the threat of foreign competitors.

This organizational superstructure, whose purpose was to carry out the moral imperatives, resulted in a radical transformation of the previous interactions of foreign laborers. Of immediate concern was the reinforcement of the illegal status of immigrant workers under the deviant label of wetback. Nevertheless, moral imperatives, even those incorporated legally and

implemented by specialized personnel, are not the only basis of motivation and rationalization of action. Others, especially political and economic interests, can be at variance with these new moral imperatives and influence behavior. When we examine such conflicting motivations we see that they may be selectively used, depending on the context of the action and the character of the actor—in particular his power. Thus, the rural entrepreneur in certain situations (e.g., harvest time) uses economic motivation to hire wetbacks with contracts calling for long hours of work and the lowest possible pay. In other situations (say, when he has unwanted workers) he uses the moral imperative to denounce wetbacks to the Border Patrol. A similar differential use of motivation occurs with other groups. It is necessary to specify the nature of motivations at play in the wetback case.

Looking at interests as a source of motivations, we shall focus on them at the juncture where they shape action; that is, at the point of interaction between wetbacks and the groups of actors discussed in this paper. A distinction will be made between group interests related to the presence of the wetback and group interests related only to each actor's role independent of the presence of the wetback. The latter would be those interests pertaining to the maintenance of the role played by actors of each group, that is, (1) the Mexican-American farm worker's role interest would be to maximize wages, (2) the farmer's (wetback employer's) role interest would be to maximize profit, (3) the lawmaker's role interest would be to provide legislation that meets the necessities of his constituencies and the country, (4) the law enforcer's (Border Patrol's) role interest would be to enforce immigration laws, (5) the moral entrepreneur's role interest would be to define good and evil for society. On the other hand, group interest related to the presence of the wetback seems to indicate a different dimension of each actor's role, as, respectively, (1) to stop the influx of wetbacks in order to avoid their competition for jobs and to increase bargaining power vis-à-vis the farmer, (2) to maximize profits by the use of the wetback cheap labor, (3) to gain political support from the farmers by protecting their interests, (4) to enforce immigration laws selectively, (5) to define protection of nationals against foreign competition as good and entrance to the United States without inspection as immoral.

This distinction of interests seems to promote

understanding of some contradictions in the wetback phenomenon, such as (1) condemning the wetback by defining him as a deviant and, at the same time, maintaining a demand for his labor force which is reflected in a steadily increasing influx of wetbacks each year (Samora 1971, pp. 195–96); (2) penalizing a person for being a wetback, but not a farmer for hiring one (U.S. Congress, 8 U.S.C., section 1324, 1952); (3) maintaining an agency for the enforcement of immigration laws and at the same time exerting budget limitations and/or political pressures to prevent successful enforcement of the law (Hadley 1956, p. 348).

These are some of the contradictions that become apparent in the wetback case, but they are nothing less than reflections of contradictions in society at large. This is particularly obvious to us when we see the conflict of interests between the farmer and Mexican-American farm worker (each tries to maximize his economical gains at the expense of the other) and when we see the presence of the wetback kept undercover as a veil hiding deeper conflict. Indeed, when the role of the wetback is introduced in agricultural production, we see a different conflict of interests taking place—namely, that between the Mexican-American worker and the wetback. The former blames the latter for lowering working conditions and standards of living.

The nature of the two conflicts should be differentiated. Whereas the conflict of interests between the Mexican-American farm worker and the farmer is determined by the position each plays in a particular mode of agricultural production, the conflict between the Mexican-American worker and the wetback is determined primarily by a set of beliefs that are not necessarily grounded in reality, namely, that wages and working conditions are determined by external laws of supply and demand independent of the employers; that the wetback *causes* low wages and low standards of living for the farm worker, etc. It is important to note the point here that the conflicts "created" by the wetback would disappear with an unrestricted enforcement of immigration laws.

Another aspect of our discussion of group interest is the power that supports each specified interest and respective action. Since the groups themselves reflect status differentials, it is the differences in power (and possible collisions of power) that give form to the interaction. Furthermore, the power of legitimization of these actions sustains the existing form against any possible transformation.

Power differences among the various actors result from their ability to manipulate or influence interaction in the direction of their interests (see Gamson 1968). In this interpretation, the wetback employer is clearly the most powerful category, since he is able to influence all other actors. On the other extreme is the wetback. He clearly appears at a disadvantage. As an outsider he has no legitimacy. He is not eligible for public assistance or for the benefits of an eventual "moral entrepreneur," since he is not eligible to stay in the country, unless he is in jail. He is also not eligible for other benefits because of the stigma of having once broken the immigration laws. This might, technically, prevent him from acquiring legal residence or citizenship in the United States. The wetback only has the original motivation which made him cross the border (survival) and a new one resulting from the deviant label (not to be caught) which becomes another element of pure survival. As an outsider with such elemental interests he dares not complain—the only possible protest comes when his survival is in jeopardy and his only course of action is to return to Mexico.

A Conceptual Addendum to Becker's Schema. Labeling theory provides us with the concept of moral entrepreneur. Applying the elements of this type to the case under analysis, we find a new type in the role of the wetback employer. His crusade is directed toward the self-serving enforcement of existing laws. The source of his crusade is the threat of the loss of cheap labor that would occur if the laws were enforced. Evidently the characteristics of this second type are the polar opposites of those of the moral entrepreneur. The imperative he singles out as a banner is economic rather than moral. The crusade he leads is supported by power and economic interest rather than moral righteousness. This type can perhaps be characterized as an *antilaw entrepreneur.* In order to be successful he associates the law enforcer and the lawmaker in his enterprise and becomes able to manipulate the law in two ways: first, by preventing its enforcement whenever he needs cheap labor; second, by stimulating its enforcement when he needs to dispose of a complaining or useless wetback.

A view of the contradictions of society apparent in the wetback case has allowed us to introduce the antilaw entrepreneur. Such a concept is useful for the understanding of deviance because it shows that violation of a law can also become the goal of an enterprise in the same sense that the creation of a law may be the goal of an enterprise. Both crusades, to be successful, require leaders holding legitimate power, although in one case they have the added legitimization of answering to a moral imperative, whereas in the other they answer to the economic interests of a specialized group. The law enforcer, the lawmaker, and a powerful group of rural entrepreneurs can launch such a crusade against the law and yet not be "labeled" as deviants.

If a Border Patrol man states firmly that to enforce the law would "ruin the fields" (Saunders and Leonard 1951, p. 68), and a lawmaker refers to specific measures in the Senate to allow the influx of wetbacks (U.S. Congress, Senate 1953), and a former vice president of the United States (John Nance Garner) says, "If they [wetback employers] get the Mexican labor it enables them to make a profit" (Jones 1965, p. 17), then the essential objectives of the enterprise are spelled out. The continuing presence of wetbacks is in no little measure an indication of the success of the antilaw entrepreneur.

Conclusion

The preceding analysis leads us to see—

1. the wetback as one who crosses the U.S.-Mexican border illegally, taking advantage of the limited enforcement of the U.S. immigration laws;
2. the interaction process in which such a man is labeled a deviant, a label that will constitute a central element of a process of exploitation;
3. the deviant label making the wetback more attractive as a worker than the Mexican-American (at the same time, paradoxically, such a label—an element of destitution—becomes what the wetback exchanges for an unstable taste of survival);
4. the labeling process in which the wetback is "created," in which interests and power are arranged in an action that we have typified as an antilaw enterprise.

And finally, a human being with the alternatives of being exploited by a country forcing him to become a deviant or of facing misery in his own country by not doing so.

REFERENCES

American G.I. Forum of Texas and Texas State Federation of Labor. 1953. *What Price Wetbacks?* Austin: American G.I. Forum of Texas and Texas State Federation of Labor (AFL).

Becker, Howard S. 1963. *Outsiders: Studies in the Sociology of Deviance*. New York: Free Press.

Bustamante, Jorge A. In press. *Don Chano: Autobiografía de un Emigrante Mexicano*. Mexico City: Instituto de Investigaciones Sociales of the National University of Mexico.

Daniels, Roger and Harry H. L. Kitano. 1970. *American Racism: Exploration of the Nature of Prejudice*. Englewood Cliffs, N.J.: Prentice-Hall.

Eckler, Ross A. and Jack Zlotnick. 1949. "Immigration and Labor Force." In Thorsten Sellin (ed.), *The Annals*. Philadelphia: American Academy of Political and Social Sciences.

Gamio, Manuel. 1930. *Mexican Immigration to the United States*. Chicago: University of Chicago Press.

Gamson, William. 1968. *Power and Discontent*. Homewood, Ill.: Dorsey.

Grebler, Leo. 1966. "Mexican Immigration to the United States." Mexican American Study Project, Advanced Report No. 2. Los Angeles: University of California.

Hadley, Eleanor M. 1956. "A Critical Analysis of the Wetback Problem." *Law and Contemporary Problems*, 21 (Spring): 334–57.

Hourwich, Isaac A. 1912. *Immigration and Labor*. New York: Putnam.

Jones, Lamar B. 1965. "Mexican American Labor Problems in Texas." Ph.D. dissertation, University of Texas.

Lemert, Edwin M. 1951. *Social Pathology*. New York: McGraw-Hill.

———. 1967. *Human Deviance, Social Control*. Englewood Cliffs. N.J.: Prentice-Hall.

McWilliams, Carey. 1968. *North from Mexico*. Westport, Conn.: Greenwood.

Marden, Charles F. and Gladys Meyer. 1968. *Minorities in American Society*. New York: American Book Co.

Mead, George H. 1918. "The Psychology of Punitive Justice." *American Journal of Sociology*, 23 (March): 577–602.

Samora, Julian, assisted by Jorge A. Bustamante and Gilbert Cardenas. 1971. *Los Mojados, the Wetback Story*. Notre Dame, Ind.: University of Notre Dame Press.

Samora, Julian and Jorge A. Bustamante. 1971. "Mexican Immigration and American Labor Demands." In *Migrant and Seasonal Farmworker Powerlessness*. Pt. 7B. Hearings, U.S. Senate, Committee on Labor and Public Welfare. Washington, D.C.: Government Printing Office.

Samora, Julian and Richard A. Lamanna. 1970. "Mexican American in a Midwest Metropolis: A Study of East Chicago." In V. Webb (ed.), *The Mexican American People: The Nation's Second Largest Minority*. New York: Free Press.

Saunders, Lyle and Olen F. Leonard. 1951. *The Wetback in the Lower Rio Grande Valley of Texas*. Inter-American Education Occasional Papers, No. 7. Austin: University of Texas.

U.S. Immigration and Naturalization Service. 1966. *Annual Report of the United States Immigration and Naturalization Service*. Washington, D.C.: Government Printing Office.

———. 1967–68. *Report of Field Operations of the Immigration and Naturalization Service*. Washington, D.C.: Government Printing Office.

U.S. Congress, Senate. 1953. Appropriation Hearings on S. 1917 before the Subcommittee of the Senate Committee of the Judiciary 83rd Cong., 1st sess., p. 123 (Senator McCarran).

Williams, Robin, Jr. 1951. *American Society: A Sociological Interpretation*. New York: Knopf.

Wittke, Carl. 1949. "Immigration Policy Prior to World War I." In Thorsten Sellin (ed.), *The Annals*. Philadelphia: American Academy of Political and Social Science.

Part II THE FORMAL REGULATION OF DEVIANCE

In addition to typing on an informal, interpersonal level, much typing of deviants occurs on a formal or official level. In fact, complex societies such as ours invariably include formal agencies whose role it is to seek out, identify, and regulate deviance. Such agencies include the police, the courts, the federal Drug Enforcement Administration, the Department of the Treasury (whose agents deal with smuggling), county and state health and welfare agencies—the list could go on and on. When these agencies of social control take action against someone adjudged deviant, the effects can be dramatic. These may include a formal confirmation of deviant typing, induction into a deviant role, and launching on a deviant career. This turning point in the deviant's life can also bring about a radical redefinition of self. What the deviant may experience as a unique personal crisis, however, is usually merely organizational routine for the agent and the agency.

The controls that such agents and agencies can impose differ significantly from those available to lay people. In terms of power, for example, the political state stands behind many agencies, while informal labelers may be no more powerful than the deviant. Likewise, the agents' control is usually legitimized by the state, whereas labeling by other people may simply represent an opposing set of norms. Finally, agents of social control usually operate according to an elaborate set of rules that provide standardized ways of dealing with deviants; other people's actions against the deviant need not be based on any plan at all.

A special perspective, composed of rules, beliefs, and practices, underlies the formal processing of deviants. In the course of their work with deviant clients, agents of social control come to adopt this perspective. As they become more familiar with the agency's perspective, agents find that they can process their deviant clients more efficiently. And, as these conceptions become routine for agents, so does their processing of clients take on a routine character.

In this part of the book, we consider the basic premises reflected in the treatment and processing of deviants by various social control agencies. We take up, in sequence, how agencies dealing with the sick and the disabled define and respond to their clients, the special perspective police use in their work, the assumptions that court personnel make about the people whom they process, and the social conditions under which lay people adopt the perspectives of agencies of social control.

Help Agencies and Their Theories

When primary group controls break down (as noted in Part I), formal agencies of social control go into action on behalf of the larger society. Criminal justice agencies (such as police, court, and corrections) collect and process those deviants said to have broken the criminal law. Other agencies, broadly classified as helping agencies, take in clients who appear to be mentally or physically ill or whose long-standing handicaps make it difficult for them to fend for themselves. People become clients of these two different sets of control agencies under different circumstances. But in both cases people who work in either type of agency develop ideas about their clientele. Thus, criminal justice agents presume their clientele intended the harm they have allegedly done to others and do not voluntarily seek their official services. By contrast, helping agents presume their clientele did not intend the harm they have done to others or to themselves and that they may voluntarily seek the services of the helping agency.

Though the circumstances of entry may be involuntary in the criminal justice case or voluntary in the helping agency case, agents in either type of agency would be hard-pressed to perform their work without a shared body of ideas about their clientele. This collection of ideas, called here agency theories, underlies a number of very important organizational tasks. Not only do these theories help in categorizing the people who have come to the official attention of the agency but they also help in specifying which agents should do what and when, how, and why such action should be taken in the course of the client's career in the agency. Perhaps most important of all are those unwritten rules—derived from agency theories—that prescribe the kinds of treatment the clients may or may not receive. In effect, an etiquette of agency–client relations obtains. And clients often do not receive services until their behavior corresponds with the category into which the agents have assigned them. Further, categorization takes place as often if not more so in helping agencies as it does in criminal justice agencies and is equally consequential.

Police Work

The police perspective—distinctly unlike other people's—is organized around "looking for trouble." Such "trouble" includes traffic violations, crimes, and observably eccentric or violent behavior. For police officers, trouble is defined by the penal code, by private citizens, and by experience with the kind of persons police define as de facto criminals.

Police culture combines legal and lay categories of deviance so as to be able to predict violations in advance. The police have advance notions of what suspects ought to look like, how they might make trouble, and how they should be typed. These routinized conceptions enable police to label suspects; thus they aid in the apprehension of deviants. In short, police perceive trouble in accordance with their working conceptions of it. Then they can regularize and deal with deviance in an orderly manner.

The Deviant in Court

Police develop their categories of deviants from contact with a variety of suspects. When they make contact with a deviant, for example, their usual concern is the mechanics of arrest. Thus one way in which police type suspects is according to how hard or easy it will be to arrest them. By contrast, court personnel employ less pragmatic categories in dealing with suspects, because their roles are abstract and symbolic in accordance with the rules of law.

Court processing involves interaction (some of it behind the scenes) among judge, prosecuting attorney, defense attorney, bailiff, and sometimes a jury. To a very large extent it depends on legal terminology, court norms, and routine conceptions of defendants. Just as police fit suspects into a system of types, the court fits defendants into routine conceptions of typical cases. The use of these routine conceptions means that some persons who fit the court's conceptions of typical cases receive a prison sentence, while others who are guilty of the same offense (but who do not fit the court's conceptions of typical cases) may get lighter sentences or not get into court at all. Court work is rapid to the extent that court personnel can collaborate to make the facts fit their ideas of what typical cases look like.

The Effects of Contact with Control Agents

When a person comes into contact with an agency of social control, the agency may view the person solely in terms of a deviant label. Initial contact with such an agency may suffice to call into question the person's "good name." Additional contact may give the person a definitely bad reputation.

Thus deviant typing may not end with the person's experience with a given agency. When meeting a stranger, for example, people look for information to help them type the stranger. If they find out that s/he has been in a prison or mental hospital, they may type the person primarily on the basis of that past experience, assuming that a person who has had contact with an agency of social control is likely to repeat the behavior that originally led to that contact. Accordingly, lay people feel less inclined to trust such a person. The agency perspective is so powerful that a deviant label, once formally applied, can long outlive any evidentiary basis. Once formally labeled, the so-called deviant becomes defined as the kind of person who probably did perform the imputed behaviors, or at least would if given a chance. Both the deviant and others may then organize their social relations around this belief.

5 HELP AGENCIES AND THEIR THEORIES

Helping agents develop a set of beliefs about their work and the clients whom they are charged with helping. These beliefs include notions about the nature of the problem, the moral character of clients presenting these problems, the kinds of help to give, and the conditions under which it may be given or withheld. The readings in this section show that regardless of the kind of help sought, agency demands and goals shape the agents' definitions of their clients and the kind of help they dispense. In the process of interaction between clients and helpers, typifications emerge which come to exert powerful influences on the way agents process those clients they have come to define as deviant.

In the first reading, Arlene Daniels describes the very special conditions under which psychiatrists will accept illness as an excuse to avoid military combat. Next, Roger Jeffery shows how English physicians in hospital emergency rooms typify some of their clients as deviant and the consequences of these typifications. Finally, Robert Scott shows how contrasting theories in two agencies for the blind affect how they deal with their clients.

The Philosophy of Combat Psychiatry

ARLENE K. DANIELS

. . . The purpose of (military) psychiatry, as for every other military support system, is to preserve the fighting strength. Psychiatrists further this purpose by refusing to support requests for release by men who want to escape from service. In the jargon of military psychiatry, the psychiatrists "support strengths" by encouraging men to be proud of themselves as adults who can take responsibility. And they "deny weakness" by refusing to see men as too weak to accept responsibility.

In combat conditions, military personnel cannot be allowed to succumb to problems which might legitimately be incapacitating to civilians. And so, the role of military psychiatrists as definers of a reality which is unpleasant but normal becomes most clear in wartime (Daniels and Clausen, 1966). The arguments they use in this definition focus upon altruistic rather than egoistic perceptions of reality. You have responsibilities to your buddies, your officers, your branch of the service, and your country. Therefore, no one should request release and ask for special treatment. Any who nonetheless do so will be interviewed by a psychiatrist who has the authority to decide whether or not each petitioner has sufficient grounds for relief from his responsibility (i.e., because of some mental disability). Since these psychiatrists are governed by the philosophy of combat psychiatry which narrowly circumscribes the definition of mental illness, it is unlikely that they will be particularly sympathetic or lenient to such suppliants.[1]

In this respect the psychiatrists are like representatives of any bureaucratic agency. They order their expectations of the clients to be serviced according to their understanding of the goals and powers of the bureaucracy. And so they attempt to fit their clients into the well-established categories. Since the psychiatrist has the authority to do so, his definition of the situation prevails in most cases.

The Mental Hygiene Approach: Strategies for Enforcing a Definition of Reality

In actual practice, the responsibility for defining the reality of combat psychiatry is most often assumed not by the psychiatrist but by his agents, "specialists," or "techs," who make the initial evaluation of those coming to the psychiatric unit. The technicians serve as screening agents who simply send some men back to duty without much comment, counsel others before and even after returning them to duty, and refer the remainder to the officers of the team for more complex decisions about treatment or disposition. Somewhat paradoxically, then, the bulk of the practice of combat psychiatry is performed not by psychiatrists (officers) but by technicians (enlisted men). It is thus mainly a medical practice turned over to the laity, performed by enlisted men for enlisted men. The officers who require attention are considered more "delicate matters" and are attended by the psychiatrists.[2]

The simplest strategy for "containing" the men (i.e., keeping them on duty) is to question their motives or intentions in requesting a psychiatric interview in the first place. Any suspicious events in their record (instances of "goldbricking" or unsatisfactory performance) may contribute to the negative interpretation of their actions. If, at this screening stage, the technician can convince the applicant that his appeal is thoroughly unworthy, the case can be closed.

Excerpt from Arlene K. Daniels, "Normal Mental Illness and Understandable Excuses: The Philosophy of Combat Psychiatry," *American Behavioral Scientist,* Vol. 14, No. 2 (November/December 1970), pp. 169–178. Copyright 1970 by Sage Publications. Reprinted by permission of Sage Publications, Inc.

[1]Generally speaking the career military psychiatrists who hold regular commissions are more wholeheartedly supportive of combat psychiatry philosophy than are the reserve officer psychiatrists on two-year commissions. But these psychiatrists are all members of the military and so, whatever their personal philosophy, they recognize the power of authorities to impose sanctions upon any psychiatrists who do not implement military policy as directed (Daniels, 1969, 1970b). Therefore, it can be assumed that the theory of military psychiatry is also practiced. In this respect the system resembles in many ways that within which the Soviet physician practices (see Field, 1960).

[2]The management of these problems, problems of command consultation, will be discussed in a forthcoming paper.

Here is how a psychiatrist explained the help his technicians gave him in this screening process at a division base camp in Vietnam in 1967:

For somebody who seems to be a malingerer, with a history of repeated shirking and sick call, they will often deal with him rather strenuously. . . . They will tell him in no uncertain terms to "cut out the crap." . . . It's obvious to them and to the patient that he's faking and often they'll return him to duty. If the patient wants to see the psychiatrist he still sees a psychiatrist. Most of them have seen the light at this point and go back to work. They weren't really serious, but they were just trying.

Thus, persons in positions of authority assume the social responsibility of establishing "the facts of the case." By their attribution of motives to the patient, they define the situation as one that the individual can endure if he wishes. Those in authority report that many patients readily accept this picture of themselves and thus most cases are successfully closed.[3]

For those who are still unconvinced, higher authority (the psychiatrist) can be requested to confirm the technician's perception of reality. The psychiatrist acts only as the possessor of an honorific status which should impress the wavering soldier, for as one psychiatrist said: "No psychiatrist in the world can differentiate between a soldier who cannot and one who will not perform" (Maskin, 1946: 190).

Some persons are not seen as immature, shirking, or manipulative, but as genuinely misunderstanding their own ability. Such conclusions are drawn from the fact that either they have no history of attempting to escape from duty, or they have injuries or illnesses which they might consider incapacitating. Here the strategy, while it involves a more conciliatory attitude toward the petitioner, also focuses on returning the man to duty as quickly as possible. A problem is recognized; but the situation is seen as tolerable. A technician provides an example of this strategy in his discussion of newcomers:

New replacements in Vietnam—I see a lot of these people. They do have psychosomatic problems as soon as they get off the boat . . . but I normally do not

send them to [the psychiatrist]. We try to handle it by getting them over it. I figure that they're going to adjust and this is part of their adjustment. They are also trying to get out of the field by remembering any sort of illness that they ever had to see whether that's going to get 'em out of it. So if we can get them over that two week period and get them into the unit . . . started to work, and forgetting about their problems and thinking about what they are doing, why that usually, I think, solves [the problems] for the new men.

In this type of situation, the established authorities show their willingness to accept the soldier's definition of himself as genuinely upset, but they deny that this upset is debilitating. They cut off any arguments for release based solely on presentation of symptoms. The world of military service is a harsh one; and so those who come to the clinic must revise their underlying assumptions or "background expectancies" (Garfinkel, 1967) about the world that they carry from civilian life. Much higher standards of endurance are taken for granted in military settings than might be the case at home. Psychiatrists and their agents reaffirm this reality when they refuse to recognize the legitimacy of illness as an excuse. They help to substantiate this reality; for if they were sympathetic or lenient in expectations of performance the military world would not, in fact, be so harsh.

To enforce their definition of the situation as one within normal tolerance limits, the psychiatrists and their agents attempt to manipulate the environment to gain reaffirmation and support. They try to keep alternative definitions of the situation from developing. First, they try to minimize the amount of time a man spends away from the world of the battlefield when he is wavering in his belief that he can soldier. Second, they try to prevent entrenchment of the idea that reasonable or justifiable excuses for *not* soldiering could possibly be present. One technician at Chu Lai in 1968 expresses both these strategies of containment:

A very frequent case will be an individual who comes back [from the field] with physical symptoms, is sent to a hospital around here, and is given extensive tests . . . which [show] nothing. . . . He is then sent back to mental hygiene and I see him back there with a consul-

---

[3] Unfortunately, it is not possible to ascertain whether this method is ultimately successful, since the measure of evaluation is simply nonreturn to that particular clinic. The possibility that such men may break down again and report to other agencies through which they are subsequently released from service has been suggested by studies of garrison troops (Datel et al., 1970). Another possibility is that men who have complained of mental illness problems may be killed in disproportionate numbers during combat (Glass, 1947). But this unfortunate possibility has never been tested.

tation by the doctors indicating some sort of functional disease. . . . He has been back [i.e., away] so long now . . . five or seven days . . . that it is very hard to get him back out to the field again. . . . [He hasn't seen a psychiatrist yet, he has just seen an ordinary physician.] So now he is [away] for quite a while and he is very hesitant to go back out again. And this is why it takes quite a bit of counseling and talking to him, to get him out there again.

From this perspective, five to seven days is a dangerous amount of time to spend away, for it gives a soldier time to realize that another reality than the battlefield exists. The hospital is also a place for the development of a counter definition of reality—a soldier's definition of his condition as illness, as something that has happened to him for which he is not responsible and thus cannot be expected to control.

The technician's argument shows the importance of using imagery to support (or deny) a particular construction of reality. He realizes that his authority may be diluted by an array of medical tests—no matter how inconclusive—for by their number they suggest medical recognition of the symptom's importance. The soldier may reason that some additional medical tests will yet uncover the illness that *he* is sure he has to provide him with his justifiable release from Vietnam. Thus the authority of the technician to deny the relevance of the illness is weakened when the patient has been allowed to leave the field for a long time. And so special efforts must be made to reassert the military definition of the situation.

If, instead of a long absence, the crucial problem is a very bad experience in the field, the technician must argue against the reasoning that the soldier has already suffered enough and now has a justifiable reason to escape. From his point of view, the technician is persuading someone to accept his responsibility and to relax so that he will be more efficient and more likely to survive when he returns to combat. From a different perspective, it could be argued that the technician is, to garble Goffman (1952), "cooling the mark in" by persuading him to return willingly to a difficult and dangerous situation.[4]

I try to put all the emphasis on him talking to me and telling me just what is the matter with him, and why he feels this way. And after he gets all this out and after he ventilates everything that he feels, then I explain to him that everybody out there feels the same way, and this anxiety and this tension and nervousness is normal. And that is not going to impair . . . it is probably going to enhance his functioning once he is forced into action. Most of the time I just try to appeal to their common sense. And try to force them to deal with the situation as it exists. . . . They are going to have to go out there again sooner or later. And once they get out there, it is not going to be as bad as they think. They are going to adjust, because they are able to adjust to any type of situation. . . . And it just takes quite a bit of talking between the two of us until we can get him [to do it].

All the preceding strategies for enforcing a definition of reality rely primarily upon the technician as the first line of defense. In this way the potential medical significance of the complaint is denied from the beginning.[5] Although psychiatrists minimize their medical connections in this way, they do not deny them altogether. Obviously some behavioral disorders will require more professional consideration than the technicians can provide. The psychiatrist will make these decisions as a medical specialist, but this will not mean that he will diagnose and treat mental illnesses as they are defined in civilian psychiatric nosology. His usual task will be to discriminate between understandable mental breakdowns (combat neuroses), which provide a reasonable excuse, and unacceptable breakdowns (character and behavior disorders, immaturity reactions) which do not (see Daniels, 1970b).

Negotiated Distinctions Between "Ordinary" and "Too Much" Trouble

Once the men are actually in combat for any length of time the strains may wear them down. Studies of the combat effectiveness of men under stress suggest that there might possibly be

---

[4] The technician has to persuade the soldier (or mark) who has already been badly frightened (or burned) that it was not as serious a danger (or loss) as he believes. And in this process, the technician must obscure the possibility that the man may not be able to return, or that his case is sufficiently marginal so that he might escape punishment if he refuses to return (or that the mark really could complain to the police and institute proceedings which would make trouble for the con man).

[5] In general, the members of the psychiatric team de-emphasize their medical contact. They speak of counseling rather than diagnosis or treatment; everyone in the service wears battle dress rather than white coats; the service is more often named Mental Hygiene than Mental Health; and it may be officially titled a division (like any other support service) rather than a clinic (with its association of hospital service).

physiological and psychological limits to the extent of time the average man can successfully remain in the combat setting (Ginzberg, 1959; Glass, 1953; Grinker and Spiegel, 1945). It also seems quite reasonable to the men that they may occasionally become hysterical or panic under the pressures they face. It is assumed that the hardships of combat life are sufficiently corrosive so that even when "physically" fit, the "mental" condition of the troops can progressively deteriorate over time. Therefore, no particular notice may be taken (no response is required) when a comrade breaks down and weeps or in other ways displays grief and rage. Such behavior is an ordinary expression in the course of war; it is not evidence of characterological weakness, immaturity, or incapacity to soldier. In fact, such displays may almost be expected from men who have fought in many battles and who are nearing their time of release. Apparently the stress of combat and the strain of anticipating release from it combine to create a terribly anxiety-provoking situation. Here is how one soldier described this process:

A few of us who were wounded returned to battle in a few weeks. And the others were sent home. You can tell now which are good soldiers when you have seen men break. They drop their weapons, lay down, and start crying. For no reason, you think. But it's just that they are tired of killing and being shot at. They are tired of seeing their friends wounded and killed. For a while you go out on patrol and make contact now and then. But you know there's a change in yourself which you have witnessed in others. You have been in combat for nine months. You are hesitant to go on . . . because the snipers, every time they fire a round, you feel they are firing at you.

This occurs when the man has less than 100 days in the country and will soon be a short timer—the two digit fidgets. . . . Can't sleep; when you should sleep you dream about dying . . . you feel alone, you think everyone is against you. . . .

When you are in camp . . . you cannot concentrate on anything and make careless mistakes that could kill you or those with you . . . then you really start getting short. Forty days till you leave. You wonder . . . if it takes 6 men to support one man in combat, why do I have to stay until I only have 20 days left to stay in the country?

This definition of the situation as intolerable uses the same criteria that the psychiatrists use in evaluating the mental deterioration in the field for which a man may be relieved from duty. These criteria include length of time in combat,

the possession of an honorable combat history, an assumption that the soldier has made a genuine attempt to continue, and a belief that the soldier is becoming progressively more disturbed and less effective. If the psychiatrist finds that these social criteria (rather than classical diagnostic categories) are met, he may use the term "combat neurosis" to suggest that a form of psychiatric illness might actually be present. In this case, the commonsense view of the combat soldier and the professional evaluation of the psychiatrist coincide, both views being compatible with understandings about average tolerance limits under stress presented in empirical studies of combat. Here is a career military psychiatrist's description of "combat neurosis":

A man should have been in combat for probably nine, ten months. There might be a little bit of range on either side. But he also has had to see some pretty severe action. He's had to see probably a lot of his friends get killed. Or he might have had to be wounded himself quite severely. . . . And he also has to be a good soldier up until that time. No problems, no character and behavior disorders at all. This man is a good man, a good soldier, is able to fight effectively, do a good job. He could be just an ordinary rifleman or a squad or platoon sergeant for that matter.

Then after experiencing the ordinary fear and anxiety that everyone in combat experiences for this period of time, finally he is triggered by this trauma of someone else getting killed, a close friend, or his unit may be overrun or himself getting severely wounded. It sets off a severe combination of anxiety, usually G.I. [gastro-intestinal] symptoms, anorexia, sometimes nausea, vomiting and bad dreams. And the nightmares are usually a recurrent type. . . . They can't sleep because their insomnia occurs. After they get enough of the bad dreams, they won't sleep by choice.

Also we find that there's a combination of this [symptomatology] with depression. Usually some guilt feelings. It's inappropriate guilt but it's guilt they feel. Maybe there's something they could have done to save their friends. . . . Or sometimes it might be a little guilt or depression that . . . after all this time they seem like they're cracking up and they can't fight effectively and they're sort of ashamed of themselves. . . .

So we have anxiety, depression, insomnia . . . G.I. symptoms, and dreams. And the anxiety is so acute that at times the guy becomes very tremulous in combat out in the field. Especially if he gets fired upon. . . . Sometimes we find the G.I. symptoms predominate. It takes just a little explosion or a rifle going off or something like that to [start] . . . severe vomiting and dry heaves. And he has to be brought back. This [symptomatology] is not dependent upon any previous psychiatric history.

This account presents a picture of a "reasonable" or "honorable" breakdown which can occur to anyone under sufficient pressure. This view requires no assumption of underlying illness or characterological weakness, only that there has been a sufficiently lengthy and successful military career prior to the event which can be seen as the cause of the breakdown. Under so much repeated, sustained, psychic, and physical punishment anyone might have broken down; there is no need to explain the situation in the traditional terminology of mental illness.

This perspective suggests that breakdown might arise after *sufficient* cause. It specifically excludes the notion that any particular encounter in wartime could be sufficient to cause breakdown (see Scott and Lyman, 1968). No single act of war or individual atrocity can be viewed as sufficiently brutalizing or terrible to induce mental incapacity. Such a view would undermine the entire picture of war as unpleasant but endurable. Should a man actually become incapacitated after such acts, a variety of other reasons for his difficulty can always be found by examining his career (Goffman, 1959).

The question of what is "enough" punishment is decided by the psychiatrist. He makes the decision according to rules that have been already formulated to a certain extent in the combat psychiatry literature from World War II. One of the best statements of how the criteria of enough punishment came to be defined on the basis of the psychiatrists' experiences in World War II is provided by Sobel (1947) in his discussion of "The 'Old Sergeant' Syndrome." Sobel suggested that men who had honorably and efficiently seen combat for long periods of time might eventually become incapacitated by all the griefs and hardships they had endured in the course of service. In effect, he was suggesting how anyone might be unable to endure any more of that kind of experience. Once their condition is recognized, it is acknowledged that such persons are "entitled" to break down, and that they are entitled to some honorable release from

pressures. But, in general, this view did not supersede more traditional psychiatric views until much later.[6]

The traditional psychiatric views have officially been abandoned in military psychiatry on the basis of experience in past wars; for a focus on symptomatology as psychiatric illness rather than understandable stress reaction presented two main problems. For the man, the psychiatric diagnosis often resulted in a mental illness label. Once the label was applied, men often found it difficult or impossible ever again to shoulder normal adult responsibilities (Ginzberg, 1959). For the military, the application of the mental illness label eventually required the federal government to assume responsibility for long-term disability payments as it would for any soldier suffering from a service-related illness. Thus, the use of illness categories encouraged lifetime dependence and created a great fiscal burden for the government (Daniels, 1970a).

Today the view that soldiers may have their breaking points is accepted in military psychiatry, and so there is less necessity for singling out as possessors of a characterological weakness those who break down after long combat experience. The significance of this view is that since there is no necessary expectation of characterological weakness, there is no reason to fear that future psychotic breaks or permanent impairment to the soldier will occur. Normal recovery should follow normal breakdown, for if there is no characterological weakness causing a collapse under severe and prolonged hardship, then there is every reason to expect spontaneous remission or remission once the situation is less oppressive. What this philosophy means in practice is that men who break down in the field are given a period of rest and sedation. They are supposed to recover quickly, forget their traumatizing experiences, and return to duty. However, if they do not recover quickly, they may be sent to some less stressful post to recover at leisure. In other words, it is reasonable to offer them some measure of escape from battle if it seems necessary to do so, even though

[6] For example, a World War II psychiatrist (Lidz, 1946a) takes the traditional psychiatric perspective in describing the dreadful circumstances under which a number of marines broke down at Guadalcanal and had to be hospitalized as psychiatric casualties. These marines had to endure months of hardship in which buddies were killed by the enemy and left to decompose in plain sight and smell around the fortifications while help never came; where fear of torture and death at the hands of the enemy was realistic and ever-present; and where defeat seemed inevitable. The symptoms now termed combat neurosis are described in men who had endured such events. Yet, in this essay and elsewhere (Lidz, 1946b), this psychiatrist places greater emphasis on prior history of neurosis, unhappiness, or family instability than he does on the view that "every soldier has his breaking point."

technically they have no illness. And so disposition of the case will stress these possibilities.

Our approach . . . is that just because he has this doesn't mean that he is no longer a good soldier. He's proven himself in battle . . . and elsewhere. What he is suffering from is a temporary reaction that's curable. And we make a big point of the fact that it is curable. And also we have to make a point of the fact that he's not going crazy. He's not going to be a psychiatric case all his life. We give him encouragement that after his treatment he can return to duty and do as good a job as he did before and then we'll treat him with some medication like Librium—20 milligrams four times a day—and make sure we give him plenty of sleeping medicine at night, like Seconal perhaps, a couple of hundred milligrams. Maybe about three days. After this we send him back to duty . . . [If his unit tells us he is not fully recovered and a recurrence of his symptoms appears] they should let us know and either arrange for a transfer with our recommendation backing theirs, or send him back to us sometime and we may be able directly to arrange a transfer to a non-combat unit.

The meaning of symptoms is thus dependent upon the combat history with which they are associated. They mean nothing without combat experience, something else when a soldier has little combat experience, and something else again when he has a history of nine or ten months of honorable and efficient service.

Possibly [a soldier] might come in with . . . symptoms but not with [the] full-blown syndrome. In the first place . . . we have to have our first criteria that the man has to have been a good soldier and have been in combat for some time before he develops this [symptomatology] in order to call this a combat neurosis. . . . If the guy comes in with anxiety and so on and maybe even some physiological symptoms after he has only been in combat for a month, we usually find that he had this right off from the first contact out in the field. And this seems to represent to us more of a kind of an immaturity reaction than anything [like] a true neurotic reaction.

When symptoms are presented within the wrong context, an entire reconstruction of the situation may be required. Not only are the symptoms given a different diagnosis but also the past history of the referral will be reexamined and then reconstructed. A contextual analysis of the situation permits the psychiatrist to find the necessary evidence in the moral career of the patient who shows symptoms too

early in his combat experience, to label him as one who has displayed immaturity reactions from the very beginning, and thus who deserves the disposition (no mental illness) he now receives (Goffman, 1959).

The diagnosis of "no mental illness" has an additional effect in that it reassures the soldier's superiors and peers that strong sanctions may properly be used to bring him into line. When the psychiatrist indicates that he sees no reasonable excuse in the case which might justify leniency for the man in question, the clear understanding that no alternative views will be tolerated creates additional pressure to accept the developing definition that "nothing is wrong" or that "nothing unusual is happening" (Emerson, 1970, 1969: 170). And since nothing is wrong, the soldier must eventually accept the world as a place where excuses are unacceptable.

REFERENCES

Becker, H. S. 1967. "Whose Side Are We On?" *Social Problems*, 14 (Winter): 239–247.

Berger, P. and T. Luckmann. 1967. *The Social Construction of Reality*. New York: Doubleday Anchor.

Blake, J. A. 1970. "The Organization as Instrument of Violence: The Military Case." *Sociological Quarterly*, 11 (Summer): 331–350.

Bloch, H. S. 1969. "Army Clinical Psychiatry in the Combat Zone 1967–1968." *American Journal of Psychiatry*, 126 (September): 289–298.

Cavan, S. 1966. *Liquor License*. Chicago: Aldine.

Daniels, A. K. 1970a. "A Sub-Specialty Within a Professional Specialty: Military Psychiatry." In E. Freidson and J. Lorber (eds.), *Reader in Medical Sociology*. New York: Atherton.

———. 1970b. "The Social Construction of Military Psychiatric Diagnoses." In H. Dreitzel (ed.), *Patterns of Communicative Behavior*. New York: Macmillan, pp. 182–205.

——— and R. E. Clausen. 1966. "Role Conflicts and Their Ideological Resolution in Military Psychiatric Practice." *American Journal of Psychiatry*, 123 (September): 280–287.

Emerson, J. 1970. "Nothing Unusual Is Happening." In T. Shibutani (ed.), *Human Nature and Collective Behavior: Papers in Honor of Herbert Blumer*. Englewood Cliffs, N.J.: Prentice-Hall.

———. 1969. "Negotiating the Serious Import of Humor." *Sociometry*, 32 (June): 169–181.

Garfinkel, H. 1967. "Studies in the Routine Grounds of Everyday Activities." In H. Garfinkel, *Studies in Ethnomethodology*. Englewood Cliffs, N.J.: Prentice-Hall, pp. 35–75.

Ginzberg, E. 1959. *The Ineffective Soldier*. New York: Columbia University Press.

Glass, A. J. 1953. "The Problem of Stress in the Combat Zone." In Army Medical Center Graduate School, *Symposium on Stress*. Washington, D.C.: Walter Reed Army Medical Center, pp. 90–102.

Goffman, E. 1959. "The Moral Career of the Mental Patient." *Psychiatry*, 22 (May): 123–142.

———. 1952. "On Cooling the Mark Out." *Psychiatry*, 15 (November): 451–463.

Grinker, R. and J. Spiegel. 1945. *Men Under Stress*. Philadelphia: Blakiston.

Lidz, T. 1946a. "Psychiatric Casualties from Guadalcanal." *Psychiatry*, 9:193–213.

———. 1946b. "Nightmares and Combat Neuroses." *Psychiatry*, 9:37–46.

Maskin, M. 1946. "Something About a Soldier," *Psychiatry*, 9:187–191.

Sobel, R. 1947. "The 'Old Sergeant' Syndrome." *Psychiatry*, 10:315–321.

Rubbish: Deviant Patients in Casualty Departments   ROGER JEFFERY

English Casualty Departments

Casualty departments have been recognised as one of the most problematic areas of the NHS [National Health Service] since about 1958, and several official and semiofficial reports were published in the following years, the most recent being a House of Commons Expenditure Committee Report.[1] The greatest public concern is voiced when departments are closed permanently, or over holiday weekends, because of shortages of staff.[2] The major criticisms have been that casualty departments have to operate in old, crowded, and ill-equipped surroundings, and that their unpopularity with doctors has meant that the doctors employed as Casualty Officers are either overworked or of poor quality. 'Poor quality' in this context seems to mean either doctors in their pre-registration year, or doctors from abroad. The normal appointment to the post of Casualty Officer (CO) is for six months, and many doctors work this period only because it is required for those who wish to sit the final examinations for FRCS [Fellow of the Royal College of Surgeons]. Although consultants have in general played very little part in the running of casualty departments (which is one reason for their poor facilities) there has been dispute over whether they should be the responsibility of orthopaedic or general surgeons: some hospitals have appointed physicians as consultants-in-charge.[3] These problems with the doctors have apparently not affected the nursing staff and in general Casualty seems to be able to attract and keep enough nurses.

The reasons for the unpopularity of Casualty work amongst doctors have usually been couched either in terms of the poor working conditions or in terms of the absence of a career structure within Casualty work. Most Casualty staff are junior doctors; very rarely are appointments made above the level of Senior House Officer, and there are very few full-time consultant appointments. Other reasons which are less frequently put forward, but seem to underlie these objections, relate more to the nature of the work, and in particular to the notion that the Casualty department is an interface between hospital and community. Prestige amongst doctors is, at least in part, related to the distance a doctor can get from the undifferentiated mass of patients, so that teaching hospital consultancies are valued because they are at the end of a series of screening mechanisms.[4] Casualty is one of these screening mechanisms, rather like general practitioners in this respect. However, they are unusual in the hospital setting in the freedom of patients to gain entrance without having seen a GP first; another low prestige area similar in this respect is the VD clinic. One of the complaints of the staff is that they are obliged, under a Ministry of Health circular, to see every patient who presents himself; and having been seen, the chances are high that the patient will then be treated. The effect of this openness is that there is a great variety of patients who present themselves, and this has hindered the development of a specialty in Casualty work. There is a Casualty Surgeons' Association, and some appointments include 'Traumatic Surgery', but it is obvious that these cover only a small selection of the patients seen in Casualty, as has been recognised by the employment of physicians as well. Casualty has been unsuited to the processes of differentiation and specialisation which have characterised the recent history of the medical

Sociology of Health and Illness, Vol. 1, No. 1 (June 1979), pp. 90–107. Reprinted by permission of Routledge & Kegan Paul Ltd.

An earlier version of this paper [entitled, *Normal Rubbish: Deviant Patients in Casualty Departments*] was presented at the Bath conference on Medical Ideologies, September 1974. I am grateful to Malcolm Johnson, Anne Murcott and Mike Smith for comments on earlier drafts.

[1] See for example, the British Orthopedic Association, 'Memorandum on Accident Services', *Journal of Bone and Joint Surgery,* Vol. 41B, No. 3, 1959, pp. 457–63; Nuffield Provincial Hospitals Trust, *Casualty Services and Their Setting,* London, O.U.P., 1960; and House of Commons Expenditure Committee, 4th Report, *Accident and Emergency Services,* London H.M.S.O. 1974. A fuller survey of this literature can be found in H. Gibson, *Rules, Routines and Records.* Ph.D. thesis, Aberdeen University, 1977.

[2] See e.g. the summary in *World Medicine,* February 1972, p. 11.

[3] Reported in the Expenditure Committee Report, op. cit. pp. xii–xiii.

[4] This is similar to Freidson's distinction between client control and colleague control; see E. Freidson, *Patients' Views of Medical Practice,* New York, Russell Sage Foundation, 1961.

profession, and this helps to explain the low prestige of the work, and the low priority it has received in hospital expenditure.

The material on which this paper is based was gathered at three Casualty departments in an English city. The largest was in the city centre, the other two were suburban; of the seven months of field work, 4½ were in the city centre. These departments would appear to be above average in terms of the criteria discussed above: all were fully staffed; only two of the seventeen doctors employed during the fieldwork period were immigrant; all were senior house officers, and one department had a registrar as well; and the working conditions were reasonable. The data presented came from either fieldwork notes or tape-recorded, open-ended interviews with the doctors.

Typifications of Patients

As Roth[5] and Strong and Davis[6] have argued, moral evaluation of patients seems to be a regular feature of medical settings, not merely amongst medical students or in mental hospitals. As Gibson[7] and Godse[8] have both pointed out, social and moral evaluations are important for the treatment given to patients defined as 'over-doses' and those defined as drunk or drug-dependent, and in the English Casualty departments I studied these categories were of considerable salience to the staff. In general, two broad categories were used to evaluate patients: good or interesting, and bad or rubbish. They were sometimes used as if they were an exhaustive dichotomy, but more generally appeared as opposite ends of a continuum.

(CO to medical students) If there's anything interesting we'll stop, but there's a lot of rubbish this morning.

We have the usual rubbish, but also a subdural haemorrhage.

On nights you get some drunken dross in, but also some good cases.

In most of this paper I shall be discussing the category of rubbish, but I shall first deal with the valued category, the good patients.

Good Patients

Good patients were described almost entirely in terms of their medical characteristics, either in terms of the symptoms or the causes of the injury. Good cases were head injuries, or cardiac arrests, or a stove-in chest; or they were RTA's (Road Traffic Accidents). There were three broad criteria by which patients were seen to be good, and each related to medical considerations.

If They Allowed the CO to Practice Skills Necessary for Passing Professional Examinations. In order to pass the FRCS examinations doctors need to be able to diagnose and describe unusual conditions and symptoms. Casualty was not a good place to discover these sorts of cases, and if they did turn up a great fuss was made of them. As one CO said, the way to get excellent treatment was to turn up at a slack period with an unusual condition. The most extreme example of this I witnessed was a young man with a severe head injury from a car accident. A major symptom of his head injury was the condition of his eyes, and by the time he was transferred to another hospital for neurological treatment, twelve medical personnel had looked into his eyes with an ophthalmoscope, and an *ad hoc* teaching session was held on him. The case was a talking point for several days, and the second hospital was phoned several times for a progress report.[9] Similar interest was shown in a man

[5] J. Roth, 'Some Contingencies of the Moral Evaluation and Control of Clientele: The Case of the Hospital Emergency Service,' *A.J.S.* Vol. 77, No. 5, March 1972. The studies of medical students which are relevant are: H. Becker *et al., Boys in White,* Chicago, University of Chicago Press, 1961; and R. K. Merton *et al.* (eds.), *The Student Physician,* Cambridge, Harvard University Press, 1957.

[6] P. Strong and A. Davis, 'Who's Who in Paediatric Encounters: Morality, Expertise and the Generation of Identity and Action in Medical Settings', in A. Davis (ed.), *Relationships Between Doctors and Patients,* Westmead, Teakfield, 1978, pp. 51–2.

[7] H. Gibson, op. cit., chapter 9.

[8] A. H. Godse, 'The Attitudes of Casualty Staff and Ambulancemen Towards Patients Who Take Drug Overdoses', *Social Science and Medicine,* Vol. 12, 5A, September 1978, pp. 341–6.

[9] This case, while not as spectacular as one reported by Sudnow, does suggest a general level of depersonalisation in British teaching hospitals rather higher than in American hospitals. See D. Sudnow, *Passing On,* New York, Prentice-Hall, 1968.

with gout, and in a woman with an abnormally slow heart beat. The general response to cases like this can be summed up in the comments of a CO on a patient with bilateral bruising of the abdomen:

This is fascinating. It's really great. I've never seen this before.

If They Allowed Staff to Practice Their Chosen Specialty. For the doctors, the specific characteristics of good patients of this sort were fairly closely defined, because most doctors saw themselves as future specialists—predominantly surgeons. They tended to accept, or conform to, the model of the surgeon as a man of action who can achieve fairly rapid results. Patients who provided the opportunity to use and act out this model were welcomed. One CO gave a particularly graphic description of this:

But I like doing surgical procedures. These are great fun. It just lets your imagination run riot really (laughs) you know, you forget for a moment you are just a very small cog incising a very small abscess, and you pick up your scalpel like anyone else (laughs). It's quite mad when you think about it but it's very satisfying. And you can see the glee with which most people leap on patients with abscesses because you know that here's an opportunity to do something.

Another one put it like this:

Anything which involves, sort of, a bit of action . . . I enjoy anything which involves bone-setting, plastering, stitching, draining pus.

For some CO's, Casualty work had some advantages over other jobs because the clientele was basically healthy, and it was possible to carry out procedures which showed quick success in terms of returning people to a healthy state.

In two of the hospitals much of this practical action was carried out by the senior nurses, and the doctors left them the more minor surgical work. These nurses too were very pleased to be able to fulfil, even if in only a minor way, the role of surgeon, and found it very rewarding.

If They Tested the General Competence and Maturity of the Staff. The patients who were most prized were those who stretched the resources of the department in doing the task they saw themselves designed to carry out—the rapid

early treatment of acutely ill patients. Many of the CO's saw their Casualty job as the first in which they were expected to make decisions without the safety net of ready advice from more senior staff. The ability to cope, the ability to make the decisions which might have a crucial bearing on whether a patient lived or died, this was something which most staff were worried about in advance. However, they were very pleased with patients who gave them this experience. The most articulate expression of this was from a CO who said:

I really do enjoy doing anything where I am a little out of my depth, where I really have to think about what I am doing. Something like a bad road traffic accident, where they ring up and give you a few minutes warning and perhaps give you an idea of what's happening . . . And when the guy finally does arrive you've got a rough idea of what you are going to do, and sorting it all out and getting him into the right speciality, this kind of thing is very satisfying, even though you don't do very much except perhaps put up a drip, but you've managed it well. And I find that very pleasing. It might be a bit sordid, the fact that I like mangled up bodies and things like this, but the job satisfaction is good.

Good patients, then, make demands which fall squarely within the boundaries of what the staff define as appropriate to their job. It is the medical characteristics of these patients which are most predominant in the discussions, and the typifications are not very well developed. Indeed, unpredictability was often stressed as one of the very few virtues of the Casualty job, and this covered not only the variability in pressure —sometimes rushed off their feet, sometimes lounging around—but also the variability between patients, even if they had superficial similarities. This is in marked contrast to 'rubbish'.

Rubbish

While the category of the good patient is one I have in part constructed from comments about 'patients I like dealing with' or 'the sort of work I like to do', 'rubbish' is a category generated by the staff themselves. It was commonly used in discussions of the work, as in the following quotes:

It's a thankless task, seeing all the rubbish, as we call it, coming through.

We get our share of rubbish, in inverted commas, but I think compared with other Casualty departments you might find we get less rubbish.

I wouldn't be making the same fuss in another job— it's only because it's mostly bloody crumble like women with insect bites.

I think the (city centre hospital) gets more of the rubbish—the drunks and that.

He'll be tied up with bloody dross down there.

Rubbish appeared to be a mutually comprehensible term, even though some staff members used other words, like dross, dregs, crumble or grot. There appeared to be some variation in the sorts of cases included under these terms, but I shall argue later that these differences related to the differential application of common criteria, rather than any substantive disagreement.

In an attempt to get a better idea of what patients would be included in the category of rubbish I asked staff what sorts of patients they did not like having to deal with, which sorts of patients made them annoyed, and why. The answers they gave suggested that staff had developed characterisations of 'normal' rubbish—the normal suicide attempt, the normal drunk, and so on—which they were thinking of when they talked about rubbish.[10] In other words, staff felt able to predict a whole range of features related not only to his medical condition but also to his past life, to his likely behaviour inside the casualty department, and to his future behaviour. These expected features of the patient could thus be used to guide the treatment (both socially and medically) that the staff decided to give the patient. Thus patients placed in these categories would tend to follow standard careers, as far as the staff were concerned, in part because of their common characteristics and in part because they were treated as if they had such common characteristics. The following

were the major categories of rubbish mentioned by the staff.

Trivia

The recurring problem of casualty departments, in the eyes of the doctors, has been the 'casual' attender. In the 19th century the infirmaries welcomed casual attenders as a way of avoiding the control of the subscribers, but since before the inauguration of the N.H.S. there have been frequent complaints about the patients who arrive without a letter from their G.P. and with a condition which is neither due to trauma nor urgent.[11]

For the staff of the casualty departments I studied, normal trivia banged their heads, their hands or their ankles, carried on working as usual, and several days later looked into Casualty to see if it was all right. Normal trivia drops in when it is passing, or if it happens to be visiting a relative in the hospital. Trivia 'didn't want to bother my doctor'. Normal trivia treats Casualty like a perfunctory service,[12] on a par with a garage, rather than as an expert emergency service, which is how the staff like to see themselves.

They come in and say 'I did an injury half an hour ago, or half a day ago, or two days ago. I'm perfectly all right, I've just come for a check-up.'

(Trivia) comes up with a pain that he's had for three weeks, and gets you out of bed at 3 in the morning.

Trivia stretches the boundaries of reasonable behaviour too far, by bringing for advice something which a reasonable person could make up his own mind about. Trivia must find Casualty a nice place to be in, else why would they come? For trivia, Casualty is a bit of a social centre: they think 'It's a nice day, I might as well go down to Casualty.' By bringing to Casualty conditions which should be taken to the G.P., trivia trivialises the service Casualty is offering, and lowers its status to that of the G.P.

[10] I am using normal in the sense that Sudnow uses it, in D. Sudnow, 'Normal Crimes', *Social Problems,* Vol. 12, Winter 1965.

[11] This topic recurs in the reports referenced in note 1 above, and in most of the research reports on casualty caseloads in the medical press. In an attempt to discourage casual attenders the Ministry of Health changed the title of the departments from 'Casualty' to 'Accident and Emergency' during the 1960s. However, most of the staff continued to call it Casualty (and I have followed their usage) and there is no evidence that the change of name has altered the nature of the case-load.

[12] See E. Goffman, *Asylums,* Harmondsworth, Penguin, 1968, especially the section 'Notes on the Vicissitudes of the Tinkering Trades'.

Drunks[13]

Normal drunks are abusive and threatening. They come in shouting and singing after a fight and they are sick all over the place, or they are brought in unconscious, having been found in the street. They come in the small hours of the night, and they often have to be kept in until morning because you never know if they have been knocked out in a fight (with the possibility of a head injury) or whether they were just sleeping it off. They come in weekend after weekend with the same injuries, and they are always unpleasant and awkward.

They keep you up all hours of the night, and you see them next day, or in outpatients, and they complain bitterly that 'the scar doesn't look nice' and they don't realise that under there you've sewn tendons and nerves, that they're bloody lucky to have a hand at all.

The person who comes along seeking admission to a hospital bed at 2 o'clock in the morning and he's rolling around and is incomprehensible, and one's got other much more serious cases to deal with but they make such a row you've got to go to them.

Overdoses[14]

The normal overdose is female, and is seen as a case of self-injury rather than of attempted suicide. She comes because her boy-friend/ husband/parents have been unkind, and she is likely to be a regular visitor. She only wants attention, she was not seriously trying to kill herself, but she uses the overdose as moral blackmail. She makes sure she does not succeed by taking a less-than-lethal dose, or by ensuring that she is discovered fairly rapidly.

In the majority of overdoses, you know, these symbolic overdoses, the sort of '5 aspirins and 5 valiums and I'm ill doctor, I've taken an overdose'.

By and large they are people who have done it time and time again, who are up, who have had treatment, who haven't responded to treatment.

Lots of the attempts are very half-hearted. They don't really mean it, they just want to make a bit of a fuss, so that husband starts loving them again and stops going drinking.

Most of the people I've met, they've either told someone or they have done it in such a way that someone has found them. I think there's very few that really wanted to, you know.

Tramps

Normal tramps can be recognised by the many layers of rotten clothing they wear, and by their smell. They are a feature of the cold winter nights and they only come to Casualty to try to wheedle a bed in the warm for the night. Tramps can never be trusted: they will usually sham their symptoms. New CO's and young staff nurses should be warned, for if one is let in one night then dozens will turn up the next night. They are abusive if they don't get their way: they should be shouted at to make sure they understand, or left in the hope that they will go away.

(Tramps are) nuisance visitors, frequent visitors, who won't go, who refuse to leave when you want them to.
(Tramps are) just trying to get a bed for the night.

These four types covered most of the patients included in rubbish, or described as unpleasant or annoying. There were some other characterisations mentioned less frequently, or which seemed to be generated by individual patients, or which seemed to be specific to particular members of staff. 'Nutcases' were in this uncertain position: there were few 'typical' features of psychiatric patients, and these were very diffuse. Nutcases might be drug addicts trying to blackmail the CO into prescribing more of their drug by threatening to attempt suicide if they do not get what they want; but in general they are just 'irrational' and present everyone with insoluble problems. Since Casualty staff tended to be primarily surgical in orientation they had little faith in the ability of the psychiatrists to achieve anything except to remove a problem from the hands of Casualty. 'Smelly', 'dirty' and 'obese' patients were also in this limbo. Patients with these characteristics were objected to, but there

---

[13]Gibson (op. cit. pp. 164–86) discusses the ways in which 'drunk' fails as a medical category since a wide variety of careers and treatments are associated with drunk patients, which tends to support the argument that this is essentially a moral category.

[14]Godse (op. cit.) suggests that there is generalised hostility towards all drug overdoses, but he elaborates his discussion with respect to three types. One of these—deliberate suicide attempts or gestures—fails to distinguish between what I call 'normal' overdoses and those believed by the staff to be serious suicide attempts. Gibson (op. cit. pp. 186–94) also reports that staff presumed that most, if not all, cases of self-poisoning were seen as acts of self-injury, wilfully and directly caused, rather than as attempts to commit suicide.

was no typical career expected for these patients: apart from the one common characteristic they were expected to be different.

As Sudnow[15] suggests, staff found it easier to create typical descriptions if they had to deal with many cases of that sort. However, it was not necessary for any one member of staff to have dealt with these cases, since the experiences of others would be shared. 'Rubbish' was a common topic of general conversations, and in this way staff could find out not only about patients who had come in while they were off duty, but also about notable cases in the past history of the department. The register of patients would also contain clues about the classification of patients this way—staff frequently vented their feelings by sarcastic comments both on the patient's record card and on the register. Again, the receptionists tended to be a repository for information of this kind, partly because they and the senior nurses had worked longest in the departments. In the departments I studied this common fund of knowledge about patients was sufficient to recognise regular visitors and tramps: other departments were reputed to keep 'black books' to achieve the same purpose.

The departments thus varied in the categories of patients typified under rubbish. The city centre hospital had all types, but only one of the suburban hospitals had tramps in any number, and neither of them had many drunks. Overdoses and trivia were, it seems, unavoidable. Comments on drunks and tramps in the suburban hospitals tended to stress their infrequency and staff had difficulty in typing them. As one CO at a suburban hospital said about drunks,

Some are dirty, but so are some ordinary people. Some are clean. Some are aggressive, some are quiet. Some are obnoxious. It's the same with ordinary people.

The features of rubbish which are attended to are not the strictly medical ones—they are left as understood. These non-medical features were not essential parts of any diagnosis, since it is not necessary to know that a man is a drunk or a tramp to see that he has cut his head. Similarly, the medical treatment of an overdose does not depend on the intentions of the patient, nor on the number of previous occasions when an overdose has been taken. The features which were attended to were more concerned with the ascription of responsibility or reasonableness. However, the staff could find out these features of patients in the course of the routine questions asked in order to establish a diagnosis.[16] Thus the questions 'when did this happen?' and 'how did this happen?' provide information not only relevant to the physical signs and symptoms which can be expected, but also to the possibility that this is trivia. 'How many pills did you take?' establishes not only the medical diagnosis but also the typicality of the overdose. Similarly, questions designed to find out whether or not the patient will follow the doctor's orders (to change the dressing, or to return to the outpatients clinic) will affect not only the orders the doctor will give but will also provide evidence about the typicality of the tramp or drunk.

Rules Broken by Rubbish

In their elaboration of *why* certain sorts of patients were rubbish, staff organised their answers in terms of a number of unwritten rules which they said rubbish had broken. These rules were in part consensual, and in part ideological. Thus some patients negotiated their status with staff in terms of these rules, while other patients rejected these rules and argued for rights even though in the eye of the staff, they might not deserve them. In so far as they were ideological, these rules can be seen as attempts by medical staff to increase their control over their clientele, so that they could spend more time on 'good' patients. The rules which the staff were trying to enforce can be seen as the obverse of professionalisation, in two senses. First, they are the obverse of attempts to specialise and to build up specialised knowledge, which implies that some areas will be excluded. Secondly, they are the obverse of attempts to increase control over the clientele, which implies that those who cannot be controlled should be excluded.[17] These rules, then, can be seen as the criteria by which staff judged the legitimacy of claims made

[15] Sudnow, 'Normal Crimes', op. cit.

[16] P. Strong and A. Davis, op. cit., p. 52.

[17] [In] research of a similar kind carried out by the author in Pakistan, doctors were both less interested in good patients and less bothered by rubbish; similarly, they had less autonomy over their working conditions.

by patients for entry into the sick role, or for medical care. I have organised them on lines similar to the classic discussion by Parsons of the sick role.[18] . . .

These . . . are rules inductively generalised from accounts given by staff.

(a) *Patients must not be responsible, either for their illness or for getting better; medical staff can only be held responsible if, in addition, they are able to treat the illness.*

The first half of this rule was broken by all normal rubbish. Drunks and tramps were responsible for their illnesses, either directly or indirectly. Drunks will continue to fall over or be involved in fights because they are drunk, and they are responsible for their drunkenness. Tramps are responsible for the illnesses like bronchitis which are a direct result of the life the tramp has chosen to lead. Normal overdoses knew what they were doing, and chose to take an overdose for their own purposes. Trivia *chose* to come to Casualty, and could be expected to deal with their illnesses themselves. All normal rubbish had within their own hands the ability to affect a complete cure, and since there was little the Casualty staff could do about it, they could not be held responsible to treat the illnesses of normal rubbish. Comments which reflected this rule included,

I don't like having to deal with drunks in particular. I find that usually they're quite aggressive. I don't like aggressive people. And I feel that, you know, they've got themselves into this state entirely through their own follies, why the hell should I have to deal with them on the NHS? So I don't like drunks, I think they are a bloody nuisance. I don't like overdoses, because I've got very little sympathy with them on the whole, I'm afraid.

(Q: Why not?)

[H]mm well you see most of them don't mean it, it's just to draw attention to themselves, you see I mean they take a nonlethal dose and they know it's not lethal.

I do feel that tramps could have been helped, and

have been helped and have rejected it. So often I feel this is brought on by themselves.

People who create a lot of trouble because of their own folly.

If patients can be held responsible, then the staff feel they have no moral obligation to treat them, though the legal obligation may remain. However, responsibility is not easily assigned. Thus some staff find it very difficult to decide about responsibility in psychiatric cases, and they express ambivalence over whether or not tramps, drunks and overdoses are 'really ill' in their underlying state. As one CO said, he did not mind treating

Anyone who is genuinely ill—I'm not talking about the psychiatric types I suppose, they're genuinely ill but the thing is I don't really understand psychiatric illness.

The staff normally felt uncertain about the existence of an illness if there was no therapy that they, or anyone else, could provide to correct the state, and it would seem that this uncertainty fostered frustration which was vented as hostility towards these patients. One example of this was in the comments on overdoses, and the distinctions made between those who really tried to commit suicide (for whom there is some respect) and the rest (viewed as immature calls for attention). This seems to be behind the following comments:

And I mean, certainly with overdoses, and sometimes you feel, if they are that determined, why not let them put themselves out of their misery.

I think it's all so unnecessary, you know, if you are going to do the job, do it properly, don't bother us!

It's the same I'm sure in any sphere, that if you're doing something and you're treating it and—say you're a plumber and the thing keeps going wrong because you haven't got the right thing to put it right, you get fed up with it, and in the end you'd much rather hit the thing over the . . . hit the thing with your hammer. Or in this case, to give up rather than go on, you know, making repeated efforts.

[18]T. Parsons [*The Social System,* New York, The Free Press, 1951]. Although Parsons never says where he developed the sick role model from, it is plausible that it comes from his discussions with doctors in his Boston study, and from his course in psychotherapy (see his footnote 2, pp. 428–9). If so, and if we reformulate the sick role in the way that I have, this may overcome some of the problems which have been pointed out by other writers: for example, the inapplicability of the sick role to chronic illness. That is, there is indeed a preference by doctors for an illness which is temporary, transitory and curable, and part of the reason for the low prestige of work with geriatric or chronic patients is that doctors are uneasy dealing with patients who do not conform to this pattern.

Similar feelings were expressed about drunks:[19]

They're jolly difficult people to deal with, there's no easy answer. Unlike someone who's got something you can put right. With them, the thing that's wrong is much more difficult to put right.

You know that whatever you do for them is only 5% of their problem, and you're not really approaching the other 95% or touching it.

(b) Patients should be restricted in their reasonable activities by the illnesses they report with.

This rule has particular point in a Casualty department, and trivia who have been able to delay coming to the department most obviously break this rule. This is implicit in the comments already reported about trivia. However, there is another aspect to this rule, which refers to the discussion of the relationship between deviance and illness, which I shall return to later. This is the requirement that the activities being followed should be reasonable, and the obvious offenders against this rule are the tramps. It applies also to other sorts of patients, who may be attributed one deviant trait ('hippy type') which then places them in the position of being an 'illegitimate aspirer to the sick role' as a generalisation from one deviant trait to a deviant character. Comments which applied this rule included:

I also like some patient relationships, providing the patient is a co-operative, pleasant, useful human being. I am afraid I get very short, very annoyed, with neurotic patients and with patients who I think are just drop-outs from society really—it's a horrible thing to say—not worth helping.

If a man has led a full productive life, he's entitled to good medical attention, because he's put a lot into society.

(Tramps) put nothing in, and are always trying to get something out.

Obviously the Protestant Ethic of work is alive and well in Casualty departments.

(c) Patients should see illness as an undesirable state.

The patients who most obviously offend against this rule are the overdoses and the tramps. The overdoses are seen to want to be ill in order to put moral pressure on someone, or to get attention. Tramps want to be ill in order to get the benefits of being a patient—a warm bed and warm meals. Trivia are also suspected of being neurotic or malingering, in order to explain why they come, as in the following comments:

In fact you get entirely indifferent, you think that everyone's neurotic, you just don't care. You just say 'you haven't got a fracture mate, you can't sue me, I haven't missed anything.' And that's all you think about, getting them out.

(d) Patients should co-operate with the competent agencies in trying to get well.

The major non-co-operative patients were the drunks and the overdoses. Drunks fail to co-operate by refusing to stay still while being sutured or examined, and overdoses fight back when a rubber tube is being forced down their throats so that their stomachs can be washed out. These are both cases where patients *refuse* to co-operate, rather than being unable to co-operate, as would be the case for patients in epileptic or diabetic fits. Similarly, they refuse to co-operate in getting 'well' because they cannot be trusted to live their lives in future in such a way that they would avoid the same injuries. The normal overdose, after all, is one who has been in time and time again, as is the normal drunk. Other patients may also offend against this rule, like skinheads who were hurt in a fight and said they were going to get their own back on their enemies:

We're wasting everybody's time by X-raying that bloke because he's only going to do it again.

However, it was noticeable that if recurrent injuries were a result of what the staff regarded as reasonable activities (such as playing rugby) similar hostility was not provoked. In general, then, patients had a duty to live their lives in order to avoid injury, to remain well, and pa-

---

[19] Similar uncertainty has been reported from America amongst a general population and amongst social workers. See H. A. Mulford and D. E. Miller, 'Measuring Community Acceptance of the Alcoholic as a Sick Person', *Quarterly Journal of Studies in Alcoholism*, Vol. 25, June 1964; and H. P. Chalfont and R. A. Kurtz, 'Alcoholics and the Sick Role: Assessments by Social Workers', *Journal of Health and Social Behaviour*, Vol. 12, March 1971.

tients who did not do this were not worth helping.

These four rules, then, seemed to cover the criteria by which normal rubbish was faulted. It can be seen that each of them required quite fine judgement about, for example, whether a patient was unco-operative by choice or because of some underlying illness. Discussions of dirty patients included an attempt to find out if they were ill and could not clean themselves, and an abusive tramp had his behaviour reinterpreted when he later had a fit—his abuse was put down to the effects of the tension preceding the fit. In other cases there was evidence of negotiation between patients and staff over how the patient was to be classified. Patients would provide evidence which did not match the normal pattern for rubbish. Certainly the staff treated differently patients who demonstrated they were abnormal overdoses or tramps. For example, respect was shown to the man who took an overdose, then slashed his wrists when he came into Casualty and finally drowned himself in the bathroom of the Casualty ward. Lesser respect was accorded to others who also made serious attempts to kill themselves. Overdoses who demonstrated that they were unlikely to repeat the behaviour were also treated better, like a thirty-year-old social worker who brought himself in and then actively assisted with the washout proceedings. Again, the clean, well-spoken tramp who had diabetes which he kept under control was helped to get somewhere other than the Salvation Army hostel to sleep for the night. Though I did not interview patients about this, there is impressionistic evidence that patients were aware of the rules which staff tried to impose, and attempted to organise their interactions with staff in order to put up a good front in terms of those rules. This was certainly the case with patients who negotiated for abnormal status, and was perhaps true for other patients. Patients with relatively minor ailments would frequently stress the accidental nature of the injury, their reasons for assessing it as serious, the reasonableness of their activities at the time of the accident, and their desire to get back to work.

Punishment

Rubbish could be punished by the staff in various ways, the most important being to increase the amount of time that rubbish had to spend in Casualty before completing treatment. In each hospital there were ways of advancing and retarding patients so that they were not seen strictly in the order in which they arrived. Good patients, in general being the more serious, could be seen immediately by being taken directly to the treatment area, either by the receptionist or by the ambulanceman. Less serious cases, including the trivia, would go first to a general waiting area. Patients there were normally left until all serious cases had been dealt with. However, during relatively busy periods these arrangements only permitted rather gross division of cases, so that the general area would also include many patients who were not regarded as trivia, and would usually contain some 'good' patients as well. In slack periods this technique was more finely used, so that if the nurse or receptionist was sure that the patient was rubbish she could delay calling the doctor.

However, the staff could also delay treatment for overdoses, tramps and drunks in a more selective fashion. Patients in these categories could be taken to relative backwaters and shut into rooms so that they could be ignored until the staff were prepared to deal with them. Sometimes staff employed a deliberate policy of leaving drunks and tramps in the hope that they would get annoyed at the delay and take their own discharge.

The other forms of punishment used were verbal hostility or the vigorous restraint of unco-operative patients. Verbal hostility was in general fairly restrained, at least in my presence, and was usually less forthright than the written comments made in the 'medical' notes, or the comments made in discussions with other staff. Vigorous treatment of patients was most noticeable in the case of overdoses, who would be held down or sat upon while the patient was forced to swallow the rubber tube used. Staff recognised that this procedure had an element of punishment in it, but defended themselves by saying that it was necessary. However, they showed no sympathy for the victim, unlike cases of accidental self-poisoning by children. Drunks and tramps who were unco-operative could be threatened with the police, who were called on a couple of occasions to undress a drunk or to stand around while a tramp was treated.

Punishment was rarely extended to a refusal to see or to treat patients, except for a few tramps who came to the department but never got themselves registered, merely sitting in the warm for a while, and for some patients who arrived in the middle of the night and were persuaded by the staff nurse on duty to come back later. The staff were very conscious of the adverse publicity raised whenever patients were refused treatment in Casualty departments, and they were also worried by the medico-legal complications to which Casualty departments are prone, and this restrained their hostility and the extent of the delay they were prepared to put patients to. A cautionary tale was told to emphasise the dangers of not treating rubbish properly, concerning a tramp who was seen in a Casualty department and discharged. A little later the porter came in and told the CO that the tramp had collapsed and died outside on the pavement. The porter then calmed the worries of the CO by saying 'It's all right, sir, I've turned him round so that it looks as though he was on his way *to* Casualty.'

Deviance and Illness

What I have argued so far is that Casualty staff classify patients broadly into good and rub-

bish patients. The features of good patients which are attended to are medical in character, whereas rubbish is described in predominantly social terms. In addition, there are typical sorts of rubbish which are picked out for particular comment, the normal trivia, normal overdoses, normal tramps and normal drunks. Staff justify their hostile typifications of those patients by arguing that they have broken most of the rules which should govern who is a legitimate aspirant for entry into patienthood. Other patients who break one or more of these rules also evoke hostile responses in staff, but are not typified in the same way. Patients who break these rules are likely to be penalised, if possible by being kept waiting longer than necessary, but the threat of legal problems ensures that they will get some diagnosis and treatment. On these grounds it seems clear to me that these patients are seen as deviant, in that they are given an unflattering label, are seen to break rules, and are liable to punishment. . . .

[I]llness is not deviant, only those who make illegitimate claims to be allowed entry to the sick role or to patienthood are deviant. . . .

The Making of Blind Men   ROBERT A. SCOTT

When a blind person first comes to an organization for the blind, he usually has some specific ideas about what his primary problems are and how they can be solved. Most new clients request services that they feel will solve or ameliorate the specific problems they experience because of their visual impairment. Many want only to be able to read better, and therefore request optical aids. Others desire help with mobility problems, or with special problems of dressing, eating, or housekeeping. Some need money or medical care. A few contact agencies for the blind in search of scientific discoveries that will restore their vision. Although the exact type of help sought varies considerably, many clients feel that the substance of their problems is contained in their specific requests. . . .

The personal conceptions that blinded persons have about the nature of their problems are in sharp contrast with beliefs that workers for the blind share about the problems of blindness. The latter regard blindness as one of the most severe of all handicaps, the effects of which are long-lasting, pervasive, and extremely difficult to ameliorate. They believe that if these problems are to be solved, blind persons must understand them and all their manifestations and willingly submit themselves to a prolonged, intensive, and comprehensive program of psychological and restorative services. *Effective socialization of the client largely depends upon changing his views about his problem.* In order to do this, the client's views about the problems of blindness must be discredited. Workers must convince him that simplistic ideas about solving the problems of blindness by means of one or a few services are unrealistic. Workers regard the client's initial definition of his problems as akin to the visible portion of an iceberg. Beneath the surface of awareness lies a tremendously complicated mass of problems that must be dealt with before the surface problems can ever be successfully solved.

Discrediting the client's personal ideas about his problems is achieved in several ways. His initial statements about why he has come to the organization and what he hopes to receive from it are euphemistically termed "the presenting problem," a phrase that implies superficiality in the client's views. During the intake interview and then later with the caseworker or psychologist, the client is encouraged to discuss his feelings and aspirations. . . . However, when concrete plans are formulated, the client learns that his personal views about his problems are largely ignored. A client's request for help with a reading problem produces a recommendation by the worker for a comprehensive psychological work-up. A client's inquiries regarding the availability of financial or medical aid may elicit the suggestion that he enroll in a complicated long-term program of testing, evaluation, and training. In short, blind persons who are acceptable to the agency for the blind will often find that intake workers listen attentively to their views but then dismiss them as superficial or inaccurate. . . . For most persons who have come this far in the process, however, dropping out is not a particularly realistic alternative, since it implies that the blind person has other resources open to him. For the most part, such resources are not available.

. . . [The] experiences a blind person has before being inducted into an agency make him vulnerable to the wishes and intentions of the workers who deal with them. The ability to withstand the pressure to act, think, and feel in conformity with the workers' concept of a model blind person is further reduced by the fact that the workers have a virtual monopoly on the rewards and punishments in the system. By manipulating these rewards and punishments, workers are able to pressure the client into rejecting personal conceptions of problems in favor of the worker's own definition of them. Much evaluative work, in fact, involves attempts to get the client to understand and accept the agency's conception of the problems of blindness. . . . In face-to-face situations, the blind person is rewarded for showing insight and subtly reprimanded for continuing to adhere to earlier notions about his problems. He is led to think that he "really" understands past and present experiences when he couches them in terms acceptable to his therapist. . . .

Psychological rewards are not the only rewards at stake in this process. A fundamental tenet of work for the blind is that a client must accept the fact of his blindness and everything implied by it before he can be effectively rehabilitated. As a result, a client must show signs of understanding his problem in the therapist's terms before he will be permitted to progress any further in the program. Since most blind persons are anxious to move along in the program as rapidly as possible, the implications of being labeled "uncooperative" are serious. Such a label prevents him from receiving basic restorative services. The uncooperative client is assigned low priority for entering preferred job programs. Workers for the blind are less willing to extend themselves on his behalf. As a result, the alert client quickly learns to become "insightful," to behave as workers expect him to.

Under these circumstances, the assumptions and theories of workers for the blind concerning blindness and rehabilitation take on new significance, for what they do is to create, shape, and mold the attitudes and behavior of the client in his role as a blind person. . . . [It] is in organizations for the blind that theories and explicit and implicit assumptions about blindness and rehabilitation become actualized in the clients' attitudes and behavior. We can therefore gain an understanding about the behavior of clients as blind people by examining the theories and assumptions about blindness and rehabilitation held by workers for the blind.

The Practice Theories of Blindness Workers

The beliefs, ideologies, and assumptions about blindness and rehabilitation that make up practice theories of work for the blind are legion. They include global and limited theories about blindness, ethical principles, commonsense ideas, and an array of specific beliefs that are unrelated, and often contradictory, to one another. Contained in this total array of ideas are two basically different approaches to the problems of blindness. The first I will call the "restorative approach"; the most complete and explicit version of this approach is contained in the writings of Father Thomas Carroll.[1] The second I will call the "accommodative approach." This approach has never been formulated into a codified practice theory; rather, it is only apparent in the programs and policies of more orthodox agencies for the blind.

The Restorative Approach

The basic premise of the restorative approach to blindness is that most blind people can be restored to a high level of independence enabling them to lead a reasonably normal life. However, these goals are attainable only if the person accepts completely the fact that he is blind, and only after he has received competent professional counseling and training. . . .

Seven basic kinds of losses resulting from blindness are identified: (1) the losses to psychological security—the losses of physical integrity, confidence in the remaining senses, reality contact with the environment, visual background, and light security; (2) the losses of the skills of mobility and techniques of daily living; (3) the communication losses, such as the loss of ease of written and spoken communication, and of information about daily events in the world; (4) the losses of appreciation, which include the loss of the visual perception of the pleasurable and of the beautiful; (5) the losses of occupational and financial status, which consist of financial security, career, vocational goals, job opportunities, and ordinary recreational activities; (6) the resulting losses to the whole personality, including the loss of personal independence, social adequacy, self-esteem, and total personality organization; and (7) the concomitant losses of sleep, of physical tone of the body, and of decision, and the sense of control over one's life.[2]

Rehabilitation, in this scheme, is the process "whereby adults in varying stages of helplessness, emotional disturbance, and dependence come to gain new understanding of themselves and their handicap, the new skills necessary for their state, and a new control of their emotions and their environment."[3] This process is not a simple one; it involves the pain and recurrent crises that accompany the acceptance of the many "deaths" to sighted life. It consists of "restorations" for each of the losses involved in

---

[1] Thomas J. Carroll, *Blindness: What It Is, What It Does, and How to Live with It,* Little, Brown & Company, Boston, 1961.

[2] *Ibid.,* pp. 14–79.

[3] *Ibid.,* pp. 96.

blindness. The final objective of total rehabilitation involves returning and integrating the blinded person in his society.

. . . The various restorations in each of these phases correspond to the losses the person has encountered. The loss of confidence in the remaining senses is restored through deliberate training of these senses; the loss of mobility is restored through training in the use of a long cane or a guide dog; the loss of ease of written communication is restored through learning braille; and so on. The goal of this process is to reintegrate the components of the restored personality into an effectively functioning whole. . . .

[In] several rehabilitation centers and general agencies . . . the ideas contained in . . . [Father Carroll's] book are used as the basis for a formal course taught to blind people while they are obtaining services. The purpose of this course is to clarify for them what they have lost because they are blind, how they must change through the course of rehabilitation, and what their lives will be like when rehabilitation has been completed. These ideas are given added weight by the fact that they are shared by all staff members who deal directly with the client and, in some agencies at least, by other nonservice personnel who have occasional contacts with clients. . . .

We cannot assume that there is a necessary correspondence between these beliefs regarding the limits and potentialities imposed by blindness and the blind client's self-image. The question of the full impact of the former on the latter is an empirical one on which there are no hard data. Our analysis of the client's "set" when he enters an agency for the blind does suggest, however, that such beliefs probably have a profound impact on his self-image. . . . [When] the client comes to an agency, he is often seeking direction and guidance and, more often than not, he is in a state of crisis. Consequently, the authority of the system makes the client highly suggestible to the attitudes of those whose help he seeks.

There is evidence that some blind people resist the pressures of the environment of agencies and centers that adopt this philosophy by feigning belief in the workers' ideas for the sake of

"making out" in the system.[4] In such cases, the impact of workers on the client's self-image will be attenuated. Despite this, he will learn only those skills made available to him by the agency or center. These skills, which the workers regard as opportunities for individual fulfillment, act also as limits. The choice of compensatory skills around which the theory revolves means the exclusion of a spectrum of other possibilities.

The Accommodative Approach

A basic premise of the restorative approach is that most blind people possess the capacity to function independently enough to lead normal lives. Rehabilitation centers and general service agencies that have embraced this approach therefore gear their entire service programs toward achieving this goal. In other agencies for the blind, no disagreement is voiced about the desirability of blind people's attaining independence, but there is considerable skepticism as to whether this is a feasible goal for more than a small fraction of the client population.[5] According to this view, blindness poses enormous obstacles to independence—obstacles seen as insurmountable by a majority of people. . . . Settings and programs are designed to accommodate the helpless, dependent blind person.

The physical environment in such agencies is often contrived specifically to suit certain limitations inherent in blindness. In some agencies, for example, the elevators have tape recorders that report the floor at which the elevator is stopping and the direction in which it is going, and panels of braille numbers for each floor as well. Other agencies have mounted over their front doors special bells that ring at regular intervals to indicate to blind people that they are approaching the building. Many agencies maintain fleets of cars to pick up clients at their homes and bring them to the agency for services. In the cafeterias of many agencies, special precautions are taken to serve only food that blind people can eat without awkwardness. In one agency cafeteria, for example, the food is cut before it is served, and only spoons are provided.

Recreation programs in agencies that have adopted the accommodative approach consist of

[4] *Information Bulletin No. 59,* University of Utah, Regional Rehabilitation Research Institute, Salt Lake City, 1968.

[5] Roger G. Barker et al., *Adjustment to Physical Handicap and Illness: A Survey of the Social Psychology of Physique and Disability,* Social Science Research Council, New York, 1953.

games and activities tailored to the disability. For example, bingo, a common activity in many programs, is played with the aid of a corps of volunteers who oversee the game, attending to anything the blind person is unable to do himself.

Employment training for clients in accommodative agencies involves instruction in the use of equipment specifically adapted to the disability. Work tasks, and even the entire method of production, are engineered with this disability in mind, so that there is little resemblance between an average commercial industrial setting and a sheltered workshop. Indeed, the blind person who has been taught to do industrial work in a training facility of an agency for the blind will acquire skills and methods of production that may be unknown in most commercial industries.

The general environment of such agencies is also accommodative in character. Clients are rewarded for trivial things and praised for performing tasks in a mediocre fashion. This superficial and overgenerous reward system makes it impossible for most clients to assess their accomplishments accurately. Eventually, since anything they do is praised as outstanding, many of them come to believe that the underlying assumption must be that blindness makes them incompetent.

The unstated assumption of accommodative agencies is that most of their clients will end up organizing their lives around the agency. Most will become regular participants in the agency's recreation programs, and those who can work will obtain employment in a sheltered workshop or other agency-sponsored employment program. The accommodative approach therefore produces a blind person who can function effectively only within the confines of the agency's contrived environment. He learns skills and behavior that are necessary for participating in activities and programs of the agency, but which make it more difficult to cope with the environment of the larger community. A blind person who has been fully socialized in an accommodative agency will be maladjusted to the larger community. In most cases, he does not have the resources, the skills, the means, or the opportunity to overcome the maladaptive patterns of behavior he has learned. He has little choice but to remain a part of the environment that has been designed and engineered to accommodate him.

This portrayal of accommodative agencies suggests that the workers in them, like those in restorative agencies, make certain assumptions about the limitations that blindness imposes, and that these assumptions are manifested in expectations about attitudes and behavior that people ought to have because they are blind. . . .

Unfortunately, no hard data are available on socialization outcomes in agencies that adopt either of the two approaches I have described. However, the materials I collected from interviews with blind people suggest that a number of discernably patterned reactions occur.[6] Some clients and trainees behave according to workers' expectations of them deliberately and consciously in order to extract from the system whatever rewards it may have. Others behave according to expectations because they have accepted and internalized them as genuine qualities of character. The former are the "expedient" blind people, and the latter are the "true believers."

Expedient blind people consciously play a part, acting convincingly the way they sense their counselors and instructors want them to act. They develop a keen sense of timing that enables them to be at their best when circumstances call for it. When the circumstances change, the façade is discarded, much as the Negro discards his "Uncle Tomisms" in the absence of whites. As a rule, the expedient blind person is one who recognizes that few alternatives are open to him in the community; his response is an understandable effort to maximize his gains in a bad situation.

True believers are blind people for whom workers' beliefs and assumptions about blindness are unquestioned ideals toward which they feel impelled earnestly to strive. While this pattern is probably found in all agencies for the blind, it is most obvious in those which embrace the accommodative approach to blindness. Clients who become true believers in such agencies actually experience the emotions that workers believe they must feel. They experience and spontaneously verbalize the proper degree of gratitude, they genuinely believe themselves to be helpless, and they feel that their world must be one of darkness and dependency.

---

[6] Most of this discussion applies to blind people who have been exposed to agencies that adopt an accommodative approach to rehabilitation. Little information could be gathered on those who have been trainees in restorative agencies, primarily because such agencies are comparatively few in number and recent in origin.

6 POLICE WORK

In occupations that routinely deal with deviants, there are often guidelines for dealing with the deviants and for compiling and using official records about them. In some occupations, such as police work, these norms are so central that they often become second nature, followed almost by rote. They prescribe how police officers should relate to deviants, as well as the form their records should take.

In the first reading Carl Werthman and Irving Piliavin describe the police perspective on juvenile delinquency. In the next reading Jennifer Hunt shows how street cops arrive at a set of shared understandings about the use of legal, normal, and brutal force. Finally, Kenneth Stoddart shows how police underpursue women heroin users while they overpursue heroin users who violate the norms of police–heroin-user interaction.

The Police Perspective on Delinquency

CARL WERTHMAN and IRVING PILIAVIN

The juvenile officer exercises a good deal of discretion in deciding how to process offenders, a discretion that far transcends the measure of ambiguity ordinarily involved in legal assessments of motivation and intent. Although a truant may not be responsible for his behavior, may be a touch rebellious, or may be acting in complete and willful disregard for law, the nature and intent of this crime are not as important to a juvenile officer as what he learns about the attitude of the offender towards the idea of the law itself. For example, if an officer decides he is dealing with a boy who is "guilty but essentially good" or "guilty but sometimes weak," the probability is high that he will decide to let the boy go with a warning about the consequences of committing this crime again. He might feel that contact with the unsavory clientele of a juvenile hall would damage an otherwise positive attitude towards the law or that moral contamination in the eyes of parents and teachers as a result of being sent to jail might weaken an otherwise firm commitment to conventional behavior. On the other hand, if the officer decides that the offender is a "punk," a "persistent troublemaker," or some other version of a thoroughly bad boy, he may well decide to make an arrest.[1]

A "delinquent" is therefore not a juvenile who happens to have committed an illegal act. He is a young person whose moral character has been negatively assessed. And this fact has led some observers to conclude that the transformation of young people into official "delinquents" is best looked at as an organizational rather than a legal process since policemen, probation officers, and juvenile court judges often base their dispositions on a host of criteria that are virtually unrelated to the nature of the specific offense.[2]

The *magnitude of an offense,* of course, can become a factor in dispositions. One responsibly planned and willfully executed robbery, rape, or assault can ruin the moral status of a juvenile indefinitely. Since 90% of the crimes committed by juveniles are minor offenses, however, this criterion is only rarely used.

The number of *previous contacts with police* has a more important effect on dispositions. These contacts are typically recorded on easily accessible files, and these files contain everything from arrests and convictions to contacts made on the flimsiest of contingent grounds. If a boy confesses to a crime and is not known to the police, he is often released. If he is caught for a third or fourth time, however, the sum total of previous contacts may be enough to affect a judgment about his moral character adversely, regardless of the nature or magnitude of the present offense and regardless of the reasons he was previously contacted. For example:

Like last night, man, me and Willy got busted for curfew. I mean I got busted for curfew. We was walkin' up the hill towards home, and these cops pull up. It was a Friday night, man, so we didn't want no trouble. When the cops ask us what we was doing and what about our names we was all nice. So then the cop gets on that radio and checks us out. There was a whole bunch of noise comin' over that box. I couldn't hear what they was sayin'. But then the cop comes out and says to Willy, "O.K., you can go." And I say, "What about me?" And the cop says, "You been in trouble before. We don't want you walkin' the streets at night. We going to take you down to the station for curfew." Then I got real mad. I almost ran. Lucky thing I didn't though. I woulda been in real trouble then.

There is even some evidence to suggest that assessments about the type and quality of *parental control* are even more important factors in dispositions than *any* of the offense-related criteria. One of the main concerns of a juvenile officer is the likelihood of future offense, and this determination is often made largely on the basis of "the kinds of parents" a boy happens to possess. Thus, the moral character of parents

[1] For a more complete discussion of police discretion in dealing with juveniles, see Irving Piliavin and Scott Briar, "Police Encounters with Juveniles," *The American Journal of Sociology,* Vol. LXX, No. 2 (Sept. 1964), pp. 209–211.

[2] The problem of discretion has been formulated and studied by Aaron Cicourel in these terms. See Aaron V. Circourel, *The Social Organization of Juvenile Justice,* New York: John Wiley & Sons, 1968.

also passes under review; and if a house appears messy, a parent is missing, or a mother is on welfare, the probability of arrest increases. Similarly, a boy with a father and two older brothers in jail is considered a different sort of person from a boy whose immediate family is not known to the police. As Cicourel points out, these judgments about family life are particularly subject to bias by attitudes related to class.[3]

See, like if you or maybe one of your brothers, say both of you been to Y.A.,[4] or your sister, every time they see you they get on your back. They know all your family. If they ever pick you up and look at your records, they automatically take you in. They see where your sister been to jail, your brother, or if you ever went to jail. And they start saying, "Your whole family is rotten. Your whole family is jailbirds." Shit like that. And this is what really make you mad, when they tell you your mother don't know how to read!

Although the family situation of a boy and his record of prior police contacts both enter into dispositions, the most important factor affecting the decision of juvenile officers is the *attitude* displayed by the offender, both during and after the confession itself. Cicourel, for example, found that juvenile officers were strongly influenced by the style and speed with which the offender confessed.[5] If a boy blurts out his misdeeds immediately, this behavior is taken as a sign that the boy "trusts" authority and is therefore "under control." If the boy proves to be a "tough nut to crack," however, he is viewed with suspicion. As soon as a juvenile is defined as "hardened," he is considered no less dangerous to society than the adult criminal.

Similarly, the boys who appear frightened, humble, penitent, and ashamed are also more likely to go free. They are often defined as "weak, troubled, and the victim of circumstances" but basically "good boys," an assessment of moral character that may win them a release.

On the other hand, if a boy shows no signs of being spiritually moved by his offense, the police deal harshly with him. Not only has he sinned against a legal rule, but he has also symbolically rejected the normative basis for conforming to it in the first place; and it is this double deviation that has fateful consequences for the way he is treated by the police. Once he gets himself defined as "the kind of person who doesn't respect the law," he becomes a perfect candidate for arrest, detention, and eventual incarceration. Most of the juvenile officers we interviewed felt that the attitude of the offender was the major determinant of dispositions in 50% of their cases, and Nathan Goldman reports that "defiance on the part of a boy will lead to juvenile court quicker than anything else."[6]

It is hardly necessary to describe the way most gang boys feel about the equity of these dispositions. One only needs to imagine the look on a boy's face when he is told that he is about to spend a year in jail for an offense committed with a friend who was sent home when he promptly confessed. . . .

In addition . . . [to type a boy] . . . the police also seem to rely on a number of physical or material *individual attributes*. Certain kinds of clothing, hair, and walking styles seem intrinsically to trigger suspicion. The general description of these styles had best be left to the boys themselves.

(Why do you think the cops pick you up all the time?) Why do they pick us up? They don't pick everybody up. They just pick up on the ones with the hats on and trench coats and conks.[7] If you got long hair and hats on, something like this one, you gonna get picked up. Especially a conk. And the way you dress. Sometimes, like if you've got on black pants, better not have on no black pants or bends[8] or Levi's.

They think you going to rob somebody. And don't have a head scarf on your head. They'll bust you for having a head scarf.[9]

(All right, so they bust you for clothes. That's one

[3] Aaron Cicourel, "Social Class, Family Structure and the Administration of Juvenile Justice," Center for the Study of Law and Society, University of California at Berkeley, Working Paper, MS.

[4] The detention facilities administered by the California Youth Authority.

[5] Cicourel, *The Social Organization of Juvenile Justice, loc. cit.*

[6] Nathan Goldman, *The Differential Selection of Juvenile Offenders for Court Appearances,* National Council on Crime and Delinquency (1963), p. 106.

[7] A "conk" is a hair straightening process used by Negroes that is similar in concept to the permanent wave.

[8] "Bends" are a form of the bell-bottom trouser which, when worn effectively, all but obscure the shoe from vision, thus creating the impression that the wearer is moving down the street with an alarmingly irresponsible shuffle.

[9] Head scarves (sometimes called "mammy rags") are worn by Negroes around the forehead to keep "conk jobs" in place.

thing. Is there anything else?) The way you walk sometimes. If you walk pimp. Don't try to walk pimp. Don't try to be cool. You know. They'll bust you for that. (Could you tell me how you walk pimp?) You know. You just walk cool like. Like you got a boss high.[10] Like you got a fix or something. Last night a cop picked me up for that. He told me I had a bad walk. He say, "You think you're bad." You know.

Finally, the police also use *themselves* as an instrument for locating suspicious people. Every time an officer makes visible contact with a citizen, the citizen is forced to confront his status in the eyes of the law, and the police soon learn to rely on hostile *looks* and furtive *glances* as signs of possible guilt. A policeman's uniform is a potent symbolic device. It sometimes has the power to turn a patrolman into a walking test of moral identity.

It should not be construed from the above discussion that the process of locating a population of potential offenders always proceeds on such slim grounds. There are a variety of "scenes" that constitute much more obvious bases for investigation. However, since policemen rarely stumble on armed men standing over dead bodies, much of their activity involves a subtle and exceedingly tenuous reading of both appearances and events. For example, when dealing with people who possess . . . indicators of suspiciousness outlined above, patrolmen may turn a screwdriver into a "deadly weapon" and a scratch on the neck into evidence of rape.

Like you be walking. Just come from working on the car or something. And if you've got a screwdriver or something in your back pocket, hell, they may beat the shit outa you. They talk about you got a burglary tool or you got a deadly weapon on you.

Remember the time when we was getting ready to go up to the gym? We came home from school one day. He had some scratches on his neck, and the cop pull over and say, "Turn around!" The cop grabbed him. I didn't say nothing. I was walking. I got to the top of the stairs and the cop holler "Turn around" at me too. So I turn around. And the cop look at my neck and he say, "Yeah. You too. You got scratches on your neck too." So he took us down to the police station. It seem like some girl way over in another district got raped. And the girl say, "I think they live over at Hunters Point and I scratched one of them on the neck." Some stuff like that.

Gang members are very much aware of their moral status in the eyes of the police. On most occasions, they are likely to know that the police

have singled them out for interrogation because of the neighborhood they live in, because of their hair styles, or perhaps because they are temporarily "out of place." They know how the police operate, and they are particularly aware of the role played by judgments about moral character in this methodology. . . .

Outcomes

If a juvenile being interrogated in the situation of suspicion refuses to proffer the expected politeness or to use the words that typically denote respect and if no offense has been discovered, a patrolman finds himself in a very awkward position. He cannot arrest the boy for insolence or defiance, since for obvious reasons no charges of this nature exist. The patrolman is thus faced with the choice of three rather unpleasant alternatives.

First, he can back down, thereby allowing his authority to evaporate. If a patrolman allows his authority to escape, however, there is no guarantee that it can be recaptured the next day or any day thereafter. Since patrolmen are structurally locked into the authority role over long periods of uninterrupted time, any fleeting defeat at the hands of a gang member has the prospect of becoming permanent. In a certain sense, then, gang members have a great deal of power. With the mere hint of impiety they can sometimes manage to strip a patrolman symbolically of his authority.

For these reasons, if a patrolman does decide to back down, he must be careful to retreat strategically by withdrawing from the encounter without a public loss of face. This is usually done by communicating to the juvenile that his innocence is fortuitous, that he is the kind of person who *could* have committed an offense, and that he owes his release to the grouchy good graces of the interrogating officer. If executed artfully, comments such as "keep your nose clean or we'll run you in next time" can pave the way out of a potentially damaging encounter. From the point of view of the boys, of course, this technique simply constitutes an additional insult to moral character.

If a patrolman chooses to press his claims to authority, however, he has only two sanctions available with which to make these claims good. On the one hand, he can attempt an arrest.

[10] "Boss" is a synonym for "good."

One day we were standing on the corner about three blocks from school and this juvenile officer comes up. He say, "Hey, you boys! Come here!" So everybody else walked over there. But this one stud made like he didn't hear him. So the cop say, "Hey punk! Come here!" So the stud sorta look up like he hear him and start walking over. But he walking over real slow. So the cop walk over there and grab him by the collar and throw him down and put the handcuffs on him, saying, "When I call you next time come see what I want!" So everybody was standing by the car, and he say, "All right you black mother fuckers! Get your ass home!" Just like that. And he handcuffed the stud and took him to juvenile hall for nothing. Just for standing there looking at him.

On the other hand, there are a variety of curfew, vagrancy, and loitering laws that can also be used to formally or officially prosecute the informal violation of norms governing deportment in the situation of suspicion.

I got arrested once when we were just riding around in a car. There was a bunch of us in the car. A police car stopped us, and it was about ten after ten when they stopped us. They started asking us our names and wanted to see our identification. Then they called in on us. So they got through calling in on us, and they just sit in the car and wait till the call came through. Then they'd bring back your I.D. and take another one. One at a time. They held me and another boy till last. And when they got to us it was five minutes to eleven. They told everybody they could go home, but they told us it didn't make no sense for us to go home because we was just riding around and we'd never make it home in five minutes. So they busted us both for curfew.

In addition to these laws, a boy can also be charged with "suspicion" of practically anything. When the police use suspicion as a charge, however, they usually try to make the specific offense as serious as possible. This is why the criminal records of many gang boys are often heavily laced with such charges as "suspicion of robbery" and "suspicion of rape."

(Could you tell me some of the things you have been busted for?) Man, I been charged with everything from suspicion of murder to having suspicious friends. I think they call it "associates!" (laughter) They got me on all kinda trash, man, and they only make but one thing stick. (What's that?) A couple of years ago they caught me stone cold sittin' behind the wheel of a '60 Pontiac. I said it belong to my uncle, but it turn out that the name of the registration was O'Shaunessee or O'Something, some old fat name like that. The cop knew there wasn't no bloods [Negroes] named things like that.

Gang boys are aware that the police have a very difficult time making these illusory charges stick. They can always succeed in sending a boy to jail for a few hours or a few days, but most of these charges are dismissed at a preliminary hearing on recommendations from probation officers. Moreover, gang members also understand the power of probation officers, and by behaving better in front of these officials they can often embarrass the local authority of patrolmen by having decisions to arrest reversed over their heads. As far as the patrolmen are concerned, then, the boys can make a mockery of false charges as a sanction against impertinence in the situation of suspicion.

Perhaps more important, however, a patrolman's sergeant also knows that most trivial or trumped-up charges are likely to be dropped, and thus the police department itself puts a premium on ability to command authority without invoking the sanction of arrest. Unlike the juvenile officer who is judged by his skills at interrogation, a patrolman's capacity to gain respect is his greatest source of pride as well as his area of greatest vulnerability. If he is forced to make too many "weak" arrests, he stands to lose prestige among his peers and superiors on the police force and to suffer humiliation at the hands of his permanent audience of tormentors on the beat.

It is largely for these reasons that many patrolmen prefer to settle a challenge to authority on the spot, an alternative that necessarily poses the prospect of violence. As William Westley has pointed out, in the last analysis the police can always try to "coerce respect."[11]

[11]The above analysis of why policemen retaliate when the legitimacy of their authority is challenged differs somewhat from Westley's analysis of why a large percentage of the policemen he studied "believed that it was legitimate to use violence to coerce respect." Westley argues that disrespectful behavior constitutes a threat to the already low "occupational status" of policemen and therefore comes as a blow to their self-esteem. Westley's hypothesis would suggest, however, that those policemen who *accepted* their low occupational status would therefore allow their authority to be challenged. Although Westley's variables no doubt affect the behavior of patrolmen, there also seems to be more at stake than status as a workman when claims to authority are ignored. In a sense the patrolman whose authority has been successfully called into question has already abdicated a sizable chunk of his honor as well as his job. See William A. Westley, "Violence and the Police," *American Journal of Sociology*, Vol. LIX (July 1953).

They don't never beat you in the car. They wait until they get you to the station. And then they beat you when the first shift comes on and they beat you when the second shift comes on. I've seen it happen. I was right there in the next cell. They had a boy. His name was Stan, and they had beat him already as soon as they brought him in. And then when they was changing shifts, you know, the detective came and looked on the paper that say what he was booked for, I think it was robbery or something like that, and they started beating on him again. See, the police are smart. They don't leave no bruises. They'll beat you somewhere where it don't show. That's the main places where they look to hit you at. And if it did show, your word wouldn't be as good as theirs. They can lie too, you know. All they have to say is that you was resisting and that's the only reason they need for doing what they do.

Resisting arrest is the one charge involving violence that seems uniquely designed to deal with improper deportment in the situation of suspicion. A policeman interviewed by Westley suggests that when the challenge to authority is not sufficiently serious to warrant this charge, the police may continue to provoke the suspect until the level of belligerence reaches proportions that legitimate invoking this category of offense.

For example, when you stop a fellow for a routine questioning, say a wise guy, and he starts talking back to you and telling you that you are no good and that sort of thing. You know you can take a man in on disorderly conduct charge, but you can practically never make it stick. So what you do in a case like this is to egg the guy on until he makes a remark where you can justifiably slap him, and then if he fights back, you can call it resisting arrest.[12]

And from a gang member's point of view:

Another reason why they beat up on you is because they always have the advantage over you. The cop might say "You done this." And you might say, "I didn't!" And he'll say, "Don't talk back to me or I'll go upside your head!" You know, and then they say they had a right to hit you or arrest you because you were talking back to an officer or resisting arrest, and you were merely trying to explain or tell him that you hadn't done what he said you'd done. One of those kinds of things. Well, that means you in the wrong when you get downtown anyway. You're always in the wrong.

Unlike encounters between gang members and patrolmen, the confrontations between gang members and juvenile officers rarely end in violence. This is because the ability to command respect is not as crucial to a juvenile officer as it is to a patrolman. A juvenile officer is not judged by his capacity to command authority on a beat, and he can therefore leave a situation in which his authority has been challenged without having to face the challenger again the next day. Since he is evaluated largely by his skill at interrogation, he rarely finds himself structurally predisposed to "coerce respect."

[12] *Ibid.*, p. 30.

Normal Force   JENNIFER HUNT

The police are required to handle a variety of peacekeeping and law enforcement tasks including settling disputes, removing drunks from the street, aiding the sick, controlling crowds, and pursuing criminals. What unifies these diverse activities is the possibility that their resolution might require the use of force. Indeed, the capacity to use force stands at the core of the police mandate (Bittner, 1980).

The bulk of the sociological literature on the use of force by police is concerned with analyzing the objective causes of "excessive" force. Some social scientists, for example, suggest that the incidence of extra-legal force correlates with characteristics of individual officers—in particular, their authoritarianism, age, or length of service (Niederhoffer, 1967; Blumberg, 1983). Others emphasize the relevance of the behavior and characteristics of the target population, including demeanor, sex, race, and class (Reiss, 1970; Friedrich, 1980; Lee, 1981). Still others investigate the legal and organizational roots of force. They are concerned with how formal rules and/or subcultural norms may influence the police officer's decision to employ force (Fyfe, 1983; Waegel, 1984).

Although representing diverse perspectives, these approaches share a similar underlying orientation to use of force by police. First, they all specify, in advance of study, formal or legal definitions of permissible force, definitions that are then used to identify deviations legally classifiable as brutal or "excessive." This procedure disregards the understandings and standards police officers actively employ in using and evaluating force in the course of their work. Second, these studies are primarily concerned with identifying the objective conditions held to determine "excessive" force defined in this way. As a result, they minimize the active role of consciousness in police decisions to use force, tending to depict such decisions as mere passive responses to external determinants.

In contrast, sociologists working within the symbolic interactionist tradition have displayed particular interest in the police officer's own assessment of what constitutes necessary force. This research has varied in how such assessments are conceptualized. Rubinstein (1973: 302), for example, suggests that police use force instrumentally to control persons whom they perceive as presenting a physical threat. In contrast, Van Maanen (1978) explores how police, in reacting to others, are highly attentive to symbolic violation of their authority, dispensing harsh treatment to categories of persons who commit such violations.

The following research departs from and seeks to extend the symbolic interactionist concern with police officers' own assessments of the use of force. It explores how police themselves classify and evaluate acts of force as either legal, normal, or excessive. Legal force is that coercion necessary to subdue, control, and restrain a suspect in order to take him into custody. Although force not accountable in legal terms is technically labelled excessive by the courts and the public, the police perceive many forms of illegal force as normal. Normal force involves coercive acts that specific "cops" on specific occasions formulate as necessary, appropriate, reasonable, or understandable. Although not always legitimated or admired, normal force is depicted as a necessary or natural response of normal police to particular situational exigencies.

Most officers are expected to use both legal and normal force as a matter of course in policing the streets. In contrast, excessive force or brutality exceeds even working police notions of normal force. . . . Brutality is viewed as illegal, illegitimate, and often immoral violence, but the police draw the lines in extremely different ways and at different points than do either the court system or the public.

These processes of assessing . . . the use of force, with special reference to the critical distinction between normal and excessive force as drawn by the police, will be explored in what follows.

The article is based on approximately eighteen

Excerpt from Jennifer Hunt, "Police Accounts of Normal Force," *Urban Life,* Vol. 13, No. 4 (January 1985), pp. 315–341. Copyright © 1985 Sage Publications. Inc. Reprinted by permission of Sage Publications, Inc.
AUTHOR'S NOTE: I am deeply indebted for both substantive and editorial assistance to Michael Brown and Robert M. Emerson. I would also like to thank Peter Manning, Bill DiFazio, Jim Birch, and Marie DeMay Della Guardia for their comments on an earlier draft of this article.

months of participant observation in a major urban police department referred to as the Metro City P.D. I attended the police academy with male and female recruits and later rode with individual officers in one-person cars on evening and night shifts in high crime districts.[1] The female officers described in this research were among the first 100 women assigned to the ranks of uniformed patrol as a result of a discrimination suit filed by the Justice Department and a policewoman plaintiff.

Normal Force

The police phrase "it's not done on the street the way that it's taught at the academy" underscores the perceived contradiction between the formal world of the police academy and the informal world of the street. This contradiction permeates the police officer's construction of his world, particularly his view of the rational and moral use of force.

In the formal world of the police academy, the recruit learns to account for force by reference to legality. He or she is issued the regulation instruments and trained to use them to subdue, control, and restrain a suspect. If threatened with great bodily harm, the officer learns that he can justifiably use deadly force and fire his revolver. Yet the recruit is taught that he cannot use his baton, jack, or gun, unnecessarily to torture, maim, or kill a suspect.

When recruits leave the formal world of the academy and are assigned to patrol a district, they are introduced to an informal world in which police recognize normal as well as legal and brutal force. Through observation and instruction, rookies gradually learn to apply force and account for its use in terms familiar to the street cop. First, rookies learn to adjust their arsenals to conform to street standards. They are encouraged to buy the more powerful weapons worn by veteran colleagues as these colleagues point out the inadequacy of a wooden baton or compare their convoy jacks to vibrators. They quickly discover that their department-issued equipment marks them as new recruits. At any rate, within a few weeks, most rookies have dispensed with the wooden baton and convoy jack and substituted them with the more powerful plastic nightstick and flat headed slapjack.[2]

Through experience and informal instruction, the rookie also learns the street use of these weapons. In school, for example, recruits are taught to avoid hitting a person on the head or neck because it could cause lethal damage. On the street, in contrast, police conclude that they must hit wherever it causes the most damage in order to incapacitate the suspect before they themselves are harmed. New officers also learn that they will earn the respect of their veteran coworkers not by observing legal niceties in using force, but by being "aggressive" and using whatever force is necessary in a given situation.

Peer approval helps neutralize the guilt and confusion that rookies often experience when they begin to use force to assert their authority. One female officer, for example, learned she was the object of a brutality suit while listening to the news on television. At first, she felt so mortified that she hesitated to go to work and face her peers. In fact, male colleagues greeted her with a standing ovation and commented, "You can use our urinal now." In their view, any aggressive police officer regularly using normal force might eventually face a brutality suit or civilian complaint. Such accusations confirm the officer's status as a "street cop" rather than an "inside man" who doesn't engage in "real police work."[3]

Whereas male rookies are assumed to be competent dispensers of force unless proven otherwise, women are believed to be physically weak, naturally passive, and emotionally vulnerable.[4]

[1] Nonetheless masculine pronouns are generally used to refer to the police in this article, because the Metro P.D. remained dominated by men numerically, in style and in tone. My fieldwork experience is discussed in detail in a forthcoming paper (Hunt, 1984).

[2] Some officers also substitute a large heavy duty flashlight for the nightstick. If used correctly, the flashlight can inflict more damage than the baton and is less likely to break when applied to the head or other parts of the body.

[3] For a discussion of the cultural distinction between "inside men" who handle desk and administrative tasks and "real cops" who work outside on the street, see Hunt (1984).

[4] As the Metro City Police Commissioner commented in an interview: "In general, they (women) are physically weaker than males. . . . I believe they would be inclined to let their emotions all to [sic] frequently overrule their good judgment . . . there are periods in their life when they are psychologically unbalanced because of physical problems that are occurring within them."

Women officers are assumed to be reluctant to use physical force and are viewed as incompetent "street cops" unitl they prove otherwise. As a result, women rookies encounter special problems in learning to use normal force in the process of becoming recognized as "real street cops." It becomes crucial for women officers to create or exploit opportunities to display their physical abilities in order to overcome sexual bias and obtain full acceptance from coworkers. As a result, women rookies are encouraged informally to act more aggressively and to display more machismo than male rookies. Consider the following incident where a young female officer reflects upon her use of force during a domestic disturbance:

And when I get there, if goddamn, there isn't a disturbance going on. So Tom comes, the guy that I went to back up. The male talks to him. I take the female and talk to her. And the drunk (cop) comes and the sergeant comes and another guy comes. So while we think we have everything settled, and we have the guy calmed down, he turns around and says to his sister, no less, that's who it is, "Give me the keys to my car!" And with that, she rips them out of her pocket and throws them at him. Now, he goes nuts. He goes into a Kung fu stance and says he's gonna kill her. The drunk cop says, "Yo, knock it off!" and goes to grab him and the guy punches him. So Mike (the drunk cop) goes down. Tommy goes to grab him and is wrestling with him. And all the cops are trying to get in there. So I ran in with my stick and I stick the guy in the head. But I just missed Tommy's face and opened him (the suspect) up. So all of a sudden everybody's grabbin' him and I'm realizing that if we get him down, he won't hurt anybody. So I pushed the sergeant out of the way and I got my stick under the guy's legs and I pulled his legs out from under him and I yelled, "Tommy, take him down." I pulled his legs and he went down and I sat on him. So Tommy says, "Well, cuff him." And I says, "I can't find my goddamned cuffs." I molested my body trying to get my cuffs. . . .

So, when I [finally] get my cuffs, we cuff him. And we're sitting there talking. And Tommy, he has no regard for me whatsoever. . . . The guy's opened up and he bled all over Tommy's shirt. And I turned around and said, "Tommy, look at your shirt. There's blood all over your shirt." He said, "Who the hell almost clobbered me?" I said, "I'm sorry Tom, that was me." He said, "You're the one that opened him up?" And I said, "Yeh. I'm sorry, I didn't mean to get so close to you." . . .

So when the sergeant came out he said, "And you, what do you mean telling me to get outta the way." He said, "Do you know you pushed me outta your way. . . ." And I said, "I didn't want you to get hurt . . . and I was afraid he was gonna kick one of you." And he says, "I still can't believe you pushed me outta your way. You were like a little dynamo." And I found after that I got respect from the sergeant. He doesn't realize it but he treated me differently after that.

Her colleagues' reactions provided informal instruction in the use of normal force, confirming that her actions under these circumstances were reasonable and even praiseworthy.

For a street cop, it is often a graver error to use too little force and develop a "shaky" reputation than it is to use too much force and be told to calm down. Thus officers, particularly rookies, who do not back up their partners in appropriate ways or who hesitate to use force in circumstances where it is deemed necessary are informally instructed regarding their aberrant ways. If the problematic incident is relatively insignificant and his general reputation is good, a rookie who "freezes" one time is given a second chance before becoming generally known as an untrustworthy partner. However, such incidents become the subject of degrading gossip, gossip that pressures the officer either to use force as expected or risk isolation. Such talk also informs rookies about the general boundaries of legal and normal force.

For example, a female rookie was accused of "freezing" in an incident that came to be referred to as a "Mexican standoff." A pedestrian had complained that "something funny is going on in the drugstore." The officer walked into the pharmacy where she found an armed man committing a robbery. Although he turned his weapon on her when she entered the premises, she still pulled out her gun and pointed it at him. When he ordered her to drop it, claiming that his partner was behind her with a revolver at her head, she refused and told him to drop his.[5] He refused, and the stalemate continued until a sergeant entered the drugstore and ordered the suspect to drop his gun.

Initially, the female officer thought she had acted appropriately and even heroically. She soon discovered, however, that her hesitation to shoot had brought into question her competence with some of her fellow officers. Although many veterans claimed that "she had a lot a balls" to take her gun out at all when the suspect already

[5] The woman officer later explained that she did not obey the suspect's command because she saw no reflection of the partner in the suspect's glasses and therefore assumed he was lying.

had a gun on her, most contended "she shoulda shot him." Other policemen confirmed that she committed a "rookie mistake"; she had failed to notice a "lookout" standing outside the store and hence had been unprepared for an armed confrontation. Her sergeant and lieutenant, moreover, even insisted that she had acted in a cowardly manner, despite her reputation as a "gung-ho cop," and cited the incident as evidence of the general inadequacy of policewomen.

In the weeks that followed, this officer became increasingly depressed and angry. She was particularly outraged when she learned that she would not receive a commendation, although such awards were commonly made for "gun pinches" of this nature. Several months later, the officer vehemently expressed the wish that she had killed the suspect and vowed that next time she would "shoot first and ask questions later." The negative sanctions of supervisors and colleagues clearly encouraged her to adopt an attitude favorable to using force with less restraint in future situations.

Reprimand, gossip, and avoidance constitute the primary means by which police try to change or control the behavior of coworkers perceived as unreliable or cowardly. Formal accusations, however, are discouraged regardless of the seriousness of the misconduct. One male rookie, for example, earned a reputation for cowardice after he allegedly had to be "dragged" out of the car during an "assist officer." Even then, he apparently refused to help the officers in trouble. Although no formal charges were filed, everyone in the district was warned to avoid working with this officer.

Indeed, to initiate formal charges against a coworker may discredit the accuser. In one incident a male rookie, although discouraged by veteran officers and even his district captain, filed charges of cowardice against a female rookie. The rookie gained the support of two supervisors and succeeded in having the case heard before the Board of Inquiry. During the trial he claimed the woman officer failed to aid him in arresting a man who presented physical resistance and had a knife on his person. In rebuttal, the woman testified that she perceived no need

to participate in a physical confrontation because she saw no knife and the policeman was hitting the suspect. In spite of conflicting testimony, she was found guilty of "Neglect of Duty." Although most veterans thought the woman was "flaky" and doubted her competence, they also felt the male rookie had exaggerated his story. Moreover, they were outraged that he filed formal charges and he quickly found himself ostracized.

At the same time that male and female rookies are commended for using force under appropriate circumstances, they are reprimanded if their participation in force is viewed as excessive or inappropriate. In this way, rookies are instructed that although many acts of coercion are accepted and even demanded, not everything goes. They thereby learn to distinguish between normal and brutal force. In the following incident, for example, a policewoman describes how she instructed a less experienced officer that her behavior was unreasonable and should be checked. Here, the new officer is chastised for misreading interactional cues and overreacting to minor affronts when treating a crazy person involved in a minor dispute as if he were a serious felon.[6]

But like I said, when I first heard about it (another fight) I'd wondered if Mary had provoked it any because we'd gone on a disturbance and it was a drunk black guy who called to complain that the kid who lived upstairs keeps walking through his apartment. The kid to me looks wacky. He's talking crazy. He's saying they shoulda sent men. What are you women going to do. Going on and on. And to me it was a bullshit job. But Mary turns around and says, "We don't have to take that from him. Let's lock him up." I said, "Mary forget it." And the kid has numchuck sticks on him and when he turned his back . . . he had them in his back pocket. So, as he's pulling away saying you're scared, like a little kid, I turned around and said, "I've got your sticks." And I go away. Mary . . . so Mary was . . . I looked at her and she was so disappointed in me . . . like I'd turned chicken on her. So I tried to explain to her, I said, "Mary, all we have is disorderly conduct. That's a summary offense. That's bullshit." I said, "Did you want to get hurt for a summary offense?" I said, "The guy was drunk who called to complain. It wasn't even a legit complaint." I said, "It's just . . . You've got to use discretion. If you

---

[6] Patrol officers do not view demented people as responsible for their acts and therefore do not hold them strictly culpable when they challenge an officer's authority (see Van Maanen, 1978: 231). In dealing with such persons, coercion other than that narrowly required for control and self-protection tends to be viewed as inappropriate and unjustifiable.

think I'm chicken think of the times when a 'man with a gun' comes over the air and I'm the first car there.'' I said, ''When it's worth it, I'll do anything. When it's not worth it, I'll back off.'' And I think she tries to temper herself some because Collette and her, they finally had a talk about why they hated each other. And Collette said to her, ''I think you're too physical. I think you look for fights.'' And I think maybe Mary hearing it twice, once from me and once from Collette, might start to think that maybe she does provoke. Instead of going up . . . I always go up to them friendly and then if they act shitty I get shitty.

In summary, when rookies leave the academy, they begin to familiarize themselves with street weapons and to gain some sense of what kinds of behavior constitute too little or too much force. They also begin to develop an understanding of street standards for using and judging appropriate and necessary force. By listening to and observing colleagues at work and by experiencing a variety of problematic interactions with the public, newcomers become cognizant of the occasions and circumstances in which to use various degrees and kinds of force. . . .

Accounting for Normal Force

. . . Police justify force [of] two analytically distinct kinds . . . situational and abstract. In the former, the officer represents force as a response in some specific situation needed to restore immediate control or to reestablish the local order of power in the face of a threat to police authority. In contrast, abstract accounts justify force as a morally appropriate response to certain categories of crime and criminals who symbolize a threat to the moral order. . . . [A]bstract justification does not highlight processes of interactional provocation and threats to immediate control, but rather legitimates force as a means of obtaining some higher moral purpose, particularly the punishment of heinous offenders. Mixed accounts involving situational and abstract justifications of force are also frequent: force may be depicted as necessary to regain control when an officer is physically assaulted; but at the same time it may also be justified as punishment appropriate to the kind of morally unworthy person who would challenge an officer's authority.

Officers . . . justify force as normal by reference to interactional situations in which an officer's authority is physically or symbolically threatened. In such accounts, the use of force is justified instrumentally—as a means of regaining immediate control in a situation where that control has become tenuous. Here, the officer depicts his primary intent for using force as a need to reestablish immediate control in a problematic encounter, and only incidentally as hurting or punishing the offender.

Few officers will hesitate to assault a suspect who physically threatens or attacks them. In one case, an officer was punched in the face by a prisoner he had just apprehended for allegedly attempting to shoot a friend. The incident occurred in the stationhouse and several policemen observed the exchange. Immediately, one officer hit the prisoner in the jaw and the rest immediately joined the brawl.

Violations of an officer's property such as his car or hat may signify a more symbolic assault on the officer's authority and self, thus justifying a forceful response to maintain control. Indeed, in the police view, almost any person who verbally challenges a police officer is appropriately subject to force.[7] In the following extract, a female officer accounts in these ways for a colleague's use of force against an escaping prisoner:

And so Susan gets on the scene (of the fight). They cuff one of the girls, and she throws her in the back seat of the car. She climbs over the back seat, jumps out of the car with cuffs on and starts running up the stairs. Susan and Jane are trying to cuff the other girl and all of a sudden Susan looks up and sees her cuffs running away. She (Jane) said Susan turned into an animal. Susan runs up the steps grabs the girl by the legs. Drags her down the five steps. Puts her in the car. Kicks her in the car. Jane goes in the car and calls her every name she can think of and waves her stick in her face.[8]

On rare occasions, women officers encounter special problems in these regards. Although most suspects view women in the same way as

---

[7] According to Van Maanen (1978: 224), such persons tend to be labeled ''assholes.'' The ''asshole,'' who symbolically challenges an officer's control and thereby defies his definition of a situation, provokes the officer's wrath and becomes a likely candidate for street justice (Van Maanen, 1978: 224).

[8] Note that this account employs both the justifications of reestablishing real and symbolic control, and the excuse of emotionally snapping out in response to this symbolic challenge and to the resulting pursuit.

policemen, some seem less inclined to accord female officers de facto and symbolic control in street encounters, and on a few occasions seem determined to provoke direct confrontations with such officers, explicitly denying their formal authority and attempting none too subtly to sexualize the encounter. Women officers, then, might use force as a resource for rectifying such insults and for establishing control over such partially sexualized interactions. Consider the following . . .

Well, the day before the lieutenant had a roll-call announcement that there had been a pursuit in one of the districts and, as a result, a fireman was killed. And he said, "Why pursue them? In court nothing is gonna happen anyway and being as it was a taxi cab that was involved it would be returned." He said, "What I'm trying to say . . ." So one of the guys said, "What's a pursuit?" He said, "Exactly."

So Goddamn, if not the next day, about three o'clock in the morning, three thirty, I heard Anne got out with a carstop at Second and Madison. And I heard Joan back her up, and she (Anne) ran the car through (the computer) and I heard, "Hold me out for TVRs (traffic tickets)." So, I'm sitting at Second Street, Second and Nassau, writing curfews up. And this silver Thunderbird (the same car) blows right by a stop sign where I'm sitting. And I look up and think to myself, "Now, do I want to get involved." And I figure, it was really belligerent doing it right in front of me. So I take off after him, put my lights on and he immediately pulls over. So he jumps out of the car. I jump out of the car right away and I say, "I'm stopping you for that stop sign you just blew through." And he says, "Aw come on, I just got stopped. I'm sick of this shit." So I said to him, "Look, I don't care how many times you got stopped." He said, "Well, I'm sick of this shit." And I said, "I'm stopping you right now for this stop sign you went through at Second and Nassau. Let me see your cards please." Then he starts making these lip smacking noises at me everytime he begins to talk. He said, (smack) "The only way you're seeing my cards is if you lock me up and the only way you're gonna lock me up is if you chase me." And I said to him, "Well, look, I will satisfy you on one account. Now go to your car because I will lock you up. . . . And just sit in your car. I'll be right with you." He smacks his lips, turns around and goes to his car and he sits. And I call a wagon at Second and Nassau. They ask me what I have. I say, "I've got one to go." So as the wagon acknowledges, the car all of a sudden tears out of its spot. And I get on the air and say, "I'm in pursuit."

And I give them a description of the car and the direction I'm going. And I heard a couple of other cars coming in and they're comin' in. And all of a sudden he pulls over about a block and a half after I started the pursuit. So I got on the air and I said, "I got him at Second and Washington." I jumped out of my car and as I jumped out he tears away again. Now I'm ready to die of embarrassment. I have to get back on the air and say no I don't have him. So I got on the air and said, "Look, he's playing games with me now. He took off again." I said, "I'm still heading South on Second street." He gets down to Lexington. He pulls over again. Well, this time I pulled the police car in front of him. I jumped out of the car and as I'm jumping out of the car I hear two female voices screaming, "Lock him up, lock him up!" I go over to the car and I hear him lock the doors. I pull out my gun and I put it right in his window. I say, "Unlock that door." Well, he looked at the gun. He nearly like to shit himself. He unlocked the door. I holster my gun. I go to grab his arms to pull him out and all of a sudden I realize Anne's got him. So we keep pulling him out of the car. Throw him on the trunk of his car and kept pounding him back down on the trunk. She's punching his head. I'm kicking him. Then I take out my blackjack. I jack him across the shoulder. Then I go to jack him in the head and I jack Anne's fingers. We're being so rough. Then the wagon comes and we're kicking the shit out of him. Trying to . . . dragging him over to the wagon. This poor sucker don't have a chance. The next thing they know is we're throwing him bodily into the wagon. And they said, "Did you search him?" We go to the wagon, drag him out again. Now we're tearing through his pockets throwing everything on the ground. Pick him up bodily again, threw him in. . . . So I straightened it out with the sergeant and he said, "By the way what were you doing?" I said, "I was in a pursuit." (He said) "A pursuit! Thank God the Lieutenant wasn't there. He said there's no such thing as a pursuit." I said, "I tried to call it another name but I couldn't think of any other name to call it. All I know of it is as a pursuit. I'm following some guy at fast speed who refuses to pull over." So I said, "What did you want me to do? Let any citizen on the street get stopped and pull away and that's the end of it?"

In this instance, a male suspect manages to convey a series of affronts to the officer's authority. These affronts become explicitly and insultingly sexual,[9] turning the challenge from the claim that "no cop will stop me" to the more gender specific one, "no woman cop will stop me." Resistance ups the ante until the suspect backs down in the face of the officer's drawn

[9] Again, such affronts arise with different frequency and have different impact depending upon gender. Although policemen are occasionally subjected to sexual insults by women and teenage girls, this kind of harassment is more commonly experienced by women and thus constitutes a special type of affront to the female officer.

revolver. The force to which the culprit was then subjected is normalized through all the accounts considered to this point—it is . . . a means to reestablish and maintain immediate and symbolic control in a highly problematic encounter and it is . . . [seen] as a natural, collective outburst following resolution of a dangerous, tension-filled incident. . . .

Police also justify the use of extreme force against certain categories of morally reprehensible persons. In this case, force is not presented as an instrumental means to regain control that has been symbolically or physically threatened. Instead, it is justified as an appropriate response to particularly heinous offenders. Categories of such offenders include: cop haters who have gained notoriety as persistent police antagonizers; cop killers or any person who has attempted seriously to harm a police officer (Westley, 1970: 131); sexual deviants who prey on children and "moral women";[10] child abusers; and junkies and other "scum" who inhabit the street. The more morally reprehensible the act is judged, the more likely the police are to depict any violence directed toward its perpetrator as justifiable. Thus a man who exposes himself to children in a playground is less likely to experience police assault than one who rapes or sexually molests a child.

"Clean" criminals, such as high level mafiosi, white-collar criminals, and professional burglars, are rarely subject to abstract force. Nor are perpetrators of violent and nonviolent street crimes who prey on adult males, prostitutes, and other categories of persons who belong on the street.[11] Similarly, the "psycho" or demented person is perceived as so mentally deranged that he is not responsible for his acts and hence does not merit abstract, punitive force (Van Maanen, 1978: 233–4).

Police justify abstract force by invoking a higher moral purpose that legitimates the violation of commonly recognized standards.[12] In one case, for example, a nun was raped by a 17-year-old male adolescent. When the police apprehended the suspect, he was severely beaten and his penis put in an electrical outlet to teach him a lesson. The story of the event was told to me by a police officer who, despite the fact that he rarely supported the use of extralegal force, depicted this treatment as legitimate. Indeed, when I asked if he would have participated had he been present, he responded, "I'm Catholic. I would have participated."

Excessive Force and Peer Responses

. . . [T]he concept of normal force is useful because it suggests that there are specific circumstances under which police officers will not condone the use of force by themselves or colleagues as reasonable and acceptable. Thus, officer-recognized conceptions of normal force are subject to restrictions of the following kinds:

1. Police recognize and honor some rough equation between the behavior of the suspect and the harmfulness of the force to which it is subject. There are limits, therefore, to the degree of force that is acceptable in particular circumstances. In the following incident, for example, an officer reflects on a situation in which a "symbolic assailant" (Skolnick, 1975: 45) was mistakenly subject to more force than he "deserved" and almost killed:

One time Bill Johnson and I, I have more respect for him than any other policeman. . . . He and I, we weren't particularly brutal. If the guy deserved it, he got it. It's generally the attitude that does it. We had a particularly rude drunk one day. He was really rude and spit on you and he did all this stuff and we even had to cuff him lying down on the hard stretcher, like you would do an epileptic. . . . We were really mad at this guy. So, what you normally do with drunks is you take them to the district cell. . . . So we were really mad. We said let's just give him one or two shots . . . slamming on the brakes and having him roll. But we didn't use our heads. He's screaming and hollering "You lousy cops" and we slammed on the brakes and we didn't use our heads and we heard the stretcher go nnnnnnBam and then nothing. We heard nothing and we realized we had put this man in with his

---

[10] For a discussion of the significance of "the moral woman," see Hunt (1984).

[11] The categories of persons who merit violence are not unique to the police. Prisoners, criminals, and hospital personnel appear to draw similar distinctions between morally unworthy persons; on the latter, see Sudnow (1967: 105).

[12] Abstract force constitutes what Emerson (1969: 149) calls a "principled justification":

Here one depicts the act as an attempt to realize some absolute moral or social value that has precedence over the value violated by the act.

head to the front so when we slammed on the brakes this stretcher. . . . I guess it can roll four foot. Well, it was his head that had hit the front of it and we heard no sounds and my God, I've never been so scared. Me and Bill we thought we killed him. So I'm saying "Bill, what are we gonna do? How are we gonna explain this one." The guy's still saying nothing. So, we went to Madison Street and parked. It's a really lonely area. And we unlocked the wagon and peeked in. We know he's in there. We were so scared and we look in and there's not a sound and we see blood coming in front of the wagon and think "Oh my God we killed this man. What am I gonna do? What am I gonna tell my family?" And to make a long story short, he was just knocked out. But boy was I scared. From then on we learned, feet first.

2. Although it is considered normal and natural to become emotional and angry in highly charged, taut encounters, officers nonetheless prefer to minimize the harmful consequences of the use of force. As a result, officers usually acknowledge that emotional reactions that might lead to extreme force should be controlled and limited by coworkers if at all possible. In the following . . . , for example, an officer justified the use of force as a legitimate means to regain situational control when physically challenged. Nonetheless, he expressed gratitude to his partner for stopping him from doing serious harm when he "snapped out" and lost control:

Well, I wasn't sure if she was a girl until I put my hand on her shoulder and realized it was a woman's shoulder. I was trying to stop her. But it happened when she suddenly kicked me in the balls. Then everything inside of me exploded and I grabbed her and pushed her against the car and started pressing her backwards and kept pressing her backwards. All of a sudden something clicked inside of me because I noticed her eyes changed and her body caved in and she looked frightened because she knew that I was gonna kill her. And I stopped. I think I stopped because Susan was on the scene. She must have said something. But anyway she (Susan) told me later that I should calm down. And I snapped at her and told her to mind her own business because she didn't know what happened. The girl kicked me in the balls. But she was right about it. I mean it was getting to me. I'd never hit a woman before.

3. Similarly, even in cases where suspects are seen as deserving some violent punishment, this force should not be used randomly and without control. Thus, in the following incident, an officer who "snapped out" and began to beat a child abuser clearly regarded his partner's attempt to stop the beating as reasonable.

We get a call "meet complainant" and I drive up and there's a lady standing out in front of the house and she's saying, "Listen officer, I don't know what the story is but the neighbors in there. They're screaming and hollering and there's kicking going on in there and I can't take it. I can't sleep. There's too much noise." Nothing unusual about that. Just a typical day in the district. So the next thing you do is knock on the door and tell them to please keep the noise down or whatever you do. You say to yourself it's probably a boy friend-girl friend fight. So I knock on the door and a lady answers just completely hysterical. And I say, "Listen, I don't know what's going on in here," but then I hear this, just this screeching. You know. And I figure well I'm going to find out what's going on so I just go past the lady and what's happening is that the husband had. . . . The kid was being potty trained and the way they were potty training this kid, this two-year-old boy, was that the boyfriend of this girl would pick up this kid and he would sit him down on top of the stove. It was their method of potty training. Well, first of all you think of your own kids. I mean afterwards you do. I mean I've never been this mad in my whole life. You see this little two-year-old boy seated on top of the stove with rings around it being absolutely scalding hot. And he's saying "I'll teach you to go. . . ." It just triggered something. An uncontrollable. . . . It's just probably the most violent I ever got. Well you just grab that guy. You hit him ten, fifteen times . . . you don't know how many. You just get so mad. And I remember my partner eventually came in and grabbed me and said, "Don't worry about it. We got him. We got him." And we cuffed him and we took him down. Yeah that was bad.

It is against this background that patrol officers identify excessive force and the existence of violence-prone peers. Some officers become known for recurrently committing acts of coercion that exceed working notions of normal force. . . . In contrast to the officer who makes a "rookie mistake" and uses excessive force from inexperience, the brutal cop does not honor the practices of normal force. Such an officer is also not effectively held in check by routine means of peer control. As a result, more drastic measures must be taken to prevent him from endangering the public and his colleagues.

One rookie gained a reputation for brutality from frequent involvement in "unnecessary" fights. One such incident was particularly noteworthy: Answering a call on a demented male with a weapon, he came upon a large man pacing the sidewalk carrying a lead pipe. The officer got out of the patrol car and yelled in a belligerent tone of voice, "What the fuck are you doing creep?" At this point "the creep" attacked the officer and tried to take away his gun. A policewoman arrived on the scene, joined the fight, called an assist, and rescued the patrolman. Although no one was hurt, colleagues felt the incident was provoked by the officer who aggressively approached a known crazy person who should have been assumed to be unpredictable and nonresponsible.

When colleagues first began to doubt this officer's competence, he was informally instructed to moderate his behavior by veteran and even rookie partners. When his behavior persisted, confrontations with fellow officers became explosive. When peers were unable to check his behavior, complaints were made to superiors. Officially, colleagues indicated they did not want to work with him because of "personality problems." Informally, however, supervisors were informed of the nature of his provocative and dangerous behavior. The sergeant responded by putting the rookie in a wagon with a responsible partner whom he thought might succeed in controlling him. When this strategy proved unsuccessful, he was eventually transferred to the subway unit. Such transfers to "punishment districts," isolated posts, "inside units," or the subway are typical means of handling police officers deemed dangerous and out of control.

As this discussion indicates, the internal control of an exceptionally or inappropriately violent police officer is largely informal. With the exception of civilian complaints and brutality suits, the behavior of such officers rarely becomes the subject of formal police documents. However, their reputations are often well known throughout the department and the rumors about their indiscretions educate rookies about how the line between normal force and brutality is drawn among working police officers.

It takes more than one incident of excessively violent behavior for a police officer to attain a brutal reputation. The violent officer is usually involved in numerous acts of aggressive behavior that are not accountable as normal force either because of their frequency or because of their substance. However, once identified as "brutal," a "head beater," and so on, an officer's use of force will be condemned by peers in circumstances in which competent officers would be given the benefit of the doubt. For example, one officer gained national notoriety during a federal investigation into a suspicious shooting. Allegedly, a local resident had thrown an axe at the patrol wagon. According to available accounts, the police pursued the suspect inside a house and the officer in question shot him in the head. Although witnesses claimed the victim was unarmed, the officer stated that he fired in self defense. The suspect reportedly attacked him with a metal pipe. This policeman had an established reputation for being "good with his hands," and many colleagues assumed he had brutally shot an unarmed man in the aftermath of a pursuit.[13] . . .

REFERENCES

Bittner, E. 1980. *The Functions of the Police in Modern Society*. Cambridge, MA: Oelgeschlager, Gunn & Hain.

Blumberg, M. 1983. "The Use of Firearms by Police Officers: The Impact of Individuals, Communities, and Race." Ph.D. dissertation. School of Criminal Justice, State University of New York at Albany.

Emerson, R. M. 1969. *Judging Delinquents: Context and Process in Juvenile Court*. Chicago: Aldine.

Friedrich, R. 1980. "Police Use of Force: Individuals, Situations, and Organizations." *The Annals*, 452: 82–97.

Fyfe, J. J. 1983. "Police Shootings: Environment, License and Individuals." Presented at the Annual Meeting of the American Society of Criminology.

Hunt, J. Forthcoming. "The Development of Rapport Through the Negotiation of Gender in Field Work Among Police." *Human Organization*.

Lee, J. A. 1981. "Some Structural Aspects of Police Deviance in Relation to Minority Groups." In C. D. Shearing (ed.), *Organizational Police Deviance*. Toronto: Butterworths.

Niederhoffer, A. 1967. *Behind the Shield: The*

---

[13] The suspect was known to other officers from prior encounters as a slightly demented cop antagonizer. Consequently, the officer's actions appeared completely unnecessary because he was not dealing with an unpredictable stranger. The suspect's neighbors depicted him as a mentally disturbed person who was deathly afraid of the police because he had been a frequent target of harassment.

Police in Urban Society. Garden City, NY: Anchor-Doubleday.

Reiss, A. J. 1970. "Police Brutality—Answers to Key Questions." In A. Niederhoffer and A. S. Blumberg (eds), *The Ambivalent Force: Perspectives on the Police*. Toronto: Xerox College Publishing.

Scott, M. B. and S. M. Lyman 1968. "Accounts." *American Sociological Review*, 33:46–62.

Skolnick, J. 1975. *Justice Without Trial*. New York: Wiley.

Sudnow, D. 1967. *Passing On: The Social Organization of Dying*. Englewood Cliffs, NJ: Prentice-Hall.

Sykes, G. M. and D. Matza 1957. *"Techniques of Neutralization: A Theory of Delinquency."* *American Sociological Review*, 22:664–70.

Van Maanen, J. 1978 "The asshole." In P. K. Manning and J. Van Maanen (eds.), *Policing: A View from the Street*. Santa Monica, CA: Goodyear.

Waegel, W. B. 1984. "The Use of Deadly Force by Police: The Effect of Statutory Change." *Crime and Delinquency*, 30:121–140.

Westley, W. A. 1970. *Violence and the Police: A Sociological Study of Law, Custom and Morality*. Cambridge, MA: MIT.

Narcotics Enforcement in a Canadian City

KENNETH STODDART

Introduction

Attempts to answer fundamental questions relating to the extent and distribution of non-medical drug use have often used some version of an officially-produced case register as a major data source, such as the one provided by Canada's Bureau of Dangerous Drugs. Traditionally the examination and analysis of official statistical records has been regarded as amongst the most valuable ways of uncovering features of the activity's volume and morphology.

During the past fifteen years, however, a considerable amount of social scientific research focussing on arrest situations and decision-making by police—major contributors to official statistics—has called into question the utility of such records in general. Basically, the discovery that police activity introduces systematic distortions rather than random, self-cancelling ones, has suggested that official statistics may be more an artifact of enforcement procedures and routines, etc. than a reliable index of community law-breaking. That this is likely the case for statistical portrayals of non-medical drug use has been claimed for a variety of jurisdictions: analyses of the Canadian situation, however, are conspicuous in their absence.

In the hope of partially filling this gap the present report offers a set of materials descriptive of some of the police activities that contribute to official portrayals of the volume and morphology of heroin use in a large city in the Canadian West. Drawing on data produced via a program of unstructured interviews with heroin users residing in Western City, this report examines the potential significance for official heroin use statistics of two police-related matters: (1) the responsiveness of crucial decision-making to certain features of narcotics violators and (2) the organization of policework.

Violator Features

As has been documented in numerous investigations, the law is *unevenly enforced* by person-nel charged with the task. Rather than as a program to be applied uniformly over all situations enforcement personnel confront the law as a scheme of interpretation that they can invoke or not invoke for a variety of reasons. Indeed, an increasing volume of research, which describes how persons are assembled by police for induction into the criminal justice process, suggests that *however* that assembly occurs, it is inadequately depicted as proceeding via the "matching" of observed conduct with prospectively defined illegal conduct. Study after study has shown that a meeting of legal specifications for arrest is merely *one of* the criteria informing the decision to arrest, not exhaustive of them. Unsurprisingly, police assembly is revealed as responsive in unknown measure to a host of other considerations. As Bittner [1] and others have suggested, policemen ". . . often make decisions based on reasons that the law probably does not recognize as valid." Some of these "reasons" relate to the policeman's perception of the violator. For example—independent of technical possibility—arrests may or may not be made because of the violator's social status in the community [2], appearance and demeanour [3], etc.

This section explores the influence of such "violator features" on two police decisions which are routine to the narcotics enforcement process: the decision to arrest and the decision to pursue a heroin user as a candidate for arrest.

There's No Way You Can Talk Them Out of It: The Restricted Relevance of Extralegal Considerations

In line with other research findings regarding decision-making in the criminal justice system and hopeful of uncovering the potential influence of violator features on official portrayals of community heroin use informants were queried about their own encounters with enforcement personnel. Perhaps not surprisingly, their accounts revealed that—unlike other kinds of violations—narcotics violations were enforced, in their words, "to the letter of the law."

"The Enforcement of Narcotics Violations in a Canadian City: Heroin Users' Perspectives on the Production of Official Statistics," *Canadian Journal of Criminology*, Vol. 23, No. 4 (October 1982), pp. 425–438.

Financial support for the research reported herein was provided by the Social and Epidemiological Research Division of the non-Medical use of Drugs Directorate (Irving Rootman, Chief). The author is solely responsible for the interpretations presented.

Indeed, some informants found *incredulous* the suggestion that police suspended the relevance of legal considerations and did not arrest a violator when it was technically possible. On occasion, variations of the question:

Have there ever been any times when they got the dope but didn't pinch you for it?

were greeted with ridicule. For example:

I: Have there ever been any times when they got the dope but didn't pinch you for it?
R: You mean just let you go or something?
I: Yeah, something like that.
R: Fuck, you gotta be kidding. Once they got it outa you you're pinched and that's it. No two ways about it, you're fuckin' pinched. You gotta be crazy to think they'd let you off just like that, fuck no, that's not the way it happens.

As suggested in the following excerpts from interviews, that such a thing was beyond the realm of possibility, was typically formulated as due to either police contempt of heroin users or the difficulty they experienced in apprehending them.

Once they've got ya, it's a good catch for them, they got some brownie points, y'know. They just don't say "well that's a bad habit you've got, sonny" and forget it cause for one thing its a lot of work for them, y'know. We put them through their paces, believe me.

The bulls hate us junkies. The more of us they pinch the happier they are.

Whatever the underlying reason, however, informants suggest that after police have obtained evidence sufficient to warrant an arrest, legal considerations are afforded priority over all others. According to this portrayal, the police systematically employ the law to decide a course of action. Informants maintained that this was the case, virtually independent of anything that one might do, say, or be. Unlike the situation with other violations, any and all features of the violator—save one, as will be indicated below—seem irrelevant vis-à-vis the decision to make an arrest for a narcotics offence. In the following excerpt from an interview, a woman recently arrested for the first time relates her "surprise" that this is the case. As she discovered, "tradi-

tional" ways of altering the probability of arrest were thoroughly ineffective:

The way the narco bulls operate is different from other kinds. They're harder . . . Like I was pinched for boosting, shoplifting a couple of times and you know I'd just start bawlin' about things. What's gonna happen to my baby if I go to jail, what's gonna happen. . . . They'd say "okay, we'll give you a break" . . . Try that with the fuckin' narco bulls and they'll tell you to shut your fuckin' mouth. There's no way you can talk them out of it.

Should a violator be "let off", it was held that it would be because of an offer to perform as an informant:

The only way they're gonna let you off once they've got you is if you offer to go rat for them.

In general, the likelihood of altering one's fate after evidence had been obtained, was received as virtually non-existent; from informants' point-of-view, ". . . there's no way you can talk them out of it." This alleged overriding priority attributed to legal considerations is a matter of some importance to those interested in the research utility of official rates of heroin use. For example, the observation that the successfully detected cohort appears to pass into official records in its intact version suggests that underreporting due to the operation of other-than-legal considerations is minimal.

Some People Have a Better Chance on the Street: Social Categories and Enforcement

Though informants asserted that legally irrelevant considerations were virtually uninfluential upon police decision-making after a successful investigation, they claimed that such considerations played an important role in determining who would be selected as a candidate for investigation in the first place. They saw the likelihood of being pursued by police as dependent on somewhat *more* than the "mere fact" that one was known to be in possession of heroin. While being in possession made one liable for pursuit, it did not guarantee it:

I: So every time you score you're taking a chance of getting pinched or at least having them come after you.
R: Oh yeah, the chance is there, but there's more to it than that, y'know.

Indeed, informants were of the opinion that not all heroin users in possession were equally likely to be selected as candidates for pursuit:

I: So does pretty well everybody have the same chance of getting followed after they score, or what?

R: Oh no, no. Some people have got a better chance on the street.

In part these differential probabilities were structured by the responsiveness of enforcement personnel to a variety of legally-irrelevant factors.

One's membership in certain *social categories* was portrayed by community members as prominent amongst those factors. For example, a heroin user identified as a "rat", i.e., a provisioner of information to the police is obviously unlikely to be selected for pursuit. As one informant puts it:

Well if somebody's rattin' to the bulls they're not gonna pinch him, are they?

It was suggested that women, too, enjoyed ". . . a better chance on the street".

I: Do the police give the women as bad a time, as rough a time as they give the men?

R: Well they're pretty rough all around, y'know. I don't think they go after the chicks as much as the guys, though. Not that they leave us alone or anything, but they don't come after us as much.

Informants were not united regarding *why* women were selected as candidates for investigation less frequently than men. Some suggested that the police perceived female heroin users as less threatening to society than their male counterparts:

Well, the bulls leave the working girls pretty much alone, usually. I guess they figure "what the fuck, they're workin' for their money, providin' a service and so on." We're not stealin' or nothin, y'know.

I guess they figure its the guys that are the ones to get 'cause of what they do, steal and the like.

Others accounted for the difference by referring to the practical problems women pose for investigative work carried out primarily by males:

A lot of girls carry dope internally, y'know, so it's a lot of trouble for the bulls. They gotta take you down to (the public safety building) and wait for a qualified doctor to come and give you an internal search. That could take hours.

What is paramount among the theories advanced to explain the lesser likelihood of pursuit enjoyed by women, however, was the notion that enforcement personnel perceived female heroin users as having "female" and not "heroin user" status. Despite their use of heroin they were understood to be *women* first and foremost. This itself was portrayed as creating a practical problem for police. Indeed, a notable feature of their regard for female heroin users in this way, it was asserted, was a reduction in the amount of physical vigour applied to obtain arrest-producing evidence. Informants attributed to police sensibilities that did not permit them to be egalitarian in their treatment of the sexes. As one informant put it:

They're not . . . they don't beat the shit outa chicks the way they do with the guys. Sure, they're rough alright, but the guys've got it worse.

Informants claimed, however, that the difference enjoyed by women in general, was enjoyed to a greater extent by particular types of women. Other types, it was told, were treated ". . . just like the guys."

Well some broads they treat just like the guys. I've seen lots with broken teeth from handcuffs going down their throats, scars. . . . They beat the shit outa them to get the dope, just like they'd do to a guy.

It was suggested that the woman who had ". . . a better chance on the street" were those with an appearance and demeanour approximating those of "ordinary", i.e. non-heroin using, women. For informants, a woman's "better chance" eroded precisely to the extent that her presentation *strayed* from the one just suggested, as:

the bulls don't mind beatin' on an old douche-bag with rotten teeth and dirty hair. Some chicks let themselves get so scraggy, its no wonder they take shit.

One informant formulated the effect of a conventional presentation as functionally equivalent to an adaptive strategy:

I: So what do you spend all that money on. Besides junk.

R: Well there's clothes and groceries. Getting my hair done and stuff. Makeup. You gotta keep yourself up, y'know.

I: Keep yourself up?

R: Yeah, its not good if you let yourself go like some chicks do.

I: Its no good to. . . .

R: Let yourself go, get . . . be a slob about yourself. I don't like gettin' that way, I never have. Its a personal thing. But if you look like shit you're gonna get treated that way too, y'know.

I: By who?

R: By everybody.

I: By the cops?

R: Oh yeah. If you look like a decent person they're not gonna bother you as much as if you walk around lookin' like a fuckin' dirty junkie asshole. Broads who do that are just askin' for it.

I: Okay, so what you're saying then is that if you look like a . . . if you look pretty good then you're not gonna get the hassle you would if you didn't. Is that right or am I missing something?

R: No, that's about it. If a chick looks good the bulls are definitely not gonna . . . they're probably not gonna give her the usual shit.

These observations appear massively relevant to research and policy decisions based on officially-located heroin users. Consider, for example, the issue of *who*—in the sense of social type—*gets assembled into official statistics*. Indeed, notation of the pre-investigation significance of such presentational considerations as demeanour, appearance, etc., underscore the fact that an *official* heroin user—as opposed to a person who "merely" uses heroin—is the product of a social judgement made by the police. To paraphrase Piliavin and Briar [3], he or she is a heroin user because someone in authority has defined him/her as one, often on the basis of the public face presented to officials rather than the kind of offence committed. Quite obviously, if similar "public faces" are being assembled,

heroin users start to look alike, a fact of no little clinical relevance.

If They Want Ya, They're Gonna Get Ya: The Particularization of Enforcement

For informants, however, category membership did not exhaust the list of extra-legal factors potentially influential upon the choice of *who* from a range of possibles might be pursued as a candidate for investigation. Indeed, they asserted the relevance of a number of other considerations. For example, they claimed that "for personal reasons", enforcement personnel singled out some heroin users for vigorous pursuit. When members of the community realized that this was the case in their situation, i.e. that they had been selected for special investigation attention, they characterized the police as "having a burn" for them:

R: . . . well if they've got a burn for you for some reason . . .

I: How do you mean have a burn?

R: Well if they really want you bad, y'know. Really want to see you pinched.

They suggested that this state-of-affairs would eventually result in their arrest, as "if they want ya, they're gonna get ya . . ."

Once they've got a burn for ya, y'might as well start sayin' goodbye to everybody 'cause you'll be in jail before ya know it. If they want ya, they're gonna get ya, no two ways about it.

Informants indicated that one could become attractive as an enforcement target for a variety of reasons. In general, their own and their colleagues' experience suggested that anything one might do to further alienate the police, i.e., ". . . to make them hate you even more than they do," stood to heighten the probability of investigative pursuit and, eventually, arrest.

If you fuck them around, treat them . . . if you don't play it right they're gonna be after you. If you do anything that . . . anything to make them hate you even more than they do, then watch out 'cause that's it for you.

It was held that further alienation of enforcement personnel could be accomplished by irritating them in any number of ways. One could, for example, make their work more difficult by interfering with it:

R: Well I did what you might call a stupid thing, what I think's a stupid thing anyway.
I: What? What kind of stupid thing did you do?
R: Well I got the narco bulls mad at me, but I couldn't help it. I couldn't just . . . I couldn't hold myself back.
I: Well what was the stupid thing?
R: Well one of my buddies—she's in here now as a matter of fact. She was gettin' roughed up a little and I was pissed off. I started screamin' at 'em, callin' them dumb fuckers and so forth. Kickin'. They told me to fuck off and mind my own business but I just got more frantic, y'know. After I thought about it I thought "Fuck, these guys are gonna be after me now for makin' them so fuckin' mad and all." So then I got pinched.
I: This last time?
R: Yeah, just before Christmas. Anyway when I got pinched one of them said "that'll teach you to keep your fuckin' nose outa other people's business." So there ya go. If I'd . . . if I'd just turned away I'd probably still be on the street, y'know.

Also, one could refuse to cooperate:

I: Have the police ever approached you, ever asked you to rat for them? Like be an informant or something?
R: Not in any kind of a formal way or nothing! Like offering me money. One time they asked me, on the street just out of the blue . . . asked me to tell them who's doin' things. I said just forget it and they said "things have been known to happen to guys like you. You'd better watch out from now on."
I: What was that supposed to mean?
R: Well they were tellin' me in so many words that they'd be watching me a little bit closer for the next while.
I: Did they?
R: Fuckin' right they did. I got jumped three times the next week.

Informants claimed that one could irritate the police—and thus potentially cause them to "have a burn for you" by, persistently frustrating their attempts at successful, arrest-producing investigation. The following excerpt from an interview provides an example:

R: I know they were after me 'cause they told me they were.
I: Oh yeah, they told you?
R: Oh yeah, it was just a matter of time. I haven't taken a pinch for years, y'know and its not 'cause they haven't tried. I just been smarter than them and they were pissed off. . . . So every time I scored I figured "well its gonna be this time, this time they're gonna get me" so I was pretty careful, y'know. And they tried but I kept outsmartin' the fuckers. "We're gonna get ya," they said, "we're gonna get ya." I was . . . hurtin' their pride I guess, always outsmartin' em like that.

Irritating the police by verbally abusing them or by suggesting the superiority of a deviant lifestyle were portrayed as making them ". . . hate you even more than they do" and thereby increasing the likelihood of being selected as a candidate for pursuit. For example:

These young kids you see on the street, they think they're smart callin' the bulls names, dirty pig and all that. All they're doin' by that is makin' it worse for themselves cause they'll be harder on 'em and bug 'em.

R: You can be on the street for a long time with no trouble then all of a sudden something happens and bingo, you're pinched.
I: Like what can happen, for example.
R: Well you do somethin' stupid. Like I started makin' fun of a bull, one bull in particular. I told him one day that I was savin' up for a downpayment on a house and he said "oh yeah, how long'll that take ya?" I said "Oh, about a month or so." And he said "fuck, it'll take you five years." So every time I saw him I said "well are ya still savin'?" Fuck he got pissed off.
I: He couldn't take a joke. . . .
R: I guess not 'cause he was sure after me for a while. I couldn't go on the street without gettin' some hassle. I was a real heatbag.

Informants indicated that the likelihood of being singled out for special investigative attention was increased by one's ignoring recent court orders:

The judge told me that I had 48 hours to get out of the Province of British Columbia and the bulls knew it, things get around. So when I scored they just naturally came right after me. Figured I'd really get the book thrown at me, what with gettin' it for possession when I shoulda been out of town.

The Organization of Policework

In addition to violator features there are, of course, numerous other considerations which influence narcotics enforcement and—ultimately—official portrayals of community drug use. This section discusses the potential impact of changes in size of the enforcement unit and quality and style of enforcement on official rates.

They're Better and There's More of Them: Asserted Changes in the Size and Quality of the Enforcement Unit

Notations of change in the rate of a given deviant behaviour presume—among other things—that the number and quality of personnel assigned to deal with the behaviour have remained static. Black [4] explains how crime rates and size of enforcement units influence each other:

Crime rates that are produced in proactive police operations, such as arrests for . . . narcotics violation, directly correlate with police manpower allocation. Until a point of total detection is reached and holding all else constant, these vice rates increase as the number of policemen assigned to vice control is increased.

The influence of enhanced *quality* of enforcement is more difficult to establish. It is the case, however, that since the early 1970's recruits to all municipal police departments in the province have been receiving narcotics investigation training through the Western Province Police College. The putative "spread" of heroin use from metropolis to hinterland thus becomes potentially more related to the diffusion of knowledge than narcotics. Some informants added documentation to this notion via their complaints about the declining number of places thought to be "safe" for engaging in drug-relevant activities. Consider the following excerpts from an interview with a drug trafficker who used to conduct business in such places . . . "before it got too hot."

I: So what happened after that?
R: Well after that I started to stay out of town pretty much. I'd take a half-a-dozen bundles

or so and go up through the Interior and places like that. There was always people lookin' for dope up here and there wasn't the heat.
I: This was when.
R: Oh, shit, 10–12 years ago or so.
I: So you'd stay out of town.
R: Yeah, I'd head up to the Interior. That was before it got too hot. The bulls are all wise now, not like before.
I: They used to be . . .
R: They didn't know what dope was, not at all. Then you could even go out to the Russell Hotel in (a municipality adjacent to Western City). Cops didn't know what was goin' on.
I: Now they do?
R: Oh yeah, they're wise all over now. Nowhere's safe anymore, like it used to be.

Undercover operations, too, were portrayed as increasingly more sophisticated. One informant insisted that ". . . the bulls are getting smarter" and documented this assertion with observations of the changed appearance and manner of personnel attempting to infiltrate the heroin community:

R: Oh yeah, the bulls are gettin' smarter, there's no doubt about it. . . . Look at the guys they send down now, the undercover bulls. They used to be big healthy lookin' assholes with size 12 shoes, hangin' around bein' a bit too pushy. Now they get these guys who look so much like dope fiends y'could never tell. Y'wonder how they ever got to be cops . . . They're cooler, too. Take their time gettin' in.

They Don't Do Things the Way They Did Before: Asserted Changes in the Style of Narcotics Enforcement

As potentially influential upon drug use statistics as the number and quality of enforcement personnel, is the *style* of enforcement. Informants were virtually unanimous in asserting that enforcement procedures and priorities had undergone dramatic stylistic revisions, that they appeared different from the way they did at an early period in the history of the local community. One informant expressed recognition of such changes in the following way:

The bulls don't do things the way they did before. Older people like me—not necessarily old but who've been around, y'know. . . . I can remember when the bulls did things very differently from the way your average one is now.

She continues, specifying the character of the stylistic changes:

Well for one thing you knew where you stood, they played by the rules. And they weren't as chickenshit about things.

Informants frequently spoke of current enforcement practices as "chickenshit" or "petty." For them, this implied an emphasis on the letter of the law, on offences of small magnitude, on ". . . things that you wouldn't get busted for before." For example, informants suggested that unlike an earlier period in the history of the local community, police would *now* attempt to arrest a person for being in possession of any heroin-using paraphernalia that might bear a minute trace of the substance—in their words, ". . . anything that might analyze. . . ."

R: The bulls are chickenshit now. They're out to pinch you for anything that might analyze—a spoon, a fit, an empty cup. That's what I got it on, a fuckin' cap for fuck sake, a fuckin' cap with hardly anythin' in it.
I: Just a cap?
R: Yeah, fuck, there was . . . I'd used better than three-quarters of it, more than that and they got it outa my purse.

Also, consider the following excerpt from an interview, wherein an informant describes the activity that resulted in her imprisonment for trafficking in narcotics:

I: So what was the offence that landed you in here this time?
R: Trafficking, they say I put out to an undercover bull.
I: But you didn't?
R: No. Its a bum rap. I just passed it to him. I wasn't puttin' out at the time. I was just with somebody when it happened.
I: Tell me what happened.
R: Well I was just in my car with this person I know and he was going to—He was putting out some stuff. This Rick guy—you've heard about him—he was gonna score from my friend. He was talkin' to him. My friend's

next to me in the passenger seat. So he takes the joint out and Rick goes around to the driver's side where I am—right out in the road—and my friend passes the joint to me and I give it to Rick. He just did that so he could get two busts at once.

Though informants characterized their adversaries as going to great lengths to enforce narcotics laws, i.e.,

the bulls'll do anything to make a pinch,

they reasonably expected enforcement to be constrained by proprieties they sometimes called the "rules of the game":

R: Its just a game, cops and junkies.
I: Games have got rules.
R: So's this one, believe me. If you don't go by the rules of the game you're fucked. Even the bulls go by rules.

In short, informants had a sense of activities that the police *would* and *would not* engage in ". . . to make a pinch." This notion was informed in part by an understanding of them as not only policemen but as well citizens, members-of-society, persons possessing sensibilities uncongenial to doing literally *anything* to enforce narcotics laws. Recently however, informants claim that the latitude of personally-congenial behaviours has widened considerably. Some related this widening to the presence in enforcement units of more *committed* personnel. In the words of an informant:

They've got bulls now who don't give a shit about nothin' except makin' pinches. Nothin' . . .

For informants, the following excerpt from an interview would exemplify this new, *liberated* enforcement style. In the late 1970's the events it relates were being spread—rumour like—throughout the heroin-using community.

I: What about this guy Fred, the narc who was just under.
R: Oh that asshole.
I: Did you ever run into him?
R: Oh, for sure. Everybody knew him. He was always around. Fuckin' earring on, just one, y'know. Big nigger hairdo. Fuckin' weird he looked. Leather jacket. Everybody knew the

prick. People figured he was solid. He even had me fooled, which is why I'm fuckin' here.

I: So everybody knew him.

R: Oh yeah. He was really into it. Only went home once in the eight fuckin' months he was on the street. That's dedication. I knew girls. . . . Well he was with a couple of girls. They were supportin' him, turnin' tricks for fuck sake. He was their old man. They were keepin' him fixed.

I: Keeping him fixed?

R: Fuck yes. He was wired up. He had to spend a whole week in the hospital afterwards. He was fuckin' wired up.

Another stylistic change cited by some informants was a refusal on the part of enforcement personnel to make "deals" with violators particularly on occasions where a detected offence involved more than one party. Solomon [5] provides an observation of the sort of deal in question:

(Name) boots in the bathroom door, knocking the girl inside into the bathtub. (Name) fishes into the sink for the needle in the midst of the scramble. They find the needle and take them both into the station. The guy had just shot up and was just about to fix his chick. He says he'll cop the rap if they let her go. The police agree to this deal.

An informant related an instance of the contemporary suspension of this practice:

I: So where's your husband now?

R: Oh he's over there (in the men's unit of the provincial prison), we got pinched together.

I: Two for the price of one.

R: Oh yeah, shit. He woulda taken the rap 'cause I was pregnant at the time, but the bulls wouldn't let him. He tried, though.

From informants' point-of-view, narcotics enforcement patterns in Western City have undergone dramatic revisions in terms of quality and style. Time and time again in interviews and casual conversation heroin users characterized current police strategies as "better" and stylistically "different" than they were at an earlier period.

That a number of changes appear to have occurred in enforcement activities is a matter of more than passing interest to those concerned

with the quality of official statistical portrayals of the volume, and volume trends of narcotics use. Indeed, the changes tend to erode one's faith in a reasonable correspondence between the portrayals and their referents. For example, the enforcement revisions appear to be *patterned,* suggesting not only the presence of systematic—rather than random and self-cancelling—error influences in the statistics, but the possibility as well that recent assertions of increases in the number of heroin users may be more an artifact of the revisions than a reflection of what is happening in the community. Taken together the changes in style and quality of enforcement provide for the appearance of an enlarged population independent of any *actual* enlargement.

The influence of enhanced quality of enforcement upon official portrayals of narcotic use is virtually self-announcing. Quite obviously, better enforcement increases the probability of arrest and thereby "builds in" an apparent increase in the number of drug users. Furthermore—as suggested earlier—it provides for the "spread" of drug-related activity to previously untainted communities.

Stylistic changes, too, suggest a potentially artificial swelling of community size. For example, the alleged refusal on the part of police to charge only one person in a multiple violator situation stands to inflate the number of arrests in unknown but potentially significant ways. Similarly, informants' characterization of enforcement personnel as newly "chickenshit" suggests not only that previously unnoticed offences are now being recorded but as well that the official records include arrests for violations that are technically but not socially valid.

Concluding Remarks

A continuing debate in the sociology of deviant behaviour concerns the degree to which official statistics accurately depict the actual volume and morphology of community deviance. At issue is not *whether* official portrayals depart from perfect correspondence with their referents: indeed, that they are somehow biased, somehow incomplete is widely acknowledged. Instead, debate centers on another question, specifically: can official statistics be taken as standing in some determinable relationship to the actual volume and morphology of a given activity or are the departures such that official statistics are essentially useless?

Commonly, sociologists have endeavoured to make the relationship determinable by attempting to identify the *source* of acknowledged bias, incompleteness, etc. Potentially more important than knowing the sources of such errors, however, is knowing their *character*. Indeed, the utility of official rates of deviant behaviour for research and policy design persists only when it can be demonstrated that factors which might erode the correspondence between such rates and their referents display a *random* character, thereby cancelling each other out.

This report has examined some of the enforcement activities that produce official portrayals of the volume and morphology of heroin use in and around a large city in the Canadian West.

Using data obtained via a program of unstructured interviews with heroin users resident in Western City, this report has described some of the ways in which police activity potentially influences official portrayals of the volume and morphology of non-medical drug use. In general, the data suggest a *pattern* and an unevenness of enforcement over time.

That the enforcement component of the narcotics environment cannot be presumed to be *static* is hardly a revelation. It remains the case, however, that many who use official statistics for research, policy, and political purposes attribute an unchanging nature to police procedures.

Recognition that a situation of uneven enforcement exists has numerous implications for users of official statistics. Some of these have been indicated here, though many more await explication. In general, however, the data presented suggest the rationality of a decreased reliance on official statistics as indicators of the extent and distribution of community heroin use.

REFERENCES

1. Bittner, Egon. 1967. "The Police on Skid-Row: A Study of Peace Keeping." *American Sociological Review, 32.*

2. Cicourel, Aaron V. 1968. *The Social Organization of Juvenile Justice.* New York: Wiley.

3. Piliavin, Irving and Scott Briar. "Police Encounters with Juveniles." *American Journal of Sociology, 70.*

4. Black, Donald J. 1970. "Production of Crime Rates," *American Sociological Review, 35.*

5. Solomon, Robert. 1970. Fieldnotes prepared for the Commission of Inquiry into the Non-Medical Use of Drugs. Unpublished manuscript.

7 THE DEVIANT IN COURT

The court is one of the important stations through which many deviants pass during their deviant careers. Like the police, court personnel have working conceptions to help them process deviants.

Reporting on the public defender, David Sudnow shows how cases are handled according to stereotypes of different kinds of crimes and criminals. In the second section Robert Emerson describes how court personnel place juveniles in particular categories. In the final section Jack Spencer shows how probation officers make sentence recommendations on the basis of defendants' answers to questions during presentence interviews.

Normal Crimes   DAVID SUDNOW

Two stances toward the utility of official classificatory schema for criminological research have been debated for years. One position, which might be termed that of the "revisionist" school, has it that the categories of the criminal law, e.g., "burglary," "petty theft," "homicide," etc., are not "homogeneous in respect to causation."[1] From an inspection of penal code descriptions of crimes, it is argued that the way persons seem to be assembled under the auspices of criminal law procedure is such as to produce classes of criminals who are, at least on theoretical grounds, as dissimilar in their social backgrounds and styles of activity as they are similar. The entries in the penal code, this school argues, require revision if sociological use is to be made of categories of crime and a classificatory scheme of etiological relevance is to be developed. Common attempts at such revision have included notions such as *"white collar* crime," and *"systematic* check forger," these conceptions constituting attempts to institute sociologically meaningful specifications which the operations of criminal law procedure and statutory legislation "fail" to achieve.

The other major perspective toward the sociologist's use of official categories and the criminal statistics compiled under their heading derives less from a concern with etiologically useful schema than from an interest in understanding the actual operations of the administrative legal system. Here, the categories of the criminal law are not regarded as useful or not, as objects to be either adopted, adapted, or ignored; rather, they are seen as constituting the basic conceptual equipment with which such people as judges, lawyers, policemen, and probation workers organize their everyday activities. The study of the actual use of official classification systems by actually employed administrative personnel regards the penal code as data, to be preserved intact; its use, both in organizing the work of legal representation, accusation, adjudication, and prognostication, and in compiling tallies of legal occurrences, is to be examined as one would examine any social activity. By sociologically regarding, rather than criticizing, rates of statistics and the categories employed to assemble them, one learns, it is promised, about the "rate producing agencies" and the assembling process.[2]

While the former perspective, the "revisionist" position, has yielded several fruitful products, the latter stance (commonly identified with what is rather loosely known as the "labelling" perspective), has been on the whole more promissory than productive, more programmatic than empirical. The present report will examine the operations of a Public Defender system in an effort to assess the warrant for the continued theoretical and empirical development of the position argued by Kitsuse and Cicourel. It will address the question: what of import for the sociological analysis of legal administration can be learned by describing the actual way the penal code is employed in the daily activities of legal representation? First, I shall consider the "guilty plea" as a way of handling criminal cases, focusing on some features of the penal code as a description of a population of defendants. Then I shall describe the Public Defender operation with special attention to the way de-

Reprinted from "Normal Crimes: Sociological Features of the Penal Code in a Public Defender Office," *Social Problems,* Vol. 12, No. 3 (Winter 1965), pp. 255–264, 269–270, by permission of the Society for the Study of Social Problems and the author.

This investigation is based on field observations of a Public Defender Office in a metropolitan California community. The research was conducted while the author was associated with the Center for the Study of Law and Society, University of California, Berkeley.

[1]D. R. Cressey, "Criminological Research and the Definition of Crimes," *American Journal of Sociology,* Vol. 61 (No. 6), 1951, p. 548. See also J. Hall, *Theft, Law and Society,* second edition, Indianapolis: Bobbs-Merrill, 1952; and E. Sutherland, *Principles of Criminology,* New York: Lippincott, 1947, p. 218. An extensive review of "typological developments" is available in D. C. Gibbons and D. L. Garrity, "Some Suggestions for the Development of Etiological and Treatment Theory in Criminology," *Social Forces,* Vol. 38 (No. 1), 1959.

[2]The most thorough statement of this position, borrowing from the writings of Harold Garfinkel, can be found in the recent critical article by J. I. Kitsuse and A. V. Cicourel, "A Note on the Official Use of Statistics," *Social Problems,*Vol. 11, No. 2 (Fall, 1963), pp. 131–139.

fendants are represented. The place of the guilty plea and penal code in this representation will be examined. Lastly, I shall briefly analyze the fashion in which the Public Defender prepares and conducts a "defense." The latter section will attempt to indicate the connection between certain prominent organizational features of the Public Defender system and the penal code's place in the routine operation of that system.

Guilty Pleas, Inclusion, and Normal Crimes

It is a commonly noted fact about the criminal court system generally, that the greatest proportion of cases are "settled" by a guilty plea.[3] In the county from which the following material is drawn, over 80 per cent of all cases "never go to trial." To describe the method of obtaining a guilty plea disposition, essential for the discussion to follow, I must distinguish between what shall be termed "necessarily-included-lesser-offenses" and "situationally-included-lesser-offenses." Of two offenses designated in the penal code, the lesser is considered to be that for which the length of required incarceration is the shorter period of time. *Inclusion* refers to the relation between two or more offenses. The "necessarily-included-lesser-offense" is a strictly legal notion:

Whether a lesser offense is included in the crime charged is a question of law to be determined solely from the definition and corpus delicti of the offense charged and of the lesser offense. . . . If all the elements of the corpus delicti of a lesser crime can be found in a list of all the elements of the offense charged, then only is the lesser included in the greater.[4]

Stated alternatively:

The test in this state of necessarily included offenses is simply that where an offense cannot be committed without necessarily committing another offense, the latter is a necessarily included offense.[5]

The implied negative is put: could Smith have committed A and not B? If the answer is yes, then B is not necessarily included in A. If the answer is no, B is necessarily included. While in a given case a battery might be committed in the course of a robbery, battery is not necessarily included in robbery. Petty theft is necessarily included in robbery but not in burglary. Burglary primarily involves the "intent" to acquire another's goods illegally (e.g., by breaking and entering); the consummation of the act need not occur for burglary to be committed. Theft, like robbery, requires that some item be stolen.

I shall call *lesser* offenses that are not necessarily but "only" *actually* included, "situationally-included-lesser-offenses." By statutory definition, necessarily included offenses are "actually" included. By actual here, I refer to the "way it occurs as a course of action." In the instance of necessary inclusion, the "way it occurs" is irrelevant. With situational inclusion, the "way it occurs" is definitive. In the former case, no particular course of action is referred to. In the latter, the scene and progress of the criminal activity would be analyzed.

The issue of necessary inclusion has special relevance for two procedural matters:

A. A man cannot be charged and/or convicted of two or more crimes any one of which is necessarily included in the others, unless the several crimes occur on separate occasions.

If a murder occurs, the defendant cannot be charged and/or convicted of both "homicide" and "intent to commit a murder," the latter of which is necessarily included in first degree murder. If, however, a defendant "intends to commit a homicide" against one person and commits a "homicide" against another, both offenses may be properly charged. While it is an extremely complex question as to the scope and definition of "in the course of," in most instances the rule is easily applied.

B. The judge cannot instruct the jury to consider as alternative crimes of which to find a

[3] See D. J. Newman, "Pleading Guilty for Considerations," *The Journal of Criminal Law, Criminology and Police Science,* Vol. 46, No. 6 (March–April, 1956), pp. 780–790. Also, M. Schwartz, *Cases and Materials on Professional Responsibility and the Administration of Criminal Justice,* San Francisco: Matthew Bender and Co., 1961, esp. pp. 79–105.

[4] C. W. Fricke, *California Criminal Law,* Los Angeles: The Legal Book Store, 1961, p. 41.

[5] People v. Greer, 30 Cal. 2d, 589.

defendant guilty, crimes that are not necessarily included in the charged crime or crimes.

If a man is charged with "statutory rape" the judge may instruct the jury to consider as a possible alternative conviction "contributing to the delinquency of a minor," as this offense is necessarily included in "statutory rape." He cannot however suggest that the alternative "intent to commit murder" be considered and the jury cannot find the defendant guilty of this latter crime, unless it is charged as a distinct offense in the complaint.

It is crucial to note that these restrictions apply only to (a) the relation between several charged offenses in a formal allegation, and (b) the alternatives allowable in a jury instruction. At any time before a case "goes to trial," alterations in the charging complaint may be made by the district attorney. The issue of necessary inclusion has no required bearing on (a) what offense(s) will be charged initially by the prosecutor, (b) what the relation is between the charge initially made and "what happened," or (c) what modifications may be made after the initial charge and the relation between initially charged offenses and those charged in modified complaints. It is this latter operation, the modification of the complaint, that is central to the guilty plea disposition.

Complaint alterations are made when a defendant agrees to plead guilty to an offense and thereby avoid a trial. The alteration occurs in the context of a "deal" consisting of an offer from the district attorney to alter the original charge in such a fashion that a lighter sentence will be incurred with a guilty plea than would be the case if the defendant were sentenced on the original charge. In return for this manipulation, the defendant agrees to plead guilty. The arrangement is proposed in this following format: "if you plead guilty to this new lesser offense, you will get less time in prison than if you plead not guilty to the original, greater charge and lose the trial." The decision must then be made whether or not the chances of obtaining complete acquittal at trial are great enough to warrant the risk of a loss and higher sentence if found guilty on the original charge. As we shall see below, it is a major job of the Public Defender, who mediates between the district attorney and the defendant, to convince his "client" that the chances of acquittal are too slight to warrant this risk.

If a man is charged with "drunkenness" and the Public Defender and Public Prosecutor (hereafter P.D. and D.A.) prefer not to have a trial, they seek to have the defendant agree to plead guilty. While it is occasionally possible, particularly with first offenders, for the P.D. to convince the defendant to plead guilty to the originally charged offense, most often it is felt that some "exchange" or "consideration" should be offered, i.e., a lesser offense charged.

To what offense can "drunkenness" be reduced? There is no statutorily designated crime that is necessarily included in the crime of "drunkenness." That is, if any of the statutorily required components of drunk behavior (its corpus delicti) are absent, there remains no offense of which the resultant description is a definition. For drunkenness there is, however, an offense that while not necessarily included is "typically-situationally-included," i.e., "typically" occurs as a feature of the way drunk persons are seen to behave—"disturbing the peace." The range of possible sentences is such that of the two offenses, "disturbing the peace" cannot call for as long a prison sentence as "drunkenness." If, in the course of going on a binge a person does so in such a fashion that "disturbing the peace" may be employed to describe some of his behavior, it would be considered as an alternative offense to offer in return for a guilty plea. A central question for the following analysis will be: in what fashion would he have to behave so that disturbing the peace would be considered a suitable reduction?

If a man is charged with "molesting a minor," there are not any necessarily included lesser offenses with which to charge him. Yet an alternative charge—"loitering around a schoolyard"—is often used as a reduction. As above, and central to our analysis the question is: what would the defendant's behavior be such that "loitering around a schoolyard" would constitute an appropriate alternative?

If a person is charged with "burglary," "petty theft" is not necessarily included. Routinely, however, "petty theft" is employed for reducing the charge of burglary. Again, we shall ask: what is the relation between burglary and petty theft and the *manner in which the former occurs* that warrants this reduction?

Offenses are regularly reduced to other offenses the latter of which are not necessarily or situationally included in the former. As I have already said the determination of whether or not offense X was situationally included in Y involves an analysis of the course of action that constitutes the criminal behavior. I must now turn to examine this mode of behavioral analysis.

When encountering a defendant who is charged with "assault with a deadly weapon," the P.D. asks: "what can this offense be reduced to so as to arrange for a guilty plea?" As the reduction is only to be proposed by the P.D. and accepted or not by the D.A., his question becomes "what reduction will be allowable?" (As shall be seen below, the P.D. and D.A. have institutionalized a common orientation to allowable reductions.) The method of reduction involves, as a general feature, the fact that the particular case in question is scrutinized to decide its membership in a class of similar cases. But *the penal code does not provide the reference for deciding the correspondence between the instant event and the general case; that is, it does not define the classes of offense types.* To decide, for purposes of finding a suitable reduction, if the instant case involves a "burglary," reference is not made to the statutory definition of "burglary." To decide what the situationally included offenses are in the instant case, the instant case is not analyzed as a *statutorily* referable course of action; rather, reference is made to a *non-statutorily* conceived class "burglary" and offenses that are typically situationally included in it, taken as a class of behavioral events. Stated again: in searching an instant case to decide what to *reduce it to,* there is no analysis of the statutorily referable elements of the instant case; instead, its membership in a class of events, the features of which cannot be described by the penal code, must be decided. An example will be useful. If a defendant is charged with burglary and the P.D. is concerned to propose a reduction to a lesser offense, he might search the elements of the burglary at hand to decide what other offenses were committed. The other offenses he might "discover" would be of two sorts: those necessarily and those situationally included. In attempting to decide those other offenses situationally included in the instant event, the instant event might be analyzed as a statutorily referable course of action. Or, as is the case with the P.D., the instant case might be analyzed to decide if it is a "burglary" in common with other "burglaries" conceived of in terms other than those provided by the statute.

Burglaries are routinely reduced to petty theft. If we were to analyze the way burglaries typically occur, petty theft is neither situationally nor necessarily included; when a burglary is committed, money or other goods are seldom illegally removed from some person's body. If we therefore analyzed burglaries, employing the penal code as our reference, and then searched the P.D.'s records to see how burglaries are reduced in the guilty plea, we could not establish a rule that would describe the transformation between the burglary cases statutorily described and the reductions routinely made (i.e., to "petty theft"). The rule must be sought elsewhere, in the character of the non-statutorily defined class of "burglaries," which I shall term *normal burglaries.*

Normal Crimes

In the course of routinely encountering persons charged with "petty theft," "burglary," "assault with a deadly weapon," "rape," "possession of marijuana," etc., the P.D. gains knowledge of the typical manner in which offenses of given classes are committed, the social characteristics of the persons who regularly commit them, the features of the settings in which they occur, the types of victims often involved, and the like. He learns to speak knowledgeably of "burglars," "petty thieves," "drunks," "rapists," "narcos," etc., and to attribute to them personal biographies, modes of usual criminal activity, criminal histories, psychological characteristics, and social backgrounds. The following characterizations are illustrative:

Most ADWs [assault with deadly weapon] start with fights over some girl.

These sex fiends [child molestation cases] usually hang around parks or schoolyards. But we often get fathers charged with these crimes. Usually the old man is out of work and stays at home when the wife goes to work and he plays around with his little daughter or something. A lot of these cases start when there is some marital trouble and the woman gets mad.

I don't know why most of them don't rob the big stores. They usually break into some cheap department store and steal some crummy item like a $9.95 record player you know.

Kids who start taking this stuff [narcotics] usually start out when some buddy gives them a cigarette and they smoke it for kicks. For some reason they always get caught in their cars, for speeding or something.

They can anticipate that point when persons are likely to get into trouble:

Dope addicts do O.K. until they lose a job or something and get back on the streets and, you know, meet the old boys. Someone tells them where to get some and there they are.

In the springtime, that's when we get all these sex crimes. You know, these kids play out in the schoolyard all day and these old men sit around and watch them jumping up and down. They get their ideas.

The P.D. learns that some kinds of offenders are likely to repeat the same offense while others are not repeat violators or, if they do commit crimes frequently, the crimes vary from occasion to occasion:

You almost never see a check man get caught for anything but checks—only an occasional drunk charge.

Burglars are usually multiple offenders, most times just burglaries or petty thefts. Petty thefts get started for almost anything—joy riding, drinking, all kinds of little things.

These narcos are usually through after the second violation or so. After the first time some stop, but when they start on the heavy stuff, they've had it.

I shall call *normal crimes* those occurrences whose typical features, e.g., the ways they usually occur and the characteristics of persons who commit them (as well as the typical victims and typical scenes), are known and attended to by the P.D. For any of a series of offense types the P.D. can provide some form of proverbial characterization. For example, *burglary* is seen as involving regular violators, no weapons, low-priced items, little property damage, lower class establishments, largely Negro defendants, independent operators, and a non-professional orientation to the crime. *Child molesting* is seen as typically entailing middle-aged strangers or lower class middle-aged fathers (few women), no actual physical penetration or severe tissue damage, mild fondling, petting, and stimulation, bad marriage circumstances, multiple offenders with the same offense repeatedly committed, a child complainant, via the mother, etc. *Narcotics* defendants are usually Negroes, not syndicated, persons who start by using small stuff, hostile with police officers, caught by some form of entrapment technique, etc. *Petty thefts* are about 50-50 Negro-white, unplanned offenses,

generally committed on lower class persons and don't get much money, don't often employ weapons, don't make living from thievery, usually younger defendants with long juvenile assaultive records, etc. *Drunkenness* offenders are lower class white and Negro, get drunk on wine and beer, have long histories of repeated drunkenness, don't hold down jobs, are usually arrested on the streets, seldom violate other penal code sections, etc.

Some general features of the normal crime as a way of attending to a category of persons and events may be mentioned:

1. The focus, in these characterizations, is not on particular individuals, but offense types. If asked "What are burglars like?" or "How are burglaries usually committed?", the P.D. does not feel obliged to refer to particular burglars and burglaries as the material for his answer.
2. The features attributed to offenders and offenses are often not of import for the statutory conception. In burglary, it is "irrelevant" for the statutory determination whether or not much damage was done to the premises (except where, for example, explosives were employed and a new statute could be invoked). Whether a defendant breaks a window or not, destroys property within the house or not, etc., does not affect his statutory classification as a burglar. While for robbery the presence or absence of a weapon sets the degree, whether the weapon is a machine gun or pocket knife is "immaterial." Whether the residence or business establishment in a burglary is located in a higher income area of the city is of no issue for the code requirements. And, generally, the defendant's race, class position, criminal history (in most offenses), personal attributes, and in particular style of committing offenses are features specifically not definitive of crimes under the auspices of the penal code. For deciding "Is this a 'burglary' case I have before me," however, the P.D.'s reference to this range of non-statutorily referable personal and social attributes, modes of operation, etc., is crucial for the arrangement of a guilty plea bargain.
3. The features attributed to offenders and offenses are, in their content, specific to the community in which the P.D. works. In other communities and historical periods the lists

would presumably differ. Narcotics violators in certain areas, for example, are syndicated in dope rackets or engage in systematic robbery as professional criminals, features which are not commonly encountered (or, at least, evidence for which is not systematically sought) in this community. Burglary in some cities will more often occur at large industrial plants, banking establishments, warehouses, etc. The P.D. refers to the population of defendants in the county as "our defendants" and qualifies his prototypical portrayals and knowledge of the typically operative social structures, "for our county." An older P.D., remembering the "old days," commented:

We used to have a lot more rapes than we do now, and they used to be much more violent. Things are duller now in. . . .

4. Offenses whose normal features are readily attended to are those which are routinely encountered in the courtroom. This feature is related to the last point. For embezzlement, bank robbery, gambling, prostitution, murder, arson, and some other uncommon offenses, the P.D. cannot readily supply anecdotal and proverbial characterizations. While there is some change in the frequencies of offense-type convictions over time, certain offenses are continually more common and others remain stably infrequent. . . . Troubles (are) created for the P.D. when offenses whose features are not readily known occur, and whose typicality is not easily constructed. . . .

5. Offenses are ecologically specified and attended to as normal or not according to the locales within which they are committed. The P.D. learns that burglaries usually occur in such and such areas of the city, petty thefts around this or that park, ADWs in these bars. Ecological patterns are seen as related to socio-economic variables and these in turn to typical modes of criminal and non-criminal activities. Knowing where an offense took place is thus, for the P.D., knowledge of the likely persons involved, the kind of scene in which the offense occurred, and the pattern of activity characteristic of such a place:

Almost all of our ADWs are in the same half a dozen bars. These places are Negro bars where

laborers come after hanging around the union halls trying to get some work. Nobody has any money and they drink too much. Tempers are high and almost anything can start happening.

6. One further important feature can be noted at this point. . . . The P.D. office consists of a staff of twelve full time attorneys. Knowledge of the properties of offense types of offenders, i.e., their normal, typical, or familiar attributes, constitutes the mark of any given attorney's competence. A major task in socializing the new P.D. deputy attorney consists in teaching him to recognize these attributes and to come to do so naturally. The achievement of competence as a P.D. is signalled by the gradual acquisition of professional command not simply of local penal code peculiarities and courtroom folklore, but, as importantly, of relevant features of the social structure and criminological wisdom. His grasp of that knowledge over the course of time is a key indication of his expertise. Below, in our brief account of some relevant organizational properties of the P.D. system, we shall have occasion to re-emphasize the competence-attesting aspects of the attorney's proper use of established sociological knowledge. Let us return to the mechanics of the guilty plea procedure as an example of the operation of the notion of normal crimes.

Over the course of their interaction and repeated "bargaining" discussions, the P.D. and D.A. have developed a set of unstated recipes for reducing original charges to lesser offenses. These recipes are specifically appropriate for use in instances of normal crimes and in such instances alone. "Typical" burglaries are reduced to petty theft, "typical" ADWs to simple assault, "typical" child molestation to loitering around a schoolyard, etc. The character of these recipes deserves attention.

The specific content of any reduction, i.e., what particular offense class X offenses will be reduced to, is such that the reduced offense may bear no obvious relation (neither situationally nor necessarily included) to the originally charged offense. The reduction of burglary to petty theft is an example. The important relation between the reduced offense and the original charge is such that the reduction from one to the other is considered "reasonable." At this point we shall only state what seems to be the general principle involved in deciding this reasonableness. The underlying premises cannot be explored at the present time, as that would involve a political analysis beyond the scope of the present report. *Both P.D. and D.A. are concerned to obtain a guilty plea wherever possible and thereby avoid a trial. At the same time, each party is concerned that the defendant "receive his due." The reduction of offense X to Y must be of such a character that the new sentence will depart from the anticipated sentence for the original charge to such a degree that the defendant is likely to plead guilty to the new charge and, at the same time, not so great that the defendant does not "get his due."*

In a homicide, while battery is a necessarily included offense, it will not be considered as a possible reduction. For a conviction of second degree murder a defendant could receive a life sentence in the penitentiary. For a battery conviction he would spend no more than six months in the county jail. In a homicide, however, "felony manslaughter," or "assault with a deadly weapon," whatever their relation to homicide as regards inclusion, would more closely approximate the sentence outcome that could be expected on a trial conviction of second degree murder. These alternatives would be considered. For burglary, a typically situationally included offense might be "disturbing the peace," "breaking and entering" or "destroying public property." "Petty theft," however, constitutes a reasonable lesser alternative to burglary as the sentence for petty theft will often range between six months and one year in the county jail and burglary regularly does not carry higher than two years in the state prison. "Disturbing the peace" would be a thirty-day sentence offense.

While the present purposes make the exposition of this calculus unnecessary, it can be noted and stressed that the particular content of the reduction does not necessarily correspond to a relation between the original and altered charge that could be described in either the terms of necessary or situational inclusion. Whatever the relation between the original and reduced charge, its essential feature resides in the spread between sentence likelihoods and the reasonableness of that spread, i.e., the balance it strikes between the defendant "getting his due" and at the same time "getting something less than he might so that he will plead guilty."

The procedure we want to clarify now, at the risk of some repetition, is the manner in which an instant case is examined to decide its membership in a class of "crimes such as this" (the category *normal crimes*). Let us start with an obvious case, burglary. As the typical reduction for burglary is petty theft and as petty theft is neither situationally nor necessarily included in burglary, the examination of the instant case is clearly not undertaken to decide whether petty theft is an appropriate statutory description. The concern is to establish the relation between the instant burglary and the normal category "burglaries" and, having decided a "sufficient correspondence," to now employ petty theft as the proposed reduction.

In scrutinizing the present burglary case, the P.D. seeks to establish that "this is a burglary just like any other." If that correspondence is not established, regardless of whether or not petty theft in fact was a feature of the way the crime was enacted, the reduction to petty theft would not be proposed. *The propriety of proposing petty theft as a reduction does not derive from its in-fact-existence in the present case, but is warranted or not by the relation of the present burglary to "burglaries," normally conceived.*

In a case of "child molestation" (officially called "lewd conduct with a minor"), the concern is to decide if this is a "typical child molestation case." While "loitering around a schoolyard" is frequently a feature of the way such crimes are instigated, establishing that the present defendant *did in fact loiter around a schoolyard* is secondary to the more general question "Is this a typical child molestation case?" What appears as a contradiction must be clarified by examining the status of "loitering around a schoolyard" as a typical feature of such child molestations. The typical character of "child molesting cases" does not stand or fall on the fact that "loitering around a schoolyard" is a feature of the way they are in fact committed. It is *not* that "loitering around a schoolyard" as a *statutorily referable behavior sequence* is part of typical "child molesting cases" but that "loitering around a schoolyard" as a *socially distinct mode of committing child molestations typifies the way such offenses are enacted.* "Strictly speaking," i.e., under the auspices of the statutory *corpus delicti*, "loitering around a schoolyard," requires *loitering, around, a schoolyard;* if one loiters around a ball park or a public recreation area, he "cannot," within a proper reading of the statute, be charged with loitering around a *schoolyard*. Yet "loitering around a school-yard," as a feature of the typical way such offenses as child molestations are committed, has the status not of a description of the way in *fact* (*fact*, statutorily decided) it occurred or typically occurs, but "the kind-of-social-activity-typically-associated-with-such-offenses." It is not its statutorily conceived features but its socially relevant‑attributes that gives "loitering around a schoolyard" its status as a feature of the class "normal child molestations." Whether the defendant loitered around a schoolyard or a ball park, and whether he loitered or "was passing by," "loitering around a schoolyard" as a reduction will be made if the defendant's activity was such that "he was hanging around some public place or another" and "was the kind of guy who hangs around schoolyards." As a component of the class of normal child molestation cases (of the variety where the victim is a stranger), "loitering around a schoolyard" typifies a mode of committing such offenses, the class of "such persons who do such things as hang around schoolyards and the like." A large variety of actual offenses could thus be nonetheless reduced to "loitering" if, as kinds of social activity, "loitering," conceived of as typifying a way of life, pattern of daily activity, social psychological circumstances, etc., characterized the conduct of the defendant. The young P.D. who would object "You can't reduce it to 'loitering'—he didn't really 'loiter,'" would be reprimanded: "Fella, you don't know how to use that term; he might as well have 'loitered'—it's the same kind of case as the others. . . ."

. . . The P.D. awaits to see if, how far, and in what ways the instant case is deviant. If the defendant is charged with burglary and a middle class establishment was burglarized, windows shattered, a large payroll sought after and a gun used, then the reduction to petty theft, generally employed for "normal burglaries," would be more difficult to arrange.

Generally, the P.D. doesn't have to discover the atypical kinds of cases through questioning. Rather, the D.A., in writing the original complaint, provides the P.D. with clues that the typical recipe, given the way the event occurred, will not be allowable. Where the way it occurs is such that it does not resemble normal burglaries and the routinely used penalty would reduce it *too far* commensurate with the way the crime

occurred, the D.A. frequently charges various situationally included offenses, indicating to the P.D. that the procedure to employ here is to suggest "dropping" some of the charges, leaving the originally charged greatest offense as it stands.

In the general case he doesn't charge all those offenses that he legally might. He might charge "child molesting" and "loitering around a schoolyard" but typically only the greater charge is made. The D.A. does so, so as to provide for a later reduction that will appear particularly lenient in that it seemingly involves a *change* in the charge. Were he to charge both molesting and loitering, he would be obliged, moreover, should the case come to trial, to introduce evidence for both offenses. The D.A. is thus always constrained not to set overly high charges or not situationally included multiple offenses by the possibility that the defendant will not plead guilty to a lesser offense and the case will go to trial. Of primary importance is that he doesn't charge multiple offenses so that the P.D. will be in the best position vis-à-vis the defendant. He thus charges the first complaint so as to provide for a "setup."

The alteration of charges must be made in open court. The P.D. requests to have a new plea entered:

P.D.: Your honor, in the interests of justice, my client would like to change his plea of not guilty to the charge of burglary and enter a plea of guilty to the charge of petty theft.
Judge: Is this new plea acceptable to the prosecution?
D.A.: Yes, your honor.

The prosecutor knows beforehand that the request will be made, and has agreed in advance to allow it.

I asked a P.D. how they felt about making such requests in open court, i.e., asking for a reduction from one offense to another when the latter is obviously not necessarily included and often (as is the case in burglary-to-petty theft) not situationally included. He summarized the office's feeling:

. . . in the old days, ten or so years ago, we didn't like to do it in front of the judge. What we used to do when we made a deal was that the D.A. would dismiss the original charge and write up a new complaint altogether. That took a lot of time. We had to re-arraign him all over again back in the muni court and everything. Besides, in the same courtroom, everyone used to know what was going on anyway. Now, we just ask for a change of plea to the lesser charge regardless of whether it's included or not. Nobody thinks twice about asking for petty theft on burglary or drunkenness on car theft, or something like that. It's just the way it's done.

Some restrictions are felt. Assaultive crimes (e.g., ADW, simple assault, attempted murder, etc.) will not be reduced to or from "money offenses" (burglary, robbery, theft) unless the latter involve weapons or some violence. Also, victimless crimes (narcotics, drunkenness) are not reduced to or from assaultive or "money offenses," unless there is some factual relation, e.g., drunkenness with a fight might turn out to be simple assault reduced to drunkenness.

For most cases that come before their courts, the P.D. and D.A. are able to employ reductions that are formulated for handling typical cases. While some burglaries, rapes, narcotics violations and petty thefts are instigated in strange ways and involve atypical facts, some manipulation in the way the initial charge is made can be used to set up a procedure to replace the simple charge-alteration form of reducing. . . .

Court Responses to Juveniles

ROBERT M. EMERSON

A Note on Total Denunciation

Consideration of the structural features of total denunciation provides additional insight into the processes of establishing moral character in the juvenile court. For a successful total denunciation must transcend routine denunciation by *foreclosing* all possible defenses and by *neutralizing* all possible sources of support.

Foreclosure of defenses available to the delinquent . . . has two related elements. First, in order to discredit moral character totally, it must be clearly demonstrated that the denounced delinquent has been given a great many "breaks" or "chances" which he has, however, rejected and spoiled. Such a demonstration is necessary to prove that the case is "hopeless," that the delinquent youth's character is so ruined as to preclude any possibility of reform. The role of the disregarded "chance" is clearly seen in the following case, where a probation officer convinces both judge and public defender to go along with his punitive recommendation by proving that the youth has received chances not even officially reported:

Two escapees from reform school were brought into court on a series of new complaints taken out by the police. Public defender argued that these complaints should be dismissed and the boys simply returned to the school. The probation officer, however, argued strongly that boys should be found delinquent on the new complaints (this would require reconsideration of their cases by the Youth Correction Authority, perhaps leading to an extension of their commitment). The probation officer described how one of his colleagues had worked hard on one of these cases earlier, giving the boy a great many chances, none of which did any good. The judge accepted the probation officer's recommendation.

After the hearing, the public defender admitted that he felt the probation officer had been right, acknowledging the validity of his picture of the character of this boy: "I did not realize he was such a bastard. . . . Apparently one of the probation officers had given him a lot of breaks. He had him on so many cases that he should be shot."

Second, it must be made to appear that the delinquent himself "messed up" the chances that he had been given. It should be established not only that the youth misbehaved on numerous occasions, but also that he did so in full knowledge of the possible consequences and with no valid excuse or extenuating circumstances. In this way, responsibility or "fault" for the imminent incarceration must fall completely on the denounced delinquent. Any official contribution to the youth's "messing up" (e.g., an official's intolerance) must be glossed over so that the delinquent bears total blame.

Court probation is in fact constructed so that responsibility for "messing up," should it occur, unavoidably falls on the delinquent. . . . Probationers are constantly warned that they will be committed if there is any further misconduct, and they are given a number of "breaks" on this condition. As one probation officer commented about a youth who had been "given a break" by the judge: "This way, if he gets committed, he knows he has it coming." Furthermore, the constant warnings and lectures against getting into trouble that occur throughout probation tend to undermine in advance the possibility of defending subsequent misbehavior. For example, it is difficult for a youth to excuse a new offense as the product of peer group influence when he has continually been warned to stay away from "bad friends."

A second key element in a successful total denunciation is the neutralization of all possible sources of support. There are several components in this neutralization. First, the assessment of discredited and "hopeless" character must be made to appear as a general consensus among all those concerned in the case. A delinquent without a spokesman—with no one to put in a good word for him—stands in a fundamentally discredited position.

Here the stance taken by the delinquent's lawyer, normally a public defender, becomes crucial. A vigorous defense and pitch by a lawyer often might dispel the appearance of consensus and weaken the denunciation. This occurs very rarely, however, because of court cooptation of the public defender. Working closely with the probation staff, the public defender comes to share their values and indexes of success and failure in delinquency cases. Consequently, he will generally concur with the court's highly negative assessments of delinquent moral character. As a public defender noted in response to a question about how he usually handled his cases in the juvenile court:

Generally I would find the probation officer handling the case and ask him: "What do you have on this kid? How bad is he?" He'll say: "Oh, he's bad!" Then he opens the probation folder to me, and I'll see he's got quite a record. Then I'll ask him, "What are you going to recommend?" He'll say, "Give him another chance. Or probation. Or we've got to put him away."

But probation officers don't make this last recommendation lightly. Generally they try to find a parent in the home, "someone who can keep him under control, someone who can watch him." But if the probation officer has given the kid a number of chances, it is a different story: "He's giving the kid chances and he keeps screwing up. . . . [Commitment will then be recommended.] And I say the kid deserves it. Before a kid goes away he's really got to be obnoxious—he will deserve it."

Adoption of probation standards for assessing delinquent character becomes crucial in total denunciation. The public defender is then in the position of arguing on behalf of a youth whose moral character has been totally discredited in his eyes and who he feels should indeed be committed. His courtroom defense will generally reflect this assessment. He will make only the most perfunctory motions of arguing that the delinquent be let off, and he will do so in a way that communicates an utter lack of conviction that this is a desirable course of action. Or, as in the following case, he will not even go through the motions of making a defense but will explicitly concur with the recommended incarceration and the grounds on which it rests:

A policeman told of finding an 11-year-old Negro boy in a laundry where a coin box had been looted. The officer reported that the boy had admitted committing the offense. Public defender waived cross-examination, and the judge found the youth delinquent.

Probation officer then delivered a rather lengthy report on the case. The boy had been sent to the Boys' Training Program and, while no great trouble, did not attend regularly. He had also recently been transferred to the Harris School and had been in trouble there. Probation officer recommended that the prior suspended sentence be revoked and the boy committed to the Youth Correction Authority.

Judge then asked the public defender if he had anything he wanted to say. Public defender: "The record more or less speaks for itself. He does not seem to have taken advantage of the opportunities the court has given him to straighten out." Then, after briefly reconferring with the probation officer, the judge ordered the commitment. Public defender waived the right of appeal.

Second, the denouncer must establish that in "messing up" and not taking advantage of the chances provided him, the denounced has created a situation in which there is *no other alternative open* but commitment to the Youth Correction Authority. In some cases, this may involve showing that the youth is so dangerous that commitment to the Authority is the only effective way he can be restrained; in others, demonstration that by his misbehavior the youth has completely destroyed all possible placements, including the one he has been in. It is only by dramatically showing in these ways that "there is nothing we can do with him" that the proposed commitment can be made to appear as an inevitable and objective necessity.

The fact that many total denunciations concentrate on proving that nothing else can be done with the case reflects the court's basic resistance to unwarrantable agency attempts to "dump" undesirable cases onto them for incarceration. The court feels that most of these institutions are too ready to give up on cases that from the court's point of view are still salvageable. To overcome this suspiciousness, the denouncer must not only present the youth's character as essentially corrupt and "hopeless," but also show that every effort has been made to work with him and every possible opportunity afforded him. The denouncer, in other words, must take pains to avoid appearing to be merely getting rid of a difficult and troublesome case simply to make his own work easier. This requires showing both that persistent efforts have been made to work with the case and that at the present time even extraordinary efforts cannot come up with anything as an alternative to incarceration.

A final aspect of demonstrating that there is no viable alternative to incarceration involves isolating the denounced delinquent from any kind of reputable sponsorship. In the usual case, where a parent acts as sponsor, successful total denunciation requires either that the parent be induced to denounce the youth and declare him fit only for incarceration or that the parent be discredited. In other cases, where the sponsor is a parental substitute, this sponsor must similarly be led to denounce the youth or be discredited. In this way, for example, sponsors who seek too aggressively to save delinquents considered overripe for commitment by other officials may encounter attacks on their motives, wisdom, or general moral character. This not only undermines the viability of any defense of character made by the sponsor, but also effectively isolates the delinquent by showing the unsuitability of his sponsorship as an alternative to commitment. . . .

Counter-denunciation

As noted earlier, the courtroom proceeding routinely comes to involve a denunciation of the accused delinquent in the course of a confrontation between him and his accusers. This fact creates the conditions for the use of *counter-denunciation* as a defensive strategy. This strategy seeks to undermine the discrediting implications of the accusation by attacking the actions, motives and/or character of one's accusers.

The underlying phenomenon in counter-denunciation has been noted in a number of other contexts. McCorkle and Korn, for example, have analyzed the concept of the "rejection of the rejectors" as a defensive reaction to imprisonment (1964, p. 520). Similarly, Sykes and Matza explain the "condemnation of the condemners" in the process of neutralization in the following terms: "The delinquent shifts the focus of attention from his own deviant acts to the motives and behaviors of those who disapprove of his violations" (1957, p. 668). The concept of counter-denunciation, in contrast, focuses on the communicative work which accomplishes this shift of attention. Furthermore, it gains relevance as a defense against attempted character discrediting. Use of this strategy, however, is extremely risky in the court setting. While counter-denunciation may appear to the delinquent as a "natural" defense as he perceives the circumstances of his case, it tends to challenge fundamental court commitments and hence, even when handled with extreme care, often only confirms the denunciation.

It is striking that counter-denunciation has the greatest likelihood of success in cases where the complainant or denouncer lacks official stature or where the initiative rests predominantly with private parties who have clearly forced official action. Under these circumstances the wrongful quality of the offense can be greatly reduced if not wholly eliminated by showing that the initiator of the complaint was at least partially to blame for the illegal act. For example:

A 16-year-old Negro boy, Johnny Haskin, was charged with assault and battery on two teenaged girls who lived near his family in a public housing project. Although a juvenile officer brought the case into court, he was clearly acting on the initiative of the two girls and their mother, for he had had no direct contact with the incident and did not testify about it. He simply put the two girls on the stand and let them tell about what happened. This was fairly confused, but eventually it appeared that Johnny Haskin had been slapping the younger sister in the hall of the project when the older girl had pulled him off. He had then threatened her with a knife. The girls admitted that there had been fighting in the hall for some time, and that they had been involved, but put the blame on Johnny for starting it. Mrs. Haskin, however, spoke up from the back of the room, and told about a gang of boys coming around to get her son (apparently justifying Johnny's carrying a knife). And Johnny himself denied that he had started the fighting, claiming that the younger girl had hit him with a bat and threatened him first.

Judge then lectured both families for fighting, and placed Johnny on probation for nine months, despite a rather long prior record.

In this case, by establishing that the girls had also been fighting, the boy was at least partially exonerated. The success of this strategy is seen in the fact that the judge lectured both families, and then gave the boy what was a mild sentence in light of his prior court record.

Similarly, the possibility of discrediting the victim, thereby invalidating the complaint, becomes apparent in the following "rape" case:

Two Negro boys, ages 12 and 13, had admitted forcing "relations" on a 12-year-old girl in a schoolyard, the police reported. After a full report on the incidents surrounding the offense, the judge asked the policemen: "What kind of girl is she?" Officer: "I checked with Reverend Frost [the girl's minister and the person instrumental in reporting this incident] and he said she was a good girl."

As the judge's query implies, the reprehensibility of this act can only be determined in relation to the assessed character of the girl victim. Had the police or the accused brought up evidence of a bad reputation or incidents suggesting "loose" or "promiscuous" behavior, the force of the complaint would have been undermined.

In the above cases, successful counter-denunciation of the complainants would undermine the moral basis of their involvement in the incident, thereby discrediting their grounds for initiating the complaint. But this merely shifts part of the responsibility for an offense onto the complaining party and does not affect the wrongful nature of the act per se. Thus, by denouncing the general character of the complainant and the nature of his involvement in the offense, the accused does not so much clear himself as diminish his guilt. If the offense involved is serious enough and the culpability of the complainant not directly related to the offense, therefore, this strategy may have little impact.

For example, in the homosexuality-tinged case of car theft . . . both the accused and his father tried to support their contention that the car owner was lying by pointing to his discredited character. But the "victim's" homosexuality had no real connection with the act of stealing the car nor with the threatened physical violence it entailed, and hence did not affect the judge's evaluation of the act and of the delinquent's character. Under these circumstances, the soiled nature of the victim simply was not considered sufficiently extenuating to dissolve the reprehensibility of the act.[1]

In general, then, a successful counter-denunciation must discredit not only the general character of the denouncer but also his immediate purpose or motive in making the complaint. Only in this way can the counter-denunciation cut the ground out from under the wrongfulness of the alleged offense. For example:

An 11-year-old Negro boy was charged with wantonly damaging the car of an older Negro man, Frankie Williams, with a BB gun. With the boy was his mother, a respectably dressed woman, a white lawyer, and a white couple who served as character witnesses.

A juvenile officer brought the case in and then called Mr. Williams up to testify. The witness told of going outside to shovel his car out of the snow several weeks previously and finding his windshield damaged in several places. He had noticed the boy at this time leaning out of the window of his house with a BB gun. Lawyer then cross-examined, getting Williams to admit that he had been bickering with the family for some time, and that a year before the mother had accused him of swearing at her son and had tried to get a court complaint against him. (Judge ruled this irrelevant after Williams had acknowledged it.) Williams seemed flustered, and grew angry under the questioning, claiming that because of the boy's shooting he would not be able to get an inspection sticker for his car.

Juvenile officer then told judge that although he had not investigated the case, his partner reported that the marks on the windshield were not consistent with a BB gun. Williams had also admitted that he had not looked for any BB pellets. On the basis of this evidence, the judge found the boy not delinquent. He then severely warned all parties in the case: "I'm going to tell you I do not want any more contests between these two families. Do you understand?"

Here, by showing that the complainant had both a selfish motive for complaining about his damaged windshield (to help get it repaired) and a grudge against the defendant and his family, as well as bringing out the lack of concrete evidence to substantiate the charge, the lawyer was able to get the complaint totally dismissed. . . .

Finally, successful counter-denunciation requires that the denounced provide a convincing account for what he claims is an illegitimate accusation. The court will reject any implication that one person will gratuitously accuse another of something he has not done. The youth in the following case can provide this kind of account:

Five young boys were charged with vandalism and with starting a fire in a public school. Juvenile officer explained that he had investigated the incident with the school principal, getting two of the boys to admit their part in the vandalism. These two boys had implicated the other three, all of whom denied the charge.

The judge then took over the questioning, trying to determine whether the three accused had in fact been in school. In this he leaned heavily on finding out why

---

[1]Note, however, that even though this denunciation succeeded, the denouncer suffered both discrediting and penalty. Immediately after the delinquency case had been decided the police took out a complaint for "contributing to the delinquency of a minor" against him, based on his admitted homosexual activities with the youth. This "contributing" case was brought before the juvenile court later that same morning, complainant and accused changed places, and the first denouncer was found guilty, primarily from what he had revealed about his behavior earlier in establishing the delinquency complaint.

the first two boys should lie. One of the accused, Ralph Kent, defended himself by saying he had not been at the school and did not know the boy who had named him. Judge asked how this boy had then been able to identify him. Kent replied that he had been a monitor at school, and one of his accusers might have seen him there. And he used to take the other accuser to the basement [lavatory] because the teacher would not trust him alone for fear he would leave the school.

The two other boys continued to deny any involvement in the incident, but could provide no reason why they should be accused unjustly. The judge told them he felt they were lying, and asked several times: "Can you give me a good reason why these boys would put you in it?" Finally he pointed toward Kent and commented: "He's the only one I'm convinced wasn't there." He then asked Kent several questions about what he did as a monitor. When it came to dispositions, Kent was continued without a finding while the four other boys were found delinquent.

In this situation an accused delinquent was able to establish his own reputable character in school (later confirmed by the probation report on his school record), the discredited character of one of his accusers, and a probable motive for their denunciation of him (resentment toward his privileges and position in school) in a few brief sentences. It should be noted, however, that this successful counter-denunciation was undoubtedly facilitated by the fact that denouncers and denounced were peers. It is incomparably more difficult for a youth to establish any acceptable reason why an adult should want to accuse and discredit him wrongfully.

Counter-denunciation occurs most routinely with offenses arising out of the family situation and involving complaints initiated by parents against their own children. Here again it is possible for the child to cast doubt on the parents' motives in taking court action, and on the parents' general character:

A Negro woman with a strong West Indian accent had brought an incorrigible child complaint against her 16-year-old daughter. The mother reported: "She never says anything to me, only to ask, 'Gimme car fare, gimme lunch money.' . . . As for the respect she gave me I don't think I have to tolerate her!" The daughter countered that her mother never let her do anything, and simply made things unbearable for her around the house. She went out nights, as her mother claimed, but only to go over to a girl friend's house to sleep.

This case was continued for several months, during which time a probation officer worked with the girl and the court clinic saw mother and daughter. The psychiatrist there felt that the mother was "very angry and cold." Eventually an arrangement was made to let the girl move in with an older sister.

In this case the daughter was effectively able to blame her mother and her intolerance for the troubled situation in the home. But in addition, counter-denunciation may also shift the focus of the court inquiry from the misconduct charged to the youth onto incidents involving the parents. This shift of attention facilitated the successful counter-denunciation in the following case:

A 16-year-old white girl from a town some distance from the city was charged with shoplifting. But as the incident was described by the police, it became clear that this offense had occurred because the girl had run away from home and needed clean clothes. Police related what the girl had said about running away: She had been babysitting at home and was visited by her boyfriend, who had been forbidden in the house. Her father had come home, discovered this, and beaten her with a strap. (The girl's face still appeared somewhat battered with a large black-and-blue mark on one cheek, although the court session occurred at least three days after the beating.) She had run away that night.

The rest of the hearing centered not on the theft but on the running away and the incident which precipitated it. After the police evidence, the judge asked the girl: "How did you get that mark on your face?" Girl: "My father hit me." Judge: "With his fist?" Girl (hesitating): "Yes, it must have been his fist." Later in the proceeding, the judge asked the girl specifically why she had run away. She emphasized that she had not tried to hide anything; the kids had been up until eleven and the boy had left his bike out front. "I didn't try to hide it. I told them he'd been there."

With this her father rose to defend himself, arguing with some agitation: ". . . His clothes were loose. Her clothes were loose. Her bra was on the floor. . . . She was not punished for the boy being in the house, but for what she did." Girl (turning toward her father): "What about my eye?" Father: "She got that when she fell out of the bed (angrily, but directed toward the judge). Girl (just as angrily): "What about the black and blue marks?" Father: "Those must have been from the strap."

The relatively high probability of successful counter-denunciation in cases arising from family situations points up the most critical contingency in the use of this protective strategy, the choice of an appropriate object. Denouncers with close and permanent relations with the denounced are particularly vulnerable to counter-denunciation, as the accusation is apt to rest solely on their word and illegitimate motives for the denunciation may be readily apparent. But again, where relations between the two parties are more distant, counter-denunciation has more chance of success where the denouncer is of more or less equivalent status with the denounced. Thus, the judge can be easily convinced that a schoolmate might unjustly accuse one from jealousy, but will reject any contention that an adult woman would lie about an attempted purse-snatching incident.

While a denounced youth has a fair chance of successfully discrediting a complainant of his own age, and some chance where the complainant is a family member, counter-denunciations directed against officials, particularly against the most frequent complainants in the juvenile court, the police, almost inevitably fail. In fact, to attempt to counterattack the police, and to a lesser extent, other officials, is to risk fundamentally discrediting moral character, for the court recoils against all attacks on the moral authority of any part of the official legal system.

One reflection of this is the court's routine refusal to acknowledge complaints of *unfair* treatment at the hands of the police. On occasion, for example, parents complain that their children were arrested and brought to court while others involved in the incident were not. Judges regularly refuse to inquire into such practices:

Two young Puerto Rican boys were charged with shooting a BB gun. After police testimony, their mother said something in Spanish, and their priest-translator explained to the judge: "What they've been asking all morning is why they did not bring the other two boys." The judge replied: "I can only deal with those cases that are before me. I can't go beyond that and ask about these other boys that are not here."

Similarly, in this same case the judge refused to inquire into a complaint of police brutality when the mother complained that one boy had been hit on the head, saying: "The question of whether he was injured is not the question for me right now."

But beyond this, the court will often go to great lengths to protect and defend the public character of the police when it is attacked during a formal proceeding. To accuse a policeman of acting for personal motives, or of dishonesty in the course of his duties, not only brings immediate sanctions from the court, but also tends to discredit basically the character of the delinquent accuser. Accusations of this nature threaten the basic ceremonial order of the court proceeding and hence the legitimacy of the legal order itself. . . .

REFERENCES

McCorkle, Lloyd W., and Richard Korn. 1964. "Resocialization Within Walls." In David Dressler (ed.), *Readings in Criminology and Penology*. New York: Columbia University Press.

Sykes, Gresham M., and David Matza. 1957. "Techniques of Neutralization: A Theory of Delinquency." *American Sociological Review*, 22:664–70.

Probation Officer–Defendant Negotiations

JACK W. SPENCER

One of the principal concerns of sociologists and criminologists has been how criminal defendants are sentenced for their crimes. Probation officers (POs) play a significant role in the sentencing process because they make sentencing recommendations to the courts. Therefore, an examination of how POs make their recommendations is crucial for a full understanding of this sentencing process. Previous research has failed to examine important aspects of the processes whereby POs arrive at these recommendations.

Historically, the dominant approach to the study of criminal behavior has been deterministic. Thus, most of the researchers and theorists in this area have been concerned with delineating the causal factors associated with the occurrence of crime (Bonger, 1916; Cloward and Ohlin, 1960; Merton, 1957; Sellin, 1938). Since the 1930s, other sociologists and criminologists have reacted to this deterministic approach by stressing the importance of examining the processes of formal social reaction to criminal behavior (Becker, 1963; Cicourel, 1968; Lemert, 1951; Schur, 1971; Tannenbaum, 1938). These theorists have argued that it is the operation of the criminal justice system which defines or labels criminal behavior. In the mid-1970s, research on the criminal justice system began to take a deterministic approach. That is, this research examined the causal factors associated with criminal justice outcomes. Much of this research was concerned with the influence of legal vs. extra-legal variables on sentencing decisions (Bernstein *et al.*, 1977; Burke and Turk, 1975; Chiricos and Waldo, 1975).

This same approach has dominated research on decision-making by POs. That is, researchers have examined the variables which determine the decision which POs make (Carter, 1967; Dembo, 1972; Hagan, 1977; Reed and King, 1966).[1] One of these decisions is the sentence recommendation that POs make to the courts. While

this approach has led to important insights it has left an important gap in our understanding of how POs arrive at these recommendations.

What has been left relatively unexamined are the *processes* whereby POs first interview defendants and then make recommendations. Previous research has found that a defendant's attitude is an important factor in these recommendations (Carter, 1967; Gross, 1967). However, we know little about the presentencing interview within which POs assess defendants' attitudes, nor how POs link this information with other factors in deciding what recommendation to make.

This paper is intended to bridge this gap. First, I discuss a set of factors—defendant's subjective orientations to criminal behavior—which includes defendants' attitudes. Next, I examine how POs assess these subjective orientations during presentence interviews. Finally, I discuss how these assessments affect the ways POs label defendants for the purpose of making sentence recommendations.

Method

In 1981, I spent nine months collecting data on the organizational processing of criminal defendants at a county probation department in the midwestern United States. This project was part of my dissertation research. The present study is based on part of that data, and consists of: (1) field notes of observations; (2) interviews with POs; and (3) tape recordings of presentencing interviews.

The probation department I studied comprised four divisions: felony, misdemeanor, juvenile, and substance-abuse. The staff consisted of a chief PO, three division heads, six POs, two substance-abuse counselors, and various support staff. I excluded the juvenile and substance-abuse division from the study early in

"Accounts, Attitudes, and Solutions: Probation Officer-Defendant Negotiations of Subjective Orientations," *Social Problems*, Vol. 30, No. 5 (June, 1983), pp. 570–581, by permission of the Society for the Study of Social Problems and the author.

[1] There are, of course, exceptions. For example, Cicourel (1968) empirically examined the routine practices of police and POs in the processing of juvenile cases. Prus and Stratton (1976) delineate a process model of how parole officers move from individual definitions to official action.

the research.[2] The chief and all the POs in the felony and misdemeanor divisions agreed to participate in the research. Before each presentencing interview I identified myself, explained the nature of my research to the defendant involved, and obtained his or her written consent to record the interaction. No defendants refused to be included in the study.

The POs were extremely helpful, allowing me access to most sources of information that I needed, offering important ethnographic data during informal conversations, and discussing particular cases which I included in the study. After a short time my presence in the department became taken for granted: I was allowed to occupy a desk while not observing presentencing interviews and, when needed, would answer the telephones and run errands.

I collected data on 23 presentencing interviews in the following manner. After obtaining written consent from the defendant, I went to a corner of the room and started the tape recorder. During the interview I noted characteristics of the defendant and salient aspects of the interaction not captured by the tape recorder, such as nonverbal behavior. After the interview was completed and the defendant had left the room, I interviewed the POs about their perception of the interaction, the defendant, and the offense.

The method I used to analyze the data closely resembles Glaser and Strauss's (1967) grounded theory approach. Thus, I formulated theoretical propositions and constructs from the data, modifying these by comparing them with subsequent data, and developing hypotheses which accounted for the relationships between these constructs. I also used Cicourel's (1975, 1978, 1980) model of discourse processes which stresses the relationship between these processes, various predicates of knowledge which participants possess, and how the participants articulate or link that knowledge with information which emerges in the interactive setting.

Defendants' Subjective Orientations

Most previous research on sentencing recommendations has divided input factors into legal and extra-legal categories, in the process either ignoring such factors as attitudes or categorizing them as extra-legal. The POs I studied considered attitudes and other related factors in making sentencing recommendations. However, such factors were relatively distinct from those traditionally designated extra-legal (e.g., race, age, employment stability) both in how they were elicited in presentencing interviews and how they affected sentence recommendations. This finding led me to formulate a third category of factors, which I call defendant's subjective orientations to their criminal behavior. I found four subjective orientations to be relevant: (1) accounts for the offenses; (2) attitudes toward the offenses; (3) attitudes toward the consequences of the offenses; and (4) attitudes toward changing their behavior. I discuss each of these in turn.

Accounts for the Offenses

According to Scott and Lyman (1968:46) an account is "a statement made by a social actor to explain unanticipated or untoward behavior." In my data the defendants' accounts consisted of two elements: the factors involved in the commission of the offense and the degree of intent involved.

There were generally two types of *factors:* motivating and causal. Motivating factors involved problematic situations in which the defendants sought to accomplish some particular goal and to which the commission of the offenses presented a solution. Causal factors, on the other hand, led to the commission of the offenses, in spite of the conscious intentions of the defendants. The degree of responsibility the defendants claimed decided the type of factor.

The amount of prior planning by the defendant determined the *degree of intent.* Relevant components of this element included the point at which defendants had decided to commit the offense and whether they had considered the method by which it would be committed. Of primary importance to the POs was whether the offense was spontaneous or calculated. Combining these two elements—the factors and the degree of intent—results in a four-fold typology of

[2] I excluded the juvenile division because of the high degree of confidentiality surrounding juvenile cases in the county. I would not have been allowed access to certain data, and POs anticipated some difficulty in obtaining consent from the juveniles' parents. Substance-abuse was excluded because its goals and focus (clinical evaluation and counseling) were distinct from the rest of the divisions' goals of sentencing recommendations and supervision. While this data would have been valuable for comparative analysis, the lack of sufficient time and other resources precluded such an expansion of the present study.

accounts, of which only two will concern us here: rational and non-rational accounts.[3]

Rational accounts were ones in which defendants claimed some degree of prior planning and in which they had been in control of their actions. For example, one rational account for shoplifting involved a defendant who claimed to have desired an item yet, lacking sufficient money, decided to steal it. *Non-rational accounts* were those in which defendants claimed they committed the offense relatively spontaneously and because of some identifiable factor which was beyond their immediate control. For example, one defendant claimed he had assaulted someone because he had been drunk and their argument had gotten "out of hand."

Defendants' accounts were important for sentencing recommendations for four reasons: (1) The POs believed planned offenses deserved more severe sanctions than those which were more spontaneous. (2) POs sometimes regarded a causal factor as a mitigating circumstance deserving a more lenient recommendation. (3) The type of account could affect the type of recommendation. For example, in some cases a claim that alcohol or drugs led to the commission of an offense encouraged the PO to recommend counseling rather than incarceration. (4) In lieu of information to the contrary, POs did not usually accept non-rational accounts since they mitigate some of the defendant's responsibility. Thus, defendants who offered rational accounts were generally viewed as cooperative and responsible; those who made (unwarranted) claims to non-rational accounts were seen as presenting a "line."

Attitudes Toward the Offense

POs generally viewed any offense which resulted in a conviction as a serious affair. For example, POs viewed with concern the theft of even a few inexpensive items from a store because such losses to stores create higher prices for customers. Similarly, pranks were defined as serious since they usually involved theft or property damage, or both.

POs regarded as relevant two basic components of defendants' attitudes toward their offense—their attitude toward the wrongfulness of the act and toward the seriousness of the act. Defendants who accepted that their behavior was wrong or illegal, and who shared the PO's definition that their behavior was serious, were viewed as holding an acceptable attitude. In addition, POs regarded defendants' attitudes as indicators of underlying character or behavior traits. Thus, defendants who exhibited acceptable attitudes were viewed as possessing some generally redeeming traits which made them less likely to commit subsequent offenses. POs viewed unacceptable attitudes, however, as cause for more severe sanctions, since they believed that such defendants were more likely to become recidivists.[4] In addition, defendants who did not even pay lip service to acceptable attitudes in presenting interviews were seen as not taking the proceedings seriously—in effect, an improper demeanor.

Attitudes Toward the Consequences

POs expected defendants to anticipate the effects of their behavior. That is, if a certain behavioral option was expected to have negative consequences, this was supposed to act as at least a partial deterrent to that behavior. Thus, POs regarded defendants' attitudes toward the consequences of their behavior as related to their likelihood of recidivism. Two sets of consequences are relevant: (1) the possible legal sanctions; and (2) the non-legal, negative effects of a criminal record on current or future endeavors. In both instances, POs considered an acceptable attitude one in which the defendant expressed concern about these consequences. This concern included both an awareness of the likelihood of the consequences and of their adverse nature.

Attitudes Toward Changing Their Behavior

POs believed that people do not engage in serious violations of the law under normal cir-

---

[3] These two types of accounts, and two others (opportunistic and pathological), form a typology of accounts obtained by intersecting the types of factors with degree of intent. Thus, an opportunistic account involved motivating factors and no prior planning, while a pathological account was one in which defendants claimed the offense was due to causal factors but in which they engaged in prior planning. While these latter two types of accounts are logical possibilities, they rarely occurred in the data and, thus, were not particularly important for this study.

[4] I am not aware of any research which addresses this issue. However, the POs held this view because unacceptable attitudes were common among defendants who were, or became, recidivists.

cumstances. The corollary of this maxim was that serious violations were the result or manifestation of some problem, to which there was an identifiable solution. In this regard, POs viewed as relevant non-legal solutions which defendants could pursue. In an important sense, POs viewed how defendants felt about these solutions as an indication of their attitudes toward changing their criminal behavior. When defendants offered non-rational accounts for their offenses, solutions were sought for the particular causal factor. For example, if an offense was caused by a defendant's alcoholism, the PO addressed solutions which the defendant could pursue and which would alleviate the problem, such as counseling. However, when rational accounts were offered, the POs located the problem in the defendant's choices of behaviors, and attention was focused on identifying more appropriate (legal) alternatives. For example, one defendant accounted for his theft of food by saying he was out of money and hadn't eaten in two days. The PO tried to point out to the defendant that there were legal alternatives available, such as welfare, which would have solved his problem. In either case, if defendants expressed a willingness to pursue a solution, they were viewed as possessing acceptable attitudes toward changing their behavior.

POs viewed as acceptable three attitudes by defendants toward changing their behavior. (1) Defendants were expected to express concern about the particular factor (causal or motivating) which had been identified. (2) They were expected to express an awareness of an appropriate solution. (3) They were expected to express a willingness to pursue these solutions—that is, demonstrate that these solutions were viewed as both feasible and desirable. POs viewed defendants who expressed these acceptable attitudes as less likely to commit further offenses, since they were more likely to solve the problem and thus change their behavior. In these cases, sentence recommendations were less severe, since legal sanctions were less necessary as a deterrent.

Negotiations Between Probation Officers and Defendants

In addition to legal and extra-legal factors, POs took into account defendants' subjective orientations to criminal behavior in deciding what sentence to recommend. POs elicited most information about legal and extra-legal factors by asking defendants simple questions. However, POs elicited information about subjective orientations in a more complex way. They engaged defendants in a process of negotiation aimed at reaching a shared agreement which at least approximated the POs' notions of propriety or acceptability. In conducting these negotiations, POs used a variety of interactional strategies to seek desired responses in each of the four subjective orientations.[5]

Accounts for the Offenses

The POs generally viewed rational accounts as more reasonable and acceptable than nonrational accounts. Therefore, when they requested accounts from defendants, their questions implied or assumed a request for a rational account. The POs used two strategies in requesting such accounts.

1. They asked a question which implied a decision-making process on the part of the defendant (D).

   PO: Why'dja decide to take the motorcycle?

2. They asked a series of indirect questions in an attempt to establish the conditions for a rational account.

   PO: You knew you were on probation when you did this.
   D: Uh huh.
   PO: Did that concern you at all? Did you think about that?

Through either of these strategies, the POs attempted to elicit a rational account from the de-

---

[5] It should be noted that these negotiations were primarily invoked by POs when defendants expressed unreasonable or unacceptable orientations. When a defendant expressed an acceptable or reasonable orientation the need for negotiation on that point was precluded and the POs introduced another topic. The majority of strategies discussed below were used by POs in attempting to change (or assess the possibility of changing) defendants' orientations when they were deemed unacceptable.

fendants. If the defendants' responses confirmed the POs' assumptions about such an account, the negotiation was concluded. However, when responses did not confirm that assumption, the negotiation took a different format.

The defendants were viewed by POs as more likely to offer a non-rational account, in the hope of mitigating some responsibility on their part. Due to this, the POs responded to such accounts with an additional request to establish specific conditions for a rational account.

> PO: Why'dja decide to take the motorcycle?
> D: Uh, its stupidity. We were messing around and then—and we didn't have no reason.
> PO: What were you gonna do with it?

If the response to this request still contained a claim to a non-rational account, the PO turned to a series of questions in an attempt to establish conditions for that type of account.

> PO: What were you gonna do with [the motorcycle]?
> D: I don't know.
> PO: How drunk or high were ya?
> D: I was still aware of what was goin on.
> PO: What did you have to drink or smoke that night?
> D: Uhm, we'd been drinking beer and smoking marijuana; and going around to different parties all that night.

Only when such conditions were established did the PO accept a non-rational account.

While the POs accepted claims to rational accounts unconditionally, claims to non-rational accounts were not so readily accepted. Further, while they made direct requests for rational accounts, requests for non-rational accounts were only approached in a piecemeal fashion which did not allow the defendant to make a singular, direct claim to that type of account.

Attitudes Toward the Offenses

While the POs defined defendants' offenses as wrong and serious enough to be concerned about, defendants did not always share this definition. The POs used four strategies in trying to obtain defendants' agreement with their definition of criminal offenses.

1. The POs would request examples of behaviors which defendants felt were subsumed under the latters' definition. The PO would then show the defendants that these behaviors were actually examples of the POs definition of the offense.

> D: I realize there's a difference between stealing and a college prank.
> PO: Give me another example of a college prank—a legitimate college prank.
> D: Another thing [people on] my [dormitory] floor have done, which I think is worse than the thing that I did, and that's paintin' a bridge outside of the front of the dorm, which is not the dorm's property. It's university property. That's permanently defacing it. I would say [this] is a college prank that was worse than the one I did.
> PO: So there's somethin' you would call a prank that you admitted was wrong. It's probably a criminal offense, yet you think they're mainly college pranks.

The effectiveness of this strategy lay in the POs ability to convince the defendants that, since these examples can be subsumed under the PO's definition, so could the defendants' current offenses.

2. The POs pointed out the seriousness of the offenses' potential or actual harm to others. For example, one defendant was convicted of shoplifting after eating candy while shopping and not paying for it.

> PO: Why didn't you pay for [the candy]?
> D: Where I come from, people do this all the time—"try it before you buy it." I've always done it. Everyone does it where I come from. No one considers it a crime. It's like spitting or littering; there's some obscure law against it.
> PO: Ya know, if everybody did that the store is out a lot of money and they're gonna pass that loss on to the customers. I'm not real happy about the prospects of paying higher prices so you can eat the candy.

This strategy pointed out to defendants that their behaviors were not isolated events, but rather had consequences for other people. In this way, the POs attempted to validate their claim to the definition of offenses as serious and wrong.

3. The POs argued that other aspects of the defendants' behaviors associated with the commission of the offenses were wrong and, in some cases, could also have been charged as criminal offenses. They did this in the hope of convincing the defendants that the acts they had been charged with were wrong and worthy of concern. For example, a teenage university student and his friends were drinking late one night. They decided to climb over the fence surrounding the university football stadium and "play some football." To prove they had been there, they decided to take a soft drink cannister back to the dormitory. The defendant was subsequently arrested and convicted of theft. Throughout the presentencing interview, the defendant steadfastly denied that what he had done was wrong or should have been charged as a criminal offense.

PO: Did ya know that you were also doing what's known as criminal trespass? What'd you do, climb over the fence?
D: Yeah. I considered that a college prank, too.
PO: Ya know that's another Class A misdemeanor. That's another year in jail if they charge you with that. You were committing a crime just by being there. Then you chose to steal something. You were drinking beer—that's another offense [since you were underage]. I mean you were doing a whole series of things here which resulted in your getting arrested.

4. The POs pointed out the potential legal consequences of a conviction. For example, one defendant presented a particularly cavalier attitude toward both his current and previous offenses. The PO seemed to think that this attitude was bolstered by the fact that the defendant had reached a plea agreement with the prosecutor. According to the agreement, in exchange for the defendant's guilty plea, the prosecutor would not argue for a severe sentence at the sentencing hearing. In addition, the PO thought the defendant "was high on something" during the interview.

PO: Do you have any prior criminal record as a juvenile?
D: Yes. I don't know what it all is. It's not very much, probably four charges—stupid charges like common nuisance, vandalism, vehicle theft, and I don't know what. Probably one or two more after that.
PO: Do you know that with a [class] C Felony you can get eight years?
D: I know.
PO: You realize if you get probation, which [there] is no guarantee you will, that plea agreement don't mean nothin' till its accepted, alright?
D: Uh huh.
PO: Only thing this plea agreement does. . . . Look, you're looking at two-to-eight [years], OK? All this plea agreement's gonna do—instead of the prosecutor getting up there and wanting your ass for eight years he's gonna stand mute. He's not gonna argue anything one way or another, but you can still be given the full amount. Do you understand that?
D: Yes, sir.
PO: Where they'll send ya ain't like boy's school. You're an adult now and you're gonna be treated as such.

The POs generally felt that this strategy was effective, even when other strategies had failed, since the prospects of incarceration and/or a substantial fine was enough "to get the attention of most of the people."

Attitudes Toward Consequences

Often the defendants had not considered the specific consequences of their convictions. The strategies the POs used in negotiating these attitudes were indirect and based on a lay version of cognitive dissonance theory (Festinger, 1957). The POs believed that if the defendants came to express acceptable attitudes "on their own, it [would] mean more to them," and they would be more inclined to act according to these acceptable attitudes than if the POs had directly presented these attitudes for their consideration. To this end the POs used two strategies.

1. The POs used defendants' expressions of an appropriate orientation to address another orientation.

D: So, I mean, I'm really scared this is on my record, 'cause I want to go to law school, ya know, like my old man, and I've heard that you can't get into law school if you have a criminal record.

PO: Does the possible sentence worry you any?

D: I couldn't care less about the sentence.

PO: Could you care less about a year of your life in jail?

D: I would be concerned about that, yes.

PO: So you are concerned about the sentence?

D: Yeah, I'm concerned about the sentence. I wanna go to school, ya know, and I don't want my dad to know.

The POs used this strategy to indicate to defendants that the attitude they expressed toward the first topic was also appropriate for the second one.

2. The POs linked background information about the defendants to the topic currently under negotiation.

PO: Have you thought about what [your conviction] is gonna do to your chances of getting into med school?

D: From the second I got out of the [store].

PO: And?

D: It's, it's gonna hurt me bad. There's a real good possibility they'd kick me out.

In this example, the defendant had been convicted of shoplifting. The PO had learned in a previous part of the interview that the defendant planned to go to medical school and used this information in negotiating his attitudes toward the consequences of his offense. This strategy was particularly effective; it pointed out to defendants that the things they valued had been placed in jeopardy by their behavior.

Attitudes Toward Changing Their Behavior

The POs used three indirect strategies in trying to get defendants to change their behavior. Which strategy the POs used was determined by the outcome of the negotiations over accounts.

1. When the POs and the defendants had reached agreement on a rational account, the POs used strategies which addressed alterna-

tive courses of action, ones which would have allowed the defendants to achieve their goal without breaking the law. In other words, the POs tried to make the defendants aware of legal (and, therefore, more desirable) alternatives to the particular courses of action they had chosen. The goal was to find solutions to the problem of the defendant's criminal behavior. A typical question in this strategy was:

PO: Think there might've been a way to avoid this?

2. When a non-rational account had been agreed upon, the POs used a strategy which allowed the defendants to consider courses of action which would alleviate or overcome the causal factor responsible for the offense. In addition, since a non-rational account mitigated some of the defendant's responsibility, the POs attempted to get the defendants to take some responsibility in solving the problem itself.

PO: Do you think alcohol is the root of your problems?

D: Yeah. I think its got a lot to do with it because I don't have no juvenile record at all or nothin'. It's only been while I've been drinking.

PO: What have you done to work on your drinking problem?

D: I tried to get away from it but I can't. It's just like on Sunday night. [The bar] opens up about noon and I can't wait to go up there and start drinkin'.

PO: If you knew this was a problem, why didn't you go get some help?

3. When no mutually satisfactory account had been agreed upon, the POs addressed this orientation in a different way. Since no problem had been identified, rather than addressing solutions, the POs addressed the defendant's risk of recidivism. They challenged the defendants to offer reasons why they would not be likely to commit a crime in the future. In this way, the defendants were asked to provide prospective accounts for their behavior.

PO: Why don't you tell me what you would like the judge to know about you; why

you did these [crimes]; and what's
to convince us you're not gonna keep
stealing. Sounds to me like you've got
sticky fingers.

D: Uhm, I know I won't do it again.

PO: Why not?

D: 'Cause ya know, I'm doin' too much
for myself now, lots of things that I
wouldn't want to lose. I have a full time
job and friends that I admire are trying
to teach me to stay out of trouble.

Negotiating Labels

[Accounts] presuppose an identifiable speaker and audience. The particular identities of the interactants
must often be established as part of the encounter in
which the account is presented. In other words, people
generate role identities for one another in social situations. . . . Every account is a manifestation of underlying negotiation of identities (Scott and Lyman,
1968:58).

I have argued that defendants' accounts of
their offenses, as well as other subjective orientations, are subject to negotiation during presentencing interviews. Analysis revealed that
these subjective orientations are one of the central components of a typology of defendants
which POs possessed and used in making sentence recommendations. I posit, therefore, that
*in the process of negotiating subjective orienta-
tions, the PO and the defendant were simultaneously negotiating the particular defendant
type that the former would use to define the latter.*

In the bureaucratic processing of defendants
this type can be conceptualized as a *label* which
POs attached to defendants for the purpose of
making sentence recommendations. Thus, the
POs did not so much process individuals as they
*processed types of individuals who had been
labeled in particular ways.* The particular label
attached to an individual defendant depended on
the POs' linking of characteristics of the individual with characteristics of the general category
or type.[6]

Ethnographic data revealed that, in making
sentence recommendations, POs used a threefold typology of criminal defendants which was
based on the defendants' risk of recidivism.

1. Low-risk defendants were usually in trouble
    with the criminal justice system for the first
    time, were between the ages of 18 and 25, and
    were either attending university or had a
    steady job. These defendants, therefore, had
    much to lose by possessing a criminal record
    and they took their current involvement with
    the courts seriously. As one PO put it,
    "These people have made one screwy mis-
    take and it's shaken them up so much we'll
    probably never see them again." For ex-
    ample, one defendant had been convicted of
    attempted theft after he had altered a sales
    receipt to obtain items he hadn't paid for.
    This defendant was unusually cooperative
    during the interview and expressed concern
    about the fact that business associates and
    local bankers would find out about the crimi-
    nal record he now possessed. His PO told
    me, "I don't think we'll see him come
    through here again. This was his first offense
    and I think it really made an impression on
    him."

2. High-risk defendants usually had at least two
    prior arrests and convictions, little formal
    education, and were seen as unwilling or un-
    able to hold a steady job. Often, they were
    perceived as not taking their involvement
    with the courts seriously. For these reasons,
    POs saw these defendants as likely to be in
    and out of trouble for much of their adult
    lives. For example, a defendant had been
    convicted of burglary and had several other
    theft-related convictions. In addition, he had
    never held a job for more than three months
    at a time. The PO who handled the case told
    me:

    This [defendant] is just too lazy to work. . . . He
    commits these burglaries because of that. I'll bet ya
    we see this guy again. He's definitely [high-risk]
    material.

3. The final category of defendants consisted of
    individuals whose risk of recidivism was
    neither definitely high nor low, but was seen
    as problematic. Some of these defendants
    had been in trouble with the law before, gen-
    erally involving minor offenses such as shop-
    lifting. Others possessed characteristics such
    as alcoholism or a "bad attitude" which POs

[6]Sudnow (1965) makes the same argument regarding public defenders and their processing of clients. He argues
that the goal of their interactions with clients is an assessment of the applicability of characteristics of "normal
crimes" with an instant case.

considered likely to be related to future criminal behavior. While there was no specific set of characteristics which defined this category of defendants, POs pointed out that what they did share was the potential for "heading for trouble." For example, a defendant had been convicted of theft and had two prior theft-related offenses. However, he also was working two jobs to pay off a student loan and return to the university. The PO described the defendant's risk of recidivism in the following way:

Its hard to tell with him. He's got these [prior offenses], but he's got these things [two jobs, a car] going for him. If he was in a situation where he could steal, I don't know.

What was important for POs was that, whatever the problem, these defendants were "workable." As one PO put it:

I spend the most time with these [defendants]. I try to make them aware of alternatives . . . or refer them for heavy-duty counseling, or do some things myself so hopefully they won't get in trouble again.

By the time POs began negotiations with defendants, they already possessed information about their criminal records and background. Thus, they had already formed initial impressions of the defendants, and had attached to them a provisional label on the basis of available information. What remained to be accomplished in the interview was to attach an unambiguous label upon which a sentence recommendation could be based.

The initial label was provisional for three reasons: (1) POs only possessed partial information about defendants. (2) Labels based on prior information could be misleading. Thus, some defendants had all the "objective" indicators of a low-risk defendant, yet may have exhibited unacceptable attitudes associated with problematic or high-risk defendants. The converse was also true. (3) In some cases the background information may have been too ambiguous to allow even a provisional labeling. For example, a defendant may have had the criminal record of a high-risk defendant, yet also have had low-risk characteristics such as a steady job or a college degree. In these cases, the determining characteristics may have been the defendants' subjective orientations.

POs used various strategies in negotiating reasonable or acceptable responses with defendants for each subjective orientation. At the aggregate level of types, however, with each verbal expression of an orientation, defendants were making claim to a certain defendant type. Thus, expressing concern about the consequences of the offense functioned as a claim to a low-risk defendant, while an unwillingness to accept the POs' definition of the offense as serious and wrong served as a claim to a high-risk defendant. These claims to defendant types were always relative to the initial impression the PO had of a defendant. A defendant initially labeled as high-risk who expressed consistently acceptable orientations was (in the eyes of the PO) making claim to a type of defendant whose risk was problematic (a change in label from high-risk to low-risk being unlikely). On the other hand, a defendant initially labeled low-risk who offered unacceptable orientations was seen as jeopardizing that label in favor of one of the others. For example, a defendant with various characteristics of a low-risk defendant (university student, relatively wealthy background, no prior record) presented consistently unacceptable orientations. After the negotiations, the PO labeled the defendant as one whose risk of recidivism was problematic, based largely on his "bad attitude."

While POs and defendants negotiated the labels that the former attached to the latter, this was not accomplished directly. Rather, it was accomplished piecemeal by negotiating the individual components of that label. Consider the following example.

PO: Didn't the time that you spent a day in jail over the [shoplifting] thing have any impact on you when you decided to steal the motorcycle? Didn't you think about that at all? Did you think about what might happen if you got caught?

D: To be truthful, as far as I remember, I didn't even think about that.

PO: You didn't even consider it. Did you realize you can go to prison for four years?

D: I do now, yes.

PO: How does that feel?

D: I wouldn't want that to happen.

PO: Do you realize that's a possibility?

D: Yes.

PO: Was it worth it?

D: No, not at all.

On the surface level, the PO and the defendant were negotiating the latter's attitude toward the consequences of his offense. However, at the aggregate level of types of defendants, the PO's strategies functioned to say, "By saying this, you are claiming to be a high-risk defendant; if you are that type, how do you feel about this?" In most cases, POs closed the negotiations when they reached a point where they could accomplish an unambiguous labeling of the defendants which made sense, given their linking of the defendant's characteristics with those characteristics of the more general type which was being assigned to the case. As Cicourel (1978:28) argues, this linking or articulation is accomplished by using abductive reasoning, that is, the ". . . inferential step that occurs in first stating and then reflecting upon a hypothesis that would choose among several possible explanations of some set of facts."

Conclusions

My findings suggest three implications for future research on POs. First, I have argued that research on POs has failed to recognize the existence of a third set of factors—defendants' subjective orientations—in sentencing recommendations. My findings suggest that POs treat the components of this set of factors in ways qualitatively different from other sets of factors. They elicited these factors in different ways. These factors affected the impression the PO formed of the defendant. They also affected the particular sentencing recommendation made by the PO. A consideration of this set of factors is important for a full explanation of the outcome of this particular aspect of the criminal justice system.

Second, my findings point to the need for research on the interaction between POs and defendants. I believe that one of the reasons subjective orientations have been largely ignored in the past is that they are only directly accessible through a detailed analysis of this discourse between POs and defendants. When such factors as attitudes have been considered in previous research, they have been treated as stable entities rather than as entities subject to manipula-

tion, as I have found. More generally, a lack of understanding about these negotiations leaves us with a lack of understanding about one of the crucial aspects of the *processes* involved in presentencing interviews.

Finally, my findings point to the need to include ethnographic data in studies of criminal justice processes. In this paper, I focused on both actual discourse processes as well as background ethnographic data. Much of my analysis would have been speculative had it not been for the insights I gained from detailed ethnographic information.[7] Knowledge of the categories POs use is crucial for understanding their actions and decisions concerning defendants and probationers, since these categories are involved in a process of typing in which POs subsume individual cases under more general categories.

REFERENCES

Becker, Howard S. 1963. *Outsiders: Studies in the Sociology of Deviance*. New York: Free Press.

Bernstein, Ilene, William Kelly, and Patricia Doyle. 1977. "Social Reactions to Deviants: The Case of Criminal Defendants." *American Sociological Review* 42(5):743–755.

Bonger, Willem. 1916. *Criminality and Economic Conditions*. Translated by Henry P. Horton. Boston: Little, Brown.

Burke, Peter and Austin Turk. 1975. "Factors Affecting Post-arrest Dispositions: A Model for Analysis." *Social Problems* 22(3):313–332.

Carter, Robert. 1967. "The Presentence Report and the Decision-making Process." *Journal of Research in Crime and Delinquency* 4(2):203–211.

Chiricos, Theodore and Gordon Waldo. 1975. "Socioeconomic Status and Criminal Sentencing: An Empirical Assessment of a Conflict Proposition." *American Sociological Review* 40(6):753–772.

Cicourel, Aaron. 1968. The Social Organization of Juvenile Justice. New York: Wiley and Sons.

———. 1975. "Discourse and Text: Cognitive and Linguistic Processes in Studies of Social Structure." *Versus: Quaderni di studi Semiotica* (September–December): 33–84.

———. 1978. "Language and Society: Cognitive, Cultural, and Linguistic Aspects of Language Use." *Social wissenschaftliche Annalen Band* 2, Seite B25–B58. Physica-Verlag, Wien.

———. 1980. "Three Models of Discourse Analysis: The Role of Social Structure." *Discourse Processes* 3(2):102–132.

[7]See Corsaro (1982) for a detailed discussion of the importance of ethnography in the analysis of discourse processes.

Cloward, Richard, and Lloyd Ohlin. 1960. *Delinquency and Opportunity: A Theory of Delinquent Gangs*. Glencoe, Ill.: Free Press.

Corsaro, William. 1982. "Something Old and Something New: The Importance of Prior Ethnography in the Collection and Analysis of Audiovisual Data." *Sociological Methods and Research* 11(2):145–166.

Dembo, Richard. 1972. "Orientations and Activities of Parole Officers." *Criminology* 10(4):193–215.

Festinger, Leon. 1957. *A Theory of Cognitive Dissonance*. Evanston, Ill.: Row, Peterson.

Glaser, Barney and Anselm Strauss. 1967. *The Discovery of Grounded Theory*. Chicago: Aldine.

Gross, Seymour. 1967. "The Prehearing Juvenile Report: Probation Officers' Conceptions." *Journal of Research in Crime and Delinquency* 4(2):212–217.

Hagan, John. 1977. "Criminal Justice in Rural and Urban Communities: A Study of the Bureaucratization of Justice." *Social Forces* 55(3):597–612.

Lemert, Edwin. 1951. *Social Pathology*. New York: McGraw-Hill.

Merton, Robert. 1957. *Social Theory and Social Structure*. Glencoe, Ill.: Free Press.

Prus, Robert and John Stratton. 1976. "Parole Revocation Decision-making: Private Typings and Official Designations." *Federal Probation* 40(1):48–53.

Reed, John and Charles King. 1966. "Factors in the Decision-making of North Carolina Probation Officers." *Journal of Research in Crime and Delinquency* 3(2):120–128.

Schur, Edwin. 1971. *Labeling Deviant Behavior*. New York: Harper & Row.

Scott, Marvin and Stanford Lyman. 1968. "Accounts." *American Sociological Review* 33(1):46–62.

Sellin, Thorsten. 1938. *Culture, Conflict, and Crime*. New York: Social Science Research Council.

Sudnow, David. 1965. "Normal Crimes: Sociological Features of the Penal Code." *Social Problems* 12(3):255–276.

Tannenbaum, Frank. 1938. *Crime and the Community*. Boston: Ginn.

8 THE EFFECTS OF CONTACT WITH CONTROL AGENTS

The careers of many deviants take them through correctional or treatment institutions. Some are arrested, charged, tried, sentenced, and sent to prison. Others are processed through a network of health and welfare agencies. Passage through such institutions can have both dramatic and subtle effects. Once it is known, for example, that a person has had contact with such institutions, other persons may regard that person as permanently suspect.

In the first reading D. L. Rosenhan shows the difficulty mental patients have in disproving the label of insanity. William Chambliss then shows that deviant labels are more often applied to lower-class than to middle-class adolescents and that this differential application markedly affects the life-chances of the adolescents. Richard Schwartz and Jerome Skolnick then show that prospective employers may discriminate against persons who have been accused of a crime, even though later found innocent; thus they illustrate how a deviant status may transcend time, organizational setting, and factual basis.

Being Sane in Insane Places   D. L. ROSENHAN

If sanity and insanity exist, how shall we know them?

The question is neither capricious nor itself insane. However much we may be personally convinced that we can tell the normal from the abnormal, the evidence is simply not compelling. It is commonplace, for example, to read about murder trials wherein eminent psychiatrists for the defense are contradicted by equally eminent psychiatrists for the prosecution on the matter of the defendant's sanity. More generally, there are a great deal of conflicting data on the reliability, utility, and meaning of such terms as "sanity," "insanity," "mental illness," and "schizophrenia" [1]. Finally, as early as 1934, Benedict suggested that normality and abnormality are not universal [2]. What is viewed as normal in one culture may be seen as quite aberrant in another. Thus, notions of normality and abnormality may not be quite as accurate as people believe they are.

To raise questions regarding normality and abnormality is in no way to question the fact that some behaviors are deviant or odd. Murder is deviant. So, too, are hallucinations. Nor does raising such questions deny the existence of the personal anguish that is often associated with "mental illness." Anxiety and depression exist. Psychological suffering exists. But normality and abnormality, sanity and insanity, and the diagnoses that flow from them may be less substantive than many believe them to be.

At its heart, the question of whether the sane can be distinguished from the insane (and whether degrees of insanity can be distinguished from each other) is a simple matter: do the salient characteristics that lead to diagnoses reside in the patients themselves or in the environments and contexts in which observers find them? . . . [T]he belief has been strong that patients present symptoms, that those symptoms can be categorized, and, implicitly, that the sane are distinguishable from the insane. More recently, however, this belief has been questioned. . . . [T]he view has grown that psychological categorization of mental illness is useless at best and downright harmful, misleading, and pejorative at worst. Psychiatric diagnoses, in this view, are in the minds of the observers and are not valid summaries of characteristics displayed by the observed [3–5].

Gains can be made in deciding which of these is more nearly accurate by getting normal people (that is, people who do not have, and have never suffered, symptoms of serious psychiatric disorders) admitted to psychiatric hospitals and then determining whether they were discovered to be sane and, if so, how. If the sanity of such pseudopatients were always detected, there would be prima facie evidence that a sane individual can be distinguished from the insane context in which he is found. . . . If, on the other hand, the sanity of the pseudopatients were never discovered, serious difficulties would arise for those who support traditional modes of psychiatric diagnosis. Given that the hospital staff was not incompetent, that the pseudopatient had been behaving as sanely as he had been outside of the hospital, and that it had never been previously suggested that he belonged in a psychiatric hospital, such an unlikely outcome would support the view that psychiatric diagnosis betrays little about the patient but much about the environment in which an observer finds him.

This article describes such an experiment. Eight sane people gained secret admission to 12 different hospitals [6]. Their diagnostic experiences constitute the data of the first part of this article; the remainder is devoted to a description of their experiences in psychiatric institutions. . . .

Pseudopatients and Their Settings

The eight pseudopatients were a varied group. One was a psychology graduate student in his 20's. The remaining seven were older and "established." Among them were three psychologists, a pediatrician, a psychiatrist, a painter, and a housewife. Three pseudopatients were women, five were men. All of them employed pseudonyms, lest their alleged diagnoses embarrass them later. Those who were in mental health professions alleged another occupation in

Reprinted from *Science*, Vol. 179 (January 1973), pp. 250–258, by permission of the publisher and author. Copyright 1973 by the American Association for the Advancement of Science.

order to avoid the special attentions that might be accorded by staff, as a matter of courtesy or caution, to ailing colleagues [7]. With the exception of myself (I was the first pseudopatient and my presence was known to the hospital administrator and chief psychologist and, so far as I can tell, them alone), the presence of pseudopatients and the nature of the research program was not known to the hospital staffs [8].

The settings were similarly varied. In order to generalize the findings, admission into a variety of hospitals was sought. The 12 hospitals in the sample were located in five different states on the East and West coasts. Some were old and shabby, some were quite new. Some were research-oriented, others not. Some had good staff-patient ratios, others were quite understaffed. Only one was a strictly private hospital. All of the others were supported by state or federal funds or, in one instance, by university funds.

After calling the hospital for an appointment, the pseudopatient arrived at the admissions office complaining that he had been hearing voices. Asked what the voices said, he replied that they were often unclear, but as far as he could tell they said "empty," "hollow," and "thud." The voices were unfamiliar and were of the same sex as the pseudopatient. . . .

Beyond alleging the symptoms and falsifying name, vocation, and employment, no further alterations of person, history, or circumstances were made. The significant events of the pseudopatient's life history were presented as they had actually occurred. Relationships with parents and siblings, with spouse and children, with people at work and in school, consistent with the aforementioned exceptions, were described as they were or had been. Frustrations and upsets were described along with joys and satisfactions. These facts are important to remember. If anything, they strongly biased the subsequent results in favor of detecting sanity, since none of their histories or current behaviors were seriously pathological in any way.

Immediately upon admission to the psychiatric ward, the pseudopatient ceased simulating *any* symptoms of abnormality. In some cases, there was a brief period of mild nervousness and anxiety, since none of the pseudopatients really believed that they would be admitted so easily. Indeed, their shared fear was that they would be immediately exposed as frauds and greatly embarrassed. Moreover, many of them had never visited a psychiatric ward; even those who had, nevertheless had some genuine fears about what might happen to them. Their nervousness, then, was quite appropriate to the novelty of the hospital setting, and it abated rapidly.

Apart from that short-lived nervousness, the pseudopatient behaved on the ward as he "normally" behaved. The pseudopatient spoke to patients and staff as he might ordinarily. Because there is uncommonly little to do on a psychiatric ward, he attempted to engage others in conversation. When asked by staff how he was feeling, he indicated that he was fine, that he no longer experienced symptoms. He responded to instructions from attendants, to calls for medication (which was not swallowed), and to dining-hall instructions. Beyond such activities as were available to him on the admissions ward, he spent his time writing down his observations about the ward, its patients, and the staff. Initially these notes were written "secretly," but as it soon became clear that no one much cared, they were subsequently written on standard tablets of paper in such public places as the dayroom. No secret was made of these activities.

The pseudopatient, very much as a true psychiatric patient, entered a hospital with no foreknowledge of when he would be discharged. Each was told that he would have to get out by his own devices, essentially by convincing the staff that he was sane. The psychological stresses associated with hospitalization were considerable, and all but one of the pseudopatients desired to be discharged almost immediately after being admitted. They were, therefore, motivated not only to behave sanely, but to be paragons of cooperation. That their behavior was in no way disruptive is confirmed by nursing reports, which have been obtained on most of the patients. These reports uniformly indicate that the patients were "friendly," "cooperative," and "exhibited no abnormal indications."

The Normal Are Not Detectably Sane

Despite their public "show" of sanity, the pseudopatients were never detected. Admitted, except in one case, with a diagnosis of schizophrenia [9], each was discharged with a diagnosis of schizophrenia "in remission." The label "in remission" should in no way be dismissed as a formality, for at no time during any hospitalization had any question been raised about any pseudopatient's simulation. Nor are there any indications in the hospital records that the pseudopatient's status was suspect. Rather, the evidence is strong that, once labeled schizophrenic, the pseudopatient was stuck with that label. If the pseudopatient was to be discharged, he must naturally be "in remission"; but he was not sane, nor, in the institution's view, had he ever been sane.

The uniform failure to recognize sanity cannot be attributed to the quality of the hospitals. . . . Nor can it be alleged that there was simply not enough time to observe the pseudopatients. Length of hospitalization ranged from 7 to 52 days, with an average of 19 days. The pseudopatients were not, in fact, carefully observed, but this failure clearly speaks more to traditions within psychiatric hospitals than to lack of opportunity.

Finally, it cannot be said that the failure to recognize the pseudopatients' sanity was due to the fact that they were not behaving sanely. While there was clearly some tension present in all of them, their daily visitors could detect no serious behavioral consequences—nor, indeed, could other patients. It was quite common for the patients to "detect" the pseudopatients' sanity. . . . "You're not crazy. You're a journalist, or a professor [referring to the continual note-taking]. You're checking up on the hospital." While most of the patients were reassured by the pseudopatient's insistence that he had been sick before he came in but was fine now, some continued to believe that the pseudopatient was sane throughout his hospitalization [10]. The fact that the patients often recognized normality when staff did not raises important questions.

Failure to detect sanity during the course of hospitalization may be due to the fact that . . . physicians are more inclined to call a healthy person sick . . . than a sick person healthy. . . . The reasons for this are not hard to find: it is clearly more dangerous to misdiagnose illness than health. Better to err on the side of caution, to suspect illness even among the healthy.

But what holds for medicine does not hold equally well for psychiatry. Medical illnesses, while unfortunate, are not commonly pejorative. Psychiatric diagnoses, on the contrary, carry with them personal, legal, and social stigmas [11]. It was therefore important to see whether the tendency toward diagnosing the sane insane could be reversed. The following experiment was arranged at a research and teaching hospital whose staff had heard these findings but doubted that such an error could occur in their hospital. The staff was informed that at some time during the following 3 months, one or more pseudopatients would attempt to be admitted into the psychiatric hospital. Each staff member was asked to rate each patient who presented himself at admissions or on the ward according to the likelihood that the patient was a pseudopatient. . . .

Judgments were obtained on 193 patients who were admitted for psychiatric treatment. All staff who had had sustained contact with or primary responsibility for the patient—attendants, nurses, psychiatrists, physicians, and psychologists—were asked to make judgments. Forty-one patients were alleged, with high confidence, to be pseudopatients by at least one member of the staff. Twenty-three were considered suspect by at least one psychiatrist. Nineteen were suspected by one psychiatrist *and* one other staff member. Actually, no genuine pseudopatient (at least from my group) presented himself during this period.

The experiment is instructive. It indicates that the tendency to designate sane people as insane can be reversed when the stakes (in this case, prestige and diagnostic acumen) are high. But what can be said of the 19 people who were suspected of being "sane" by one psychiatrist and another staff member? Were these people truly "sane?" . . . There is no way of knowing. But one thing is certain: any diagnostic process that lends itself so readily to massive errors of this sort cannot be a very reliable one.

The Stickiness of Psychodiagnostic Labels

Beyond the tendency to call the healthy sick —a tendency that accounts better for diagnostic behavior on admission than it does for such behavior after a lengthy period of exposure—the data speak to the massive role of labeling in psychiatric assessment. Having once been labeled schizophrenic, there is nothing the pseudopatient can do to overcome the tag. The tag profoundly colors others' perceptions of him and his behavior.

From one viewpoint, these data are hardly surprising, for it has long been known that elements are given meaning by the context in which they occur. . . . Once a person is designated abnormal, all of his other behaviors and characteristics are colored by that label. Indeed, that label is so powerful that many of the pseudopatients' normal behaviors were overlooked entirely or profoundly misinterpreted. Some examples may clarify this issue.

Earlier I indicated that there were no changes in the pseudopatient's personal history and current status beyond those of name, employment, and, where necessary, vocation. Otherwise, a veridical description of personal history and circumstances was offered. Those circumstances were not psychotic. How were they made consonant with the diagnosis of psychosis? Or were those diagnoses modified in such a way as to bring them into accord with the circumstances of the pseudopatient's life, as described by him?

As far as I can determine, diagnoses were in no way affected by the relative health of the circumstances of a pseudopatient's life. Rather, the reverse occurred: the perception of his circumstances was shaped entirely by the diagnosis. A clear example of such translation is found in the case of a pseudopatient who had had a close relationship with his mother but was rather remote from his father during his early childhood. During adolescence and beyond, however, his father became a close friend, while his relationship with his mother cooled. His present relationship with his wife was characteristically close and warm. Apart from occasional angry exchanges, friction was minimal. The children had rarely been spanked. Surely there is nothing especially pathological about such a history. . . . Observe, however, how such a history was translated in the psychopathological context, this from the case summary prepared after the patient was discharged.

This white 39-year-old male . . . manifests a long history of considerable ambivalence in close relationships, which began in early childhood. A warm relationship with his mother cools during his adolescence. A distant relationship to his father is described as becoming very intense. Affective stability is absent. His attempts to control emotionality with his wife and children are punctuated by angry outbursts and, in the case of the children, spankings. And while he says that he has several good friends, one senses considerable ambivalence embedded in those relationships also. . . .

The facts of the case were unintentionally distorted by the staff to achieve consistency with a popular theory of the dynamics of a schizo-phrenic reaction [12]. Nothing of an ambivalent nature had been described in relations with parents, spouse, or friends. . . . Clearly, the meaning ascribed to his verbalizations (that is, ambivalence, affective instability) was determined by the diagnosis: schizophrenia. An entirely different meaning would have been ascribed if it were known that the man was "normal."

All pseudopatients took extensive notes publicly. Under ordinary circumstances, such behavior would have raised questions in the minds of observers, as, in fact, it did among patients. Indeed, it seemed so certain that the notes would elicit suspicion that elaborate precautions were taken to remove them from the ward each day. But the precautions proved needless. The closest any staff member came to questioning these notes occurred when one pseudopatient asked his physician what kind of medication he was receiving and began to write down the response. "You needn't write it," he was told gently. "If you have trouble remembering, just ask me again."

If no questions were asked of the pseudopatients, how was their writing interpreted? Nursing records for three patients indicate that the writing was seen as an aspect of their pathological behavior. . . . Given that the patient is in the hospital, he must be psychologically disturbed. And given that he is disturbed, continuous writing must be a behavioral manifestation of that disturbance, perhaps a subset of the compulsive behaviors that are sometimes correlated with schizophrenia.

One tacit characteristic of psychiatric diagnosis is that it locates the sources of aberration within the individual and only rarely within the complex of stimuli that surrounds him. Consequently, behaviors that are stimulated by the environment are commonly misattributed to the patient's disorder. For example, one kindly nurse found a pseudopatient pacing the long hospital corridors. "Nervous, Mr. X?" she asked. "No, bored," he said.

The notes kept by pseudopatients are full of patient behaviors that were misinterpreted by well-intentioned staff. Often enough, a patient would go "berserk" because he had, wittingly or unwittingly, been mistreated by, say, an attendant. A nurse coming upon the scene would rarely inquire even cursorily into the environmental stimuli of the patient's behavior. Rather, she assumed that his upset derived from his pathology, not from his present interactions with other staff members. . . . [N]ever were the staff found to assume that one of themselves or the structure of the hospital had anything to do with a patient's behavior. One psychiatrist pointed to a group of patients who were sitting outside the cafeteria entrance half an hour before lunchtime. To a group of young residents he indicated that such behavior was characteristic of the oral-acquisitive nature of the syndrome. It seemed not to occur to him that there were very few things to anticipate in a psychiatric hospital besides eating.

A psychiatric label has a life and an influence of its own. Once the impression has been formed that the patient is schizophrenic, the expectation is that he will continue to be schizophrenic. When a sufficient amount of time has passed, during which the patient has done nothing bizarre, he is considered to be in remission and available for discharge. But the label endures beyond discharge, with the unconfirmed expectation that he will behave as a schizophrenic again. Such labels, conferred by mental health professionals, are as influential on the patient as they are on his relatives and friends, and it should not surprise anyone that the diagnosis acts on all of them as a self-fulfilling prophecy. Eventually, the patient himself accepts the diagnosis, with all of its surplus meanings and expectations, and behaves accordingly [5]. . . .

Powerlessness and Depersonalization

Eye contact and verbal contact reflect concern and individuation; their absence, avoidance and depersonalization. The data I have presented do not do justice to the rich daily encounters that grew up around matters of depersonalization and avoidance. I have records of patients who were beaten by staff for the sin of having initiated verbal contact. During my own experience, for example, one patient was beaten in the presence of other patients for having approached an attendant and told him, "I like you." Occasionally, punishment meted out to patients for misdemeanors seemed so excessive that it could not be justified by the most radical interpretations of psychiatric canon. Nevertheless, they appeared to go unquestioned. Tempers were often short. A patient who had not heard a call for medication would be roundly excoriated, and the morning attendants would

often wake patients with, "Come on, you m-----f-----s, out of bed!"

Neither anecdotal nor "hard" data can convey the overwhelming sense of powerlessness which invades the individual as he is continually exposed to the depersonalization of the psychiatric hospital. . . .

Powerlessness was evident everywhere. The patient is deprived of many of his legal rights by dint of his psychiatric commitment [13]. He is shorn of credibility by virtue of his psychiatric label. His freedom of movement is restricted. He cannot initiate contact with the staff, but may only respond to such overtures as they make. Personal privacy is minimal. Patient quarters and possessions can be entered and examined by any staff member, for whatever reason. His personal history and anguish is available to any staff member (often including the "grey lady" and "candy striper" volunteer) who chooses to read his folder, regardless of their therapeutic relationship to him. His personal hygiene and waste evacuation are often monitored. The [toilets] may have no doors.

At times, depersonalization reached such proportions that pseudopatients had the sense that they were invisible, or at least unworthy of account. Upon being admitted, I and other pseudopatients took the initial physical examinations in a semipublic room, where staff members went about their own business as if we were not there.

On the ward, attendants delivered verbal and occasionally serious physical abuse to patients in the presence of other observing patients, some of whom (the pseudopatients) were writing it all down. Abusive behavior, on the other hand, terminated quite abruptly when other staff members were known to be coming. Staff are credible witnesses. Patients are not.

A nurse unbuttoned her uniform to adjust her brassiere in the presence of an entire ward of viewing men. One did not have the sense that she was being seductive. Rather, she didn't notice us. A group of staff persons might point to a patient in the dayroom and discuss him animatedly, as if he were not there.

One illuminating instance of depersonalization and invisibility occurred with regard to medications. All told, the pseudopatients were administered nearly 2100 pills. . . . Only two were swallowed. The rest were either pocketed or deposited in the toilet. The pseudopatients were not alone in this. Although I have no precise records on how many patients rejected their medications, the pseudopatients frequently found the medications of other patients in the toilet before they deposited their own. As long as they were cooperative, their behavior and the pseudopatients' own in this matter, as in other important matters, went unnoticed throughout.

Reactions to such depersonalization among pseudopatients were intense. Although they had come to the hospital as participant observers and were fully aware that they did not "belong," they nevertheless found themselves caught up in and fighting the process of depersonalization. . . .

The Consequences of Labeling and Depersonalization

Whenever the ratio of what is known to what needs to be known approaches zero, we tend to invent "knowledge" and assume that we understand more than we actually do. We seem unable to acknowledge that we simply don't know. The needs for diagnosis and remediation of behavioral and emotional problems are enormous. But rather than acknowledge that we are just embarking on understanding, we continue to label patients "schizophrenic," "manic-depressive," and "insane," as if in those words we had captured the essence of understanding. The facts of the matter are that we have known for a long time that diagnoses are often not useful or reliable, but we have nevertheless continued to use them. We now know that we cannot distinguish insanity from sanity. It is depressing to consider how that information will be used.

Not merely depressing, but frightening. How many people, one wonders, are sane but not recognized as such in our psychiatric institutions? How many have been needlessly stripped of their privileges of citizenship, from the right to vote and drive to that of handling their own accounts? How many have feigned insanity in order to avoid the criminal consequences of their behavior, and, conversely, how many would rather stand trial than live interminably in a psychiatric hospital—but are wrongly thought to be mentally ill? How many have been stigmatized by well-intentioned, but nevertheless erroneous, diagnoses? . . . [P]sychiatric diagnoses are rarely found to be in error. The label sticks, a mark of inadequacy forever.

Finally, how many patients might be "sane" outside the psychiatric hospital but seem insane in it—not because craziness resides in them, as it were, but because they are responding to a bizarre setting, one that may be unique to institutions which harbor nether people? Goffman [4] calls the process of socialization to such institutions "mortification"—an apt metaphor that includes the processes of depersonalization that have been described here. And while it is impossible to know whether the pseudopatients' responses to these processes are characteristic of all inmates—they were, after all, not real patients—it is difficult to believe that these processes of socialization to a psychiatric hospital provide useful attitudes or habits of response for living in the "real world."

REFERENCES AND NOTES

1. P. Ash, *J. Abnorm. Soc. Psychol.* 44, 272 (1949); A. T. Beck, *Amer. J. Psychiat.* 119, 210 (1962); A. T. Boisen, *Psychiatry* 2, 233 (1938); N. Kreitman, *J. Ment. Sci.* 107, 876 (1961); N. Kreitman, P. Sainsbury, J. Morrisey, J. Towers, J. Scrivener, *ibid.*, p. 887; H. O. Schmitt and C. P. Fonda, *J. Abnorm. Soc. Psychol.* 52, 262 (1956); W. Seeman, *J. Nerv. Ment. Dis.* 118, 541 (1953). For an analysis of these artifacts and summaries of the disputes, see J. Zubin, *Annu. Rev. Psychol.* 18, 373 (1967); L. Phillips and J. G. Draguns, *ibid.*, 22, 447 (1971).

2. R. Benedict, *J. Gen. Psychol.* 10, 59 (1934).

3. See in this regard H. Becker, *Outsiders: Studies in the Sociology of Deviance* (Free Press, New York, 1963); B. M. Braginsky, D. D. Braginsky, K. Ring, *Methods of Madness: The Mental Hospital as a Last Resort* (Holt, Rinehart & Winston, New York, 1969); G. M. Crocetti and P. V. Lemkau, *Amer. Sociol. Rev.* 30, 577 (1965); E. Goffman, *Behavior in Public Places* (Free Press, New York, 1964); R. D. Laing, *The Divided Self: A Study of Sanity and Madness* (Quadrangle, Chicago, 1960); D. L. Phillips, *Amer. Sociol. Rev.* 28, 963 (1963); T. R. Sarbin, *Psychol. Today* 6, 18 (1972); E. Schur, *Amer. J. Sociol.* 75, 309 (1969); T. Szasz, *Law, Liberty and Psychiatry* (Macmillan, New York, 1963); *The Myth of Mental Illness: Foundations of a Theory of Mental Illness* (Hoeber Harper, New York, 1963). For a critique of some of these views, see W. R. Gove, *Amer. Sociol. Rev.* 35, 873 (1970).

4. E. Goffman, *Asylums* (Doubleday, Garden City, N.Y., 1961).

5. T. J. Scheff, *Being Mentally Ill: A Sociological Theory* (Aldine, Chicago, 1966).

6. Data from a ninth pseudopatient are not incorporated in this report because, although his sanity went undetected, he falsified aspects of his personal history, including his marital status and parental relationships. His experimental behaviors therefore were not identical to those of the other pseudopatients.

7. Beyond the personal difficulties that the pseudo-patient is likely to experience in the hospital, there are legal and social ones that, combined, require considerable attention before entry. For example, once admitted to a psychiatric institution, it is difficult, if not impossible, to be discharged on short notice, state law to the contrary notwithstanding. I was not sensitive to these difficulties at the outset of the project, nor to the personal and situational emergencies that can arise, but later a writ of habeas corpus was prepared for each of the entering pseudopatients and an attorney was kept "on call" during every hospitalization. I am grateful to John Kaplan and Robert Bartels for legal advice and assistance in these matters.

8. However distasteful such concealment is, it was a necessary first step to examining these questions. Without concealment, there would have been no way to know how valid these experiences were; nor was there any way of knowing whether whatever detections occurred were a tribute to the diagnostic acumen of the staff or to the hospital's rumor network. Obviously, since my concerns are general ones that cut across individual hospitals and staffs, I have respected their anonymity and have eliminated clues that might lead to their identification.

9. Interestingly, of the 12 admissions, 11 were diagnosed as schizophrenic and one, with the identical symptomatology, as manic-depressive psychosis. This diagnosis has a more favorable prognosis, and it was given by the only private hospital in our sample. On the relations between social class and psychiatric diagnosis, see A. B. Hollingshead and F. C. Redlich, *Social Class and Mental Illness: A Community Study* (Wiley, New York, 1958).

10. It is possible, of course, that patients have quite broad latitudes in diagnosis and therefore are inclined to call many people sane, even those whose behavior is patently aberrant. However, although we have no hard data on this matter, it was our distinct impression that this was not the case. In many instances, patients not only singled us out for attention, but came to imitate our behaviors and styles.

11. J. Cumming and E. Cumming, *Community Ment. Health* 1, 135 (1965); A. Farina and K. Ring, *J. Abnorm. Psychol.* 70, 47 (1965); H. E. Freeman and O. G. Simmons, *The Mental Patient Comes Home* (Wiley, New York, 1963); W. J. Johannsen, *Ment. Hygiene* 53, 218 (1969); A. S. Linsky, *Soc. Psychiat.* 5, 166 (1970).

12. For an example of a similar self-fulfilling prophecy, in this instance dealing with the "central" trait of intelligence, see R. Rosenthal and L. Jacobson, *Pygmalion in the Classroom* (Holt, Rinehart & Winston, New York, 1968).

13. D. B. Wexler and S. E. Scoville, *Ariz. Law Rev.* 13, 1 (1971).

The Saints and the Roughnecks

WILLIAM J. CHAMBLISS

Eight promising young men—children of good, stable, white upper-middle-class families, active in school affairs, good pre-college students— were some of the most delinquent boys at Hanibal High School. While community residents and parents knew that these boys occasionally sowed a few wild oats, they were totally unaware that sowing wild oats completely occupied the daily routine of these young men. The Saints were constantly occupied with truancy, drinking, wild driving, petty theft and vandalism. Yet not one was officially arrested for any misdeed during the two years I observed them.

This record was particularly surprising in light of my observations during the same two years of another gang of Hanibal High School students, six lower-class white boys known as the Roughnecks. The Roughnecks were constantly in trouble with police and community even though their rate of delinquency was about equal with that of the Saints. What was the cause of this disparity? The result? The following consideration of the activities, social class and community perceptions of both gangs may provide some answers.

The Saints from Monday to Friday

The Saints' principal daily concern was with getting out of school as early as possible. The boys managed to get out of school with minimum danger that they would be accused of playing hookey through an elaborate procedure for obtaining "legitimate" release from class. The most common procedure was for one boy to obtain the release of another by fabricating a meeting of some committee, program or recognized club. Charles might raise his hand in his 9:00 chemistry class and ask to be excused—a euphemism for going to the bathroom. Charles would go to Ed's math class and inform the teacher that Ed was needed for a 9:30 rehearsal of the drama club play. The math teacher would recognize Ed and Charles as "good students" involved in numerous school activities and would permit Ed to leave at 9:30. Charles would return to his class, and Ed would go to Tom's English class to obtain his release. Tom would

engineer Charles' escape. The strategy would continue until as many of the Saints as possible were freed. After a stealthy trip to the car (which had been parked in a strategic spot), the boys were off for a day of fun.

Over the two years I observed the Saints, this pattern was repeated nearly every day. There were variations on the theme, but in one form or another, the boys used this procedure for getting out of class and then off the school grounds. Rarely did all eight of the Saints manage to leave school at the same time. The average number avoiding school on the days I observed them was five.

Having escaped from the concrete corridors the boys usually went either to a pool hall on the other (lower-class) side of town or to a cafe in the suburbs. Both places were out of the way of people the boys were likely to know (family or school officials), and both provided a source of entertainment. The pool hall entertainment was the generally rough atmosphere, the occasional hustler, the sometimes drunk proprietor and, of course, the game of pool. The cafe's entertainment was provided by the owner. The boys would "accidentally" knock a glass on the floor or spill cola on the counter—not all the time, but enough to be sporting. They would also bend spoons, put salt in sugar bowls and generally tease whoever was working in the cafe. The owner had opened the cafe recently and was dependent on the boys' business which was, in fact, substantial since between the horsing around and the teasing they bought food and drinks.

The Saints on Weekends

On weekends, the automobile was even more critical than during the week, for on weekends the Saints went to Big Town—a large city with a population of over a million, 25 miles from Hanibal. Every Friday and Saturday night most of the Saints would meet between 8:00 and 8:30 and would go into Big Town. Big Town activities included drinking heavily in taverns or nightclubs, driving drunkenly through the streets, and committing acts of vandalism and playing pranks.

Reprinted by permission of Transaction, Inc., from *Society*, Vol. 11, No. 1 (November/December 1973), pp. 24– 31. Copyright © 1973 by Transaction, Inc.

By midnight on Fridays and Saturdays the Saints were usually thoroughly high, and one or two of them were often so drunk they had to be carried to the cars. Then the boys drove around town, calling obscenities to women and girls; occasionally trying (unsuccessfully so far as I could tell) to pick girls up; and driving recklessly through red lights and at high speeds with their lights out. Occasionally they played "chicken." One boy would climb out the back window of the car and across the roof to the driver's side of the car while the car was moving at high speed (between 40 and 50 miles an hour); then the driver would move over and the boy who had just crawled across the car roof would take the driver's seat.

Searching for "fair game" for a prank was the boys' principal activity after they left the tavern. The boys would drive alongside a foot patrolman and ask directions to some street. If the policeman leaned on the car in the course of answering the question, the driver would speed away, causing him to lose his balance. The Saints were careful to play this prank only in an area where they were not going to spend much time and where they could quickly disappear around a corner to avoid having their license plate number taken.

Construction sites and road repair areas were the special province of the Saints' mischief. A soon-to-be-repaired hole in the road inevitably invited the Saints to remove lanterns and wooden barricades and put them in the car, leaving the hole unprotected. The boys would find a safe vantage point and wait for an unsuspecting motorist to drive into the hole. Often, though not always, the boys would go up to the motorist and commiserate with him about the dreadful way the city protected its citizenry.

Leaving the scene of the open hole and the motorist, the boys would then go searching for an appropriate place to erect the stolen barricade. An "appropriate place" was often a spot on a highway near a curve in the road where the barricade would not be seen by an oncoming motorist. The boys would wait to watch an unsuspecting motorist attempt to stop and (usually) crash into the wooden barricade. With saintly bearing the boys might offer help and understanding.

A stolen lantern might well find its way onto the back of a police car or hang from a street lamp. Once a lantern served as a prop for a reenactment of the "midnight ride of Paul Revere" until the "play," which was taking place at 2:00 A.M. in the center of a main street of Big Town, was interrupted by a police car several blocks away. The boys ran, leaving the lanterns on the street, and managed to avoid being apprehended.

Abandoned houses, especially if they were located in out-of-the-way places, were fair game for destruction and spontaneous vandalism. The boys would break windows, remove furniture to the yard and tear it apart, urinate on the walls and scrawl obscenities inside.

Through all the pranks, drinking and reckless driving the boys managed miraculously to avoid being stopped by police. Only twice in two years was I aware that they had been stopped by a Big City policeman. Once was for speeding (which they did every time they drove whether they were drunk or sober), and the driver managed to convince the policeman that it was simply an error. The second time they were stopped they had just left a nightclub and were walking through an alley. Aaron stopped to urinate and the boys began making obscene remarks. A foot patrolman came into the alley, lectured the boys and sent them home. Before the boys got to the car one began talking in a loud voice again. The policeman, who had followed them down the alley, arrested this boy for disturbing the peace and took him to the police station where the other Saints gathered. After paying a $5.00 fine, and with the assurance that there would be no permanent record of the arrest, the boy was released.

The boys had a spirit of frivolity and fun about their escapades. They did not view what they were engaged in as "delinquency," though it surely was by any reasonable definition of that word. They simply viewed themselves as having a little fun and who, they would ask, was really hurt by it? The answer had to be no one, although this fact remains one of the most difficult things to explain about the gang's behavior. Unlikely though it seems, in two years of drinking, driving, carousing and vandalism no one was seriously injured as a result of the Saints' activities.

The Saints in School

The Saints were highly successful in school. The average grade for the group was "B," with two of the boys having close to a straight "A" average. Almost all of the boys were popular and many of them held offices in the school. One of the boys was vice-president of the student body one year. Six of the boys played on athletic teams.

At the end of their senior year, the student body selected ten seniors for special recognition as the "school wheels"; four of the ten were Saints. Teachers and school officials saw no problem with any of these boys and anticipated that they would all "make something of themselves."

How the boys managed to maintain this impression is surprising in view of their actual behavior while in school. Their technique for covering truancy was so successful that teachers did not even realize that the boys were absent from school much of the time. Occasionally, of course, the system would backfire and then the boy was on his own. A boy who was caught would be most contrite, would plead guilty and ask for mercy. He inevitably got the mercy he sought.

Cheating on examinations was rampant, even to the point of orally communicating answers to exams as well as looking at one another's papers. Since none of the group studied, and since they were primarily dependent on one another for help, it is surprising that grades were so high. Teachers contributed to the deception in their admitted inclination to give these boys (and presumably others like them) the benefit of the doubt. When asked how the boys did in school, and when pressed on specific examinations, teachers might admit that they were disappointed in John's performance, but would quickly add that they "knew he was capable of doing better," so John was given a higher grade than he had actually earned. How often this happened is impossible to know. During the time that I observed the group, I never saw any of the boys take homework home. Teachers may have been "understanding" very regularly.

One exception to the gang's generally good performance was Jerry, who had a "C" average in his junior year, experienced disaster the next year and failed to graduate. Jerry had always been a little more nonchalant than the others about the liberties he took in school. Rather than wait for someone to come get him from class, he would offer his own excuse and leave. Although he probably did not miss any more classes than most of the others in the group, he did not take the requisite pains to cover his absences. Jerry

was the only Saint whom I ever heard talk back to a teacher. Although teachers often called him a "cut up" or a "smart kid," they never referred to him as a troublemaker or as a kid headed for trouble. It seems likely, then, that Jerry's failure his senior year and his mediocre performance his junior year were consequences of his not playing the game the proper way (possibly because he was disturbed by his parents' divorce). His teachers regarded him as "immature" and not quite ready to get out of high school.

The Police and the Saints

The local police saw the Saints as good boys who were among the leaders of the youth in the community. Rarely, the boys might be stopped in town for speeding or for running a stop sign. When this happened the boys were always polite, contrite and pled for mercy. As in school, they received the mercy they asked for. None ever received a ticket or was taken into the precinct by the local police.

The situation in Big City, where the boys engaged in most of their delinquency, was only slightly different. The police there did not know the boys at all, although occasionally the boys were stopped by a patrolman. Once they were caught taking a lantern from a construction site. Another time they were stopped for running a stop sign, and on several occasions they were stopped for speeding. Their behavior was as before: contrite, polite and penitent. The urban police, like the local police, accepted their demeanor as sincere. More important, the urban police were convinced that these were good boys just out for a lark.

The Roughnecks

Hanibal townspeople never perceived the Saints' high level of delinquency. The Saints were good boys who just went in for an occasional prank. After all, they were well dressed, well mannered and had nice cars. The Roughnecks were a different story. Although the two gangs of boys were the same age, and both groups engaged in an equal amount of wild-oat sowing, everyone agreed that the not-so-well-dressed, not-so-well-mannered, not-so-rich boys were heading for trouble. Townspeople would say, "You can see the gang members at the drugstore night after night, leaning against the storefront (sometimes drunk) or slouching around inside buying cokes, reading magazines, and probably stealing old Mr. Wall blind. When they are outside and girls walk by, even respectable girls, these boys make suggestive remarks. Sometimes their remarks are downright lewd."

From the community's viewpoint, the real indication that these kids were in for trouble was that they were constantly involved with the police. Some of them had been picked up for stealing, mostly small stuff, of course, "but still it's stealing small stuff that leads to big time crimes." "Too bad," people said. "Too bad that these boys couldn't behave like the other kids in town; stay out of trouble, be polite to adults, and look to their future."

The community's impression of the degree to which this group of six boys (ranging in age from 16 to 19) engaged in delinquency was somewhat distorted. In some ways the gang was more delinquent than the community thought; in other ways they were less.

The fighting activities of the group were fairly readily and accurately perceived by almost everyone. At least once a month, the boys would get into some sort of fight, although most fights were scraps between members of the group or involved only one member of the group and some peripheral hanger-on. Only three times in the period of observation did the group fight together: once against a gang from across town, once against two blacks and once against a group of boys from another school. For the first two fights the group went out "looking for trouble"—and they found it both times. The third fight followed a football game and began spontaneously with an argument on the football field between one of the Roughnecks and a member of the opposition's football team.

Jack had a particular propensity for fighting and was involved in most of the brawls. He was a prime mover of the escalation of arguments into fights.

More serious than fighting, had the community been aware of it, was theft. Although almost everyone was aware that the boys occasionally stole things, they did not realize the extent of the activity. Petty stealing was a frequent event for the Roughnecks. Sometimes they stole as a group and coordinated their efforts; other times they stole in pairs. Rarely did they steal alone.

The thefts ranged from very small things like paperback books, comics and ballpoint pens to expensive items like watches. The nature of the thefts varied from time to time. The gang would go through a period of systematically lifting items from automobiles or school lockers. Types of thievery varied with the whim of the gang. Some forms of thievery were more profitable than others, but all thefts were for profit, not just thrills.

Roughnecks siphoned gasoline from cars as often as they had access to an automobile, which was not very often. Unlike the Saints, who owned their own cars, the Roughnecks would have to borrow their parents' cars, an event which occurred only eight or nine times a year. The boys claimed to have stolen cars for joy rides from time to time.

Ron committed the most serious of the group's offenses. With an unidentified associate the boy attempted to burglarize a gasoline station. Although this station had been robbed twice previously in the same month, Ron denied any involvement in either of the other thefts. When Ron and his accomplice approached the station, the owner was hiding in the bushes beside the station. He fired both barrels of a double-barreled shotgun at the boys. Ron was severely injured; the other boy ran away and was never caught. Though he remained in critical condition for several months, Ron finally recovered and served six months of the following year in reform school. Upon release from reform school, Ron was put back a grade in school, and began running around with a different gang of boys. The Roughnecks considered the new gang less delinquent than themselves, and during the following year Ron had no more trouble with the police.

The Roughnecks, then, engaged mainly in three types of delinquency: theft, drinking and fighting. Although community members perceived that this gang of kids was delinquent, they mistakenly believed that their illegal activities were primarily drinking, fighting and being a nuisance to passersby. Drinking was limited among the gang members, although it did occur, and theft was much more prevalent than anyone realized.

Drinking would doubtless have been more prevalent had the boys had ready access to liquor. Since they rarely had automobiles at their disposal, they could not travel very far, and the bars in town would not serve them. Most of the boys had little money, and this, too, inhibited their purchase of alcohol. Their major source of liquor was a local drunk who would buy them a fifth if they would give him enough extra to buy himself a pint of whiskey or a bottle of wine.

The community's perception of drinking as prevalent stemmed from the fact that it was the most obvious delinquency the boys engaged in. When one of the boys had been drinking, even a casual observer seeing him on the corner would suspect that he was high.

There was a high level of mutual distrust and dislike between the Roughnecks and the police. The boys felt very strongly that the police were unfair and corrupt. Some evidence existed that the boys were correct in their perception.

The main source of the boys' dislike for the police undoubtedly stemmed from the fact that the police would sporadically harass the group. From the standpoint of the boys, these acts of occasional enforcement of the law were whimsical and uncalled for. It made no sense to them, for example, that the police would come to the corner occasionally and threaten them with arrest for loitering when the night before the boys had been out siphoning gasoline from cars and the police had been nowhere in sight. To the boys, the police were stupid on the one hand, for not being where they should have been and catching the boys in a serious offense, and unfair on the other hand, for trumping up "loitering" charges against them.

From the viewpoint of the police, the situation was quite different. They knew, with all the confidence necessary to be a policeman, that these boys were engaged in criminal activities. They knew this partly from occasionally catching them, mostly from circumstantial evidence ("the boys were around when those tires were slashed"), and partly because the police shared the view of the community in general that this was a bad bunch of boys. The best the police could hope to do was to be sensitive to the fact that these boys were engaged in illegal acts and arrest them whenever there was some evidence that they had been involved. Whether or not the boys had in fact committed a particular act in a particular way was not especially important. The police had a broader view: their job was to stamp out these kids' crimes; the tactics were not as important as the end result.

Over the period that the group was under observation, each member was arrested at least once. Several of the boys were arrested a number of times and spent at least one night in jail. While most were never taken to court, two of the boys were sentenced to six months' incarceration in boys' schools.

The Roughnecks in School

The Roughnecks' behavior in school was not particularly disruptive. During school hours they did not all hang around together, but tended instead to spend most of their time with one or two other members of the gang who were their special buddies. Although every member of the gang attempted to avoid school as much as possible, they were not particularly successful and most of them attended school with surprising regularity. They considered school a burden— something to be gotten through with a minimum of conflict. If they were "bugged" by a particular teacher, it could lead to trouble. One of the boys, Al, once threatened to beat up a teacher and, according to the other boys, the teacher hid under a desk to escape him.

Teachers saw the boys the way the general community did, as heading for trouble, as being uninterested in making something of themselves. Some were also seen as being incapable of meeting the academic standards of the school. Most of the teachers expressed concern for this group of boys and were willing to pass them despite poor performance, in the belief that failing them would only aggravate the problem.

The group of boys had a grade point average just slightly above "C." No one in the group failed either grade, and no one had better than a "C" average. They were very consistent in their achievement or, at least, the teachers were consistent in their perception of the boys' achievement.

Two of the boys were good football players. Herb was acknowledged to be the best player in the school and Jack was almost as good. Both boys were criticized for their failure to abide by training rules, for refusing to come to practice as often as they should, and for not playing their best during practice. What they lacked in sportsmanship they made up for in skill, apparently, and played every game no matter how poorly they had performed in practice or how many practice sessions they had missed.

Two Questions

Why did the community, the school and the police react to the Saints as though they were good, upstanding, nondelinquent youths with bright futures but to the Roughnecks as though they were tough, young criminals who were headed for trouble? Why did the Roughnecks and the Saints in fact have quite different careers after high school—careers which, by and large, lived up to the expectations of the community?

The most obvious explanation for the differences in the community's and law enforcement agencies' reactions to the two gangs is that one group of boys was "more delinquent" than the other. Which group *was* more delinquent? The answer to this question will determine in part how we explain the differential responses to these groups by the members of the community and, particularly, by law enforcement and school officials.

In sheer number of illegal acts, the Saints were the more delinquent. They were truant from school for at least part of the day almost every day of the week. In addition, their drinking and vandalism occurred with surprising regularity. The Roughnecks, in contrast, engaged sporadically in delinquent episodes. While these episodes were frequent, they certainly did not occur on a daily or even a weekly basis.

The difference in frequency of offenses was probably caused by the Roughnecks' inability to obtain liquor and to manipulate legitimate excuses from school. Since the Roughnecks had less money than the Saints, and teachers carefully supervised their school activities, the Roughnecks' hearts may have been as black as the Saints', but their misdeeds were not nearly as frequent.

There are really no clear-cut criteria by which to measure qualitative differences in antisocial behavior. The most important dimension of the difference is generally referred to as the "seriousness" of the offenses.

If seriousness encompasses the relative economic costs of delinquent acts, then some assessment can be made. The Roughnecks probably stole an average of about $5.00 worth of goods a week. Some weeks the figure was considerably higher, but these times must be balanced against long periods when almost nothing was stolen.

The Saints were more continuously engaged in delinquency but their acts were not for the most part costly to property. Only their vandalism and occasional theft of gasoline would so qualify. Perhaps once or twice a month they would siphon a tankful of gas. The other costly items were street signs, construction lanterns and the like. All of these acts combined probably did not quite average $5.00 a week, partly because much of the stolen equipment was abandoned and presumably could be recovered. The difference in cost of stolen property between the two groups was trivial, but the Roughnecks probably had a slightly more expensive set of activities than did the Saints.

Another meaning of seriousness is the potential threat of physical harm to members of the community and to the boys themselves. The Roughnecks were more prone to physical violence; they not only welcomed an opportunity to fight; they went seeking it. In addition, they fought among themselves frequently. Although the fighting never included deadly weapons, it was still a menace, however minor, to the physical safety of those involved.

The Saints never fought. They avoided physical conflict both inside and outside the group. At the same time, though, the Saints frequently endangered their own and other people's lives. They did so almost every time they drove a car, especially if they had been drinking. Sober, their driving was risky; under the influence of alcohol it was horrendous. In addition, the Saints endangered the lives of others with their pranks. Street excavations left unmarked were a very serious hazard.

Evaluating the relative seriousness of the two gangs' activities is difficult. The community reacted as though the behavior of the Roughnecks was a problem, and they reacted as though the behavior of the Saints was not. But the members of the community were ignorant of the array of delinquent acts that characterized the Saints' behavior. Although concerned citizens were unaware of much of the Roughnecks' behavior as well, they were much better informed about the Roughnecks' involvement in delinquency than they were about the Saints'.

Visibility

Differential treatment of the two gangs resulted in part because one gang was infinitely more visible than the other. This differential visibility was a direct function of the economic standing of the families. The Saints had access to automobiles and were able to remove themselves from the sight of the community. In as routine a decision as to where to go to have a milkshake after school, the Saints stayed away from the mainstream of community life. Lacking transportation, the Roughnecks could not make it to the edge of town. The center of town was the only practical place for them to meet since their homes were scattered throughout the town and any noncentral meeting place put an undue hardship on some members. Through necessity the Roughnecks congregated in a crowded area where everyone in the community passed frequently, including teachers and law enforcement officers. They could easily see the Roughnecks hanging around the drugstore.

The Roughnecks, of course, made themselves even more visible by making remarks to passersby and by occasionally getting into fights on the corner. Meanwhile, just as regularly, the Saints were either at the cafe on one edge of town or in the pool hall at the other edge of town. Without any particular realization that they were making themselves inconspicuous, the Saints were able to hide their time-wasting. Not only were they removed from the mainstream of traffic, but they were almost always inside a building.

On their escapades the Saints were also relatively invisible, since they left Hanibal and travelled to Big City. Here, too, they were mobile, roaming the city, rarely going to the same area twice.

Demeanor

To the notion of visibility must be added the difference in the responses of group members to outside intervention with their activities. If one of the Saints was confronted with an accusing policeman, even if he felt he was truly innocent of a wrongdoing, his demeanor was apologetic and penitent. A Roughneck's attitude was almost the polar opposite. When confronted with a threatening adult authority, even one who tried to be pleasant, the Roughneck's hostility and disdain were clearly observable. Sometimes he might attempt to put up a veneer of respect, but it was thin and was not accepted as sincere by the authority.

School was no different from the community at large. The Saints could manipulate the system by feigning compliance with the school norms. The availability of cars at school meant that once free from the immediate sight of the teacher, the boys could disappear rapidly. And

this escape was well enough planned that no administrator or teacher was nearby when the boys left. A Roughneck who wished to escape for a few hours was in a bind. If it were possible to get free from class, downtown was still a mile away, and even if he arrived there, he was still very visible. Truancy for the Roughnecks meant almost certain detection, while the Saints enjoyed almost complete immunity from sanctions.

Bias

Community members were not aware of the transgressions of the Saints. Even if the Saints had been less discreet, their favorite delinquencies would have been perceived as less serious than those of the Roughnecks.

In the eyes of the police and school officials, a boy who drinks in an alley and stands intoxicated on the street corner is committing a more serious offense than is a boy who drinks to inebriation in a nightclub or a tavern and drives around afterwards in a car. Similarly, a boy who steals a wallet from a store will be viewed as having committed a more serious offense than a boy who steals a lantern from a construction site.

Perceptual bias also operates with respect to the demeanor of the boys in the two groups when they are confronted by adults. It is not simply that adults dislike the posture affected by boys of the Roughneck ilk; more important is the conviction that the posture adopted by the Roughnecks is an indication of their devotion and commitment to deviance as a way of life. The posture becomes a cue, just as the type of the offense is a cue, to the degree to which the known transgressions are indicators of the youths' potential for other problems.

Visibility, demeanor and bias are surface variables which explain the day-to-day operations of the police. Why do these surface variables operate as they do? Why did the police choose to disregard the Saints' delinquencies while breathing down the backs of the Roughnecks?

The answer lies in the class structure of American society and the control of legal institutions by those at the top of the class structure. Obviously, no representative of the upper class drew up the operational chart for the police which led them to look in the ghettoes and on streetcorners—which led them to see the demeanor of lower-class youth as troublesome and that of upper-middle-class youth as tolerable. Rather, the procedures simply developed from experience—experience with irate and influential upper-middle-class parents insisting that their son's vandalism was simply a prank and his drunkenness only a momentary "sowing of wild oats"—experience with cooperative or indifferent, powerless, lower-class parents who acquiesced to the laws' definition of their son's behavior.

Adult Careers of the Saints and the Roughnecks

The community's confidence in the potential of the Saints and the Roughnecks apparently was justified. If anything, the community members underestimated the degree to which these youngsters would turn out "good" or "bad."

Seven of the eight members of the Saints went on to college immediately after high school. Five of the boys graduated from college in four years. The sixth one finished college after two years in the army, and the seventh spent four years in the air force before returning to college and receiving a B.A. degree. Of these seven college graduates, three went on for advanced degrees. One finished law school and is now active in state politics, one finished medical school and is practicing near Hanibal, and one boy is now working for a Ph.D. The other four college graduates entered submanagerial, managerial or executive training positions with larger firms.

The only Saint who did not complete college was Jerry. Jerry had failed to graduate from high school with the other Saints. During his second senior year, after the other Saints had gone on to college, Jerry began to hang around with what several teachers described as a "rough crowd"—the gang that was heir apparent to the Roughnecks. At the end of his second senior year, when he did graduate from high school, Jerry took a job as a used-car salesman, got married and quickly had a child. Although he made several abortive attempts to go to college by attending night school, when I last saw him (ten years after high school) Jerry was unemployed and had been living on unemployment for almost a year. His wife worked as a waitress.

Some of the Roughnecks have lived up to community expectations. A number of them were headed for trouble. A few were not.

Jack and Herb were the athletes among the Roughnecks and their athletic prowess paid off handsomely. Both boys received unsolicited athletic scholarships to college. After Herb received his scholarship (near the end of his senior year), he apparently did an about-face. His demeanor became very similar to that of the Saints. Although he remained a member in good standing of the Roughnecks, he stopped participating in most activities and did not hang on the corner as often.

Jack did not change. If anything, he became more prone to fighting. He even made excuses for accepting the scholarship. He told the other gang members that the school had guaranteed him a "C" average if he would come to play football—an idea that seems far-fetched, even in this day of highly competitive recruiting.

During the summer after graduation from high school, Jack attempted suicide by jumping from a tall building. The jump would certainly have killed most people trying it, but Jack survived. He entered college in the fall and played four years of football. He and Herb graduated in four years, and both are teaching and coaching in high schools. They are married and have stable families. If anything, Jack appears to have a more prestigious position in the community than does Herb, though both are well respected and secure in their positions.

Two of the boys never finished high school. Tommy left at the end of his junior year and went to another state. That summer he was arrested and placed on probation on a manslaughter charge. Three years later he was arrested for murder; he pleaded guilty to second degree murder and is serving a 30-year sentence in the state penitentiary.

Al, the other boy who did not finish high school, also left the state in his senior year. He is serving a life sentence in a state penitentiary for first degree murder.

Wes is a small-time gambler. He finished high school and "bummed around." After several years he made contact with a bookmaker who employed him as a runner. Later he acquired his own area and has been working it ever since. His position among the bookmakers is almost identical to the position he had in the gang; he is always around but no one is really aware of him. He makes no trouble and he does not get into any. Steady, reliable, capable of keeping his mouth closed, he plays the game by the rules, even though the game is an illegal one.

That leaves only Ron. Some of his former

friends reported that they had heard he was "driving a truck up north," but no one could provide any concrete information.

Reinforcement

The community responded to the Roughnecks as boys in trouble, and the boys agreed with that perception. Their pattern of deviancy was reinforced, and breaking away from it became increasingly unlikely. Once the boys acquired an image of themselves as deviants, they selected new friends who affirmed that self-image. As that self-conception became more firmly entrenched, they also became willing to try new and more extreme deviances. With their growing alienation came freer expression of disrespect and hostility for representatives of the legitimate society. This disrespect increased the community's negativism, perpetuating the entire process of commitment to deviance. Lack of a commitment to deviance works the same way. In either case, the process will perpetuate itself unless some event (like a scholarship to college or a sudden failure) external to the established relationship intervenes. For two of the Roughnecks (Herb and Jack), receiving college athletic scholarships created new relations and culminated in a break with the established pattern of deviance. In the case of one of the Saints (Jerry), his parents' divorce and his failing to graduate from high school changed some of his other relations. Being held back in school for a year and losing

his place among the Saints had sufficient impact on Jerry to alter his self-image and virtually to assure that he would not go on to college as his peers did. Although the experiments of life can rarely be reversed, it seems likely in view of the behavior of the other boys who did not enjoy this special treatment by the school that Jerry, too, would have "become something" had he graduated as anticipated. For Herb and Jack outside intervention worked to their advantage; for Jerry it was his undoing.

Selective perception and labelling—finding, processing and punishing some kinds of criminality and not others—means that visible, poor, nonmobile, outspoken, undiplomatic "tough" kids will be noticed, whether their actions are seriously delinquent or not. Other kids, who have established a reputation for being bright (even though underachieving), disciplined and involved in respectable activities, who are mobile and monied, will be invisible when they deviate from sanctioned activities. They'll sew their wild oats—perhaps even wider and thicker than their lower-class cohorts—but they won't be noticed. When it's time to leave adolescence most will follow the expected path, settling into the ways of the middle class, remembering fondly the delinquent but unnoticed fling of their youth. The Roughnecks and others like them may turn around, too. It is more likely that their noticeable deviance will have been so reinforced by police and community that their lives will be effectively channelled into careers consistent with their adolescent background.

Legal Stigma
RICHARD D. SCHWARTZ and JEROME H. SKOLNICK

Legal thinking has moved increasingly toward a sociologically meaningful view of the legal system. Sanctions, in particular, have come to be regarded in functional terms.[1] In criminal law, for instance, sanctions are said to be designed to prevent recidivism by rehabilitating, restraining, or executing the offender. They are also said to deter others from the performance of similar acts and, sometimes, to provide a channel for the expression of retaliatory motives. In such civil actions as tort or contract, monetary awards may be intended as retributive and deterrent, as in the use of punitive damages, or may be regarded as a *quid pro quo* to compensate the plaintiff for his wrongful loss.

While these goals comprise an integral part of the rationale of law, little is known about the extent to which they are fulfilled in practice. Lawmen do not as a rule make such studies, because their traditions and techniques are not designed for a systematic examination of the operation of the legal system in action, especially outside the courtroom. Thus, when extra-legal consequences—e.g., the social stigma of a prison sentence—are taken into account at all, it is through the discretionary actions of police, prosecutor, judge, and jury. Systematic information on a variety of unanticipated outcomes, those which benefit the accused as well as those which hurt him, might help to inform these decision makers and perhaps lead to changes in substantive law as well. The present paper is an attempt to study the consequences of stigma associated with legal accusation. . . .

The Effects of a Criminal Court Record on the Employment Opportunities of Unskilled Workers

In [a] field experiment, four employment folders were prepared, the same in all respects except for the criminal court record of the applicant. In all of the folders he was described as a thirty-two year old single male of unspecified race, with a high school training in mechanical trades, and a record of successive short term jobs as a kitchen helper, maintenance worker, and handyman. These characteristics are roughly typical of applicants for unskilled hotel jobs in the Catskill resort area of New York State where employment opportunities were tested.[2]

The four folders differed only in the applicant's reported record of criminal court involvement. The first folder indicated that the applicant had been convicted and sentenced for assault; the second, that he had been tried for assault and acquitted; the third, also tried for assault and acquitted, but with a letter from the judge certifying the finding of not guilty and reaffirming the legal presumption of innocence. The fourth folder made no mention of any criminal record.

A sample of one hundred employers was utilized. Each employer was assigned to one of four "treatment" groups.[3] To each employer only one folder was shown; this folder was one of the four kinds mentioned above, the selection of the folder being determined by the treatment

---

Reprinted from "Two Studies of Legal Stigma," *Social Problems,* Vol. 10 (Fall 1962), pp. 133–38, by permission of the Society for the Study of Social Problems and the authors.

[1] Legal sanctions are defined as changes in life conditions imposed through court action.

[2] The generality of these results remains to be determined. The effects of criminal involvement in the Catskill area are probably diminished, however, by the temporary nature of employment, the generally poor qualifications of the work force, and the excess of demand over supply of unskilled labor there. Accordingly, the employment differences among the four treatment groups found in this study are likely, if anything to be *smaller* than would be expected in industries and areas where workers are more carefully selected.

[3] Employers were not approached in pre-selected random order, due to a misunderstanding of instructions on the part of the law student who carried out the experiment during a three and one-half week period. Because of this flaw in the experimental procedure, the results should be treated with appropriate caution. Thus, chi-squared analysis may not properly be utilized. (For those used to this measure, $P < .05$ for Table 1.)

group to which the potential employer was assigned. The employer was asked whether he could "use" the man described in the folder. To preserve the reality of the situation and make it a true field experiment, employers were never given any indication that they were participating in an experiment. So far as they knew, a legitimate offer to work was being made in each showing of the folder by the "employment agent."

The experiment was designed to determine what employers would do in fact if confronted with an employment applicant with a criminal record. The questionnaire approach used in earlier studies[4] seemed ill-adapted to the problem since respondents confronted with hypothetical situations might be particularly prone to answer in what they considered a socially acceptable manner. The second alternative—studying job opportunities of individuals who had been involved with the law—would have made it very difficult to find comparable groups of applicants and potential employers. For these reasons, the field experiment reported here was utilized.

Some deception was involved in the study. The "employment agent"—the same individual in all hundred cases—was in fact a law student who was working in the Catskills during the summer of 1959 as an insurance adjuster. In representing himself as being both an adjuster and an employment agent, he was assuming a combination of roles which is not uncommon there. The adjuster role gave him an opportunity to introduce a single application for employment casually and naturally. To the extent that the experiment worked, however, it was inevitable that some employers should be led to believe that they had immediate prospects of filling a job opening. In those instances where an offer to hire was made, the "agent" called a few hours later to say that the applicant had taken another job. The field experimenter attempted in such instances to locate a satisfactory replacement by contacting an employment agency in the area. Because this procedure was used and since the jobs involved were of relatively minor consequence, we believe that the deception caused little economic harm.

As mentioned, each treatment group of twenty-five employers was approached with one type of folder. Responses were dichotomized: those who expressed a willingness to consider the applicant in any way were termed positive, those who made no response or who explicitly refused to consider the candidate were termed negative. Our results consist of comparisons between positive and negative responses, thus defined, for the treatment groups.

Of the twenty-five employers shown the "no record" folder, nine gave positive responses. Subject to reservations arising from chance variations in sampling, we take this as indicative of the "ceiling" of jobs available for this kind of applicant under the given field conditions. Positive responses by these employers may be compared with those in the other treatment groups to obtain an indication of job opportunities lost because of the various legal records.

Of the twenty-five employers approached with the "convict" folder, only one expressed interest in the applicant. This is a rather graphic indication of the effect which a criminal record may have on job opportunities. Care must be exercised, of course, in generalizing the conclusions to other settings. In this context, however, the criminal record made a major difference.

From a theoretical point of view, the finding leads toward the conclusion that conviction constitutes a powerful form of "status degradation"[5] which continues to operate after the time when, according to the generalized theory of justice underlying punishment in our society, the individual's "debt" has been paid. A record of conviction produces a durable if not permanent loss of status. For purposes of effective social control, this state of affairs may heighten the deterrent effect of conviction—though that remains to be established. Any such contribution to social control, however, must be balanced against the barriers imposed upon rehabilitation of the convict. If the exprisoner finds difficulty in securing menial kinds of legitimate work, further crime may become an increasingly attractive alternative.[6]

Another important finding of this study concerns the small number of positive responses

---

[4] Sol Rubin, *Crime and Juvenile Delinquency,* New York: Oceana, 1958, pp. 151–56.

[5] Harold Garfinkel, "Conditions of Successful Degradation Ceremonies," *American Journal of Sociology,* 61 (March, 1956), pp. 420–24.

[6] Severe negative effects of conviction on employment opportunities have been noted by Sol Rubin, *Crime and Juvenile Delinquency,* New York: Oceana, 1958. A further source of employment difficulty is inherent in licensing

elicited by the "accused but acquitted" applicant. Of the twenty-five employers approached with this folder, three offered jobs. Thus, the individual accused but acquitted of assault has almost as much trouble finding even an unskilled job as the one who was not only accused of the same offense, but also convicted.

From a theoretical point of view, this result indicates that permanent lowering of status is not limited to those explicitly singled out by being convicted of a crime. As an ideal outcome of American justice, criminal procedure is supposed to distinguish between the "guilty" and those who have been acquitted. Legally controlled consequences which follow the judgment are consistent with this purpose. Thus, the "guilty" are subject to fine and imprisonment, while those who are acquitted are immune from these sanctions. But deprivations may be imposed on the acquitted, both before and after victory in court. Before trial, legal rules either permit or require arrest and detention. The suspect may be faced with the expense of an attorney and a bail bond if he is to mitigate these limitations on his privacy and freedom. In addition, some pre-trial deprivations are imposed without formal legal permission. These may include coercive questioning, use of violence, and stigmatization. And, as this study indicates, some deprivations not under the direct control of the legal process may develop or persist after an official decision of acquittal has been made.

Thus two legal principles conflict in practice. On the one hand, "a man is innocent until proven guilty." On the other, the accused is systematically treated as guilty under the administration of criminal law until a functionary or official body—police, magistrate, prosecuting attorney or trial judge—decides that he is entitled to be free. Even then, the results of treating him as guilty persist and may lead to serious consequences.

The conflict could be eased by measures aimed at reducing the deprivations imposed on the accused, before and after acquittal. Some legal attention has been focused on pre-trial deprivations. The provision of bail and counsel, the availability of habeas corpus, limitations on the admissibility of coerced confessions, and civil actions for false arrest are examples of measures aimed at protecting the rights of the accused before trial. Although these are often limited in effectiveness, especially for individuals of lower socioeconomic status, they at least represent some concern with implementing the presumption of innocence at the pre-trial stage.

By contrast, the courts have done little toward alleviating the post-acquittal consequences of legal accusation. One effort along these lines has been employed in the federal courts, however. Where an individual has been accused and exonerated of a crime, he may petition the federal courts for a "Certificate of Innocence" certifying this fact.[7] Possession of such a document might be expected to alleviate post-acquittal deprivations.

Some indication of the effectiveness of such a measure is found in the responses of the final treatment group. Their folder, it will be recalled, contained information on the accusation and acquittal of the applicant, but also included a letter from the judge addressed "To whom it may concern" certifying the applicant's acquittal and reminding the reader of the presumption of innocence. Such a letter might have had a boomerang effect, by reemphasizing the legal involvement of the applicant. It was important, therefore, to determine empirically whether such a communication would improve or harm the chances of employment. Our findings indicate that it increased employment opportunities, since the letter folder elicited six positive responses. Even though this fell short of the nine responses to the "no record" folder, it doubled the number for the "accused but acquitted" and created a significantly greater number of job offers than those elicited by the convicted record.

statutes and security regulations which sometimes preclude convicts from being employed in their pre-conviction occupation or even in the trades which they may have acquired during imprisonment. These effects, may, however, be counteracted by bonding arrangement, prison associations, and publicity programs aimed at increasing confidence in, and sympathy for, exconvicts. See also, B. F. McSally, "Finding Jobs for Released Offenders," *Federal Probation,* 24 (June, 1960), pp. 12–17; Harold D. Lasswell and Richard C. Donnelly, "The Continuing Debate over Responsibility: An Introduction to Isolating the Condemnation Sanction," *Yale Law Journal,* 68 (April, 1959), pp. 869–99; Johs Andenaes, "General Prevention—Illusion or Reality?" *J. Criminal Law, Criminology and Police Science,* 43 (July–August, 1952), pp. 176–98.

[7] 28 United States Code, Secs, 1495, 2513.

TABLE 1.   Effect of Four Types of Legal Folder on Job Opportunities (in per cent)

	No Record	Acquitted With Letter	Acquitted Without Letter	Convicted	Total
	(N = 25)	(N = 25)	(N = 25)	(N = 25)	(N = 100)
Positive response	36	24	12	4	19
Negative response	64	76	88	96	81
Total	100	100	100	100	100

This suggests that the procedure merits consideration as a means of offsetting the occupational loss resulting from accusation. It should be noted, however, that repeated use of this device might reduce its effectiveness.

The results of the experiment are summarized in Table 1. The differences in outcome found there indicate that various types of legal records are systematically related to job opportunities. It seems fair to infer also that the trend of job losses corresponds with the apparent punitive intent of the authorities. Where the man is convicted, that intent is presumably greatest. It is less where he is accused but acquitted and still less where the court makes an effort to emphasize the absence of a finding of guilt. Nevertheless, where the difference in punitive intent is ideally greatest, between conviction and acquittal, the difference in occupational harm is very slight. . . .

Part III DEVIANT SUBCULTURES

Despite popular stereotype, deviant careers are not unilinear; nor do they have fixed and inevitable stages. Some people who commit deviant acts may never be typed as deviant and/or may discontinue those acts, while others may become "hard-core" career deviants. And even those who do become career deviants may do so through widely different routes. Thus there is no single natural history of deviant careers; there are many career histories. One hypothetical deviant career might proceed as follows. A person lives in a culture where certain acts are viewed as deviant. This person is believed, rightly or wrongly, to have committed such deviance. Someone (e.g., teacher, neighbor) types the person as a certain type of deviant. The person comes to the attention of an official agency (e.g., juvenile authorities) and becomes an official case. This social processing propels the person into organized deviant life (e.g., the person is now a "hoodlum"—ostracized by "good kids" and accepted only in disreputable circles). Finally, in self-redefinition, the person assumes the deviant role (i.e., actually becomes a "hood"), thus confirming the initial typing.

This, however, is only one developmental model. Another hypothetical deviant career (which is probably more characteristic of certain kinds of deviance such as professional crime) might proceed along opposite lines. First, the person defines himself or herself as a certain kind of deviant, then enters a deviant world to confirm that identity, comes to official notice, becomes an official case, and engages in more persistent and patterned deviations, thus reinforcing the system of social types. Still other types of deviant careers may require different models. In fact, deviant careers vary so widely that a person might enter the deviance process at any one of the various stages and move forward, backward, or out of the process completely.

Perhaps a visual image will help. Suppose we visualize deviant careers as a long corridor. Each segment of the corridor represents one stage in a deviant career, with doors that allow people to directly enter into or exit from that stage. Some people can enter the deviance corridor from a side door, without previous experience in a deviant career. Others can leave by a side door, thus terminating their deviant careers. Finally, there are some who will enter at one end of the corridor and proceed through all the stages to the other end. The following diagram shows how the traffic of deviance may flow.

The deviance corridor

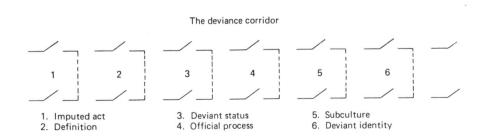

1. Imputed act 3. Deviant status 5. Subculture
2. Definition 4. Official process 6. Deviant identity

The dotted lines represent the invisible boundaries marking stages of a person's deviant career. At each of these symbolic boundaries there are defining agents who speed certain people farther along the corridor and usher others out the side doors or back to where they started.

The rate and direction of a person's progress through the corridor are based largely on the person's responses to others' symbolic definitions of him or her. In addition to conventional people, those who type and respond to the deviant often include members of the deviant subculture; thus these people can be an important influence in solidifying a person's deviant career.

The fact that a person has been assigned a deviant label does not mean that s/he will automatically be drawn into a deviant subculture. Nonetheless, dilettantes in deviance and career deviants alike are likely to become involved with a deviant subculture at some time. Thus Part III of this book examines the rise and nature of deviant subcultures. It then goes on to examine how people enter deviant worlds, and how they learn subcultural traditions. Finally, it considers social variations within and among deviant subcultures.

The Rise and Nature of Deviant Subcultures

A subculture is apt to come into being when people are in contact with one another, suffer a common fate, and have common interests. These common interests generally arise from their social situation and are shared because these people face more or less the same dilemma.

The general dilemma for the persons who ultimately become involved in deviant subcultures is that they want to continue activities that the society labels deviant but at the same time they want to avoid punishment. When enough people become aware that they share such a problem, a deviant subculture can arise to provide a solution.

When these people are especially concerned with continuing their activities, the deviant group forms on the basis of a common attraction; an example would be the gay subculture. When people are thrust together because of official typing, on the other hand, the deviant group forms on the basis of shared punishment; the prison subculture is one example. Finally, if it is merely by chance that the persons engage together in deviant activities, they do not actually form a subculture. Race riots provide an example.

Entry and Acculturation

Entry refers to the ways in which a person comes to participate in and gain admittance to a deviant subculture. *Acculturation* refers to the new ways and meanings a person acquires from that subculture. Entry can be clearly defined (where a person clearly is or is not a member of the subculture), or it can be rather loose in character. Likewise, acculturation can be highly specialized or casual and offhand. Like colleges, subcultures vary in how hard they are to get into and how hard they are to stay in. Much of this depends on the complexity of the activities involved, on how much commitment others in the subculture expect from newcomers, and on how much they must rely on them for their own safety and welfare. With a team of pickpockets, for example, entry and socialization are rigorous. On the other hand, admission and socialization to a Skid Row bottle gang are relatively simple. Here all a person needs is a few coins to "go in on a bottle," and there is relatively little to learn.

Subcultural Variations

Some deviants become highly involved in deviant subcultures, but this is not true for all deviants. Within a particular subculture (e.g., a youth subculture) some people may be highly immersed while others (e.g., weekend visitors) may participate only occasionally. Also, some forms of deviance lend themselves to more involvement in a subculture than do others. Because they have to be highly mobile, check forgers, for example, may be marginal to any kind of social group, conventional or deviant. Skid Row drunks, on the other hand, are freer to immerse themselves in a subculture. In addition, covert deviants (e.g., "closet queens") are generally less engulfed in an unconventional way of life and engage in the deviant subculture sporadically and secretly. Overt deviants (e.g., gay activists) ordinarily find themselves more involved in an unconventional way of life that stipulates a regular schedule of activities and a circle of intimate and deviant acquaintances.

Sanctions that deviants bring against one another are also important. Social control operates in deviant ways of life just as it does in the conventional world. How well do deviant groups control members? In general, it seems that in some subcultures (e.g., organized crime) members are subject to more social control than in others (e.g., the gay subculture). Also, it seems that within a subculture more social control is exerted over some members (e.g., a novice) than over others (e.g., a leader in the group).

Subcultures have beliefs, values, and norms that are supposed to regulate conduct. These prescriptions contribute to a form of social order. Deviant groups vary in the extent to which they organize their activities and define them by subcultural rules: some have elaborate rules that specify beliefs and actions; others have simpler codes. A simple, tightly organized code leads to one set of consequences, a complex, loosely organized code to another. In addition, some deviant subcultures have rules and beliefs that protect and dignify their members while others spawn normlessness, induce exploitation, and set deviants against one another.

Within a subculture some members show more commitment to the deviant way of life than do others. How dependent the person is on the deviant subculture, the person's identity, how much the person shares the viewpoints of others in the subculture —all these seem to be factors influencing a person's commitment to the subculture.

9 THE RISE AND NATURE OF DEVIANT SUBCULTURES

In most cases a so-called deviant is not unique or alone. There are often many other people who have been similarly typed; they may also have been similarly punished (e.g., imprisoned) for their alleged deviance and thus further differentiated from conventional society. If such people come into contact with one another, they may form their own subculture, thereby gaining acceptance and support. Also, when they are interested in continuing their "deviant ways," a subculture may arise to offer good opportunities for them to do so. These conditions and others discussed in the readings to follow, then, may lead to the rise of deviant subcultures.

In the first reading Earl Rubington points out that deviants develop through the process of social interaction a set of shared solutions to the various problems they face. This body of problem-solving devices—what they think and do—make up their subculture. In the second reading J. L. Simmons describes the sociological character of these groups. In the final reading Lewis Yablonsky illustrates Simmons' points with research on delinquent gangs.

Theory of Deviant Subcultures   EARL RUBINGTON

"Subculture," as a concept, has gained widespread currency in lay as well as sociological circles. Usually it refers to beliefs, values, and norms which are different from, yet supportive of, conventional traditions. Ethnic groups in the United States, who eat different foods, are bilingual, and dress differently, are examples. Beliefs, values, and norms shared by people who violate conventional traditions have come to be referred to as "deviant subcultures." Hippies, punks, Skid Row bums, and junkies are some examples of persons who are seen to be in deviant subcultures.

Three questions about deviant subcultures which sociologists have raised are: Under what social conditions do these subcultures come into existence? How do they function for those people who participate in them? And how do people who behave the same way yet are not in the subculture differ from those who are? Albert K. Cohen[1] has perhaps done the most to develop some systematic answers to such questions. We turn now to a brief exposition of his views.

Albert Cohen says that all behavior is problem-solving. The genesis of deviant subcultures follows from that general principle; that is, people in a given social situation face social-psychological problems of adjustment. Given an appropriate sequence of events, a subculture can emerge. The result of its emergence, of course, is that it provides a solution to the common problem experienced by all people in the situation. The reason why there aren't more subcultures, conventional or deviant, follows from a natural history model of how subcultures emerge.

As Cohen sees it, there are five stages in the development of a subculture: (1) experiencing a problem, (2) communicating about it with someone else in the same situation, (3) interacting on the basis of the problem, (4) developing a solution, and (5) sustaining and passing on the tradition.

Experiencing a problem is a necessary but not sufficient condition for the development of a subculture. Although people without problems are not likely to create and sustain a special subculture, experiencing a problem cannot lead to the emergence of a subculture if people do not talk about their common problem. If they do communicate with one another about their shared problem, then the chances of the next step (namely, that they will come to interact with one another on the basis of their shared problem) being taken become that much better. Out of this focused interaction, they come to forge a solution to their common problem. They apply their solution, it works, and soon a few others in the same situation join up with them. The last stage comes when they practice and pass on the tradition they have just developed.

According to Cohen (1955), the delinquent subculture emerged in the following way. First, working class youth came to sense difficulties in their competition for status in school. Their parents could not train them as well to compete for the middle class values the school distributed. A few of them began talking about the way they felt. Soon others came to express similar feelings. In the course of subsequent meetings, they focused in their interaction on their common fate. Unable to compete successfully for these values, they rejected them, turned them around, and became malicious, negativistic, and nonutilitarian. A few of them hit upon some joint activities that captured their imagination, such as breaking school windows after school was out. This activity only led to similar kinds of negativistic acts. It soon became a pattern, and after a while they found a number of recruits who wanted to join up with them and engage in similar activities. In effect, they invented a new game—juvenile delinquency—in which they were able to achieve status.

Critics argue that Cohen's theory requires all gang participants to respond to the same set of unconscious motives when they form a delinquent gang. Kitsuse and Dietrick (1959), for example, argue that a reactive theory of delinquent subculture formation is more plausible; that is, when working class youths engage in delinquent behavior, they are responding to an almost

Slightly revised excerpt from Earl Rubington, "Deviant Subcultures," in Michael Rosenberg, Robert A. Stebbins, and Allan Turowetz (eds.), *The Sociology of Deviance*, New York: St. Martin's Press, pp. 57–60. Copyright © 1982 by St. Martin's Press, Inc., and used with permission of the publisher.

[1] Albert K. Cohen, *Delinquent Boys: The Culture of the Gang,* New York: The Free Press, 1955.

infinite variety of motives for participation. The sense of rejection and alienation from middle class values, they say, happens after these youths have been caught, punished, and stigmatized. The common fate they experience is that of being singled out and treated as deviants by their teachers and classmates. According to Kitsuse and Dietrick, the punitive reaction isolates them from middle-class values and their representatives in schools and thrusts them into the company of all the others who have been tarred with the same brush. The rejection of middle-class values follows from sharing the common fate of social punishment and becomes the basis for delinquent gang formation. Unlike Cohen, Kitsuse and Dietrick argue that the shared status problem has little to do with failure to compete for success and status in the school's social system. Rather, having now been defined as outsiders by the authorities, they react with group vengeance against their social punishment. These actions only trigger another acting out—social punishment cycle. In the interaction between authorities and youth, the delinquent subculture is born.

Whether the deviant subculture arises out of deviant motivation or in response to a process of social differentiation, Cohen's main point still holds. In either case, people who feel rejected, as well as people who have actually experienced rejection, have an acute problem of social-psychological adjustment. Under whatever conditions the deviant subculture emerges, people who share in it sustain it and live by it so long as it helps them to manage these problems.

A deviant subculture, then, consists of a body of shared solutions to the problems of social deviance. Three areas in which a variety of problems may develop include the act, partners, and the consequences of the act. A subculture of deviants of whatever kind will make available to its constituents ways of organizing and executing the deviant act, a set of rules of associating with one's partners in deviance, and some means for either avoiding or managing the consequences of deviance. The subculture of drug addicts provides a useful example (Rubington, 1967).

Once addicted, drug users require another shot some four hours after their last injection, if they are to avoid severe withdrawal symptoms. Awareness of this necessity generates a set of fairly regular activities. The cycle of activities the addict engages in includes obtaining a supply of drugs, having the drug experience, managing the aftermath, and then starting the cycle all over again. The cycle begins with a "hustle." This includes selling drugs, engaging in prostitution, and stealing goods and then fencing them for money. Once the addict has the price, the next step is to "cop" (obtain a supply of drugs). The third step is to find a "shooting gallery" (a place where one can take drugs in safety) and then "fix" (inject the dose). The fourth step is either "going on the nod" (falling asleep) or just "feeling normal." After a few hours, the cycle is reactivated, and the addict goes out to "hustle," "cop," and "fix" all over again.

At each juncture of the cycle, addicts go through all of the steps required before they can administer the needed dosage. In the process, there are always problems connected with obtaining drugs, interacting with an assortment of role-partners, and avoiding capture. Through the process of interaction with other addicts, they learn, share, and employ a set of collective solutions to every one of these problems, all of which are contingent on their status as drug addicts.

Addict subculture, learned in intimate interaction with other addicts, provides solutions to problems that arise at any of the phases of the addict's cycle of activities. Thus the behavior patterns center on the administration of drugs in order to obtain the desired drug experience. The norms specify rules for how to conduct oneself when in the company of other addicts, dealers, undercover agents, the police, and so on. . . . And the ideology contains justifications for the drug experience, along with a body of ideas about the social world of nonusers. In addition, it is the main repository of collective definitions of the range of situations in which addicts may expect to find themselves. In summary, then, the beliefs, values, and norms of the addict subculture provide information on how to think, feel, and act like an addict. This subculture affords to each of its participants answers to the central question of drug addiction: what to think, feel, say, and do while having drug experiences and coping with their social and psychological consequences.

Culture for deviants such as drug addicts is essentially the same as it is for conventional people. The main difference, of course, is that the content of deviant subcultures is illegal, immoral, or both. The content provides knowledge and skills on how to execute deviant activities and further the interests of those who engage in such activities. Because the activities are stigmatized, those who engage in them place themselves in opposition to the dominant culture. Their resistance to conventionality requires them to develop justifications for their activities. The ideology of the deviant subculture supplies these justifications. Without them, it is questionable whether these actions could continue, given the necessity that people understand the meaning of their own conduct.

The major difference between social deviants and solitary deviants is that social deviants draw upon a stock of collective solutions to the problems their deviance creates for them. By contrast, solitary deviants proceed by trial-and-error and fashion private solutions to the problems of deviance. Being a member of a group, albeit a deviant one, the social deviant experiences the benefits as well as the costs of group membership. As with all groups, however, the benefits of membership are contingent on the members paying the price of conformity. Considering the hazards attached to the situation of most social deviants, they are usually more than willing to pay this price. The group, as is the case with any group, prescribes norms for its members to follow. By adhering to the group's code of conduct, members satisfy their deviant motives.

Solitary deviants lack guidelines, not to mention social support. Lacking both a membership and a reference group of similarly situated other people, they also lack a set of consistent definitions for the range of unpredictable and hazardous situations in which they may become implicated. In these isolated circumstances, solitary deviants cannot achieve consensus about the meaning of their activities and how best to pursue their interest in deviance.

The Nature of Deviant Subcultures

J. L. SIMMONS

. . . "Deviant subculture" is a stripped-down scientific abstraction for a very real and concrete thing—most deviants live in connection with other deviants and "sympathizers," even if this be only half a dozen people in a little Midwestern town. And such subcultures evolve their own little communities or social worlds, each with its own local myths (the county attorney goes easy with us cause he's an old head himself), its own legendary heroes (remember Max—what a crazy one he was), its own honorary members (Blaine the druggist or Sophie at the cafe), its own scale of reputations (Garth's all right, he's just a little slow about some things), and its own social routine (probably see you at the Totem later on tonight).

The term is useful because it points to something important; deviants tend to get together. There are deviant traditions and ideologies, deviant prestige systems, commitment and conformity to deviant codes, deviant recruitment and missionary work, and deviant utopian dreams.

But the social scientists have also been taken in by their own word game. My conclusion from field research with two rural delinquent gangs, a health food coterie, two mystic groups, several beatnik and hippie groups, and various student fringe groups is that "deviant subcultures" are in actuality far from the tightly-knit, highly cohesive, clearly structured entities they are pictured to be in social science literature, police records, or the press. These misconceptions are projected onto what, in reality, is usually no more than a bunch of people with ever-shifting, overlapping relationships. Such groups are amorphous and quite unstable through time. Goals and purposes, moral codes, and even memberships are often only semi-conscious. Commitment and loyalties to the group wax and wane, and they are seldom dependable. I recall the remark of a mischievous teenager in Cedar Rapids, Iowa: "I had no idea I belonged to a delinquent gang until the cops told me."

The notion of "deviant subculture," therefore, is itself a stereotype which is partly true but also false in several important respects. Lewis Yablonsky's concept, "near-group"—a collectivity of people whose degree of cohesion and organization falls somewhere between a mob and a true group—applies, I think, far more accurately to the realities of deviants associating together. There are shared understandings among the participants, but their interpersonal relations are also shot through with many misunderstandings and miscarried intentions. Any "organization" is usually informal, uncrystallized and unstable beyond a few weeks.

With a few notable exceptions, such as the Hell's Angels, the commitment of the participants to one another and to the group as a whole is tenuous and half-hearted. For individual "members" it varies. On one occasion it may be an intense brotherhood; on the next the individuals may be willing to sell each other out to save themselves or to obtain some small personal gain. (Sometimes this personal gain may be no more than the undivided attention of a reporter or a bit of flattery from an investigator.)

Membership itself is often vague, and the line between "us" and "them" wavers and changes. . . . The dichotomy of members and nonmembers is oversimple; usually a few core members are unequivocally committed, a larger circle of part-time members drift back and forth between conventionality and deviance, and an even larger circle are only tangentially acquainted or involved. These last two circles, and sometimes even the few at the core, constantly move in and out of the subculture. They are occupied with a variety of conventional as well as deviant activities and commitments. Rather than being the essential part of their lives, the deviance may be only a casual weekend thing or the result of an occasional spree.

The supposed members are often not very clear in their own minds on what the group is about, who else is in it, and what it attempts to accomplish. And different members will give conflicting views on these matters.

Even leadership and other designations of functions are vague and constantly changing. Factionalism and incessant internal shifts in personal status are the rule rather than the exception. Internal statuses tend to be negotiated and temporary, so control of individual members by the group isn't really all that extensive.

These vagaries are why drug use or black radicalism or homosexuality can't be eradicated by dealing with the supposed leaders. There are eminent people in these and similar fringe movements but there is no "head to lop off." A teacher in one of the depressed schools of Wichita, Kansas, exclaimed after the assassination of Martin Luther King, "Good, that'll be the end of all this trouble and unrest." I could only feel sorry for her on various counts.

We mustn't, however, err in the opposite direction by suggesting that the whole subculture notion is false. A deviant's closer associates are statistically most likely to be other fringe people. There are discernible deviant social worlds, partially insulated and estranged from the society at large, each with its subterranean traditions, its own literature and slang, its own beliefs and ways of looking at things. All these things exist but in varying degrees, not as hard and fast characteristics.

The ambivalence of the participants is the main thing that keeps deviant subcultures from becoming more solid. Most members are of two minds about deviating and most of them still have many conventional commitments. My observations suggest that the vast majority of deviants inhabit dual worlds of deviance/conventionality and when things aren't going well in the one they turn to the other. They vacillate between the two as situations and opportunities shift. . . .

A visible deviant group is the symptom and surface of some larger and more widespread fringe drift within the society. The Women's Christian Temperance Union, for instance, was only the organized spearhead of a Prohibition backlash against the perceived moral decline of urbanism—the Prohibition mood was felt by far more people than were members of this organization, and it spread beyond a fight against liquor into action against illicit drugs, sex, political liberalism and so on. Delinquent gangs were only the more spectacular aspects of the failure of the huge metropolis to take humane care of its inhabitants. The hippies are only the more far out examples of the pervasive unrest and disillusionment of a whole generation of youth with standard-brand America. And the Black Panthers are but a more vocal and visible swell on the surface of a deep militant thrust of twenty million blacks for a place in the sun.

Sometimes changes in these fringe drifts will leave particular deviant groups aground to flounder and finally expire for lack of underlying support. This seems to be the fate of the old Marxist radicals in the United States, younger radicals have gone beyond Communism as well as capitalism. . . .

More often there is a number of different . . . groups expressing a range of different positions in the fringe drift. Most such groups are more fleeting and unstable than the underlying deviant subcultural drift that spawned them. Wife-swapping clubs, sexual freedom leagues . . . are only facets of the erotic revolution in our time.

Societal condemnation gives powerful support to the creation and continuation of those deviant groups. Even when the members don't altogether agree with or even like each other they are thrown together because they may have nowhere else to turn for help and support. But just about everything else is against them. Unlike conventional associations, deviant groups must solve their internal conflicts and problems without any supports from the larger society. . . .

The Delinquent Gang as a Near-Group

LEWIS YABLONSKY

. . . Some recent sociological theory and discourse on gangs suffers from distortions of gang structure to fit a group rather than a near-group conception. Most gang theorizing begins with an automatic assumption that gangs are defined sociological groups. Many of these misconceived theories about gangs in sociological treatises are derived from the popular and traditional image of gangs held by the general public as reported in the press, rather than as based upon empirical scientific investigation. The following case material reveals the disparities between popular reports of gang war behavior and their organization as revealed by more systematic study.

The official report of a gang fight, which made headlines in New York papers as the biggest in the city's history, detailed a gang war between six gangs over a territorial dispute.[1] The police, social workers, the press, and the public accepted a defined version of groups meeting in battle over territory. Research into this gang war incident, utilizing a near-group concept of gangs, indicates another picture of the situation.

N.Y. Daily News
NIP 200—PUNK FIGHT NEAR COLUMBIA CAMPUS
by Grover Ryder and Jack Smee
A flying squad of 25 cops, alerted by a civilian's tip, broke up the makings of one of the biggest gang rumbles in the city's turbulent teen history last night at the edge of Columbia University campus on Morningside Heights.

N.Y. Herald Tribune
POLICE SEIZE 38, AVERT GANG BATTLE—RIVERSIDE PARK RULE WAS GOAL
Police broke up what they said might have been "a very serious" battle between two juvenile factions last night as they intercepted thirty-eight youths.

N.Y. Times
GANG WAR OVER PARK BROKEN BY POLICE
The West Side police broke up an impending gang fight near Columbia University last night as 200 teenagers were massing for battle over exclusive rights to the use of Riverside Park.

N.Y. Journal-American
6-GANG BATTLE FOR PARK AVERTED NEAR GRANT'S TOMB COPS PATROL TROUBLE SPOT
Police reinforcements today patrolled Morningside Heights to prevent a teen-aged gang war for "control" of Riverside Park.

World-Telegram and Sun
HOODLUM WAR AVERTED AS COPS ACT FAST
38 to 200 Seized Near Columbia
by Richard Graf
Fast police action averted what threatened to be one of the biggest street gang fights in the city's history as some 200 hoodlums massed last night on the upper West Side to battle over "exclusive rights" to Riverside Park.

Depth interviews with 40 gang boys, most of whom had been arrested at the scene of the gang fight, revealed a variety of reasons for attendance at the battle. There were also varied perceptions of the event and the gangs involved reported simply in the press as "gangs battling over territory." Some of the following recurring themes were revealed in the gang boys' responses.

Estimates of the number of gang boys present varied from 80 to 5,000.

Gang boys interviewed explained their presence at the "battle" as follows:

I didn't have anything to do that night and wanted to see what was going to happen.

Those guys called me a Spic and I was going to get even. [He made this comment even though the "rival" gangs were mostly Puerto Ricans.]

They always picked on us. [The "they" is usually a vague reference.]

I always like a fight; it keeps up my rep.

My father threw me out of the house; I wanted to get somebody and heard about the fight.

Reprinted from *Social Problems*, Vol. 7, No. 2 (Fall 1959), pp. 108–117, by permission of the Society for the Study of Social Problems and the author. This is a revised version of a paper delivered at The Eastern Sociological Meetings in New York City, April 11, 1959. [A larger version of the theory of near-groups and gang data presented in this paper can be found in *The Violent Gang*, Baltimore, Md.: Penguin Books, 1966.]

[1]New York newspaper headlines—June 11, 1955.

The youth who was responsible for "calling on" the gang war—the reputed Balkan Gang leader—presented this version of the event:

That night I was out walkin' my dog about 7:30. Then I saw all these guys coming from different directions. I couldn't figure out what was happening. Then I saw some of the guys I know and I remembered we had called it on for that night.

I never really figured the Politicians [a supposed "brother Gang" he had called] would show.

Another boy added another dimension to "gang war organization":

How did we get our name? Well, when we were in the police station, the cops kept askin' us who we were. Jay was studying history in school—so he said how about the Balkans. Let's call ourselves the Balkans.' So we told the cops—we're the Balkans—and that was it.

Extensive data revealed this was not a case of two organized groups meeting in battle. The press, public, police, social workers, and others projected group conceptions onto a near-group activity. Most of the youths at the scene of the gang war were, in fact, participating in a kind of mob action. Most had no real concept of belonging to any gang or group; however, they were interested in a situation which might be exciting and possibly a channel for expressing some of their aggressions and hostilities. Although it was not necessarily a defined war, the possibilities of a stabbing or even a killing were high—with a few hundred disturbed and fearful youths milling around in the undefined situation. The gang war was not a social situation of two structured teen-aged armies meeting on a battlefield to act out a defined situation; it was a case of two near-groups in action.

Another boy's participation in this gang war further reveals its structure. The evening of the fight he had nothing to do, heard about this event and decided that he would wander up to see what was going to happen. On his way to the scene of the rumored gang fight he thought it might be a good idea to invite a few friends "just to be on the safe side." This swelled the final number of youths arriving at the scene of the gang fight, since other boys did the same. He denied (and I had no reason to disbelieve him) belonging to either of the gangs and the same applied to his friends. He was arrested at the scene of "battle" for disorderly conduct and weapon-carrying.

I asked him why he had carried a knife and a zip gun on his person when he went to the gang fight if he did not belong to either of the reputed gangs and intended to be merely a "peaceful observer." His response: "Man, I'm not going to a rumble without packin'." The boy took along weapons for self-defense in the event he was attacked. The possibilities of his being attacked in an hysterical situation involving hundreds of youths who had no clear idea of what they were doing at the scene of a gang fight was, of course, great. Therefore, he was correct (within his social framework) in taking along a weapon for self-protection.

These characteristic responses to the situation when multiplied by the numbers of others present characterize the problem. What may be a confused situation involving many aggressive youths (belonging to near-groups) is often defined as a case of two highly mechanized and organized gang groups battling each other with definition to their activities.

In another "gang war case" which made headlines, a psychotic youth acted out his syndrome by stabbing another youth. When arrested and questioned about committing the offense, the youth stated that he was a member of a gang carrying out retaliation against another gang, which was out to get him. He attributed his assault to gang affiliation.

The psychotic youth used the malleable near-group, the gang, *as his psychotic syndrome*. Napoleon, God, Christ, and other psychotic syndromes, so popular over the years, may have been replaced on city streets by gang membership. Not only is it a convenient syndrome, but some disturbed youths find their behavior as rational, accepted, and even aggrandized by many representatives of society. Officials such as police officers and social workers, in their interpretation of the incident, often amplify this individual behavior by a youth into a group gang war condition because it is a seemingly more logical explanation of a senseless act.

In the case of the Balkans, the societal response of viewing them as a group rather than a near-group solidified their structure. After the incident, as one leader stated it, "lots more kids wanted to join."

Another gang war event further reveals the near-group structure of the gang. On the night of July 30, 1957, a polio victim named Michael

Farmer was beaten and stabbed to death by a gang varyingly known as the Egyptian Kings and the Dragons. The boys who participated in this homicide came from the upper West Side of Manhattan. I had contact with many of these boys prior to the event and was known to others through the community program I directed. Because of this prior relationship the boys cooperated and responded openly when I interviewed them in the institutions where they were being held in custody.[2]

Responses to my interviews indicated the near-group nature of the gang. Some of the pertinent responses which reveal this characteristic of the Egyptian King gang structure are somewhat demonstrated by the following comments made by five of the participants in the killing. (These are representative comments selected from over ten hours of recorded interviews.)

I was walking uptown with a couple of friends and we ran into Magician [one of the Egyptian King gang leaders] and them there. They asked us if we wanted to go to a fight, and we said yes. When he asked me if I wanted to go to a fight, I couldn't say no. I mean, I could say no, but for old time's sake, I said yes.

Everyone was pushin' and I pulled out my knife. I saw this face—I never seen it before, so I stabbed it.

He was laying on the ground lookin' up at us. Everyone was kicking, punching, stabbing. I kicked him on the jaw or someplace; then I kicked him in the stomach. That was the least I could do was kick 'im.

They have guys watching you and if you don't stab or hit somebody, they get you later. I hit him over the head with a bat. [Gang youths are unable to articulate specific individuals of the vague "they" who watch over them.]

I don't know how many guys are in the gang. They tell me maybe a hundred or a thousand. I don't know them all. [Each boy interviewed had a different image of the gang.]

These comments and others revealed the gang youths' somewhat different perceptions and rationale of gang war activity. There is a limited consensus of participants as to the nature of the gang war situations because the gang structure—the collectivity which defines gang war

behavior—is amorphous, diffuse, and malleable.

Despite the fact of gang phenomena taking a diffuse form, theoreticians, social workers, the police, the press, and the public autistically distort gangs and gang behavior toward a gestalt of clarity. The rigid frame of perceiving gangs as groups should shift to the fact of gangs as near-groups. This basic redefinition is necessary if progress is to be made in sociological diagnosis as a foundation for delinquent gang prevention and correction. . . .

Near-Group Structure

Research into the structure of 30 groups revealed three characteristic levels of membership organization. In the center of the gang, on the first level, are the most psychologically disturbed members—the leaders. It is these youths who require and need the gang most of all. This core of disturbed youths provides the gang's more cohesive force. In a gang of some 30 boys there may be five or six who are central or core members because they desperately need the gang in order to deal with their personal problems of inadequacy. These are youths always working to keep the gang together and in action, always drafting, plotting, and talking gang warfare. They are the center of the near-group activity.

At a second level of near-group organization in the gang, we have youths who claim affiliation to the gang but only participate in it according to their emotional needs at given times. For example, one of the Egyptian Kings reported that if his father had not given him a "bad time" and kicked him out of the house the night of the homicide, he would not have gone to the corner and become involved in the Michael Farmer killing. This second-level gang member's participation in the gang killing was a function of his disturbance on that particular evening. This temporal gang need is a usual occurrence.

At a third level of gang participation, we have peripheral members who will join in with gang activity on occasion, although they seldom identify themselves as members of the gang at times.

---

[2]The research and interviewing at this time was combined with my role as consultant to the Columbia Broadcasting System. I assisted in the production of a gang war documentary narrated by Edward R. Murrow, entitled "Who Killed Michael Farmer?" The documentary tells the story of the killing through the actual voices of the boys who committed the act.

This type of gang member is illustrated by the youth who went along with the Egyptian Kings on the night of the Farmer killing, as he put it "for old time's sake." He just happened to be around on that particular evening and went along due to a situational condition. He never really "belonged" to the gang nor was he defined by himself or others as a gang member.

The size of gangs is determined in great measure by the emotional needs of its members at any given point. It is not a measure of actual and live membership. Many of the members exist only on the thought level. In the gang, if the boys feel particularly hemmed in (for paranoid reasons), they will expand the number of their near-group. On the other hand, at other times when they feel secure, the gang's size is reduced to include only those youths known on a face-to-face basis. The research revealed that, unlike an actual group, no member of a near-group can accurately determine the number of its membership at a particular point in time.

For example, most any university department member will tell you the number of other individuals who comprise the faculty of their department. It is apparent that if there are eight members in a department of psychology, each member will know each other member, his role, and the total number of members of the department. In contrast, in examining the size of gangs or near-group participation, the size increases in almost direct relationship to the lack of membership clarity. That is, the second- and third-level members are modified numerically with greater ease than the central members. Third level members are distorted at times to an almost infinite number.

In one interview, a gang leader distorted the size and affiliations of the gang as his emotional state shifted. In an hour interview, the size of his gang varied from 100 members to 4,000, from five brother gangs or alliances to 60, from about ten square blocks of territorial control to include jurisdiction over the five boroughs of New York City, New Jersey, and part of Philadelphia.

Another characteristic of the gang is its lack of role definition. Gang boys exhibit considerable difficulty and contradiction in their roles in the gang. They may say that the gang is organized for protection and that one role of a gang is to fight. How, when, whom, and for what reason he is to fight are seldom clear. The rights, duties, and obligations associated with the gang member's role in the gang varies from gang boy to gang boy.

One gang boy may define himself as a protector of the younger boys in the neighborhood. Another defines his role in the gang as "We are going to get all those guys who call us Spics." Still other gang boys define their participation in the gang as involuntarily forced upon them, through their being "drafted." Moreover, few gang members maintain a consistent function or role within the gang organization.

Definition of membership is vague and indefinite. A youth will say he belongs one day and will quit the next without necessarily telling any other gang member. I would ask one gang boy who came into my office daily whether he was a Balkan. This was comparable to asking him, "How do you feel today?"

Because of limited social ability to assume rights, duties, and obligations in constructive solidified groups, the gang boy attaches himself to a structure which requires limited social ability and can itself be modified to fit his momentary needs. This malleability factor is characteristic of the near-group membership. As roles are building blocks of a group, diffuse role definitions fit in adequately to the near-group which itself has diverse and diffuse objectives and goals. The near-group, unlike a true group, has norms, roles, functions, cohesion, size, and goals which are shaped by the emotional needs of its members.

Gang Leadership Characteristics

Another aspect of near-groups is the factor of self-appointed leadership, usually of a dictatorial, authoritarian type. In interviewing hundreds of gang members one finds that many of them give themselves some role of leadership. For example, in the Egyptian Kings, approximately five boys defined themselves as "war counsellors." It is equally apparent that, except on specific occasions, no one will argue with this self-defined role. Consequently, leadership in the gang may be assumed by practically any member of the gang if he so determines and emotionally needs the power of being a leader at the time. It is not necessary to have his leadership role ratified by his constituents.

Another aspect of leadership in the gang is the procedure of "drafting" or enlisting new members. In many instances, this pattern of coercion to get another youth to join or belong to the gang becomes an end in itself, rather than a means to an end. In short, the process of inducing, coercing, and threatening violence upon another youth, under the guise of getting him to join, is an important gang leader activity. The gang boy is not truly concerned with acquiring another gang member, since the meaning of membership is vague at best; however, acting the power role of a leader forcing another youth to do something against his will becomes meaningful to the "drafter."

Gang Functions

In most groups some function is performed or believed to be performed. The function which it performs may be a constructive one, as in an industrial organization, a P.T.A. group, or a political party. On the other hand, it may be a socially destructive group, such as a drug syndicate, a group of bookies, or a subversive political party. There is usually a consensus of objectives and goals shared by the membership, and their behavior tends to be essentially organized group action.

The structure of a near-group is such that its functions not only vary greatly and shift considerably from time to time, but its primary function is unclear. The gang may on one occasion be organized to protect the neighborhood; on another occasion, to take over a particular territory, and on still another, it may be organized in response to or for the purpose of racial discrimination.

The function of near-groups, moreover, is not one which is clearly understood, known, and communicated among all of its members. There is no consensus in this near-group of goals, objectives, or functions of the collectivity—much near-group behavior is individualistic and flows from emotional disturbance.

A prime function of the gang is to provide a channel to act out hostility and aggression to satisfy the continuing and momentary emotional needs of its members. The gang is a convenient and malleable structure quickly adaptable to the needs of emotionally disturbed youths, who are unable to fulfill the responsibility and demands required for participation in constructive groups. He belongs to the gang because he lacks the social ability to relate to others and to as-

sume responsibility for the relationship, not because the gang gives him a "feeling of belonging."

Because of the gang youth's limited "social ability," he constructs a social organization which enables him to relate and to function at his limited level of performance. In this structure norms are adjusted so that the gang youth can function and achieve despite his limited ability to relate to others.

An example of this is the function of violence in the near-group of the gang. Violence in the gang is highly valued as a means for the achievement of reputation or "rep." This inversion of societal norms is a means for quick upward social mobility in the gang. He can acquire and maintain a position in the gang through establishing a violent reputation.

The following comments by members of the Egyptian Kings illustrate this point:

If I would of got the knife, I would have stabbed him. That would have gave me more of a build-up. People would have respected me for what I've done and things like that. They would say, "There goes a cold killer."

It makes you feel like a big shot. You know some guys think they're big shots and all that. They think, you know, they got the power to do everything they feel like doing.

They say, like, "I wanna stab a guy," and the other guy says, "Oh, I wouldn't dare to do that." You know, he thinks I'm acting like a big shot. That's the way he feels. He probably thinks in his mind, "Oh, he probably won't do that." Then, when we go to a fight, you know, he finds out what I do.

Momentarily, I started to thinking about it inside: den I have my mind made up I'm not going to be in no gang. Then I go on inside. Something comes up den here come all my friends coming to me. Like I said before, I'm intelligent and so forth. They be coming to me—then they talk to me about what they gonna do. Like, "Man, we'll go out here and kill this guy." I say, "Yeah." They kept on talkin' and talkin'. I said, "Man, I just gotta go with you." Myself, I don't want to go, but when they start talkin' about what they gonna do, I say, "So, he isn't gonna take over my rep. I ain't gonna let him be known more than me." And I go ahead just for selfishness.

The near-group of the gang, with its diffuse and malleable structure, can function as a convenient vehicle for the acting out of varied individual needs and problems. For the gang leader it can be a super-powered organization through which (in his phantasy) he dominates and controls "divisions" of thousands of members. For gang members, unable to achieve in more demanding social organizations, swift and sudden violence is a means for quick upward social mobility and the achievement of a reputation. For less disturbed youths, the gang may function as a convenient temporary escape from the dull and rigid requirements of a difficult and demanding society. These are only some of the functions the near-group of the gang performs for its membership.

Near-Group Theory and Social Problems

The concept of the near-group may be of importance in the analysis of other collectivities which reflect and produce social problems. The analysis of other social structures may reveal similar distortions of their organization. To operate on an assumption that individuals in interaction with each other, around some function, with some shared mutual expectation, in a particular normative system as always being a group formation is to project a degree of distortion onto certain types of collectivities. Groups are social structures at one end of a continuum; mobs are social structures at another end; and at the center are near-groups which have some of the characteristics of both, and yet are characterized by factors not found fully in either.

In summary, these factors may include the following:

1. Individualized role definition to fit momentary needs.
2. Diffuse and differential definitions of membership.
3. Emotion-motivated behavior.
4. A decrease of cohesiveness as one moves from the center of the collectivity to the periphery.
5. Limited responsibility and sociability required for membership and belonging.

6. Self-appointed and disturbed leadership.
7. A limited consensus among participants of the collectivities' functions or goals.
8. A shifting and personalized stratification system.
9. Shifting membership.
10. The inclusion in size of phantasy membership.
11. Limited consensus of normative expectations.
12. Norms in conflict with the inclusive social system's prescriptions.

Although the gang was the primary type of near-group appraised in this analysis, there are perhaps other collectivities whose structure is distorted by autistic observers. Their organization might become clearer if subjected to this conceptual scheme. Specifically, in the area of criminal behavior, these might very well include adult gangs varyingly called the "Mafia," the "National Crime Syndicate," and so-called International Crime Cartels. There are indications that these social organizations are comparable in organization to the delinquent gang. They might fit the near-group category if closely analyzed in this context, rather than aggrandized and distorted by mass media and even Senate Committees.

Other more institutionalized collectivities might fit the near-group pattern. As a possible example, "the family in transition" may not be in transition at all. The family, as a social institution, may be suffering from near-groupism. Moreover, such standardized escape hatches of alcoholism, psychoses, and addictions may be too prosaic for the sophisticated intellectual to utilize in escaping from himself. For him, the creation and perpetuation of near-groups requiring limited responsibility and personal commitment may be a more attractive contemporary form of expressing social and personal pathology. The measure of organization or disorganization of an inclusive social system may possibly be assessed by the prevalence of near-group collectivities in its midst. The delinquent gang may be only one type of near-group in American society.

10 GETTING INTO DEVIANT SUBCULTURES

Getting into deviant subcultures is rarely simple or automatic. People usually have to come into frequent contact with deviants and have some lengthy exposure to their traditions before gaining initial acceptance. In addition, factors that initially bring people into contact with deviants are often not the same ones that sustain that contact.

In the first reading Martin Weinberg deals with how people become nudists and how segmental that involvement remains. Charles McCaghy and James Skipper then describe occupational conditions that are conducive to getting involved in lesbianism. In the last reading John Lofland highlights the processes by which people gradually become converted to a religious cult.

Becoming a Nudist   MARTIN S. WEINBERG

In order to better understand deviant life-styles and the meanings they have for those engaged in them, it is often useful to conceptualize a life-style as a career, consisting of various stages. We can then study the interpersonal processes that draw and sustain people at each of these various stages. In this way, we can appreciate the motivations, perceptions, and experiences that characterize involvement in that way of life at various points in time—e.g., these may differ for novices, "veterans," etc.

Using such a career model, this paper deals with the interpersonal processes and phases involved in nudist camp membership. Specifically, it deals with the processes by which people come to contemplate a visit to a nudist camp, attend for the first time, and then continue attending over a period of time. The data come from three sources—101 interviews with nudists in the Chicago area; two successive summers of participant observation in nudist camps; and 617 mailed questionnaires completed by nudists located throughout the United States and Canada.[1]

Prenudist Attitudes Toward Nudism

Most people seldom give much thought to the subject of nudism.[2] Responses in the interviews indicated that nudism is not a prominent object of thought even for many persons who will later become nudists. Thus when nudist members were asked what they had thought of nudism before visiting a camp, many stated that they had never really given it any thought. Until their initial experience, the interviewees' conceptions of nudism had been vague stereotypes, much like those held by the general public. In the words of a now active nudist:

I never gave it too much thought. I thought it was a cult—a nut-eating, berry-chewing bunch of vegetarians, doing calisthenics all day, a gymno-physical society. I thought they were carrying health to an extreme, being egomaniacs about their body.

Many of those who had thought about the subject conceived of nudists' camps as more exclusive, luxurious, and expensive than they actually are. Others had different conceptions:

I'm afraid I had the prevailing notion that they were undignified, untidy places populated (a) by the very poor, and (b) by languishing bleached blonds, and (c) by greasy, leering bachelors.

Table 1 sums up the attitudes that nudists reported themselves to have taken before their affiliation.

The Initial Interest in Nudism

If prenudist attitudes are of the nature indicated by Table 1, how does one become interested enough to make a first visit to a nudist camp? As shown in Table 2, the highest percentage of men mentioned magazines as the source of their interest, and the next largest source was other persons (exclusive of parents or parents-in-law). For women, the pattern was different; the highest percentage were first informed about nudism by their husbands. In 78 percent of the families, the husband had been more interested

Reprinted by special permission of The William Alanson White Psychiatric Foundation, Inc., from *Psychiatry: Journal for the Study of Interpersonal Processes,* Vol. 29, No. 1 (February 1966), pp. 15–24. Copyright 1966 by The William Alanson White Psychiatric Foundation, Inc.

This investigation was supported in part by a Public Health Service fellowship (No. 7–F1–MH–14, 660–01A1 BEH) from the National Institute of Mental Health, and in part by contributions from Mr. O. B. E. and from the National Nudist Council.

[1] Interviews were the primary source of data, and all of the quotations and quantifications in this paper, unless otherwise specified, are drawn from interviews. All known nudists in the vicinity of Chicago were contacted for an interview; the mean interview time was three and one-half hours. Approximately one hundred camps were represented in the interviews and questionnaires. A detailed discussion of my methodology may be found in "Sex, Modesty, and Deviants," Ph.D. Dissertation, Northwestern University, June, 1965.

[2] This statement is based on the results of a questionnaire study of social response to nudism.

TABLE 1.   Prenudist Attitudes Toward Nudism*

Attitude	Percentage of Interviewees
Positive	35
Live and let live	16
Negative	19
Very negative	1
Does not know	29

*For coding purposes, "positive" was defined as a desire to participate in nudism or to become a nudist. "Live and let live" included those who did not desire participation in nudism, but did not think ill of those who did participate; however, some of these respondents would have imposed social distance from nudists, and some would not.

TABLE 2.   Source of Initial Interest in Nudism

Source	Male	Female
Magazines	47%	14%
Movies	6	6
Newspapers	6	0
Spouse	0	47
Parents or parents-in-law	2	8
Other person	31	23
Medical advice from physician	0	2
Other source	8	0

in visiting a camp. In all other cases both spouses had equally wanted to go. There were no cases in which the wife had wanted to go more than the husband.

The fact that the overwhelming majority of women became interested in nudism through their relationships with other people, rather than through the mass media which played such an important part with men, was reflected in the finding that interpersonal trust had to be sustained in order to evoke the women's interest.[3] This was indicated in the content of many interviews. The interviews also indicated that commonsense justifications and "derivations"[4] were important in overcoming the women's anxieties.

The following quotation is from an interview with a woman who became interested in nudism after being informed about it by a male friend. Here she was describing what her feelings would have been prior to that time. (In this quotation, as in others in this paper, Q is used to signify a neutral probe by the interviewer that follows the course of the last reply—such as "Could you tell me some more about that?" or "How's that?" or "What do you mean?" Other questions by the interviewer are given in full.)

. . . [Whether or not I would go to a nudist camp would] depend on who asked me. If a friend, I probably would have gone along with it. . . . [Q] If an acquaintance, I wouldn't have been interested. [Q] I don't know, I think it would depend on who was asking me to go. [Q] If it was someone you liked or had confidence in, you'd go along with it. If you didn't think they were morally upright you probably wouldn't have anything to do with it.

A man described how he had persuaded his wife to become interested in nudism:

I expected difficulty with my wife. I presented it to her in a wholesome manner. [Q] I had to convince her it was a wholesome thing, and that the people there were sincere. . . . [Q] That they were sincere in efforts to sunbathe together and had only good purposes in mind when they did that. [Q] All the things that nudism stands for: a healthy body and a cleansed mind by killing sex curiosities.

The anxieties that enter into the anticipation of public nudity were described in the following interview excerpts:

I was nervous. . . . [Q] It's different. It's not a daily practice. . . . I'm heavy, that added to the nervousness.

They said they were ashamed of their builds. They think everyone there is perfection. [Q] They think everyone will look at them.

He [a friend] said he'd never go, but that he could understand it. He saw nothing wrong in it. [Q] He said he wouldn't want other men looking at his wife.

Even though they had enough confidence to make the decision to visit a camp, the respondents did not necessarily anticipate becoming nudists themselves. For many the first trip was merely a joke, a lark, or a new experience, and

---

[3] My thanks are due to James L. Wilkins for initially pointing this pattern out in his analysis of the additional data on the response of college students to nudists.

[4] For a discussion of Pareto's concept of derivation, see Talcott Parsons, *The Structure of Social Action* (second edition); Glencoe, Ill., Free Press, 1949; pp. 198 *ff.*

TABLE 3.   Motivations for the First Visit to a Nudist Camp

Motivation	Male	Female
Curiosity over what it was like	33%	25%
Sexual curiosity	16	2
To satisfy spouse or relative	2	38
Combination of curiosity and to satisfy spouse	0	13
For relaxation	2	4
For health	12	6
To sunbathe	8	2
To make friends	6	0
Other	21	10

the main motivation was curiosity. They visited the camp as one might make a trip to the zoo, to see what it was like and what kind of characters would belong to such a group. There was also curiosity, on the part of many of the respondents, about seeing nude members of the opposite sex.

The original thought was that we were going to see a bunch of nuts. It was a joke going out there.

I thought they must be a little nutty. Eccentric. I didn't think there'd be so many normal people. . . . [Q] I felt that people that are nudists are a little bohemian or strange. [Q] I don't feel that way now. I thought we'd be the only sane people there. I thought it was kind of an adventure. . . . [Q] I like feeling I'm doing something unusual that no one knows about. It's a big secret. . . . [Q] The novelty, the excitement of driving up in the car; no one knew we were going. . . .

Table 3 presents the motivations given by interviewees for their first trip to a nudist camp.

The First Visit

The first trip to camp was frequently accompanied by extreme nervousness. Part of this might be attributed simply to the experience of entering a new group. The visitors did not know the patterns common to the group, and they were uncertain about their acceptance by group members. For example, a nudist said, referring to his participation in a nudist camp in which he was not well known:

I guess I'm a little nervous when I get there, 'cause I'm not recognized as a member of the group.[5]

But, in the instance of a first visit to a nudist camp, this anxiety on entering a new group was considerably heightened by the unknown nature of the experience that lay ahead. Mead, in his discussion of the "social psychology of the act," has described how people, in planning an action, imaginatively rehearse it and its anticipated consequences.[6] The nudist camp, however, presents a totally unfamiliar situation; the person planning a visit has no past of similar situations, and usually no one has effectively described the situation to him in advance. This gap in effective imagination produces apprehension, anxiety, and nervousness.

[On the trip up] I was very nervous. [Q] Because the idea was foreign. [Q] . . . The unknown factor. Just seeing a lot of people without clothes on is an unusual situation. Different or new experiences make one nervous.

You're nervous and apprehensive. You don't know what to expect. . . . I was very nervous. . . . I thought of everything under the sun. . . . I didn't know what to expect.

I felt a little inferior at first, because I had no knowledge of nudist camps. . . . I started to enjoy myself, but I couldn't quite feel comfortable. [Q] In the nude. In front of a lot of people. A lack of confidence, self-confidence. [Q] By not having a complete knowledge. I really didn't know what to expect.

I was afraid of the unknown. I didn't know what to expect. If we had known nudists, I wouldn't have had those fears.

[5] It is this very fact of an established social system, however, that prevents a disruption of social order in nudist camps. Traditions and norms are stabilized, and even neophytes who think of themselves as leader-types are forced to fall into the pattern or be rejected. (For a small-group experiment that studies this phenomenon, see Ferenc Merei, "Group Leadership and Institutionalization," *Human Relations* [1949] 2:23–39.) In another paper I have shown how some of these traditions function to sustain a nonsexual definition of the nudist situation. See Martin S. Weinberg, "Sexual Modesty, Social Meanings, and the Nudist Camp," *Social Problems* (1965) 12:311–318.

[6] Anselm Strauss, editor, *The Social Psychology of George Herbert Mead;* Chicago, Univ. of Chicago Press, 1956; p. xiii.

In most instances, the initial nervousness dissipated soon after the newcomer's arrival. Forty-six percent of the interviewees said that they were not nervous at all after arriving at camp. An additional 31 percent felt at ease in less than three hours. Thus most visitors adjusted rapidly to the nudist way of life. Seventy-one percent of those interviewed reported that *no* major adjustment was necessary. Sixteen percent of the residual group reported that undressing for the first time, or becoming used to being nude, was the only adjustment. Of these people who had to adjust, only 15 percent found the adjustment to be difficult.

I really was afraid and shy and I didn't feel too well. We had discussed going, but when the time came to go I couldn't sleep that night. . . . Once we got nude then everything just seemed to come natural. I was surprised at how at ease I felt.

A variety of other response patterns, which I shall not discuss in detail, were characteristic of the initial visit. For example, one pattern related to the visitor's socioeconomic position.[7] Because facilities in many camps are relatively primitive, those used to more comfortable circumstances were likely to be disappointed. One professional man said:

I was disappointed to see it was as rustic and unkempt as it was. . . . If people wore clothes and nothing else changed it would be a fourth-class resort. [Q] Everything there is shabby and not well cared for.

The Adoption of Nudism as a Way of Life

Coaching and Social Validation

The newcomers to camps received no formal indoctrination in the nudist perspective, but acquired it almost imperceptibly as the result of a subtle social process. Informal coaching, either prior to or after arrival, appears to have eased adjustment problems.[8]

My husband said the men are gentlemen. He told me I'd have fun, like play in the sun, play games, and swim.

She didn't want to undress. . . . [Q] I tried to talk to her and her husband did; she finally got convinced. [Q] I told her you feel better with them off, and that no one will pay any attention.

The consensus of 95 percent of the interviewees was that, as one of them put it, "Things run along very smoothly when you first become a nudist." Asked if they ever had any doubts that becoming a nudist was the right decision, once they had made up their minds, 77 percent reported that they had never had any doubts. Fourteen percent had doubts at the time of the interview. The following quotations illustrate the process of social validation that tends to quell doubts:[9]

I do and I don't [have doubts], because of my religion. [Q] Nobody knows about it, and I wonder about that. [Q] Whether it's the right thing. But as I read the pamphlets [nudist literature] I realize it's up to the individual. God made Adam and Eve and they had no clothes. You don't have to be ashamed of your body. Some are fat and some are thin, but it doesn't matter; it's your personality that matters. I don't know, if my minister found out, I'd defend it. We don't use bad language. Sometimes I wonder, but down underneath I think it's all right. We've just been taught to hide our bodies. Sometimes I wonder, but then I think what the pamphlets say. [Q: *At what time do you have these doubts?*] When I'm in church. [Q] Yes, when I get to thinking about religion. Not very often. Sometimes I just wonder. [Q: *Do you ever have these doubts while at camp?*] No, I forget about everything. I'm having too much fun. I remind myself that this is something good for the children. My children won't become Peeping Toms or sex maniacs.

---

[7] At the time of the interviews, the interviewers, making a commonsense judgment, placed 54 percent of the nudist respondents in the lower-middle class. This was the modal and median placement.

[8] For a discussion of "coaching" relationships, see Anselm Strauss, *Mirrors and Masks: The Search for Identity;* New York, Free Press, 1959; pp. 109–118.

[9] By "social validation," I mean the process by which the subjective comes to be considered objective—that is, true. The views of others (especially those considered to have more extensive knowledge) provide a social yardstick by which to measure truth. Pareto reaches a similar view of objectivity. Note the following statement: ". . . we apply the term 'logical actions' to actions that logically conjoin means to ends not only from the standpoint of the subject performing them, but from the standpoint of other persons who have more extensive knowledge—in other words, to actions that are logical both subjectively and objectively in the sense just explained." See Vilfredo Pareto, *The Mind and Society,* Vol. 1; New York, Harcourt, Brace, 1935; p. 77.

[At first] I felt ridiculous. I thought all those people looked so funny. [*Q: Why's that?*] All your life you've seen people with their clothes on; now they all have them off. After a while, you feel ridiculous with your clothes on. [*Q*] I liked the people. They were all very nice. They came from nice families. It couldn't just be something anyone would do, or just people from a lower class.

The nudist way of life becomes a different reality, a new world:

It seems like a different world from the world we live in every day. No washing, ironing, worries. You feel so free there. The people are friendly there, interested in each other. But not nosy. You can relax among them more easily than in the city.

And this new reality imposes a different meaning on the everyday life of the outside world:

My daughter told us today the boys and girls don't sit together at school, but it makes no difference to her. Several times they're out playing and the boys get excited when they see their panties. My children don't understand that. They have a different state of mind toward different sexes.

Motives for Becoming a Nudist

Persons who became nudists—that is, became members of a camp and conceived of themselves as nudists—usually demonstrated an autonomy of motives,[10] in the sense that their motives for doing so differed from their motives for first visiting a camp. That is to say, participation in different stages of the "nudist career" were usually characterized by different sets of motives. Hence the curiosity that had often been the overriding motive for initial visits was satisfied, and the incentive for affiliating with a nudist camp was based on the person's experiences at the camp, experiences which may not have been anticipated before visiting the camp.[11] It should be noted, however, that the decision was sometimes prompted by the owner's insistence that visitors join if they wished to return. As Table 4 shows, there was a considerable change, after the first visit, in the pattern of male versus female desire to attend the camp.

The following quotations are illustrative of the

TABLE 4. Comparative Desires of Male and Female Members of Couples to Visit a Nudist Camp*

	Male Wanted to Go More	Male and Female Wanted to Go Equally	Female Wanted to Go More
First visit	79%	21%	0%
Return visits	40	51	9

*Two unmarried couples are included in these data.

autonomous motives of respondents for the first and subsequent visits:

[*Q: What was your main reason for wanting to attend camp the first time?*] Curiosity. [*Q*] To see how people behave under such circumstances, and maybe also looking at the girls. [*Q*] Just that it's interesting to see girls in the nude. [*Q: What is the main reason you continue to attend?*] I found it very relaxing. [*Q*] It's more comfortable to swim without a wet suit, and not wearing clothes when it's real warm is more comfortable and relaxing.

[I went up the first time] to satisfy my husband. He wanted me to go and I fought it. But he does a lot for me, so why not do him a favor. [She had told him that people went to nudist camps only for thrills and that she would divorce him before she would go. Although he talked her into it, she cried all the way to camp. Asked why she continued to attend, she looked surprised and replied:] Why, because I thoroughly enjoy it!

This last quotation describes a common pattern for women, which appears also in the following recollection:

[I went the first time] because my husband wanted me to go. [*Q: What is the main reason that you continue to attend?*] Because we had fun . . . and we met a lot of nice people.

The interviewees were asked what they liked most about nudism, with the results shown in Table 5. Three of the benefits cited are of special sociological interest—the concept of nudist freedom, the family-centered nature of the recre-

[10] This concept was developed by Gordon Allport, "The Functional Autonomy of Motives," *Amer. J. Psychology* (1937) 50:141–156.

[11] Attendance is usually confined to summer weekends, and sexual curiosity may arise again between seasons.

TABLE 5. What Interviewees Liked Most About Nudism

	Percent of Sample Mentioning the Item
Friendliness, sociability	60%
Relaxation, getting away from the city	47
Enjoyment of outdoors and sports	36
Freedom	31
Sunbathing	26
Physical health	26
Children becoming informed about the human body	11
Mental health	8
Economical vacations	4
Family recreation, keeping family together	4
Seeing people nude	1
Other aspects	15

ation, and the emphasis on friendliness and sociability.

"Freedom." Echoing the nudist ideology, many respondents mentioned "freedom"—using the term in various contexts—as a major benefit. There were varied definitions of this freedom and its meaning for the participant. Some defined it in terms of free body action, of being unhindered by clothing.

Nudism . . . gives me an opportunity to be in the sunshine and fresh air. Also to take a swim nude gives me free expression of body. [Q] I'm not hindered by clothes, a freedom of body movement and I can feel the water all over my body.

Nothing was binding; no socks, no tight belt, nothing clothing-wise touching me.

You don't have garter belts or bras. Your body can breathe.

With perspiration your clothes start to bind and you develop rashes. [Q] You just feel more relaxed when you're nude, and more comfortable from hot, sticky clothing.

Others interpreted freedom from clothing in a different way:

Freedom from a convention of society. It's a relief to get away from it. [Q] A physical relief in that wearing clothes is something you must do. I hate wearing a choking tie at a dinner party, but I have to because it is a society convention.

You don't have to dress appropriate for the occasion. You aren't looking for the smartest slacks and sports clothes.

The freedom. . . . You don't have to worry about the way you're dressed. You don't try to outdo someone with a thirty-dollar bathing suit.

For others, freedom meant the absence of routine and restraint:

A nudist camp has a lot more freedom [than a summer resort]. You do just as you want. . . . [Q] Just to do what you want to do, there is nothing you have to do. At a resort you have to participate in activities.

The freedom. [Q] You can do as you please. [Q] I can read or just lay in the sun.

The freedom. [Q] You can go any place you want in the camp. You can walk anywhere nude.

The range of conceptions of freedom is indicated by the following examples:

I felt free in the water. No one staring at you.

I like the complete freedom of . . . expression. With nudist people, I find them more frank and outspoken, not two-faced. You don't have to be cagey and worry about saying the wrong thing.

Feeling free with your body. [Q] I can't really explain it. Feeling more confident, I guess.

The varying constructions of nudist freedom support Schutz's model of man as a common-sense actor.[12] According to Schutz, man lives very naively in his world; clear and distinct experiences are mixed with vague conjectures, and "cookbook" descriptions of experiences are uncritically adopted from others. When these standard descriptions are vague, and are called into question—for example, by an interviewer who asks what is meant by "freedom"—a wide variety of constructions is elicited from respondents. Nudists, as devotees to a "cause," resemble other commonsense actors in their frequent inability to understand their stock answers critically.

[12] See Alfred Schutz, "The Dimensions of the Social World," in *Collected Papers, II: Studies in Social Theory*, edited by Arvid Broderson; The Hague, Martinus Nijhoff, 1964; pp. 48 *ff.*

Family Cohesion. As shown in Table 5, some respondents gave, as the feature of nudism they like most, its function in providing family recreation. One of the interview sample expressed this as follows:

Nudism tends to keep the family together. In the non-nudist society the family tends to split into different organizations; all have different interests. You can still do different things in camp, but you still have a common interest. And all your plans are made together.

One would expect that nudism would lead to family cohesiveness, as a result of this common interest, and also as a result of a tendency for the family members to conceal their nudist involvements in their dealings with the outside world. In regard to the element of secrecy, Simmel has pointed out how a group's intensified seclusion results in heightened cohesiveness.[13] Participation in nudism did not, however, always lead to increased family cohesiveness. For example, if one spouse did not appreciate the experience, the family's continued participation resulted in increased strain. And although nudist ideology claims that nudist participation brings the family closer together, 78 percent of the interviewees, and 82 percent of the questionnaire respondents, reported no change in their family relationships.

Relationships with Others. Friendliness and sociability were the characteristics of the nudist experience mentioned most often by interviewees. In addition, nudists extended the concept of "family" to include fellow nudists; they cited a "togetherness" that is rare in the clothed society. Some insight into this cohesiveness was displayed in the following remarks by an interviewee:

Camaraderie and congeniality . . . comes in any minority group that supports an unpopular position. [Q] Feelings develop by these in-groups because you are brought together by one idea which you share. On the street you may run into people you share no ideas with.

The interviewees were asked how the camp situation would change if everything remained constant except that clothes were required. Most of them anticipated that their bond would be dissolved.

They would lose the common bond. They have a bond that automatically is a bond. They are in a minority. They are glad you're here. You are welcome there; they're glad you're one of us.

I think the people would be less friendly. When you're all nude you feel the same as them. You all came here to be nude. . . . [Q] Everybody feels the other is the same; you have something in common to be doing this unusual thing.

A number of interviewees, supporting the nudist contention that social distinctions diminish in the nudist camp, believed that class distinctions would reappear if clothing were donned.[14] A 19-year-old respondent cited both class and age distinctions:

You would have . . . your classes, and age. [Q] I wouldn't feel as close to B and G.

There is a great age difference. Knowing them this way, though, gives us a common bond. You just don't think about their ages or anything else about them.

Several blue-collar workers remarked that one of the things they liked about nudism was that, without their uniforms or customary clothes, they and their families could associate with a better class of people. Status striving decreases with the removal of these important props of impression management.

[If everyone in the camp wore clothes] everything I detest about country clubs I've seen would immediately become manifest. Namely: (1) social climbing with all its accompanying insincerity and ostentation; (2) wolves tracking down virgins; (3) highly formalized activities such as golf; (4) gambling and drinking; (5) embarrassment of having to swim under the appraising gaze of a gallery full of people sipping cocktails. This is the paradox, the curious thing; it doesn't embarrass me to swim at . . . [a nudist camp] whereas I can't be coaxed into the swimming pool at the country club in my hometown. [Q] I think that the reason is the fact that so much in that country club is so calculated to make tableaux or pictures, in which

---

[13] Kurt H. Wolff, *The Sociology of Georg Simmel;* New York, Free Press, 1950; see Part IV.

[14] For discussions of clothes as "sign equipment," see Erving Goffman, "Symbols of Class Status," *British J. Sociology* (1951) 2:294–304; and *The Presentation of Self in Everyday Life;* Garden City, N.Y., Doubleday, 1959; pp. 24 *ff.* Also see Gregory Stone, "Appearance and the Self," in *Human Behavior and Social Processes: An Interactionist Approach,* edited by Arnold Rose; Boston, Houghton Mifflin, 1962; pp. 86–118.

only the young and the handsome can really be a part. That's terribly true.

Another interviewee, when asked what he liked most about social nudism, replied:

It is the best way to relax. [Q] Once you take your clothes off, people are on the same basis. [Q] Everyone is a person. There are no distinctions between a doctor or a mechanic because of clothing. [Q] . . . It's hard to describe. It's just that all have an equal basis, no distinctions because of clothing. That helps you to relax.

Although these statements may be somewhat idealized, the nudist camp does effectively break down patterns common to country clubs, resorts, and other settings in the outside society. Sex, class, and power lose much of their relevance in the nudist camp, and the suspension of the barriers they create effects a greater unity among the participants. This is not to say, however, that there is no social hierarchy—a point to which I shall return shortly.

The suspension of clothing modesty reinforces the atmosphere of "one big family" in another way. Clothing modesty is a *ceremony* of everyday life that sustains a nonintimate definition of relationships, and with its voluntary suspension relationships are usually defined as closer in character. However, for this to occur, trust must not be called into question, and each person must take for granted that he is differentiated from other social objects. Camp relationships usually meet these conditions. For example, they are differentiated from relationships elsewhere; being undressed in front of others is still out of the ordinary, since nudists do not appear nude among outsiders.

The social effect was significant enough to prompt members to describe the nudist way of life as a discovery that had brought new meaning to their lives. The experience provided many of them with "a sense of belonging." As one respondent put it:

. . . you feel like you're part of a whole family. You feel very close. That's how I feel.

The feeling of being part of "one big family" was, of course, more common to the smaller camps. But even in the large camps, participants in camp activities felt themselves to be a part of a special group.

As I have suggested, however, the "togetherness" of nudists is exaggerated. Personality clashes, cliques, and intergroup disagreements exist, and social stratification remains in evidence. In the words of an unmarried neophyte:

Sometimes I think there is a hierarchy at . . . [a large nudist camp]. [Q] In any organization there are cliques. [Q] These cliques I believe are formed by seniority. [Q] Those who have been there the longest. [Q: *What makes you think this?*] Something that is in the air. [Q] Just an impression you get. It's hard to say; it's just a feeling. [Q] As a newcomer I felt not at ease. [Q] There is an air of suspicion; people are not really friendly. [Q] They are not really unfriendly, just suspicious, I suppose, of single men. . . . They suspect single men are coming for Peeping Tom purposes. [Q] Just to see the nude women. . . . Single men, I think, are the lowest class at camp.

This attitude was borne out in the interviews with other single men; rarely did they describe nudism in *gemeinschaftlich* terms. The meaning of a person's experiences still depends on his social position.

Furthermore, it is doubtful that many people find a Utopia in nudism. The nudists interviewed were asked how seriously they felt that they would be affected if nudist camps were closed. As Table 6 shows, 30 percent of the interviewees considered that they would be relatively unaffected. When they were asked to identify their three best friends, almost half of the inter-

TABLE 6.   The Degree to Which the Closing of Nudist Camps Would Affect Interviewees*

Closing Camps Would Affect Respondent	Percent of Respondents
Very much	43
Somewhat	26
Not too much	17
Not at all	13

*Vague categories, such as those presented in this table, were occasionally used for their descriptive value in grossly delineating some point. In this case, respondents were asked to classify themselves (after completing their open-end response). In other cases, the coders used a large group of indicators in constructing such gross scales. Although these scales lacked intrinsic rigor, reliability between coders was high.

TABLE 7. Social Involvement with Other Nudists*

Best Friends Who Are Nudists	Degree of Social Involvement					
	Very Low	Moderately Low	Neither High Nor Low	Moderately High	Very High	Totals
None	13	9	12	5	7	46 (47%)
One	3	2	6	9	5	25 (26%)
Two		1	3	3	10	17 (18%)
Three					9	9 (9%)
Total	16	12	21	17	31	97 (100%)
	(16%)	(12%)	(22%)	(18%)	(32%)	

*The data on the number of best friends who are nudists were drawn from the replies of interviewees. The degree of social involvement was rated by coders on the basis of the following instructions: Code the degree of social involvement with nudists throughout the year on the basis of answers to Question 40 (b and c). Think of this as a scale or continuum: (1) Very low involvement (no contact at all); (2) moderately low involvement (just write or phone occasionally); (3) neither low nor high involvement (get together every couple of months—or attend New Year's party or splash party together); (4) moderately high involvement (visit once a month); (5) very high involvement (visit every week or two).

viewees did not name another nudist.[15] Table 7 details this information, as well as the degree of social involvement with other nudists, as rated by coders.

Nudists and the Clothed Society

Nudists envision themselves as being labeled deviant by members of the clothed society. In both the interviews and the questionnaires, the respondents were asked to conceptualize the view of nudists taken by the general public, and by their parents. No consistent difference was found between the views of the two groups, as described by the nudists.[16] Approximately one-third of the respondents conceptualized a live-and-let-live attitude on the part of parents and public. Two-thirds conceptualized a negative or very negative attitude.

They think we're fanatics. [Q] That we go overboard on something. That we're out of line.

If I went by what the guys say at work, you'd have to be pretty crazy, off your head a little bit. [Q] They

think you almost have to be . . . a sex fiend or something like that. They think there's sex orgies, or wife-swapping, or something.

They think we're a bunch of nuts. [Q] They just think that anyone who runs around without clothes is nuts. If they stopped to investigate, they'd find we weren't.

People think the body should be clothed and not exposed at any time. They associate that with vulgarity, indecency, and abnormality. [Q] Vulgarity is something that is unacceptable to the general public. [Q] Indecency in this respect would be exposing portions of the body which normally we hide. [Q] Abnormality? Well, the general public feels it's abnormal for the body to be undressed around other people, in a social group.

TABLE 8. Frequency of Informal Group Participation

	Nudists	General Population
At least twice a week	17%	30%
Every 4 or 5 days	4	35
Once a week	12	16
Less often or never	67	19

[15] Although 59 percent of the interviewees had been nudists for over two years, and 27 percent of this group had been nudists for over ten years, involvement did not appear to be particularly high. Also, an estimated 17 percent of the membership drops out every year.

[16] Although a positive versus negative differentiation of parents and general public was not found, there was a difference in the character of the typifications involved. In the case of parents, the typifications were derived from a history of experiences with an acting personality and were relatively concrete. In contrast, typifications of the general public were highly anonymous. Because such a collectivity could never be experienced directly, there was a much larger region of taken-for-granteds. This is due to the great number of substrata typifications underlying the general whole. This phenomenon is discussed by Alfred Schutz (see footnote 12).

TABLE 9.   Frequency of Association with Several Types of Informal Groups

	Relatives		Friends		Neighbors		Co-workers	
	Nudists	General Population	Nudists	General Population	Nudists	General Population	Nudists	General Population
At least once a week	38%	51%	49%	29%	26%	30%	17%	13%
A few times a month	16	13	21	20	11	9	10	8
About once a month	11	13	8	19	6	9	7	15
Less often	34	23	20	32	56	52	63	65

The fact that nudists were able to participate in a group which they viewed as stigmatized (and also the sense of belonging they claimed to have found in nudism) suggested that nudists might be isolated in the larger society. If they were isolated they could more easily participate in such a deviant group, being insulated from social controls.

A comparison of nudist interviewees with a sample of the general population[17] did show the nudists to fall substantially below the general population in frequency of informal association,[18] as shown in Table 8. Further, while members of the general population got together most often with relatives, nudists got together most often with friends,[19] as Table 9 indicates. The fact that 34 percent of the nudist sample got together with relatives less than once a month may reflect a considerable insulation from informal controls, since it is relatives who would probably provide the greatest pressure in inhibiting participation in such deviant groups.[20]

The degree to which nudists were isolated in the clothed society was found to be related to the length of time they had been nudists. As

TABLE 10.   Social Isolation of Nudists According to Their Length of Time in Nudism

Degree of Social Isolation*	Years in Nudism			
	1–2	3–5	6–9	10 and Over
Moderately or very isolated	22%	38%	44%	54%
Neither isolated nor active	39	31	25	35
Very or moderately active	39	31	32	12

* As rated by coders.

shown in Table 10, the longer a person had been in nudism, the more likely he was to be isolated. This may be interpreted in different ways. For example, there may be a tendency to become more isolated with continued participation, perhaps to avoid sanctions. (Yet, in regard to formal organizations nudists did *not* drop out or become less active.) Or, in the past it is likely that nudism was considered even more deviant than it is today and therefore it may have

---

[17] In this comparison, Axelrod's data on a sample of the general population in the Detroit area were used. See Morris Axelrod, "Urban Structure and Social Participation," *Amer. Sociol. Review* (1956) 21:13–18.

[18] A major limitation in this comparison, however, is that Axelrod has collapsed frequencies of association that are less than once a week into the category of "less often or never."

[19] Axelrod finds this greater participation with friends only for members of his sample with high income or high educational or social status.

[20] Also the absolute frequency of association with friends includes association with nudist friends. This reduces the apparent social-control function of their friendship associations.

Curiously, members of the nudist sample belonged to more formal organizations than did members of Axelrod's sample of the general population. The comparison was as follows: Membership in no group—general population, 37 percent; nudists, 18 percent. One group—general population, 31 percent; nudists, 27 percent. Two groups—general population, 16 percent; nudists, 19 percent.

appealed primarily to more isolated types of people.

Regardless of which interpretation is correct, as previously discussed, many nudists found a sense of belonging in nudism.[21]

People are lonely. It gives them a sense of belonging.

Until I started going out . . . [to camp] I never felt like I was part of a crowd. But I do out there. I was surprised. [*Q*] Well, like I said, I was never part of a crowd . . . I had friends, but never outstanding. My wife and I were [camp] King and Queen.

However, while the nudist experience helps solve this life problem for some, it creates this same problem for others. For the latter group, nudism may only ease the problem that it creates—that is, the isolation that results from concealing one's affiliation with a deviant group.[22]

---

[21] Some nudists also viewed themselves as members of an elite, superior to clothed society because they had suspended the body taboo.

[22] For a discussion of information control, see Erving Goffman, *Stigma: The Management of Spoiled Identity;* Englewood Cliffs, N.J., Prentice-Hall, 1963; pp. 41–104.

Occupational Predispositions and Lesbianism

CHARLES H. McCAGHY and JAMES K. SKIPPER, JR.

In recent publications Simon and Gagnon (1967a and b) contend that too frequently students of deviant behavior are prepossessed with the significance of the behavior itself and with the "exotic" trappings which accompany it. One finds exhaustive accounts of the demographic characteristics of deviants, the variety of forms their behavior may take, and the characteristics of any subculture or "community," including its argot which emerge as a direct consequence of a deviant status. Furthermore, Simon and Gagnon chide researchers for being locked into futile searches for ways in which inappropriate or inadequate socialization serves to explain their subject's behavior.

Simon and Gagnon argue that these research emphases upon descriptions of deviant behavior patterns and their etiology provide an unbalanced and misleading approach to an understanding of deviants. Deviants do or, at least, attempt to accommodate themselves to the "conventional" world, and they play many roles which conform to society's expectations. Yet, for the most part, deviants' learning and playing of nondeviant or conventional roles are either ignored by researchers or interpreted strictly as being influenced by a dominant deviant role. The focus of most research obscures the fact that with few exceptions a deviant role occupies a minor portion of the individuals' behavior spectrums. What is not recognized is the influence which commitments and roles of a nondeviant nature have upon deviant commitments and roles. To illustrate their contention, Simon and Gagnon discuss how homosexual behavior patterns are linked with the identical concerns and determinants which influence heterosexuals: aging problems, identity problems, making a living, management of sexual activity, etc. The authors argue convincingly for damping concern over ultimate causes of homosexuality and for concentrating on factors and contingencies shaping the homosexual role. In their words: "Patterns of adult homosexuality are consequent upon the social structures and values that surround the homosexual after he becomes, or conceives himself as, homosexual rather than

upon original and ultimate causes" (Simon and Gagnon, 1967b:179).

Since past research on homosexuals has been dominated by an emphasis upon the sexual feature of their behavior and its consequences, it is fitting that Simon and Gagnon draw attention to linking deviant with nondeviant behaviors or roles. However, since in their scheme the choice of sexual object is taken as given, a complementary perspective is still needed to gain an understanding of the process by which individuals engage in homosexual behavior. We suggest a structural approach. Because sexual behavior, deviant or not, emerges out of the context of social situations, it would seem that the structure of certain situations might contribute to becoming involved in homosexual behavior and to the formation of a homosexual self-concept. We are not suggesting such structures as "ultimate" causes; rather, we are saying that different social structures may provide conditions, learning patterns, and justifications differentially favorable to the occurrence of homosexual contacts and self-concepts. This is not strictly a matter of etiology, then, but an epidemiological concern over differential incidences of deviance, regardless of how episodic or pervasive homosexual behavior may be for an individual case.

A pertinent, albeit extreme, example here is the incidence of homosexual behavior occurring among incarcerated populations. A large proportion of prisoners can be identified as "jailhouse turnouts": those whose homosexual behavior is limited to within an institutional setting (Sykes, 1965:72, 95–99; Ward and Kassebaum, 1965:76, 96). Evidence indicates that contingencies and opportunities inherent in the prison setting are related to the onset and possible continuation of homosexual behavior. There is no question that for some prisoners homosexual behavior emerges as an adaptation to the prison structure which not only curtails avenues of heterosexual release, but deprives inmates of meaningful affective relationships they would otherwise have (Gagnon and Simon, 1968b; Giallombardo, 1966:133–157).

We have little reliable information concerning

Reprinted from Charles H. McCaghy and James K. Skipper, Jr., "Lesbian Behavior as an Adaptation to the Occupation of Stripping," *Social Problems,* Vol. 17, No. 2 (Fall 1969), pp. 262–70, by permission of the Society for the Study of Social Problems and the authors.

the incidence of homosexuality among various populations outside the setting of total institutions.[1] Most researchers agree that homosexuals will be found across the entire socioeconomic spectrum (Kinsey *et al.,* 1948:639–655, Kinsey *et al.,* 1953:459–460, 500; Gerassi, 1966, Leznoff and Westley, 1956). There is, however, continual speculation that relatively high proportions of male homosexuals are contained in certain occupational groups such as dancers, hair dressers, etc. Assuming this speculation to be correct it is still unclear which is prior: occupational choice or commitment to homosexual behavior. The sociological literature is replete with examples of how occupation influences other aspects of social life; there is no apparent reason why choice of sexual objects should necessarily vary independently. This is not to say that occupations are as extreme as total institutions in their control over life situations regarding sexual behavior. We do suggest that *some* occupations, like the prison setting, may play a crucial role in providing pressures, rationales, and opportunities leading to involvement, in, if not eventual commitment to, homosexual behavior.

In the course of conducting a study of the occupational culture of stripping, we found that homosexual behavior was an important aspect of the culture which apparently stemmed less from any predisposition of the participants than from contingencies of the occupation.

Nature of the Research

The principal research site was a midwestern burlesque theater which employed a different group of four touring strippers each week. With the permission and support of the theater manager, two male researchers were allowed access to the backstage dressing room area during and after afternoon performances. The researchers were introduced to each new touring group by the female stage manager, a person whom the girls trusted. After the stage manager presented them as "professors from the university who are doing an anthology of burlesque," the researchers explained that they were interested in how persons became strippers and what these persons thought about stripping as an occupation. After this, the researchers bided their time with small talk, card playing, and general questions to the girls about their occupation.[2] The purposes of this tactic were to allow the researchers to survey the field for respondents.

The primary data were gathered through in-depth interviews with 35 strippers.[3] Although there was no systematic method of selecting respondents from each touring group, an attempt was made to obtain a range of ages, years in the occupation, and salary levels. There were only four cases of outright refusals to be interviewed, one coming after the girl had consulted with a boyfriend. In six cases no convenient time for the interview could be arranged because the potential subjects were "busy." It was impossible in these instances to determine whether the excuses really constituted refusals. In general, the researchers found the girls eager to cooperate and far more of them wanted to be interviewed than could be accommodated.

The interviews, lasting an average of an hour and a half, were conducted in bars, restaurants, and, on occasion, backstage. Although difficult at times, the interviewing took place in a manner in which it was not overheard by others. In all but one case, two researchers were present. Interviews were also conducted with others, both male and female, whose work brought them in contact with strippers: the theater manager, union agent, and sales persons selling goods to strippers backstage. The interviews were semistructured and designed to elicit information on

---

[1] Estimates of the proportion of males having homosexual contacts during imprisonment range between 30 and 45 percent, depending on the institution, characteristics of the population, and length of sentences (Gagnon and Simon, 1968b:25). In one women's institution researchers estimated that 50 percent of the inmates had at least one sexual contact during their imprisonment (Ward and Kassebaum, 1965:92).

[2] Data concerning stripteasers and the occupation of stripping may be found in a paper by Skipper and McCaghy (1969).

[3] The social characteristics of the interviewed sample of strippers are as follows: All were white and ranged in age from 19 to 45, with 60 percent between the ages of 20 and 30. On the Hollingshead (1957) two-factor index of social position, ten came from families in classes I and II, nine from class III, and 12 from classes IV and V. (Family background data were not obtained in four cases.) Their range of education was from seven to 16 years: 22 had graduated from high school, eight of whom had at least one year of college.

background, the process of entering the occupation, and aspects of the occupational culture.

Incidence of Homosexuality

Ideally, in order to posit a relationship between the occupation and homosexual contacts it would be necessary to establish that the incidence of such behavior is relatively higher among strippers than in other female occupations. However, statistics comparing rates of homosexuality among specific female occupational groups are simply not available. Ward and Kassebaum (1965:75, 148–149) did find as part of female prison lore that lesbianism is prominent among models and strippers. In our research the restricted sample and relatively brief contact with the subjects did not allow us to ascertain directly the extent of homosexual behavior among strippers. We were, however, able to gauge the salience of such behavior in the occupation by asking the subjects to estimate what proportion of strippers had homosexual contacts. Estimates ranged from 15 to 100 percent of the girls currently being at least bisexual in their contacts; most responses fell within the 50 to 75 percent range. We also have evidence, mostly self-admissions, that nine of the thirty-five respondents (26 percent) themselves engaged in homosexual behavior while in the occupation, although in no case did we request such information or have prior evidence of the respondents' involvement. We did make some attempt to include subjects in the sample whom we suspected were maintaining relatively stable homosexual relationships. But these deliberate efforts were futile. In two cases strippers known to be traveling with unemployed and unrelated female companions refused to be interviewed, saying they were "too busy."

Despite our inability to fix an exact proportion of strippers who had engaged in homosexuality, it is clear from the subjects' estimates and their ensuing discussions that such behavior is an important facet of the occupation. The estimates of 50 to 75 percent are well above Kinsey's finding that 19 percent of his total female sample had physical sexual contact with other females by age 40 (1953:452–453). This difference is further heightened when we consider that a large majority of our sample (69 percent) were or had been married, Kinsey found that only three percent of married and nine percent of previously married

females had homosexual contacts by age 40 (1953:453–454).

Conditions Contributing to Homosexuality

More relevant to the hypothesis of this paper, however, are the conditions of the occupation which our subjects claimed were related to the incidence of homosexual behavior, whatever its magnitude. It was evident from their discussions that a great part, if not most, of such behavior could be attributed to occupational conditions. Specifically, conditions supportive of homosexual behavior in the stripping occupation can be classified as follows: (1) isolation from affective social relationships; (2) unsatisfactory relationships with males; and (3) an opportunity structure allowing a wide range of sexual behavior.

Isolation from Affective Social Relationships. Evidence from our research indicates that in general strippers have difficulty maintaining permanent affective social relationships, judging by their catalogues of marital difficulties and lack of persons whom they say they can trust. Aside from such basic inabilities, it is apparent that the demands of the occupation as a touring stripper make it exceedingly difficult for the girls to establish or maintain immediate affective relationships, even on a temporary basis. The best way to demonstrate this is to describe their working hours. Generally, strippers on tour spend only one week in each city and work all seven days from Friday through Thursday evening. They must be in the next city by late Friday morning for rehearsal. Their working day usually begins with a show about 1 P.M. and ends around 11 P.M., except on Saturday when there may be a midnight show. Although the girls' own acts may last only about 20 minutes in each of four daily shows, they also perform as foils in the comedians' skits. As a consequence, the girls usually are restricted to the theater every day from 1 to 11 P.M. except for a two and a half hour dinner break. After the last show most either go to a nearby nightclub or to their hotel rooms to watch television. Many girls spend over 40 weeks a year on tour.

Such working conditions effectively curtail the range of social relationships these girls might otherwise have. It should not be surprising that a nearly universal complaint among strippers is the loneliness they encounter while on tour. One girl claimed: "When you are lonely enough you will try anything." By itself this loneliness is not necessarily conducive to homosexual activities since, aside from other girls in the troupe, there is isolation from females as well as from males. But strippers find that contacts with males are not only limited but often highly unsatisfactory in content, and homosexuality can become an increasingly attractive alternative.

Unsatisfactory Relationships with Males. As stated above, women prisoners claim that lesbianism is very frequent among strippers. Data from our research tends to confirm this rumor. There is also some evidence that homosexual behavior is relatively frequent among prostitutes (Ward and Kassebaum, 1965:126–132). It is a curious paradox that two occupations dedicated to the sexual titillation of males would contain large numbers of persons who frequently obtain their own gratification from females. Tempting as it may be to turn to some exotic psychoanalytic explanations concerning latent homosexuality, the reasons may not be so covert. Ward and Kassebaum (1965:126–132) and others (Benjamin and Masters, 1964:245–246n) note that among prostitutes homosexual behavior may result less from inclination or predisposition than from continual experiences which engender hostility toward males in general.

A recurring theme in our interviews was strippers' disillusionment with the male of the species. This disillusionment often begins on stage when the neophyte first witnesses audience reactions which prove shocking even to girls who take off their clothes in public. Due to lighting conditions the stripper is unable to see beyond the second row of seats but from these front rows she is often gratuitously treated to performances rivaling her own act: exhibitionism and masturbation. There is no question that strippers are very conscious of this phenomenon for they characterize a large proportion of their audience as "degenerates." This term, incidentally, occurred so often in the course of our interviews it could be considered part of the stripper argot. Strippers know that "respectable" people attend their performances, but they are usually out in the dark where they cannot be seen. Furthermore, a sizeable proportion of these "respectables" are perceived by strippers to be "couples," hence most of the unattached male audience is suspect.

There is no indication that strippers on tour have more off-stage contact with their audience than does any other type of performer. But the precedent set by the males in rows one and two persists for strippers even in their off-stage contacts with men. They find that their stage identifications as sex objects are all too frequently taken at face value. Initially, strippers may find this identification flattering but many eventually become irritated by it. As one subject put it:

If a guy took me out to dinner and showed me a good time, I'd sleep with him. But most of them just call up and say "Let's fuck."

When checking into hotels while on tour most girls register under their real rather than their stage name. Several girls pointed out to us that the purpose of this practice was to eliminate being phoned by their admirers. Furthermore, many of the girls avoid identifying themselves in public as strippers, preferring to call themselves dancers, entertainers, and the like. This enables them not only to steer clear of a pariah label but to minimize unwelcome sexual reactions which they feel the name "stripper" engenders.

When strippers do form relatively prolonged liaisons with males during the course of their stripping career, chances are good that they will result in another embittering experience. In some cases the man will insist that the girl abandon the occupation, something she may not be inclined to do; hence a breakup occurs. But more frequently the girls find themselves entangled with males who are interested only in a financial or sexual advantage. One of our male informants closely connected with the stripping profession claimed, "You know the kind of jerks these girls tie up with? They're pimps, leeches, or weirdos." This, of course is an oversimplification; yet the strippers themselves confirm that they seem to be involved with more than their share of rough, unemployed males who are more than happy to enjoy their paycheck.

Strippers probably are not without fault themselves in their difficulties with heterosexual relationships; in our sample of 35 we found that of the 24 who had ever been married, 20 had experienced at least one divorce. It is evident, however, that their problems are compounded by the exploitive males who gravitate toward them. Under these circumstances contacts with lesbians are often seen as respites from importunate males. One subject claimed that although she did not care to engage in homosexual activities she would frequently go to a lesbian bar where she could "have a good time and not be bothered." Another said that lesbians are the only ones who "treat you like a person." As one reasoned:

Strippers go gay because they have little chance to meet nice guys. They come in contact with a lot of degenerate types. If they do meet a nice guy chances are he will ask them to stop stripping. If he doesn't he's likely to be a pimp. So the girls got to turn to a woman who understands them and their job. It is very easy for them to listen to the arguments of lesbians who will tell them basically that men are no good and women can give them better companionship.

Our argument should in no way be interpreted to mean that most strippers are anti-male or have completely severed all contacts with males. From our research it appears that the "career" homosexual is the exception among strippers. At best, the majority can be described as bisexual. The point is that experiences gained in the course of their occupation promote the homosexual aspect by generating caution and skepticism where relationships with males are concerned. Limited contacts with males plus the wariness which accompanies these contacts can be instrumental in severely curtailing the sexual activity of strippers outside of prostitution. Thus an opportunity for a warm, intimate relationship unaccompanied by masculine hazards becomes increasingly attractive. According to one of our subjects, when faced by the lesbian ploy, "Men are no good; I can do things for you they can't," many strippers find themselves persuaded at least temporarily.

Opportunity Structure Allowing a Wide Range of Sexual Behavior. The final occupational condition contributing to the incidence of homosexual behavior among strippers involves the existence of both opportunities and tacit support for such behavior. As male researchers we found it difficult to fathom the opportunities available for female homosexual activities. Our respondents pointed out, however, that there is no want in this regard. Strippers on tour have easy access to information on the location of gay bars in any city they play; furthermore, the reception strippers receive in these bars is especially hospitable. More immediate opportunities are available, obviously, with the presence of homosexuals in the touring group itself. The

group which, of necessity, spends most of the day together provides the novice stripper with at least an opportunity for sexual experimentation without the risks inherent in becoming involved with complete strangers.

There is some indication also that some strippers experienced in homosexual behavior are not particularly quiescent when obtaining partners. One subject informed us that she avoids touring with certain groups simply because homosexual contacts within the group are an expected mode of behavior and noncompliance is punished by ostracism. She claimed that being on tour was boring enough without having the other girls refusing to talk or associate with her. In this same vein, several of our subjects stated that certain older and established women in the occupation actively recruit partners with promises of career rewards. We were at first skeptical of such "casting couch" tactics among strippers, but the same stories and names recurred so often from such diverse sources that the possibility cannot be ignored.

We do not wish to over-dramatize the pressures placed on the girls by others to engage in lesbian practices. No doubt such pressures do occur, but sporadically. More important is the fact that opportunities for homosexual contacts occur in an atmosphere of permissiveness toward sexual behavior which characterizes the workday philosophy of strippers. The strippers' principal salable product is sex; the music, dancing, and costumes are only accessories. The real product becomes, over time, effectively devoid of any exclusiveness and is treated with the same detachment as grocers eventually view their radishes. For some strippers sexual contacts are regarded not only with detachment but with a sense of indifference:

I usually don't get kicks out of other women, not really, but there are times. Sometimes you come home and you are just too tired to work at it. Then it's nice to have a woman around. You can lay down on the floor, relax, watch T.V. and let her do it.

Add to this a sense of cynicism regarding sexual mores. Sexual behavior is generally not characterized by strippers as right or wrong by any universal standard but in terms of its presumed incidence in the general society; many of our respondents firmly expressed their view that lesbianism and prostitution are easily as common among women outside the occupation as among strippers. One respondent reasoned:

Strippers are no different in morality than housewives, secretaries, waitresses, or anybody else. There is a certain amount of laxity of behavior which would occur in anybody, but with the occupational hazard of being lonely and moving from town to town, well, that's the reason.

The end effect of such attitudes is that no stigma is attached to either homosexual behavior or prostitution among strippers as long as the participants are discreet, do not bother others, and do not allow their activities to interfere with the stability of the touring group.[4] It appears, then, that strippers work in a situation where opportunities for homosexuality are not only available but where social pressures restricting sexual choice to males are minimal or nonexistent.

Summary

Previous research indicates that most homosexual careers, male or female, begun outside the total institutional setting involve enlistment rather than a system of recruitment through peer group or subcultural pressures (Gagnon and Simon, 1968a:116, 118). As sociologists however, we must not lose sight of the importance of situational conditions as explanatory variables for understanding rates of deviant behavior. We have attempted to demonstrate how sexual behavior may be an adaptation to social factors immediately impinging upon the actors; specifically, we have argued that the stripping occupation may be analogous to the prison setting in that its structural characteristics contribute to the incidence of homosexual behavior.

REFERENCES

Benjamin, Harry and R. E. L. Masters. 1964. *Prostitution and Morality*. New York: Julian Press.

Gagnon, John H. and William Simon. 1968a. "Sexual Deviance in Contemporary America." *The Annals of the American Academy of Political and Social Science*, 376 (March): 106–122. 1968b. "The Social Meaning of Prison Homosexuality." *Federal Probation*, 32 (March): 23–29.

Gerassi, John. 1966. *The Boys of Boise: Furor, Vice, and Folly in an American City*. New York: Macmillan.

Giallombardo, Rose. 1966. *Society of Women: A Study of a Woman's Prison*. New York: Wiley.

Hollingshead, August B. 1957. *Two Factor Index of Social Position*. New Haven: Yale University (mimeographed).

Kinsey, Alfred C., Wardell B. Pomeroy, and Clyde E. Martin. 1948. *Sexual Behavior in the Human Male*. Philadelphia: Saunders.

Kinsey, Alfred C., Wardell B. Pomeroy, Clyde E. Martin, and Paul H. Gebhard. 1953. *Sexual Behavior in the Human Female*. Philadelphia: Saunders.

Leznoff, Maurice, and William A. Westley. 1956. "The Homosexual Community." *Social Problems*, 3 (April): 257–263.

Simon, William, and John H. Gagnon. 1967a. "Femininity in the Lesbian Community." *Social Problems*, 15 (Fall): 212–221. 1967b. "Homosexuality: The Formulation of a Sociological Perspective." *Journal of Health and Social Behavior*, 8 (September): 177–185.

Skipper, James K., Jr., and Charles H. McCaghy. 1969. "Stripteasers and the Anatomy of a Deviant Occupation." Paper read at American Sociological Association meetings in San Francisco (September).

Sykes, Gresham M. 1965. *The Society of Captives: A Study of a Maximum Security Prison*. New York: Atheneum.

Ward, David A., and Gene G. Kassebaum. 1965. *Women's Prison: Sex and Social Structure*. Chicago: Aldine.

[4]One perceptive respondent even questioned the rationality of the legal definition of prostitution: There is a very hazy line between what people call prostitution and just going to bed with a man. What is the difference between taking $50 for it, or receiving flowers, going out to dinner, and then the theater, and then getting laid? One has preliminaries, otherwise there is no difference. There is a payment both ways.

Conversion to the Doomsday Cult

JOHN LOFLAND

The logical and methodological structure of . . . [this] analysis is based on a developmental conception.[1] That is, I will offer a series of more or less successively accumulating factors, which in their total combination would seem to account for conversion to the DP's [Divine Precepts]. Seven such factors will be presented, all of which together seem both necessary and sufficient causes for conversion to occur. . . .

A Model of Conversion

To account for the process by which persons come to be world savers for the DP, I shall be concerned with two types of conditions or factors. The first type, which may be called *predisposing conditions,* comprises attributes of persons *prior* to their contact with the cult. . . .

The second type of conditions concerns . . . the contingencies of social situations. By *situational contingencies* I refer to those conditions that develop through direct confrontation and interaction between the potential convert and DP members, conditions that can lead to the successful recruitment of persons already well disposed toward the enterprise. Many of those who qualified for conversion on the basis of predispositional factors entered into interpersonal relationships with the DP's, but because the proper situational conditions were not met, they did not convert.

Let us now turn to a discussion of each of the factors operating within these two classes.

Tension

It would seem that no model of human conduct entirely escapes some concept of tension, strain, frustration, deprivation, or the like, as a factor in accounting for action. And not surprisingly, even the most cursory examination of the life situations of converts over the years before they embraced the DP reveals that they labored under what they at least *perceived* to be considerable tension.

This tension is best characterized as a felt discrepancy between some imaginary, ideal state of affairs and the circumstances in which they actually saw themselves. It is suggested that such acutely felt tension is a necessary, but far from sufficient condition for conversion. It provides some disposition to act. But tension may be resolved in a number of ways (or remain unresolved). Hence to know that these people were in a tension situation says little about *what* action they might take. . . .

It would appear that problems we find among [pre-converts] . . . are not *qualitatively* different or distinct from those presumably experienced by a significant, albeit unknown, proportion of the general population. Their peculiarity, if any, appears to be *quantitative;* that is, preconverts felt their problems to be acute and experienced high levels of tension concerning them over rather long periods of time.

It might in fact be said that from the point of view of an outside observer, their circumstances were in general not massively oppressive. One can probably find among the general population large numbers of people laboring under tensions that would seem to be considerably more acute and prolonged.

Perhaps the strongest qualitative characterization of tension supportable by the data is that pre-converts felt themselves frustrated in their various aspirations and *experienced* the tension rather more acutely and over longer periods than most do. . . .

Types of Problem-Solving Perspectives

On the basis of the first factor alone, only those without enduring, acute tensions are ruled out as potential DP converts. Since conversion is hardly the only response to problems, it is important to ask what else these people could have done, and why they didn't.

It seems likely that there were very few converts to the DP's for the simple reason that people have a number of conventional and readily available alternative ways of defining and coping

From John Lofland, *Doomsday Cult: A Study of Conversion, Proselytization, and Maintenance of Faith,* Englewood Cliffs, N.J.: Prentice-Hall, © 1966. Excerpt from pp. 31–62. Reprinted by permission of the author.

[1]Cf. Ralph Turner, "The Quest for Universals in Sociological Research," *American Sociological Review,* Vol. XVIII (December, 1953), 604–611; Howard S. Becker, *Outsiders* (New York: The Free Press of Glencoe, Inc., 1963), esp. pp. 22–25; and, Neil J. Smelser, *Theory of Collective Behavior* (New York: The Free Press of Glencoe, Inc., 1963), pp. 12–21.

with their problems. By this I mean that they have alternative perspectives, or rhetorics, that specify the nature and sources of problems and offer some program for their resolution. There are many such alternatives in modern society, but I shall briefly describe three particular types: the *psychiatric,* the *political,* and the *religious.* In the first, the origin of problems is typically traced to the psyche, and manipulation of the self is advocated as a resolution to problems. Political solutions, mainly radical, locate the sources of problems in the social structure and advocate its reorganization as a solution. The religious perspective tends to see both sources and solutions to difficulties as emanating from an unseen, and in principle unseeable, realm.

The first two rhetorics are both secular and are the most often used in contemporary society. It is no longer appropriate to regard recalcitrant and aberrant actors as possessed of devils. Indeed, modern religious institutions, in significant measure, offer secular, frequently psychiatric rhetorics concerning problems in living. The predominance of secular definitions of tension is a major source of loss of potential converts to the DP. Most people with acute tensions "get the psychiatric word" especially, either by defining themselves as grist for its mill or by being forced into it. Several persons met other conditions of the model but had adopted a psychiatric definition of their tensions and failed to convert. . . .

All pre-converts seemed surprisingly uninformed about conventional psychiatric and political perspectives for defining their problems. Perhaps largely because of their backgrounds (many were from small towns and rural communities), they had long been accustomed to defining the world in religious terms. Although conventional religious outlooks had been discarded by all pre-converts as inadequate, "spiritless," "dead," etc., prior to contact with the DP's, *the general propensity to impose religious meaning on events had been retained.*

Even within these constrictions in the available solutions for acutely felt problems, a number of alternative responses still remain. First, it must be recognized that people can persist in stressful situations and do little or nothing to reduce their discomfort. This is something that students of social life too often tend to underestimate. . . .

Second, people often take specifically problem-directed action to change those portions of their lives that are troublesome, without at the same time adopting a different world view to interpret them. . . .

Third, there exists a range of maneuvers that "put the problem out of mind." In general these constitute compensations for, or distractions from, problems in living. Such maneuvers include addiction to the mass media, preoccupation with childrearing, or immersion in work. More spectacular bypass routes are alcoholism, suicide, promiscuity, and the like. . . .

In any event, it may be assumed not only that many people with tensions explore these strategies, but also that some succeed and hence become unavailable as potential DP recruits.[2]

Religious Seekership

Whatever the reasons, pre-converts failed in their attempts to find a successful way out of their difficulties through any of the strategies outlined above. Thus their need for solutions persisted, and their problem-solving perspective was restricted to a religious outlook. However, all pre-converts found that conventional religious institutions failed to provide adequate solutions. Subsequently, each came to see himself as a seeker, a person searching for some satisfactory system for interpreting and resolving his discontent. Given their generally religious view of the world, all pre-converts had, to a greater or lesser extent, defined themselves as looking for an adequate religious perspective and had taken some action to achieve this end.

Some went from church to church and prayer group to prayer group, routing their religious seeking through relatively conventional institutions. . . .

The necessary attributes of pre-converts stated thus far could all have persisted for some time before these people encountered the DP and can be thought of as background factors, or predispositions. Although they appeared to have arisen and been active in the order specified, they are important here as accumulated and

---

[2]It perhaps needs to be noted that this discussion is confined to isolating the elements of the conversion sequence. Extended analysis would have to give attention to the factors that *in turn* bring each conversion condition into existence—that is, to develop a theory for each of the seven elements, specifying the conditions under which they develop. On the form that this would likely take see Ralph Turner's discussion of "the intrusive factor," *op. cit.,* 609–611.

simultaneously active factors during the development of succeeding conditions.

The Turning Point

We now turn to situational factors in which timing becomes significant. The first of these is the striking universal circumstance that at the time when they first encountered the DP, all pre-converts had reached or were about to reach what they perceived as a turning point in their lives. That is, each had come to a moment when old lines of action were complete, had failed, or had been or were about to be disrupted, and when they were faced with the opportunity or necessity for doing something different with their lives.[3] . . .

Turning points in general derived from having recently migrated, lost or quit a job . . . or graduated from, failed in, or quit an educational institution. Perhaps because most converts were young adults, turning points involving educational institutions were relatively frequent. . . .

The significance of . . . [the] various kinds of turning points lies in their having produced an increased awareness of and desire to take some action on their problems, *combined with a new opportunity to do so*. Turning points were circumstances in which old obligations and lines of action had diminished, and new involvements had become desirable and possible.

Cult-Affective Bonds

We come now to the moments of contact between a potential recruit and the DP's. In order for persons who meet all four of the previously activated steps to be further drawn down the road to full conversion, an affective bond must develop or already exist between the potential recruit and one or more of the DP members. The development or presence of some positive, emotive, interpersonal response seems necessary to bridge the gap between first exposure to the message and coming to accept its truth. That is, persons developed affective ties with the group or some of its members while they still regarded the DP perspective as problematic, or even "way out." In a manner of speaking, final conversion was coming to accept the opinions of one's friends.[4] . . .

It is particularly important to note that conversions frequently moved through *pre-existing* friendship pairs or nets. . . .

The building of bonds that were unsupported by previous friendships with a new convert often took the form of a sense of instant and powerful rapport with a believer. . . .

It is suggested, then, that although potential converts might have difficulty in taking up the DP perspective, when the four previous conditions *and* an affective tie were present, they came to consider the DP seriously and to begin to accept it as their personal construction of reality.

Extra-Cult-Affective Bonds

It may be supposed that non-DP associates of the convert-in-process would not be entirely neutral to the now live possibility of his taking up with the DP's. We must inquire, then, into the conditions under which extra-cult controls in the form of emotional attachments are activated, and how they restrain or fail to restrain persons from DP conversion.

By virtue of recent migration, disaffection with geographically distant families and spouses, and very few proximate, extra-cult acquaintances, a few converts were "social atoms" in the classic sense. For them extra-cult attachments were irrelevant. . . .

More typically, converts were effectively without opposition because, although they were acquainted with persons, no one was intimate enough with them to become aware that a conversion was in progress, or, if they knew, did not feel that there was a sufficient mutual attachment to justify intervention. . . .

Ironically, in many cases positive extra-cult attachments were to other religious seekers, who, even though not yet budding converts themselves, provided impetus to continue inves-

[3] Everett C. Hughes, *Men and Their Work* (New York: The Free Press of Glencoe, Inc., 1958), Chap. 1; Anselm Strauss, "Transformations of Identity," in Arnold Rose, ed., *Human Behavior and Social Processes* (Boston: Houghton Mifflin Company, 1962), pp. 67–71. Cf. the oft-noted "cultural dislocation" and migration pattern found in the background of converts to many groups, especially cults.

[4] Cf. Tamotsu Shibutani, *Society and Personality* (Englewood Cliffs, N.J.: Prentice-Hall, Inc., 1961), pp. 523–532, 588–592. Edgar Schein reports that in prison "the most potent source of influence in coercive persuasion was the identification which arose between a prisoner and his more reformed cellmate" [*Coercive Persuasion* (New York: W. W. Norton & Company, Inc., 1961), p. 277]. See also Alan Kerckhoff, Kurt Back, and Norman Miller, "Sociometric Patterns in Hysterical Contagion," *Sociometry*, Vol. XXVIII (March, 1965), 2–15.

tigation or entertainment of the DP rather than exercising a countervailing force. Indeed, such extra-cult persons might only be slightly behind their friend or friends in their own conversion process. . . .

In the relatively few cases where there were positive attachments between conventional extra-cult persons and a convert-in-process, control was minimized or not activated because of geographical distance and intentional avoidance of contact or communication about the topic during the period when the convert was solidifying his faith. . . .

When there were emotional attachments to extra-cult, nonseeking persons, and when these persons were physically present and cognizant of the incipient transformation, conversion became a nip and tuck affair. Pulled upon by competing emotional loyalties and their discordant versions of reality, pre-converts were thrown into intense emotional strain. . . .

When extra-cult bonds withstood the period of affective and ideological flirtation with the DP's, conversion failed to be consummated. However, most converts did not seem to have the kind of external affiliations in which the informal control over belief that is exerted among close friends could be exercised. They were so effectively unintegrated into any network of conventional people that for the most part they could simply fall out of relatively routine society virtually unnoticed and take their co-seeker friends (if any) with them.

Intensive Interaction

The combination of the six previous factors seems sufficient to bring a person to *verbal conversion* to the DP, but one more contingency must be met if he is to become a deployable agent,[5] or what I have termed a *total convert*.

. . . [Most,] but not all, verbal converts ultimately put their lives at the disposal of the cult. It is suggested that such commitment took place as a result of intensive interaction with DP's and failed to result when such interaction was absent. By intensive interaction is meant actual daily, and even hourly physical accessibility to DP total converts. Such intense exposure offers the opportunity to reinforce and elaborate upon the initial, tentative assent that has been granted the DP world view. It is in such prolonged association that the perspective comes alive as a device for interpreting the moment-to-moment events in the verbal convert's life.

The DP doctrine has a variety of resources for explaining the most minor everyday events and for relating them to a cosmic battle between good and evil spirits in a way that places the convert at the center of this war. Since all DP interpretations point to the imminence of the end, to participate in these explanations of daily life is more and more to come to see the necessity of one's personal participation as a totally committed agent in this cosmic struggle.[6]

The need to make other converts and to support the cause in all ways was the main theme of verbal exchanges between the tentatively accepting and the total converts—and, indeed, among the total converts themselves. Without this close association with those already totally committed, such an appreciation of the need for one's transformation into a total convert failed to develop. In recognition of this fact, the DP's gave greatest priority to attempting to get verbal converts (and even the merely interested) to move into the cult's communal dwellings. . . .

Thus it is that verbal conversion and resolutions to reorganize one's life for the DP's are not automatically translated into total conversion. One must be intensively exposed to the group supporting these new standards of conduct. The DP's did not find proselytizing, the primary task of total converts, a very easy activity to perform. But in the presence of people who supported one another and balmed their collective wounds, such a transformation became possible. Those who accepted the truth of the doctrine but lacked intensive interaction with the core group remained partisan spectators and failed to play an active part in the battle to usher in God's kingdom. . . .

Concluding Remark

In view of the character of the set of conditions outlined, it might be wondered what competitive advantage the DP's had over other unusual religious groups. In terms of background

---

[5] On the concept of the "deployable agent" or "deployable personnel" in social movements, see Philip Selznick, *The Organizational Weapon* (New York: The Free Press of Glencoe, Inc., 1959), pp. 18–29.

[6] Cf. Schein, *op. cit.*, pp. 136–139, 280–282.

conditions, I am suggesting that they had little, if any, advantage. In terms of situational conditions, their advantage lay merely in the fact that they got there and actually made their pitch, developed affective bonds, and induced people into intensive interaction. As with so much in life one may say that "there but for the grace of God go I"—within the limits of the conditions specified. It is to be hoped that the present effort will contribute to dispelling the tendency to think that there must be some deep, almost mystical connection between world views and their carriers. Like conceptions which hold that criminals and delinquents must be different from others, so our thinking about other types of deviants has too often assumed some extensive characterological conjunction between participant and pattern of participation.

11 LEARNING THE CULTURE

Deviant subcultures have their own distinctive traditions; these include ways of thinking, feeling, and behaving. Newcomers must learn these traditions, and deviant groups must work to sustain their ideas against the countervailing influences of the dominant culture.

In the first selection Barbara Heyl describes a brothel specifically devoted to training new prostitutes. Next, Martin Weinberg describes the norms nudists learn and how these norms sustain the official nudist perspective. Kenneth Stoddart then shows how LSD users learn from members of their drug-using community how to interpret and control the drug experience.

The Training of House Prostitutes

BARBARA SHERMAN HEYL

Although the day of the elaborate and conspicuous high-class house of prostitution is gone, houses still operate throughout the United States in a variety of altered forms. The business may be run out of trailers and motels along major highways, luxury apartments in the center of a metropolis or run-down houses in smaller, industrialized cities. (Recent discussions of various aspects of house prostitution include: Gagnon and Simon, 1973:226–27; Hall, 1973:115–95; Heyl, 1974; Jackson, 1969:185–92; Sheehy, 1974:185–204; Stewart, 1972; and Vogliotti, 1975:25–80.) Madams sometimes find themselves teaching young women how to become professional prostitutes. This paper focuses on one madam who trains novices to work at the house level. I compare the training to Bryan's (1965) account of the apprenticeship of call girls and relate the madam's role to the social organization of house prostitution.

Bryan's study of thirty-three Los Angeles call girls is one of the earliest interactionist treatments of prostitution. His data focus on the process of entry into the occupation of call girl and permit an analysis of the structure and content of a woman's apprenticeship. He concluded that the apprenticeship of call girls is mainly directed toward developing a clientele, rather than sexual skills (1965:288, 296–7). But while Bryan notes that pimps seldom train women directly, approximately half of his field evidence in fact derives from pimp-call girl apprenticeships. Thus, in Bryan's study (as well as in subsequent work on entry into prostitution as an occupation) there is a missing set of data on the more typical female

trainer-trainee relationship and on the content and process of training at other levels of the business in nonmetropolitan settings. This paper attempts to fill this gap.

Ann's Turn-Out Establishment

A professional prostitute, whether she works as a streetwalker, house prostitute, or call girl, can usually pick out one person in her past who "turned her out," that is, who taught her the basic techniques and rules of the prostitute's occupation.[1] For women who begin working at the house level, that person may be a pimp, another "working girl," or a madam. Most madams and managers of prostitution establishments, however, prefer not to take on novice prostitutes, and they may even have a specific policy against hiring turn-outs (see Erwin (1960:204–5) and Lewis (1942:222)). The turn-out's inexperience may cost the madam clients and money; to train the novice, on the other hand, costs her time and energy. Most madams and managers simply do not want the additional burden.

It was precisely the madam's typical disdain for turn-outs that led to the emergence of the house discussed in this paper—a house specifically devoted to training new prostitutes. The madam of this operation, whom we shall call Ann, is forty-one years old and has been in the prostitution world twenty-three years, working primarily at the house level. Ann knew that pimps who manage women at this level have difficulty placing novices in houses. After oper-

From "The Madam as Teacher: The Training of House Prostitutes," *Social Problems,* Vol. 24, No. 5 (June 1977), pp. 545–551, 554–555, and in *The Madam as Entrepreneur* by Barbara Sherman Heyl (New Brunswick, NJ: Transaction Books, 1979), pp. 113–128. Reprinted with permission of the Society for the Study of Social Problems and the author.

AUTHOR'S NOTE: This study analyzes the training provided by one madam for women entering house prostitution in a moderate-sized city. The data include taped training sessions, observations of the madam's teaching techniques, and repeated interviews with the madam. The content and structure of the training is compared to that reported in Bryan's (1965) study of the apprenticeship of call girls. The madam's training reflects aspects of the social organization of house prostitution, especially the close interaction of prostitutes in the house that requires a common set of work rules and practices. This paper is a revised version of "The Training of House Prostitutes," presented at the Annual Meeting of the American Sociological Association, San Francisco, 28 August 1975.

[1] This situation-specific induction into prostitution may be contrasted with the "smooth and almost imperceptible" transition to the status of poolroom "hustler" noted by Polsky (1969:80–81).

ating several houses staffed by professional prostitutes, she decided to run a school for turn-outs partly as a strategy for acquiring a continually changing staff of young women for her house. Pimps are the active recruiters of new prostitutes, and Ann found that, upon demonstrating that she could transform the pimps' new, square women into trained prostitutes easily placed in professional houses, pimps would help keep her business staffed.[2] Ann's house is a small operation in a middle-sized, industrial city (population 300,000), with a limited clientele of primarily working-class men retained as customers for ten to fifteen years and offered low rates to maintain their patronage.

Although Ann insists that every turn-out is different, her group of novices is remarkably homogeneous in some ways. Ann has turned out approximately twenty women a year over the six years while she has operated a training school. Except for one Chicano, one black and one American Indian, the women were all white. They ranged in age from eighteen to twenty seven. Until three years ago, all the women she hired had pimps. Since then, more women are independent (so-called "outlaws"), although many come to Ann sponsored by a pimp. That is, in return for being placed with Ann, the turn-out gives the pimp a percentage of her earnings for a specific length of time. At present eighty percent of the turn-outs come to Ann without a long term commitment to a pimp. The turn-outs stay at Ann's on the average of two to three months. This is the same average length of time Bryan (1965:290) finds for the apprenticeship in his call-girl study. Ann seldom has more than two or three women in training at any one time. Most turn-outs live at the house, often just a large apartment near the older business section of the city.

The Content of the Training

The data for the following analysis are of three kinds. First, tape recordings from actual training sessions with fourteen novices helped specify the structure and content of the training provided. Second, lengthy interviews with three of the novices and multiple interviews with Ann were conducted to obtain data on the training during the novice's first few days at the house before the first group training sessions were conducted and recorded by Ann. And third, visits to the house on ten occasions and observations of Ann's interaction with the novices during teaching periods extended the data on training techniques used and the relationship between madam and novice. In addition, weekly contact with Ann over a four-year period allowed repeated review of current problems and strategies in training turn-outs.

Ann's training of the novice begins soon after the woman arrives at the house. The woman first chooses an alias. Ann then asks her whether she has ever "Frenched a guy all the way," that is, whether she has brought a man to orgasm during the act of fellatio. Few of the women say they have. By admitting her lack of competence in a specialized area, the novice has permitted Ann to assume the role of teacher. Ann then launches into instruction on performing fellatio. Such instruction is important to her business. Approximately eighty percent of her customers are what Ann calls "French tricks." Many men visit prostitutes to receive sexual services, including fellatio, their wives or lovers seldom perform. This may be particularly true of the lower- and working-class clientele of the houses and hotels of prostitution (Gagnon and Simon, 1973:230). Yet the request for fellatio may come from clients at all social levels; consequently, it is a sexual skill today's prostitute must possess and one she may not have prior to entry into the business (Bryan, 1965:293; Winick and Kinsie, 1971:180, 207; Gray, 1973:413).

Although Ann devotes much more time to teaching the physical and psychological techniques of performing fellatio than she does to any other sexual skill, she also provides strategies for coitus and giving a "half and half"— fellatio followed by coitus. The sexual strategies taught are frequently a mixture of ways for stimulating the client sexually and techniques of self-protection during the sexual acts. For example, during coitus, the woman is to move her hips "like a go-go dancer's" while keeping her feet on the bed and tightening her inner thigh

[2] In the wider context of the national prostitution scene, Ann's situation reflects the "minor league" status of her geographical location. In fact, she trains women from other communities who move on to the more lucrative opportunities in the big city. See the stimulating applications of the concept of "minor league" to the study of occupations in Faulkner (1974).

muscles to protect herself from the customer's thrust and full penetration. Ann allows turn-outs to perform coitus on their backs only, and the woman is taught to keep one of her arms across her chest as a measure of self-defense in this vulnerable position.

After Ann has described the rudimentary techniques for the three basic sexual acts—fellatio, coitus, and "half and half"—she begins to explain the rules of the house operation. The first set of rules concerns what acts the client may receive for specific sums of money. Time limits are imposed on the clients, roughly at the rate of $1 per minute; the minimum rate in this house is $15 for any of the three basic positions. Ann describes in detail what will occur when the first client arrives: he will be admitted by either Ann or the maid; the women are to stand and smile at him, but not speak to him (considered "dirty hustling"); he will choose one of the women and go to the bedroom with her. Ann accompanies the turn-out and the client to the bedroom and begins teaching the woman how to check the man for any cuts or open sores on the genitals and for any signs of old or active venereal disease. Ann usually rechecks each client herself during the turn-out's first two weeks of work. For the first few days Ann remains in the room while the turn-out and client negotiate the sexual contract. In ensuing days Ann spends time helping the woman develop verbal skills to "hustle" the customer for more expensive sexual activities.

The following analysis of the instruction Ann provides is based on tape recordings made by Ann during actual training sessions in 1971 and 1975. These sessions took place after the turn-outs had worked several days but usually during their first two weeks of work. The tapes contain ten hours of group discussion with fourteen different novices. The teaching tapes were analyzed according to topics covered in the discussions, using the method outlined in Barker (1963) for making such divisions in the flow of conversation and using Bryan's analysis of the call girl's apprenticeship as a guide in grouping the topics. Bryan divides the content of the training of call girls into two broad dimensions, one philosophical and one interpersonal (1965: 291–4). The first emphasizes a subcultural value system and sets down guidelines for how the novice *should* treat her clients and her colleagues in the business. The second dimension follows from the first but emphasizes actual behavioral techniques and skills.

The content analysis of the taped training sessions produced three major topics of discussion and revealed the relative amount of time Ann devoted to each. The first two most frequently discussed topics can be categorized under Bryan's dimension of interpersonal skills; they were devoted to teaching situational strategies for managing clients. The third topic resembles Bryan's value dimension (1965:291–2).

The first topic stressed physical skills and strategies. Included in this category were instruction on how to perform certain sexual acts and specification of their prices, discussion of particular clients, and instruction in techniques for dealing with certain categories of clients, such as "older men" or "kinky" tricks. This topic of physical skills also included discussion of, and Ann's demonstration of, positions designed to provide the woman maximum comfort and protection from the man during different sexual acts. Defense tactics, such as ways to get out of a sexual position and out of the bedroom quickly, were practiced by the novices. Much time was devoted to analyzing past encounters with particular clients. Bryan finds similar discussions of individual tricks among novice call girls and their trainers (1965:293). In the case of Ann's turn-outs these discussions were often initiated by a novice's complaint or question about a certain client and his requests or behavior in the bedroom. The novice always received tips and advice from Ann and the other women present on how to manage that type of bedroom encounter. Such sharing of tactics allows the turn-out to learn what Gagnon and Simon call "patterns of client management" (1973:231).

Ann typically used these discussions of bedroom difficulties to further the training in specific sexual skills she had begun during the turn-out's first few days at work. It is possible that the addition of such follow-up sexual training to that provided during the turn-out's first days at the house results in a more extensive teaching of actual sexual skills than that obtained either by call girls or streetwalkers. Bryan finds that in the call-girl training—except for fellatio—"There seems to be little instruction concerning sexual techniques as such, even though the previous sexual experience of the trainee may have been quite limited" (1965:293). Gray (1973:413) notes that her sample of streetwalker turn-outs were rarely taught specific work strategies:

They learned these things by trial and error on the job. Nor were they schooled in specific sexual techniques: usually they were taught by customers who made the specific requests.

House prostitution may require more extensive sexual instruction than other forms of the business. The dissatisfied customer of a house may mean loss of business and therefore loss of income to the madam and the prostitutes who work there. The sexually inept streetwalker or call girl does not hurt business for anyone but herself; she may actually increase business for those women in the area should dissatisfied clients choose to avoid her. But the house depends on a stable clientele of satisfied customers.

The second most frequently discussed topic could be labeled: client management—verbal skills. Ann's primary concern was teaching what she calls "hustling." "Hustling" is similar to what Bryan terms a "sales pitch" for call girls (1965:292), but in the house setting it takes place in the bedroom while the client is deciding how much to spend and what sexual acts he wishes performed. "Hustling" is designed to encourage the client to spend more than the minimum rate.[3] The prominence on the teaching tapes of instruction in this verbal skill shows its importance in Ann's training of novices.

On one of the tapes Ann uses her own turning-out experience to explain to two novices (both with pimps) why she always teaches hustling skills as an integral part of working in a house.

Ann as a Turn-out[4]

Ann: Of course, I can remember a time when I didn't know that I was supposed to hustle. So that's why I understand that it's difficult to *learn* to hustle. When I turned out it was $2 a throw. They came in. They gave me their $2. They got a hell of a fuck. And that was it.

Then one Saturday night I turned *forty-four* tricks! And Penny [the madam] used to put the number of tricks at the top of the page and the amount of money at the bottom of the page—she used these big ledger books. Lloyd [Ann's pimp] came in at six o'clock and he looked at that book and he just *knew* I had made all kinds of money. Would you believe I had turned forty-two $2 tricks and two $3 tricks—because two of 'em got generous and gave me an extra buck! [Laughs] I got my ass whipped. And I was so tired—I thought I was going to die—I was 15 years old. And I got my ass whipped for it. [Ann imitates an angry Lloyd:] "Don't you know you're supposed to ask for more money?!" No, I didn't. Nobody told me that. All they told me was it was $2. So that is learning it the *hard* way. I'm trying to help you learn it the *easy* way, if there is an easy way to do it.

In the same session Ann asks one of the turn-outs (Linda, age eighteen) to practice her hustling rap.

Learning the Hustling Rap

Ann: I'm going to be a trick. You've checked me. I want you to carry it from there. [Ann begins role-playing: she plays the client; Linda, the hustler.]
Linda: [mechanically] What kind of party would you like to have?
Ann: That had all the enthusiasm of a wet noodle. I really wouldn't *want* any party with that because you evidently don't want to give me one.
Linda: What kind of party would you *like* to have?
Ann: I usually take a half and half.
Linda: Uh, the money?
Ann: What money?
Linda: The money you're supposed to have! [loudly] 'Cause you ain't gettin' it for free!
Ann: [upset] Linda, if you *ever,* ever say that in my joint . . . Because that's fine for street

---

[3] The term "hustling" has been used to describe a wide range of small-time criminal activities. Even within the world of prostitution, "hustling" can refer to different occupational styles; see Ross' description of the "hustler" who "is distinguished from ordinary prostitutes in frequently engaging in accessory crimes of exploitation," such as extortion or robbery (1959:16). The use of the term here is thus highly specific, reflecting its meaning in Ann's world.

[4] The indented sections (for example, "Ann as a Turn-out" and "Learning the Hustling Rap") are transcriptions from the teaching tapes. Redundant expressions have been omitted, and the author's comments on the speech tone or delivery are bracketed. Words italicized indicate emphasis by the speaker.

hustling. In street hustling, you're going to *have* to hard-hustle those guys or they're not going to come up with anything. Because they're going to *try* and get it for free. But when they walk in here, they *know* they're not going to get it for free to begin with. So try another tack—just a little more friendly, not quite so hard-nosed. [Returning to role-playing:] I just take a half and half.

Linda: How about fifteen [dollars]?

Ann: You're leading into the money too fast, honey. Try: "What are you going to spend?" or "How much money are you going to spend?" or something like that.

Linda: How much would you like to spend?

Ann: No! Not "like." 'Cause they don't *like* to spend anything.

Linda: How much *would* you like to spend?

Ann: Make it a very definite, positive statement: "How much are you going to spend?"

Ann considers teaching hustling skills her most difficult and important task. In spite of her lengthy discussion on the tapes of the rules and techniques for dealing with the customer sexually, Ann states that it may take only a few minutes to "show a girl how to turn a trick." A substantially longer period is required, however, to teach her to hustle. To be adept at hustling, the woman must be mentally alert and sensitive to the client's response to what she is saying and doing and be able to act on those perceptions of his reactions. The hustler must maintain a steady patter of verbal coaxing, during which her tone of voice may be more important than her actual words.

In Ann's framework, then, hustling is a form of verbal sexual aggression. Referring to the problems in teaching novices to hustle, Ann notes that "taking the aggressive part is something women are not used to doing; particularly young women." No doubt, hustling is difficult to teach partly because the woman must learn to discuss sexual acts, whereas in her previous experience, sexual behavior and preferences had been negotiated nonverbally (see Gagnon and Simon, 1973:228). Ann feels that to be effective, each woman's "hustling rap" must be her own—one that comes naturally and will strike the clients as sincere. All of that takes practice. But Ann is aware that the difficulty in learning to hustle stems more from the fact that it involved inappropriate sex-role behavior. Bryan concludes that it is precisely this aspect of soliciting

men on the telephone that causes the greatest distress to the novice call girl (1965:293). Thus, the call girl's income is affected by how much business she can bring in by her calls, that is, by how well she can learn to be socially aggressive on the telephone. The income of the house prostitute, in turn, depends heavily on her hustling skills in the bedroom. Ann's task, then, is to train the novice, who has recently come from a culture where young women are not expected to be sexually aggressive, to assume that role with a persuasive naturalness.

Following the first two major topics—client management through physical and verbal skills—the teaching of "racket" (prostitution world) values was the third-ranking topic of training and discussion on the teaching tapes. Bryan notes that the major value taught to call girls is "that of maximizing gains and minimizing effort, even if this requires transgressions of either a legal or moral nature" (1965:291). In her training, however, Ann avoids communicating the notion that the novices may exploit the customers in any way they can. For example, stealing or cheating clients is grounds for dismissal from the house. Ann cannot afford the reputation among her tricks that they risk being robbed when they visit her. Moreover, being honest with clients is extolled as a virtue. Thus, Ann urges the novices to tell the trick if she is nervous or unsure, to let him know she is new to the business. This is in direct contradiction to the advice pimps usually give their new women to hide their inexperience from the trick. Ann asserts that honesty in this case usually means that the client will be more tolerant of mistakes in sexual technique, be less likely to interpret hesitancy as coldness, and be generally more helpful and sympathetic. Putting her "basic principle" in the form of a simple directive, Ann declares: "Please the trick, but at the same time get as much money for pleasing him as you possibly can." Ann does not consider hustling to be client exploitation. It is simply the attempt to sell the customer the product with the highest profit margin. That is, she would defend hustling in terms familiar to the businessman or sales manager.

That Ann teaches hustling as a value is revealed in the following discussion between Ann and Sandy—a former hustler and long-time friend of Ann. Sandy, who married a former trick and still lives in town, has come over to the house to help instruct several novices in the hustling business.

Whores, Prostitutes and Hustlers

Ann: [To the turn-outs:] Don't get up-tight that you're hesitating or you're fumbling, within the first week or even the first five years. Because it takes that long to become a good hustler. I mean you can be a whore in one night. There's nothing to that. The first time you take money you're a whore.

Sandy: This girl in Midtown [a small, Midwestern city] informed me—I had been working there awhile—that I was a "whore" and she was a "prostitute." And I said: "Now what the hell does that mean?" Well the difference was that a prostitute could pick her customer and a whore had to take anybody. I said: "Well honey, I want to tell you something. I'm neither one." She said: "Well, you *work*." I said: "I know, but I'm a *hustler*. I make *money* for what I do."

Ann: And this is what I turn out—or try to turn out—hustlers. Not prostitutes. Not whores. But hustlers.

For Ann and Sandy the hustler deserves high status in the prostitution business because she has mastered a specific set of skills that, even with many repeat clients, earn her premiums above the going rate for sexual acts.

In the ideological training of call girls Bryan finds that "values such as fairness with other working girls, or fidelity to a pimp, may occasionally be taught" (1965:291–2); the teaching tapes revealed Ann's affirmation of both these virtues. When a pimp brings a woman to Ann, she supports his control over that woman. For example, if during her stay at the house, the novice breaks any of the basic rules—by using drugs, holding back money (from either Ann or the pimp), lying or seeing another man—Ann will report the infractions to the woman's pimp. Ann notes: "If I don't do that and the pimp finds out, he knows I'm not training her right, and he won't bring his future ladies to me for training." Ann knows she is dependent on the pimps to help supply her with turn-outs. Bryan, likewise, finds a willingness among call-girls' trainers to defer to the pimps' wishes during the apprenticeship period (1965:290).

Teaching fairness to other prostitutes is particularly relevant to the madam who daily faces the problem of maintaining peace among competing women at work under one roof. If two streetwalkers or two call girls find they cannot get along, they need not work near one another.

But if a woman leaves a house because of personal conflicts, the madam loses a source of income. To minimize potential negative feelings among novices, Ann stresses mutual support, prohibits "criticizing another girl," and denigrates the "prima donna"—the prostitute who flaunts her financial success before the other women.

In still another strategy to encourage fair treatment of one's colleagues in the establishment, Ann emphasizes a set of rules prohibiting "dirty hustling"—behavior engaged in by one prostitute that would undercut the business of other women in the house. Tabooed under the label of "dirty hustling" are the following: appearing in the line-up partially unclothed; performing certain disapproved sexual positions, such as anal intercourse; and allowing approved sexual extras without charging additional fees. The norms governing acceptable behavior vary from house to house and region to region, and Ann warns the turn-outs to ask about such rules when they begin work in a new establishment. The woman who breaks the work norms in a house, either knowingly or unknowingly, will draw the anger of the other women and can be fired by a madam eager to restore peace and order in the house.

Other topics considered on the tapes—in addition to physical skills, "hustling" and work values—were instruction on personal hygiene and grooming, role-playing of conversational skills with tricks on topics not related to sex or hustling ("living room talk"), house rules not related to hustling (such as punctuality, no perfume, no drugs), and guidelines for what to do during an arrest. There were specific suggestions on how to handle personal criticism, questions and insults from clients. In addition, the discussions on the tapes provided the novices with many general strategies for becoming "professionals" at their work, for example, the importance of personal style, enthusiasm ("the customer is always right"), and sense of humor. In some ways these guidelines resemble a beginning course in salesmanship. But they also provide clues, particularly in combination with the topics on handling client insults and the emphasis on hustling, on how the house prostitute learns to manage a stable and limited clientele and cope psychologically with the repetition of the clients and the sheer tedium of the physical work (Hughes, 1971:342–5).

. . . Although Ann feels strongly that training

is required to become a successful hustler at the house level, the function served by the training can be seen more as a spin-off of the structure of the occupation at that level: madams of establishments will often hire only trained prostitutes. Novices who pose as experienced hustlers are fairly easily detected by those proficient in the business working in the same house; to be found out all she need do is violate any of the expected norms of behavior: wear perfume, repeatedly fail to hustle any "over-money" or engage in dirty hustling. The exposure to racket values, which the training provides, may be more critical to the house prostitute than to the call girl. She must live and work in close contact with others in the business. Participants in house prostitution are more integrated into the prostitution world than are call girls, who can be and frequently are "independent"—working without close ties to pimps or other prostitutes. Becoming skilled in hustling is also less important for the call girl, as her minimum fee is usually high, making hustling for small increments less necessary. The house prostitute who does not know how to ask for more money, however, lowers the madam's income as well—another reason why madams prefer professional prostitutes.

The training of house prostitutes, then, reflects two problems in the social organization of house prostitution: (1) most madams will not hire untrained prostitutes; and (2) the close interaction of prostitutes operating within the confines of a house requires a common set of work standards and practices. These two factors differentiate house prostitution from call-girl and streetwalking operations and facilitate this madam's task of turning novices into professional prostitutes. The teaching madam employs a variety of coaching techniques to train turn-outs in sexual and hustling skills and to expose them to a set of occupational rules and values. Hers is an effort to prepare women with conventional backgrounds for work in the social environment of a house of prostitution where those skills and values are expected and necessary.

REFERENCES

Barker, Roger G. (ed.). 1963. *The Stream of Behavior: Explorations of Its Structure and Content.* New York: Appleton-Century-Crofts.

Bryan, James H. 1965. "Apprenticeships in Prostitution." *Social Problems,* 12 (Winter): 287–297.

———. 1966. "Occupational Ideologies and Individual Attitudes of Call Girls." *Social Problems,* 13 (Spring): 441–450.

Erwin, Carol. 1960. *The Orderly Disorderly House.* Garden City, N.Y.: Doubleday.

Faulkner, Robert R. 1974. "Coming of Age in Organizations: A Comparative Study of Career Contingencies and Adult Socialization." *Sociology of Work and Occupations,* 1 (May): 131–173.

Gagnon, John H. and William Simon. 1973. *Sexual Conduct: The Social Sources of Human Sexuality.* Chicago: Aldine.

Gray, Diana. 1973. "Turning-out: A Study of Teenage Prostitution." *Urban Life and Culture,* 1 (January): 401–425.

Hall, Susan. 1973. *Ladies of the Night.* New York: Trident Press.

Heyl, Barbara S. 1974. "The Madam as Entrepreneur." *Sociological Symposium,* 11 (Spring): 61–82.

Hughes, Everett C. 1971. "Work and Self." In *The Sociological Eye: Selected Papers.* Chicago: Aldine-Atherton, pp. 338–347.

Jackson, Bruce. 1969. *A Thief's Primer.* Toronto, Ontario: Macmillan.

Kinsey, Alfred C., Wardell B. Pomeroy, and Clyde E. Martin. 1948. *Sexual Behavior in the Human Male.* Philadelphia: W. B. Saunders.

Lewis, Gladys Adelina (ed.). 1942. *Call House Madam: The Story of the Career of Beverly Davis.* San Francisco: Martin Tudordale.

Polsky, Ned. 1969. *Hustlers, Beats and Others.* Garden City, N.Y.: Doubleday.

Ross, H. Laurence. 1959. "The 'Hustler' in Chicago." *Journal of Student Research,* 1: 13–19.

Sheehy, Gail. 1974. *Hustling: Prostitution in Our Wide-Open Society.* New York: Dell.

Stewart, George I. 1972. "On First Being a John." *Urban Life and Culture,* 1 (October): 255–274.

Vogliotti, Gabriel R. 1975. *The Girls of Nevada.* Secaucus, New Jersey: Citadel Press.

Winick, Charles and Paul M. Kinsie. 1971. *The Lively Commerce: Prostitution in the United States.* Chicago: Quadrangle Books.

The Nudist Management of Respectability

MARTIN S. WEINBERG

Public nudity is taboo in our society. Yet there is a group who breach this moral rule. They call themselves "social nudists."

A number of questions may be asked about these people. For example, how can they see their behavior as morally appropriate? Have they constructed their own morality? If so, what characterizes this morality and what are its consequences?[1]

This article will attempt to answer these questions through a study of social interaction in nudist camps. The data come from three sources: two summers of participant observation in nudist camps; 101 interviews with nudists in the Chicago area; and 617 mailed questionnaires completed by nudists in the United States and Canada.[2]

The Construction of Situated Moral Meanings: The Nudist Morality

The construction of morality in nudist camps is based on the official interpretations that camps provide regarding the moral meanings of public heterosexual nudity. These are (1) that nudity and sexuality are unrelated, (2) that there is nothing shameful about the human body, (3) that nudity promotes a feeling of freedom and natural pleasure, and (4) that nude exposure to the sun promotes physical, mental, and spiritual well-being.

This official perspective is sustained in nudist camps to an extraordinary degree, illustrating the extent to which adult socialization can affect traditional moral meanings. (This is especially true with regard to the first two points of the nudist perspective, which will be our primary

concern since these are its "deviant" aspects.) The assumption in the larger society that nudity and sexuality are related, and the resulting emphasis on covering the sexual organs, make the nudist perspective a specifically situated morality. My field work, interview, and questionnaire research show that nudists routinely use a special system of rules to create, sustain, and enforce this situated morality.

Strategies for Sustaining a Situated Morality

The first strategy used by the nudist camp to anesthetize any relationship between nudity and sexuality[3] involves a system of organizational precautions regarding who can come into the camp. Most camps, for example, regard unmarried people, especially single men, as a threat to the nudist morality. They suspect that singles may indeed see nudity as something sexual. Thus, most camps either exclude unmarried people (especially men), or allow only a small quota of them. Camps that do allow single men may charge them up to 35 percent more than they charge families. (This is intended to discourage single men, but since the cost is still relatively low compared with other resorts, this measure is not very effective. It seems to do little more than create resentment among the singles, and by giving formal organizational backing to the definition that singles are not especially desirable, it may contribute to the segregation of single and married members in nudist camps.)

Certification by the camp owner is another requirement for admission to camp grounds, and

Reprinted from *Sex Research: Studies from the Kinsey Institute* by Martin S. Weinberg, pp. 217–232. Copyright © 1976 by Oxford University Press, Inc. Reprinted by permission.

[1] In my previous papers, I have dealt with other questions that are commonly asked about nudists. How persons become nudists is discussed in my "Becoming a Nudist," *Psychiatry,* XXIX (February, 1966), 15–24. A report on the nudist way of life and social structure can be found in my article in *Human Organization,* XXVI (Fall, 1967), 91–99.

[2] Approximately one hundred camps were represented in the interviews and questionnaires. Interviews were conducted in the homes of nudists during the off season. Arrangements for the interviews were initially made with these nudists during the first summer of participant observation; selection of respondents was limited to those living within a one-hundred-mile radius of Chicago. The questionnaires were sent to all members of the National Nudist Council. The different techniques of data collection provided a test of convergent validation.

[3] For a discussion of the essence of such relationships, see Alfred Schutz, *Collected Papers: The Problem of Social Reality,* Maurice Natanson, ed. (The Hague: Nijhoff, 1962), I, 287 ff.

three letters of recommendation regarding the applicant's character are sometimes required. These regulations help preclude people whom members regard as a threat to the nudist morality.

[The camp owner] invited us over to see if we were *desirable* people. Then after we did this, he invited us to camp on probation; then they voted us into camp. [Q: Could you tell me what you mean by desirable people?] Well, not people who are inclined to drink, or people who go there for a peep show. Then they don't want you there. They feel you out in conversation. They want people for mental and physical health reasons.

Whom to admit [is the biggest problem of the camp]. [Q][4] Because the world is so full of people whose attitudes on nudity are hopelessly warped. [Q: Has this always been the biggest problem in camp?] Yes. Every time anybody comes, a decision has to be made. [Q] . . . The lady sitting at the gate decides about admittance. The director decides on membership.

A limit is sometimes set on the number of trial visits a non-member may make to camp. In addition, there is usually a limit on how long a person can remain clothed. This is a strategy to mark guests who may not sincerely accept the nudist perspective.

The second strategy for sustaining the nudist morality involves norms of interpersonal behavior. These norms are as follows:

No Staring. This rule controls overt signs of overinvolvement. As the publisher of one nudist magazine said, "They all look up to the heavens and never look below." Such studied inattention is most exaggerated among women, who usually show no recognition that the male is unclothed. Women also recount that they had expected men to look at their nude bodies, only to find, when they finally did get up the courage to undress, that no one seemed to notice. As one woman states: "I got so mad because my husband wanted me to undress in front of other men that I just pulled my clothes right off thinking everyone would look at me." She was amazed (and appeared somewhat disappointed) when no one did.

The following statements illustrate the constraints that result:

[Q: Have you ever observed or heard about anyone staring at someone's body while at camp?] I've heard stories, particularly about men that stare. Since I heard these stories, I tried not to, and have even done away with my sunglasses after someone said, half-joking, that I hide behind sunglasses to stare. Toward the end of the summer I stopped wearing sunglasses. And you know what, it was a child who told me this.

[Q: Would you stare . . . ?] Probably not, 'cause you can get in trouble and get thrown out. If I thought I could stare unobserved I might. They might not throw you out, but it wouldn't do you any good. [Q] The girl might tell others and they might not want to talk to me. . . . [Q] They disapprove by not talking to you, ignoring you, etc.

[Someone who stares] wouldn't belong there. [Q] If he does that he is just going to camp to see the opposite sex. [Q] He is just coming to stare. [Q] You go there to swim and relax.

I try very hard to look at them from the jaw up—even more than you would normally.[5]

No Sex Talk. Sex talk, or telling "dirty jokes," is uncommon in camp. The owner of a large camp in the Midwest stated: "It is usually expected that members of a nudist camp will not talk about sex, politics, or religion." Or as one single male explained: "It is taboo to make sexual remarks here." During my field work, it was rare to hear "sexual" joking such as one hears at most other types of resort. Interview respondents who mentioned that they had talked about sex qualified this by explaining that such talk was restricted to close friends, was of a "scientific nature," or, if a joke, was a "cute sort."

Asked what they would think of someone who breached this rule, respondents indicated that

---

[4][Q] is used to signify a neutral probe by the interviewer that follows the course of the last reply, such as "Could you tell me some more about that?" or "How is that?" or "What do you mean?" Other questions by the interviewer are given in full.

[5]The King and Queen contest, which takes place at conventions, allows for a patterned evasion of the staring rule. Applicants stand before the crowd in front of the royal platform, and applause is used for selecting the winners. Photography is allowed during the contest, and no one is permitted to enter the contest unless willing to be photographed. The major reason for this is that this is a major camp event, and contest pictures are used in nudist magazines. At the same time, the large number of photographs sometimes taken by lay photographers (that is, not working for the magazines), makes many nudists uncomfortable by calling into question a nonsexual definition of the situation.

such behavior would cast doubt on the situated morality of the nudist camp:

One would expect to hear less of that at camp than at other places. [Q] Because you expect that the members are screened in their attitude for nudism—and this isn't one who prefers sexual jokes.

I've never heard anyone swear or tell a dirty joke out there.

No. Not at camp. You're not supposed to. You bend over backwards not to.

They probably don't belong there. They're there to see what they can find to observe. [Q] Well, their mind isn't on being a nudist, but to see so and so nude.

No Body Contact. Although the extent to which this is enforced varies from camp to camp, there is at least some degree of informal enforcement in nearly every camp. Nudists mention that they are particularly careful not to brush against anyone or have any body contact for fear of how it might be interpreted:

I stay clear of the opposite sex. They're so sensitive, they imagine things.

People don't get too close to you. Even when they talk. They sit close to you, but they don't get close enough to touch you.

We have a minimum of contact. There are more restrictions [at a nudist camp]. [Q] Just a feeling I had. I would openly show my affection more readily someplace else.

And when asked to conceptualize a breach of this rule, the following response is typical:

They are in the wrong place. [Q] That's not part of nudism. [Q] I think they are there for some sort of sex thrill. They are certainly not there to enjoy the sun.

Also, in photographs taken for nudist magazines, the subjects usually have only limited body contact. One female nudist explained: "We don't want anyone to think we're immoral." Outsiders' interpretations, then, can also constitute a threat.

Associated with the body contact taboo is a prohibition of nude dancing. Nudists cite this as a separate rule. This rule is often talked about by members in a way that indicates organizational strain—that is, the rule itself makes evident that a strategy is in operation to sustain their situated morality.

This reflects a contradiction in our beliefs. But it's self-protection. One incident and we'd be closed.

No Alcoholic Beverages in American Camps. This rule guards against breakdowns in inhibition, and even respondents who admitted that they had "snuck a beer" before going to bed went on to say that they fully favor the rule.

Yes. We have [drunk at camp]. We keep a can of beer in the refrigerator since we're out of the main area. We're not young people or carousers. . . . I still most generally approve of it as a camp rule and would disapprove of anyone going to extremes. [Q] For common-sense reasons. People who overindulge lose their inhibitions, and there is no denying that the atmosphere of a nudist camp makes one bend over backwards to keep people who are so inclined from going beyond the bounds of propriety.

Anyone who drinks in camp is jeopardizing their membership and they shouldn't. Anyone who drinks in camp could get reckless. [Q] Well, when guys and girls drink they're a lot bolder—they might get fresh with someone else's girl. That's why it isn't permitted, I guess.

Rules Regarding Photography. Photography in a nudist camp is controlled by the camp management. Unless the photographer works for a nudist magazine, his (or her) moral perspective is sometimes suspect. One photographer's remark to a woman that led to his being so typed was, "Do you think you could open your legs a little more?"

Aside from a general restriction on the use of cameras, when cameras are allowed, it is expected that no pictures will be taken without the subject's permission. Members blame the misuse of cameras especially on single men. As one nudist said: "You always see the singles poppin' around out of nowhere snappin' pictures." In general, control is maintained, and any infractions that take place are not blatant or obvious. Overindulgence in picture-taking communicates an overinvolvement in the subjects' nudity and casts doubt on the assumption that nudity and sexuality are unrelated.

Photographers dressed only in cameras and light exposure meters. I don't like them. I think they only go out for pictures. Their motives should be questioned.

Photographers for nudist magazines recognize the signs that strain the situated morality that characterizes nudist camps. As one such photographer commented:

I never let a girl look straight at the camera. It looks too suggestive. I always have her look off to the side.

Similarly, a nudist model showed the writer a pin-up magazine to point out how a model could make a nude picture "sexy"—through the use of various stagings, props, and expressions—and in contrast, how the nudist model eliminates these techniques to make her pictures "natural." Although it may be questionable that a nudist model completely eliminates a sexual perspective for the non-nudist, the model discussed how she attempts to do this.

It depends on the way you look. Your eyes and your smile can make you look sexy. The way they're looking at you. Here, she's on a bed. It wouldn't be sexy if she were on a beach with kids running around. They always have some clothes on too. See how she's "looking" sexy? Like an "oh dear!" look. A different look can change the whole picture.

Now here's a decent pose. . . . Outdoors makes it "nature." Here she's giving you "the eye," or is undressing. It's cheesecake. It depends on the expression on her face. Having nature behind it makes it better. Don't smile like "come on honey!" It's that look and the lace thing she has on. . . . Like when you half-close your eyes, like "oh baby," a Marilyn Monroe look. Art is when you don't look like you're hiding it halfway.

The element of trust plays a particularly strong role in socializing women to the nudist perspective. Consider this in the following statements made by another model for nudist magazines. She and her husband had been indoctrinated in the nudist ideology by friends. At the time of the interview, however, the couple had not yet been to camp, although they had posed indoors for nudist magazines.

[Three months ago, before I was married] I never knew a man had any pubic hairs. I was shocked when I was married. . . . I wouldn't think of getting undressed in front of my husband. I wouldn't make love with a light on, or in the daytime.

With regard to being a nudist model, this woman commented:

None of the pictures are sexually seductive. [Q] The pose, the look—you can have a pose that's completely nothing, till you get a look that's not too hard to do. [Q: How do you do that?] I've never tried. By putting on a certain air about a person; a picture that couldn't be submitted to a nudist magazine—using _____ [the nudist photographer's] language. . . . [Q: Will your parents see your pictures in the magazine?] Possibly. I don't really care. . . . My mother might take it all right. But they've been married twenty years and she's never seen my dad undressed.[6]

No Accentuation of the Body. Accentuating the body is regarded as incongruent with the nudist morality. Thus, a woman who had shaved her pubic area was labeled "disgusting" by other members. There was a similar reaction to women who sat in a blatantly "unladylike" manner.

I'd think she was inviting remarks. [Q] I don't know. It seems strange to think of it. It's strange you ask it. Out there, they're not unconscious about their posture. Most women there are very circumspect even though in the nude.

For a girl, . . . [sitting with your legs open] is just not feminine or ladylike. The hair doesn't always cover it. [Q] Men get away with so many things. But, it would look dirty for a girl, like she was waiting for something. When I'm in a secluded area I've spread my legs to sun, but I kept an eye open and if anyone came I'd close my legs and sit up a little. It's just not ladylike.

You can lay on your back or side, or with your knees under your chin. But not with your legs spread apart. It would look to other people like you're there for other reasons. [Q: What other reasons?] . . . To stare and get an eyeful . . . not to enjoy the sun and people.

No Unnatural Attempts at Covering the Body. "Unnatural attempts" at covering the body are ridiculed since they call into question the assumption that there is no shame in exposing any area of the body. If such behavior occurs early in one's nudist career, however, members usually have more compassion, assuming that the person just has not yet fully assimilated the new morality.

It is how members interpret the behavior, however, rather than the behavior per se, that determines whether covering up is disapproved.

---

[6] I was amazed at how many young female nudists described a similar pattern of extreme clothing modesty among their parents and in their own married life. Included in this group was another nudist model, one of the most photographed of nudist models. Perhaps there are some fruitful data here for cognitive-dissonance psychologists.

If they're cold or sunburned, it's understandable. If it's because they don't agree with the philosophy, they don't belong there.

I would feel their motives for becoming nudists were not well founded. That they were not true nudists, not idealistic enough.

A third strategy that is sometimes employed to sustain the nudist reality is the use of communal toilets. Not all the camps have communal toilets, but the large camp where I did most of my field work did have such a facility, which was marked, "Little Girls Room and Little Boys Too." Although the stalls had three-quarter-length doors, this combined facility still helped to provide an element of consistency; as the owner said, "If you are not ashamed of any part of your body or any of its natural functions, men and women do not need separate toilets." Thus, even the physical ecology of the nudist camp was designed to be consistent with the nudist morality. For some, however, communal toilets were going too far.

I think they should be separated. For myself it's all right. But there are varied opinions, and for the satisfaction of all, I think they should separate them. There are niceties of life we often like to maintain, and for some people this is embarrassing. . . . [Q] You know, in a bowel movement it always isn't silent.

The Routinization of Nudity

In the nudist camp, nudity becomes routinized; its attention-provoking quality recedes, and nudity becomes a taken-for-granted state of affairs. Thus, when asked questions about staring ("While at camp, have you ever stared at anyone's body? Do you think you would stare at anyone's body?") nudists indicate that nudity generally does not invoke their attention.

Nudists don't care what bodies are like. They're out there for themselves. It's a matter-of-fact thing. After a while you feel like you're sitting with a full suit of clothes on.

To nudists the body becomes so matter-of-fact, whether clothed or unclothed, when you make it an undue point of interest it becomes an abnormal thing.

[Q: What would you think of someone staring?] I would feel bad and let down. [Q] I have it set up on a high standard. I have never seen it happen. . . . [Q] Because it's not done there. It's above that; you don't stare. . . . If I saw it happen, I'd be startled. There's no inclination to do that. Why would they?

There are two types—male and female. I couldn't see why they were staring. I wouldn't understand it.

In fact, these questions about staring elicit from nudists a frame of possibilities in which what is relevant to staring is ordinarily not nudity itself. Rather, what evokes attention is something unusual, something the observer seldom sees and thus is not routinized to.[7]

There was a red-haired man. He had red pubic hair. I had never seen this before. . . . He didn't see me. If anyone did, I would turn the other way.

Well, once I was staring at a pregnant woman. It was the first time I ever saw this. I was curious, her stomach stretched, the shape. . . . I also have stared at extremely obese people, cripples. All this is due to curiosity, just a novel sight. [Q] . . . I was discreet. [Q] I didn't look at them when their eyes were fixed in a direction so they could tell I was.

[Q: While at camp have you ever stared at someone's body?] Yes. [Q] A little girl. She had a birthmark on her back, at the base of her spine.

[Q: Do you think you would ever stare at someone's body while at camp?] No. I don't like that. I think it's silly. . . . What people are is not their fault if they are deformed.

I don't think it would be very nice, very polite. [Q] I can't see anything to stare at, whether it's a scar or anything else. [Q] It just isn't done.

I've looked, but not stared. I'm careful about that, because you could get in bad about that. [Q] Get thrown out by the owner. I was curious when I once had a perfect view of a girl's sex organs, because her legs were spread when she was sitting on a chair. I sat in the chair across from her in perfect view of her organs. [Q] For about ten or fifteen minutes. [Q] Nobody noticed. [Q] It's not often you get that opportunity.[8]

[Q: How would you feel if you were alone in a secluded area of camp sunning yourself, and then noticed that other nudists were staring at your body?] I would think I had some mud on me. [Q] . . . I would just ask them why they were staring at me. Probably I

---

[7]Cf. Schutz, *op. cit.*, p. 74.

[8]For some respondents, the female genitals, because of their hidden character, never become a routinized part of camp nudity; thus their visible exposure does not lose an attention-provoking quality.

was getting sunburn and they wanted to tell me to turn over, or maybe I had a speck of mud on me. [Q] These are the only two reasons I can think of why they were staring.

In the nudist camp, the arousal of attention by nudity is usually regarded as *unnatural*. Thus, staring is unnatural, especially after a period of grace in which to adjust to the new meanings.

If he did it when he was first there, I'd figure he's normal. If he kept it up I'd stay away from him, or suggest to the owner that he be thrown out. [Q] At first it's a new experience, so he might be staring. [Q] He wouldn't know how to react to it. [Q] The first time seeing nudes of the opposite sex. [Q] I'd think if he kept staring, that he's thinking of something, like grabbing someone, running to the bushes and raping them. [Q] Maybe he's mentally unbalanced.

He just sat there watching the women. You can forgive it the first time, because of curiosity. But not every weekend. [Q] The owner asked him to leave.

These women made comments on some men's shapes. They said, "He has a hairy body or ugly bones," or "Boy his wife must like him because he's hung big." That was embarrassing. . . . I thought they were terrible. [Q] Because I realized they were walking around looking. I can't see that.

Organizations and the Constitution of Normality

The rules-in-use of an organization *and the reality they sustain* form the basis on which behaviors are interpreted as "unnatural."[9] Overinvolvement in nudity, for example, is interpreted by nudists as unnatural (and not simply immoral). Similarly, erotic stimuli or responses, which breach the nudist morality, are defined as unnatural.

They let one single in. He acted peculiar. . . . He got up and had a big erection. I didn't know what he'd do at night. He might molest a child or anybody. . . . My husband went and told the owner.

I told you about this one on the sundeck with her legs spread. She made no bones about closing up. Maybe it was an error, but I doubt it. It wasn't a normal position. Normally you wouldn't lay like this. It's like standing on your head. She had sufficient time and there were people around.

She sat there with her legs like they were straddling a horse. I don't know how else to describe it. [Q] She was just sitting on the ground. [Q] I think she's a dirty pig. [Q] If you sit that way, everyone don't want to know what she had for breakfast. [Q] It's just the wrong way to sit. You keep your legs together even with clothes on.

[Q: Do you think it is possible for a person to be modest in a nudist camp?] I think so. [Q] If a person acts natural. . . . An immodest person would be an exhibitionist, and you find them in nudism too. . . . Most people's conduct is all right.

When behaviors are constituted as *unnatural,* attempts to understand them are usually suspended, and reciprocity of perspectives is called into question. (The "reciprocity of perspectives" involves the assumption that if one changed places with the other, one would, for all practical purposes, see the world as the other sees it.[10])

[Q: What would you think of a man who had an erection at camp?] Maybe they can't control themselves. [Q] Better watch out for him. [Q] I would tell the camp director to keep an eye on him. And the children would question that. [Q: What would you tell them?] I'd tell them the man is sick or something.

[Q: What would you think of a Peeping Tom—a nonnudist trespasser?] They should be reported and sent out. [Q] I think they shouldn't be there. They're sick. [Q] Mentally. [Q] Because anyone who wants to look at someone else's body, well, is a Peeping Tom, is sick in the first place. He looks at you differently than a normal person would. [Q] With ideas of sex. [A trespasser] . . . is sick. He probably uses this as a source of sexual stimulation.

Such occurrences call into question the taken-for-granted character of nudity in the nudist camp and the situated morality that is officially set forth.

Inhibiting Breakdowns in the Nudist Morality

Organized nudism promulgates a nonsexual perspective toward nudity, and breakdowns in that perspective are inhibited by (1) controlling erotic actions and (2) controlling erotic reac-

---

[9]Compare Harold Garfinkel, "A Conception of, and Experiments with, 'Trust' as a Condition of Stable Concreted Actions," in O. J. Harvey, ed., *Motivation and Social Interaction* (New York: Ronald, 1963).

[10]See: Schutz, *op. cit.,* I, 11, for his definition of reciprocity of perspectives.

tions. Nudity is partitioned off from other forms of "immodesty" (e.g., verbal immodesty, erotic overtures). In this way, a person can learn more easily to attribute a new meaning to nudity.[11] When behaviors occur that reflect other forms of "immodesty," however, nudists often fear a voiding of the nonsexual meaning that they impose on nudity.

This woman with a sexy walk would shake her hips and try to arouse the men. . . . [Q] These men went to the camp director to complain that the woman had purposely tried to arouse them. The camp director told this woman to leave.

Nudists are sensitive to the possibility of a breakdown in the nudist morality. Thus, they have a low threshold for interpreting acts as "sexual."

Playing badminton, this teenager was hitting the birdie up and down and she said. "What do you think of that?" I said, "Kind of sexy." _____ [the president of the camp] said I shouldn't talk like that, but I was only kidding.

Note the following description of "mauling":

I don't like to see a man and a girl mauling each other in the nude before others. . . . [Q: Did you ever see this at camp?] I saw it once. . . . [Q: What do you mean by mauling?] Just, well, I never saw him put his hands on her breasts, but he was running his hands along her arms.

This sensitivity to "sexual" signs also sensitizes nudists to the possibility that certain of their own acts, although not intended as "sexual," might nonetheless be interpreted that way.

Sometimes you're resting and you spread your legs unknowingly. [Q] My husband just told me not to sit that way. [Q] I put my legs together.

Since "immodesty" is defined as an unnatural manner of behavior, such behaviors are easily interpreted as being motivated by "dishonorable" intent. When the individual is thought to be in physical control of the "immodest" behavior and to know the behavior's meaning within the nudist scheme of interpretation, sexual intentions are assigned. Referring to a quotation that was presented earlier, one man said that a woman who was lying with her legs spread may have been doing so unintentionally, "but I doubt it. [Q] It wasn't a normal position. Normally you wouldn't lay like this. It's like standing on your head."

Erotic reactions, as well as erotic actions, are controlled in camp. Thus, even when erotic stimuli come into play, erotic responses may be inhibited.

When lying on the grass already hiding my penis, I got erotic thoughts. And then one realizes it can't happen here. With fear there isn't much erection.

Yes, once I started to have an erection. Once. [Q] A friend told me how he was invited by some young lady to go to bed. [Q] I started to picture the situation and I felt the erection coming on; so I immediately jumped in the pool. It went away.

I was once in the woods alone and ran into a woman. I felt myself getting excited. A secluded spot in the bushes which was an ideal place for procreation. [Q] Nothing happened, though.

When breaches of the nudist morality do occur, other nudists' sense of modesty may inhibit sanctioning. The immediate breach may go unsanctioned. The observers may feign inattention or withdraw from the scene. The occurrence is usually communicated, however, via the grapevine, and it may reach the camp director.

We were shooting a series of pictures and my wife was getting out of her clothes. _____ [the photographer] had an erection but went ahead like nothing was happening. [Q] It was over kind of fast. . . . [Q] Nothing. We tried to avoid the issue. . . . Later we went to see _____ [the camp director] and _____ [the photographer] denied it.

[If a man had an erection] people would probably pretend they didn't see it.

[Q: What do you think of someone this happens to?] They should try to get rid of it fast. It don't look nice. Nudists are prudists. They are more prudish. Because they take their clothes off they are more careful. [Q] They become more prudish than people with clothes. They won't let anything out of the way happen.

As indicated in the remark, "nudists are prudists," nudists may at times become aware of the fragility of their situated moral meanings.

---

[11]This corresponds with the findings of learning-theory psychologists.

At _____ [camp], this family had a small boy no more than ten years old who had an erection. Mrs. _____ [the owner's wife] saw him and told his parents that they should keep him in check, and tell him what had happened to him and to watch himself. This was silly, for such a little kid who didn't know what happened.

Deviance and Multiple Realities

There are basic social processes that underlie responses to deviance. Collectivities control thresholds of response to various behaviors, determining the relevance, meaning, and importance of the behavior. In the nudist camp, as pointed out previously, erotic overtures and erotic responses are regarded as unnatural, and reciprocity of perspectives is called into questions by such behaviors.

We thought this single was all right, until others clued us in that he had brought girls up to camp. [Then we recalled that] . . . he was kind of weird. The way he'd look at you. He had glassy eyes, like he could see through you.[12]

Such a response to deviance in the nudist camp is a result of effective socialization to the new system of moral meanings. The deviant's behavior, on the other hand, can be construed as reflecting an ineffective socialization to the new system of meanings.

I think it's impossible [to have an erection in a nudist camp]. [Q] In a nudist camp you must have some physical contact and a desire to have one.

He isn't thinking like a nudist. [Q] The body is wholesome, not . . . a sex object. He'd have to do that—think of sex.

Sex isn't supposed to be in your mind, as far as the body. He doesn't belong there. [Q] If you go in thinking about sex, naturally it's going to happen. . . . You're not supposed to think about going to bed with anyone, not even your wife.

As these quotes illustrate, the unnaturalness or deviance of a behavior is ordinarily determined by relating it to an institutionalized scheme of interpretation. Occurrences that are "not understandable" in the reality of one collectivity may, however, be quite understandable in the reality of another collectivity.[13] Thus, what are "deviant" occurrences in nudist camps probably would be regarded by members of the clothed society as natural and understandable rather than unnatural and difficult to understand.

Finally, a group of people may subscribe to different and conflicting interpretive schemes. Thus, the low threshold of nudists to anything "sexual" is a function of their marginality; the fact that they have not completely suspended the moral meanings of the clothed society is what leads them to constitute many events as "sexual" in purpose.

---

[12] For a study of the process of doublethink, see James L. Wilkins, "Doublethink: A Study of Erasure of the Social Past," unpublished doctoral dissertation, Northwestern University, 1964.

[13] Cf. Schutz, op. cit., pp. 229 ff.

The Facts of Life About LSD   KENNETH STODDART

Kinds of Dope

Participants in the community under study maintained that a grasp of LSD's location in the local schema of pharmacological classification was central to the achievement of desirable experiences with the substance. For them, any encountered drug was classifiable into one of two categories, namely "mind drugs" and "body drugs." As one experienced user put it: "When you get right down to it there's only two kinds of drugs. Anything's gotta be a mind drug or a body drug." Such substances as heroin, barbiturates, amphetamines, and so forth, are classified as "body drugs" while LSD, mescaline, and so forth, are properly spoken of as "mind drugs."

Single Versus Multiple Determinants

Obviously, mind and body drugs are named by reference to the principal locus of their effects, that is, "mind" and "body." But they are contrasted by users in a way less obvious and more important than locus. Through their talk about past drug experiences, their planning of future ones, their advice given to colleagues, and their common talk about a variety of topics, participants in the . . . community revealed that the most significant difference between the two categories of substance resides in the manner in which their effects are generated. While "body drug" effects were seen as effects produced primarily by the action of drug upon ingestor, "mind drug" effects were understood as not merely the result of such action, but instead as the result of a number of determining factors, some irrelevant to that action. A grasp of the fact of multiple determining factors, a knowledge of them, and attendance to them were seen by participants in the pub scene community as

central to the achievement of desirable experiences with LSD.

User-asserted Determinants of the Character of the LSD Experience

Users endorse as significant in the determination of the character of an LSD experience at least five relatively distinct sets of circumstances. The following discussion will reveal that only one (chemical composition) makes reference to features of the drug ingested: the remainder formulate as relevant features of the user —his "state of mind," recent history of general drug use, and cumulative experience with LSD and features of the setting in which the drug experience takes place.

State of Mind

Included in the . . . corpus of knowledge about drugs is the notion that the effects of psychedelic substances are related to their ingestor's "state of mind" or "psychological condition." The determinant significance of one's "head" is expressed via the attribution of the quality of a psychedelic experience to "What people think when they take acid. What's in their head when they drop." Specifically, it is asserted that LSD intensifies a felt state of mind and heightens the experience of it without engendering an alteration of its "basic nature." A self-styled "connoisseur" of the substance put it this way: "Acid doesn't change the way you're feeling, like other dope does. It just makes you feel more that way." Basing their reasoning in this belief, . . . drug users claim that they attenuate the possibility of an adverse reaction or "bad trip" if they ingest LSD when—and only when—in a "good frame of mind."[1] An ex-

Excerpt from Kenneth Stoddart, "The Facts of Life about Dope: Observations of a Local Pharmacology," *Urban Life and Culture,* Vol. 3, No. 2 (July 1974), pp. 182–204. Copyright © 1974 Sage Publications, Inc. Reprinted by permission of Sage Publications, Inc.
AUTHOR'S NOTE: Financial support for the research reported herein was provided by the Commission of Inquiry into the Non-Medical Use of Drugs, Gerald LeDain, O.C., Chairman.

[1] In contrast, as the following suggests, marijuana is regarded as an *antidote* to depression: "Henri told Rory and I that he was quite depressed because of a recent fight with Joan, the love of his life. Rory put his hand on Henri's shoulder and said: 'Look, I'll get us a joint. That'll make you feel better. There's nothing like a few tokes on some good grass to make a guy feel right again.' Henri nodded in agreement and Rory went to look for 'the guy who's selling joints for four-bits a piece.' "

pressed "desire" to drop acid can be lent a rational appearance by referring to a felt experience of joy or happiness:

Henri told me that he'd just met the girl he wanted to marry. I ordered two beers to celebrate the occasion. When they came, Henri raised his glass in a toast to "Fran, the girl of my dreams." He sighed dramatically and remarked that he wished he had some acid to drop. I asked him why he wanted to drop acid at this particular moment and he said: "I feel great because I'm in love and the trip would be beautiful for me."

The asserted relationship between state of mind and the expected effects of LSD ingestion was encountered as advice extended by drug users to colleagues who voiced the intention to drop acid at what was construed to be a "bad psychological time."

Gerry had been commenting that I "looked sad" or "worried about something." I told him that I had a few things on my mind and assured him that it was nothing serious. Later, I purchased a tablet of apparently high-grade "Pink Berkeley" acid from Gino, a dealer well-known for the quality of his merchandise. As I was examining the tablet, Gerry said he hoped I was going to "wait a little while" before taking it. I looked at him rather quizzically and asked him why it should matter whether I took the acid now or later. He put his hand on my shoulder and said, in what appeared to be a sincere, concerned manner: "It's just that you shouldn't be dropping acid when you're uptight. I wouldn't want you to freak out on us or have a bummer."

Jocko was going on and on about how poorly life had been going for him since he lost his job, how depressed he was, how the future looked no brighter than the present, and so forth. When he finished his rather sorry-sounding recitation, Jocko shrugged his shoulders and announced that he felt like getting "some good acid" to "take all this shit off my mind." At this point, Lou—who had been listening sympathetically to Jocko's woes—said to him: "You're just asking for a bad trip if you drop now, with your head in that kind of shape. Wait till you're feeling better about things. Now is a bad psychological time."

Thus, their understanding of the likely consequences of ingesting LSD when in a depressed or anxious state of mind advises drug users to postpone ingestion until such states of mind "pass." . . . It is further claimed that LSD is thoroughly incompatible with the "character structure" possessed by some people. Thus, one can say of a colleague known to have experienced an inordinate number of "bad trips":

"He's the kind of person who shouldn't do acid. His head's fucked."

Setting

The film EASY RIDER (Fonda et al., 1970: 103) contains a scene wherein one of the central characters is extended this advice: "When you get to the right place, with the right people—quarter this." Such advice, occasioned by the gift of what turned out to be a tablet of LSD or some other hallucinogenic chemical, is illustrative of the culturally-asserted relationship between setting and quality of drug experience. That is: in the community under study, the effects of psychedelic substances are seen as partially dependent upon the social and physical aspects of the setting in which they are experienced. Or, as one young drug user commented: "Half of acid is where you're at and who you're with. The place and the people." As noted earlier, . . . drug users entertain a conception of psychedelic substances in general, and LSD in particular, as intensifiers of the received world. Consistent with that understanding, they maintain that the likelihood of an adverse reaction or "bad trip" is dramatically increased if they experience the effects of such substances in settings that are, for whatever reason, received as "bad": "If you drop in a bad situation, you're just asking for it. You're bound to have a bad trip because acid just brings out what's around you." And conversely, a pleasant trip can be anticipated if the substance is experienced in a "good" situation. . . .

. . . Drug users characterize settings as good or bad places to trip relative to the anxiety they would encounter there while operating "normally" and in accordance with the view of LSD as an experience-intensifier. Thus:

Any place you like ordinarily (that is, when not under the influence of LSD) is a good place to drop 'cause you're gonna like it even better when you're tripping. And the other way around. The places you hate get worse.

I told Freddie that he was "wasting" his acid trip by having it in the dark and dingy Alcatraz beer-parlor. This place, I noted, is surely the worst in the world for experiencing acid. Freddie said that I was nuts and informed me that "This is a great place to trip. I can really get off here. All my friends are with me and there's nice music on the juke-box. It's great."

The drug user's corpus of knowledge specifies as well the relevance of a setting's social features. One . . . [user] stated their relevance in the following manner:

The people you're with can make or break a trip. There's some people I just wouldn't trip with because they're complete assholes. They just get me by the way they act and it unnerves me.

Indeed, the behavior of other persons in a setting is a feature that . . . drug users insist is a determinant of any setting's anxiety-producing potential. Thus, as the following suggests, a setting conceived of as "good" on other grounds may be avoided as a place to have a psychedelic experience because of what the drug user knows about the behavior of the people who routinely populate it:

In his enumeration of things that had "changed" in Pacific City since the beginning of the summer, Henri made reference to the demise of two local beaches as "good places to crop acid." He said that those places had been "spoiled by all the bikers and greasers who go down there and hassle people." . . .

Experience

The following report introduces a further "fact" that is included in the . . . corpus of knowledge about psychedelic drugs and their effects:

I was standing in front of the beer parlor watching Singh as he attempted to sell LSD to passersby. Two long-haired males in their mid-teens responded to his solicitations and asked him the price of his acid and whether it was "good stuff." With regard to their latter question, Singh told them that he'd been dropping acid "for years" and was able to "really get off on a tab of this stuff." His customers decided that they'd take one tablet, saying that it would probably be sufficient to get them both "off" since they'd only dropped acid a few times. Yes, agreed Singh, half a tab each should be more than enough. After they left, Singh told me that "a full tab of this stuff would freak anybody who wasn't really used to acid."

The field-note describes the common belief that the amount of LSD required to produce recognizably psychedelic effects varies directly with any person's experience with the substance.[2] Or: "The more acid you take, the more you need

to take to get off. People who've taken a lot of acid need more to get off than before."

Pub scene drug users offer two interpretations of this phenomenon. According to both interpretations, frequent use of LSD creates within the user a situation that permits the full experience of its effects only when the amount ingested is larger than amounts ingested in the recent past. The interpretations collide on the issue of whether the effects actually diminish. In one interpretation, the effects of LSD are regarded as merely appearing to diminish. What "really" diminishes, it is held, is the frequent user's appreciation of those effects. The following field-notes, wherein acid-users report they increased their per-occasion dosage because they were "used to" or tired of the effects of previous amounts, are illustrative of these interpretations.

Rory joined us at our table and, much to everyone's surprise, bought a round of beer. He told us that he'd panhandled seven dollars at the bus depot and wanted to share it with us by buying some beer. Also, he said he wanted to buy two tabs of acid and treat himself to a "really fine trip." "Why two tabs?" I asked. "Can't you get off on one?" Rory said that yes, he *could* get off on one tab but it was "kind of boring" to him. "I've had so many trips that one tab is just like nothing to me."

Henri told me that for the first ten-or-so times he dropped acid one tab was enough to produce an interesting experience. Since that time, though, he claims that he's had to increase his dose twice to one-and-a-half and then to two, which he takes now in order to have "a halfway decent trip." He said that after a while "your head gets used to what happens when you take one tab."

In the second interpretation of the necessity of increasing dosage, the effects of LSD are seen as actually diminishing as a consequence of frequent use. One young drug user referred to this attenuation as a "loss of sensitivity" and offered the common claim that it is the result of a concentration of acid "in the brain": "What it is is that you lose your sensitivity to the chemicals in acid that make you trip. Acid builds up in your brain and you get sort of immune to it so it takes more and more to get you off." Such a concen-

---

[2] Marijuana is regarded in exactly the opposite fashion: it is held that the more experience one has with it, the less grass it takes to get "stoned." Thus, it is common for experienced users to claim intoxication after inhaling only a small quantity of marijuana, and equally as common for novices to fail to get "stoned" after smoking a large quantity. See Becker (1963). In passing it is interesting to note that in social worlds where alcohol is the main drug of intoxication, these persons who become "stoned" on small amounts are negatively regarded.

tration of LSD, resulting in "immunity," is frequently cited as the reason motivating increased dosage. . . .

Chemical Composition

From the point of view of . . . drug users, the character of an LSD experience—considered in all its phases—is partially dependent upon the proportion and kind of adulterant mixed with the "acid" they ingest. Members "know" the acid they purchase in the illicit marketplace will be "impure" insofar as it has been adulterated with a variety of other substances. It is expected that anything offered for sale as "acid" will regularly be a combination of LSD and amphetamine. Furthermore, they expect that what is bought as "acid" will occasionally contain LSD in combination with atropine or strychnine. The following notes report . . . claims and expectations regarding the presence of such substances and the chemical composition of "acid" in general.

In the course of asking various people about the local availability of speed I was told repeatedly that "most of the speed is in the acid." Barry, a former speedfreak, held this belief so strongly that he refused, since voluntarily "quitting" speed, to drop acid. He said that "the acid you can buy around here" makes him "yenny for bigger and better things," meaning that the amphetamine-content of LSD make him desirous of the substance of his former "addiction." According to Barry, he'd drop acid if and only if he could obtain it from a "reliable medical source." "It's impossible to buy street acid without speed," he added.

Grace was telling Rory, Bert, and I that her first acid trip consisted mainly of "seeing brightness" in colors and little else. She said that she was expecting much more, given all she'd heard of acid's powers. Rory asked if she'd experienced a rush and Grace replied that she did indeed. Rory told her that what she dropped was probably a combination of atropine and speed, with no acid at all. Grace said she was "pissed off" at being burned by a guy she knew. Rory said that at least she got a trip out of it and added that "a lot of acid has got atropine in it, to make the visual part of it better."

I was approached by a dealer whose face was familiar and asked if I wanted to buy some acid. I told him that I'd just bought a tab from somebody. The dealer wanted to know "who?" I told him I didn't know, and, as he left our table he said "It's probably full of rat poison." Rory laughed. I asked him "what's this about rat poison?" He replied: "Well, sometimes you get a tab of acid that's a little heavy on the strychnine, you know."

. . . [D]rug users believe that one can recognize the adulterant mixed with the acid by the type of "down" and/or "rush" it produces: "Henry told me that all the acid offered for sale around the Pacific City pubs was 'loaded with speed.' He said that he knew this because 'the rush is so strong it almost explodes your heart' and the down brings with it severe depression and the shakes." The character of the psychedelic experience, too, is held to be indicative of the chemical composition of the substance ingested:

According to many of the people around the beer parlor, a lot of the acid is merely atropine, speed, and a filler compound. They say that they can tell it's mainly atropine because the trip it produces is thoroughly visual. Acid, they say, would give an experience that was tactile and auditory as well as visual.

Prior to actually ingesting whatever acid they purchase "on the street," however, the dealer's testimony is the only information pub scene drug users have regarding its chemical composition. They recognize that dealers often misrepresent their wares and suggest that one "know" a dealer before making a purchase from him:

Rory told me that I shouldn't have bought acid from a "guy I'd never seen before." He said that "the only smart way to do it" is to "buy from Lou, or somebody else who's always around so if something goes wrong you'll know who to see." According to Rory, if I find myself burned or poisoned I've only got myself to blame.

The preceding comments are not intended to suggest that the members of the community under study prefer "pure" LSD and seek to avoid its adulterated versions. In their ordinary talk, . . . drug users contrast "good acid" with "bad acid" not in terms of the presence or absence of adulterants but in terms of the relative proportion of those adulterants. That is, "good acid" is not necessarily "pure" or unadulterated, for it is held that "To be any good, acid's gotta have something in it beside acid." Thus, acid may be regarded as good because it contains the "right amount" of speed:

Why, I asked, is the brand of acid known as "Pink Berkeley" so highly regarded by all? "Well," said Harvey, "real Pink Berkeley has got just the right amount of speed in it." He went on to tell me that it gives you a nice rush and doesn't "let you down hard" at the end of the trip.

Or the "right amount" of strychnine:

I wondered aloud about the kind of chemist who would adulterate his acid with rat poison. Bobby told me that it was really nothing to worry about unless you ingested some acid that contained it in a large quantity. Rat poison, he said, despite its toxicity, contributes to the experience insofar as it makes the trip "more physical." A little rat poison, said Bobby, "makes for a fine rush."

Drug Interaction

. . . [D]rug users maintain that the effects of LSD are partially dependent upon the kind and quantity of other substances ingested immediately prior to or during an anticipated psychedelic experience. In their common talk and behavior they expressed a special concern for the "mixing" of LSD and those substances thought to inhibit or diminish its effects. Given the high cost of acid relative to their financial resources, members were anxious to avoid substances they saw as attenuating its effects and thereby "wasting" a trip.

Virtually without exception, . . . drug users mix LSD and beer. It is held that drinking beer shortly before or after dropping acid will put one in a physically and psychologically "relaxed" state, thus enabling him to have a better psychedelic experience. Such a belief, as illustrated in the following field-note is consistent with the culturally-asserted relationship between "state of mind" and the quality of the trip:

Alex put the tab of acid in his mouth and washed it down with a gulp of the beer he'd been drinking. He raised his glass in a toast "to a good trip" and emptied it. Alex told me that it was good to drink "a bit of beer" before you get off on acid because it relaxes you and makes you "less uptight."

Similarly, beer or any depressant is recommended as an aid to those who find the final or "down" phase of an acid trip particularly disquieting. The user whose claims are reported above followed such a strategy:

Alex talked further about beer, and told me that he generally has a few glasses when he's coming down from acid. He said that "the down you get from the acid around here is like a speed down" and added that he experienced severe nervousness towards the end of an LSD trip. The beer, said Alex, "makes me feel better." I asked him if a downer would do the same

thing and he told me that it would, laughingly adding that "beer tastes better."

. . . [D]rug users believe, however, that alcoholic beverages and barbiturates consumed in large quantities will inhibit the effects of LSD:

An interview in a public park with David, a former pub scene regular, was interrupted by one of his hobo-alcoholic friends. Upon hearing that we were talking about acid, he told us that he took it once and "it didn't do anything for me." Laughing, David pushed him over on the grass and said: "You were probably sloshed out of your head when you dropped it. Acid doesn't work when you've got too much booze in your body." Later, I asked David to explain this statement to me. He told me that "too much booze or too many downers" tend to "numb your body and head" making one "not feel acid."

While . . . drug users attempt in general to avoid substances whose interaction with LSD diminishes or blocks its effects, there are some situations wherein such attenuation is deliberately sought. For example, the experiencing of a bad trip is seen as an occasion calling for the ingestion of a "downer":

I told Rick that I was curious about taking acid, but had so far avoided it because of a fear of having a bad trip. Rick said that that was always a possibility, but nothing to be really afraid of. He said that you can bring yourself out of any bad trip by dropping a couple of downers.

While depressants such as alcohol and barbiturates are seen as at most "blocking" or "neutralizing" any effects of LSD, other substances are understood as specifically incompatible with acid. Speed is one of these and, as indicated below, the mixing of it with acid is portrayed as the "cause" of some people's bad trips:

I asked Henri why he thought Bert had such a bad trip two evenings ago. He told me that one of the reasons was "probably" the fact that Bert had injected himself with speed while he was getting off on the acid.

Joan, who earlier told us that she'd dropped a tab of "white lightening" acid, came over to our table and said that her former boyfriend had taken her into "the men's can" and injected her with speed. Eileen was standing behind Joan shaking her head in a somewhat disgusted and definitely disapproving manner. Later, when Joan was in the midst of a particularly adverse reaction, Eileen said that it was "all she could expect, mixing acid and speed like that."

Concluding Remarks

Participant observation in a community where drug use was a focal concern detected a corpus of knowledge about LSD and its effects that members of the community appreciated and attended to as *factual*. The corpus was encountered by the researcher (and presumably by "ordinary" participants as well) in a variety of ways: as advice given by experienced drug users to their novice counterparts . . . , as grounds for "timing" the ingestion of LSD relative to diverse objective factors, as explanations of good or bad experiences with LSD, and so on.

Over the course of time, participants' talk revealed a conception of LSD effects as effects whose character was determined by a number of diverse factors. Indeed, far from being seen as merely "programmed" by the action of drug upon ingestor—as is the case with "body drugs"—the character of the LSD experience is understood by users as variably constituted by a *variety* of personal and environmental factors.

The corpus of knowledge described in this report proposes for participants in the community studied a set of *facts* about the effects of LSD and the contingencies bearing on their generation. For those who appreciate it *as* factual the corpus they call the "facts of life about dope" is understood as constituting the truth about LSD and LSD effects and hence as formulating a set of conditions properly attended to by all those who wish to consume LSD *rationally,* that is, with the hope of achieving desirable outcomes.

REFERENCES

Becker, H. S. 1963. "Becoming a Marijuana User." In *Outsiders: Studies in the Sociology of Deviance.* New York: Free Press.

Fonda, P. et al. 1970. *Easy Rider.* New York: Dell.

12 SUBCULTURAL VARIATIONS

While some deviants engage in solitary deviance, many are involved in deviance for which there is a definite subculture—what we call *subcultural deviance*. Even among those engaging in subcultural deviance, though, there is a great deal of variation. The deviants may differ in their backgrounds and social situations. Some may participate in the subculture more than others. And they may differ in the activities, both deviant and conventional, that they engage in. Associated with these variations are other differences—e.g., in the ways people perform deviant roles.

In this chapter the selections explore some of these subcultural variations. In the first reading Laud Humphreys describes various forms of participation in one sector of the homosexual subculture and the social situations related to these different forms of participation. Paul Higgins then shows the character of two distinct social segments in the deaf community—those who use sign language and those who don't. Finally, Ann Cordilia shows the different ways in which inmates adapt to the prison environment.

A Typology of Tearoom Participants

LAUD HUMPHREYS

At shortly after five o'clock on a weekday evening, four men enter a public restroom in the city park. One wears a well-tailored business suit; another wears tennis shoes, shorts and teeshirt; the third man is still clad in the khaki uniform of his filling station; the last, a salesman, has loosened his tie and left his sports coat in the car. What has caused these men to leave the company of other homeward-bound commuters on the freeway? What common interest brings these men, with their divergent backgrounds, to this public facility?

They have come here not for the obvious reason, but in a search for "instant sex." Many men—married and unmarried, those with heterosexual identities and those whose self-image is a homosexual one—seek such impersonal sex, shunning involvement, desiring kicks without commitment. Whatever reasons—social, physiological or psychological—might be postulated for this search, the phenomenon of impersonal sex persists as a widespread but rarely studied form of human interaction.

There are several settings for this type of deviant activity—the balconies of movie theaters, automobiles, behind bushes—but few offer the advantages for these men that public restrooms provide. "Tearooms," as these facilities are called in the language of the homosexual subculture, have several characteristics that make them attractive as locales for sexual encounters without involvement. . . .

Tearoom activity attracts a large number of participants—enough to produce the majority of arrests for homosexual offenses in the United States. Now, employing data gained from both formal and informal interviews, we shall consider what these men are like away from the scenes of impersonal sex. "For some people," says Evelyn Hooker, an authority on male homosexuality, "the seeking of sexual contacts with other males is an activity isolated from all other aspects of their lives." Such segregation is apparent with most men who engage in the homosexual activity of public restrooms; but the degree and manner in which "deviant" is

isolated from "normal" behavior in their lives will be seen to vary along social dimensions.

For the man who lives next door, the tearoom participant is just another neighbor—and probably a very good one at that. He may make a little more money than the next man and work a little harder for it. It is likely that he will drive a nicer car and maintain a neater yard than do other neighbors in the block. Maybe, like some tearoom regulars, he will work with Boy Scouts in the evenings and spend much of his weekend at the church. It may be more surprising for the outsider to discover that most of these men are married.

Indeed, 54 percent of my research subjects are married and living with their wives. From the data at hand, there is no evidence that these unions are particularly unstable; nor does it appear that any of the wives are aware of their husbands' secret sexual activity. Indeed, the husbands choose public restrooms as sexual settings partly to avoid just such exposure. I see no reason to dispute the claim of a number of tearoom respondents that their preference for a form of concerted action that is fair and impersonal is largely predicated on a desire to protect their family relationships.

Superficial analysis of the data indicates that the maintenance of exemplary marriages—at least in appearance—is very important to the subjects of this study. In answering questions such as "When it comes to making decisions in your household, who generally makes them?" the participants indicate they are more apt to defer to their mates than are those in the control sample. They also indicate that they find it more important to "get along well" with their wives. In the open-ended questions regarding marital relationships, they tend to speak of them in more glowing terms. . . .

In most cases, fellatio is a service performed by an older man upon a younger. In one encounter, for example, a man appearing to be around 40 was observed as insertee with a man in his twenties as insertor. A few minutes later, the man of 40 was being sucked by one in his

Reprinted from Laud Humphreys, *Tearoom Trade: Impersonal Sex in Public Places* (Chicago: Aldine Publishing Company, 1970), pp. 1–2, 104–105, 108–130; copyright © 1970 by R. A. Laud Humphreys. Reprinted by permission of the author and Aldine • Atherton, Inc.

fifties. Analyzing the estimated ages of the principal partners in 53 observed acts of fellatio, I arrived at these conclusions: the insertee was judged to be older than the insertor in 40 cases; they were approximately the same age in three; and the insertor was the older in ten instances. The age differences ranged from an insertee estimated to be 25 years older than his partner to an insertee thought to be ten years younger than his insertor.

Strong references to this crisis of aging are found in my interviews with cooperating respondents, one of whom had this to say:

Well, I started off as the straight young thing. Everyone wanted to suck my cock. I wouldn't have been caught dead with one of the things in my mouth! . . . So, here I am at 40—with grown kids—and the biggest cocksucker in [the city]!

Similar experiences were expressed, in more reserved language, by another man, some 15 years his senior:

I suppose I was around 35—or 36—when I started giving out blow jobs. It just got so I couldn't operate any other way in the park johns. I'd still rather have a good blow job any day, but I've gotten so I like it the way it is now.

Perhaps by now there is enough real knowledge abroad to have dispelled the idea that men who engage in homosexual acts may be typed by any consistency of performance in one or another sexual role. Undoubtedly, there are preferences: few persons are so adaptable, their conditioning so undifferentiated, that they fail to exercise choice between various sexual roles and positions. Such preferences, however, are learned, and sexual repertories tend to expand with time and experience. This study of restroom sex indicates that sexual roles within these encounters are far from stable. They are apt to change within an encounter, from one encounter to another, with age, and with the amount of exposure to influences from a sexually deviant subculture.

It is to this last factor that I should like to direct the reader's attention. The degree of contact with a network of friends who share the actor's sexual interests takes a central position in mediating not only his preferences for sex role, but his style of adaptation to—and rationalization of—the deviant activity in which he participates. There are, however, two reasons why I have not classified research subjects in terms of their participation in the homosexual subculture. It is difficult to measure accurately the degree of such involvement; and such subcultural interaction depends upon other social variables, two of which are easily measured.

Family status has a definitive effect on the deviant careers of those whose concern is with controlling information about their sexual behavior. The married man who engages in homosexual activity must be more cautious about his involvement in the subculture than his single counterpart. As a determinant of life style and sexual activity, marital status is also a determinant of the patterns of deviant adaptation and rationalization. Only those in my sample who were divorced or separated from their wives were difficult to categorize as either married or single. Those who had been married, however, showed a tendency to remain in friendship networks with married men. Three of the four were still limited in freedom by responsibilities for their children. For these reasons, I have included all men who were once married in the "married" categories.

The second determining variable is the relative autonomy of the respondent's occupation. A man is "independently" employed when his job allows him freedom of movement and security from being fired; the most obvious example is self-employment. Occupational "dependence" leaves a man little freedom for engaging in disreputable activity. The sales manager or other executive of a business firm has greater freedom than the salesman or attorney who is employed in the lower echelons of a large industry or by the federal government. The sales representative whose territory is far removed from the home office has greater independence, in terms of information control, than the minister of a local congregation. The majority of those placed in both the married and unmarried categories with *dependent* occupations were employed by large industries or the government.

Median education levels and annual family incomes indicate that those with dependent occupations rank lower on the socioeconomic scale. Only in the case of married men, however, is this correlation between social class and occupational autonomy strongly supported by the ratings of these respondents on Warner's Index of Status Characteristics. Nearly all the married men with dependent occupations are of the upper-lower or lower-middle classes, whereas those with independent occupations are of the upper-middle or upper classes. For single men, the social class variable is neither so easily identifiable nor so clearly divided. Nearly all single men in the sample can be classified only as "vaguely middle class."

As occupational autonomy and marital status remain the most important dimensions along which participants may be ranked, we shall consider four general types of tearoom customers: (1) married men with dependent occupations, (2) married men with independent occupations, (3) unmarried men with independent occupations, and (4) unmarried men with dependent occupations. As will become evident with the discussion of each type, I have employed labels from the homosexual argot, along with pseudonyms, to designate each class of participants. This is done not only to facilitate reading but to emphasize that we are describing persons rather than merely "typical" constructs.

Type I: Trade

The first classification, which includes 19 of the participants (38 percent), may be called "trade," since most would earn that appellation from the gay subculture. All of these men are, or have been, married—one was separated from his wife at the time of interviewing and another was divorced.

Most work as truck drivers, machine operators or clerical workers. There is a member of the armed forces, a carpenter, and the minister of a Pentecostal church. Most of their wives work, at least part time, to help raise their median annual family income to $8,000. One in six of these men is black. All are normally masculine in appearance and mannerism. Although 14 have completed high school, there are only three college graduates among them, and five have had less than 12 years of schooling.

George is representative of this largest group of respondents. Born of second-generation German parentage in an ethnic enclave of the midwestern city where he still resides, he was raised as a Lutheran. He feels that his father (like George a truck driver) was quite warm in his relationship with him as a child. His mother he describes as a very nervous, asthmatic woman and thinks that an older sister suffered a nervous breakdown some years ago, although she was

never treated for it. Another sister and a brother have evidenced no emotional problems.

At the age of 20 he married a Roman Catholic girl and has since joined her church, although he classifies himself as "lapsed." In the 14 years of their marriage, they have had seven children, one of whom is less than a year old. George doesn't think they should have more children, but his wife objects to using any type of birth control other than the rhythm method. With his wife working part time as a waitress, they have an income of about $5,000.

"How often do you have intercourse with your wife?" I asked. "Not very much the last few years," he replied. "It's up to when she feels like giving it to me—which ain't very often. I never suggest it."

George was cooking hamburgers on an outdoor grill and enjoying a beer as I interviewed him. "Me, I like to come home," he asserted. "I love to take care of the outside of the house . . . like to go places with the children—my wife, she doesn't."

With their mother at work, the children were running in and out of the door, revealing a household interior in gross disarray. George stopped to call one of the smaller youngsters out of the street in front of his modest, suburban home. When he resumed his remarks about his wife, there was more feeling in his description:

My wife doesn't have much outside interest. She doesn't like to go out or take the kids places. But she's an A-1 mother. I'll say that! I guess you'd say she's very nice to get along with—but don't cross her! She gets aggravated with me—I don't know why. . . . Well, you'd have to know my wife. We fight all the time. Anymore, it seems we just don't get along—except when we're apart. Mostly, we argue about the kids. She's afraid of having more. . . . She's afraid to have sex but doesn't believe in birth control. I'd just rather not be around her! I won't suggest having sex anyway—and she just doesn't want it anymore.

While more open than most in his acknowledgment of marital tension, George's appraisal of sexual relations in the marriage is typical of those respondents classified as Trade. In 63 percent of these marriages, the wife, husband or both are Roman Catholic. When answering questions about their sexual lives, a story much like George's emerged: at least since the birth of the last child, conjugal relations have been very rare.

These data suggest that, along with providing an excuse for diminishing intercourse with their wives, the religious teachings to which most of these families adhere may cause the husbands to search for sex in the tearooms. Whatever the causes that turn them unsatisfied from the marriage bed, however, the alternate outlet must be quick, inexpensive and impersonal. Any personal, ongoing affair—any outlet requiring money or hours away from home—would threaten a marriage that is already shaky and jeopardize the most important thing these men possess, their standing as father of their children.

Around the turn of the century, before the vice squads moved in (in their never-ending process of narrowing the behavioral options of those in the lower classes), the Georges of this study would probably have made regular visits to the two-bit bordellos. With a madam watching a clock to limit the time, these cheap whore-houses provided the same sort of fast, impersonal service as today's public restrooms. I find no indication that these men seek homosexual contact as such; rather, they want a form of orgasm-producing action that is less lonely than masturbation and less involving than a love relationship. As the forces of social control deprive them of one outlet, they provide another. The newer form, it should be noted, is more stigmatizing than the previous one—thus giving "proof" to the adage that "the sinful are drawn ever deeper into perversity."

George was quite affable when interviewed on his home territory A year before, when I first observed him in the tearoom of a park about three miles from his home, he was a far more cautious man. Situated at the window of the restroom, I saw him leave his old station wagon and, looking up and down the street, walk to the facility at a very fast pace. Once inside, he paced nervously from door to window until satisfied that I would serve as an adequate lookout. After playing the insertor role with a man who had waited in the stall farthest from the door, he left quickly, without wiping or washing his hands, and drove away toward the nearest exit from the park. In the tearoom he was a frightened man, engaging in furtive sex. In his own back yard, talking with an observer whom he failed to recognize, he was warm, open and apparently at ease.

Weighing 200 pounds or more, George has a protruding gut and tattoos on both forearms. Although muscular and in his mid-thirties, he would not be described as a handsome person. For him, no doubt, the aging crisis is also an identity crisis. Only with reluctance—and perhaps never—will he turn to the insertee role. The threat of such a role to his masculine self-image is too great. Like others of his class with whom I have had more extensive interviews, George may have learned that sexual game as a teenage hustler, or else when serving in the army during the Korean War. In either case, his socialization into homosexual experience took place in a masculine world where it is permissible to accept money from a "queer" in return for carefully limited sexual favors. But to use one's own mouth as a substitute for the female organ, or even to express enjoyment of the action, is taboo in the Trade code.

Moreover, for men of George's occupational and marital status, there is no network of friends engaged in tearoom activity to help them adapt to the changes aging will bring. I found no evidence of friendship networks among respondents of this type, who enter and leave the restrooms alone, avoiding conversation while within. Marginal to both the heterosexual and homosexual worlds, these men shun involvement in any form of gay subculture. Type I participants report fewer friends of any sort than do those of other classes. When asked how many close friends he has, George answered: "None. I haven't got time for that."

It is difficult to interview the Trade without becoming depressed over the hopelessness of their situation. They are almost uniformly lonely and isolated: lacking success in either marriage bed or work, unable to discuss their three best friends (because they don't have three); en route from the din of factories to the clamor of children, they slip off the freeways for a few moments of impersonal sex in a toilet stall.

Such unrewarded existence is reflected in the portrait of another marginal man. A jobless Negro, he earns only contempt and sexual rejection from his working wife in return for baby-sitting duties. The paperback books and magazines scattered about his living room supported his comment that he reads a great deal to relieve boredom. (George seldom reads even the newspaper and has no hobbies to report.) No wonder that he urged me to stay for supper when my interview schedule was finished. "I really wish you'd stay awhile," he said. "I haven't talked to anyone about myself in a hell of a long time!"

Type II: Ambisexuals

A very different picture emerges in the case of Dwight. As sales manager for a small manufacturing concern, he is in a position to hire men who share his sexual and other interests. Not only does he have a business associate or two who share his predilection for tearoom sex, he has been able to stretch chance meetings in the tearoom purlieu into long-lasting friendships. Once, after I had gained his confidence through repeated interviews, I asked him to name all the participants he knew. The names of five other Type II men in my sample were found in the list of nearly two dozen names he gave me.

Dwight, then, has social advantages in the public restrooms as well as in society at large. His annual income of $16,000 helps in the achievement of these benefits, as does his marriage into a large and distinguished family and his education at a prestigious local college. From his restroom friends Dwight learns which tearooms in the city are popular and where the police are clamping down. He even knows which officers are looking for payoffs and how much they expect to be paid. It is of even greater importance that his attitudes toward—and perceptions of—the tearoom encounters are shaped and reinforced by the friendship network in which he participates.

It has thus been easier for Dwight to meet the changing demands of the aging crisis. He knows others who lost no self-respect when they began "going down" on their sexual partners, and they have helped him learn to enjoy the involvement of oral membranes in impersonal sex. As Tom, too, moves into this class of participants, he can be expected to learn how to rationalize the switch in sexual roles necessitated by the loss of youthful good looks. He will cease thinking of the insertee role as threatening to his masculinity. His socialization into the Ambisexuals will make the orgasm but one of a number of kicks.

Three-fourths of the married participants with independent occupations were observed, at one time or another, participating as insertees in fellatio, compared to only one-third of the Trade. Not only do the Type II participants tend to switch roles with greater facility, they seem inclined to search beyond the tearooms for more exotic forms of sexual experience. Dwight, along with others in his class, expresses a liking for anal intercourse (both as insertee and insertor), for group activity, and even for mild

forms of sadomasochistic sex. A friend of his once invited me to an "orgy" he had planned in an apartment he maintains for sexual purposes. Another friend, a social and commercial leader of the community, told me that he enjoys having men urinate into his mouth between acts of fellatio.

Dwight is in his early forties and has two sons in high school. The school-bound offspring provide him with an excuse to leave his wife at home during frequent business trips across the country. Maintaining a list of gay contacts, Dwight is able to engage wholeheartedly in the life of the homosexual subculture in other cities—the sort of involvement he is careful to avoid at home. In the parks or over cocktails, he amuses his friends with lengthy accounts of these adventures.

Dwight recounts his first sexual relationship with another boy at the age of "nine or ten":

My parents always sent me off to camp in the summer, and it was there that I had my sexual initiation. This sort of thing usually took the form of rolling around in a bunk together and ended in our jacking each other off. . . . I suppose I started pretty early. God, I was almost in college before I had my first woman! I always had some other guy on the string in prep school—some real romances there! But I made up for lost time with the girls during my college years. . . . During that time, I only slipped back into my old habits a couple of times—and then it was a once-only occurrence with a roommate after we had been drinking.

Culminating an active heterosexual life at the university, Dwight married the girl he had impregnated. He reports having intercourse three or four times a week with her throughout their 18 married years but also admits to supplementing that activity on occasion: "I had the seven-year-itch and stepped out on her quite a bit then." Dwight also visits the tearooms almost daily:

I guess you might say I'm pretty highly sexed [he chuckled a little], but I really don't think that's why I go to tearooms. That's really not sex. Sex is something I have with my wife in bed. It's not as if I were committing adultery by getting my rocks off—or going down on some guy—in a tearoom. I get a kick out of it. Some of my friends go out for handball. I'd rather cruise the park. Does that sound perverse to you?

Dwight's openness in dealing with the more sensitive areas of his biography was typical of upper-middle and upper-class respondents of both the participant and control samples. Actual refusals of interviews came almost entirely from lower-class participants; more of the cooperating respondents were of the upper socioeconomic ranks. In the same vein, working-class respondents were most cautious about answering questions pertaining to their income and their social and political views.

Other researchers have encountered a similar response differential along class lines, and I realize that my educational and social characteristics encourage rapport with Dwight more than with George. It may also be assumed that sympathy with survey research increases with education. Two-thirds of the married participants with occupational independence are college graduates.

It has been suggested, however, that another factor may be operative in this instance: although the upper-class deviants may have more to lose from exposure (in the sense that the mighty have farther to fall), they also have more means at their disposal with which to protect their moral histories. Some need only tap their spending money to pay off a member of the vice squad. In other instances, social contacts with police commissioners or newspaper publishers make it possible to squelch either record or publicity of an arrest. One respondent has made substantial contributions to a police charity fund, while another hired private detectives to track down a blackmailer. Not least in their capacity to cover for errors in judgment is the fact that their word has the backing of economic and social influence. Evidence must be strong to prosecute a man who can hire the best attorneys. Lower-class men are rightfully more suspicious, for they have fewer resources with which to defend themselves if exposed.

This does not mean that Type II participants are immune to the risks of the game but simply that they are bidding from strength. To them, the risks of arrest, exposure, blackmail or physical assault contribute to the excitement quotient. It is not unusual for them to speak of cruising as an adventure, in contrast with the Trade, who engage in a furtive search for sexual relief. On the whole, then, the action of Type II respondents is apt to be somewhat bolder and their search for "kicks" less inhibited than that of most other types of participants.

Dwight is not fleeing from an unhappy home life or sexless marriage to the encounters in the parks. He expresses great devotion to his wife and children: "They're my whole life,"

he exclaims. All evidence indicates that, as father, citizen, businessman and church member, Dwight's behavior patterns—as viewed by his peers—are exemplary.

Five of the 12 participants in Dwight's class are members of the Episcopal church. Dwight is one of two who were raised in that church, although he is not as active a churchman as some who became Episcopalians later in life. In spite of his infrequent attendance to worship, he feels his church is "just right" for him and needs no changing. Its tradition and ceremony are intellectually and esthetically pleasing to him. Its liberal outlook on questions of morality round out a religious orientation that he finds generally supportive.

In an interview witnessed by a friend he had brought to meet me, Dwight discussed his relationship with his parents: "Father ignored me. He just never said anything to me. I don't think he ever knew I existed." [His father was an attorney, esteemed beyond the city of Dwight's birth, who died while his only son was yet in his teens.] "I hope I'm a better father to my boys than he was to me," Dwight added.

"But his mother is a remarkable woman," the friend interjected, "really one of the most fabulous women I've met! Dwight took me back to meet her—years ago, when we were lovers of a sort. I still look forward to her visits."

"She's remarkable just to have put up with me," Dwight added:

Just to give you an idea, one vacation I brought another boy home from school with me. She walked into the bedroom one morning and caught us bare-assed in a 69 position. She just excused herself and backed out of the room. Later, when we were alone, she just looked at me—over the edge of her glasses—and said: "I'm not going to lecture you, dear, but I do hope you don't swallow that stuff!"

Although he has never had a nervous breakdown, Dwight takes "an occasional antidepressant" because of his "moodiness." "I'm really quite moody, and I go to the tearooms more often when my spirits are low." While his periods of depression may result in increased tearoom activity, his deviant behavior does not seem to produce much tension in his life:

I don't feel guilty about my little sexual games in the park. I'm not some sort of sick queer. . . . You might think I live two lives; but, if I do, I don't feel split in two by them.

Unlike the Trade, Type II participants recognize their homosexual activity as indicative of their own psychosexual orientations. They think of themselves as bisexual or ambisexual and have intellectualized their deviant tendencies in terms of the pseudopsychology of the popular press. They speak often of the great men of history, as well as of certain movie stars and others of contemporary fame, who are also "AC/DC." Erving Goffman has remarked that stigmatized Americans "tend to live in a literally-defined world." This is nowhere truer than of the subculturally oriented participants of this study. Not only do they read a great deal about homosexuality, they discuss it within their network of friends. For the Dwights there is subcultural support that enables them to integrate their deviance with the remainder of their lives, while maintaining control over the information that could discredit their whole being. For these reasons they look upon the gaming encounters in the parks as enjoyable experiences.

Type III: Gay Guys

Like the Ambisexuals, unmarried respondents with independent occupations are locked into a strong subculture, a community that provides them with knowledge about the tearooms and reinforcement in their particular brand of deviant activity. This open participation in the gay community distinguishes these single men from the larger group of unmarrieds with dependent occupations. These men take the homosexual role of our society, and are thus the most truly "gay" of all participant types. Except for Tim, who was recruited as a decoy in the tearooms by the vice squad of a police department, Type III participants learned the strategies of the tearooms through friends already experienced in this branch of the sexual market.

Typical of this group is Ricky, a 24-year-old university student whose older male lover supports him. Ricky stands at the median age of his type, who range from 19 to 50 years. Half of them are college graduates and all but one other are at least part-time students, a characteristic that explains their low median income of $3,000. Because Ricky's lover is a good provider, he is comfortably situated in a midtown apartment, a more pleasant residence than most of his friends enjoy.

Ricky is a thin, good-looking young man with certain movements and manners of speech that might be termed effeminate. He is careful of his appearance, dresses well, and keeps an immaculate apartment, furnished with an expensive stereo and some tasteful antique pieces. Seated on a sofa in the midst of the things his lover has provided for their mutual comfort, Ricky is impressively self-assured. He is proud to say that he has found, at least for the time being, what all those participants in his category claim to seek: a "permanent" love relationship.

Having met his lover in a park, Ricky returns there only when his mate is on a business trip or their relationship is strained. Then Ricky becomes, as he puts it, "horny" and he goes to the park to study, cruise and engage in tearoom sex:

The bars are o.k.—but a little too public for a "married" man like me. . . . Tearooms are just another kind of action, and they do quite well when nothing better is available.

Like other Type III respondents, he shows little preference in sexual roles. "It depends on the other guy," Ricky says, "and whether I like his looks or not. Some men I'd crawl across the street on my knees for—others I wouldn't piss on!" His aging crisis will be shared with all others in the gay world. It will take the nightmarish form of waning attractiveness and the search for a permanent lover to fill his later years, but it will have no direct relationship with the tearoom roles. Because of his socialization in the homosexual society, taking the insertee role is neither traumatic for him nor related to aging.

Ricky's life revolves around his sexual deviance in a way that is not true of George or even of Dwight. Most of his friends and social contacts are connected with the homosexual subculture. His attitudes toward and rationalization of his sexual behavior are largely gained from this wide circle of friends. The gay men claim to have more close friends than do any other type of control or participant respondents. As frequency of orgasm is reported, this class also has more sex than any other group sampled, averaging 2.5 acts per week. They seem relatively satisfied with this aspect of their lives and regard their sexual drive as normal—although Ricky perceives his sexual needs as less than most.

One of his tearoom friends has recently married a woman, but Ricky has no intention of following his example. Another of his type, asked about marriage, said: "I prefer men, but I would make a good *wife* for the right *man*."

The vocabulary of heterosexual marriage is commonly used by those of Ricky's type. They speak of "marrying" the men they love and want to "settle down in a nice home." In a surprising number of cases, they take their lovers "home to meet mother." This act, like the exchange of "pinky rings," is intended to provide social strength to the lovers' union.

Three of the seven persons of this type were adopted—Ricky at the age of six months. Ricky told me that his adoptive father, who died three years before our interview, was "very warm and loving. He worked hard for a living, and we moved a lot." He is still close to his adoptive mother, who knows of his sexual deviance and treats his lover "like an older son."

Ricky hopes to be a writer, an occupation that would "allow me the freedom to be myself. I have a religion [Unitarian] which allows me freedom, and I want a career which will do the same." This, again, is typical: all three of the Unitarians in the sample are Type III men, although none was raised in that faith; and their jobs are uniformly of the sort to which their sexual activity, if exposed, would present little threat.

Although these men correspond most closely to society's homosexual stereotype, they are least representative of the tearoom population, constituting only 14 percent of the participant sample. More than any other type, the Rickys seem at ease with their behavior in the sexual market, and their scarcity in the tearooms is indicative of this. They want personal sex—more permanent relationships—and the public restrooms are not where this is to be found.

That any of them patronize the tearooms at all is the result of incidental factors: they fear that open cruising in the more common homosexual market places of the baths and bars might disrupt a current love affair; or they drop in at a tearoom while waiting for a friend at one of the "watering places" where homosexuals congregate in the parks. They find the anonymity of the tearooms suitable for their purposes, but not inviting enough to provide the primary setting for sexual activity.

Type IV: Closet Queens

Another dozen of the 50 participants interviewed may be classified as single deviants with dependent occupations, "closet queens" in homosexual slang. Again, the label may be applied to others who keep their deviance hidden, whether married or single, but the covert, unmarried men are most apt to earn this appellation. With them, we have moved full circle in our classifications, for they parallel the Trade in a number of ways:

1. They have a few friends, only a minority of whom are involved in tearoom activity.
2. They tend to play the insertor role, at least until they confront the crisis of aging.
3. Half of them are Roman Catholic in religion.
4. Their median annual income is $6,000; and they work as teachers, postmen, salesmen, clerks—usually for large corporations or agencies.
5. Most of them have completed only high school, although there are a few exceptionally well-educated men in this group.
6. One in six is black.
7. Not only are they afraid of becoming involved in other forms of the sexual market, they share with the Trade a relatively furtive involvement in the tearoom encounters.

Arnold will be used as the typical case. Only 22, Arnold is well below the median age of this group; but in most other respects he is quite representative, particularly in regard to the psychological problems common to Type IV.

A routine interview with Arnold stretched to nearly three hours in the suburban apartment he shares with another single man. Currently employed as a hospital attendant, he has had trouble with job stability, usually because he finds the job unsatisfactory. He frequently is unoccupied.

Arnold: I hang around the park a lot when I don't have anything else to do. I guess I've always known about the tearooms . . . so I just started going in there to get my rocks off. But I haven't gone since I caught my lover there in September. You get in the habit of going; but I don't think I'll start in again—unless I get too desperate.

Interviewer: Do you make the bar scene?

Arnold: Very seldom. My roommate and I go out together once in a while, but everybody there seems to think we're lovers. So I don't really operate in the bars. I really don't like gay people. They can be so damned bitchy! I really like women better than men—except for sex. There's a lot of the female in me, and I feel more comfortable with women than with men. I understand women and like to be with them. I'm really very close to my mother. The reason I don't live at home is because there are too many brothers and sisters living there. . . .

Interviewer: Is she still a devout Roman Catholic?

Arnold: Well, yes and no. She still goes to Mass some, but she and I go to seances together with a friend. I am studying astrology and talk it over with her quite a bit. I also analyze handwriting and read a lot about numerology. Mother knows I am gay and doesn't seem to mind. I don't think she really believes it though.

Arnold has a health problem: "heart attacks," which the doctor says are psychological and which take the form of "palpitations, dizziness, chest pain, shortness of breath and extreme weakness." These attacks, which began soon after his father's death from a coronary two years ago, make him feel as if he were "dying and turning cold." Tranquilizers were prescribed for him, "but I threw them out, because I don't like to become dependent on such things." He quoted a book on mental control of health that drugs are "unnecessary, if you have proper control."

He also connects these health problems with his resentment of his father, who was mentally ill:

Arnold: I don't understand his mental illness and have always blamed him for it. You might say that I have a father complex and, along with that, a security complex. Guess that's why I always run around with older men.

Interviewer: Were any of your brothers gay?

Arnold: Not that I know of. I used to have sex with the brother closest to my age when we were little kids. But he's married now, and I don't think he is gay at all. It's just that most of the kids I ran around with always jacked each other off or screwed each other in the ass. I just seemed to grow up with it. I can't remember a time when I didn't find men attractive. . . . I used to have terrible crushes on my gym teachers, but nothing sexual ever came of it. I just worshipped them, and

wanted to be around them all the time. I had coitus with a woman when I was 16—she was 22. After it was over, she asked me what I thought of it. I told her I would rather masturbate. Boy, was she pissed off! I've always liked older men. If they are under 30, I just couldn't be less interested. . . . Nearly all my lovers have been between 30 and 50. The trouble is that *they* always want sex—and sex isn't really what I want. I just want to be with them—to have them for friends. I guess it's part of my father complex. I just want to be loved by an older man.

Few of the Type IV participants share Arnold's preference for older men, although they report poorer childhood relationships with their fathers than do those of any other group. As is the case with Arnold's roommate, many closet queens seem to prefer teenage boys as sexual objects. This is one of the features that distinguishes them from all other participant types. Although scarce in tearooms, teenagers make themselves available for sexual activity in other places frequented by closet queens. A number of these men regularly cruise the streets where boys thumb rides each afternoon when school is over. One closet queen from my sample has been arrested for luring boys in their early teens to his home.

Interaction between these men and the youths they seek frequently results in the sort of scandal feared by the gay community. Newspaper reports of molestations usually contain clues of the closet queen style of adaptation on the part of such offenders. Those respondents whose lives had been threatened by teenage toughs were generally of this type. One of the standard rules governing one-night-stand operations cautions against becoming involved with such "chicken." The frequent violation of this rule by closet queens may contribute to their general disrepute among the bar set of the homosexual subculture, where "closet queen" is a pejorative term.

One Type IV respondent, an alcoholic whose intense self-hatred seemed always about to overflow, told me one night over coffee of his loneliness and his endless search for someone to love:

I don't find it in the tearooms—although I go there because it's handy to my work. But I suppose the [hustler's hangout] is really my meat. I just want to love every one of those kids!

Later, this man was murdered by a teenager he had picked up.

Arnold, too, expressed loneliness and the need for someone to talk with. "When I can really sit down and talk to someone else," he said, "I begin to feel real again. I lose that constant fear of mine—that sensation that I'm dying."

Styles of Deviant Adaptation

Social isolation is characteristic of Type IV participants. Generally, it is more severe even than that encountered among the Trade, most of whom enjoy at least a vestigial family life. Although painfully aware of their homosexual orientations, these men find little solace in association with others who share their deviant interests. Fearing exposure, arrest, the stigmatization that might result from a participation in the homosexual subculture, they are driven to a desperate, lone-wolf sort of activity that may prove most dangerous to themselves and the rest of society. Although it is tempting to look for psychological explanations of their apparent preference for chicken, the sociological ones are evident. They resort to the more dangerous game because of a lack of both the normative restraints and adult markets that prevail in the more overt subculture. To them, the costs (financial and otherwise) of operating among street corner youths are more acceptable than those of active participation in the gay subculture. Only the tearooms provide a less expensive alternative for the closet queens.

I have tried to make it impossible for any close associate to recognize the real people behind the disguised composites portrayed in this article. But I have worked equally hard to enable a number of tearoom players to see themselves in the portrait of George, and others to find their own stories in those of Dwight, Ricky or Arnold. If I am accurate, the real Tom will wonder whether he is trade or ambisexual; and a few others will be able to identify only partly with Arnold or Ricky.

My one certainty is that there is no single composite with whom all may identify. It should now be evident that, like other next door neighbors, the participants in tearoom sex are of no one type. They vary along a number of possible continua of social characteristics. They differ widely in terms of sexual career and activity, and even in terms of what that behavior means to them or what sort of needs it may fulfill. Acting in response to a variety of pressures toward deviance (some of which we may never ascertain), their adaptations follow a number of lines of least resistance.

In delineating styles of adaptation, I do not intend to imply that these men are faced with an array of styles from which they may pick one or even a combination. No man's freedom is that great. They have been able to choose only among the limited options offered them by society. These sets of alternatives, which determine the modes of adaptation to deviant pressures, are defined and allocated in accordance with major sociological variables: occupation, marital status, age, race, amount of education. That is one meaning of social probability.

Outsiders in a Hearing World   PAUL C. HIGGINS

Much of everyday life is based on the assumption that people can hear and speak. We communicate through telephones, radios, television, intercom systems and loudspeakers. Warning signals are often buzzers, sirens or alarms. Time is structured by bells and whistles. And, of course, people talk. Our world is an oral-aural one in which deaf people are typically left out (Higgins, 1978). They are *outsiders* in a hearing world (Becker, 1963). And like other outsiders, they are likely to create and maintain their own communities in order to survive and even thrive within an often hostile world.

In this article I explore the deaf community. Unlike many other disabled populations—who often only establish self-help groups (Sagarin, 1969)—the deaf are not merely a statistical aggregate. For example, 85% of deaf people who lost their hearing before the age of 19 have hearing-impaired spouses (Schein and Delk, 1974: 40).[1] Through marriage, friendships, casual acquaintances, clubs, religious groups, magazines published by and for themselves and sign language, the deaf create and maintain communities in the hearing world. Though scattered throughout a metropolitan area, members of the deaf community primarily confine their social relations to other members (Schein, 1968: 74). Membership within those deaf communities and the organization of the relationships among members are the foci of this article. Each of these aspects of deaf communities revolves around the deaf being outsiders in a hearing world.

Methods

This article is part of a larger study in Chicago which investigated the identity, interaction and community of the deaf in a hearing world (Higgins, 1977). I draw on materials from in-depth interviews with 75 hearing-impaired people and 15 counselors or friends of the deaf. My sample was developed through a snowballing technique. Two well-known deaf people in Chicago provided me with names of deaf people. I contacted those people who in turn provided me other names and so on. I supplemented my interviews with observations of a club for the deaf in Chicago, a winter carnival sponsored by a deaf-run organization and several meetings and outings of a senior citizen's club for the deaf in Chicago. National publications by and for the deaf, published writings of deaf individuals and articles or monographs about the deaf proved helpful. My research and analysis was primarily limited to the white deaf community. I soon learned that there was little interaction between white and black deaf. They form separate communities.

As I will discuss later, members of the deaf community are often suspicious and wary of hearing people (just as outsiders in general are of "normals"). They are reluctant to share their lives with the hearing. I overcame that potential reluctance in several ways. First, my parents are deaf. I am a "wise" hearing person (Goffman, 1963). Several people I interviewed knew them and therefore were happy to talk with me. Others approached me at a club for the deaf because of my name. One hearing woman of deaf parents told me that her husband was concerned that I would be interviewing her while she was alone. She told her husband that I had deaf parents (though she did not know them personally) and therefore everything would be alright. Second, I was mistaken for being deaf during my research due to my signing skills, though I did not intentionally try to pass as deaf. Finally, by contacting potential respondents through referrals (snowball technique) or through having first met them at a club for the deaf, I reduced

Excerpt from Paul C. Higgins, "Outsiders in a Hearing World—The Deaf Community," *Urban Life,* Vol. 8, No. 1 (April 1979), pp. 3–22. Copyright © 1979 Sage Publications, Inc. Reprinted by permission of Sage Publications, Inc.

[1] Ghettos for the blind have existed in the past in China and in many European cities. In 1935, a prominent worker in the field of blindness proposed establishing self-contained communities of the blind (Chevigny and Braverman, 1950). Few blind people, though, have blind spouses (Best, 1934).

A predominantly self-contained village of 400 physically disabled adults has been created by rehabilitation specialists in the Netherlands (Zola, unpublished). To what extent it is a community and to what extent it is merely an extension of a long-term care facility is not clear.

potential problems of establishing my identity and intentions. Only five people refused to be interviewed and two of those may never have received my letter asking to meet them.

It is a lack of trust which typically has led outsiders to distort the information they give to members of the larger society. For example, black respondents give more "docile" and "subservient" replies to white interviewers than to black interviewers (Sattler, 1970: 151). Through all the ways noted above, I believe I gained the trust of those members of the deaf community who shared their lives with me.

Membership

More than 13 million people in America have some form of hearing impairment. Almost 2 million are deaf. Of those 2 million approximately 410,000 are "prevocationally" deaf; they suffered their hearing losses before the end of adolescence (Schein and Delk, 1974).[2] It is from this latter group, the prevocationally deaf, that members of deaf communities are likely to come. I neither met nor heard of members of the Chicago-area deaf community who lost their hearing after adolescence. Surely some exist, but they are few. It will become evident later why that is so.

Deafness is not a sufficient condition for membership in deaf communities, though some degree of hearing impairment is a necessary condition as I will examine later. Deafness does not make "its members part of a natural community" (Furth, 1973: 2). Membership in deaf communities must be *achieved*. It is not an ascribed status (Markowicz and Woodward, 1975). Membership in a deaf community is achieved through (1) *identification* with the deaf world, (2) *shared experiences* of being hearing impaired, and (3) *participation* in the community's activities. Without all three characteristics one cannot be nor would one choose to be a member of a deaf community.

Identification

A deaf community is in part a "moral" phenomenon. It involves:

a sense of identity and unity with one's group and a feeling of involvement and wholeness on the part of the individual [Poplin, 1972: 7].

A deaf woman, her hearing impaired since childhood, dramatically describes the realization in her late teens and early twenties that she was part of the deaf world:

I didn't think I was very deaf myself. But when I saw these people (at a deaf organization) I knew I belonged to their world. I didn't belong to the hearing world. Once you are deaf, you are deaf, period. If you put something black in white paint, you can't get the black out. Same with the deaf. Once you are deaf, you're always deaf.

While it is problematic both physiologically and in terms of identification that "once you are deaf, you are always deaf," the woman's remarks express her commitment to the deaf world.[3] Whether members dramatically realize it or not, what is important is their commitment to and identification with the deaf. Other members, who attended schools and classes for the deaf since childhood and continued their interaction in the deaf world as adults, may, on looking back, find no dramatic moment when they realized that they had become part of a deaf community.

Members of the deaf community feel more comfortable with deaf people than they do with hearing people. They feel a sense of belonging. A young deaf woman explained:

At a club for the deaf, if I see a deaf person whom I don't know, I will go up to that person and say, "Hi! What's your name?" I would never do that to a hearing person.

Not all deaf or hearing-impaired people, though, identify with the deaf world. Those who

---

[2] Prevocationally deaf people were defined as those "who could not hear and understand speech and who had lost (or never had) that ability prior to 19 years of age" (Schein and Delk, 1974: 2). A self-report hearing scale was used to determine the respondent's hearing ability. Schein (1968) discusses the factors (e.g., chronicity, age of onset and degree of loss) involved in defining deafness and examines previous definitions.

[3] Most "coming out" among homosexuals, a process of defining oneself as gay, seems to occur in interaction with other homosexuals. Gays too feel that being gay is a permanent condition (Dank, 1971; Warren, 1974).

lost their hearing later in life through an accident, occupational hazard or presbycusis (i.e., aging process) do not seek to become members of deaf communities. Rather, as Goffman (1963) notes, they are likely to stigmatize members of deaf communities in the same way that those with normal hearing stigmatize them. Others, impaired from birth or from an early age, may never have developed such an identification. They probably had hearing parents and were educated in schools for the hearing. Some may participate in activities of deaf communities, but are not members. They are tolerated, though not accepted by the members. While audiologically they are deaf, socially they are not.

A hearing-impaired man, who participates in a deaf religious organization, but is not part of the deaf community, explained his self-identity in the following way:

In everyday life I consider myself a hearing person. (His hearing impaired wife interjected that she did too.) I usually forget it that I have a hearing problem. Sometimes I'm so lost (absorbed) in the hearing world; I mean I don't even realize I have a hearing problem. It seems automatic. I don't know what it is. I feel I'm hearing people to the deaf and hearing. I don't feel hearing impaired not even if I have a hard time to understand somebody. Still I don't feel I'm deaf because I couldn't hear you or understand you.

This man and his hearing-impaired wife are on the fringe of the deaf community. They participate in some community activities "just to show that we care" and "because they (the deaf) need help."

Hearing-impaired people like this man and his wife are often a source of both ill feelings and amusement for members of deaf communities. They are a source of ill feelings because their behavior does not respect the identity of the deaf community. Thus, this same hearing-impaired man was severely criticized for having someone at a board meeting of a religious group interpret his spoken remarks into sign language rather than signing himself. As I will explain later, signing skill and communication preference are indications of one's commitment to the deaf community. Those who are opposed to signing or who do not sign are not members of the community.

They are a source of amusement for trying to be what members of deaf communities feel they are not—hearing. A deaf couple were both critical and amused at the attempt of the same hear-

ing-impaired man's wife to hide her deafness. As they explained:

A hearing woman who signs well came up to her (the wife) at a religious gathering, and assuming that she was deaf, which she is, began to sign to her. The wife became flustered, put her own hands down and started talking.

Such hearing-impaired people serve as examples that members of deaf communities use in explaining to others what their community is like and in reaffirming to themselves who they are. These hearing-impaired people help to define for the members the boundary of their community and their identity as deaf people. The members reject the feelings of these "misguided" hearing-impaired people; feelings which deny their deafness. And in rejection, the members affirm who they are and what their community is.

Shared Experiences

In developing an identification with the deaf world, members of deaf communities share many similar experiences. Those experiences relate particularly to the everyday problems of navigating in a hearing world (Higgins, 1978) and to being educated in special programs for the deaf.

Since childhood, members of deaf communities have experienced repeated frustration in making themselves understood, embarrassing misunderstandings and the loneliness of being left out by family, neighborhood acquaintances and others. Such past and present experiences help to strengthen a deaf person's identification with the deaf world. A *typical* instance of these experiences, remarkable only because it is so routine, was described by a deaf man:

Most of my friends are deaf. I feel more comfortable with them. Well, we have the same feelings. We are more comfortable with each other. I can communicate good with hearing people, but in a group, no. For example, I go bowling. Have a league of hearing bowlers. Four of them will be talking, talking, talking and I will be left out. Maybe if there was one person I would catch some by lipreading, but the conversation passes back and forth so quickly. I can't keep up. I just let it go; pay attention to my bowling. Many things like that.

Yet, to be a member of a deaf community, one need not actually be deaf. Some members have lesser degrees of hearing impairment. As children, though, they were processed through educational programs for the deaf. These children were not necessarily mislabeled, though certainly some were. Rather, often no local programs for "hard of hearing" children were available. Children with various degrees of impairment were educated together. Through such processing, these children developed friendships with deaf children and an identification with the deaf world. As adults, they moved comfortably into deaf communities. With amplification these members of deaf communities are often able to use the telephone successfully, if also somewhat haltingly. Some converse with hearing people reasonably well. Yet, due to that childhood processing as deaf, these hearing-impaired people choose to live their lives within deaf communities. Audiologically they are not deaf; socially they are (Furfey and Harte, 1964, 1968; Schein, 1968).

Other members of a deaf community may have once been deaf, but through surgery or fortuitous circumstances they have regained some hearing. Though no longer severely hearing impaired, they remain active in the deaf community where their identity as a person developed. A dramatic case is that of a now slightly hearing-impaired man. He went to the state school for the deaf in Illinois. His childhood friends were deaf. During World War II, though, he regained much of his hearing while working in a munitions plant; the loud blasts from testing the bombs apparently improved his hearing. Consequently, his speech also improved. Only his modest hearing aid indicates that he has a slight impairment. Yet his wife is deaf, most of their friends are deaf, and he is active in a state organization for the deaf. As he explained:

(As your speech got better, did you continue to associate with your deaf friends in _____ town?) Oh, yeh, I'm more involved with the deaf community now than I was back then (WW II). To me they are still my family. I feel more at home when I walk into a room with 1,000 deaf people; more so than walking into a room with 1,000 hearing people, non-deaf. I feel at home. I can relate to them. We had something in common; our childhood, our education, our problems, and all that.

Since membership in a deaf community is based on shared experiences of being deaf and identification with the deaf world, it is difficult for hearing individuals to be members of such communities. A deaf woman put it simply: "Hearing people are lost in the deaf world just as deaf people are lost in the hearing world."

Outsiders are often wary and resentful of "normals": blacks of whites, gays of straights and so on. Likewise, deaf people are skeptical of hearing people's motives and intentions. A deaf man remarked:

When a hearing person starts to associate with the deaf, the deaf begin to wonder why that hearing person is here. What does that hearing person want?

When a "hard of hearing" woman, who for years had associated exclusively with the hearing, started a north shore club for the deaf, her motives and behavior were questioned by some of the deaf members. I was warned myself by two deaf leaders to expect such skepticism and resistance by members of the deaf community. I encountered little in my research, but having deaf parents and clearly establishing my intentions probably allayed members' suspicions.

Outsider communities may grant courtesy membership to "wise" people who are not similarly stigmatized (Goffman, 1963). These individuals are "normal," yet they are familiar with and sympathetic to the conditions of outsiders. For example, gay communities grant courtesy membership to "wise" heterosexuals: heterosexual couples or single females known as "fag hags" (Warren, 1974: 113). Researchers are often granted that status. Yet, that courtesy membership represents only a partial acceptance by the outsiders of the "normals."

Some hearing individuals are courtesy members of deaf communities. They may be educators, counselors, interpreters or friends of the deaf. Often they have deafness in their families: deaf parents, siblings, children or even spouses. Yet, their membership is just that, a courtesy, which recognizes the fundamental fact that no matter how empathetic they are, no matter that there is deafness in their families, they are not deaf and can never "really" know what it means to be deaf.[4]

---

[4] While members of deaf communities grant courtesy membership to "wise" hearing people, those members often subtly indicate that those hearing people are still not "one of them" (Markowicz and Woodward, 1975). When signing to a hearing person, the deaf may slow the speed of their signing or speak while signing. They would rarely do that when communicating with a fellow member.

Not surprisingly, hearing-impaired individuals who through their actions and attitudes would otherwise be part of a deaf community may be rejected by some members because they hear and speak too well. A hearing-impaired woman who speaks well and with amplification uses the telephone, who went to a state school for the deaf since childhood and to a college for the deaf and who is married to a deaf man is such an individual.

Yet, hearing-impaired people like that woman do receive some acceptance from those members who tend to reject them. They are called upon to act as go-betweens with the hearing world. This clearly differentiates these impaired people from the hearing. As the hearing-impaired woman, mentioned above noted:

They (deaf people) can rely on me to do the talking for them (e.g., telephoning). And in that sense they do accept me because I am somebody who can help them. Because they don't really want to turn around to a hearing person and ask them to do something.

The hearing and speech ability of this hearing-impaired woman creates a barrier between her and some members of the deaf community, but simultaneously allows her some acceptance by those who reject her. She is almost hearing; therefore, some members reject her. She is not quite hearing, though; therefore, members will rely on her for help in navigating through the hearing world. It is often only with greatest reluctance that members of deaf communities rely on hearing people for such assistance.[5]

Participation

Active participation in the deaf community is the final criteria for being a member. Participation, though, is an outgrowth of identification with the deaf world and of sharing similar experiences in being hearing impaired. In that respect, then, it is the least important characteristic for being a member of the deaf community. Yet the deaf community is not merely a symbolic community of hearing-impaired people who share similar experiences. It is also created through marriages, friendships, acquaintances, parties, clubs, religious organizations and published materials. The activities provide the body of the community, whereas the identification and shared experiences provide the soul.

Thus, a deaf couple, who lived in the Chicago area for years, were not warmly received when they began to attend a deaf, Protestant congregation. The members of the congregation wondered where they had been all these years. Members interpreted that lack of participation as a lack of identification with themselves and a lack of commitment to the deaf community.

Participation, though, varies among the members of deaf communities. Involvement in community activities is tempered by outside commitments such as work, family and traveling time to and from activities as well as individual preference. More importantly, what activities one participates in and with whom one associates help to organize relationships among members of the deaf community.

Social Organization

While normals may often treat outsiders as a homogeneous group, the outsiders themselves create distinctions among one another. Gays distinguish among "elite," "career" and "deviants" (Warren, 1972). Lower-class blacks may vilify middle-class blacks for being Uncle Toms (Pettigrew, 1964). The deaf community, too, is heterogeneous. Through differential participation with other members and in various activities of the deaf community, members organize their relationships with one another.

Members of the deaf community use several major characteristics in organizing relationships with one another. Some of these characteristics operate in much the same way as in the hearing world. Outsiders, whether they be deaf or not, live within a larger world. Some are not born as outsiders, but only later acquire that status. All are socialized to some degree within the dominant culture. Consequently, communities of outsiders and their subculture are continuous with the dominant culture of the larger society (Plummer, 1975: 157). Therefore, it is not surprising that some characteristics which members of the dominant culture use to differentiate each other are also used by members of communities of outsiders. Sex, race, religion and sophistication

[5]This desire of the deaf to be independent from and their skeptical attitude toward help offered by the hearing has been documented in the more general situation of disabled-nondisabled relations (Ladieu et al., 1947).

(as often indicated by educational attainment) differentiate members in the deaf community as they do in the hearing world. Consequently, they will not receive special attention here.

Age, however, adds a special dimension to deaf communities. Unlike ethnic or racial outsiders, there are few deaf children in the deaf community. Less than 10% of deaf people have deaf parents (Schein and Delk, 1974: 35). Consequently, deaf communities are actually adult deaf communities. As children, most members of the community were probably isolated in a hearing world except while attending educational programs for the deaf. The same holds true today, though deaf children may participate in such activities as religious worship where deaf adults are present. The intriguing question becomes: how are deaf children and adolescents socialized into the adult deaf community? I did not address this issue which clearly needs attention.

Communication

Other characteristics which members of an outsider community use to organize their relationships with one another are related to their unique position within the dominant world. For example, within the black community skin color has played an important but diminishing role (Udry et al., 1971). Within the deaf community, communication preference and skill, the relative emphasis that members give to signing and speaking, is an important basis on which relationships are organized. I will examine this characteristic closely, because it is crucial for understanding the deaf community in a hearing world.

There are two general modes of communication used among the deaf. One is called the oral method; the other is the manual method. The oral method in its "purest" form is composed of speaking and lipreading. Manual communication is sign language and fingerspelling. Put very simply, sign language is a concept-based language of signs (i.e., various movements of the hands in relationship to one another and to the body in which the hands themselves take various shapes) that has a different structure from English, but one that is not yet fully understood

(Stokoe et al., 1975). Within the deaf community there are oralists and manualists who I will refer to as *speakers* and *signers*.[6]

Speakers. Speakers rely primarily on speaking and lipreading when communicating with fellow oralists. When communicating with signers, they may often accompany their speaking with signs, but they do not sign fluently. Those who are "pure" oralists in philosophy or communicative behavior are not part of the deaf community. A small number of these "pure" oralists are members of an oral association of the deaf; whereas, others go it alone in the hearing world (Oral Deaf Adults Section Handbook, 1975). Of course, the distinction between a "pure" oralist and a speaker is arbitrary. Speakers may accept as a member of the community an oralist who signers reject as too orally oriented to be a fellow member. Speakers are likely to have had hearing parents and attended day schools and classes for the deaf where signing was not permitted.

Signers. Signers sign and fingerspell when communicating to their deaf friends. For many signers their first language is sign language. They are native signers. Some have unintelligible speech and poor lipreading skills. Yet, others speak and lipread well, even better than speakers. Signers, though, prefer signing as compared to speech or lipreading when communicating with one another. Rarely will they use their voices or even move their mouths with other signers. Those who do may be teased. Signers reason that speaking and lipreading are for navigating in the hearing world, but they are not necessary among fellow signers.

Varieties of sign language exist. Many of those are due to the mixing of sign language and English. American Sign Language is least influenced by English. The use of varieties of sign language displays the social organization of the deaf community. The more educated the deaf individual is, the more likely that individual will be familiar with varieties which approximate English. Varieties of sign language which approximate English are more likely to be used at formal

---

[6]It is difficult to estimate the relative proportion of oralists and manualists within deaf communities. Both the relative membership within the oral and manual divisions of a deaf fraternal organization (in Chicago) and the proportion of the prevocationally, adult deaf population who use signs (Schein, 1968; Schein and Delk, 1974) indicate that oralists are a numerical minority within deaf communities. Further, their numbers are likely to decline in the future as signing becomes more extensively employed in educational programs for the deaf.

occasions (e.g., at a conference) than at informal ones. Social, educational, regional and ethnic (particularly black-white) variations in signing exist much as they do in English (Stokoe and Battison, 1975).

Becoming a signer follows no single path. Those who have deaf parents who sign most likely grew up as signers themselves. Others became signers in residential schools. Although signing often was not permitted in the classrooms of such schools, it was often allowed outside of the classrooms in the dorms and on the playgrounds. After leaving *oral* day school programs, many deaf individuals began to use signs which they learned from deaf adults. The hand rapping and monetary fines which were (and in some cases still are) administered to them when they were caught using their hands to communicate were not forgotten. The frustration and bitterness from failing to understand and to learn through the oral approach is still felt.[7] Consequently, these converts are often the most adamantly opposed to oral education because they are the self-perceived victims of it.

Others who did not immediately seek out signers often found that their speech and lipreading skills did not gain them easy entrance into the hearing world. They were misunderstood and in turn misunderstood hearing people. Such experiences influenced these deaf individuals to become signers.

Cleavage Between Signers and Speakers

Signers and speakers are members of the same deaf community. They may attend the same religious organization, social club or community gala. They also marry one another. In such marriages the speaker typically becomes a signer. Yet, through their feelings toward each other and their differential involvement with each other, strong divisions and at times antagonisms are created. That cleavage within the deaf community relates historically to the deaf's position within a hearing world. Particularly, it is an outgrowth of how educators of the deaf have traditionally felt it best to teach deaf children.

Historically, throughout the United States and especially in Chicago, Boston, and a few other places, the oral method of instruction has been dominant in schools and classes for the deaf.

Only since the early 1970s has the Chicago area begun to emphasize manual communication in the classroom. The combination of the two approaches along with writing and any other effective means of communication has been called total communication (O'Rourke, 1972).

The oral philosophy was stressed in the hope and desire that deaf children, trained in such a method, would be able to move easily into the hearing world as adults. Perhaps more importantly, it was also stressed due to the fear that deaf children were allowed to sign and fingerspell with one another, especially in often isolated residential schools, then as adults they would marry one another and form deaf communities within, but apart from the hearing world. Alexander Graham Bell, whose wife was deaf and who was an influential supporter of the oral philosophy, voiced such fears in an 1883 paper, "Upon the Formation of a Deaf Variety of the Human Race" (Boese, 1971). This emphasis of hearing educators on oralism and their suppression of signing among deaf children has not gone unnoticed by the deaf.

Through formal organizations as well as friendships and informal relations, signers and speakers organize the deaf community according to communication skill and preference. For example, a national fraternal organization for the deaf has several divisions in the Chicago area. One is attended by speakers; the other two by signers. Though the oral division has a dwindling membership, its members insist on being separate from the larger, manually oriented divisions. Further, respondents noted that most, if not all, of their friends had similar communication preferences as their own, be they manual or oral. Each group is not quite comfortable with the other's mode of communication. Speakers explain that it is difficult to follow fast signers, especially when the signers do not move their mouths. Signers complain that it is difficult to lipread the oralists or understand their modest or minimal signing.

The conflict between signing and speaking also disrupts family relationships. It is not unusual for deaf children who sign to communicate little with their parents who do not sign. As adults, their relationships with their parents may be bitter. Deaf siblings, too, can be divided by

---

[7]On academic achievement tests, deaf children score several years behind their hearing counterparts (Trybus and Karchmer, 1977).

communication differences. For example, two deaf sisters in the Chicago area rarely see each other. Both grew up in the oral tradition but the older married a speaker while the younger married a signer. The younger sister has retained her oral skills, but has become more involved with signers. Rather than join the oral fraternal division at her sister's request, she remains in the larger, manual division where her friends are.

Although signing is not a basis for membership in deaf communities, it is clearly an outgrowth of becoming a member.[8] Signing is an indication of one's identity as a deaf person and one's commitment to the deaf world. It is perhaps the most obvious indication to hearing people that one is deaf. Because deafness is a relatively invisible impairment, deaf people would often go unnoticed in everyday, impersonal activities except for their signing to one another. Also, signing often attracts stares, unflattering imitations and ridicule from the hearing. Therefore, "pure" oralists are viewed by members of deaf communities, particularly by signers, as outsiders to the deaf world. Further, some signers wonder if speakers are ashamed of being deaf. Signers may interpret the speakers' not fully embracing signing as an indication that speakers are either trying to hide their deafness or are still hopelessly under the influence of misguided, hearing educators. Either way, the speakers' commitment to the deaf world becomes questioned. That commitment is partially based on the conviction that hearing people have too long dominated deaf people's lives; in education, in jobs, in even telling them how to communicate with each other.

Conclusion

Within the larger society, outsiders often create and maintain communities. Some of these communities are located within well-defined geographical areas of the city: ethnic neighborhoods, black ghettos or Mexican-American barrios. Other communities of outsiders may not be quite so geographically bounded. Through marriages (both legal and symbolic), friendships, clubs, formal organizations, publications and a special argot, outsiders who are scattered throughout a metropolitan area *create* their community. The deaf community is such a creation.

Membership in deaf communities, though, is neither granted to nor sought by all who are deaf. Rather, it is achieved through identification with the deaf world, shared experiences of being hearing impaired and involvement with other members. Most people who are audiologically deaf never become members. Some with lesser degrees of hearing impairment have been members for as long as they can remember.

Although the deaf community may appear to be homogeneous to the hearing, members of the community create distinctions among one another. These distinctions are used in organizing relationships within the community. Some of these distinguishing characteristics, such as sex, are used within the hearing world as well. Yet, due to the unique (historical and present) position of the deaf as outsiders in a hearing world, members of the community distinguish among one another based on communication preference. Signers and speakers find it easier to communicate with those who have preferences similar to their own. More importantly, speaking to fellow members is a vestige of the hearing's domination of and paternalism toward the deaf. Therefore, not fully embracing and using sign language may call into question one's identification with and commitment to the deaf community.

Within deaf communities the members seldom face the difficulties and frustrations which arise when they navigate through the hearing world. A sense of belonging and wholeness is achieved which is not found among the hearing. *Among fellow members there is no shame in being deaf* and being deaf does not mean being odd or different. Deafness is taken for granted. Within deaf communities those who cannot "turn a deaf ear" now become the outsiders.

[8] Some researchers have viewed deaf communities as language communities where American Sign Language use is necessary for membership (Markowicz and Woodward, 1975; Schlesinger and Meadow, 1972). This approach is too restrictive because it excludes speakers as well as many signers who are not ASL users from being members of deaf communities. Yet, speakers, nonnative signers and native signers associate with each other, marry one another and recognize each other as part of the same community while also maintaining distinctions among one another.

REFERENCES

Becker, H. S. 1963. *Outsiders: Studies in the Sociology of Deviance*. New York: Free Press.

Best, H. 1934. *Blindness and the Blind in the United States*. New York: Macmillan.

Boese, R. J. 1971. "Native Sign Language and the Problem of Meaning." Ph.D. dissertation, University of California—Santa Barbara (unpublished).

Chevigny, H. and S. Braverman. 1950. *The Adjustment of the Blind*. New Haven, CT: Yale Univ. Press.

Dank, B. M. 1971. "Coming Out in the Gay World." *Psychiatry*, 34: 180–197.

Furfey, P. H. and T. J. Harte. 1968. *Interaction of Deaf and Hearing in Baltimore City, Maryland*. Washington, DC: Catholic University Press.

———. 1964. *Interaction of Deaf and Hearing in Frederick County, Maryland*. Washington, DC: Catholic University of America Press.

Furth, H. G. 1973. *Deafness and Learning: A Psychosocial Approach*. Belmont, CA: Wadsworth.

Goffman, E. 1963. *Stigma: Notes on the Management of Spoiled Identity*. Englewood Cliffs, NJ: Prentice-Hall.

Higgins, P. C. 1978. "Encounters Between the Disabled and the Nondisabled: Bringing the Impairment Back In." American Sociological Association Meetings, San Francisco.

———. 1977. "The Deaf Community: Identity and Interaction in a Hearing World." Ph.D. dissertation, Northwestern University (unpublished).

Ladieu, G., E. Haufman, and T. Dembo. 1947. "Studies in Adjustment to Visible Injuries: Evaluation of Help by the Injured." *Journal of Abnormal and Social Psychology*, 42: 169–192.

Markowicz, H. and J. Woodward. 1975. "Language and the Maintenance of Ethnic Boundaries in the Deaf Community." Conference on Culture and Communication, Temple University, March 13–15.

Oral Deaf Adults Section Handbook. 1975. Washington, DC: Alexander Graham Bell Association for the Deaf.

O'Rourke, T. J. (ed.). 1972. *Psycholinguistics and Total Communication: The State of the Art*. Washington, DC: American Annals of the Deaf.

Pettigrew, T. F. 1964. *A Profile of the Negro American*. Princeton, NJ: D. Van Nostrand.

Plummer, K. 1975. *Sexual Stigma: An Interactionist Account*. London: Routledge and Kegan Paul.

Poplin, D. E. 1972. *Communities: A Survey of Theories and Methods of Research*. New York: Macmillan.

Sagarin, E. 1969. *Odd Man In: Societies of Deviants in America*. Chicago: Quadrangle.

Sattler, J. M. 1970. "Racial 'Experimenter Effects' in Experimentation, Testing, Interviewing, and Psychotherapy." *Psychological Bulletin*, 73: 137–160.

Schein, J. D. 1968. *The Deaf Community: Studies in the Social Psychology of Deafness*. Washington, DC: Gallaudet College Press.

Schein, J. D. and M. T. Delk, Jr. 1974. *The Deaf Population of the United States*. Silver Spring, MD: National Association of the Deaf.

Schlesinger, H. S. and K. P. Meadow. 1972. *Sound and Sign: Childhood Deafness and Mental Health*. Berkeley: Univ. of California Press.

Stokoe, W. C. and R. M. Battison. 1975. "Sign Language, Mental Health, and Satisfying Interaction." First National Symposium on the Mental Health Needs of Deaf Adults and Children. Chicago: David T. Siegel Institute for Communicative Disorders, Michael Reese Hospital and Medical Center, June 12–14.

Stokoe, W. C., C. G. Casterline, and C. G. Croneberg (eds.). 1975. *A Dictionary of American Sign Language on Linguistic Principles*. Washington, DC: Gallaudet College Press.

Trybus, R. J. and M. A. Karchmer. 1977. "School Achievement Scores of Hearing Impaired Children: National Data on Achievement Status and Growth Patterns." *American Annals of the Deaf*, 122(2): 62–69.

Udry, J. R., K. E. Bauman, and C. Chase. 1971. "Skin Color, Status, and Mate Selection." *American Journal of Sociology*, 76: 722–733.

Warren, C. A. B. 1974. *Identity and Community in the Gay World*. New York: Wiley.

———. 1972. "Observing the Gay Community." In J. D. Douglas (ed.), *Research on Deviance*. New York: Random House, pp. 139–163.

Zola, I. K. "To Find the Missing Piece." (Unpublished.)

Patterns of Living with Other Convicts

ANN CORDILIA

Relating to people requires a variety of skills normally learned through interaction. These skills, which include the management of everyday interaction, of intimacy and of reciprocal obligations, differ in content from one setting to another. Therefore, the interaction skills a person has learned in one setting may be inadequate or inappropriate in another.

Convicts learn a unique style of interaction. They live in forced separation from people outside prison and in forced intimacy with other inmates chosen by the prison system. The literature describing interactions among convicts centers around the contradictory themes of cohesion and alienation [1]. The theme of inmate cohesion is based on the idea that an "inmate code" exists that demands that prisoners distance themselves from staff and show loyalty to other convicts. The theme of alienation focuses upon the description of roles in inmate culture that stem from the exploitation or rejection of other inmates. Recent studies of inmate society have introduced doubt about the cohesiveness of inmate subculture. Inmate solidarity is said to have declined because prisoners are transferred more frequently, staff are becoming more rehabilitation oriented, gang activity has increased, and the power of the administration to reward inmates has grown [2].

Data from our study strongly support the argument that inmates feel alienated from living with each other. According to Kassebaum et al., prisoners view getting along with other inmates as the most difficult problem in adjusting to prison [3]. Inmates in our sample share this strongly negative view.

Fear of Other Inmates

Sykes describes prison as a world where "the assaults of fellow prisoners are a greater danger than the barbarity of the captors." While not every inmate feels in constant danger, most express at least some fear of violence; as one inmate put it, "There are vicious people in prison and they use knives on other people." Some inmates, especially those involved in homosexuality or the drug trade, or who have been committed for particular crimes such as child abuse and sexual assault, are more exposed to violence. Like the following inmate who was convicted of child molestation, they may live in perpetual fear.

C. has had trouble with the other inmates because of the charges against him. He says that they have wanted to kill him since he got to prison and he hasn't known whether he would live from one day to the next. He feels that the guards can't protect him. Once an inmate came into his room and threw the TV out the window. Somebody else left him a note saying, "We know what you're in for. We know you're no good. We're going to kill you." Inmates also pushed him and gave him body punches. Last summer, he was in his room and a drunk inmate came in and insulted him. C. said to leave him alone and the inmate punched him.

Inmates also express fear of nonphysical harm, such as betrayal or exploitation. They feel both that the prison structure promotes such exploitation and that it is in the nature of other inmates to exploit people. Inmates often charge that the prison administration rewards inmates who inform on other inmates ("the only ones who get the breaks are the snitches"). Since they are uncertain who is an informer, they tend to be suspicious of everyone.

Prison is full of rats, people who would rat on you for a furlough or a privilege. . . . People have been told that if they rat on who lights fires, they will be taken care of by the Board. So some people will rat. And it's hard to know who are the rats.

They also claim that inmates by their very nature routinely exploit each other.

The majority of cons try to work some game on people. They try to con them into doing something they wouldn't ordinarily do maybe just out of laziness. Everyone does it. If you see somebody with a little bit of weakness, you play on that weakness.

From Ann Cordilia, *The Making of an Inmate: Prison as a Way of Life.* Cambridge, MA: Schenkman, 1983, pp. 13–29.

Rejection of Other Inmates

A second set of commonly expressed attitudes revolves around identification with or rejection of other inmates. The literature on inmate culture stresses the psychological aspect of inmate solidarity, that is, that inmates identify with other inmates and distance themselves from staff. This helps inmates to deal with their rejection by society; they respond by accepting each other and rejecting their rejectors. As described above, observers are now finding a decline in inmate solidarity. Our interviews confirm this. The inmates not only lacked psychological solidarity with each other, but were explicitly rejecting. Rather than reflecting the cohesiveness described in the prison literature, their feelings were closer to what Goffman describes among patients in mental hospitals [4]:

... instead of clinging together to uphold their patient status against the traditional world, they sought in cliques and dyads to define themselves as normal and to define many of the other patients as crazy.

Some inmates reject their peers because they do not think of themselves as truly criminal. According to Irwin, two types of inmates tend to fall into this category [5]. They are the middle-class offender who sees his crime as resulting from a psychological problem, and the "lower-class man," who committed a violent crime he considers an accident resulting from a set of unlucky circumstances. These men view themselves as different from the run of inmates in prison and object to being categorized with them. Six of the interviewees in my sample did not consider themselves to be criminals like the other inmates. The following quote, from an inmate who was imprisoned as a first offender for killing a man in a fight, expresses his feelings of distance from "criminal" inmates:

The institution looks at all the inmates and considers that they are all criminal. This hurts because I know I'm not a real criminal. I'm not saying that some people shouldn't be in jail. There are some people who have criminal instincts, maybe killer instincts. When you come to this place, if you're not strong, that instinct may develop in you. But I don't feel that way. I've been here twenty-four months and I'm fighting all the way.

Other inmates reject their peers because they believe that inmates in general are "losers," inferior in various ways to people outside of prison. Generally, they distinguish themselves as different from the average inmate.

In prison, the average person has a ninth-grade education. . . . They are not too smart. They react instead of act. But I am able to see the plays before they come.

M. says that he is annoyed by a lot of people in prison. "They come in and strut around and say 'I'm a bad s.o.b. I'm in here for armed robbery.' They tell you about the nice Cadillacs they had on the street. Then in the next breath, they'll bum a cigarette. They're a bunch of phonies."

The majority of people in prison are into petty things. They don't think about big jobs. They have the same m.o. all the time. They are careless, they don't care, they don't want to help themselves. . . . The majority of inmates are third or fourth offenders. You give anything good to these cons and they will fuck it up.

Many inmates reserve their strongest condemnation for certain segments of the inmate population, such as Blacks (in the case of White prisoners), the young, or people who have committed particular crimes. One of the main groups rejected by other inmates are people imprisoned for sexual crimes, especially for molesting children. As one inmate put it:

Some guys are in here for molesting little kids. When we hear that, a couple of us guys get him in a room and punch him out. . . . I hate anyone who did anything to kids, or raped a woman, or mugged an old woman, or any woman for that matter.

Given these negative attitudes, inmates naturally dislike living in close quarters with each other. Most inmates spend their work day with other inmates and, unless they choose to be in their cells, they are also with other inmates during recreational time. Some inmates, however, choose to be locked in their cells for free periods and for long parts of the weekend just to be alone for a while. Even in cells, however, they can still hear other inmates, their voices, their music, and their television. This lack of privacy and the dislike many inmates have for each other often combine to lead to violence, as the following case illustrates:

C. likes country and western music. His dislike for soul music and for Blacks is ever-increasing because of personal problems with another inmate living in the cell next to him. The other inmate is Black. C. says that he is constantly playing loud music. This became so annoying to him that it ended up in a physical confrontation between both of them. C. was threatened by the other inmate with bodily harm and believes that the incident has not been resolved yet. He says that he thinks the other inmate's friends may burn out his cell.

Inmates as Friends

Despite their hostility toward each other, inmates need other inmates. They are physically and psychologically isolated from people on the outside, so they must turn to their peers for human contact. Inmates often mention that, whatever the problems of relating to other inmates, it is easier to do time if you have friends, that one of the few pleasures accessible to inmates is friendship.

In here, you get to know everybody in your house well. You eat together and spend your evenings together. It's hard to do time if you're isolated. All you have in here is your stereo, TV, joints, and friends.

Some prisoners appreciate their fellow inmates because they contrast them with people on the outside who they feel have betrayed them. It is common in prison for outside friends not to visit and to lose contact with inmates. Inmates may then feel that their only option is to look inside the prison for friends. The following quotation from a young drug dealer whose friends never came to visit illustrates these feelings:

As far as I'm concerned, I don't have any friends on the street any more. All those assholes gave me up the day I walked into the joint. Before, when I was on the street, they all would ask for dope from me and like a fool I'd give it to them. But not any more. There's one guy out there now, Billy, who better stay out of my way. In fact, I'd like to rearrange his face just for the hell of it. I don't know where I'm going to live when I leave here. I know if I run into them on the street that the shit will fly. You want to know something, the only friends I have are here in the joint.

In contrast to people on the outside, inmates live in forced close proximity with each other. While this leads to conflict, it can also lead to intimacy. After living very closely with someone for a number of years, inmates often feel that they know that person better than anyone they know on the outside.

G. says that he would trust his friends in prison more than those on the outside. "When you live next to a guy for two years, you know everything there is to know about him—when he pisses, when he shits, if he snores."

While no inmate in my sample expressed the idea described by Irwin that "cons are my people," some inmates do distinguish groups within the inmate population with whom they can identify. Prisoners usually identify with inmates who are similar to them; middle-class first offenders with other middle-class first offenders; drug addicts with other drug addicts, etc. Sometimes the groups with which inmates identify are very small, for example, a few members of an AA group; in other instances, they are rather large, as illustrated by the following quote from a professional thief:

E. says that there are a lot of "weirdos" in prison, both among the guards and the cons. He also says that there are some good guys, especially among the thief population. He claims that out of the five hundred men in the prison there are probably about a hundred thieves.

Inmates, therefore, react to living with other convicts with fear and mistrust; they do not identify with convicts as a group and resent the forced closeness and lack of privacy. At the same time, they often distinguish a group or type of convict toward whom they do feel friendly. They may prefer convicts to people on the outside who have betrayed them; forced physical closeness sometimes leads to psychological intimacy; and inmates recognize that doing time is easier if one has friends. With this in mind, let us look at how inmates treat the convict population as a whole and at how they treat their particular friends.

Relating to the Inmate Population

In the literature we find two approaches to the way inmates interact with one another. The first assumes that bonds of loyalty unite inmates, that inmates adopt a code that restrains them from harming each other. The second approach, perhaps best expressed by Korn and McCorkle, views prison interaction as basically exploitative and oriented toward acquiring power over other inmates [6]:

The dominating value of the inmate social system seems to be the possession and exercise of coercive power. There are probably no relationship functions which have escaped the influence of this factor.

Interviewees expressed great mistrust of other inmates. They clearly saw relationships among the mass of convicts as exploitative and felt very little solidarity with them as a group:

In prison you prey on weakness. I've done it myself. Everyone does it to a degree. The rule is that the strong shall survive and the weak shall fall by the wayside.

Although inmate interactions were not invariably hostile and exploitative, prisoners always mentioned such problems. The exploitation and conflict in prison occur in certain patterns and it is to these particular patterns that the inmate must learn to adjust. One of the major conflict patterns, which will be referred to here as the "dominance game," was described as follows by Sykes [7]:

. . . the inmate is acutely aware that sooner or later he will be "tested"—that someone will "push" him to see how far they can go and that he must be prepared to fight for the safety of his person and his possessions. If he should fail, he will thereafter be an object of contempt, constantly in danger of being attacked by other inmates who view him as an obvious victim.

According to Toch, inmates seek to build their sense of manliness by establishing their own superiority over other inmates [8]. The payoff in this game is sometimes actual sexual domination of the victim; most often, however, it is simply the imposition of the aggressor's will on the victim, the appropriation of the victim's possessions, or at minimum getting the victim to show fear.

New inmates are informally oriented to prison partly through exposure to this dominance game. The game is used as a means of placing the new inmate, or "fish," somewhere on the dominance hierarchy.

While M. was in jail awaiting transfer to prison, the old timers told him what to expect. They told him that the other cons would try to "make a faggot out of you" and this led him to be very apprehensive. "When I first got there [to prison], a big Mexican kid approached me. I said, 'Sure, let's get it on. Let's go to my room.' We were walking down the tier and we passed a broom closet. I grabbed a wringer out of it and beat the kid from the third to the first tier."

Older inmates, even those who have established their reputations, may have to reestablish them when transferred to a new institution or when meeting up with a new group of inmates. The following describes the experience of a fifty-year-old inmate who has spent most of his adult life in prison.

When C. first arrived at the prison, he was surrounded by a group of young inmates, the oldest of whom was twenty-nine. They told him that he was going to do their tailoring for them. C. says that he just stood there and took it for a while and then decided that he didn't have to take it because he was old enough to be their father. He took the smallest guy and punched him and said, "Who's next?"

Some inmates never learn to deal with the dominance game; they are placed low on the dominance hierarchy, are prey to manipulation by other inmates, and perhaps spend their time in protective custody. Most inmates, however, learn at least to some degree to deal with the situation by remaining constantly on guard and by responding aggressively to challenges. When they are with convicts who are not their particular friends, inmates must learn to be vigilant. They come to suspect friendly gestures, such as being given a gift of cigarettes, as preludes to attempts at dominance. The donor of the gift may later reinterpret it as a loan and demand repayment; occasionally sexual favors will be sought as repayment; more commonly, return of the principal with interest or submission to the control of the lender is demanded. Small aggressive gestures, such as being bumped while walking down the corridor, cannot be passed off as accidents, since they may be ritualized insults, the toleration of which will lead to escalation. In short, the inmate must learn to control any tendency to respond to people with trust and openness and to remain emotionally mobilized for attack.

Inmates also must learn to respond to aggression by immediate retaliation. Often inmates feel that the appropriate response to a challenge is through violent massive retaliation that would appear to people outside of prison to be far out of proportion to the initial attack. Here are two inmates' views of the necessity for alertness to aggression and readiness to retaliate:

M. says that a person has to be very ready to fight in prison. If someone betrays you, you can't let him get away with it. If you do, everybody else will start to pick on you. If anybody puts you down in front of other people, unless you tell him where to go, the other cons will say, "How come you let him do that to you?" If someone steals a pack of cigarettes off you, you have to be ready to kill him or at least hurt him so bad that he can't harm you.

O. says that prison has changed him. He tries to control himself, but says, "I can be vicious if I'm pushed." He carries scissors on him and says that he wouldn't hurt anyone but would stab someone if they messed with him.

Many inmates realize how prison has changed their interaction style and that what is vital in prison will not do on the outside.

Z. says that he has learned how to live in prison. "If somebody gives you guff, then you knock them down. You're not supposed to do that on the outside."

However, this style may be difficult for the inmate to drop once he is freed. As Toch has pointed out, "The difficulty with role-playing is that the line between the staged self and the real self can dissolve. Men who see themselves as gentle can become prisoners of aggressor roles they play" [9]. Inmates often feel that they have become overly aggressive, mistrustful and full of hate and that these changes have gotten out of their control.

D. feels that he has "learned to be really an animal." In the clothing factory, a guy kidded him and D. "flew off the handle" until he realized that the guy was trying to be friendly.

R. says that he has difficulty relating to people. When inmates kid him about [the interviewer's] visits, he gets infuriated, even though he knows that they are only kidding.

W. says that prison has made him what he is today. "People have treated me like dirt, so whenever anyone does something nice, I get suspicious. . . . Hatred is second nature in prison. I've seen guys stabbed and been mad at them for bleeding on the floor."

M. described a prison he was in in Arizona. He referred to it as a "school for gladiators" where inmates killed, robbed and maimed. He said that this violence left great scars on him. He doesn't like the way he is now, the way he hates. "This is not my real self. My real self is easy-going."

Other inmates actually learn to prefer the aggressive interaction style in prison. They are more comfortable with inmates who are open about their hostility and ready to use violence than with people on the outside whom they view as more devious about expressing anger. Here is an inmate who compares the behavior of "crooks" and "Square Johns."*

B. says that he is not used to dealing with "Square Johns." "They are a bunch of sick bastards. When you are dealing with a con, you know what is expected of you, what is going to happen when you do something wrong. He may confront you about it or, if it is really wrong, he may do something about it. But the Square Johns are two-faced. They say one thing to your face and another thing behind your back. Crooks at least are honest that way. . . . There are a lot of confrontations in prison. One con will say, "Go screw yourself" and the other will say, "Go fuck yourself" and it ends there, or maybe they will confront each other about it. But a Square John won't do that; he goes right to the man.

Relating to Inmate Friends

While inmates express almost complete alienation from the convict population as a whole, they sometimes develop ties to individual inmates. Clemmer describes four types of inmates according to their friendship patterns: the complete clique man, comprising 18 percent of the inmate population, who has close ties to two or three other inmates; the group man, comprising about 40 percent of the inmate population, who is friendly with other inmates but limits his involvement; the semisolitary man, comprising about 40 percent of the inmate population, who is civil to other inmates but not involved with them; and the complete solitary man, comprising about 3 percent of the inmate population, who is completely cut off from other inmates. A more recent study by Toch minimizes the extent of close ties among inmates, stressing that "memberships in groups are temporal and artificial, and where groups may be friendly, there are few friends." Other researchers have shown

*The interviewee uses the term "Square John" to refer to people who have never been in prison rather than, as it has generally been used in the literature, to refer to middle-class inmates.

that inmates tend to choose friends who share criminal histories and attitudes [10].

Though they reject the majority of their fellows, the inmates we interviewed often chose a small group as friends. All but one inmate in our sample fit into the group man or semisolitary man categories described by Clemmer, that is, they had guarded friendships or at least friendly interactions with a few other inmates.

As compared to relationships on the outside, relationships among inmates are limited in content, commitment and reciprocal obligations. This pattern stems from the situation in which inmates find themselves, which makes it safer and more comfortable to become somewhat involved, but not highly involved.

Getting into Trouble

These contradictory forces are revealed when inmates discuss "getting into trouble." Being highly involved with other inmates is a sure way to get into trouble; yet, if an inmate is isolated, he will be unprotected in times of trouble.

In orientation sessions, prison staff warn new convicts that having inmate friends can lead to trouble. Inmates generally believe this. Getting into trouble may have hardly concerned them in the past when there was little the prison system could do to reward them for compliance; today, however, when the administration can offer early release, furloughs and transfers to better facilities, getting into trouble carries a high personal cost that most inmates wish to avoid.

Relationships with other inmates can cause trouble in several ways. The nature of peer influence on inmates is shown in the fact that they tend to express more antisocial norms when they are in the presence of friends than when they are alone [11]. Thus, fear of losing face in front of friends can lead an inmate to take risks he would not otherwise take.

> . . . if a guard tells you to do something, you have to decide whether to do it or to tell the guard to screw. If you are with friends and you are afraid that they are going to think you are a chump, you may tell the guard to screw. But if you want to get paroled as soon as possible, you do what the guard tells you to.

If an inmate has friends, he may feel obligated to do favors for them that may expose him to the risk of punishment by the administration. Commonly sought favors include hiding contraband, smuggling in money or drugs, and appropriating

some article from the prison supply. In the following quote, the interviewer describes an incident in which an inmate reluctantly acquiesced to his friends' expectation that he smuggle in contraband for them.

> M. was called over by another inmate. When he returned, he told me that he was supposed to sneak in a vial of pills that the other inmate's visitors had brought. He said that he planned to bring it in inside his pants and that he was really "uptight." When I asked why he had to be the one to bring it in, he explained that he was in a kind of clique, and only three of them were outside with visitors and the other two were visibly high, so it was up to him.

Convicts are particularly afraid that their friends might entangle them in violence. If an inmate has friends, he may feel obligated to defend them if they are attacked; this is dangerous because it may involve both personal injury and punishment by the administration.

> G. says that he has gotten to know a number of inmates well, but hasn't gotten close to anyone. "If you get involved and somebody attacks a friend, then you have to get into a fight and pretty soon it's war. I don't want any of that."

While having inmate friends may expose the inmate to trouble, if he is isolated, he will be alone if he gets into trouble. If he needs a favor of some kind, he will have no one to ask unless he has friends; and if he is threatened with violence, he will have no one to call to his aid. The inmate quoted below describes his reliance on friends for protection coupled with his reluctance to get friends involved.

> The Blacks in prison stick together and for some reason the Whites do not. If you get in a hassle with a Black, he will come back for you with fifteen other Blacks. All you will have on your side is three or four of your best buddies and they don't really want to get involved. So you are caught in a bind; you really don't want to get them involved but you don't want to get killed either.

While most inmates describe themselves as potential victims and claim that they need other inmates for protection, some inmates value the fact that having friends allows them to be violent toward others. The inmate quoted below contrasts his situation in one prison where he was isolated with his status in another where he was a member of "the toughest gang."

I was in prison six or seven times and in jail thirty or forty times. These were mostly Black jails. I watched myself there and kept to myself. Then I wound up in a White prison. There were gangs up there of White guys. What's more, I got picked out to be a tough guy and I got involved with some of the guys who were in the toughest gang. I wasn't scared anymore. At first I went to the extreme. I started getting violent. . . . It was a stupid thing to do, childish or whatever. But I learned something from it. I gained a lot of confidence.

Trust vs. Mistrust

Another theme inmates mention when they discuss their choices of friendship patterns is trust. Many inmates have more confidence in other inmates than they do in their friends outside of prison. They often feel betrayed because friends do not visit or because they find it hard to have confidence in people with whom they have occasional contact at best and whose daily actions they can hardly see. In contrast, they are physically close to other convicts and can observe their words and actions every day. This physical closeness can generate a certain degree of trust. Still, inmates usually have a large reservoir of mistrust of other inmates. Some feel that inmates are naturally untrustworthy and exploitative; others feel that the prison by its very structure encourages inmates to betray each other. Inmates thus often feel enough trust to cautiously befriend each other, but not enough to develop relationships that would empower their friends to harm them. They therefore prefer not to reveal any vulnerability or weakness, to conceal any facts that could be used against them and to resist being dependent on friends. Inmates do this at a heavy cost to themselves for, as Toch documents, they feel a need for trust, emotional feedback, and relationships where they can express fear and vulnerability, and they are cut off from people on the outside with whom they could fulfill these needs [12]. When they develop their friendship patterns, inmates make compromises based on the degree of trust and mistrust they feel and on the strength of their friendship needs. Sometimes inmates deal with the situation by making friends but not trusting them, as the following quote illustrates:

C. says that Bobby is his best friend in prison, but he really doesn't tell him anything personal about himself as he fears he will tell others. C. says that I [the interviewer] am really the only person he can talk to.

Other inmates face conflicts between mistrust and the desire for closeness. This conflict was experienced very strongly by the inmate quoted below who reveals that while he looks upon his friend almost as a brother, experience has taught him that he cannot let his guard down.

M. says that in prison a person is very dependent on friends. You eat and work together. To him, his "partner" is almost like a brother. "When he hurts, I hurt. But still, I can't let my guard down. If you let your guard down, you lose control. . . . Every time I've let my guard down, I've been shit on."

Emotional Commitment

Emotional commitment is a third theme inmates mention in relation to their choice of friendship patterns. These men desire involvement in emotionally committed relationships. Few have the emotional commitment they want with people outside of prison. Accordingly, it would seem that they would be motivated to develop with other inmates the kind of close bonds found among males in institutions such as the army and the police force. Inmates, however, generally do not want this.

Inmates offer three reasons for their desire to remain emotionally distant from their peers. One is that they want to leave the prison situation behind as soon as possible and strong ties with other inmates will keep them connected to prison. Like the junior executive who eschews close relationships with other junior executives since they might hinder his rise in the firm [13], some inmates fear that close association with other inmates will tend to keep them in the "same old bag." In addition, inmates often view other inmates as doomed to fail; they fear emotional commitment because they do not want to suffer the pain of witnessing the failure of the person to whom they are committed. Third, inmates feel that neither they nor their friends are in control of their lives. The prison system decides when inmates will be separated and when they will be brought together and the emotional costs of being separated from friends by transfer or release may outweigh the benefits of commitment. One inmate explained why it was essential to "do your own time" and not to get too deeply involved with other inmates:

You may get close to someone in prison and he is switched to some other prison; you want to feel, "OK, nothing has changed, life goes on as before." Of course, you feel bad when friends leave, but it really doesn't make a difference.

Thus, while inmates desire emotional closeness, their ambition to cut their ties with the prison system, their desire to distance themselves from failure, and their lack of control over their situation raise the cost of involvement and lead many inmates to "hang loose" emotionally.

In the following passage an inmate combines elements of these themes to explain his formula for relating to other inmates:

R. told me that he knew how to "do easy time." He says that "you basically have to keep to yourself; you get up in the morning, eat, do your job, see your friends at lunch, talk about old times, go to sleep at two in the afternoon, eat dinner, maybe play softball or read. Sometimes there's something special like ordering sausages and cooking them up and making subs." Everything is very routine and you "kind of just float through. The day kind of slips by." He said that the biggest difference between prison and the outside is that on the outside you have to be with people and in prison you get used to being alone, because that's how you have to be in prison. I asked him what he meant when he said that you have to be alone in prison. He replied that it meant two things: first, that the amount of hours you spend with your friends is small and second, that you have to "do your own time." He illustrated the second point as follows. "For instance, if a guy has a father figure in prison, somebody whom they imitate and admire, this is bad; this is not doing your own time. When you're in prison, you always have to make decisions and they have to be your own decisions. For instance, if a guard tells you to do something, you have to decide whether to do it or to tell the guard to screw. If you are with friends and you are afraid they are going to think you are a chump, maybe you'll tell the guard to screw. But if you want to get paroled as soon as possible, you do what the guard tells you to do. But you can only do that if you are doing your own time. Also, you may get close to someone in prison and he is switched to some other prison; you want to just feel, 'OK, nothing has changed; life goes on as before.' Of course you feel bad when friends leave, but it really doesn't make a difference. Also, if someone you know gets into trouble, you don't want to have to get into trouble yourself; maybe he's pulling some ragtime and you don't want to get involved. He may ask you and you say, 'Hey man, do your own time.' "

The Nature of Prison Friendship

In comparison to friendships on the outside, prison relationships are very limited. The mutual obligations that inmate friends honor are restricted. While the right to call upon friends for protection from fellow inmates or from the authorities is frequently invoked, help is often refused or given reluctantly. Inmates more willingly do small favors for friends, such as delivering messages or, in the case of kitchen workers, giving them extra food when they pass on the chow line. In addition, prisoners are often willing to share some of their material possessions, especially food, with friends.

Friendship in prison is limited to the present. Commitment to continue friendships into the future is conspicuously absent. As Toch notes, "In prison there are . . . few alliances that extend beyond the immediate situation" [14]. Rather, there is a strong sense that no obligation will hold for the future, particularly if one or both inmates are transferred or released.

Finally, the emotional exchanges within prison friendships are meager. Inmates remain psychologically isolated; they do not reveal themselves or make themselves vulnerable even in close relationships.

Glaser has noted that the main reason inmates give for wanting friends in prison is the desire for sociability [15]. Such was the case for the inmates we interviewed. Most inmates feel that they must have friends with whom they can pass the time of day or talk with at meals or during their free time. For some inmates, friendship consists simply of exchanging greetings or engaging in occasional short conversations. Others, who are more socially involved, regularly converse with their friends and perhaps sit with them at meals. Still others spend much of their free time in the company of inmate friends and share with them some of the pleasures that are available in prison. As one inmate describes it:

There are a good bunch of guys [on my floor]. We eat together, we rag each other. Sometimes we get food sent in from the outside and make special dishes in the kitchen.

Young inmates tend to be most sociable and often bring a playful, carefree tone to their relationships. The following description is from a nineteen-year-old inmate:

M. has a friend named Z. who is eighteen. He says that they share food, grass and money. They play softball every night and when the weather is good, they sun themselves on the "beach" [a grassy strip to which inmates have access]. M. related, as a funny story, an incident in which he and Z. were in the basement smoking when a guard came down and caught them. When the guard said, "What do you have in your hand?" Z. stepped in front of M. and M. ate the "roaches" [marijuana].

Young inmates sometimes enjoy horseplay together as the following description from a twenty-year-old inmate reveals:

L. is leaving prison in a few days. He says he will probably be given a "party" by his friends. About ten guys will jump him and cover him with shaving cream and punch him a few times. Some guys also get a cold shower. He pointed out another guy whose arm was black and blue from a "party" the night before. I asked L. if there was a chance that someone who didn't like him could use this as a chance to get even, but he said no, because he'd have ten guys on him if he did that.

Skills

Unfortunately, inmate friendships teach few skills applicable to life on the outside. The skills inmates learn are appropriate for relationships that are oriented only toward the present, which involve few mutual obligations and which are conducted in an emotionally defensive way. These skills may impede relationships with men outside of prison; however, since for many inmates relationships in prison are the only important ones in their lives and the only settings in which they can learn how to interact, it is important to consider how severely crippling such limited skills will be when the inmate is released and attempts to establish a family and carry on relationships with a wife and children. Having spent so much time in prison, many inmates either have never learned the appropriate skills or have not used them for so long that they lack the ability to handle relationships that demand emotional involvement, trust, commitment for the future, and a multitude of reciprocal obligations.

REFERENCES

1. Gresham Sykes. 1968. *The Society of Captives.* New York: Atheneum. Gresham Sykes and Sheldon Messinger. 1960. "The Inmate Social System." In Richard Cloward et al. (eds.), *Theoretical Studies in the Social Organization of the Prison.* New York: Social Science Research Council, pp. 5–19. Donald Clemmer, 1958. *The Prison Community.* New York: Holt, Rinehart and Winston.

2. John Irwin. 1970. *The Felon.* Englewood Cliffs, N.J.: Prentice-Hall, pp. 65–67. Oscar Grusky. 1959. "Organizational Goals and the Behavior of Informal Leaders." *American Journal of Sociology,* 65: 59. Bernard Berk. 1966. "Organization Goals and Inmate Organization." *American Journal of Sociology,* 71: 522. David Street, Robert Vinter, and Charles Perrow. 1966. *Organization for Treatment.* New York: Free Press. James B. Jacobs. 1977. *Stateville.* Chicago: The University of Chicago Press, pp. 137–174. Gene Kassebaum, David Ward, and Daniel Wilner. 1971. *Prison Treatment and Parole Survival.* New York: Wiley, p. 330.

3. Kassebaum, p. 30.

4. Erving Goffman. 1961. *Asylums.* New York: Doubleday Anchor, p. 302.

5. Irwin, pp. 29–34.

6. Lloyd McCorkle and Richard Korn. 1954. "Resocialization Within the Walls." *Annals of the Academy of Political and Social Science,* 293 (May): 90.

7. Sykes, pp. 77–78.

8. Hans Toch. 1977. *Living in Prison.* New York: Free Press, p. 143.

9. Toch, p. 155.

10. Clemmer, pp. 113–120; Toch, pp. 194–198; and Irwin, pp. 66–84.

11. Richard Cloward. 1955. In H. L. Witmer and R. Kotinsky, *New Perspectives for Research on Juvenile Delinquency.* Washington, D.C.: U.S. Govt. Printing Office, pp. 80–91.

12. Toch, Chap. 4.

13. Rosabeth Kanter. 1977. *Men and Women of the Corporation.* New York: Basic Books, p. 116.

14. Toch, p. 195.

15. Daniel Glaser. 1969. *The Effectiveness of a Prison and Parole System.* New York: Bobbs-Merrill, pp. 18–21.

Part IV DEVIANT IDENTITY

When a person asks "Who am I?" there are private answers as well as public ones. The private answers—how a person views him/herself—form one's *personal* identity. The public answers—the image others have of the person—provide one's *social* identity. There is sometimes little consistency between the two. Con men, for example, may studiously present social identities that diverge widely from their true, personal identities. Thus they assume social identities that their personal identities, if known, would discredit. This is true for covert deviants generally. When in the company of heterosexuals, for example, the secret homosexual may ridicule or condemn homosexuality, or pretend to be interested in the opposite sex, in order to achieve a heterosexual social identity. The task of harmonizing one's personal and social identities is hard enough for conventional people. For certain kinds of deviants, particularly secret deviants, it is even more complex.

A deviant social identity may lead to a deviant personal identity when a person finds it prudent to accept a publicly attributed deviant status. This passive style of bringing personal and social identities together probably produces relatively little identity conflict. When a person identified as a deviant refuses to take on a deviant personal identity, however, greater identity problems are likely to result.

Social identities may be devised by the person or by others. Spies, for example, consciously devise and enact their own deceptive social identities. Public relations people, gossips, and agents of social control, on the other hand, often cast other people into social identities that may or may not conform to their personal identities.

In a complex, urban society where many people relate to a wide assortment of new, previously unknown people, the opportunity for taking on a new social identity comes up all the time. Similarly, the chance of being cast by someone else into a new social identity is also more likely. In addition, the possibility of having multiple social identities, with different identities for different audiences, also arises. In such a society, then, people often find it difficult to develop a single, coherent social identity; they may also find it difficult to harmonize their personal and social identities. In fact, attempts to manage this problem may produce the very deceitfulness that is presumed to be characteristic of so many deviants.

Because a social identity as a conforming person is usually preferred to a deviant social identity, most deviants need to practice some duplicity. The steady practice of duplicity may enable the deviant to avert conflict between his or her various positions and roles. On the other hand, duplicity may cause such a strain that the deviant gives it up. For example, Edwin Lemert found that with regard to the systematic check forger the need to assume many legitimate social roles and social identities produces a heavy strain;[1] constant impersonations are not easy to maintain. Hence, paradoxi-

---

[1] Edwin M. Lemert, *Human Deviance, Social Problems, and Social Control*, second edition, Englewood Cliffs, N.J.: Prentice-Hall, 1972, pp. 162–182.

cally, discovery and arrest actually solve an identity problem for the forger. In prison the forger at least has an authentic social identity. The strains confronting the systematic check forger typify the kinds of identity problems that many deviants must come to terms with in one way or another.

In this part of the book we examine the issue of deviant identity more specifically. First we consider the process of acquiring a deviant identity. Then we look at the ways a person sustains a particular identity. Finally, we consider the conditions under which a person is most likely to change a deviant identity.

Acquiring a Deviant Identity

People acquire deviant identities in what is often a long drawn-out interactive process. For example, a person performs a deviant act for the very first time and then others respond to the act, usually with some form of social punishment. If the deviant act is repeated, the chances are that the social penalties will be repeated and may even increase. These social penalties, in turn, can alienate the alleged deviant; if the deviant act is repeated again, it may now be done with a degree of defiance. In time, then, a vicious circle tends to evolve. This cycle continues until others have come to expect a pattern of systematic deviant behavior from the "deviant"; in effect they have assigned that person to a deviant role. Reciprocally, the person who is now expected to perform a deviant role comes to see himself or herself in the same terms and may begin to devise ways of continuing the deviant line of action without getting caught. Thus, we see how the interactive process works: the alleged deviant *act* produces the negative *social response* which in time elicits the deviant *social role*, which in turn after a while culminates in the person's adopting a deviant *identity*. The initial deviance, as proposed by Edwin Lemert, is referred to as *primary deviance*, and the deviant role and identity that develop as a result of people's reactions to the initial deviance, *secondary deviance*.[2]

Acquiring a deviant identity follows no consistent pattern, since a reduction in either the frequency of the deviant acts or the severity of the responses of others can diminish the chances of adopting a deviant identity. Reductions in either or both may prevent assignment to a deviant role and the reciprocal deviant self-definition. Increases in either or both, on the other hand, can increase the chances of the social acquisition of a deviant identity.

Several social and cultural conditions affect the process by which people assume deviant identities. These include factors that influence the performance of deviant acts, responses of others, and the definitions of various deviant roles. For example, social responses to initial deviant acts can be extremely effective in discouraging a future career in deviance. Social responses have this effect when they call attention to the marked discrepancy between the deviant act and the kind of person most likely

[2] Edwin M. Lemert, *Social Pathology*, New York: McGraw-Hill, 1951, p. 76.

to perform the role, on the one hand, and the identity of the person on the other hand. Thus, middle-class housewives caught in the act of shoplifting see themselves as being treated as if they were thieves. Being caught awakens them for the first time to the way their families and friends would regard their actions if they knew of them. This awakening usually is sufficient to discourage them from future thievery because they do not see themselves as "thieves."

Usually, when a person embarks on a deviant activity such as shoplifting for the very first time, he or she does not think too much about getting caught. At the same time, the person may justify the act in one way or another. Some justifications before the fact hamper a self-definition as deviant. People who embezzle money, for example, may not define their actions as stealing. Instead, they often tell themselves that they are only borrowing the money and will repay it at the earliest opportunity. Seeing themselves as borrowers, not thieves, embezzlers can justify taking the money.

On the other hand, occasionally a person acquires a deviant identity *before* taking on a deviant role. For example, male adolescents who are aware of a sexual interest in men and who grow up in an environment which defines homosexuality negatively may come to regard themselves as "sick" or "queer." In their case, though they have a personal and secret deviant identity, they may refrain from engaging in any form of homosexual behavior. Hence, they cannot be said to have assumed a homosexual role, though they do have a personal identity as homosexual. We might speculate that the greater the stigma, the more likely it is that a deviant identity can exist without either deviant acts or a deviant role to support it.

People may also engage in a deviant act and expect a severely negative social reaction, only to find that this reaction does not occur. Without a negative social reaction, there is much less chance of being officially labeled as deviant. As a result, although the act has occurred, there is no significant social response to thrust the person into the role of deviant and thereby evoke the reciprocal deviant identity that goes with such a role-assignment.

Thus, the responses of others are crucial when it comes to acquiring a deviant identity. Frequently these others are family or friends. Or they can be agents of social control, such as police officers, teachers, social workers, doctors, or priests. Sometimes, they can be fellow deviants. For instance, a person might experiment with heroin. In an initial act of experimenting with drugs in the company of others, the novice may see himself or herself as merely satisfying a curiosity about the effects of the drug. But later on, drug-using friends may tell the novice that the way to cure withdrawal distress is to take more heroin. The novice may now be on his way or her way to becoming a drug addict, along with its correlative deviant identity, acts, and roles. In this last instance, the responses of deviant others redefine the novice's situation for him/her.

Managing Deviant Identity

In order to sustain a deviant social identity and membership in a deviant group, new members have to incorporate the group's signs and symbols into their own personal styles and to behave according to deviant norms even when they may not especially want to. The novice's deviant identity may then be confirmed by the group. A deviant who fails to learn the appropriate ways probably will not be truly accepted as a member of the group.

Attempts at being a deviant can fail if the audience refuses to confirm the person's deviant social identity. Then there is no effective audience to reward the person's deviant actions or to confirm his/her self-typing. A jack-of-all-trades offender, for instance, may be considered too inept or "unprofessional" to be accepted into more skillful criminal circles. An audience—conformist or deviant—will not confirm the social identity desired by a person who has obviously miscast him/herself, who does not look the part.

Some deviant statuses imply more than one audience, and the various audiences may demand different, sometimes contradictory, roles on the part of the deviant. Deviants with multiple audiences will have problems of identity unless they can clearly understand which audience they are confronting and which role is required at a particular time. It is often the case, for example, that "front ward" patients in mental hospitals are expected by fellow inmates to act "normal," while they are expected by outsiders to act "sick" and in need of treatment.

It should be noted that deviants can often choose among deviant identities, and this is often one facet of managing a deviant identity. This means that there can be "imposters" who sustain deviant identities as well as "imposters" who sustain conventional identities. Some epileptics, for example, try to pass as alcoholics because they see alcoholism as less stigmatized than epilepsy. As long as these pseudo-alcoholics have only limited contact with genuine alcoholics, their secret is probably safe.

To sustain a deviant identity and membership in a deviant group, then, it is necessary to act like other members of the group. Some social conditions are more conducive to this than others. For example, becoming more involved with other deviants and avoiding contact with nondeviants facilitates developing the deviant identity and maintaining the deviant role. It also makes it easier to cast off conventional traits and loyalties. Thus a deviant identity is easier to sustain under these optimum conditions.

Persons who wish to conceal their deviant identity also confront both role and self-problems. As Erving Goffman has pointed out, they can seek to control information about their identity or, if already known about, try to control the tension possible in their face-to-face contacts with others.[3] Stutterers, for instance, may solve these role problems by hiding the fact that they stutter, revealing it on their own terms, or refusing to acknowledge the fact that they are stuttering. And, similarly, when control agents seek to assign a deviant identity, the person at risk of being so designated may try to neutralize the deviant identity. As Gresham Sykes and David Matza have pointed out with regard to delinquency, juveniles may deny responsibility for the behavior, any injury or harm to anyone, or the existence of any victim who really matters. In addition, the delinquent may cite an appeal to higher loyalties (e.g., that his behavior showed loyalty to his friends), or he may condemn the persons' condemning him (e.g., as being hypocrites).[4]

The Transformation of Deviant Identity

As suggested above, some deviants have trouble managing a deviant identity. Fitting social positions, roles, and self-concepts together is too hard or undesirable. Thus the deviant may face an identity crisis that can become the turning point in his or her deviant career. Nonetheless, it is not necessarily true that most deviants are unhappy and wish to renounce their deviance. Conventional stereotypes of deviants suggest as much, but the facts are otherwise. If people can successfully conceal their deviance, for example, they can continue to enjoy their deviance without "paying the price."

A profound identity crisis usually becomes one of the conditions for transforming a deviant identity back to a more conventional one. Discovery, or recurrent feelings of remorse, can produce the crisis, impelling the person to contemplate making some radical changes in his/her life. In such a crisis the mechanisms that successfully sustain a deviant identity usually show signs of breaking down, which in turn intensifies the crisis.

As already noted, assuming and maintaining a deviant identity is not an easy matter. Renouncing one is even more difficult. Even if a deviant experiences an extreme identity crisis, that person may not succeed in transforming his/her deviant identity to a more conventional one. Three factors imperil successful transformation: lack of practice in conventional roles, continued distrust by conventional people, and pressure from fellow deviates to return to their group. Time spent in deviance is time spent away from the conventional world. Legitimate skills may fall into disuse; for example, the alcoholic toolmaker who returns to his craft after years of heavy drinking and unemployment may find that he cannot pick up where he left off. The ex-convict's difficulty in finding work may exemplify the continued suspicion and disapproval that deviants arouse in the larger society. Finally, fellow deviants may press

---

[3] Erving Goffman, *Stigma*, Englewood Cliffs, N.J.: Prentice-Hall, 1963.
[4] Gresham M. Sykes and David Matza, "Techniques of Neutralization: A Theory of Delinquency," *American Sociological Review*, 22 (December, 1957), pp. 667–670.

one to continue former deviations; thus the drug addict, on release from a hospital, may be quickly surrounded by former friends who are eager to supply a free fix.

Deviants who want to return to a more conventional way of life ordinarily have the best chance of success if they join a primary group with similar intentions. The best-known example of such a primary group is Alcoholics Anonymous. The group members reward the ex-drinker for making changes toward conventionality, and they confirm his/her new social identity as a nondrinker. These conditions encourage the deviant to return to conventional life. Such social and cultural supports are not available, however, to many deviants who might want to return to conformity.

13 ACQUIRING A DEVIANT IDENTITY

One important factor in the development of a deviant identity is how other people respond to an alleged deviant act. These other people may be deviants, or they may be conventional friends or family. They may also be official social control agents. In all cases their responses to the would-be deviant have considerable influence on whether the person goes on to a bona fide deviant role and adopts the deviant identity that goes with it.

In the first reading Richard Troiden describes the stages men go through on the way to adopting a homosexual identity. Next, Manuel Crespo shows how entry into a career as a school skipper can become the social basis for ultimately dropping out of school. Finally, Mary Owen Cameron describes how amateur shoplifters, when they are caught, generally quit shoplifting because neither they nor the people close to them think of them as being "the thieving type."

Becoming Homosexual RICHARD R. TROIDEN

In the pages that follow, an ideal-typical model of gay identity acquisition is presented. Data obtained from interviews conducted on a sample of male homosexuals provide empirical support for the model. The model is by no means definitive; rather, it is intended to provide a meaningful framework within which to describe and better understand just how it is that many men who adopt homosexuality as a way of life begin to engage in homosexual behavior, decide to designate their sexual attractions as homosexual, define themselves as homosexual in the sense of an identity, start associating with other homosexuals, and enter into homophile love (as well as sexual) relationships.

According to Warren's (1972) informants, the concept of gay identity contains the components of same-sex sexual activity, same-sex sexual attraction, self-identification as homosexual, involvement in the homosexual subculture, and same-sex romantic attachments. Here, these identities are viewed as being acquired in four stages: sensitization, dissociation and signification, coming out, and commitment.

Method

As a means of ascertaining the ways in which gay men come to realize and decide they are gay, I undertook an interview study of a sample of male homosexuals. The sample was collected by means of the "snowball" technique: contacting men known to me, interviewing them, and then asking each to supply the names of other men willing to be interviewed. Using this technique, 150 men were interviewed, 50 in each of three areas: New York City, Suffolk County (a suburban to semirural area about 50 miles from New York), and Minneapolis, Minnesota. All of the respondents were white. All

were between the ages of 20 and 40; slightly more than half ($N = 77$) were in their 20s, and the remainder ($N = 73$) were in their 30s (or exactly 40 years old). Over a third (36%) had no college education; a third (34%) had attended college; and roughly a third (30%) had at least some graduate school experience. Since many studies of homosexual populations have concentrated on men who frequent gay bars, I sought to incorporate non-gay-bar-goers into the sample. Roughly half ($N = 78$) were bar-goers, and half ($N = 72$) were not. A bar-goer was defined as someone who went to a gay bar for sexual and/or social purposes more than once per month during the previous year.

The Model

Stage 1: Sensitization[1]

As the name *sensitization* implies, it is during this stage that men gain experiences which *later* serve as sources for interpreting their feelings as homosexual. The stage is divided into an early (prior to age 13) and a late (age 13–17) phase, and its hallmark is a sense of apartness from more conventional peers.

Most informants reported that during the early part of the stage they were only dimly aware, if aware at all, of the nature of their sexual orientation. Altman (1971) suggests that prior to adolescence many boys gain certain types of experiences that may later serve as sources for interpreting their sexual feelings as homosexual. Plummer (1975) singles out for special attention events located in social, genital, and emotional spheres as predisposing young men to later self-identification of themselves as homosexual. Unfortunately, Plummer does not specify exactly when those experiences are gained.

Data will be presented which indicate that ex-

Reprinted by special permission of The William Alanson White Psychiatric Foundation, Inc. Excerpt from Richard R. Troiden, "Becoming Homosexual: A Model of Gay Identity Acquisition," *Psychiatry: Journal for the Study of Interpersonal Processes,* vol. 42 (November 1979), pp. 362–373. Copyright © 1979 by The William Alanson White Psychiatric Foundation, Inc.

This work is based in part on research aided by a grant from the National Institute of Mental Health, grant number 1 R01 MH 28155–01.

[1]The terms *sensitization* and *signification* are borrowed from Plummer (1975).

periences in these areas produced a sense of difference during childhood (prior to age 13) that crystallized into a distinct sense of *sexual* dissimilarity during high school, usually before informants reached age 17. It is not so much childhood experiences themselves, then, but the *meanings* which later came to be attributed to them that are important in the acquisition of gay identities. These results also indicate that a majority of the sample recalled engaging in their first homosexual contacts to orgasm during the latter part of this stage.

Of the interviewees, 72% experienced a sense of apartness during preadolescence. The following comments convey the content of this stage:

A Student: I never felt as if I fit in. I don't know why for sure. I felt different. I thought it was because I was more sensitive.

A College Instructor: I felt different due to my interest in school, ineptness at sports, and the like.

A Minister: I felt intimidated by my peers . . . I envied their athletic skills.

A Waiter: I was fascinated by the male body and decided that I wanted to be a dancer. My friends often teased me about it but it didn't upset me all that much because I was good at other sports, too. On a certain level, however, I felt that my fascination with the male body was somehow wrong, but I couldn't tell you why I felt this way.

The comments of all informants are summarized in Table 1. As the table indicates, the most frequently recalled sources of a childhood sense of difference were: alienation, reasons unknown (22%); feelings of gender inadequacy (19%); and warmth and excitement in the presence of other males (15%). The references to alienation and gender inadequacy show that childhood *social* experiences played a greater role in sensitizing a person for subsequent self-definition as homosexual than did preadolescent experiences gained in the spheres of *genitality* (same-sex relations) and *emotionality* (warmth and excitement).

However, this is not to say that feelings of alienation, gender inadequacy, or warmth and excitement either cause or are indicative of homosexuality. Nor is the claim being made that homosexuality causes the emergence of such feelings. Moreover, the assertion is *not* made that a childhood sense of difference is experienced only by persons who later become homosexual, or that differences need necessarily exist between the overt behavior of young males who later acquire gay identities and those who do not. It is quite possible that during their childhood many males who later develop *heterosexual* commitments also feel estranged, for various reasons, from other males.

What *is* suggested here is that homosexual and heterosexual males may differ in terms of the *meanings* they later come to attribute to a childhood sense of apartness. The same childhood

TABLE 1. In What Ways Did You Feel Different During Your Childhood Years?[1]

	Responses	
	%	*No.*
A general sense of alienation; no specific reason	22	30
A sense of gender inadequacy	19	27
Experiences warmth and excitement in presence of other males	15	21
Did not share many interests in common with male age-mates	14	20
Effeminacy	9	13
Awareness of and fascination with male body	6	8
A medical or physical disability	6	8
Was a self-designated homosexual	4	6
Experienced guilt over sexual activity with other males	2	3
Other	2	3
	99	139[2]

[1] As used here, "childhood" refers to the time prior to the 13th birthday.

[2] Responses were obtained from the 108 informants who experienced a sense of difference during childhood. In this and the following tables, the number of responses exceeds the number of informants because of multiple responses.

TABLE 2.   In What Ways Did You Feel Different During Your High School Years?[1]

	Responses	
	%	No.
Less interested than peers in members of the opposite sex	40	71
Felt "unduly" interested in persons of the same sex	14	25
As a consequence of sexual activity with other males	11	19
A sense of gender inadequacy	11	20
Opposite-sex sexual relations were somewhat unsatisfying; something seemed to be missing	9	16
Was a self-designated homosexual	4	7
Alienation	3	6
Homosexual activity was more satisfying than heterosexual activity	2	4
Other	5	9
	99	177[2]

[1] As used here, "high school years" refers to events which occurred between a person's 13th birthday and graduation from high school.

[2] Responses were obtained from the 149 informants who felt a sense of difference during their adolescence.

feelings which the adolescent heterosexual may come to redefine as the initial signs of, for instance, artistic sensitivity may be reinterpreted by the teen-aged male who later becomes homosexual as the first stirrings of homosexual interest. Childhood experiences gained in social, emotional, and genital realms, then, came to be *invested* with homosexual meanings when informants were adolescents. Thus, the reinterpretation of past events as indicating a homosexual potential appears to be a necessary condition for the eventual adoption of a gay identity.

In the later phase of the sensitization stage, during their high school years, usually prior to their 17th birthday, almost all—99%—of the males experienced a sense of *sexual* difference. Informants recollected that a global sense of apartness during childhood crystallized into a subjectively experienced sense of sexual difference during middle adolescence. Reasons offered by informants for this solidification are listed in Table 2. Unlike the childhood sense of difference that mainly grew out of *social* experiences, the grounds for feelings of sexual difference during adolescence stemmed primarily from the spheres of *emotionality* and *genitality:* less opposite-sex interest than other males (40%), undue interest—as defined by informants—in other young men (14%), sexual activity with other males (11%), and gender inadequacy (11%) were the most frequently cited. These responses are significant considering that nearly two-thirds, or 98 of the 150 interviewees, engaged in their first homosexual activity to or-

gasm during this stage, at a mean age of 14.9. This indicates that an important aspect of the process of becoming homosexual involves learning to recognize and define one's feelings as homosexual.

Stage 2: Dissociation and Signification

The hallmark of this stage—*dissociation*—consists of the partitioning in consciousness of sexual feelings and/or activity from sexual identity. Rather than diminishing a growing awareness of "possible" homosexual tendencies, dissociation has the ironic effect of *signifying* these feelings. That is, the very act of dissociation serves to *re-present* to those who practice it that which they are attempting to dissociate—namely, the implications which their same-sex sexual interest or activity may hold regarding the fundamental character of their sexual orientations.

The suspicion that one "might" be homosexual is used to mark the outset of the stage, a point suggested in Plummer's thesis on "becoming" homosexual. The mean age at which participants in this study started questioning their heterosexuality—that is, could no longer take their "straightness" as given—was 17.1. Of the 150 informants, 148 remembered having passed through a period in their lives when they thought they "might" be homosexual but could not tell for sure.

The following comments are fairly representative of the forms dissociation assumed for these men:

A Hotel Desk Clerk: I went into service at 17, mainly to get away from home. That's where I finished high school. Anyway, when I was in service I started to realize that I felt a sexual attraction for other men, that I was as strongly attracted to men as I was to women. I was engaged to be married at the time, so I passed the attraction off as being due to the circumstances—the loneliness and the lack of female companionship. I rationalized my feelings as indicating feelings of deep friendship. But I couldn't seem to stop thinking about it. The possibility that I might be gay terrified me.

A Waiter: Before I was publicly labeled a faggot, I realized that I wasn't very interested in women. I had had enough experiences with girls to realize that while I was aroused by them, I was also aroused by males and wanted to have sex with them. However, I thought this was something I'd outgrow in time, something that would straighten itself out as I matured.

An Auto Mechanic: I had a sexual experience with a neighbor. We got drunk together and we ended up masturbating each other. I felt guilty and ashamed. I knew that the activity was homosexual, but I refused to label myself as gay. I rationalized it away as sexual experimentation and curiosity. Even so, I still worried about it. I didn't like to think that I could enjoy homosexual activity, which suggested homosexual inclinations. I decided that I'd try not to think about my attraction toward men, that if I didn't think about it, it might go away.

Dissociation or the separation of identity from activity and/or feelings is reflected in the examples presented above, where there is a seeming need to explain ("something I'd outgrow"), excuse ("due to . . . loneliness and the lack of female companionship"), or justify ("sexual experimentation and curiosity") the implications which one's acts or feelings have regarding the nature and direction of one's sexual identity.

Table 3 summarizes the circumstances that led informants to question the nature of their sexual feelings. Sexual doubts were prompted by experiences subjects defined as more explicitly homosexual than those which had earlier led them to believe they were merely sexually different. Events most frequently reported as having provided grounds for suspecting homosexual interests were: becoming sexually aroused by another male (24%) and physically enjoyable homosexual experiences or fantasies (23%). Although the homosexual component in these feelings and behavior was recognized during this stage, no degree of permanence was attributed to it. Put somewhat differently, even though informants questioned their sexual feelings, they neither effortlessly nor immediately defined them as decidedly homosexual. Most males attributed a temporary status to the sensations, as a glance at Table 4 will show. Sexual attractions were not labeled as definitely homosexual because they were interpreted as a phase of development that would eventually pass (54%), or because interviewees believed they shared little or nothing in common with homosexuals as a group (22%). In short, the idea that one might possibly

TABLE 3. What Led You to Question the Nature of Your Sexual Orientation?

	Responses	
	%	No.
Becoming sexually aroused by another male or beginning to view other males in sexual terms	24	40
A physically enjoyable homosexual experience or homosexual fantasies	23	39
The desire to repeat a homosexual experience	18	31
Reading or learning about homosexuality	16	28
Heterosexual interests or emotional involvements seemed less strong than those exhibited by male peers	11	19
Developing a "crush" on or an emotional attachment for another male	7	12
Other	1	1
	100	170*

*Responses were obtained from the 148 informants who reported that for a time in their lives they thought that they might be homosexual but couldn't tell for sure.

TABLE 4.   When You Thought You Might Be Gay, What Kept You from Labeling Your Feelings as Such?

	Responses	
	%	*No.*
Viewed feelings as indicating a phase	54	89
Inaccurate knowledge regarding homosexuality led to believe that little was shared in common with homosexuals as a group	22	36
Did not reciprocate sexually (e.g., was passive partner in fellatio) or viewed homosexual activity as an expedient means of sexual release	7	12
No history of homosexual experience or a history of heterosexual experience	8	13
Viewed feelings as indicating tendencies	3	5
Viewed feelings as indicating bisexuality	2	4
Other	3	5
	99	164*

*Responses were obtained from the 148 informants who did not label these feelings as gay even though they suspected they "might" be homosexual.

be homosexual was ego-dystonic for these men at this point in their lives.

Stage 3: Coming Out

The events included within the stage of *coming out* occur relatively close together. Thus, for heuristic purposes, the decision to label one's sexual feelings as definitely homosexual is used to mark the outset of this stage. Self-definition as homosexual, initial involvement in the homosexual subculture, and redefinition of homosexuality as a positive and viable lifestyle alternative are viewed as making up the content of this stage. While the commencement of homosexual activity on a regular basis (one or more times per week) is associated with the stage (the mean age was 21.0), a majority of the sample (68%) experienced homosexual contacts to orgasm one or more times prior to labeling themselves as homosexual. For this reason, changes in the conception of one's identity and of one's view of

homosexuality and homosexuals—rather than homosexual behavior—are seen as crucial to this stage.

Some disagreement exists among both social scientists and members of the gay community as to what is meant by the term "coming out."[2] The ways in which participants in this study defined "coming out" are presented in Table 5. Some disagreement existed among interviewees about the meaning of coming out, with 51% maintaining that coming out refers to the act of defining oneself to oneself as homosexual. This definition is used here.[3]

The decision to label sexual feelings as definitely homosexual is used to mark the transition to this stage; the mean age at which this occurred was 19.7. However, approximately two-thirds of the interviewees ($N = 93$) *did not* designate themselves as homosexual—that is, arrive at homosexual self-definitions—at the time they designated their feelings as such. The

[2] Gagnon and Simon refer to coming out as "that point in time when there is self-recognition by the individual of his identity as a homosexual and the first major exploration of the homosexual community" (1967, p. 131). Hooker's homosexual subjects attributed a somewhat different meaning to the term; they saw it as a "debut . . . of a person who believes himself to be homosexual but who has struggled against it. [Coming out occurs] when he identifies himself publicly for the first time as a homosexual in the presence of other homosexuals by his appearance in a [gay] bar" (1965, p. 99). Still another meaning of the term is offered by the homosexual respondents who took part in Dank's study of coming out in the gay world; his informants tended to use the term to mean only "identifying oneself [to oneself] as being homosexual" (1971, p. 181). Last, Plummer notes that the term can mean something else altogether when used by members of the Gay Liberation Movement, for whom "it means 'going public'— letting oneself be seen in the 'straight' world as homosexual" (1975, p. 147).

[3] The data contained in Table 5 provide some empirical support for each of the definitions of coming out discussed in footnote 2. Of the men interviewed, 51% essentially agreed with the definition offered by Dank's respondents, and 27% attributed to the term a meaning similar to that formulated by Gagnon and Simon. Further, if one can presume that the decision to start actively seeking out other males as sexual partners involved initial forays into social settings reputedly frequented by homosexuals, it could be said that 9% of the interviewees saw coming out in terms somewhat similar to the definitions offered by Hooker.

TABLE 5.   What Does the Term "Coming Out" Mean?*

	Responses	
	%	No.
To admit to oneself a homosexual preference, or decide that one is, essentially, homosexual	31	77
To admit to oneself a homosexual preference *and* to begin to practice homosexual activity	27	41
To start actively seeking out other males as sexual partners	9	13
First homosexual experience as a young adult (i.e., after middle teens)	8	12
A homosexual experience that triggers self-designation as homosexual	1	2
Other	3	5
	99	150

*Informants were asked to define what the term "coming out" meant to them—that is, how they would use the term.

reasons for labeling sexual feelings but not sexual identities as homosexual are listed in Table 6. The most frequently cited reasons for not labeling sexual identities as homosexual were: Homosexual attractions were seen as a phase (34%), as indicating bisexuality (28%), or as a manifestation of homosexual tendencies or inclinations (13%). Thus, these data indicate that many respondents recalled having experienced at least some degree of confusion regarding the nature of their sexual identities in the twilight of their teens. It will be shown that this uncertainty was for the most part eliminated once these men were able to gain accurate knowledge regarding homosexuals and homosexuality.

The mean age at which homosexual self-designation occurred was 21.3. The following comment illustrates the types of circumstances that encouraged self-definition as homosexual:

A Waiter: I met a straight guy when I was in college. He also was studying dance. As our friendship developed, I realized that I was falling in love with him and that I had never cared for anyone as deeply as I cared for him. I think he suspected the way I felt for him but I'm not sure. One night we were out drinking with a bunch of guys at a college bar. We both got rather high and when we returned to the dorm I went with him to his room. It was the beginning of a very beautiful night. I walked over to him, put my arms around him, and kissed him. He reciprocated. We eventually mutually masturbated each other. He is now married and has a family. This incident led a fateful resignation on my part that I was irrevocably gay. Due to the beauty of the experience, however, I was able to rid myself of any doubts I had regarding my being a

TABLE 6.   When You Labeled Your Feelings as Homosexual, What Kept You from Labeling Yourself as Such?

	Responses	
	%	No.
Viewed feelings as indicating a phase	34	35
Viewed feelings as indicating bisexuality	28	29
Viewed feelings as indicating tendencies	13	14
Inaccurate knowledge regarding homosexuality led to belief that little was shared in common with homosexuals as a group	12	12
No history of homosexual experience or a history of heterosexual experience	7	7
Did not reciprocate sexually (e.g., was passive partner in fellatio) or viewed homosexual activity as an expedient means of sexual release	5	5
Other	2	2
	101	104*

*Responses were obtained from the 93 informants who did not label themselves as homosexual at the same time they labeled their sexual feelings as homosexual.

TABLE 7.   What Circumstances Surrounded Your Decision to Label Yourself as Being Essentially Homosexual?

	Responses	
	%	No.
Knowing or meeting other gays socially	33	65
Deciding to put oneself to the "test" by seeking out homosexual contacts to see if this was what was "really" desired	17	33
A physically or emotionally enjoyable homosexual experience	17	34
Fell in love with another male	16	31
A chance homosexual experience or chance entry into a gay social contact such as a homosexual bar	8	16
Realizing that the label "homosexual" applied to oneself as a consequence of reading about or learning of the existence of homosexuals	6	12
Reciprocated sexually	3	6
Other	2	3
	102	200

homosexual as negating the possibility of being a good person.

The circumstances in which informants arrived at homosexual self-definitions are summarized in Table 7. Meeting other gay men was the most common circumstance leading to homosexual self-definition. Males who "tested" themselves differed from males who concluded they were homosexual after a meaningful homophile experience. The former decided to determine their sexual preferences after undergoing an intense psychological struggle, often of protracted duration, during which they attempted to suppress their homosexual feelings. Over time, however, these men decided that any form of sexual identity—heterosexual, bisexual, or homosexual—would be preferable to the sexual ambiguity and confusion they were experiencing. Accordingly, they put themselves to the test—that is, they actively sought out homosexual experiences in order to determine whether or not their inclinations were in fact homosexual. The sense of urgency or need to decide once and for all who and what they were sexually was for the most part absent in the life histories of those men who decided they were homosexual as a consequence of a chance homosexual encounter which they found fulfilling. When these men—as young adults—had the opportunity to engage in homosexual activity, they simply did so, decided they liked it, and consequently defined themselves as homosexual.

The findings presented here partially replicate the results obtained in Dank's (1971) study of

homosexual identity. He also found the mean age of self-designation as homosexual to be 21. In addition, males who took part in this study tended to arrive at homosexual self-definitions in social contexts quite similar to those reported by Dank's respondents. However, these results differ from Dank's with respect to the role played by love as a generating force to homosexual self-definition. Falling in love rather than initiating a love affair with another male enabled a number of informants in this study to arrive at homosexual self-definitions.

Initial involvement in the homosexual subculture also occurred during this stage. When asked, "Which came first, beginning to think of yourself as homosexual or associating with other homosexuals?," 52% of the informants stated both occurred at roughly the same time, 41% said homosexual self-definition took place at least six months prior to interactions with other gays, and 7% claimed they had associated with other gays at least six months before self-labeling.

Once again, this finding is quite similar to Dank's results. Of his respondents, 50% defined themselves as homosexual when they began associating with other homosexuals. The mean age at which participants in this research started associating with other gays—that is, started to involve themselves in the homosexual subculture—was 21.8, in comparison with the mean age for self-designation as homosexual, 21.3. Thus, self-definition and initial subcultural involvement took place quite closely together. However, following the interactionist tradition of George H. Mead, Dank and Warren point out that the real significance of subcultural exposure resides in the impact it has on an individual's sense of identity and his attitudes toward homosexuality.

The opportunity to gain information about homosexuality that runs contrary to society's stereotypes led the men who took part in this study to see both themselves and homosexuality in a positive light. According to self-reports, 87% changed their attitudes about themselves roughly one year after becoming self-defined homosexuals. Self-conceptions were reportedly altered by 6% at approximately the same time as self-designation. Only 11 males experienced no change at all. Of the men who experienced attitude change, 46% viewed the change as positive, leading to a firmer sense of identity, 20% maintained they achieved higher levels of self-acceptance and happiness, and 11% claimed they felt less guilty or anxious about their sexual-emotional preferences. The change in self-image was related by 44% to exposure to the gay world or making a gay friend(s).

In addition to changes in self-image and identity, time spent in the gay world altered the views these men held toward homosexuality. The meaning of the cognitive category *homosexual* was transformed (Dank). Before arriving at homosexual self-definitions, nearly all—94%—of the respondents recalled having viewed homosexuality as a form of mental illness. When interviewed, only two men looked upon homosexuality as a "sickness." The rest saw it as a variation from the norm. When asked how these changes in attitudes were brought about, the vast majority (88%) claimed their favorable views stemmed from gaining the opportunity to meet homosexuals with interests and attitudes similar to their own—men who, like themselves, appear to be heterosexual. In short, differential association elicited and reinforced a positive sense of identity and served as a barrier to and/or neutralized the highly negative images of homosexuals held by dominant groups in American society.

Stage 4: Commitment

Following Warren, the taking of a lover—that is, the fusion of gay sexuality and emotionality

into a meaningful whole—was used to signify the outset of the stage of *commitment*. Commitment is indicated when homosexuality is adopted as a way of life—that is, when men express contentment with their life situations, see no reason to change, or believe nothing is to be gained by choosing bisexuality or heterosexuality.

The taking of a lover *confirms* gay identity. In terms of the perspective of Warren's informants, an individual whose sexual activity is exclusively homosexual, who has been sexually active with other males for an extended period of time, say 20 or 30 years, but who has never entered a love relationship with another male or interacted with other gays socially, would be viewed as possessing a *homosexual* rather than gay identity. Without a romantic involvement—that is, never having had a lover and social interaction with other gays—the individual is defined as lacking a *gay* identity:[4]

The romantic-sexual act fusion . . . serves as a highly significant benchmark symbol of converted self-identity for many . . . members [of the gay community] who . . . indicate that [the linking] of romantic-sex acts . . . differentiates the "true" homosexual from the one who is simply experimenting. [Warren, 1972, p. 223]

The assertion that love relationships are usually initiated in the post-coming-out period has a basis in fact. Current evidence (Gagnon and Simon, 1973) suggests that large numbers of male homosexuals are more likely to enter into love relations after, rather than at the same time as, they label themselves as homosexual. Gagnon and Simon suggest that once familiar with the sexual side of the gay scene, many homosexual men may begin to personalize their sexual encounters, seeking persons from whom social, emotional, and intellectual as well as sexual gratification can be obtained. The data derived from this research bear out this suggestion. When asked, "At the present time do you want a lover (given your own definition of the term)?," 91% replied yes. Further, 76% of the informants answered yes to the question, "Have you ever had a lover?," and an additional 12% indicated they had been in love with another man and would have gladly entered into a love relation-

---

[4] The assertion that the fusion of sexuality and emotionality is a necessary condition for identity development is not new (see Erikson, 1956).

ship had the other person been willing. The men who initiated one or more love relationships entered their first love affair at a mean age of 23.9—approximately 2½ years *after* the mean age of homosexual self-definition.

Contrary to Warren's conception, however, the process of becoming committed to homosexuality as a way of life is seen here as involving more than the taking of a lover. Although a foundation for commitment is laid during the coming-out stage, when men redefine homosexuality as a legitimate life-style alternative, they can still see heterosexuality or bisexuality as more viable and rewarding. In a similar vein, while many men may come to accept a gay identity, they may still place a higher premium on heterosexual or bisexual identities. That is, men may vary in the extent to which they are satisfied with their identities.

Therefore, one's present identity has implications for the future, since today's identity can provide the foundation for tomorrow's interactions. In fact, the degree of satisfaction an individual expresses about his present identity as a future identity is a measure of his commitment to that identity (Hammersmith and Weinberg, 1973). Thus *commitment* to identity differs from *acceptance,* in that commitment presupposes a reluctance to abandon the identity even if given the opportunity to do so. When asked, "To what extent would you say you are accepting of and comfortable with your homosexuality?," 88% of the sample said they were accepting, 11% replied they were somewhat accepting, and only one person stated he was somewhat unaccepting. No one claimed to be completely unaccepting.

When asked, "At this time would you say you are more, less, or about as happy as you were prior to arriving at a homosexual self-definition?," 91% indicated they were more happy, 8% stated they were about as happy, and only one person said he was less happy. Gaining a sense of identity (47%) and a clearer sense of what is desired both sexually and emotionally (13%) were the most frequently mentioned reasons for higher levels of happiness. Thus, perceived levels of happiness increased with the crystallization of a sense of identity.

An increased sense of identity, however, does not necessarily guarantee commitment to that identity. Similarly, increased happiness resulting from a firmer sense of identity does not warrant the presupposition that the newly acquired identity is necessarily the most highly valued one for that person. A compromise might well be involved. In certain instances, *any* conception of identity might be viewed as an improvement over no sense of identity, or over feelings of ambiguity and uncertainty regarding an identity. Some males could feel happier after defining themselves as homosexual and yet remain convinced they would be even more contented living as heterosexuals. Therefore, to be judged as committed, the homosexual should value homosexuality at least as much as, and perhaps more than, the bisexual or heterosexual alternatives, and elect to remain homosexual if faced with the opportunity to abandon his homosexuality.

When respondents were asked if they would choose to remain homosexual if given the chance to abandon the homosexual option, 91% stated they would not become heterosexual even if they knew of a proven method to accomplish this change; 10 indicated they would change; and 3 replied they didn't know what they would do.

The most frequently mentioned reasons for not becoming heterosexual were: contentment and happiness with a homosexual preference (52%); the belief that nothing would be gained by a change of sexual orientation (24%); and a clearly expressed preference for the gay life (14%). These data, then, seem to show that the majority of the males who participated in this research endeavor saw homosexuality as more personally meaningful and rewarding than heterosexuality. One could, therefore, conclude that most of these males are committed homosexuals. In short, given the definition presented here, the vast majority of these men could be described as having acquired gay identities.

Some disagreement, however, exists as to what constitutes the essential element of gay experience. I take exception to Warren's contention that distinctness, a sense of being different or set apart from more conventional persons, is an inescapable consequence of adopting a gay identity. While distinctness probably is acutely experienced at the time of self-definition as homosexual and for some time after—while the experience of being gay is still novel—the effects of time and experience probably distance gays from their unconventionality, thereby decreasing their feelings of distinctness.

When informants were asked, "In what ways

do you think homosexuals are similar to and different from heterosexuals?," they most frequently saw homosexuals as differing from heterosexuals only in sexual behavior and preference (65%). Since the mean age of self-definition as homosexual for the participants in this study was 21.3 and the mean age of these males when interviewed was 30, it is suggested that the effects of time and experience in the gay world provided an opportunity to become distanced from the homosexual role. Such distance might account for the relative lack of overriding feelings of distinctness. Indeed, Martin Weinberg (1970) found indirect evidence for this assertion. He found increasing age to be associated with greater self-acceptance and decreased involvement in the gay community, with corresponding increases in time spent with heterosexuals.

Perhaps the disparity between these results and Warren's can partly be explained by one of the sources upon which she rests her case. She draws heavily upon testimony presented in Donald Webster Cory's *The Homosexual in America*. This work, a combination of autobiography, first-person accounts, testimony, and social commentary, was written (under a pseudonym) by a one-time homosexual who "converted" to heterosexuality. Published in 1951, Cory's work was a contribution insofar as it broke the taboo of silence that had so long surrounded the topic of homosexuality. However, to assume that a 1951 work by a man who decided to relinquish his gay identity can be used in the 1970s to describe the essence of gay identity for men who have no desire to abandon their identities seems, at best, somewhat risky.

Conclusions

A number of comments are in order on the model of gay identity development outlined and supported in this paper. First, gay identities are not viewed as being acquired in an absolute, fixed, or final sense. One of the main assumptions of this model is that identity is never fully acquired, but is always somewhat incomplete, forever subject to modification.

Nor is the model meant to convey the idea that gay identity development is inevitable for those who experience the first stages. Rather, each stage is viewed as making the acquisition of a gay identity more probable, but not as an inevi-

table determinant. As some persons progress through these stages, some steps may be merged or glossed over, bypassed, or realized simultaneously. A kind of shifting effect is probably involved, with some males "drifting away" at various points prior to stage four. It is quite possible that as adolescents, young adults, or even as adults, a relatively large number of males consciously "test" the extent to which they may be sexually attracted to other men. As a consequence of such sexual experimentation, a substantial number of males may decide that homosexuality is not for them and choose to leave the scene entirely. It is therefore quite likely that only a tiny portion of American males who practice homosexual behavior ever take on gay identities. Those who do acquire them exhibit the following characteristics: homosexual behavior, homosexual attractions, homosexual self-conceptions, social as well as sexual affiliations with the gay world, and same-sex romantic attachments.

Perhaps the most striking conclusion that can be drawn regarding the process of acquiring a gay identity is its tenuous character. For a majority of the sample, the route to gay identity was fraught with ambiguity, confusion, and uncertainty. For only a small minority was the gay identity taken on rapidly.

Regarding the reliability of the model, I wish to end this paper with a comment made by David Matza:

The aim of writing is to create coherence. The risk is that coherence will be imposed on actual disorder and a forgery thus produced. No way of avoiding that risk exists, since to write [or speak] is to take on the task of bringing together or organizing materials. Thus the only legitimate question about a work is the measure of imposition or the amount of forgery, the only offsetting compensation the possibility of entertainment or illumination. [1969, p. 2]

I hope that this model will be viewed as an attempt to illuminate the process whereby gay identities are acquired.

REFERENCES

Altman, D. 1971. *Homosexual*. London: Outerbridge and Dienstfrey.

Cory, D. W. 1951. *The Homosexual in America: A Subjective Approach*. New York: Greenberg.

Dank, B. M. 1971. "Coming Out in the Gay World," *Psychiatry* 34:180–197.

Erikson, E. H. 1956. "The Problem of Ego Identity," *Journal of the American Psychoanalytic Association*, 4:56–121.

Gagnon, J. H. and W. Simon. 1973. *Sexual Conduct*. Chicago: Aldine.

Gagnon, J. H. and W. Simon. 1967. "Homosexuality: The Formulation of a Sociological Perspective," *Journal of Health and Social Behavior* 8:177–185.

Hammersmith, S. K., and M. S. Weinberg. 1973. "Homosexual Identity: Commitment, Adjustments, and Significant Others," *Sociometry*, 36:56–78.

Hooker, E. 1965. "Male Homosexuals and Their 'Worlds.' " In J. Marmor (ed.), *Sexual Inversion*. New York: Holt, Rinehart and Winston.

Matza, D. 1969. *Becoming Deviant*. Englewood Cliffs, N.J.: Prentice-Hall.

Plummer, K. 1975. *Sexual Stigma*. London: Routledge and Kegan Paul.

Troiden, R. R. 1977. "Becoming Homosexual: Research on Acquiring a Gay Identity." Doctoral dissertation, State University of N.Y., Stony Brook.

Warren, C. A. B. 1974. *Identity and Community in the Gay World*. Wiley-Interscience (doctoral dissertation, University of Southern California).

Weinberg, M. S. 1970. "The Male Homosexual: Age-Related Variations in Social and Psychological Characteristics." *Social Problems*, 17:527–537.

Weinberg, T. S. 1977. "Becoming Homosexual: Self Discovery, Self-Identity, and Self-Maintenance." Doctoral dissertation, University of Connecticut.

The School Skipper   MANUEL CRESPO

. . . The data for this paper were gathered in 1972 during an eight month period of participant observation and interviewing in an urban, French-speaking, comprehensive high school situated in a low-income area in Montreal. This school had, at the moment of the study, an enrollment of around fourteen hundred students, and was the only comprehensive school in the district.

Forty-five students were interviewed for a period ranging from forty-five minutes to an hour and a half. The interviewees were chosen from those students who had been absent twenty-one days or more during the academic year.[1] Interviews and more informal talks with the teachers, administrative officers, and secretarial personnel were also included data. Finally, information was gathered from the skippers' academic dossiers, as well as from those of non-skippers and dropouts. The non-skipper population consisted of a random sample drawn from the entire population—skippers excluded; the dropouts were those students who had quit school during the 1971–72 academic year.

Although the material cited in this paper comes from conversations and observations during the research stage, the insights and my confidence in the adequacy of the material are the result of a rather long period of participant observation prior to the research itself, when I was a secondary-school teacher. At that time I had some ideas concerning the impact of school organization on students' behaviour, and also some knowledge of teachers' motivations and attitudes toward lower track students. Therefore, when the themes appeared in conversation in the actual research, I could easily recognize them in the context of what I already knew.

The Career of the School Skipper

The career of the school skipper begins for all practical purposes with the first time he or she skips school.[2] Once a student has actually skipped school, he is in a position to consider whether or not the activity is worth doing again. This paper specifically elaborates the considerations and processes by which a student may try skipping and then abandon it, may get into skipping in a more systematic way and then change his mind, or may become, in the course of systematic skipping, increasingly marginal to school life.

Skipping School for the First Time

It is the purpose of this section to account for two seemingly disparate observations: the accidental character of the initial act of skipping as it is described by students, and the heavy concentration of skipping among students in the lower academic tracks.

When students are asked how they came to skip school for the first time, they mention a variety of circumstances ranging from long-term hospitalization to an early morning headache. Some, but not many, mention more specifically school-related reasons. There is no striking pattern to the circumstances they report; these are simply a variety of contingencies which have produced the same result.

R: But tell me, how did it happen that suddenly you became a skipper?[3]
S: Well, my father beats me often. . . . So I stayed three weeks at the hospital; after that, I started to like skipping.
R: When was the first time you missed?
S: It was during the first strike. We'd come and they'd send us home. One morning I came to school and there were classes, but I returned home.
R: When do you skip?
S: It's when I'm in a bad mood.
R: Why are you sometimes in a bad mood?

Excerpt from Manuel Crespo, "Career of the School Skipper," in *Decency and Deviance: Studies in Deviant Behavior,* Jack Haas and Bill Shaffir (eds.). Toronto: McClelland and Stewart, 1974, pp. 129–145.

[1] This is an arbitrary official criterion for defining a chronic absentee. It happened that almost all the students (92 per cent) chosen among those with at least twenty-one days of absence were skippers.

[2] Girls . . . account for 45 per cent of all skippers. From now on, however, for convenience's sake, pronouns will be used in the masculine form.

[3] Since all the quotes have been translated from French to English, the flow and meaning is therefore somewhat altered.

S: It's because I go to bed too late, after looking at the late movie.

S: It was in Grade 5; I had my leg in a cast for two months because of an infection, and then I took a taste to missing school.

R: After that, did you continue missing?

S: Yes.

R: When did you start skipping?

S: In Grade 7.

R: At the beginning of the year, or what?

S: Sometime near May, when the nice weather arrived.

R: How did it happen?

S: A bunch of girls asked me to skip with them and I accepted. After that, I began to like it. I didn't like getting up in the morning . . .

R: How did you start skipping?

S: It was because in a math course I didn't understand anything . . . so, I started not coming.

A student account of skipping would therefore not suggest any particular pattern of skipping and would certainly not suggest a causal or prior relationship between experiences in school and skipping. Yet, even making a generous allowance for errors in the reporting system (errors which could not easily be related to the academic tracks of various students)[4] skippers are overrepresented in the lower tracks.[5] As evidence, 71 per cent of all skippers—as compared with 49 per cent of non-skippers—are located in tracks C and D. In other words, an account of skipping based on student interviews would describe the accidental and contingent origins of skipping, while an account constructed from other data would describe the systematic and school-related origins of skipping.

There are a number of ways in which a discrepancy like this can be accounted for; most of these essentially discount what students say as epiphenomenal. The object here, however, is not to *discount* the affinity between being in a lower track and skipping school, but to account for it in ways which mesh with the students' own descriptions of school and skipping. There are two ways to see this affinity.

First, in what ways does a student's lower track position prepare him for considering skipping? Simply by being in a track in which skipping is concentrated, students are more likely to know others who skip and, in fact, to be invited to skip. More importantly, students who do not find school rewarding are more prepared to consider missing it. In this sense, the tracking system provides the invitational edge to the activity of skipping.

R: What do skippers dislike about school?

S: You know, we're always sitting down, we read, we write on the board, it's boring; we're like in a prison. Outside, it's freedom, lots of air, we walk around . . .

S: I don't get anything from school; it's always the same thing: same teachers, same courses; we don't learn anything. Even when we change class, it's always the same; it's dull, we don't learn anything. Nobody gets anything from school.

These quotes also point to another way in which the affinity between being in a lower track and skipping school can be understood. If being in school offers the lower-track student little satisfaction, the out-of-school skipping experience may only serve to emphasize this fact. The following quote shows in more detail the contrasts between a student's experiences in and out of school, and implies that a student may, in fact, learn more out of school than in it.

---

[4]The absence accounting system, even if it did not function well, was applied evenly to all tracks. Bias may be the result either of teacher's choice or of the secretary's choice: the former for not counting as absent some students, the latter for failing to record the absences. Both attitudes, though possible, did not seem to operate differentially with respect to academic track. With the exception of the daily call of skippers' and absentees' parents (which the secretary sometimes omitted), she performed the remaining duties in an accurate manner, as sustained observation revealed. She could not exercise bias because she knew only the names and numbers of 'foyers' (administrative groupings of students), and not the academic tracks of particular students. Teachers had to send the absences slip to the secretary; they either sent it or failed to send it; they did not seem to have preferences in reporting absences for one track or another, or for some particular students rather than others.

[5]The tracking system was devised as a means of individualizing the learning process. Since individuals differ in intellectual abilities and rhythms of learning, the grouping of students by their abilities was considered the best way for adjusting teaching to individuals. Each grouping constitutes a track, and the system comprises four tracks: enriched, regular, alleviated, and practical. These are arranged in order of the capacities they presumably demand. For purposes of the present research these tracks will be called respectively from top to bottom: A, B, C, and D.

R: What do your friends think of school?

S: They say they don't learn anything here at school, and that they learn better elsewhere, on the street. Let's say they go and walk around, they talk with the men, and they show them things . . .

R: How?

S: They walk around and meet men, let's say a man making a desk; so he shows him how we do it, we take plywood, when they have time on their hands, they'll be able to make a desk; but here at school they don't learn anything. One of my chums is in refrigeration, he shows me something he has learned and it's always interesting. Here at school, we don't learn much; outside we learn a lot.

This interpretation would suggest that many students try skipping, but that lower-track students are more likely to continue skipping. There is evidence that many students have at one time or another skipped school, even fairly systematically. Among the non-skippers in this school (non-skippers at the time of this study are defined in accordance with the school's official criterion—that is, students with fewer than twenty-one absences for the year), for example, 11 per cent of those who had attendance records in their dossiers from previous years had reached the twenty-one absences mark in at least one of their previous years. Presumably, an even greater number of these "non-skippers" have at one time or another skipped school, but not often enough or noticeably enough to hit the twenty-one absences mark. An interesting implication of this observation, particularly in conjunction with qualitative data from students, is that students may try out skipping and then abandon it, either after several experiences or after having skipped over a considerable span of time.

"Getting into" Skipping and "Getting out of" Skipping

Once a student has skipped school for the first time, he is in a position to consider whether or not the activity is worth doing again. Students' considerations have generally to do with three matters: the fear of being caught; the enjoyment derived from skipping; and the assessment of school's relevance for the more long-term future. In relation to each of these matters, students' considerations did not occur individually, but involved the support or lack of support of other skippers.

The first problem a skipping student faces is the fear of getting caught. Interviews reveal that potential skippers are afraid when they start skipping, and that, after a while, they overcome it. This stage is crucial for if they do not overcome this fear, they are unlikely to continue skipping.

R: How can students keep on skipping in spite of the school's supervision?

S: Because they're not afraid.

R: You, why did you become a regular attender?

S: Because me, I'm afraid.

R: Do you skip?

S: I used to, not much.

R: Why?

S: Ah well, it wasn't interesting . . . not that, but I was afraid of getting caught. When I came back to school I thought everybody was looking at me . . . so, I didn't want to continue. My friends weren't afraid; they told me, "They won't get you, you'll see," . . . but I had no confidence.

The company of other skippers serves to reduce this fear. "Experienced" skippers tell the newcomer to take it easy and to control his imagination, for it is not as difficult as he thinks to skip unnoticed: teachers are not at every corner ready to pick him up.

S: At first, when I started skipping I saw teachers everywhere. I thought I'd get caught at every street corner. My chums used to tell me not to be afraid, but I was afraid just the same.

R: And that lasted long?

S: Not really, after a week I wasn't afraid any more.

As part of learning how to cope with their fears of getting caught, skippers learn from one another how to skip with relative safety. Those who skip alone are more easily caught, and they may attribute this to their possible lack of sophistication, a sophistication experienced through the company of other skippers.

S: This year I skipped. I went to the hospital and I missed biology. Next day, I didn't go, I didn't feel like it, but I got caught.

R: How did you get caught?

S: The teacher had noticed that I wasn't present and told Mr._____ (director). He called me through the intercom and told me that if I did it again, that he'd suspend me from school for two weeks.

R: Do the heavy skippers get caught?

S: The others, they don't get caught. They come into the classroom as if nothing had happened and they go to their place; the teacher doesn't say anything to them for having skipped.

Skippers must also find the activity enjoyable. It is evident that those who do not overcome the fear of getting caught do not have much "fun" skipping. Also, if being in school is more interesting, more fun than being out of school, or if skipping is *"platte,"*[6] students are not likely to continue it.

R: What do you do when you skip?

S: We walk around, we don't do anything, it's very boring walking around all the time. We're much better off at school.

The company of others is an important feature of whether or not one has fun. The common pattern of skipping involves the presence of at least one friend with whom even the simplest things become really enjoyable.

R: What do you do when you skip?

S: O.K., we start off and go toward the park . . . there we sit down. . . .

R: Even when it's cold?

S: Yes, we tell jokes, we laugh; after that, we take the metro.

Affiliation with skippers can also make it difficult to say no to a skipping invitation, particularly if one is known to have skipped.

S: Sometimes we don't feel like going, but we go just the same so that, when we'll want to go, we can ask them to come with us.

R: How do students skip?

S: Sometimes, there are some who want to skip and say to others "Come with us." The others, not to look like cowards, will follow them.

R: So you think that sometimes the guys just follow?

S: They want to show off, and that they're not scared.

An analysis of skipping shows that after Grade 9 there is a dramatic drop in its occurrence. How can this be accounted for? To begin with, the drop coincides with the cessation of compulsory education. At fifteen years of age, the student is no longer compelled to attend school. Furthermore, the completion of school life, which in the junior years was so distant, is now in sight; and the element of choice makes it possible to see the future as one's own.

R: You see on this list that there is a radical change, as far as skipping is concerned, between students in Grades 7, 8, 9, and those in Grades 10 and 11. What has happened to make students of Grades 10 and 11 skip less?

S: What happens in Grades 10 and 11 is that those who skip, we see them quit school. At the beginning of the year, we see students who start missing school and suddenly we learn that they've found a job. . . . We're not obliged to come to school, so if we do, we're necessarily interested in finishing; before that, we didn't think of what we were going to do. Now we're beginning to see. . . . In Grades 7, 8, 9, we don't know what we're doing in school.

The "reality" of the future—that is, the possibility of shaping it according to one's own will—is facilitated by the school curriculum. Students can at this point take new courses which lead directly to that future.

At the end of Grade 9, each student chooses what particular orientation he or she would like to pursue. These students are registered in what is called the Long Professional Course. It is open to all Grade nines, but the recruitment is particularly high among students from track C.[7]

Starting in Grade 10, students can choose an occupational orientation. They can learn a trade and feel that they are directly preparing them-

[6]French slang word for boring, tedious.

[7]In 1971–72, according to the division chief, almost 100 per cent of the Long Professional Course was composed of students from track C.

selves to enter the labour market; upon leaving school, girls can obtain a secretarial training.

The experience of work, which for some skippers becomes the decisive element in dropping out, is for others an occasion for a different sort of reflection and a consequent decision to continue.

S: Me, I worked during the summer, so I became more serious and I saw it was better to be at school.

Their future is now patent in the knowledge that they may have difficulty getting ahead without a school degree. They may compare themselves with other workers in the job situation, and see themselves as they will be in a few years, should they cease going to school.

S: When I was working last summer, I met people who were pretty ignorant and I told myself, "It's not a place for me." I had what?—a Grade 9, so I went back for studying.

R: Do you think you'll skip this year?

S: I haven't skipped yet. During the summer I saw that I was earning $1.25 per hour, and my friend was earning $2.35 and we were doing the same thing . . . so I told myself, "If I continue and get my Grade 11 diploma, I will earn the same salary."

R: That made you think, the fact that you weren't getting the same salary?

S: That's it. My friend who gave up school, who was skipping with me last year, doesn't realize it because on his floor everybody got $1.25. But I was mixed up with others who earned more than me. Suppose that you and I, we present ourselves to work, they'll pay a bigger salary to the one who has more studies, they'll even take him before one who has less. My chum, they took him; at the beginning he was supposed to have a steady job, but they slacked him two months after. So he finds himself poor jobs of $1.25 and he's happy. Me, if I saw others earn more than me, I wouldn't be happy; suppose I wanted

to buy a car, I wouldn't be able to and the others could buy it a good two months before me.

Sheer chronological age may also serve to bring the future closer.

R: Do the boys of Grades 10 and 11 skip?

S: They skip less.

R: Why, according to you?

S: It's that they want to keep on; there isn't much time left and they want to continue their studies to have a diploma.

R: And the Grades 7, 8, 9?

S: They don't think about the future too much. In Grades 10 and 11 we think of what we'll do to be happy later. In Grades 7, 8, 9 we don't care about the future, we don't know what we're going to do.

R: But you're in Grade 8.

S: But look, it's like I was in Grade 10. I passed three years in Grade 8. My chum also, last year he skipped and this year he's gone up to Grade 9, and he doesn't skip. It's the same thing, he would be in Grade 10.

R: So, it's a matter of age?

S: We pass from child to adolescent. When we're in 7, 8, 9, we don't think of what we're going to be.

This student stopped skipping and although he is not in Grade 10, he would be had he not tripled Grade 8. He now views school as a means for achieving some social success; but when he was younger he did not.

In Grade 10 and 11, although there are two more years of high school, skippers see this time as being compressed; they have wasted so much time that, in order to catch up, they feel they cannot miss school any longer.[8]

S: In Grade 10 we tell ourselves that we'll succeed better because I have only one year left and if I raise my marks, perhaps I'll be placed in regular.

S: Grade 10 is important because after there's

[8] The idea of future recuperation does not appear to have real grounds in the senior section of this comprehensive school. If one considers the future academic orientation of students who graduated in 1971, it is obvious that, in general, the students see the Grade 11 diploma as terminal. A survey done on 93 or the 137 graduates of the 1970–71 academic year shows that only 25 per cent of them orient their future toward a university diploma. For the rest, the high school is terminal. The survey does not give data of future orientation by tracks, but one can reasonably suppose that the greatest proportion of this 25 per cent is composed of tracks A and B students. There are no data for 1972 graduates. Nevertheless, there are no reasonable grounds for suspecting a dramatic change in their future orientation.

Grade 11, and either we work or we go to college. Those in Grade 7, 8, 9 tell themselves they still have many years to catch up.

R: Do you think that or did those in 7, 8, 9 tell you?

S: They've told me, and I think so too.

Very often skipping friends abandon skipping at about the same time. Although the interviews do not clearly indicate a joint decision to return to normal attendance, the fact of the common "conversion" suggests that some talk has taken place among them concerning the relation between attendance and obtaining a school degree.

The three considerations described—the fear of being caught; the enjoyment derived, or not; and the assessment of school's importance—may lead a student who has tried skipping to abandon it. However, the first two may also lead the skipper to continue skipping and, in fact, to become a systematic skipper.

The Amplification of Deviance

The consequences of systematic skipping go beyond that of material missed due to absence from class. While a student's knowledge, and even the relevant matter of his reputation, could be handled effectively during the times he is in fact in class, skippers' strategies for not getting caught tend to amplify the consequences of missing classes. One way that skippers cover the fact of their having skipped is to maintain a very low profile in class. The disinterested and anonymous impression they maintain merely suggests to the teachers that they are just part of that general body of bored and mediocre students. Furthermore, if they should make an active attempt to catch up or to understand what is going on by asking the teacher to explain something, the teacher will often suggest that the best way to understand is to come regularly, that the subject has been explained, and that there is not time. Should the student want an explanation, he must see the teacher after school. Seeing teachers after school hours is not a customary activity for a great number of students, especially for skippers. They never stay after school hours, unless they are being punished. They see the referral, then, as a polite way of refusing to teach them.

A more radical amplification of the consequences of systematic skipping is provided in the link between the tracking system and skipping. The treatment of lower-track skippers takes on aspects of the teachers' more general treatment of and feelings about lower-track students. Teachers assigned to lower-track students believe that those students are the worst the system contains and that teaching them requires a lot of energy and patience. They do not happily accept an assignment to lower tracks. As one female teacher explained:

Last year, I was all right. I had regular and enriched students. This year, it's more difficult: I was given two classes in the alleviated track. It's different; when I finish my day, I'm glad. Last year, it wasn't the same. I was glad to come to school. This year, it's a big effort.

The same comment, but from the other side—tracks A and B—was made by a male teacher:

This year, I've got the cream. They are little boys who want to learn. There are a few frictions, but not serious ones; we get along well together. I give them some work and right away, they start doing it. It's generally very well done. I don't have any difficulties with them.

As assignments are based on seniority—though the administrative officer in charge may deny it—young teachers and newcomers have to teach students from tracks C and D.[9] Lower-track students therefore become in the eyes of these teachers indicators of their own low status.

The treatment of lower-track students—the comments on their performance, the comparisons made with higher-track students, and the aggressive behaviour toward them—does not fail to have an affect on them.

R: Why do young people become skippers?

S: They come in and the teacher tells them, "What are you coming here for? To be like that, it's much better that you stay home!"

---

[9]The same administrative officer denied that some teachers were assigned exclusively to lower tracks. This assertion was not accurate either. Late transfers from another school were often assigned to what remained, that is, to lower tracks. Only 18 per cent of mathematics teachers, and none of the French teachers (the survey covers 70 per cent of all these teachers) had an even assignment, that is, an assignment with equal numbers of higher and lower tracks.

And the student stays home! He's not interested in having these things said to him.

It has been suggested above that the first acts of skipping provide students with comparisons between their experiences being in school—experiences significantly determined by their lower-track status—and their experiences out of school. Skipping can clarify, organize, and thus amplify the experience of being in a lower track. In other words, the combined effect of being in a lower track and skipping escalates the sense that school, and being there, is useless.

S: It's strange, sir, we're here like in nothing. . . .
R: What do you mean?
S: We're apart, . . . the teachers don't ask us questions: when we're in the shops, they watch us as if we were going to commit a crime . . . the courses are not the same as the others'. . . .
S: What's the use, sir, of coming to school? It doesn't lead anywhere, the alleviated course; and if on top of that we have poor results. . . . Do you know what an employer thinks when we go see him and show him our report card, and he sees "alleviated"? With the alleviated course we're blocked; we can't go far.

Since they play an important part in the process by which a skipper becomes increasingly marginal to school life, the effects of the school's attempts to control skipping should be considered. When the director of students comes to know about the frequent absences of a particular student, he initiates a set of actions intended to get the student back in school. Generally, he first tries to talk with the student in order to find out the real reason for the absences. When the interview fails, as it often does, he calls the parents to inform them about the student's behaviour. If there is no change, he has the secretary send a letter to the parents.

The letter is a special form which notifies the parents that student X has been absent for a precise number of days and provides a space allowing the parents to write the reason for the absences. It is rare to find in the parents' responses an incrimination of the student's behaviour.

Generally, parents give sickness and babysitting as reasons for the absences.

When there is no answer to the official form, or when absences continue to be frequent, the director of students refers the case to the controller, whose duty is to contact the student's family in order to find some way of getting the student back to school. Basically, the controller's activities consist of a series of telephone calls and visits to homes. The reports to the director frequently state that the student concerned is willing to return to school. In other cases, the controller may try to intimidate parents, reminding them that there is a law to protect children and that family allowances may be suspended if they do not send their children to school.

The effectiveness of the controller's action is doubtful. The majority of the skippers visited by the controller continue to skip school as frequently as before. This is evident when one compares the date of the controller's report and the absentees' cards.[10]

It is clear, therefore, that although these efforts do not contribute directly to the marginalization of students, they do not contribute much in the other direction either; that is, these efforts do not succeed in integrating students back into the school.

The second line of response to the systematic skipper contributes directly to his marginalization from the school. It is perhaps ironic that the most severe measure a school can take against a student—suspension—enforces skipping while presumably being a measure for controlling it.

R: O.K., they don't like a teacher, a course or the school. . . . What is it exactly they don't like?
S: They don't give a damn about the school. There are even students who miss for two days and if they're caught, they're suspended for a month, so they're proud of that. . . . When they come back, they get suspended again by missing again!

The irony of this response is not unobserved by students themselves. As one student, who was suspended for, among other things, skipping and who refused to return to school when his time of exclusion expired, pointed out:

[10]There is a card for each student. Every day the secretary in charge of absences sorts the absentees' cards and marks the absences in the appropriate place.

They kicked me out of school: they didn't want me. . . . I found a good job and they came to get me back. They're all crazy in this school!

The third line of response is not one taken directly by the school, but by the police—generally, by its Youth Division. Police activity concerning skippers consists essentially in patrolling the streets of the neighbourhood and asking suspects if they are still students. They sometimes force skippers to return to school at once, by picking them up and bringing them *manu militari* to the school.

The police play an important part in the skipper's universe: some characteristics of skipping, namely the number of participants and the place of the activity, are geared to avoid police vigilance. The reason for this importance lies perhaps in the fact that, although police do not mistreat skippers, being picked up by the police and particularly being brought back to school by them is highly noticeable and generates a more serious impression (for oneself and others) of one's deviant status.

The processes in which school skippers are involved do not end, at least in the school under study, only in skipping. As a consequence of the processes just described, skippers become more and more identified with a version of themselves as marginal to school life. When they become fully identified with this version, dropping out becomes sensible to them.

Among the skippers that dropped out during the year under study, 60 per cent were registered in the lower tracks. If one considers not only the skippers registered in the lower tracks, but also those with at least one subject in a lower-track level, the percentage rises to 82 per cent.[11] Such a high percentage is indicative of the impact of marginalization in the final outcome of the skipper's career.

Many skippers felt that they did not have the qualities required to fit into the school setting. They considered themselves different from other students.

R: How do you succeed in your classes?
S: Not too well. . . .

R: Are there girls who get better marks than you?
S: Yes, the teacher's pets, the little squares, they're always studying. . . .
R: Do they skip?
S: Never, they're much too scared!
R: Do the "squares," as you call them, make fun of you?
S: Never! I sure would like to see that! No, they're scared; they're always busy working. If we talk to them, they say, "Let me work." . . . They're sick!

Much of systematic skipping can be treated as commitment to a certain line of activity. The student becomes committed to skipping through the fun he has doing it; through the contrast it provides with his experiences in school; through the obligations and pleasures he shares with skipping friends; and through the several difficulties skipping generates for the possibility of catching up. These are commitments which may be reversed; but they may also become the material for confirming a view of self as unfit for school. At this point systematic skipping becomes a matter of identification rather than commitment, as students become more and more identified with a version of themselves as marginal to school life. When the skipper finally views himself in the same terms as the school views him, he drops out.

School skipping in this comprehensive school may be understood then in terms of a deviant career. The trajectory of the career moves from an accidental beginning to a final confirmation of marginal identity expressed by dropping out, unless skippers' considerations about the activity lead them to abandon it. Between the beginning and the most logical outcome—dropping out—the potential skipper constructs his deviation within the context of the school.

There is a patent irony in organizational processes: the official ideology claims that the aim of the new comprehensive school, and of the tracking system, is to individualize teaching in order to process most effectively the majority of students through the secondary level of education. This ideology, however, plays an active part in marginalizing and extruding students from school. . . .

---

[11] It is worth noting that profiles of skippers and dropouts have several traits in common. They have a similar past history of absenteeism; their respective distributions by tracks, although not exactly the same (skipping does not necessarily precede *all* dropping out), bear definite resemblances; in academic performance dropouts are closer to skippers than to non-skippers. However, dropouts are not found exclusively (as skippers) in the lowest economic strata of this school.

Identity and the Shoplifter

MARY OWEN CAMERON

It seems probable that most adult pilferers start their careers as children or adolescents in groups where the techniques of successful pilfering are learned from other more experienced children. Later as group activity is abandoned some of the group members continue the practices they learned as adolescents. The lavish displays of merchandise which department stores exhibit to encourage "impulse buying" are, for the experienced pilferer, there for the taking.

Adult women pilferers, generally belonging to families of rather modest income, enter department stores with a strong sense of the limitations of their household budgets. They do not steal merchandise which they can rationalize purchasing: household supplies, husband's clothes, children's wear. But beautiful and luxury goods for their personal use can be purchased legitimately only if some other member of the family is deprived. Although pilferers often have guilt feelings about their thefts, it still seems to them less wrong to steal from a rich store than to take from the family budget. Pilferers seem to be, thus, narcissistic individuals in that they steal for their own personal use, but, on the other hand, they do not use the limited family income for their own luxury goods.

Pilferers differ in one outstanding respect, at least, from other thieves: They generally do not think of themselves as thieves. In fact, even when arrested, they resist strongly being pushed to admit their behavior is theft. This became very clear as I observed a number of interrogations of shoplifters by the store detective staff, and it was supported in conversations with the detectives who drew on their own wider experience. It is quite often difficult for the store staff to convince the arrested person that he has actually been arrested, even when the detectives show their licenses and badges. Again and again store police explain to pilferers that they are under arrest as thieves, that they will, in the normal course of events, be taken in a police van to jail, held in jail until bond is raised, and tried in a court before a judge and sentenced. Much of the interview time of store detectives is devoted to establishing this point; in making the pilferer understand that what happens to him from the time of his arrest is a legal question, but it is still a question for decision, first of all, by the store staff.

Store detectives use the naivete of pilferers as an assistance in arrest procedures while the pilferer is in the presence of legitimate customers on the floor of the store. The most tactful approach possible is used. The store detective will say, for example, "I represent the store office, and I'm afraid the office will have to see what's in your shopping bag. Would you care to come with me, please?" If the pilferer protests, the detective adds, "You wouldn't want to be embarrassed in front of all these people, would you? In the office we can talk things over in private."

Edwards states that the method of making an arrest is important in preventing excitement and even disorder.

A gentle approach will usually disarm any shoplifter, amateur or professional, while a rough seizure or loud accusation may immediately put him on the defensive. At other times it may result in a nervous or hysterical condition accompanied by an involuntary discharge which may be embarrassing to both the arrestor and the arrested.[1]

Inbau adds the thought that the gentle approach is helpful too in forestalling suits for false arrest.

The finesse with which defendant accosts plaintiff is a definite factor also affecting the temper with which the court approaches a case. The defendant acting in good faith with probable cause, whose attitude is quite, non-threatening, and deferential to the plaintiff's feelings can weather an honest mistake much more cheaply than otherwise. At the most it may induce a court to find there was no imprisonment at all. At the least, it will relieve the defendant of punitive damages and reduce the amount of actual damages.[2]

[1] Loren Edwards, *Shoplifting and Shrinkage Protection for Stores* (Springfield, Ill.: Charles C Thomas, 1958), p. 134.

[2] Inbau, Fred E., "Protection and Recapture of Merchandise from Shoplifters," *Illinois Law Review.* Vol. 46, No. 6, 1952.

The "deference" of the arresting detective combined with the already existing rationalizations of the pilferer sustain in him the belief that whereas his behavior might be reprehensible, the objects taken were, after all, not of great value, he would be glad to pay for them and be on his way. "Yes, I took the dress," one woman sobbed as she was being closely interrogated, "but that doesn't mean I'm a thief."

Arrest forces the pilferer to think of himself as a thief. The interrogation procedure of the store is specifically and consciously aimed at breaking down any illusions the shoplifter may have that his behavior is regarded as merely "naughty" or "bad." The breakdown of illusions is, to the store detective staff, both a goal in itself and a means of establishing the fact that each innocent-appearing pilferer, is not in fact, a professional thief "putting on an act." In the interrogation the shoplifter is searched for other stolen merchandise and for identification papers. Pockets and pocketbooks are thoroughly examined. All papers, letters, tickets, bills, etc., are read in detail in spite of considerable protest from the arrested person. Each person is made to explain everything he has with him. If suspect items such as public locker keys, pawn tickets, etc., are found, he will have to explain very thoroughly indeed and agree to have the locker examined and the pawned merchandise seen to avoid formal charge. In any event, once name, address, and occupation have been established (and for women, the maiden name and names in other marriages), the file of names and identifying material of all persons who have, in the past years, been arrested in any of the State Street department stores is consulted. The shoplifter is questioned at length if similarities of names or other identifying data are encountered.

While identification and prior record are being checked, store detectives, persons in charge of refunds, and even experienced sales clerks may be summoned to look at the arrested person to determine if he has been previously suspected of stealing merchandise or has been noted as behaving suspiciously.

In the course of all this investigation, it becomes increasingly clear to the pilferer that he is considered a thief and is in imminent danger of being hauled into court and publicly exhibited as such. This realization is often accompanied by a dramatic change in attitudes and by severe emotional disturbance. Occasionally even hysterical semi-attempts at suicide result.

The professional shoplifter who has been arrested and knows he is recognized, on the other hand, behaves quite differently. He does, of course, make every effort possible to talk his way out of the situation. But once he finds that this is impossible, he accepts jail and its inconveniences as a normal hazard of his trade.

"This is a nightmare," said one woman pilferer who had been formally charged with stealing an expensive handbag. "It can't be happening to me! Why, oh why can't I wake up and find that it isn't so," she cried later as she waited at a store exit, accompanied by a city and a store policeman, for the city police van to arrive. "Whatever will I do? Please make it go away," she pleaded with the officer. "I'll be disgraced forever. I can never look anyone in the face again."

Pilferers expect no "in-group" support for their behavior. As they become aware of the possible serious consequences of their arrest (trial, jail, etc.), pilferers obviously feel isolated from all supporting relationships. Store detectives report that the most frequent question women ask is, "Will my husband have to know about this?" Men, they say, express immediate fear that their employers will be informed of their arrest when questions about employment are raised. Children are apprehensive of parental reaction. Edwards says,

The composure of juveniles being detained has never ceased to amaze me, that is, until notified that they must tell a parent of their misdemeanor. Then the tears flow and pleadings begin. The interviewer must be firm in his denial that notification will "kill" the parent, and he must sell the child on the idea that any deviation from accepted practice must be discussed with the person most interested in his welfare.[3]

Pilferers feel that if their family or friends learn about their arrest they will be thoroughly disgraced. The fear, shame, and remorse expressed by arrested pilferers could not be other than genuine and a reflection of their appraisal of the attitudes they believe others will take toward them. One woman was observed who, thoroughly shaken as the realization of her predicament began to appear to her, interrupted her protestations of innocence from time to time,

---

[3] Edwards, *op. cit.,* pp. 135–136.

overwhelmed at the thought of how some particular person in her "in-group" would react to her arrest. Her conversation with the interrogator ran somewhat as follows: "I didn't intend to take the dress. I just wanted to see it in daylight. [She had stuffed it into a shopping bag and carried it out of the store.] Oh, what will my husband do? I *did* intend to pay for it. It's all a mistake. Oh, my God, what will my mother say! I'll be glad to pay for it. See, I've got the money with me. Oh, my children! They can't find out I've been *arrested!* I'd never be able to face them again."

Pilferers not only expect no in-group support, but they feel that they have literally *no* one to turn to. The problem of being embroiled in a wholly unfamiliar legal situation is obviously not only frightening but unexpected. Apparently they had anticipated being reprimanded; they had not anticipated being searched by a licensed detective, identified, etc., and on the whole, placed in a position in which the burden of argument for keeping out of jail is theirs.

The contrast in behavior between the pilferer and the recognized and self-admitted thief is striking. The experienced thief either already knows what to do or knows precisely where and how to find out. His emotional reactions may involve anger directed at himself or at features in the situation around him, but he is not at a loss for reactions. He follows the prescribed modes of behavior, and knows, either because of prior experience or through the vicarious experiences of acquaintances, what arrest involves by way of obligations and rights. He has some familiarity with bonding practice and either already has or knows how to find a lawyer who will act for him. *Because the adult pilferer does not think of himself, prior to his arrest, as a thief and can conceive of no in-group support for himself in that role, his arrest forces him to reject the role* (at least insofar as department store shoplifting is concerned). The arrest procedure, even though not followed by prosecution, is in itself sufficient to cause him to redefine his situation. He is, of course, informed that subsequent arrest by any store will be followed by immediate prosecution and probably by a considerable jail sentence. But since this does not act as a deterrent to the self-admitted thief nor could this kind of admonition deter the compulsive neurotic, neither the fear of punishment nor the objective severity of the punishment in itself is the crucial point in relation to the change from criminal to law-abiding behavior. Rather the threat to the person's system of values and prestige relationships is involved. Social scientists who have investigated criminal activities which have subcultural support are unanimous in pointing out the persistence of criminal activity, the high rate of recidivism and the resistance to reform shown by law violators. Pilfering seems to be the other side of the coin. Not having the support of a criminal subculture, pilferers are very "reformable" individuals. If the findings of this study are substantiated by studies of other offenses in which the offenders are similarly without support of a criminal subculture, there would be a strong argument in favor of keeping pilferers out of jail lest they receive there the kinds of knowledge and emotional support they need to become "successful" commercial thieves. Crime prevention would seem best achieved by helping the law violators retain their self-image of respectability while making it clear to them that a second offense will really mean disgrace.

14 MANAGING DEVIANT IDENTITY

Once a deviant identity has been acquired, problems can arise in managing it. Deviants must decide how much to integrate their social identities with their personal identities in various social situations. With other deviants it is often wise to be open about one's deviance; with nondeviants it is seldom so. How deviants manage their deviant identities affects how they fare in their deviant careers—how long these careers last, how successful they are, and whether and how the deviants can ever terminate them.

In the first reading Michael Petrunik and Clifford Shearing describe how stutterers cope with their disability by concealing, revealing, or disavowing stuttering. Next David Davis illustrates how the bailbondsman's work, which presupposes a deviant identity, makes for two styles of stigma management. Then Diana Scully and Joseph Marolla explain how convicted rapists use a variety of excuses and justifications to disavow their social identities as rapists. Finally, Albert Reiss describes how teenage youths can engage in homosexual activity without assuming a homosexual identity.

Stutterers' Practices

MICHAEL PETRUNIK
and CLIFFORD D. SHEARING

. . . Stuttering is a puzzling disorder of human communication which has defied explanation and cure for thousands of years (Van Riper, 1971:2). According to survey estimates in Europe and North America, stutterers constitute about 1 percent of the school-age population, regardless of language or dialect (Bloodstein, 1981:79; Van Riper, 1971:39). Although systematic data are not available—there are only impressionistic accounts from anthropologists—stuttering appears to be less common in non-western, non-industrial societies.[1] Stuttering typically appears between two and nine years of age. There is some evidence that stuttering has a genetic basis; it tends to appear in successive generations of the same family and frequently in identical twins (Bloodstein, 1981:94). Stuttering is more common among males than females, by a ratio of three or four to one (Bloodstein, 1981:86). Only about one fifth of those who stutter in early childhood continue to stutter into adulthood (Bloodstein, 1981:86; Van Riper, 1971:45).

Stuttering, as visible behavior, refers to interruptions in speech involving the prolongation or repetition of sounds or words, pauses between words or syllables, and "blocking" on words, sometimes accompanied by extraneous sounds such as grunts, facial grimaces, body movements, and postural freezing as the person struggles to "get the word out." These speech difficulties can range from a split second to, in the worst cases, about a minute (Bloodstein, 1981:3).

Like other perceived impairments, stuttering interferes with "the etiquette and mechanisms of communication" (Goffman, 1963:103) and disrupts the "feedback mechanics of spoken interaction" (1963:49). Depending on the social context, the culture, and the health and social status of the speakers (Petrunik, 1977:37), persons who unintentionally and chronically deviate from fluency standards are likely to be defined as stutterers and subjected to various penalizing social reactions, including pity, condescension, embarrassment, amusement, ridicule, and impatience (Johnson, 1959:239; Lemert, 1967:135).

The extent and frequency of stuttering varies. No one stutters all the time. Indeed, there are some situations in which virtually all stutterers are fluent, for example, when singing, speaking in unison with others (including other stutterers), and speaking to themselves, animals, and infants. In addition, stutterers are often more fluent when speaking with a drawl, accent, or different pitch (Petrunik, 1977:34, 71). Some individuals stutter on some words or sounds but not others. ("I can never say 'g's." "I always stutter on the word 'coffee'.") Setting is also important. Many stutter more during telephone conversations than they do in face-to-face conversation; others find speaking to strangers particularly difficult; still others are more fluent in formal than informal situations, or vice versa. Stutterers have good periods and bad periods. ("Some days I wake up and I'm fine, other days I'm in for hell all day.") There are even some actors and entertainers who stutter but who are fluent when playing a role or facing an audience.

Studying the ways stutterers cope with their stuttering offers valuable insights into how people manage perceived disabilities (Friedson, 1965) and the potential stigma associated with them by highlighting processes that are usually taken for granted, and thus obscured (Davis, 1961). This strategy of using the specific to identify the general has recently been employed by Kitsuse (1980) who has used the "coming out of the closet" metaphor to examine the processes which establish new and legitimate identities. Schneider and Conrad (1980) have developed

From "Fragile Facades: Stuttering and the Strategic Manipulation of Awareness," *Social Problems,* Vol. 31, No. 2 (December 1983), pp. 125–138 by permission of the Society for the Study of Social Problems and the authors.

[1] A good summary is provided in Bloodstein (1981:103). Some observers have reported an absence of stuttering among certain North American Midwest Indian tribes such as the Utes, the Shoshone, and the Bannock (Johnson, 1944, 1944b; Snidecor, 1947). Other studies (Clifford, 1965; Lemert, 1967: 135; Sapir, 1915; Stewart, 1959; Van Riper, 1946) have noted that this is by no means true for all North American Indian tribes. Both Lemert and Stewart found that tribes (particularly those on the Pacific Northwest coast of Canada) which encouraged competition and stricter child-rearing practices, and which placed more emphasis on self-control, reported more instances of stuttering. Lemert (1967:146) also offered a similar explanation for a higher incidence of stuttering among Japanese than Polynesians.

Kitsuse's analysis by using epilepsy to examine how persons manage discreditable information where there is "no clear identity to move to or from" (1980:32) and where "no 'new' readily available supportive . . . subculture exists" (1980:33).

Both Kitsuse, and Schneider and Conrad, focus on identity rather than interactional order, and on calculated and planned management rather than moment-to-moment strategies. We broaden this analysis by examining: (1) how people coordinate the requirements of creating acceptable identities *and* orderly interaction; (2) how they integrate management strategies thought out in advance with those selected on a moment-to-moment basis; and (3) how the subjective experience of disability together with the reactions of others, shape the management process (Higgins, 1980; Petrunik, 1983). Stuttering has three features which facilitate an examination of these issues. First, stuttering is a potentially stigmatizing disability that disrupts interaction. Second, because stutterers experience speech as a function over which they exercise partial but precarious control, their management of speech is both spontaneous and premeditated. Third, the experience of stuttering is critical for how stutterers, and others, define and manage stuttering. . . . We examine the central importance of stuttering as a reality experienced by the stutterer. We then examine a variety of strategies which stutterers use to manipulate awareness of their stuttering and present the fragile facade of normal speech. Although we refer throughout to Goffman's (1963) analysis of stigma management as a benchmark in demonstrating how an understanding of stuttering contributes to a more general understanding of stigma, we go beyond Goffman and those who have extended his work, such as Conrad and Schneider, in emphasizing the importance of the experiential domain for sociological analysis. . . .

The Experience of Stuttering

I suppose that the hope of every stutterer is to awaken some morning and find that his disability has vanished. There is just enough promise of this in his experience to make it seem possible. There are days when, for some reason, the entangled web of words trips him only occasionally. In such periods of relief, he may peer back into his other condition and puzzle over the nature of the oppressive "presence" . . . [hoping that it] is a transitory aberration which might fade and vanish. . . . One feels that only an added will-power, some accretion of psychic rather than physical strength, should be necessary for its conquest. Yet, try as I might, I could not take the final step. I had come up against some invisible power which no strength of will seemed to surmount (Gustavson, 1944:466).

Like normal speakers, stutterers believe speech is something that should be intentionally controlled. Yet, somehow their words are mysteriously blocked or interrupted. Stutterers experience stuttering as the work of an alien inner force (often referred to in the third person as "it") which takes control of their speech mechanism. Stuttering is something which stutterers feel happens *to* them, not something they do: "somebody else is in charge of my mouth and I can't do anything about it" (Van Riper, 1971:158).

In coping with this subjective reality, stutterers use three general strategies: concealment, openness, and disavowal. Concealment strategies involve three principal tactics: avoidance, circumvention, and camouflage. These tactics allow most stutterers to avoid being seen as stutterers part of the time and a few to become secret stutterers. Openness tactics include: treating stuttering as unproblematic, struggle with the "it," and voluntary disclosure. Disavowal—which often calls for the tacit co-operation of others—involves the pretense that stuttering is not occurring when it is obvious that it is. We discuss in turn each of these strategies and their tactics.

Concealment

Avoidance

The simplest way to conceal stuttering is to avoid speaking. Many stutterers select occupations they think will minimize speaking. Others avoid situations in which they fear stuttering will embarrass them.

I never went to the dances at school because I was afraid of stuttering and looking silly. Because I didn't go, I didn't learn to dance or mix socially. I always felt bad when people would ask me if I was going to a dance or party. I would make up some excuse or say that I didn't want to go. I felt that people thought I was some sort of creep because I didn't go. Each time I wouldn't go because of my fears, I felt even weirder.

Stutterers avoid specific types of encounters. Instead of using the telephone they will write a letter, "drop in on someone," or go to a store to see if it has the item they want. Stutterers avoid particular words, substituting "easy" words for "hard" ones. Word substitution sometimes results in convoluted phrasing in which nothing seems to be addressed directly.

If I didn't dodge and duck, I wouldn't be able to carry on a conversation. If I didn't circumlocute, I wouldn't be able to get certain words out at all. Unless I'm coming in through the back door and taking a run at it, I'd never get it out.

Where this tactic proves difficult or impossible, stutterers may structure conversations so others say the troublesome words for them. One way of doing this is by feigning forgetfulness:

You know what I mean, what was it we were talking about this morning, you know, John has one, it's ah, this is annoying, it's right on the tip of my tongue. . . .

Another tactic is to structure the situation so that someone else will be called upon to do the talking. For example, most stutterers fear they will stutter on their name (Petrunik, 1982:306). To avoid introducing themselves when they meet strangers, stutterers sometimes arrange their entry so that someone who knows them will proceed them into the situation. They then rely on the social conventions governing introductions to compel the other person to introduce them. Similarly, stutterers often fear placing orders in restaurants because here, too, word substitution is difficult. To cope with this situation, stutterers may encourage others to order before them; as soon as an item they would like—or at least find acceptable—is mentioned, they can use words they feel more confident with to duplicate the other person's order: "me too" or "same here." With close associates such cooperation may take on the character of finely tuned team work.

When we were visiting friends of ours and I was having blocks, my wife would sometimes get what seemed to be a slightly anxious look and would quietly supply the word. She did this in a way that seemed so natural to me that I wondered if the others noticed it.

While the willing cooperation of others, especially intimates, has been well documented (Goffman, 1963:55, 97) a study of stuttering draws attention to how others may unknowingly be coopted to conceal a potential stigma.

Circumvention and Camouflage

Stutterers sometimes use tactics based on timing and rhythm to outsmart the "it." Using these tactics requires a knowledge of both the etiquette of conversation and the patterns of one's own stuttering. Some speak quickly, for example, "building up" momentum to get "past" or "over" "difficult words." Others rhythmically pace their speech with the aid of coordinated hand and/or leg movements. Some arrange their sentences so that "easy" words precede "hard" ones, to establish a "flow" which carries them uneventfully over "trouble spots." Others arrange their speech so that "difficult" sounds are said on falling (or rising) pitches. Still others find that changing their tone of voice, or speaking in dialect or with an accent, is helpful.

A similar tactic involves delaying saying a troublesome word until the stutterer feels "it" no longer threatens to control speech and the word is ready to "come out." One way of doing this is to introduce starters and fillers (well, like, er, ah, um) into speech, to postpone troublesome words until the moment when they can be said. One stutterer, for example, was walking along a street when a stranger asked him for directions: "Where is the Borden Building?" A sudden panic gripped the stutterer. He knew exactly where the building was but, to permit him to wait for a moment when "it" could be caught off guard, he responded: "Well, let me see [pause with quizzical expression] oh, ah, near . . . let me see . . . near, I think Spadina and, ah, College." A variant of this tactic involves rearranging words. The late British humorist and stutterer, Patrick Campbell, gave an example of this in a television interview. While travelling on a London bus, he feared he would not be able to say, "May I have a ticket to Marble Arch?" without stuttering. So, when the conductor approached, he said instead, "May I have a ticket to that arch which is of marble made?"—which he executed fluently.

Where stutterers fail to outwit the "it" they may attempt to camouflage their problem by, for example, visually isolating others from evidence of their stuttering. A teacher who stutters accomplished this by writing on the blackboard just as he was about to stutter, thereby disguising a "block" as a pause to write.

Secret Stutterers

Most stutterers avoid detection only part of the time. However, some stutterers manage to maintain the identity of a "normal speaker" virtually all the time. They define themselves as stutterers not because they stutter in secret, like Becker's (1963:11) "secret deviants," but because they confront and respond to an inner propensity to stutter. Some stutterers report going for years without overtly stuttering. This fact— that a deviant identity can exist in the absence of visible deviant behavior—adds weight to Jack Katz's (1972) critique of those conceptions of labeling which focus exclusively on deviance as behavior and ignore deviance as an inner essence imputed to individuals. Goffman's (1963:56) refusal to recognize that stigmatized people may define themselves in terms of an inner essence and "that what distinguishes an individual from others is the core of his being" has limited his ability to comprehend how both stigmatized and "normal" people perceive their differences and the consequences of this for defining their "real" or "natural" groupings (1963:112). Some speech pathologists, on the other hand, have long recognized that stigmatized people define themselves on the basis of their subjective experience. They refer to secret stutterers as interiorized, indicating that stuttering can be an internal experience as well as an external appearance (Douglass and Quarrington, 1952:378).

Interiorized stutterers place great importance on preserving a social identity and will go to extraordinary lengths to preserve it. For example, a self-employed businessman in his early forties concealed his stuttering from his first wife. He confided in his second wife, but continued to conceal his stuttering from his children. At work, he had his secretary handle potentially troublesome situations. He would, for example, have her make certain phone calls for him. He claimed he would lose business if his stuttering became known. At one time he fired a secretary who had been working with him for a number of years because he thought her facial expressions showed that she had noticed him stuttering. He took great care not to drink too much or become fatigued so that he would not lose control over his speech. He preferred to entertain at home rather than to go out because he felt he could better regulate his drinking at home.

Successful interiorized stutterers develop a particular sensitivity to the intricacies of syntax. They "become 'situation conscious' [and display] special aliveness to the contingencies of acceptance and disclosure, contingencies to which normals will be less alive" (Goffman, 1963:111).

Avoiding stuttering has many costs. Some tactics exclude the stutterer from fully participating in social life as a "normal person," infringing on the very status the stutterer wishes to preserve. The interactional costs may be relatively trivial (not eating what one really wants in a restaurant, or saying something quite different from what one intended), or far more consequential (depriving oneself of a social life or not pursuing a desired occupation).

Because I wasn't normal I thought I couldn't do normal things like get married. I avoided going to parties, because I didn't want to feel bad, and then I felt bad because I didn't go and wasn't meeting people and having a good social life.

Similarly, the consequences for social identity may be relatively benign (being defined as "quiet" or "shy") or even somewhat flattering (being a "good listener" or a "strong silent type"). On the other hand, avoiding interaction may result in derogatory characterizations ("nervous," "odd," "rude," "affected," "silly," "strange," or "retarded").[2] A border crossing incident illustrates how avoidance can be interpreted as evidence of impropriety:

The border guard asked me where I was born. Because I was afraid I would stutter on "Nova Scotia," I hesitated and started to "ah" and "um" to him. "Let me see now . . . it's the . . . uh, Maritimes . . . uh . . ." and so on. The outcome of all this evasion was that they made a thorough search of my car and even threatened to slit my seat covers.

The importance which stutterers give to the costs of concealment determines the tactics they use. Some people will do almost anything to avoid stuttering; others prefer to stutter in some situations rather than face the consequences of concealment.

---

[2] See Goffman (1963:94) for a parallel between stutterers and the hard of hearing.

On the first day [of the Kerr course] we were gathering at the motel and going through the ritual of introductions. One man put his hand out to me and said, "My name is . . . uh . . . actually . . . my name is Jim." Afterwards one of the other men in the group who had a highly noticeable stutter shook his head and said, in an aside to me, "What a fool! I'd rather stammer my head off than avoid like that. It looks ridiculous. People must think he's crazy!"

Openness

Unproblematic Stuttering

Unlike interiorized stutterers, those with visible and audible speech disruptions find that some audiences become so familiar with their stuttering that they no longer have anything to conceal. ("All my friends know I stutter. I can't hide my stuttering long enough.") These stutterers simply go ahead and speak without thinking about the consequences. As a result, particularly when speaking with persons who know their problem, they can be barely conscious of their stuttering.

With Evelyn, if you asked me, I never stutter. If there was a tape recorder going it might show that I was stuttering. But I don't notice it and it doesn't bother me. I don't have any trouble talking to her on the phone unless others are there.

At the same time those who know stutterers well seem less conscious of their stuttering. Spouses and friends remarked:

You know, since I've got to know you well, I hardly ever notice your stuttering.

You know, sometimes I forget he stutters.

I notice his stuttering only when others are present. I'm more conscious of it. At other times, I don't care.

Goffman (1963:81) argues that friends are less aware of a stigmatized person's problem because they are more familiar with the stigma. In the case of stuttering, however, what is critical is its obtrusiveness—"how much it interferes with the flow of interaction" (Goffman, 1963:49)—rather than mere visibility. When stutterers are with friends they feel less con-

strained to meet the exacting requirements which talk requires in other circumstances, because both parties develop idiosyncratic rules which enable them to become less dependent on such things as precise timing. For example, in telephone conversations between stutterers and their friends silences can cease to be interpreted as cues indicating the end of a speaking turn or a break in the telephone connection.

Once such understandings are developed stutterers feel less pressure to account for their problems or to work at concealing and controlling the "it"; thus, the sense of stuttering as a subjective presence wanes. For stutterers who learn to speak fluently by meticulously learning a new set of speech behaviors (Webster, 1975), the experience of stuttering as an "it" may fade away because with their speech under control there is no longer any need to account for stuttering.[3]

Struggling with the "It"

Stutterers who find it difficult to conceal their stuttering face the additional problem of how to converse with people who take interruptions in the speech of stutterers as a signal to resume talking themselves. Stutterers attempt to avoid this by making two claims: first, that they are competent persons who understand the conventions of talk; and second, that they have not relinquished their speaking turn—even though they are lapsing into unusually long silences—and should be permitted to continue speaking uninterrupted. These claims are important to the stutterer because together they provide the basis for participation in conversation and for maintaining an acceptable identity. One way stutterers make these claims is by confronting a block "head on" and trying to force out the word or sound: a typical pattern is a deep breath followed by muscle tension and visible strain as the stutterer attempts to "break through" the interruption and regain control of speech. The late Japanese novelist Yukio Mishima (1959:5) vividly described this phenomenon: "When a stutterer is struggling desperately to utter his first sound he is like a little bird that is trying to extricate itself from thick lime."

By making visible the "I/it" conflict through struggle, stutterers demonstrate to those they

---

[3] While fluency can be achieved and the sense of stuttering as an "it" can disappear, the continued maintenance of fluency is quite another matter. Time and again those who have achieved fluency—through whatever means—find themselves relapsing, even years later (Perkins, 1979; Sheehan, 1979, 1983).

are conversing with that they have not given up their speaking turn and are doing their utmost to limit the interruption in their speech. This process of externalizing stuttering enables stutterers to share with others their experience of stuttering as a mysterious intrusive force. By demonstrating that their deviation from the conventions of speech is not intentional (Blum and McHugh, 1971; Goffman, 1963:128, 143; Mills, 1940) they hope to persuade others to bear with them and not to regard them as outsiders who reject, or do not understand, the norms others adhere to. The struggle that stutterers engage in is the "stigma symbol" (Goffman, 1963:46) that others recognize as stuttering. Struggle feeds into the troubles stutterers are trying to remedy in a classic vicious circle: stuttering is in part a product of attachment to the very social conventions that stutterers struggle to avoid breaking.

This analysis is supported by evidence that some members of the British upper classes view stuttering (or stammering as it is referred to in Britain) as a mark of distinction (Kazin, 1978:124; Shenker, 1970:112). They openly cultivate stuttering as a display of their superior social status and expect others to wait at their convenience. These persons make no apology for their stuttering and accordingly do not struggle with it to demonstrate its involuntary character. Consequently, their stuttering typically takes the form of a "slight stammer" characterized by relaxed repetitions and hesitations without any of the facial distortions associated with struggle.

Voluntary Disclosure

Like concealment, struggle also involves costs. Stuttering presents the listener with the problem of knowing how to sustain an interaction punctuated with silences, prolongations, and facial contortions. As one observer noted:

What am I supposed to do when a stutterer is struggling to say something? Should I help him by saying the word—because I usually know what he is trying to say—or am I supposed to wait? Then if you wait, what do you do? Am I supposed to watch him struggling? It can be awful. And then there is just no knowing what to do with the time. It can be a long wait. It's embarrassing.

One way stutterers deal with this, and with the fear of exposure in the case of concealment, is by voluntarily disclosing their stuttering (Van Riper, 1971:211) in much the same manner as epileptics (Schneider and Conrad, 1980).

The person who has an unapparent, negatively valued attribute often finds it expedient to begin an encounter with an unobtrusive admission of his own failing, especially with persons who are uninformed about him (Goffman, 1967:29).

Stutterers who make public speeches may begin by referring to their problem so their audiences won't be unduly shocked. One university professor started off each term by talking about his stuttering and inviting students to ask questions about it. Another began his courses by deliberately stuttering, so that he would not create expectations of fluency that he might later fail to meet.

Stutterers sometimes indicate the involuntary nature of their disability by apologizing or by noting that their present stuttering is worse than usual. Through such tactics they, in effect, argue that the stigmatized and normal categories represent poles of a continuum, and that they are much further toward the normal end of this continuum than their present behavior would suggest. In doing so, stutterers typically take advantage of the fact that while struggling with some sound or word they can often make fluent asides which display their relative normality.

We went to the shh—shh—(s's always give me trouble)shh—show last night.

I was talking to K—K—en (Wow! I had a hard time on that one) and he was saying. . . .

Other stutterers put listeners at ease with retrospective accounts such as, "Boy, I'm having a hard time today. I must be really tired."

Sometimes humor is used to anticipate and defuse confusion or embarrassment. One stutterer told people at informal gatherings to "go ahead and talk amongst yourselves if I take too long about saying anything." A teacher attempted to put his students at ease by inviting them to "take advantage of my stuttering to catch up on your note-taking."

Other stutterers use humor to claim more desirable identities for themselves.

I use humor a lot now. If I'm having a problem, I'll make a comment like, "Boy, it's a problem having a big mouth like mine and not being able to use it." When I'm having a hard time getting out a word in a store I'll say something like, "Three tries for a quarter." Once a waitress started guessing when I blocked giving my order and kept on guessing and guessing wrong. Every so often, I would smile and say, "You just keep guessing." Everyone was laughing but they were laughing at her, not me.

Stutterers may also take a more aggressive stance. By pitting themselves against the listener, they indicate that they refuse to allow others to use their stuttering to belittle them. One of our respondents referred to this as the "fuck you, Mac" approach.

I challenge the listener. I can make a game out of it. I look them straight in the eye and in my mind tell them to "fuck off." I might stutter like hell, but so what. It doesn't make them any better than me.

In using this strategy stutterers attempt to disavow the implications that they suspect others will draw about their lack of control over speech by displaying "cool." This strategy draws its impetus from the fear that many stutterers have that they will be seen as nervous and easily ruffled persons when they perceive themselves as normal persons in every respect other than their inability to control speech.

Another non-apologetic, but less aggressive, strategy that is occasionally used is one in which the stutterer systematically attempts to redefine stuttering as a "new and proud identity" (Schneider and Conrad, 1980:32) and to use this new identity as a means of getting stuttering "out of the closet" (M. Katz, 1968; Lambidakis, 1972). Some of our respondents reported that talking about their problem to new acquaintances proved to be a good way of gaining rapport. Revealing one's weakness to another can be a way of appearing honest, frank, and "more human." Others claimed that their efforts to overcome their "handicap" had strengthened their character. A few (e.g. Van Riper, Sheehan, and Douglass) have even used their personal experience of stuttering professionally, in therapy and research, to gain knowledge and rapport with patients and/or subjects. Even in occupations such as sales or journalism, where stuttering might ordinarily be seen to be a great handicap, some stutterers have used stuttering to their advantage. A Canadian journalist was said to have "disarmed" those he interviewed with his stuttering so that they were sympathetic toward him and unusually frank. A salesman had his business cards printed: "B-B-Bob G-G-Goldman the stuttering Toyota salesman."

Public figures sometimes use their stuttering as a trademark and a means to success. Some examples are the comedian "Stuttering Joe" Frisco, the humorist Patrick Campbell, and the country and western singer Mel Tillis. In his autobiography, Campbell (1967:212) reports how his stuttering on British television made him famous:

While making the ginger ale commercials I looked upon my stammer as a nuisance that would have to be played down as much as possible if we weren't to have endless takes. . . . Although I didn't care to think about this aspect of it too much I did realize that my stammer fitted rather neatly into their campaign, the essence of which was never to mention the word 'Schweppes', but merely to mention the first syllable 'sch—', and that was quite enough for me in every way.

It wasn't until nearly a year later [when asked to advertise butter] that I realized my mistake. [Again Campbell tried to control his stuttering. The producer called him aside and said] "I don't know quite how to put this—but could we have a little more of your trademark on the word 'butter'?" . . . I'd been trying to suppress the very thing it seemed that everyone wanted.

Reflecting on his "asset," Campbell claimed that while he tried to put the best possible light on it, he never really became proud of his identity as a stutterer. The frequent and fleeting gains did not offset the losses that recurred day after day.

If I was offered by some miraculous overnight cure the opportunity never to stammer again, I'd accept it without hesitation, even though it meant the end for me of television (1967:213).

Disavowal

While stutterers sometimes try to put listeners at their ease by drawing attention to themselves, there are often circumstances in which they prefer to define their stuttering out of existence. To do this successfully, they need the tacit cooperation of their listeners. Both parties must share the assumption that the embarrassment and awkwardness associated with stuttering and attempts to control it are best dealt with by acting as if the stuttering were not happening. This provides a "phantom normalcy" (Goffman, 1963:122). By overlooking stuttering, both parties act as if "nothing unusual is happening" (Emerson, 1970) rather than acknowledge something which would require a response for which no shared guidelines exist. This tactic leaves intact the stutterer's status as a normal and competent person and the other's as a decent and tactful person who avoids needlessly embarrassing others. Tactful overlooking, as Safilios-Rothschild (1970:129) has suggested, is normatively prescribed:

Regardless of any degree of aversion felt toward the disabled, the non-disabled are normatively not permitted to show these negative feelings in any way and their fear of making a verbal or a non-verbal "slip" indicating their emotions renders the interaction quite formal and rigid.

The importance of tacit disavowal of stuttering is indicated by the anxiety some stutterers feel when they enter a situation where they know it cannot, or will not, be ignored. Conversations with little children are one example.

Children give me the hardest time. They know something is wrong and they don't hide it. My little nephew embarrassed me terribly in front of the family. He said "your mouth moves funny." I tried to explain to him that I had something wrong with my mouth just like other people had something wrong with their ears or their eyes.

Another example is where stutterers are forced to watch and listen to themselves or others stuttering. Just as many fat people avoid scales and mirrors (Himelfarb and Evans, 1974:222), many stutterers shun mirrors and audio and video tape recorders. Similarly, stutterers are often uncomfortable watching others stutter. We witnessed stutterers in the speech clinic cover their faces with their hands or even walk out of the room rather than witness another person stutter. These attempts to distance themselves from stuttering appeared in some cases to be experienced as a disassociation of the body and the self through a loss or blurring of self-awareness. Stutterers talked of "slipping out of the situation" at the moment of stuttering and not being aware of what they or others were doing when they "returned." During these periods, stutterers experience a "time out" (Goffman, 1967:30; Scott and Lyman, 1968) from the situation. Time appears to stop so that when speech resumes it is as if the block did not occur. This sense of time having stopped, and of stuttering occurring outside the situation, is symbolized by the frozen poses stutterers sometimes adopt at the mo-

ment of stuttering: gestures are stopped, only to be resumed once speech continues. For example, one stutterer regularly "blocked" on a word just as he was about to tap the ash off his cigarette with his finger. During the few seconds he was "caught" in his block, his finger remained poised, frozen an inch or so above his cigarette. When he released the sound, the finger would simultaneously tap the ash into the ashtray.

Stutterers and their listeners manage time outs cooperatively by severing eye contact. Normally, people who are conversing indicate their attentiveness by facial expressions and eye contact, thereby reaffirming that they are listening and involved in the interaction. By breaking eye contact at the moment of stuttering, stutterers and their listeners jointly disengage from the conversation and exclude stuttering from the interaction. The moment fluent speech returns engagement is reestablished through a renewal of eye contact; the participants confirm their mutual subterfuge by acting as if nothing had happened. During time outs listeners may also confirm their disengagement by doing something unrelated, such as assuming an air of nonchalance, shuffling papers, glancing through a magazine or a book, fiddling with an object, or surveying the immediate surroundings. These signals indicate that the participants are not "in" the conversation.

While struggling to "get a word out" stutterers may avert their faces or hide their mouths with their hands. This phenomenon reveals an apparent difference in the social significance of sight and hearing. During this obscuring of the sight of stuttering, as with the time out, both parties are presumably aware that stuttering is taking place, and indeed that the stutterer is doing her or his best to "get past the block" and resume the conversation. Yet, at the same time, stuttering is denied. It is as if through the "thin disguises" (Goffman, 1963:81) which contradictory appearances provide it is possible to establish opposing social claims and thus "have one's cake and eat it too."

Time out, besides resolving the interactional problem of how to respond to stuttering, protects or hides one's vulnerability; it's much like the common response of averting your eyes when you accidentally see someone naked. Stutterers are, in a sense, "naked" at the moment of stuttering; they are without a mask, their front is crumbling and their "raw self" exposed (Goffman, 1963:16). Averting their eyes is a cue to the other to look away from the stutterer's "nakedness," thus saving both from embarrassment. The stutterers we interviewed expressed this sense of "nakedness" or vulnerability with descriptions such as "weak," "helpless," "like a little kid," and "with my shell removed." Some even said that at the point of stuttering they felt transparent. This can be related to the saying that the eyes are the mirror of the soul, which stems from the belief that the eyes reflect one's true feelings even though the rest of one's face may camouflage them.

Loss of eye contact gives stutterers time to recover their composure, manage the "unsatisfactory" image that has emerged, and, if possible, project a new image. Listeners have their own self to consider. Because they too may be held partly responsible for the stutterer's embarrassment, they can use loss of eye contact to indicate that they did not intend the embarrassment to happen and, above all, that they are not amused or uncomfortable.

While the tactic of mutual disavowal is usually a situational one the comment of one stutterer we interviewed indicates that in some cases it can be much more pervasive:

Ever since I was a young child I can't remember my parents ever directly mentioning stuttering. It seemed obvious that they saw me stuttering, and they knew I stuttered, but they never said anything. The only incident I can remember is my father singing "K-K-Katy" a couple of times. I felt badly about that. Nothing direct was ever said, even by my brothers. My younger brother always gave me a lot of trouble. But he never mentioned stuttering once. I wondered if my parents told them not to say anything. My parents did make lots of references to me as nervous, sensitive, or different, and were always saying they were going to take me to the doctor for my nerves. But except for brief references on very few occasions, they never mentioned anything about stuttering.

In such cases, the disavowal of stigma is extended across entire situations. This requires others to tacitly agree to ignore the stigma in all encounters with the stigmatized person.

Discussion

Our study of stuttering provides a vehicle to elaborate upon and extend the work of Davis, Goffman, Schneider and Conrad, and others on the strategic manipulation of awareness to manage potential stigma. The implications of our analysis also extend beyond stigma management to a consideration of the importance of the experiential dimension for the construction of social order. Because the stutterer finds problematic what others take for granted, the stutterer's social world is the world of everyman writ large.

In our consideration of stuttering we have developed three major lines of argument. First, our analysis shows the importance of considering subjective experience as well as behavior when studying the management of identity and the construction of interactional order. Stutterers engage in the ongoing creation of a subjective reality which at once shapes, and is shaped by, the management strategies they employ to regulate awareness of their disability and claim or disown identities. This consideration of the subjective experience of stuttering supports Jack Katz's (1972) argument that deviance theory should recognize that people sometimes perceive deviance as an inner essence independent of behavior. In addition, our analysis extends rather than simply elaborates upon Goffman's work, for though he writes of "ego" or "felt" identity, which he defines as "the subjective sense of [the stigmatized person's] own situation" (1963:105), he does not develop this concept.

Second, we have shown that the management of potential stigma can involve strategies conceived of, and executed, on a moment-to-moment basis, in addition to the premeditated strategies that have attracted most sociologists' attention. Advance planning was usually necessary where stutterers tried to conceal their problem through role avoidance. In speaking situations, management became more spontaneous: stutterers selected strategies in the light of opportunities and difficulties which arose in the course of interaction. In both cases, concealment strategies were marked by a high level of self-consciousness. When stutterers used openness or disavowal, however, only voluntary disclosure was consciously employed. Both struggling to overcome the "it" and time outs were non-calculated, though, especially in the latter case, stutterers were quick to recognize these tactics as coping and "restorative measures" (Goffman, 1963:128) once they were brought to their attention.

Finally, we have called attention to the fact that stutterers, like other stigmatized persons, seek to manage two interrelated, yet analytically distinguishable, problems. They are concerned both with preserving an acceptable identity and with preserving orderly interaction so that they can get on with the business of living. In exploring this issue we have shown how stutterers sometimes find themselves in situations in which it is not possible to simultaneously achieve both these objectives and thus are required to choose between them. The repertoire of tactics stutterers develop, and by implication the limits they place on their involvement in social life, depend on the importance they attach to these objectives.

REFERENCES

Becker, Howard S. 1963. *Outsiders: Studies in the Sociology of Deviance*. New York: The Free Press.

Bloodstein, Oliver. 1981. *A Handbook on Stuttering*. Chicago: National Easter Seal Society.

Blum, Alan and Peter McHugh. 1971. "The Social Ascription of Motives." *American Sociological Review*, 36 (February):98–109.

Campbell, Patrick. 1967. *My Life and Easy Times*. London: Anthony Blond.

Clifford, S. 1965. "Stuttering in South Dakota Indians." *Central States Speech Association Journal*, 26 (February):59–60.

Davis, Fred. 1961. "Deviance Disavowal: The Management of Strained Interaction by the Visibly Handicapped." *Social Problems*, 9 (Fall):120–132.

Douglass, Ernest, and Bruce Quarrington. 1952. "Differentiation of Interiorized and Exteriorized Secondary Stuttering." *Journal of Speech and Hearing Disorders*, 17 (December):377–385.

Emerson, Joan. 1970. "Nothing Unusual is Happening." In Thomas Shibutani (ed.), *Human Nature and Collective Behavior*. Englewood Cliffs, N.J.: Prentice-Hall, pp. 208–223.

Freidson, Eliot. 1965. "Disability as Social Deviance." In Marvin Sussman (ed.), *Sociology and Rehabilitation*. Washington, D.C.: American Sociological Association, pp. 71–99.

Goffman, Erving, 1963. *Stigma*. Englewood Cliffs, N.J.: Prentice-Hall.

———. 1967. *Interaction Ritual*. Garden City, N.Y.: Doubleday-Anchor.

Gustavson, Carl. 1944. "A Talisman and a Convalescence." *Quarterly Journal of Speech*, 30(1):465–471.

Higgins, Paul C. 1980. "Social Reaction and the Physically Disabled: Bringing the Impairment Back In." *Symbolic Interaction*, 3 (Spring):139–156.

Himelfarb, Alex and John Evans. 1974. "Deviance Disavowal and Stigma Management: A Study of Obesity." In Jack Haas and Bill Shaffir (eds.), *Decency and Deviance*. Toronto: McClelland and Stewart, pp. 221–232.

Johnson, Wendell. 1944a. "The Indian Has No Word for It: Part 1, Stuttering in Children." *Quarterly Journal of Speech*, 30 (October):330–337.

———. 1944b. "The Indian Has No Word for It: Part 2, Stuttering in Adults." *Quarterly Journal of Speech*, 30 (December):456–465.

———. 1959. *The Onset of Stuttering*. Minneapolis: University of Minneapolis Press.

Katz, Jack. 1972. "Deviance, Charisma, and Rule-defined Behavior." *Social Problems*, 20(2):186–202.

Katz, Murray. 1968. "Stuttering Power." *Journal of the Council of Adult Stutterers* (January):5.

Kazin, Alfred. 1978. *New York Jew*. New York: Random House.

Kitsuse, John I. 1980. "Coming Out All Over: Deviants and the Politics of Social Problems." *Social Problems*, 28 (October):1–13.

Lambidakis, Elenore. 1972. "Stutterers' Lib." *Journal of the Council of Adult Stutterers* (Winter):4–6.

Lemert, Edwin. 1967. *Human Deviance, Social Problems and Social Control*. Englewood Cliffs, N.J.: Prentice-Hall.

Mills, C. Wright. 1940. "Situated Action and Vocabularies of Motives." *American Sociological Review*, 5 (December): 904–913.

Mishima, Yukio. 1959. *The Temple of the Golden Pavilion*. New York: A.A. Knopf.

Perkins, William. 1979. "From Psychoanalysis to Discoordination." In Hugo Gregory (ed.), *Controversies About Stuttering Therapy*. Baltimore: University Park Press, pp. 97–129.

Petrunik, Michael. 1974. "The Quest for Fluency: Fluency Variations and the Identity Problems and Management Strategies of Stutterers." In Jack Haas and Bill Shaffir (eds.), *Decency and Deviance*. Toronto: McClelland and Stewart, pp. 201–220.

———. 1977. "The Quest for Fluency: A Study of the Identity Problems and Management Strategies of Adult Stutterers and Some Suggestions for an Approach to Deviance Management." Unpublished Ph.D. dissertation, University of Toronto.

———. 1980. "Stutterers Adaptations to Non-avoidance Therapy: Primary/Secondary Deviance Theory as a Professional Treatment Ideology." Paper presented at the annual meetings of the Society for the Study of Social Problems, New York, August.

———. 1982. "Telephone Troubles: Interactional Breakdown and Its Management by Stutterers and Their Listeners." *Symbolic Interaction*, 5 (Fall):299–310.

———. 1983. "Being Deviant: A Critique of the Neglect of the Experiential Dimension in Sociological Constructions of Deviance." Paper presented at the annual meetings of the Society for the Study of Social Problems, Detroit, August.

Safilios-Rothschild, Constantina. 1970. *The Sociol-*

ogy and Social Psychology of Disability and Rehabilitation. New York: Random House.

Sapir, Edward. 1915. *Abnormal Types of Speech in Nootka*. Canadian Geological Survey, Memoir 62, Anthropological Series No. 5. Ottawa: Government Printing Bureau.

Schneider, Joseph W. and Peter Conrad. 1980. "In the Closet with Illness: Epilepsy, Stigma Potential, and Information Control." *Social Problems*, 28 (October):32–44.

Scott, Marvin B. and Stanford Lyman. 1968. "Accounts." *American Sociological Review*, 33 (February):44–62.

Sheehan, Joseph. 1979. "Current Issues on Stuttering Recovery." In Hugo Gregory (ed.), *Controversies About Stuttering Therapy*. Baltimore: University Park Press, pp. 175–209.

———. 1983. "Invitation to Relapse." *The Journal*, National Council on Stuttering (Summer):16–20.

Shenker, Israel. 1970. "Stammer Becomes Fashionable." *Globe and Mail* (Toronto), November 12:12.

Snidecor, John. 1947. "Why the Indian Does Not Stutter." *Quarterly Journal of Speech*, 33 (December):493–495.

Stewart, Joseph. 1959. "The Problem of Stuttering in Certain North American Societies." *Journal of Speech and Hearing Disorders* (Monograph Supplement 6):1–87.

Van Riper, Charles. 1946. "Speech Defects among the Kalabash." *Marquette County Historical Society*, 8 (December):308–322.

———. 1971. *The Nature of Stuttering*. Englewood Cliffs, N.J.: Prentice-Hall.

Webster, Ronald. 1975. *The Precision Fluency Shaping Program: Speech Reconstruction for Stutterers*. Roanoke, Virginia: Communication Development Corporation.

The Bailbondsman   DAVID S. DAVIS

Introduction

. . . Everett Hughes in his essay "Good People and Dirty Work" writes of how the extermination of Jews in Nazi Germany was dirty work carried out by a small group of individuals so that the rest of German society, most of whom supported this activity, could remain distant from it and maintain a conception of themselves as good. Hughes implies the pathological and defective may be found among those who do the dirty work in society. Hughes (1964: 34) writes, "that we have a sufficient pool or fund of personalities warped toward perverse punishment and cruelty to do any amount of dirty work that the good people may be inclined to countenance." Others have argued that stigmatized occupations attract certain kinds of individuals who, because of their psychological or social characteristics contribute to the occupation's reputation (see Saunders [1981] for discussion of this point). However, given that there is an "unwillingness to think about the dirty work done [and] complicated mechanisms by which the individual mind keeps unpleasant or intolerable knowledge from consciousness (Hughes, 1964: 27)" it could be argued that the definition of dirty workers as warped and perverse serves as a further distancing mechanism for the "good". Instead, perhaps, we should consider the possibility that many dirty workers are really no different from the good people; that they are good people *doing* dirty work. To strip them of their respectability by defining them as disrespectable (Ball, 1970) strengthens the respectability of others.

The theme of 'dirty work' has been picked up by those who study occupations (Blau, 1982; Goldman, 1981; Killian, 1981, Saunders, 1981; Simoni and Ball, 1977; Jacobs and Retsky, 1975). In particular, some sociologists have been interested in the "manner in which the socially deviant do the 'necessary' but unacknowledged 'dirty work' for the 'good people' whose re-

spectability must keep them above such things" (Simoni and Ball, 1977: 361). The performance of what is perceived as dirty work plays a crucial part in an individual's self identity, since occupation has become the main determinant of status and prestige (Goldschalk, 1979; Hughes, 1951). Being a dirty worker can make claims to self worth difficult.

Ball (1970: 329) notes that "respectability is a central concern of actors in the problematic dramas of mundane life." Respectability is not a generic characteristic of an individual or group, but is a product of social relationships. Ball distinguishes between the *"unrespectable"* who agree with the audience's perception of them as not lacking meriting respect, and the *"disreputable"* who reject the way in which they are perceived. In this paper we examine a group of dirty workers, some of whom are *unrespectable* and some of whom are *disrespectable*. We show how these different perceptions of self result in different social consequences. In particular, there is a tendency for the *disrespectable* to become socially isolated.

There have been only a few sociologists who have examined social isolation. Lemert (1953), for instance, in his discussion of solitary check forgers finds that their lack of integration, "is reflected in self-attitudes in which many refer to themselves as 'black-sheep' or as a kind of Dr. Jekyll-Mr. Hyde person" (p. 148). In prison, the check forger is marginal to and is isolated from the other prisoners. Similarly, Wulbert (1965) accounts for the lack of organized collective behavior in mental hospitals and the opposite in prisons by an absence of inmate pride in the former and its presence in the latter. Inmate pride for mental patients would require an acceptance of their inmate status. If, by attitude, we mean "a process of individual consciousness which determines activity" (Thomas and Znaniecki, 1918:21–22) for both systematic

"Good People Doing Dirty Work: A Study of Social Isolation," *Symbolic Interaction,* Vol. 7, No. 2 (Fall 1984), pp. 233–247.

The author would like to acknowledge the substantive comments of Robert Scott as well as the comments and editorial suggestions of Gary Alan Fine, Michael Radelet, and Harold Finestone. This study was prepared with the partial support of the National Institute of Mental Health (USPHS-MH14538) and the National Institute of Handicapped Research (NIHR-G00806802) although neither agency is responsible for the views presented.

check forgers and institutionalized mental patients the reason for their social isolation must be sought, in part, in their *self attitudes*.

Schneider and Conrad (1980) in their study of epileptics present their subjects as being isolated from one another. The authors state that the "very desire to lead conventional and stigma-free lives further separates and isolates them from each other" (p. 42). Here the authors intimate that the reason for their isolation must be sought in the epileptic's *attitude toward conventional society*.

Goffman (1963:107–108) devotes a short discussion to the actor who finds it difficult to affiliate with like others:

Whether closely aligned with his own kind or not, the stigmatized individual may exhibit identity ambivalence when he attains a close sight of his own kind behaving in a stereotyped way, flamboyantly or pitifully acting out the negative attributes imputed to them. The sight may repel him, since after all he supports the norms of the wider society, but his social and psychological identification with these offenders holds him to what repels him, transforming repulsion into shame, and then transforming ashamedness itself into something of which he is ashamed. In brief, he can neither embrace his group nor let it go.

While not socially isolated, this actor is somehow stuck between his tainted fellows and conventional society. He embraces the values and norms of conventional society, recognizes he violates them, but is repelled by his fellows. Part of the source of this ambivalence, for Goffman, is found in the actor's *attitude to like others*.

Faced with an inability to pass amidst conventional society and rejected by it, it would, from this work, appear that social isolation could result from a combination of three attitudes held by the discredited actor. First, a self attitude that the perception of himself as lacking in moral worth is unjustified: that he is not what he is said to be. Second, an attitude to like others that, to some extent, the attribution of stigma to the members of the group to which he belongs has at least some justification. Third, an attitude of acceptance toward conventional society's values and norms. Faced by rejection by members of conventional society, yet believing that he rightly belongs to it, it would make sense for the actor to reject affiliation with like others or other discredited actors when he believes them to lack respect. To associate with them would undermine his attempt to be seen as respectable. The crucial variable here is the actor's belief that he is unjustifiably being defined as a dirty worker, that he is being falsely accused. While this belief would not seem to necessarily result in social isolation, its presence would appear to increase the probability that social isolation will occur.

The following study examines a set of socially isolated stigmatized individuals and traces that adaptation to their consciousness of self as falsely accused. These individuals are bailbondsmen (also called bondsmen): those who work for a living by charging fees to get defendants out of jail prior to trial. They are contrasted with avowedly dishonest bailbondsmen (the unrespected), and compared as well with members of several other discredited occupations and statuses.

Methods

Twenty-five bailbondsmen (one of whom was female), in and surrounding a county in a Northeastern state, were given unstructured interviews in sessions totalling from one to six hours. Two additional bondsmen in this area were intensively interviewed. One set of these interviews lasted 26 hours over ten sessions and the other lasted 18 hours over seven sessions. In addition to the interviews, over 100 hours were spent in participant observation and observing bondsmen as they worked in their offices, court rooms and work related travel.

Using interview data, observations, and reputational data, bondsmen were classified as considering themselves "honest," meaning that engaging in dishonest, illegal, or unethical behavior as part of their routine work activities was seen by them to be rare and "dishonest," [and the "dishonest"] meaning that engaging in dishonest, illegal, or unethical behavior was seen by them to be part of and common to their work routine. For the latter, to have not engaged in those activities would have meant radically changing that routine. Among the dishonest activities observed and self-reported by bondsmen were: the bribing of lawyers, judges and policemen; recommending lawyers to defendants; soliciting cases from lawyers; withholding security deposits from defendants; having foreknowledge of crimes; and failing to report cash receipts as income. As part of this classification procedure most of the bondsmen were asked the following question about each of the bondsmen interviewed: "Do you consider [name of bondsman] to be honest or dishonest?" Bailbondsmen also rated themselves as either honest or dishonest. There was a high degree of agreement between ratings based on interviews and observations, and the bondsmens' ratings of themselves and others (Davis, 1982). Twenty-one bondsmen were classified as "honest" and six bondsmen were classified as "dishonest". To obtain additional information about bondsmen, the author attended a state regulated bailbondsman course, became a bondsman and conducted a national mail survey of bondsmen.

The survey consisted of a random sample of 307 bailbondsmen in 48 communities around the United States. The sample was stratified by the number of bailbondsmen per community. The sampling frame was bailbondsmen advertisements in the telephone yellow pages, which yielded names of 3120 bailbondsmen. Thirty-seven questionnaires were returned as "addressee unknown" and "not deliverable as addressed". Eighty-one bondsmen responded for a 33 percent response rate. There was no follow up.

This survey should not be taken to constitute a reliable random sample of bailbondsmen. For one thing, the universe of bailbondsmen may be quite different from those who advertise in the yellow pages, although from this study it appears that most bailbondsmen do advertise in the yellow pages. The most systematic bias may arise from the low response rate. The survey was a source of data that supplemented the other data collected.

The Bailbondsman

The bailbondsman is an individual who, for a fee, will post bail for an accused defendant and thereby achieve that defendant's release from custody. In return the bailbondsman assumes the risk of forfeiting the entire bail amount should the defendant fail to appear for trial. There are approximately 4200 bailbondsmen in the United States (DeRhoda, 1979; Lazar Institute, 1981). The results of the mail survey indicate eighty-two percent of bondsmen are male (n = 66) and eighty-seven percent are white (n = 70). The mean age of the respondents was 47.8. Bondsmen are most likely to work alone. Thirty-three (89%, missing data = 44) of the respondents worked in low prestige jobs prior to

becoming bondsmen, jobs only slightly higher in prestige than their fathers'. However, twenty-two percent (n = 8, missing data = 45) of the respondents had fathers who were bailbondsmen (Davis, 1982).

Bailbondsmen as Disrespected

Like many other occupations of low status in the occupational systems of which they are a part, the occupation of bailbondsmen lacks respect. An advocate of pawnbrokers describes the general problem of these low status occupations in the following passage (Levine, 1913:14; see also, Hartnett, 1981):

In every trade there are practitioners whose business methods react unfavorably upon their fellow tradesmen. Public opinion is very prone to condemn all in the trade as equally delinquent, making little discrimination between the honest and the dishonest. This attitude is one from which the pawnbroker has most unjustly suffered . . . Experience has taught them that the innocent as well as the guilty will suffer at the hands of an unthinking public.

The image of the "heavy-set, cigar chomping, sinister" (Wice, 1974:50) bailbondsmen has never been a good one. In 1905 a former Police Chief of New York, William McAdoo (1905:80–81) wrote about them:

They threaten the destruction of honest police captains . . . they hound and prosecute an officer who interferes with their schemes or lessens their profits; they drive good and honest policemen into being bad ones; they have a price for every man on the force . . . The sergeant at the desk is often only their tool; and the Captain and his plainsclothesmen and other officers have in many cases made arrests only to furnish victims and money for these unspeakable scoundrels. There should be a law against the professional bondsman.

Most of what has been written about bondsmen emerges from both a reform minded perspective and the journalistic muckraking tradition. These approaches seek to present the occupation as dysfunctional for the criminal justice system and the bailbondsman as corrupt and criminal. Goldfarb (1965:101–102), for instance, pictures bondsmen as:

. . . undesirable persons, former felons, and generally repugnant characters. Some bondsmen are colorful Runyonesque characters. Some are legitimate businessmen. But too many are "low-lives" whose very presence contaminates the business profession. . . . (V)ery frequently, if not generally, the bailbondsman is an unappealing and useless member of society. He lives on the law's inadequacy and his fellowmen's troubles. He gives nothing in return, or so little as to serve no overriding utilitarian purposes.

The bailbond system is seen to be corrupted by the individuals who become bailbondsmen. This corruption then spreads to other parts of the criminal justice system. Similar views have been echoed by investigatory committees (for instance, see U.S. Task Force on Law Enforcement, 1970), newspapers and magazines (for instance, see the recent expose in *Cleveland Plain Dealer* [1980] and other authors: see Roth, 1962; Breslin, 1963; Freed and Wald, 1964; Foote, 1966; Barnes, 1969; Smith and Ehrmann, 1974; Thomas, 1976). Bailbondsmen have been the constant object of vilifying attacks and moral crusades. Smith and Ehrmann (1974:36, 36) wrote that, "the real evil in the [bail] situation is not the matter of easy bail, but the disreputable bondsman . . . so far as it may be impossible to eliminate the professional bondsman, his business should be regulated like that of the 'Loan Sharks' in many jurisdictions." The *Cleveland Plain Dealer* (1980) presented bailsbondsmen as "parasites who feed off the misfortunes of others." They, "feed on legal system, get fat on misery."

Bailbondsmen possess what Saunders (1981: 43) has defined as occupational stigma.

Occupational stigma is a discrediting attribute accorded to individuals or groups who are performing certain occupationally identifiable roles . . . by other individuals or groups within a community, representing an actual threat to full social acceptance for the socially disgraced (by reason of their work function) who are perceived as negatively departing from the work norm of those engaged in 'respectable' occupational activities.

Awareness of Stigma

Bailbondsmen believe that conventional society perceives them as odious and they believe conventional society rejects association with them as a consequence of that perception. Both bailbondsmen who considered themselves to be respectable businessmen and those who consider themselves justly accused evinced this be-

lief.[1] As one bondsman who considered himself to be falsely accused responded to the mail survey:

Bailbondsmen, unlike other professionals, must start out with the opinion that they are crooks. It is a near impossibility for a bondsman, no matter how honest he is, to prove he is an honest businessman.

Another bondsman responded in an interview saying, "When people know you are a bondsman they don't want you in their house."

Workers in other dirty work occupations reveal a similar awareness. A garbageman interviewed in Perry's (1978:108) study of his occupation reported the following:

People don't want to have anything to do with you. They ask you what you do. You tell them, and they right away think you make so much money. It's . . . okay, but it's not more than they get. . . . Maybe it is all in my head, but it seems like they go to the other side of the street if they see you coming.

In another study of garbagemen, Saunders (1981:32) reports one as saying, "I know chaps who change their clothes because they do not want their neighbors to know what work they do." And Bleackley (1929:xviii) describes the particular stigma of the hangman:

(T)he necessity to perform unpleasant duties in other walks of life does not involve a social stigma. The occupations of the dentist and the dustman, the butcher, the sanitary inspector and the man midwife are frequently of an unsavoury description and yet we do not ostracise these persons in consequence. The surgeon kills many more people every year than 'Jack Ketch,' but the reason we refrain from placing him beyond the pale is not because, unlike the hangman's work, it is not done on purpose. He happens to belong to a trade that is not taboo, whereas 'Jack Ketch' does not.

Attitude to and Association with Like Others

Structurally, the relationship between bondsmen is primarily a competitive one, as they compete for a limited number of bailbonds within a geographically defined area. This may account, in part, for the antipathy between them. However, this antipathy is not universal. It is mani-

---

[1] While most members of the public may have only a superficial knowledge of bailbondsmen, the bailbondsman is in daily association with those individuals in part responsible for creating their disparaged image.

fested, for the most part, by those bondsmen who consider themselves to be respectable and honest. As two of these bondsmen said:

Ali Baba and his forty thieves would rank second to other bondsmen.

Most bondsmen are shit. They have no morals. They are not stand up straight guys. Half of them aren't worth a damn.

Interaction between these bondsmen was limited to the requirements of their work. Indicative, was the comment of one in an interview:

Look, I don't like to have too much to do with them [bondsmen]. I like to be around a better class of people if they'll let me.

This contrasted with the six bailbondsmen classified as "dishonest" who were interviewed and observed. They did not show antipathy to like others. Two of these six bailbondsmen were good friends. They each spoke about seeing each other socially outside the work setting. They also, upon occasion, participated in illegal activities together. An additional two of these bondsmen spoke of being friendly with other bondsmen (in other counties). None of the six bondsmen was averse to associating with other bondsmen.

Although bondsmen represent a discredited group which is the frequent object of attack by respectable society, organizations of bondsmen to counter these attacks appear to be rare, have low membership, and little commitment from most members (Davis, 1982). None of the bondsmen interviewed were members of such an organization.

The falsely accused bondsman, while recognizing individual bondsmen as respectable, attempts to separate himself from bondsmen as a whole. He sees himself as a particularly respectable businessman. Dishonest bondsmen on the other hand, tend to see themselves and other bondsmen as quite alike. One said, "We are in this boat together—all part of the swill."

Browne (1973:58) found a similar response among used car salesmen who, "are quick to point out the difference between themselves and their kind of operation as contrasted with other used car salesmen and their less scrupulous, less honest kind of operation." This is despite the fact that Browne (p. 58) finds that "(t)hey are almost always operating well within the

law. . . ." Similarly, an 18th century writer (Anonymous, 1745:4) describes pawnbrokers as rejecting association with others. They are "a Sett of Men that never associate with any other tradesmen. . . ."

Bailbondsmen have the opportunity to affiliate with discredited individuals apart from other bondsmen; clients of bondsmen and their acquaintances. However the falsely accused bondsmen interviewed and observed distanced themselves from their clients and their world. As one of these bondsmen said:

To me it's strictly business. I don't want to be bothered by people like that. I wouldn't want them in my house either. It happens to be a lousy business I am in.

And another remarked:

They're [clients] the lowest of the low. I wouldn't go near them except to get their money or help them.

By contrast, five of the six avowedly dishonest bondsmen were firmly enmeshed in a social network consisting of individuals who engaged in criminal activity on a frequent basis. Their relationships with them were both of a business and social nature.

Gold (1964:27) describes attitudes among janitors that are very similar to those of "disrespectable" bondsmen:

Janitors are keenly aware of their occupation's lowly reputation in the community. Yet, as individuals, they develop self-conceptions of the sort that ordinarily would be found in members of established middle-class occupations. How, then, does the janitor reconcile his self conceptions with corresponding social conceptions of janitors? He uses a simple, clear-cut device. After comparing himself with occupational associates, he tends to agree that the community is right in its evaluation of *them*, but that *he* is "different." He agrees that other janitors are unprincipled, disorderly, and irresponsible. However, he, the individual janitor, belongs to the category of practitioners who are morally sound, capable, and responsible.

Attitude to and Association with Conventional Society

Bailbondsmen routinely encounter rejection from respectable society. Bailbondsmen have described how this rejection may occur in the workplace:

Judges think bondsmen are lower than whale shit. They think we socialize with criminals. A judge would never lower himself to talk to a bondsman.

And outside the workplace:

When people know you are a bondsman they don't want you in their house.

Pine (1977:38), in his study of funeral directors has found a similar tendency for them to be rejected:

Another problem for funeral directors is the occasional banning of funeral homes from certain community areas. Even in the absence of zoning regulations, funeral homes have been closed or forced to move when they were offensive to neighbors in residential areas. Also troublesome is that the funeral home ban may extend to the funeral director himself . . . (F)uneral directors have been denied membership in organizations solely because of their occupation.

The falsely accused bailbondsman is aware of how he is perceived by respectable society. Respectable society forms, in a sense, the bailbondsman's "looking glass self" (Cooley, 1964:183–184). He believes respectable society both perceives him and judges him as dishonest and sleazy. But respectable society also forms his normative reference group. It is with them that he identifies and aspires to belong. To condemn conventional society as being as evil as the bailbondsman would be to corrupt his own aspiration to be accepted as respectable; it would bring him closer to the world of the stigmatized which he shuns. Rather he aligns himself with respectable society. The falsely accused sees respectable society as no better than he is and at the same time compares himself favorably to it. Thus, he not only points to the illegal activities of respectable people, but, in addition, sees his normal work activities on an equal footing with high status occupations. As one respondent wrote to illustrate the first point that dirty workers are to be found in all occupations:

I would suggest there are so many bad apples in other professions . . . a couple of educators used federal money to lobby and defame the profession (of bondsmen) because of some unethical men. There are many excellent men in the field. There are many excellent men in the field that are outstanding citizens. There are bad insurance agents, bad salesmen, bad students, just bad plain citizens, and bad politicians. . . . There are many corrupt police, courts, and other enforcement people, and the percentage is fairly high from what I see.

And in demonstrating the second point, that bailbonding is not dirty work, another respondent wrote:

It must be remembered that we are normally well educated and well versed in many professions. We, to operate successfully, must have in many respects the knowledge of attorneys, police officers, investigators, collection agencies, car salesmen, court clerks, judges and loan officers and bankers.

The falsely accused bailbondsman justifies his work as socially valuable. He sees himself as a good person *doing* dirty work. A bailbondsman said:

I feel that having bailbondsmen are a service to the community because all persons that are locked up cannot make a bond. And we try to be selective, but be kind where there is reason, even though persons may be involved with drugs, alcohol, and other habits. We also save the taxpayer money when he does not show in court. We stand the loss and have to find the missing person, and keep a record of those that do not show, and will see that other bondsmen will not take the same person out.

The falsely accused bondsman embraces conventional values of honesty, compassion, monetary success, professionalism. In interviews falsely accused bondsmen remarked:

I treat my business as a career and handle it with care, compassion and brains. The reason I became a bondsman was there wasn't any here. Lots of blacks were getting arrested and nobody seemed to care. I got into it as a civil thing. This was a good will thing. I made money too. We all know that it's for the dollars. . . . You must be honest with the person, go according with the law, be honest with yourself.

Like the janitors described in Gold's (1964) study, the bailbondsman's "conceptions of himself are thoroughly wrapped up in his work. He is aware that society judges him, and that he judges himself, largely by the work he does. He is consciously trying to achieve higher status through public recognition of higher work status" (p. 21).

Social Isolation

The falsely accused bondsmen tend to lead lives of social isolation. Following Seeman's

(1972) definition of social isolation, these bondsmen have a "low expectancy for inclusion and social acceptance, expressed typically in feelings of loneliness or feelings of rejection and repudiation."

These feelings have been detailed earlier in the paper. But there are other indicators of social isolation that we can point to. Only five of the twenty-one falsely accused bondsmen said they were members of community organizations, although, only two were active members. When I asked a bondsman why he was not a member of any organization he said:

First of all, I haven't got the time for such stuff. Then I tried joining one once but they didn't like the idea of a bondsman being a member, I guess.

We find that for the falsely accused bondsman work activities are structured so that very little time is available for non-work activity:

What social contacts do you make? A college professor meets people that is his equal or better than you. You don't have to worry about your social life. If a bailbondsman wants to live a clean life and not associate with these people, he's limited. And then your time, you're working so many hours that you don't have time to go out and socialize. Your life passes you by and what do you end up with?

The twenty-one falsely accused bailbondsmen studied worked a mean of 76 hours a week. The six dishonest bailbondsmen worked, as bailbondsmen, a mean of 36 hours a week.

Many of the avowedly dishonest bondsmen saw their work as bondsmen as less central to their overall activities. One individual, for instance, could be said to have become a bondsman because of his involvement with others in criminal activity. He was active in many illegal activities prior to becoming a bondsman (fencing cars, running numbers, and gambling). Many of his friends and associates were also engaged in these and other illegal activities. He saw becoming a bondsman as an opportunity to make money regardless of whether it was done legally. His contacts with criminals, he believed would be useful to him. Three of these bondsmen professed to have grown up with others who routinely engaged in criminal

activity. The first job of one of these individuals prior to becoming a bondsman was to pay off bondsmen and lawyers for professional criminals who wanted cases fixed and for other services. Another commented, "The only people I knew were criminals."[2] As bondsmen, except for social isolation, immersion in a stigmatized subculture remained their most viable option. As one of these bondsmen commented during an interview:

You know, I got my friends: car thieves, robbers, bad guys. But that's all I got. I'm stuck with them and they're stuck with me.

Unlike the falsely accused bondsmen, it is not respectable society that is their reference group, but the world peopled by professional and petty criminals. The falsely accused bondsman finds it difficult to join or embrace the straight world because it often will not have him. Yet to embrace the world of the stigmatized is not a solution either. To associate with his fellow bondsmen (some of whom are dishonest and all of whom are generally believed to be dishonest) would be to confirm and strengthen, in the eyes of his audience, their original evaluation of him, thus furthering the difficulty of becoming respectable. The falsely accused bondsman does not feel he is doing anything wrong. Rather, he feels wronged. The image he presents of himself as respectable clashes with the way he believes he is viewed by respectable society. Rather than immersing himself in a stigmatized subculture or forming, with other bondsmen, a subculture of the stigmatized or an organization of the stigmatized (solutions that would belie his self image of respectability) he often chooses social isolation.

Occupants of similarly disparaged work roles also report feelings of social isolation. Sanson the executioner (1881:xii, 19) describes his life in Paris:

I have lived for twelve years under a name which is not mine, reaping with something like shame the friendship and good will which I constantly fear to be dispelled by the discovery of my former avocations. . . . A glance at (my ancestor) was sufficient to identify him as the executioner; men, women, and children recoiled from him.

---

[2]These bondsmen can be seen in one way as the archetypal deviant who is immersed in a subculture. However, they also illustrate the problem with that literature: the difficulty in determining whether their immersion in a deviant subculture was an adaptation to social reaction or a factor in producing their initial rule breaking.

In an 1924 pamphlet an anonymous writer describes the plight of the pawnbroker (Anonymous, 1824):

Perhaps no class of men ever were greater sufferers from this cause (that honorable people dislike them) than the persons I am advocating. Owing to it, their personal intercourse, and friendly communication with society have been interrupted; clouds of suspicion have been raised without any cause, and evils believed which never existed.

Their profession has been deemed dishonourable—their hearts callous—their sentiments illiberal; and, though I may be bold to say, many of them, in their walk of life, have been and are, considered persons of the most irreproachable character, yet the excellency of their conduct scarcely ever did more than remove the odium from themselves in the general circle to which they are confined, while the general prejudice has grown stronger from age, and more inveterate by repetition.

Similarly, Saunders (1981) in his study of lower grade workers in service organizations found that janitors and nightwatchmen are often isolates.

There were good reasons why many of the falsely accused bondsmen became socially isolated. Some of these reasons arise from the structure of the occupation itself which limits available options. Because bondsmen constantly have clients "out on the street" it is difficult to stop being a bondsman once one has become established in the occupation. Thus, it is difficult to resume or assume the role of the conformist.[3] At the same time, to pursue a livelihood as a bondsman, the individual must make it known that he is one; to advertise himself. This makes "passing" a difficult option to pursue. In addition, although there is some degree of cooperation between bondsmen, it is essentially a highly competitive business. Often resources are scarce and demand is low. Bondsmen also often work alone or in small partnerships. This may be less a result of animosity than economic rationality. As Robinson (1935:50) has argued, in conditions where there is a high degree of uncertainty, small firms are likely to be more successful than large ones. Organizational alliances become difficult to forge under these circumstances. However, these structural reasons cannot be seen as sufficient explanations for the

social isolation of the falsely accused bondsman. As we pointed out, there are good reasons why we should expect organizations of bondsmen to form. In addition, we have seen that their dishonest counterparts are not socially isolated. The social isolation of the falsely accused is an adaptation to their dilemma of believing themselves to be respectable, desiring to be perceived and accepted as respectable, and encountering rejection from respectable society.

Conclusion

The social categories to which bailbondsmen, janitors, garbagemen, the mentally ill, and others belong are stigmatized. That is, these individuals by virtue of their membership in these social categories are perceived as blemished and defective. Further, as a result of this perception, they encounter rejection by conventional society. Rather than accept this view of themselves some of them attempt to be and define themselves as respectable and conformist. The falsely accused's knowledge and perception that like others may be engaged in discrediting behavior may make him wary of association with other members he believes may bring ill repute upon him in his quest for respectability. Given structural conditions that make other forms of adaptation (neutralization, passing, and "rehabilitation") difficult, this may result in his social isolation between conventional and stigmatized worlds.

Stonequist (1942:297), in his discussion of the marginal man, alludes to a similar phenomenon:

The marginal man is the individual who lives in, or has ties of kinship with, two or more interacting societies between which there exists sufficient incompatibility to render his own adjustment to them difficult or impossible.

The social isolate is this marginal man. His isolation is made possible by three elements: (1) rejection or hostility from conventional society; (2) a belief on the part of the actor that he is being unjustly excluded from that society; and (3) an attitude toward like others and other stigmatized individuals that sees them as rightfully rejected.

---

[3] Gold (1964:43) found that for similar reasons janitors who see retirement "as the termination of distasteful work . . . rarely reach their goal."

We can see that if the actor can see like others as sharing in what he sees as his injustice that he may likely affiliate with them. One has only to point to the many organizations of discredited groups. But for each of these groups there are probably individuals who lie outside and isolated from them. While among Jews there are countless organizations and subcultural supports there is still the Wandering Jew (Stonequist, 1942:307):

They (the individual marginal Jew) . . . are divided in their social allegiance, drawn forward by the Gentile world but uncertain of its hospitality, restrained by sentiments of loyalty to the Jewish world but repelled by its restrictions. They are self-conscious and feel inferior because their social status is in question. They are the partly assimilated, the partly accepted, the real Wandering Jews, at home neither in the ghetto nor in the world outside the ghetto.

Believing oneself to be falsely accused and isolating oneself from like others and discredited others results in a paradoxical and ironic situation. If being truly accused is likely to result in affiliation with stigmatized others in a situation where one is provided with social support, believing oneself to be falsely accused may result in a social role that lacks social support. The actor who considers himself "innocent" may suffer isolation as a result. The actor who considers himself correctly stigmatized may find himself in a more positive social position. Further, this social isolation makes it more difficult to neutralize the stigma and, at the same time, makes it easier to stigmatize the actor. The inability of the falsely accused bailbondsmen to organize and protest the attributions made against them, in turn, made it easier for the attributions to be made regardless of their validity.

This conception of self and its relationship to others can be seen to have a direct bearing on the very creation of stigma; who, how, and why some individuals and groups are successfully discredited. Under some circumstances (for instance, when members of a group are competing with one another) it may be easier to discredit certain groups of individuals when those individuals *deny* the validity of that definition. Denial of stigma may then result in increased difficulty in neutralizing the stigma.

REFERENCES

Anonymous. 1745. *A Plain Answer To a Late Pamphlet Entitled The Business of Pawnbroking Stated and Defended.* London: George Woodfall.

Anonymous. 1824. *An Apology for the Pawnbrokers Most Respectfully Addressed to the Members of Both Houses of Parliament, the Judges of the Land and the Justices of the Peace Throughout the Kingdom.* Leadenhall Street: S. McDowell.

Ball, Donald W. 1970. "The Problematics of Respectability." In Jack D. Douglas (ed.), *Deviance and Respectability: The Social Construction of Moral Meanings.* New York: Basic, pp. 326–371.

Barnes, Fred. 1969. "The Professional Bondsman: Life Isn't What It Used to Be." *Sunday Magazine, Washington Star,* August 17.

Blau, Judith. 1982. "Prominence in a Network of Communication: Work Relations in a Children's Psychiatric Hospital." *Sociological Quarterly,* 23:235–251.

Bleackley, Horace. 1929. *The Hangmen of England.* London: Chapman and Hall.

Breslin, Jimmy. 1963. "Best Bet for Bail: A Good Crook." *Life* (March 23):15–16.

Browne, Joy. 1973. *The Used-Car Game: A Sociology of the Bargain.* Lexington, Mass.: Heath.

Cooley, Charles Horton. 1964. *Human Nature and the Social Order.* New York: Schocken Books.

Cleveland Plain Dealer. 1980. "Bailbondsmen Here Feed on Legal System, Get Fat on Misery." August 3, Section A:1.

Davis, David Scott. 1982. *Deviance and Social Isolation: The Case of the Falsely Accused.* Unpublished Ph.D. dissertation, Princeton University.

DeRhoda. 1979. "Whither the Bailbondsman." *Law Journal,* 1:19.

Foote, Caleb (ed.). 1966. *Studies in Bail.* Philadelphia: University of Pennsylvania Press.

Freed, Donald and Patricia Wald. 1964. "Bail in the United States: 1964." Working Papers for the National Conference on Bail and Criminal Justice, Washington, D.C.

Goffman, Erving. 1963. *Stigma.* Englewood Cliffs, N.J.: Prentice-Hall.

Gold, Raymond L. 1964. "In the Basement-the Apartment-Building Janitor." In Peter Berger (ed.), *The Human Shape of Work.* New York: Macmillan, pp. 1–49.

Goldfarb, Ronald. 1965. *Ransom: A Critique of the American Bail System.* New York: Harper & Row.

Goldman, Marion S. 1981. "Book review of Robert Prus and Styllianos Irini. Hookers; Rounders, and Desk Clerks: The Social Organization of a Hotel Community." *Sociology of Work and Occupations,* 8:381–384.

Goldschalk, J. J. 1979. "Foreign Labour and Dirty Work." *The Netherlands' Journal of Sociology,* 15:1–11.

Hartnett, Catherine. 1981. "The Pawnbroker: Banker of the Poor?" In Israel L. Barak-Glantz and C. Ronald Huff (eds.), *The Mad, the Bad, and the Different: Essays in Honor of Simon Dinitz*. Lexington, Mass.: Lexington Books, pp. 149–155.

Hughes, Everett C. 1951. "Work and Self." In John H. Rohrer and Muzafer Sherif (eds.), *Social Psychology at the Crossroads*. New York: Harper & Row, pp. 313–323.

————. 1964. "Good People and Dirty Work." In Howard Becker (ed.), *The Other Side*. New York: Free Press, pp. 23–26.

Jacobs, James B. and Harold C. Retsky. 1975. "Prison Guard." *Urban Life*, 4:5–29.

Killian, Lewis M. 1981. "The Sociologists Look at the Cuckoo's Nest: The Misuse of Ideal Types." *The American Sociologist*, 16:230–239.

Lazar Institute. 1981. *Advisory Panel Meeting on Bail Bonding Study*. Washington, D.C., April 10.

Lemert, Edwin. 1953. "An Isolation Closure Theory of Check Forgery." *Journal of Criminal Law, Criminology, and Police Science*, 44(3):296–307.

Levine, S. 1913. *The Business of Pawnbroking: A Guide and a Defense*. New York: D. Halpern.

McAdoo, William. 1905. *Guarding a Great City*. New York: Harper & Row.

Perry, S. E. 1978. *San Francisco Scavengers: Dirty Work and the Pride of Ownership*. Berkeley: University of California Press.

Pine, V. 1977. *Caretaker of the Dead: The American Funeral Director*. New York: Irvington.

Robinson, E. 1935. *The Structure of Competitive Industry*. London: Nisbet.

Roth, J. 1962. "Bondsman Looks Back Wistfully to Days of Reliable Criminals." *New York Times* (September 20):35.

Sanson, Henry (ed.) 1881. *Memoirs of the Sansons*. Picadilly: Chatto and Windus.

Saunders, Conrad. 1981. *Social Stigma of Occupations: The Lower Grade Worker in Service Organizations*. Westmead: Gower.

Schneider, Joseph and Peter Conrad. 1980. "In the Closet with Illness: Epilepsy, Stigma Potential and Information Control." *Social Problems*, 28(1):32–44.

Seeman, Melvin. 1972. "Alienation and Engagement." In Angus Campbell and Phillip E. Converse (eds.), *The Human Meaning of Social Change*. New York: Russell Sage, pp. 467–527.

Simoni, Joseph J. and Richard A. Ball. 1977. "The Mexican Medicine Huckster: He Must Be Doing Something Right." *Sociology of Work and Occupations*, 4:343–365.

Smith, Reginald H. and Herbert B. Ehrmann. 1974. "The Municipal Court in Cleveland." In John Robertson (ed.), *Rough Justice: Perspectives on Lower Criminal Courts*. Boston: Little Brown, pp. 26–59.

Stonequist, Everett. 1942. "The Marginal Character of the Jews." In Isacque Graeber and Steuart Brett (eds.), *Jews in a Gentile World: The Problems of Anti-Semitism*. Westport, Conn.: Greenwood.

Thomas, Wayne. 1976. *Bail Reform in America*. Berkeley: University of California Press.

Thomas, William Isaac and Florian Znaniecki. 1918. *The Polish Peasant in Europe and America*. Vol. 1. Chicago: University of Chicago Press.

U.S. Task Force on Law and Law Enforcement. 1970. *The Rule of Law: An Alternative to Violence*. Nashville: Aurora Publishers.

Wice, Paul. 1974. *Freedom for Sale: A National Study of Pretrial Release*. Lexington, Mass.: Lexington Books.

Wulbert, Roland. 1965. "Inmate Pride in Total Institutions." *American Journal of Sociology*, 71(1): 1–9.

Rapists' Vocabulary of Motives

DIANA SCULLY and JOSEPH MAROLLA

Psychiatry has dominated the literature on rapists since "irresistible impulse" (Glueck, 1925:323) and "disease of the mind" (Glueck, 1925:243) were introduced as the causes of rape. Research has been based on small samples of men, frequently the clinicians' own patient population. Not surprisingly, the medical model has predominated: rape is viewed as an individualistic, idiosyncratic symptom of a disordered personality. That is, rape is assumed to be a psychopathologic problem and individual rapists are assumed to be "sick." However, advocates of this model have been unable to isolate a typical or even predictable pattern of symptoms that are causally linked to rape. Additionally, research has demonstrated that fewer than 5 percent of rapists were psychotic at the time of their rape (Abel *et al.,* 1980).

We view rape as behavior learned socially through interaction with others; convicted rapists have learned the attitudes and actions consistent with sexual aggression against women. Learning also includes the acquisition of culturally derived vocabularies of motive, which can be used to diminish responsibility and to negotiate a non-deviant identity.

Sociologists have long noted that people can, and do, commit acts they define as wrong and, having done so, engage various techniques to disavow deviance and present themselves as normal. Through the concept of "vocabulary of motive," Mills (1940:904) was among the first to shed light on this seemingly perplexing contradiction. Wrong-doers attempt to reinterpret their actions through the use of a linguistic device by which norm-breaking conduct is socially interpreted. That is, anticipating the negative consequences of their behavior, wrong-doers attempt to present the act in terms that are both culturally appropriate and acceptable.

Following Mills, a number of sociologists have focused on the types of techniques employed by actors in problematic situations (Hall and Hewitt, 1970; Hewitt and Hall, 1973; Hewitt and Stokes, 1975; Sykes and Matza, 1957). Scott and Lyman (1968) describe excuses and justifications, linguistic "accounts" that explain and remove culpability for an untoward act after it has been committed. *Excuses* admit the act was bad or inappropriate but deny full responsibility, often through appeals to accident, or biological drive, or through scapegoating. In contrast, *justifications* accept responsibility for the act but deny that it was wrong—that is, they show in this situation the act was appropriate. *Accounts* are socially approved vocabularies that neutralize an act or its consequences and are always a manifestation of an underlying negotiation of identity.

Stokes and Hewitt (1976:837) use the term "aligning actions" to refer to those tactics and techniques used by actors when some feature of a situation is problematic. Stated simply, the concept refers to an actor's attempt, through various means, to bring his or her conduct into alignment with culture. Culture in this sense is conceptualized as a "set of cognitive constraints—objects—to which people must relate as they form lines of conduct" (1976:837), and includes physical constraints, expectations and definitions of others, and personal biography. Carrying out aligning actions implies both awareness of those elements of normative culture that are applicable to the deviant act and, in addition, an actual effort to bring the act into line with this awareness. The result is that deviant behavior is legitimized.

This paper presents an analysis of interviews we conducted with a sample of 114 convicted, incarcerated rapists. We use the concept of accounts (Scott and Lyman, 1968) as a tool to organize and analyze the vocabularies of motive which this group of rapists used to explain themselves and their actions. An analysis of their ac-

Excerpt from "Convicted Rapists' Vocabulary of Motive: Excuses and Justifications," *Social Problems,* Vol. 31, No. 5 (June 1984), pp. 530–544 by permission of the Society for the Study of Social Problems and the authors. This research was supported by a grant (R01 MH33013) from the National Center For the Prevention and Control of Rape, National Institute of Mental Health. The authors thank the Virginia Department of Corrections for their cooperation and assistance in this research.

counts demonstrates how it was possible for 83 percent (n = 114)[1] of these convicted rapists to view themselves as non-rapists.

When rapists' accounts are examined, a typology emerges that consists of admitters and deniers. Admitters (n = 47) acknowledged that they had forced sexual acts on their victims and defined the behavior as rape. In contrast, deniers[2] either eschewed sexual contact or all association with the victim (n = 35),[3] or admitted to sexual acts but did not define their behavior as rape (n = 32).

The remainder of this paper is divided into two sections. In the first, we discuss the accounts which the rapists used to justify their behavior. In the second, we discuss those accounts which attempted to excuse the rape. By and large, the deniers used justifications while the admitters used excuses. In some cases, both groups relied on the same themes, stereotypes, and images: some admitters, like most deniers, claimed that women enjoyed being raped. Some deniers excused their behavior by referring to alcohol or drug use, although they did so quite differently than admitters. Through these narrative accounts, we explore convicted rapists' own perceptions of their crimes.

Methods and Validity

From September, 1980, through September, 1981, we interviewed 114 male convicted rapists who were incarcerated in seven maximum or medium security prisons in the Commonwealth of Virginia. All of the rapists had been convicted of the rape or attempted rape (n = 8) of an adult woman, although a few had teenage victims as well. Men convicted of incest, statutory rape, or sodomy of a male were omitted from the sample.

Twelve percent of the rapists had been convicted of more than one rape or attempted rape, 39 percent also had convictions for burglary or robbery, 29 percent for abduction, 25 percent for sodomy, and 11 percent for first or second de-

gree murder. Eighty-two percent had a previous criminal history but only 23 percent had records for previous sex offenses. Their sentences for rape and accompanying crimes ranged from 10 years to an accumulation by one man of seven life sentences plus 380 years; 43 percent of the rapists were serving from 10 to 30 years and 22 percent were serving at least one life term. Forty-six percent of the rapists were white and 54 percent were black. Their ages ranged from 18 to 60 years; 88 percent were between 18 and 35 years. Forty-two percent were either married or cohabitating at the time of their offense. Only 20 percent had a high school education or better, and 85 percent came from working-class backgrounds. Despite the popular belief that rape is due to a personality disorder, only 26 percent of these rapists had any history of emotional problems. When the rapists in this study were compared to a statistical profile of felons in all Virginia prisons, prepared by the Virginia Department of Corrections, rapists who volunteered for this research were disproportionately white, somewhat better educated, and younger than the average inmate.

All participants in this study were volunteers. We sent a letter to every inmate (n = 3500) at each of the seven prisons. The letters introduced us as professors at a local university, described our research as a study of men's attitudes toward sexual behavior and women, outlined our procedures for ensuring confidentiality, and solicited volunteers from all criminal categories. Using one follow-up letter, approximately 25 percent of all inmates, including rapists, indicated their willingness to be interviewed by mailing an information sheet to us at the university. From this pool of volunteers, we constructed a sample of rapists based on age, education, race, severity of current offenses, and previous criminal records. Obviously, the sample was not random and thus may not be representative of all rapists.

Each of the authors—one woman and one man—interviewed half of the rapists. Both au-

---

[1] These numbers include pretest interviews. When the analysis involves either questions that were not asked in the pretest or that were changed, they are excluded and thus the number changes.

[2] There is, of course, the possibility that some of these men really were innocent of rape. However, while the U.S. criminal justice system is not without flaw, we assume that it is highly unlikely that this many men could have been unjustly convicted of rape, especially since rape is a crime with traditionally low conviction rates. Instead, for purposes of this research, we assume that these men were guilty as charged and that their attempt to maintain an image of non-rapist springs from some psychological or sociologically interpretable mechanism.

[3] Because of their outright denial, interviews with this group of rapists did not contain the data being analyzed here and, consequently, they are not included in this paper.

thors were able to establish rapport and obtain information. However, the rapists volunteered more about their feelings and emotions to the female author and her interviews lasted longer.

All rapists were given an 89-page interview, which included a general background, psychological, criminal, and sexual history, attitude scales, and 30 pages of open-ended questions intended to explore their perceptions of their crimes, their victims, and themselves. Because a voice print is an absolute source of identification, we did not use tape recorders. All interviews were hand recorded. With some practice, we found it was possible to record much of the interview verbatim. While hand recording inevitably resulted in some lost data, it did have the advantage of eliciting more confidence and candor in the men.

Interviews with the rapist lasted from three hours to seven hours; the average was about four-and-one-half hours. Most of the rapists were reluctant to end the interview. Once rapport had been established, the men wanted to talk, even though it sometimes meant, for example, missing a meal.

Because of the reputation prison inmates have for 'conning,' validity was a special concern in our research. Although the purpose of the research was to obtain the men's own perceptions of their acts, it was also necessary to establish the extent to which these perceptions deviated from other descriptions of their crimes. To establish validity, we used the same technique others have used in prison research: comparing factual information, including details of the crime, obtained in the interview with pre-sentence reports on file at the prisons (Athens, 1977; Luckenbill, 1977; Queen's Bench Foundation, 1976). Pre-sentence reports, written by a court worker at the time of conviction, usually include general background information, a psychological evaluation, the offender's version of the details of the crime, and the victim's or police's version of the details of the crime. Using these records allowed us to clarify two important issues: first, the amount of change that had occurred in rapists' accounts from pre-sentencing to the time when we interviewed them; and, second, the amount of discrepancy between rapists' accounts, as told to us, and the

victims' and/or police versions of the crime, contained in the pre-sentence reports.

The time between pre-sentence reports and our interviews (in effect, the amount of time rapists had spent in prison before we interviewed them) ranged from less than one year to 20 years; the average was three years. Yet despite this time lapse, there were no significant changes in the way rapists explained their crimes, with the exception of 18 men who had denied their crimes at their trials but admitted them to us. There were no cases of men who admitted their crime at their trial but denied them when talking to us.

However, there were major differences between the accounts we heard of the crimes from rapists and the police's and victim's versions. Admitters (including deniers turned admitters) told us essentially the same story as the police and victim versions. However, the admitters subtly understated the force they had used and, though they used words such as *violent* to describe their acts, they also omitted reference to the more brutal aspects of their crime.

In contrast, deniers' interview accounts differed significantly from victim and police versions. According to the pre-sentence reports, 11 of the 32 deniers had been acquainted with their victim. But an additional four deniers told us they had been acquainted with their victims. In the pre-sentence reports, police or victim versions of the crime described seven rapes in which the victim had been hitchhiking or was picked up in a bar; but deniers told us this was true of 20 victims. Weapons were present in 21 of the 32 rapes according to the pre-sentence reports, yet only nine men acknowledged the presence of a weapon and only two of the nine admitted they had used it to threaten or intimidate their victim. Finally, in at least seven of the rapes, the victim had been seriously injured,[4] but only three men admitted injury. In two of the three cases, the victim had been murdered; in these cases the men denied the rape but not the murder. Indeed, deniers constructed accounts for us which, by implicating the victim, made their own conduct appear to have been more appropriate. They never used words such as *violent*, choosing instead to emphasize the sexual component of their behavior.

---

[4] It was sometimes difficult to determine the full extent of victim injury from the pre-sentence reports. Consequently, it is doubtful that this number accurately reflects the degree of injuries sustained by victims.

It should be noted that we investigated the possibility that deniers claimed their behavior was not criminal because, in contrast to admitters, their crimes resembled what research has found the public define as a controversial rape, that is, victim an acquaintance, no injury or weapon, victim picked up hitchhiking or in a bar (Burt, 1980; Burt and Albin, 1981; Williams, 1979). . . . [T]he crimes committed by deniers were only slightly more likely to involve these elements.

This contrast between pre-sentence reports and interviews suggests several significant factors related to interview content validity. First, when asked to explain their behavior, our sample of convicted rapists (except deniers turned admitters) responded with accounts that had changed surprisingly little since their trials. Second, admitters' interview accounts were basically the same as others' versions of their crimes, while deniers systematically put more blame on the victims.

Justifying Rape

Deniers attempted to justify their behavior by presenting the victim in a light that made her appear culpable, regardless of their own actions. Five themes run through attempts to justify their rapes: (1) women as seductresses; (2) women mean "yes" when they say "no"; (3) most women eventually relax and enjoy it; (4) nice girls don't get raped; and (5) guilty of a minor wrongdoing.

Women as Seductresses
Men who rape need not search far for cultural language which supports the premise that women provoke or are responsible for rape. In addition to common cultural stereotypes, the fields of psychiatry and criminology (particularly the subfield of victimology) have traditionally provided justifications for rape, often by portraying raped women as the victims of their own seduction (Albin, 1977; Marolla and Scully, 1979). For example, Hollander (1924:130) argues:

Considering the amount of illicit intercourse, rape of women is very rare indeed. Flirtation and provocative conduct, i.e. tacit (if not actual) consent is generally the prelude to intercourse.

Since women are supposed to be coy about their sexual availability, refusal to comply with a man's sexual demands lacks meaning and rape appears normal. The fact that violence and, often, a weapon are used to accomplish the rape is not considered. As an example, Abrahamsen (1960:61) writes:

The conscious or unconscious biological or psychological attraction between man and woman does not exist only on the part of the offender toward the woman but, also, on her part toward him, which in many instances may, to some extent, be the impetus for his sexual attack. Often a women [sic] unconsciously wishes to be taken by force—consider the theft of the bride in Peer Gynt.

Like Peer Gynt, the deniers we interviewed tried to demonstrate that their victims were willing and, in some cases, enthusiastic participants. In these accounts, the rape became more dependent upon the victim's behavior than upon their own actions.

Thirty-one percent (n = 10) of the deniers presented an extreme view of the victim. Not only willing, she was the aggressor, a seductress who lured them, unsuspecting, into sexual action. Typical was a denier convicted of his first rape and accompanying crimes of burglary, sodomy, and abduction. According to the pre-sentence reports, he had broken into the victim's house and raped her at knife point. While he admitted to the breaking and entry, which he claimed was for altruistic purposes ("to pay for the prenatal care of a friend's girlfriend"), he also argued that when the victim discovered him, he had tried to leave but she had asked him to stay. Telling him that she cheated on her husband, she had voluntarily removed her clothes and seduced him. She was, according to him, an exemplary sex partner who "enjoyed it very much and asked for oral sex.[5] Can I have it now?" he reported her as saying. He claimed they had spent hours in bed, after which the victim had

---

[5] It is worth noting that a number of deniers specifically mentioned the victim's alleged interest in oral sex. Since our interview questions about sexual history indicated that the rapists themselves found oral sex marginally acceptable, the frequent mention is probably another attempt to discredit the victim. However, since a tape recorder could not be used for the interviews and the importance of these claims didn't emerge until the data was being coded and analyzed, it is possible that it was mentioned even more frequently but not recorded.

told him he was good looking and asked to see him again. "Who would believe I'd meet a fellow like this?" he reported her as saying.

In addition to this extreme group, 25 percent (n = 8) of the deniers said the victim was willing and had made some sexual advances. An additional 9 percent (n = 3) said the victim was willing to have sex for money or drugs. In two of these three cases, the victim had been either an acquaintance or picked up, which the rapists said led them to expect sex.

Women Mean "Yes" When They Say "No"

Thirty-four percent (n = 11) of the deniers described their victim as unwilling, at least initially, indicating either that she had resisted or that she had said no. Despite this, and even though (according to pre-sentence reports) a weapon had been present in 64 percent (n = 7) of these 11 cases, the rapists justified their behavior by arguing that either the victim had not resisted enough or that her "no" had really meant "yes." For example, one denier who was serving time for a previous rape was subsequently convicted of attempting to rape a prison hospital nurse. He insisted he had actually completed the second rape, and said of his victim: "She semi-struggled but deep down inside I think she felt it was a fantasy come true." The nurse, according to him, had asked a question about his conviction for rape, which he interpreted as teasing. "It was like she was saying, 'rape me'." Further, he stated that she had helped him along with oral sex and "from her actions, she was enjoying it." In another case, a 34-year-old man convicted of abducting and raping a 15-year old teenager at knife point as she walked on the beach, claimed it was a pickup. This rapist said women like to be overpowered before sex, but to dominate after it begins.

A man's body is like a coke bottle, shake it up, put your thumb over the opening and feel the tension. When you take a woman out, woo her, then she says "no, I'm a nice girl," you have to use force. All men do this. She said "no" but it was a societal no, she wanted to be coaxed. All women say "no" when they mean "yes" but its a societal no, so they won't have to feel responsible later.

Claims that the victim didn't resist or, if she did, didn't resist enough, were also used by 24 percent (n = 11) of admitters to explain why, during the incident, they believed the victim was willing and that they were not raping. These rapists didn't redefine their acts until some time after the crime. For example, an admitter who used a bayonet to threaten his victim, an employee of the store he had been robbing, stated:

At the time I didn't think it was rape. I just asked her nicely and she didn't resist. I never considered prison. I just felt like I had met a friend. It took about five years of reading and going to school to change my mind about whether it was rape. I became familiar with the subtlety of violence. But at the time, I believe that as long as I didn't hurt anyone it wasn't wrong. At the time, I didn't think I would go to prison, I thought I would beat it.

Another typical case involved a gang rape in which the victim was abducted at knife point as she walked home about midnight. According to two of the rapists, both of whom were interviewed, at the time they had thought the victim had willingly accepted a ride from the third rapist (who was not interviewed). They claimed the victim didn't resist and one reported her as saying she would do anything if they would take her home. In this rapist's view, "She acted like she enjoyed it, but maybe she was just acting. She wasn't crying, she was engaging in it." He reported that she had been friendly to the rapist who abducted her and, claiming not to have a home phone, she gave him her office number—a tactic eventually used to catch the three. In retrospect, this young man had decided, "She was scared and just relaxed and enjoyed it to avoid getting hurt." Note, however, that while he had redefined the act as rape, he continued to believe she enjoyed it.

Men who claimed to have been unaware that they were raping viewed sexual aggression as a man's prerogative at the time of the rape. Thus they regarded their act as little more than a minor wrongdoing even though most possessed or used a weapon. As long as the victim survived without major physical injury, from their perspective, a rape had not taken place. Indeed, even U.S. courts have often taken the position that physical injury is a necessary ingredient for a rape conviction.

Most Women Eventually Relax and Enjoy It

Many of the rapists expected us to accept the image, drawn from cultural stereotype, that once the rape began, the victim relaxed and enjoyed it.[6] Indeed, 69 percent (n = 22) of deniers justified their behavior by claiming not only that the victim was willing, but also that she enjoyed herself, in some cases to an immense degree. Several men suggested that they had fulfilled their victims' dreams. Additionally, while most admitters used adjectives such as "dirty," "humiliated," and "disgusted," to describe how they thought rape made women feel, 20 percent (n = 9) believed that their victim enjoyed herself. For example, one denier had posed as a salesman to gain entry to his victim's house. But he claimed he had had a previous sexual relationship with the victim, that she agreed to have sex for drugs, and that the opportunity to have sex with him produced "a glow, because she was really into oral stuff and fascinated by the idea of sex with a black man. She felt satisfied, fulfilled, wanted me to stay, but I didn't want her." In another case, a denier who had broken into his victim's house but who insisted the victim was his lover and let him in voluntarily, declared "She felt good, kept kissing me and wanted me to stay the night. She felt proud after sex with me." And another denier, who had hid in his victim's closet and later attacked her while she slept, argued that while she was scared at first, "once we got into it, she was ok." He continued to believe he hadn't committed rape because "she enjoyed it and it was like she consented."

Nice Girls Don't Get Raped

The belief that "nice girls don't get raped" affects perception of fault. The victim's reputation, as well as characteristics or behavior which violate normative sex role expectations, are perceived as contributing to the commission of the crime. For example, Nelson and Amir (1975) defined hitchhike rape as a victim-precipitated offense.

In our study, 69 percent (n = 22) of deniers and 22 percent (n = 10) of admitters referred to their victims' sexual reputation, thereby evoking the stereotype that "nice girls don't get raped."

They claimed that the victim was known to have been a prostitute, or a "loose" woman, or to have had a lot of affairs, or to have given birth to a child out of wedlock. For example, a denier who claimed he had picked up his victim while she was hitchhiking stated, "To be honest, we [his family] knew she was a damn whore and whether she screwed one or 50 guys didn't matter." According to pre-sentence reports this victim didn't know her attacker and he abducted her at knife point from the street. In another case, a denier who claimed to have known his victim by reputation stated:

If you wanted drugs or a quick piece of ass, she would do it. In court she said she was a virgin, but I could tell during sex [rape] that she was very experienced.

When other types of discrediting biographical information were added to these sexual slurs, a total of 78 percent (n = 25) of the deniers used the victim's reputation to substantiate their accounts. Most frequently, they referred to the victim's emotional state or drug use. For example, one denier claimed his victim had been known to be loose and, additionally, had turned state's evidence against her husband to put him in prison and save herself from a burglary conviction. Further, he asserted that she had met her current boyfriend, who was himself in and out of prison, in a drug rehabilitation center where they were both clients.

Evoking the stereotype that women provoke rape by the way they dress, a description of the victim as seductively attired appeared in the accounts of 22 percent (n = 7) of deniers and 17 percent (n = 8) of admitters. Typically, these descriptions were used to substantiate their claims about the victim's reputation. Some men went to extremes to paint a tarnished picture of the victim, describing her as dressed in tight black clothes and without a bra; in one case, the victim was portrayed as sexually provocative in dress and carriage. Not only did she wear short skirts, but she was observed to "spread her legs while getting out of cars." Not all of the men

---

[6]Research shows clearly that women do not enjoy rape. Holmstrom and Burgess (1978) asked 93 adult rape victims, "How did it feel sexually?" Not one said they enjoyed it. Further, the trauma of rape is so great that it disrupts sexual functioning (both frequency and satisfaction) for the overwhelming majority of victims, at least during the period immediately following the rape and, in fewer cases, for an extended period of time (Burgess and Holmstrom, 1979; Feldman-Summers et al., 1979). In addition, a number of studies have shown that rape victims experience adverse consequences prompting some to move, change jobs, or drop out of school (Burgess and Holmstrom, 1974; Kilpatrick et al., 1979; Ruch et al., 1980; Shore, 1979).

attempted to assassinate their victim's reputation with equal vengeance. Numerous times they made subtle and offhand remarks like, "She was a waitress and you know how they are."

The intent of these discrediting statements is clear. Deniers argued that the woman was a "legitimate" victim who got what she deserved. For example, one denier stated that all of his victims had been prostitutes; pre-sentence reports indicated they were not. Several times during his interview, he referred to them as "dirty sluts," and argued "anything I did to them was justified." Deniers also claimed their victim had wrongly accused them and was the type of woman who would perjure herself in court.

Only a Minor Wrongdoing

The majority of deniers did not claim to be completely innocent and they also accepted some accountability for their actions. Only 16 percent (n = 5) of deniers argued that they were totally free of blame. Instead, the majority of deniers pleaded guilty to a lesser charge. That is, they obfuscated the rape by pleading guilty to a less serious, more acceptable charge. They accepted being over-sexed, accused of poor judgment or trickery, even some violence, or guilty of adultery or contributing to the delinquency of a minor, charges that are hardly the equivalent of rape.

Typical of this reasoning is a denier who met his victim in a bar when the bartender asked him if he would try to repair her stalled car. After attempting unsuccessfully, he claimed the victim drank with him and later accepted a ride. Out riding, he pulled into a deserted area "to see how my luck would go." When the victim resisted his advances, he beat her and he stated:

I did something stupid. I pulled a knife on her and I hit her as hard as I would hit a man. But I shouldn't be in prison for what I did. I shouldn't have all this time [sentence] for going to bed with a broad.

This rapist continued to believe that while the knife was wrong, his sexual behavior was justified.

In another case, the denier claimed he picked up his under-age victim at a party and that she voluntarily went with him to a motel. According to pre-sentence reports, the victim had been abducted at knife point from a party. He explained:

After I paid for a motel, she would have to have sex but I wouldn't use a weapon. I would have explained. I spent money and, if she still said no, I would have forced her. If it had happened that way, it would have been rape to some people but not to my way of thinking. I've done that kind of thing before. I'm guilty of sex and contributing to the delinquency of a minor, but not rape.

In sum, deniers argued that, while their behavior may not have been completely proper, it should not have been considered rape. To accomplish this, they attempted to discredit and blame the victim while presenting their own actions as justified in the context. Not surprisingly, none of the deniers thought of himself as a rapist. A minority of the admitters attempted to lessen the impact of their crime by claiming the victim enjoyed being raped. But despite this similarity, the nature and tone of admitters' and deniers' accounts were essentially different.

Excusing Rape

In stark contrast to deniers, admitters regarded their behavior as morally wrong and beyond justification. They blamed themselves rather than the victim, although some continued to cling to the belief that the victim had contributed to the crime somewhat, for example, by not resisting enough.

Several of the admitters expressed the view that rape was an act of such moral outrage that it was unforgivable. Several admitters broke into tears at intervals during their interviews. A typical sentiment was,

I equate rape with someone throwing you up against a wall and tearing your liver and guts out of you. . . . Rape is worse than murder . . . and I'm disgusting.

Another young admitter frequently referred to himself as repulsive and confided:

I'm in here for rape and in my own mind, its the most disgusting crime, sickening. When people see me and know, I get sick.

Admitters tried to explain their crime in a way that allowed them to retain a semblance of moral integrity. Thus, in contrast to deniers' justifications, admitters used excuses to explain how they were compelled to rape. These excuses appealed to the existence of forces outside of the rapists' control. Through the use of excuses, they attempted to demonstrate that either intent was absent or responsibility was diminished. This allowed them to admit rape while reducing the threat to their identity as a moral person. Excuses also permitted them to view their behavior as idiosyncratic rather than typical and, thus, to believe they were not "really" rapists. Three themes run through these accounts: (1) the use of alcohol and drugs; (2) emotional problems; and (3) nice guy image.

The Use of Alcohol and Drugs

A number of studies have noted a high incidence of alcohol and drug consumption by convicted rapists prior to their crime (Groth, 1979; Queen's Bench Foundation, 1976). However, more recent research has tentatively concluded that the connection between substance use and crime is not as direct as previously thought (Ladouceur, 1983). Another facet of alcohol and drug use mentioned in the literature is its utility in disavowing deviance. McCaghy (1968) found that child molesters used alcohol as a technique for neutralizing their deviant identity. Marolla and Scully (1979), in a review of psychiatric literature, demonstrated how alcohol consumption is applied differently as a vocabulary of motive. Rapists can use alcohol both as an excuse for their behavior and to discredit the victim and make her more responsible. We found the former common among admitters and the latter common among deniers.

Alcohol and/or drugs were mentioned in the accounts of 77 percent (n = 30) of admitters and 84 percent (n = 21) of deniers and both groups were equally likely to have acknowledged consuming a substance—admitters, 77 percent (n = 30); deniers, 72 percent (n = 18). However, admitters said they had been affected by the substance; if not the cause of their behavior, it was at least a contributing factor. For example, an admitter who estimated his consumption to have been eight beers and four "hits of acid" reported:

Straight, I don't have the guts to rape. I could fight a man but not that. To say, "I'm going to do it to a woman," knowing it will scare and hurt her, takes guts or you have to be sick.

Another admitter believed that his alcohol and drug use,

. . . brought out what was already there but in such intensity it was uncontrollable. Feelings of being dominant, powerful, using someone for my own gratification, all rose to the surface.

In contrast, deniers' justifications required that they not be substantially impaired. To say that they had been drunk or high would cast doubt on their ability to control themself or to remember events as they actually happened. Consistent with this, when we asked if the alcohol and/or drugs had had an effect on their behavior, 69 percent (n = 27) of admitters, but only 40 percent (n = 10) of deniers, said they had been affected.

Even more interesting were references to the victim's alcohol and/or drug use. Since admitters had already relieved themselves of responsibility through claims of being drunk or high, they had nothing to gain from the assertion that the victim had used or been affected by alcohol and/or drugs. On the other hand, it was very much in the interest of deniers to declare that their victim had been intoxicated or high: that fact lessened her credibility and made her more responsible for the act. Reflecting these observations, 72 percent (n = 18) of deniers and 26 percent (n = 10) of admitters maintained that alcohol or drugs had been consumed by the victim. Further, while 56 percent (n = 14) of deniers declared she had been affected by this use, only 15 percent (n = 6) of admitters made a similar claim. Typically, deniers argued that the alcohol and drugs had sexually aroused their victim or rendered her out of control. For example, one denier insisted that his victim had become hysterical from drugs, not from being raped, and it was because of the drugs that she had reported him to the police. In addition, 40 percent (n = 10) of deniers argued that while the victim had been drunk or high, they themselves either hadn't ingested or weren't affected by alcohol and/or drugs. None of the admitters made this claim. In fact, in all of the 15 percent (n = 6) of cases where an admitter said the victim was drunk or high, he also admitted to being similarly affected.

These data strongly suggest that whatever role alcohol and drugs play in sexual and other types of violent crime, rapists have learned the advantage to be gained from using alcohol and drugs as an account. Our sample were aware that their victim would be discredited and their own behavior excused or justified by referring to alcohol and/or drugs.

Emotional Problems

Admitters frequently attributed their acts to emotional problems. Forty percent (n = 19) of admitters said they believed an emotional problem had been at the root of their rape behavior, and 33 percent (n = 15) specifically related the problem to an unhappy, unstable childhood or a marital-domestic situation. Still others claimed to have been in a general state of unease. For example, one admitter said that at the time of the rape he had been depressed, feeling he couldn't do anything right, and that something had been missing from his life. But he also added, "being a rapist is not part of my personality." Even admitters who could locate no source for an emotional problem evoked the popular image of rapists as the product of disordered personalities to argue they also must have problems:

The fact that I'm a rapist makes me different. Rapists aren't all there. They have problems. It was wrong so there must be a reason why I did it. I must have a problem.

Our data do indicate that a precipitating event, involving an upsetting problem of everyday living, appeared in the accounts of 80 percent (n = 38) of admitters and 25 percent (n = 8) of deniers. Of those experiencing a precipitating event, including deniers, 76 percent (n = 35) involved a wife or girlfriend. Over and over, these men described themselves as having been in a rage because of an incident involving a woman with whom they believed they were in love.

Frequently, the upsetting event was related to a rigid and unrealistic double standard for sexual conduct and virtue which they applied to "their" woman but which they didn't expect from men, didn't apply to themselves, and, obviously, didn't honor in other women. To discover that the "pedestal" didn't apply to their wife or girlfriend sent them into a fury. One especially articulate and typical admitter described his feeling as follows. After serving a short prison term for auto theft, he married his "childhood sweetheart" and secured a well-paying job. Between his job and the volunteer work he was doing with an ex-offender group, he was spending long hours away from home, a situation that had bothered his wife. In response to her request, he gave up his volunteer work, though it was clearly meaningful to him. Then, one day, he discovered his wife with her former boyfriend

"and my life fell apart." During the next several days, he said his anger had made him withdraw into himself and, after three days of drinking in a motel room, he abducted and raped a stranger. He stated:

My parents have been married for many years and I had high expectations about marriage. I put my wife on a pedestal. When I walked in on her, I felt like my life had been destroyed, it was such a shock. I was bitter and angry about the fact that I hadn't done anything to my wife for cheating. I didn't want to hurt her [victim], only to scare and degrade her.

It is clear that many admitters, and a minority of deniers, were under stress at the time of their rapes. However, their problems were ordinary—the types of upsetting events that everyone experiences at some point in life. The overwhelming majority of the men were not clinically defined as mentally ill in court-ordered psychiatric examinations prior to their trials. Indeed, our sample is consistent with Abel *et al.* (1980) who found fewer than 5 percent of rapists were psychotic at the time of their offense.

As with alcohol and drug intoxication, a claim of emotional problems works differently depending upon whether the behavior in question is being justified or excused. It would have been counter-productive for deniers to have claimed to have had emotional problems at the time of the rape. Admitters used psychological explanations to portray themselves as having been temporarily "sick" at the time of the rape. Sick people are usually blamed for neither the cause of their illness nor for acts committed while in that state of diminished capacity. Thus, adopting the sick role removed responsibility by excusing the behavior as having been beyond the ability of the individual to control. Since the rapists were not "themselves," the rape was idiosyncratic rather than typical behavior. Admitters asserted a non-deviant identity despite their self-proclaimed disgust with what they had done. Although admitters were willing to assume the sick role, they did not view their problem as a chronic condition, nor did they believe themselves to be insane or permanently impaired. Said one admitter, who believed that he needed psychological counseling: "I have a mental disorder, but I'm not crazy." Instead, admitters viewed their "problem" as mild, transient, and curable. Indeed, part of the appeal of this excuse was that not only did it relieve responsibility, but, as with alcohol and drug addiction, it allowed the rapist to "recover." Thus, at the time of their interviews, only 31 percent (n = 14) of admitters indicated that "being a rapist" was part of their self-concept. Twenty-eight percent (n = 13) of admitters stated they had never thought of themselves as rapists, 8 percent (n = 4) said they were unsure, and 33 percent (n = 16) asserted they had been a rapist at one time but now were recovered. A multiple "exrapist," who believed his "problem" was due to "something buried in my subconscious" that was triggered when his girlfriend broke up with him, expressed a typical opinion:

I was a rapist, but not now. I've grown up, had to live with it. I've hit the bottom of the well and it can't get worse. I feel born again to deal with my problems.

Nice Guy Image

Admitters attempted to further neutralize their crime and negotiate a non-rapist identity by painting an image of themselves as a "nice guy." Admitters projected the image of someone who had made a serious mistake but, in every other respect, was a decent person. Fifty-seven percent (n = 27) expressed regret and sorrow for their victim indicating that they wished there were a way to apologize for or amend their behavior. For example, a participant in a rape-murder, who insisted his partner did the murder, confided, "I wish there was something I could do besides saying 'I'm sorry, I'm sorry.' I live with it 24 hours a day and, sometimes, I wake up crying in the middle of the night because of it."

Schlenker and Darby (1981) explain the significance of apologies beyond the obvious expression of regret. An apology allows a person to admit guilt while at the same time seeking a pardon by signalling that the event should not be considered a fair representation of what the person is really like. An apology separates the bad self from the good self, and promises more acceptable behavior in the future. When apologizing, an individual is attempting to say: "I have repented and should be forgiven," thus making it appear that no further rehabilitation is required.

The "nice guy" statements of the admitters reflected an attempt to communicate a message consistent with Schlenker's and Darby's analysis of apologies. It was an attempt to convey that rape was not a representation of their "true" self. For example,

It's different from anything else I've ever done. I feel more guilt about this. It's not consistent with me. When I talk about it, it's like being assaulted myself. I don't know why I did it, but once I started, I got into it. Armed robbery was a way of life for me, but not rape. I feel like I wasn't being myself.

Admitters also used "nice guy" statements to register their moral opposition to violence and harming women, even though, in some cases, they had seriously injured their victims. Such was the case of an admitter convicted of a gang rape:

I'm against hurting women. She should have resisted. None of us were the type of person that would use force on a woman. I never positioned myself on a woman unless she showed an interest in me. They would play to me, not me to them. My weakness is to follow. I never would have stopped, let along pick her up without the others. I never would have let anyone beat her. I never bothered women who didn't want sex; never had a problem with sex or getting it. I loved her—like all women.

Finally, a number of admitters attempted to improve their self-image by demonstrating that, while they had raped, it could have been worse if they had not been a "nice guy." For example, one admitter professed to being especially gentle with his victim after she told him she had just had a baby. Others claimed to have given the victim money to get home or make a phone call, or to have made sure the victim's children were not in the room. A multiple rapist, whose pattern was to break in and attack sleeping victims in their homes, stated:

I never beat any of my victims and I told them I wouldn't hurt them if they cooperated. I'm a professional thief. But I never robbed the women I raped because I felt so bad about what I had already done to them.

Even a young man, who raped his five victims at gun point and then stabbed them to death, attempted to improve his image by stating:

Physically they enjoyed the sex [rape]. Once they got involved, it would be difficult to resist. I was always gentle and kind until I started to kill them. And the killing was always sudden, so they wouldn't know it was coming.

Summary and Conclusions

Convicted rapists' accounts of their crimes include both excuses and justifications. Those who deny what they did was rape justify their actions; those who admit it was rape attempt to excuse it or themselves. This study does not address why some men admit while others deny, but future research might address this question. This paper does provide insight on how men who are sexually aggressive or violent construct reality, describing the different strategies of admitters and deniers.

Admitters expressed the belief that rape was morally reprehensible. But they explained themselves and their acts by appealing to forces beyond their control, forces which reduced their capacity to act rationally and thus compelled them to rape. Two types of excuses predominated: alcohol/drug intoxication and emotional problems. Admitters used these excuses to negotiate a moral identity for themselves by viewing rape as idiosyncratic rather than typical behavior. This allowed them to reconceptualize themselves as recovered or "exrapists," someone who had made a serious mistake which did not represent their "true" self.

In contrast, deniers' accounts indicate that these men raped because their value system provided no compelling reason not to do so. When sex is viewed as a male entitlement, rape is no longer seen as criminal. However, the deniers had been convicted of rape, and like the admitters, they attempted to negotiate an identity. Through justifications, they constructed a "controversial" rape and attempted to demonstrate how their behavior, even if not quite right, was appropriate in the situation. Their denials, drawn from common cultural rape stereotypes, took two forms, both of which ultimately denied the existence of a victim.

The first form of denial was buttressed by the cultural view of men as sexually masterful and women as coy but seductive. Injury was denied by portraying the victim as willing, even enthusiastic, or as politely resistant at first but eventually yielding to "relax and enjoy it." In these accounts, force appeared merely as a seductive technique. Rape was disclaimed: rather than harm the woman, the rapist had fulfilled her dreams. In the second form of denial, the victim was portrayed as the type of woman who "got what she deserved." Through attacks on the victim's sexual reputation and, to a lesser degree,

her emotional state, deniers attempted to demonstrate that since the victim wasn't a "nice girl," they were not rapists. Consistent with both forms of denial was the self-interested use of alcohol and drugs as a justification. Thus, in contrast to admitters, who accentuated their own use as an excuse, deniers emphasized the victim's consumption in an effort to both discredit her and make her appear more responsible for the rape. It is important to remember that deniers did not invent these justifications. Rather, they reflect a belief system which has historically victimized women by promulgating the myth that women both enjoy and are responsible for their own rape.

While admitters and deniers present an essentially contrasting view of men who rape, there were some shared characteristics. Justifications particularly, but also excuses, are buttressed by the cultural view of women as sexual commodities, dehumanized and devoid of autonomy and dignity. In this sense, the sexual objectification of women must be understood as an important factor contributing to an environment that trivializes, neutralizes, and, perhaps, facilitates rape.

Finally, we must comment on the consequences of allowing one perspective to dominate thought on a social problem. Rape, like any complex continuum of behavior, has multiple causes and is influenced by a number of social factors. Yet, dominated by psychiatry and the medical model, the underlying assumption that rapists are "sick" has pervaded research. Although methodologically unsound, conclusions have been based almost exclusively on small clinical populations of rapists—that extreme group of rapists who seek counseling in prison and are the most likely to exhibit psychopathology. From this small, atypical group of men, psychiatric findings have been generalized to all men who rape. Our research, however, based on volunteers from the entire prison population, indicates that some rapists, like deniers, viewed and understood their behavior from a popular cultural perspective. This strongly suggests that cultural perspectives, and not an idiosyncratic illness, motivated their behavior. Indeed, we can argue that the psychiatric perspective has contributed to the vocabulary of motive that rapists use to excuse and justify their behavior (Scully and Marolla, 1984).

Efforts to arrive at a general explanation for rape have been retarded by the narrow focus of the medical model and the preoccupation with clinical populations. The continued reduction of such complex behavior to a singular cause hinders, rather than enhances, our understanding of rape.

REFERENCES

Abel, Gene, Judith Becker, and Linda Skinner. 1980. "Aggressive Behavior and Sex." *Psychiatric Clinics of North America*, 3(2):133–151.

Abrahamsen, David. 1960. *The Psychology of Crime*. New York: Wiley.

Albin, Rochelle. 1977. "Psychological Studies of Rape." *Signs*, 3(2):423–435.

Athens, Lonnie. 1977. "Violent Crimes: A Symbolic Interactionist Study." *Symbolic Interaction*, 1(1):56–71.

Burgess, Ann Wolbert and Lynda Lytle Holmstrom. 1974. *Rape: Victims of Crisis*. Bowie: Robert J. Brady.

———. 1979. "Rape: Sexual Disruption and Recovery." *American Journal of Orthopsychiatry*, 49(4): 648–657.

Burt, Martha. 1980. "Cultural Myths and Supports for Rape." *Journal of Personality and Social Psychology*, 38(2):217–230.

Burt, Martha and Rochelle Albin. 1981. "Rape Myths, Rape Definitions, and Probability of Conviction." *Journal of Applied Psychology*, 11(3):212–230.

Feldman–Summers, Shirley, Patricia E. Gordon, and Jeanette R. Meagher. 1979. "The Impact of Rape on Sexual Satisfaction." *Journal of Abnormal Psychology*, 88(1):101–105.

Glueck, Sheldon. 1925. *Mental Disorders and the Criminal Law*. New York: Little Brown.

Groth, Nicholas A. 1979. *Men Who Rape*. New York: Plenum Press.

Hall, Peter M. and John P. Hewitt. 1970. "The Quasi-theory of Communication and the Management of Dissent." *Social Problems*, 18(1):17–27.

Hewitt, John P. and Peter M. Hall. 1973. "Social Problems, Problematic Situations, and Quasi-theories." *American Sociological Review*, 38(3):367–374.

Hewitt, John P. and Randall Stokes. 1975. "Disclaimers." *American Sociological Review*, 40(1):1–11.

Hollander, Bernard. 1924. *The Psychology of Misconduct, Vice, and Crime*. New York: Macmillan

Holmstrom, Lynda Lytle and Ann Wolbert Burgess. 1978. "Sexual Behavior of Assailant and Victim During Rape." Paper presented at the annual meetings of the American Sociological Association, San Francisco, September 2–8.

Kilpatrick, Dean G., Lois Veronen, and Patricia A.

Resnick. 1979. "The Aftermath of Rape: Recent Empirical Findings." *American Journal of Orthopsychiatry*, 49(4):658–669.

Ladouceur, Patricia. 1983. "The Relative Impact of Drugs and Alcohol on Serious Felons." Paper presented at the annual meetings of the American Society of Criminology, Denver, November 9–12.

Luckenbill, David. 1977. "Criminal Homicide as a Situated Transaction." *Social Problems*, 25(2):176–187.

McCaghy, Charles. 1968. "Drinking and Deviance Disavowal: The Case of Child Molesters." *Social Problems*, 16(1):43–49.

Marolla, Joseph, and Diana Scully. 1979. "Rape and Psychiatric Vocabularies of Motive." In Edith S. Gomberg and Violet Franks (eds.), *Gender and Disordered Behavior: Sex Differences in Psychopathology*. New York: Brunner/Mazel, pp. 301–318.

Mills, C. Wright. 1940. "Situated Actions and Vocabularies of Motive." *American Sociological Review*, 5(6):904–913.

Nelson, Steve and Menachem Amir. 1975. "The Hitchhike Victim of Rape: A Research Report." In Israel Drapkin and Emilio Viano (eds.), *Victimology: A New Focus*. Lexington, KY: Lexington Books, pp. 47–65.

Queen's Bench Foundation. 1976. *Rape: Prevention and Resistance*. San Francisco: Queen's Bench Foundation.

Ruch, Libby O., Susan Meyers Chandler, and Richard A. Harter. 1980. "Life Change and Rape Impact." *Journal of Health and Social Behavior*, 21(3):248–260.

Scott, Marvin and Stanford Lyman. 1968. "Accounts." *American Sociological Review*, 33(1):46–62.

Schlenker, Barry R. and Bruce W. Darby. 1981. "The Use of Apologies in Social Predicaments." *Social Psychology Quarterly*, 44(3):271–278.

Scully, Diana and Joseph Marolla. 1984. "Rape and Psychiatric Vocabularies of Motive: Alternative Perspectives." In Ann Wolbert Burgess (ed.), *Handbook on Rape and Sexual Assault*. New York: Garland Publishing. Forthcoming.

Shore, Barbara K. 1979. *An Examination of Critical Process and Outcome Factors in Rape*. Rockville, MD: National Institute of Mental Health.

Stokes, Randall and John P. Hewitt. 1976. "Aligning Actions." *American Sociological Review*, 41(5):837–849.

Sykes, Gresham M. and David Matza. 1957. "Techniques of Neutralization." *American Sociological Review*, 22(6):664–670.

Williams, Joyce. 1979. "Sex Role Stereotypes, Women's Liberation, and Rape: A Cross-cultural Analysis of Attitude." *Sociological Symposium*, 25 (Winter):61–97.

The Social Integration of Queers and Peers
ALBERT J. REISS, JR.

. . . An attempt is made in this paper to describe the sexual relations between "delinquent peers" and "adult queers" and to account for its social organization. This transaction is one form of homosexual prostitution between a young male and an adult male fellator. The adult male client pays a delinquent boy prostitute a sum of money in order to be allowed to act as a fellator. The transaction is limited to fellation and is one in which the boy develops no self-conception as a homosexual person or sexual deviator, although he perceives adult male clients as sexual deviators, "queers" or "gay boys." . . .

The Data

Information on the sexual transaction and its social organization was gathered mostly by interviews, partly by social observation of their meeting places. Though there are limitations to inferring social organization from interview data (particularly when the organization arises through behavior that is negatively sanctioned in the larger society), they provide a convenient basis for exploration.

Sex histories were gathered from 18.6 per cent of the 1008 boys between the ages of 12 and 17 who were interviewed in the Nashville, Tennessee, SMA for an investigation of adolescent conforming and deviating behavior. These represent all of the interviews of one of the interviewers during a two-month period, together with interviews with all Nashville boys incarcerated at the Tennessee State Training School for Boys. . . .

How Peers and Queers Meet

Meetings between adult male fellators and delinquent boys are easily made, because both know how and where to meet within the community space. Those within the common culture know that contact can be established within a relatively short period of time, if it is wished. The fact that meetings between peers and queers can be made easily is muted evidence of the organized understandings which prevail between the two populations.

There are a large number of places where the boys meet their clients, the fellators. Many of these points are known to all boys regardless of where they reside in the metropolitan area. This is particularly true of the central city locations where the largest number of contact points are found within a small territorial area. Each community area of the city, and certain fringe areas, inhabited by substantial numbers of lower-class persons, also have their meeting places, generally known only to the boys residing in the area.

Queers and peers typically establish contact in public or quasi-public places. Major points of contact include street corners, public parks, men's toilets in public or quasi-public places such as those in transportation depots, parks or hotels, and "second" and "third-run" movie houses (open around the clock and permitting sitting through shows). Bars are seldom points of contact, perhaps largely because they are plied by older male hustlers who lie outside the peer culture and groups, and because bar proprietors will not risk the presence of under-age boys.

There are a number of prescribed modes for establishing contact in these situations. They permit the boys and fellators to communicate intent to one another privately despite the public character of the situation. The major form of establishing contact is the "cruise," with the fellator passing "queer-corners" or locations until his effort is recognized by one of the boys. A boy can then signal—usually by nodding his head, a hand gesticulation signifying OK, following, or responding to commonly understood introductions such as "You got the time?"— that he is prepared to undertake the transaction. Entrepreneur and client then move to a place where the sexual activity is consummated, usually a place affording privacy, protection and hasty exit. "Dolly," a three-time loser at the State Training School, describes one of these prescribed forms for making contact:

Reprinted from *Social Problems,* Vol. 9, No. 2 (Fall, 1961), pp. 102, 104, 106–109, 112–119, by permission of the Society for the Study of Social Problems and the author.

Well, like at the bus station, you go to the bathroom and stand there pretendin' like . . . and they're standin' there pretendin' like . . . and then they motions their head and walks out and you follow them, and you go some place. Either they's got a car, or you go to one of them hotels near the depot or some place like that . . . most any place.

Frequently contact between boys and fellators is established when the boy is hitchhiking. This is particularly true for boys' first contacts of this nature. Since lower-class boys are more likely than middle-class ones to hitch rides within a city, particularly at night when such contacts are most frequently made, they perhaps are most often solicited in this manner.

The experienced boy who knows a "lot of queers," may phone known fellators directly from a public phone, and some fellators try to establish continued contact with boys by giving them their phone numbers. However, the boys seldom use this means of contact for reasons inherent in their orientation toward the transaction, as we shall see below.

We shall now examine how the transaction is facilitated by these types of situations and the prescribed modes of contact and communication. One of the characteristics of all these contact situations is that they provide a *rationale* for the presence of *both* peers and queers in the *same* situation or place. This rationale is necessary for both parties, for were there high visibility to the presence of either and no ready explanation for it, contact and communication would be far more difficult. Public and quasi-public facilities provide situations which account for the presence of most persons since there is relatively little social control over the establishment of contacts. There is, of course, some risk to the boys and the fellators in making contact in these situations since they are generally known to the police. The Morals Squad may have "stakeouts," but this is one of the calculated risks and the communication network carries information about their tactics.

A most important element in furnishing a rationale is that these meeting places must account for the presence of delinquent boys of es-sentially lower-class dress and appearance who make contact with fellators of almost any class level. This is true despite the fact that the social settings which fellators ordinarily choose to establish contact generally vary according to the class level of the fellators. Fellators of high social class generally make contact by "cruising" past streetcorners, in parks, or the men's rooms in "better" hotels, while those from the lower class are likely to select the public bath or transportation depot. There apparently is some general equation of the class position of boys and fellators in the peer-queer transaction. The large majority of fellators in the delinquent peer-queer transaction probably are from the lower class ("apes"). But it is difficult to be certain about the class position of the fellator clients since no study was made of this population.

The absence of data from the fellator population poses difficulties in interpreting the contact relationship. Many fellators involved with delinquent boys do not appear to participate in any overt or covert homosexual groups, such as the organized homosexual community of the "gay world."[1] The "gay world" is the most visible form of organized homosexuality since it is an organized community, but it probably encompasses only a small proportion of all homosexual contact. Even among those in the organized homosexual community, evidence suggests that the homosexual members seek sexual gratification outside their group with persons who are essentially anonymous to them. Excluding homosexual married couples, Leznoff and Westley maintain that there is ". . . a prohibition against sexual relationships within the group. . . ."[2] Ross indicates that young male prostitutes are chosen, among other reasons, for the fact that they protect the identity of the client.[3] Both of these factors tend to coerce many male fellators to choose an anonymous contact situation.

It is clear that these contact situations not only provide a rationale for the presence of the parties to the transaction but a guarantee of anonymity. The guarantee does not necessarily restrict social visibility as both the boys and the fellators may recognize cues (including, but not necessarily, those of gesture and dress) which

---

[1] See, for example, Maurice Leznoff and William A. Westley, "The Homosexual Community," *Social Problems,* 4 (April, 1956), pp. 257–263.

[2] *Ibid.,* p. 258.

[3] H. Laurence Ross, "The 'Hustler' in Chicago," *The Journal of Student Research,* 1 (September, 1959), p. 15.

lead to mutual role identification.[4] But anonymity is guaranteed in at least two senses; anonymity of presence is assured in the situation and their personal identity in the community is protected unless disclosed by choice.

There presumably are a variety of reasons for the requirement of anonymity. For many, a homosexual relationship must remain a secret since their other relationships in the community—families, business relationships, etc.—must be protected. Leznoff and Westley refer to these men as the "secret" as contrasted with the "overt" homosexuals,[5] and in the organized "gay world," they are known as "closet fags." For some, there is also a necessity for protecting identity to avoid blackmail.[6] Although none of the peer hustlers reported resorting to blackmail, the adult male fellator may nonetheless hold such an expectation, particularly if he is older or of high social class. Lower-class ones, by contrast, are more likely to face the threat of violence from adolescent boys since they more often frequent situations where they are likely to contact "rough trade."[7] The kind of situation in which the delinquent peer-queer contact is made and the sexual relationship consummated tends to minimize the possibility of violence.

Not all male fellators protect their anonymity; some will let a boy have their phone number and a few "keep a boy." Still, most fellators want to meet boys where they are least likely to be victimized, although boys sometimes roll queers by selecting a meeting place where by prearrangement, their friends can meet them and help roll the queer, steal his car, or commit other acts of violence. Boys generally know that fellators are vulnerable in that they can't report their victimization. Parenthetically, it might be mentioned that these boys are not usually aware of their own institutional invulnerability to arrest. An adolescent boy is peculiarly invulnerable to arrest even when found with a fellator since the mores define the boy as exploited.[8]

Situations of personal contact between adolescent boys and adult male fellators also provide important ways to *communicate intent* or to carry out the transaction *without* making the contact particularly visible to others. The wall writings in many of these places are not without their primitive communication value, e.g., "show it hard," and places such as a public restroom provide a modus operandi. The entrepreneur and his customer in fact can meet with little more than an exchange of non-verbal gestures, transact their business with a minimum of verbal communication and part without a knowledge of one another's identity. In most cases, boys report "almost nothing" was said. The sexual transaction may occur with the only formal transaction being payment to the boy. . . .

Norms Governing the Transaction

Does the peer society have any norms about personal relations with fellators? Or, does it simply induct a boy into a relationship by teaching him how to effect the transaction? The answer is that there appear to be several clear-cut norms about the relations between peers and queers, even though there is some deviation from them.

The first major norm is that *a boy must undertake the relationship with a queer solely as a way of making money; sexual gratification cannot be actively sought as a goal in the relationship.* This norm does not preclude a boy from sexual gratification by the act; he simply must not seek this as a goal. Put another way, a boy cannot admit that he failed to get money from the transaction unless he used violence toward the fellator and he cannot admit that he sought it as a means of sexual gratification.

---

[4]The cues which lead to the queer-peer transaction can be subtle ones. The literature on adult male homosexuality makes it clear that adult males who participate in homosexual behavior are not generally socially visible to the public by manner and dress. Cf., Jess Stearn, *The Sixth Man*, New York: Macfadden Publications, 1962, Chapters 1 and 3.

[5]*Op. cit.,* pp. 260–261.

[6]Ross notes that, failing in the con-man role, some hustlers resort to extortion and blackmail since they provide higher income. See Ross, *op. cit.,* p. 16. Sutherland discusses extortion and blackmail of homosexuals as part of the practice of professional thieves. The "muzzle" or "mouse" is part of the role of the professional thief. See Edwin Sutherland, *The Professional Thief*, Chicago: University of Chicago Press, 1937, pp. 78–81. See also the chapter on "Blackmail" in Jess Stearn, *op. cit.,* Chapter 16.

[7]Jess Stearn, *op. cit.,* p. 47.

[8]Albert J. Reiss, Jr., "Sex Offenses: The Marginal Status of the Adolescent," *Law and Contemporary Problems,* 25 (Spring, 1960), pp. 322–324 and 326–327.

The importance of making money in motivating a boy to the peer-queer transaction is succinctly stated by Dewey H.:

This guy in the Rex Theatre came over and sat down next to me when I was 11 or 12, and he started to fool with me. I got over and sat down another place and he came over and asked me, didn't I want to and he'd pay me five bucks. I figured it was *easy money* so I went with him . . . I didn't do it before that. That wasn't too long after I'd moved to South Nashville. I was a pretty good boy before that . . . not real good, but I never ran with a crowd that got into trouble before that. But, I met a lot of 'em there. (Why do you run with queers?) It's *easy money* . . . like I could go out and break into a place when I'm broke and get money that way . . . but that's harder and *you take a bigger risk* . . . with a queer it's *easy money.*

Dewey's comments reveal two important motivating factors in getting money from queers, both suggested by the expression, "easy money." First, the money is easy in that it can be made quickly. Some boys reported that when they needed money for a date or a night out, they obtained it within an hour through the sexual transaction with a queer. All the boy has to do is go to a place where he will be contacted, wait around, get picked up, carried to a place where the sexual transaction occurs, and in a relatively short period of time he obtains the money for his service.

It is easy money in another and more important sense for many of these boys. Boys who undertake the peer-queer transaction are generally members of career-oriented delinquent groups. Rejecting the limited opportunities for making money by legitimate means or finding them inaccessible, their opportunities to make money by illegitimate means may also be limited or the risk may be great. Theft is an available means, but it is more difficult and involves greater risk than the peer-queer transaction. Delinquent boys are not unaware of the risks they take. Under most circumstances, delinquents may calculate an act of stealing as "worth the risk." There are occasions, however, when the risk is calculated as too great. These occasions occur when the "heat" is on the boy or when he can least afford to run the risk of being picked up by the police, as is the case following a pickup by the police, being put on probation or parole, or being warned that incarceration will follow the next violation. At such times, boys particularly calculate whether they can afford to take the risk. Gerald L., describing a continuing relationship with a fellator who gave him his phone number, reflects Dewey's attitude toward minimizing risk in the peer-queer transaction: "So twie'd after that when I was gettin' real low and couldn't risk stealin' and gettin' caught, I called him and he took me out and blowed me." Here is a profit with no investment of capital and a minimum of risk in social, if not in psychological, terms.

The element of risk coupled with the wish for "easy money" enters into our understanding of the peer-queer relationship in another way. From a sociological point of view, the peer-queer sexual transaction occurs between two major types of deviators—"delinquents" and "queers." Both types of deviators risk negative sanctions for their deviant acts. The more often one has been arrested or incarcerated, the more punitive the sanctions from the larger social system for both types of deviators. At some point, therefore, both calculate risks and seek to minimize them, at least in the very short-run. Each then becomes a means for the other to minimize risk.

When the delinquent boy is confronted with a situation in which he wants money and risks little in getting it, how is he to get it without working? Illegitimate activities frequently provide the "best" opportunity for easy money. These activities often are restricted in kind and number for adolescents and the risk of negative sanctions is high. Under such circumstances, the service offered a queer is a chance to make easy money with a minimum of risk.

Opportunities for sexual gratification are limited for the adult male fellator, particularly if he wishes to minimize the risk of detection in locating patrons, to avoid personal involvement and to get his gratification when he wishes it. The choice of a lower-class male, precisely because of his class position somewhat reduces the risk. If the lower-class male also is a delinquent, the risk is minimized to an even greater degree.

This is not to say that the parties take equal risks in the situation. Of the two, the fellator perhaps is less able to minimize his risk since he still risks violence from his patron, but much less so if a set of expectations arise which control the use of violence as well. The boy is most able to minimize his risk since he is likely to be defined as "exploited" in the situation if caught.

Under special circumstances, boys may substitute other gratifications for the goal of money, provided that these gratifications do not include sexual gratification as a major goal. These special circumstances are the case where an entire gang will "make a night (or time) of it" with one or more adult male fellators. Under these circumstances, everyone is exempted from the subcultural expectations about making money from the fellator because everyone participates and there is no reason for everyone (or anyone) to make money. For the group to substitute being given a "good time" by a "queer" for the prescribed financial transaction is, of course, the exception which proves the rule.

Several examples of group exemption from the prescribed norm of a financial gain were discovered. Danny S., leader of the Black Aces, tells of his gang's group experiences with queers: "There's this one guy takes us to the Colonial Motel out on Dickerson Pike . . . usually it's a bunch of us boys and we all get drunk and get blowed by this queer . . . we don't get any money then . . . it's more a drinking party." The Black Aces are a fighting gang and place great stress on physical prowess, particularly boxing. All of its members have done time more than once at the State Training School. During one of these periods, the school employed a boxing instructor whom the boys identified as "a queer," but the boys had great respect for him since he taught them how to box and was a game fighter. Danny refers to him in accepting terms: "He's a real good guy. He's fought with us once or twice and we drink with him when we run into him. . . . He's taken us up to Miter Dam a coupla times, he's got a cabin up there on the creek and he blows us. . . . But mostly we just drink and have a real good time." These examples illustrate the instrumental orientation of the gang members. If the expense of the gang members getting drunk and having a good time are borne by a "queer," each member is released from the obligation to receive cash. The relationship in this case represents an exchange of services rather than that of money for a service.

The second major norm operating in the rela-

tionship is that *the sexual transaction must be limited to mouth-genital fellation. No other sexual acts are generally tolerated.*[9] The adult male fellator must deport himself in such a way as to re-enforce the instrumental aspects of the role relationship and to insure affective neutrality.[10] For the adult male fellator to violate the boy's expectation of "getting blowed," as the boys refer to the act, is to risk violence and loss of service. Whether or not the boys actually use violent means as often as they say they do when expectations are violated, there is no way of knowing with precision. Nevertheless, whenever boys reported they used violent means, they always reported some violation of the subcultural expectations. Likewise, they never reported a violation of the subcultural expectations which was not followed by the use of violent means, unless it was clearly held up as an exception. Bobby A. expresses the boys' point of view on the use of violent means in the following exchange: "How much did you usually get?" "Around five dollars; if they didn't give that much, I'd beat their head in." "Did they ever want you to do anything besides blow you?" "Yeh, sometimes . . . like they want me to blow them, but I'd tell them to go to hell and maybe beat them up."

Boys are very averse to being thought of in a queer role or engaging in acts of fellation. The act of fellation is defined as a "queer" act. Most boys were asked whether they would engage in such behavior. All but those who had the status of "punks" denied they had engaged in behavior associated with the queer role. Asking a boy whether he is a fellator meets with strong denial and often with open hostility. This could be interpreted as defensive behavior against latent homosexuality. Whether or not this is the case, strong denial could be expected because the question goes counter to the subcultural definitions of the peer role in the transaction.

A few boys on occasion apparently permit the fellator to perform other sexual acts. These boys, it is guessed, are quite infrequent in a de-

[9] It is not altogether clear why mouth-genital fellation is the only sexual act which is tolerated in the peer-queer transaction. The act seems to conform to the more "masculine" aspects of the role than do most, but not all possible alternatives. Ross has suggested to me that it also involves less bodily contact and therefore may be less threatening to the peers' self-definitions. One possible explanation therefore for the exclusiveness of the relationship to this act is that it is the most masculine alternative involving the least threat to peers' self-definition as nonhustler and nonhomosexual.

[10] Talcott Parsons in *The Social System* (New York: The Free Press, 1951, Chapter III) discusses this kind of role as ". . . the segregation of specific instrumental performances, both from expressive orientations other than the specifically appropriate rewards and from other components of the instrumental complex." (p. 87).

linquent peer population. Were their acts known to the members of the group, they would soon be defined as outside the delinquent peer society. Despite the limitation of the peer-queer sexual transaction to mouth-genital fellation, there are other sexual transactions which the peer group permits members to perform under special circumstances. They are, for example, permitted to perform the *male* roles in "crimes against nature," such as in pederasty ("cornholing" to the boys), bestiality (sometimes referred to as buggery) and carnal copulation with a man involving no orifice (referred to as "slick-legging" among the boys) provided that the partner is roughly of the same age and not a member of the group and provided also that the boys are confined to the single-sex society of incarcerated delinquent boys. Under no circumstances, however, is the female role in carnal copulation acceptable in any form. It is taboo. Boys who accept the female role in sexual transactions occupy the lowest status position among delinquents. They are "punks."

The third major norm operating on the relationship is that *both peers and queers, as participants, should remain affectively neutral during the transaction.* Boys within the peer society define the ideal form of the role with the fellator as one in which the boy is the entrepreneur and the queer is viewed as purchasing a service. The service is a business deal where a sexual transaction is purchased for an agreed upon amount of money. In the typical case, the boy is neither expected to enjoy or be repulsed by the sexual transaction; mouth-genital fellation is accepted as a service offered in exchange for a fee. It should be kept in mind that self-gratification is permitted in the sexual act. Only the motivation to sexual gratification in the transaction is tabooed. But self gratification must occur without displaying either positive or negative affect toward the queer. In the prescribed form of the role relationship, the boy sells a service for profit and the queer is to accept it without show of emotion.

The case of Thurman L., one of three brothers who are usually in trouble with the law, illustrates some aspects of the expected pattern of affective neutrality. Thurman has had a continuing relationship with a queer, a type of relationship in which it would be anticipated that affective neutrality would be difficult to maintain. This relationship continued, in fact, with a 21-year-old "gay" until the man was "sent to the pen." When queried about his relationship with this man and why he went with him, Thurman replied:

Don't know . . . money and stuff like that I guess. (What do you mean? . . . stuff like that?) Oh, clothes. . . . (He ever bought you any clothes?) Sure, by this one gay. . . . (You mind being blowed?) No. (You like it?) Don't care one way or the other. I don't like, and I don't not like it. (You like this one gay?) Nope, can't say that I liked anythin' about him. (How come you do it then?) Well, the money for one thing. . . . I need that. (You enjoy it some?) Can't say I do or don't.

More typical than Thurman's expression of affective neutrality is the boy who accepts it as "OK" or, "It's all right; I don't mind it." Most frequent of all is some variant of the statement: "It's OK, but I like the money best of all." The definition of affective neutrality fundamentally requires only that there be no positive emotional commitment to the queer *as a person.* The relationship must be essentially an impersonal one, even though the pure form of the business relationship may seldom be attained. Thus, it is possible for a boy to admit self-gratification without admitting any emotional commitment to the homosexual partner.

Although the peer group prescribes affective neutrality toward the queer in the peer-queer transaction, queers must be regarded as low prestige persons, held in low esteem, and the queer role is taboo. The queer is most commonly regarded as "crazy, I guess." Some boys take a more rationalistic view "They're just like that, I guess" or, "They're just born that way." While there are circumstances under which one is permitted to like a particular fellator, as in the case of all prejudices attached to devalued status, the person who is liked must be the exception which states the rule. Though in many cases both the boy and the fellator are of very low class origins, and in many cases both are altogether repulsive in appearance, cleanliness and dress by middle-class standards, these are not the standards of comparison used by the boys. The deviation of the queers from the boy's norms of masculine behavior places the fellator in the lowest possible status, even "beneath contempt." If the fellator violates the expected affective relationship in the transaction, he may be treated not only with violence but with contempt as well. The seller of the service ultimately reserves the right to set the conditions for his patrons.

Some boys find it difficult to be emotionally neutral toward the queer role and its occupants; they are either personally offended or affronted by the behavior of queers. JDC is an instance of a boy who is personally offended by their behavior; yet he is unable to use violence even when expectations governing the transaction are violated. He does not rely very much on the peer-queer relationship as a source of income. JDC expresses his view: "I don't really go for that like some guys; I just do it when I go along with the crowd. . . . You know. . . . That, and when I do it for money. . . . And I go along. . . . But . . . I hate queers. They embarrass me." "How?" "Well, like you'll be in the lobby at the theatre, and they'll come up and pat your ass or your prick right in front of everybody. I just can't go for that—not me." Most of the boys wouldn't either, but they would have resorted to violent means in this situation.

Two principal types of boys maintain a continuing relationship with a known queer. A few boys develop such relationships to insure a steady income. While this is permitted within peer society for a short period of time, boys who undertake it for extended periods of time do so with some risk, since in the words of the boys, "queers can be got too easy." The boy who is affectively involved with a queer or his role is downgraded in status to a position, "Ain't no better'n a queer." There are also a few boys affectively committed to a continuing relationship with an adult male homosexual. Such boys usually form a strong dependency relationship with him and are kept much as the cabin boys of old. This type of boy is clearly outside the peer society of delinquents and is isolated from participation in gang activity. The sociometric pattern for such boys is one of choice into more than one gang, none of which is reciprocated.

Street-hustlers are also downgraded within the peer society, generally having reputations as "punk kids." The street-hustler pretty much "goes it alone." Only a few street-hustlers were interviewed for this study. None of them was a member of an organized delinquent group. The sociometric pattern for each, together with his history of delinquent activity, placed them in the classification of nonconforming isolates.

A fourth major norm operating on the peer-queer relationship serves as a primary factor in stabilizing the system. This norm holds that *violence must not be used so long as the relationship conforms to the shared set of expectations between queers and peers*. So long as the fellator conforms to the norms governing the transaction in the peer-queer society, he runs little risk of violence from the boys.

The main reason, perhaps, for this norm is that uncontrolled violence is potentially disruptive of any organized system. All organized social systems must control violence. If the fellator clients were repeatedly the objects of violence, the system as it has been described could not exist. Most boys who share the common expectations of the peer-queer relationship do not use violent means unless the expectations are violated. To use violence, of course, is to become affectively involved and therefore another prescription of the relation is violated.

It is not known whether adult male fellators who are the clients of delinquent entrepreneurs share the boys' definition of the norm regarding the use of violence. They may, therefore, violate expectations of the peer society through ignorance of the system rather than from any attempt to go beyond the set of shared expectations.

There are several ways the fellator can violate the expectations of boys. The first concerns money: refusal to pay or paying too little may bring violence from most boys. Fellators may also violate peer expectations by attempting to go beyond the mouth-genital sexual act. If such an attempt is made, he is usually made an object of aggression as in the following excerpt from Dolly's sex history:

(You like it?) It's OK. I don't mind it. It feels OK. (They ever try anything else on you?) They usually just blow and that's all. (Any ever try anything else on you?) Oh sure, but we really fix 'em. I just hit 'em on the head or roll 'em . . . throw 'em out of the car. . . . Once a guy tried that and we rolled him and threw him out of the car. Then we took the car and stripped it (laughs with glee).

Another way the fellator violates a boy's expectations is to introduce considerable affect into the relationship. It appears that affect is least acceptable in two forms, both of which could be seen as "attacks on his masculinity." In one form, the queer violates the affective neutrality requirement by treating the adolescent boy as if he were a girl or in a girl's role during the sexual transaction, as for example, by speaking to him in affectionate terms such as "sweetie." There are many reasons why the feminine sex role is unacceptable to these lower-class boys, including the fact that such boys place considerable emphasis on being "tough" and masculine. Walter Miller, for example, observes that:

. . . The almost compulsive lower class concern with "masculinity" derives from a type of compulsive reaction-formation. A concern over homosexuality runs like a persistent thread through lower class culture—manifested by the institutionalized practice of "baiting queers," often accompanied by violent physical attacks, an expressed contempt for "softness" or frills, and the use of the local term for "homosexual" as a general pejorative epithet (e.g., higher class individuals or upwardly mobile peers are frequently characterized as "fags" or "queers").[11]

Miller sees violence as part of a reaction-formation against the matriarchal lower-class household where the father often is absent. For this reason, he suggests, many lower-class boys find it difficult to identify with a male role, and the "collective" reaction-formation is a cultural emphasis on masculinity. Violence toward queers is seen as a consequence of this conflict. Data from our interviews suggest that among career-oriented delinquents, violation of the affective neutrality requirement in the peer-queer relationship is at least as important in precipitating violence toward "queers." There are, of course, gangs which were not studied in this investigation which "queer-bait" for the express purposes of "rolling the queer."

The other form in which the fellator may violate the affective neutrality requirement is to approach the boy and make suggestive advances to him when he is with his age-mates, either with girls or with his peer group when he is not located for "business." In either case, the sexual advances suggest that the boy is not engaged in a business relationship within the normative expectations of the system, but that he has sexual motivation as well. The delinquent boy is expected to control the relationship with his customers. He is the entrepreneur "looking" for easy money or at the very least he must appear as being merely receptive to business; this means that he is receptive only in certain situations and under certain circumstances. He is not in business when he is with girls and he is not a businessman when he is cast in a female role. To

be cast in a female role before peers is highly unacceptable, as the following account suggests:

This gay comes up to me in the lobby of the Empress when we was standin' around and starts feelin' me up and callin' me Sweetie and like that . . . and, I just couldn't take none of that there . . . what was he makin' out like I was a queer or somethin' . . . so I jumps him right then and there and we like to of knocked his teeth out.

The sexual advance is even less acceptable when a girl is involved:

I was walkin' down the street with my steady girl when this gay drives by that I'd been with once before and he whistles at me and calls, "Hi Sweetie." . . . And, was I mad . . . so I went down to where the boys was and we laid for him and beat on him 'til he like to a never come to . . . ain't gonna take nothin' like that off'n a queer.

In both of these instances, not only is the boys' masculinity under attack, but the affective neutrality requirement of the business transaction is violated. The queer's behavior is particularly unacceptable, however, because it occurs in a peer setting where the crucial condition is the maintenance of the boy's status within the group. A lower-class boy cannot afford to be cast in less than a highly masculine role before lower-class girls nor risk definition as a queer before peers. His role within his peer group is under threat even if he suffers *no* anxiety about masculinity. Not only the boy himself but his peers perceive such behavior as violating role expectations and join him in violent acts toward the fellator to protect the group's integrity and status.

If violence generally occurs only when one of the major peer norms has been violated, it would also seem to follow that *violence is a means of enforcing the peer entrepreneurial norms of the system.* Violence or the threat of violence is thus used to keep adult male fellators in line with the boys' expectations in his customer role. It represents social control, a punishment meted out to a fellator who violates the cultural expectation. Only so long as the fellator seeks gratification from lower-class boys in a casual pick-up or continuing relationship where he pays money for a

---

[11] Walter Miller, "Lower-Class Culture as a Generating Milieu of Gang Delinquency," *The Journal of Social Issues,* 14, No. 3 (1958), p. 9.

"blow-job" is he reasonably free from acts of violence.

There is another, and perhaps more important reason for the use of violence when the peer defined norms of the peer-queer relationship are violated. The formally prescribed roles for peers and queers are basically the roles involved in all institutionalized forms of prostitution, the prostitute and the client. But in most forms of prostitution, whether male or female, the hustlers perceive of themselves in hustler roles, and furthermore the male hustlers also develop a conception of themselves as homosexual whereas *the peer hustler in the peer-queer relationship develops no conception of himself either as prostitute or as homosexual.*

The fellator risks violence, therefore, if he threatens the boy's self-conception by suggesting that the boy may be homosexual and treats him as if he were.

Violence seems to function, then, in two basic ways for the peers. On the one hand, it integrates their norms and expectations by controlling and combatting behavior which violates them. On the other hand, it protects the boy's self-identity as nonhomosexual and reinforces his self-conception as "masculine."

The other norms of the peer society governing the peer-queer transaction also function to prevent boys in the peer-queer society from defining themselves as homosexual. The prescriptions that the goal is money, that sexual gratification is not to be sought as an end in the relationship, that affective neutrality be maintained toward the fellator and that only mouth-genital fellation is permitted, all tend to insulate the boy from a homosexual self-definition. So long as he conforms to these expectations, *his "significant others" will not define him as homosexual;* and this is perhaps the most crucial factor in his own self-definition. The peers define one as homosexual not on the basis of homosexual *behavior* as such, but on the basis of participation in the homosexual *role,* the "queer" role. The reactions of the larger society, in defining the *behavior* as homosexual is unimportant in their own self-definition. What is important to them is the reactions of their peers to violation of peer group norms which define roles in the peer-queer transaction.

15 TRANSFORMING DEVIANT IDENTITY

Over the course of time deviance sometimes proves to be more punishing than rewarding. People whose deviance is self-destructive (e.g., alcoholics, drug addicts) are especially apt to try to relinquish their deviant ways and identity. But terminating a deviant career is no easy matter. The conditions for successfully transforming a deviant identity are narrow and exacting. They include the development of a conventional lifestyle and identity, support from deviants and nondeviants alike, and opportunities to adopt conventional ways. Without these conditions, a transformation of identity is unlikely.

In the first reading Barbara Laslett and Carol Warren present an instance of a positive use for secondary deviation. They demonstrate that a condition of weight control by overweight women may be acceptance of a deviant identity as "obese." Harrison Trice and Paul Michael Roman then analyze the factors involved in the success of Alcoholics Anonymous. Finally, Neal Shover analyzes some of the temporal as well as interpersonal contingencies that combine to help ordinary property offenders renounce their criminal careers.

Losing Weight   BARBARA LASLETT
and CAROL A. B. WARREN

Fatness, or as it is more politely called in our society "obesity,"[1] is both a medical and a social problem, since in our society the fat are stigmatized. However, unlike other forms of deviant behavior such as check forgery and shoplifting, obesity is not against the law. Reaction to this deviant status and behavior cannot, therefore, be channeled through the criminal justice system as a means of control.

One purpose of this analysis is to explore the sociological dimensions of obesity as a type of deviance by applying the concept of stigma, as developed by Goffman (1963), to the strategies used by one voluntary weight loss organization[2] to combat obesity. In this organization, efforts to change the behavior of fat people so that they would become thin included, as a central feature, the application of stigmatizing labels. The insights which this analysis provides will then be used to specify variation in the meanings, uses and consequences of applying stigmatizing labels.

The use of stigma as a strategy for changing behavior from deviant to normal presents a challenge to labeling theory in general and in particular, to Lemert's (1967) theory of secondary deviation which assumes that further deviance follows from the application of stigmatizing labels. We will argue that the social labeling involved in stigmatization may also be used to change behavior in the opposite direction, i.e., toward normalcy. If this is true, then whether a stigmatizing label has a positive or negative effect on behavior will depend on other features of

the situation than the labeling process alone. The empirical example upon which this analysis is based presents some suggestions of what these features may be, and they will be discussed in the concluding section of the paper.

Stigma and Obesity

Stigma, as Goffman (1963:3) puts it, is "an attribute that is deeply discrediting." In Lemert's terms, it is a negative label. Goffman distinguishes three types of stigma: (1) perceived "blemishes of individual character," such as criminality, (2) the "tribal stigma of race, nation and religion" and (3) "abominations of the body—various physical deformities." Obesity is one type of "abomination of the body" which is particularly affected by cultural definitions. Not only do physiologically based definitions of obesity vary, but definitions of beauty—where obesity may or may not be discrediting—are particularly liable to cultural and historical variation.[3] In our society, although slimness is a general societal ideal, definitions of fat and slim vary according to social class, ethnicity, age and geographical area. Adolescents are more inclined to view themselves as fat than are adults, females more than males, and people of higher socio-economic status more than lower status (Dwyer et al. 1970). Fatness can also affect socio-economic opportunities: in New York, the extremely obese may go on welfare permanently since they are regarded as essentially unemploy-

Reprinted from "Losing Weight: The Organizational Promotion of Behavior Change," *Social Problems,* Vol. 23, No. 1 (October, 1975), pp. 69–80 by permission of the Society for the Study of Social Problems and the authors.

An earlier version of this paper was read at the 1973 meetings of the Pacific Sociological Association, Scottsdale, Arizona. This research was supported by the Social Science Research Institute, University of Southern California.

[1] Under the more technical rubric "obesity," two types of problem are included: overfat and overweight. A person can be slender and overfat, and overweight but not overfat. For example, a football player may weigh more than ideal for his height, as specified by life insurance company tables, but his body may not have any excess fat over muscle. A slender, sedentary person may, in contrast, have an excess of fat cells in his or her body and be "overfat" but not overweight. We use the terms "fat" and "obese" interchangeably to refer to persons who are perceived as too large by significant others and who perceive themselves that way as well.

[2] Permission to use the name of the organization studied was denied. Therefore, we refer only to the "weight loss organization" in the discussion.

[3] In classical Hawaiian culture, for example, a man's wealth, and a woman's beauty, were both measured by the amount of fat accumulated.

able, and in one California city, teachers may not be more than 25% overweight.[4]

Goffman (1963:3-4) emphasizes that while stigma might be seen in terms of individual characteristics, "a language of relationships, not attributes is really needed." The social meaning of obesity is derived in interaction with others, not from the attribute alone. It is for this reason that Goffman's further distinction of discrediting features that are or are not visible to others is relevant to the study of obesity.

For stigmatization to occur, the discrediting attribute must be known by the others with whom interaction takes place. Some stigmatizing attributes, like criminality and homosexuality, are not immediately apparent. Goffman (1963:4) refers to those persons whose stigma is invisible as *discreditable*. Other attributes, such as obesity, provide visible cues to stigma: their bearers are *discredited*. The obese cannot "pass" as thin; they must either lose weight or remain stigmatized.

Obesity as a source of stigma in contemporary American society has been documented in both the popular and professional literature (Stuart and Davis, 1972; Allon, 1973). Dwyer et al. (1970) point out that "normal" persons (using the term as Goffman does, to contrast with the stigmatized) stereotype fat persons as weak willed, ugly, awkward and immoral and the fat themselves have negative self-images to match the stereotypes. Fat people in contemporary American society, therefore, are the subject of the stigmatizing labels used by others and themselves.[5]

The Labeling Perspective

The labeling perspective defines deviance and normalcy in terms of the reactions of social audiences.[6] Lemert (1967:41) extends this perspective to the theory of secondary deviation.

The essence of the theory of secondary deviation is contained in two propositions, one explicit and one implicit: (1) Further deviance is promoted by audience labeling of persons as deviant, and (2) the "further deviance" promoted by labeling is made up of a deviant identity, deviant behavior, and a deviant way of life *which vary together*. This study questions these propositions by showing that *the use of negative or stigmatizing labels, in this case the label "fat," can be used to promote the normalization of deviant behavior, i.e., to make fat people thin*. Additionally, we question the logically assumed connection between identity, behavior and way of life.

Methodology

The data were collected in six months of systematic participant observation by the two authors in two different groups of the organization's weekly meetings. We observed three lecturers and several hundred members in interaction. One of the authors had been a long-term member of the organization (for over three years), and could provide additional informal data on more than 6 other lecturers. The other author joined the organization for the purpose of the research.

Each observer participated as a member, and it was only as a member that access to the organization was permitted. Leaders of the weight loss organization itself suggested the tactic of becoming a member when a representative denied our request for permission to do overt research. The authors were therefore in the unusual situation of doing secret research with the implicit permission of the institution involved.

The lack of overt permission did present certain problems for data collection. Each observer attempted to take notes in the field on the content of the weekly meetings. During one meet-

---

[4]Occupational health standards of such large-scale employers as the Los Angeles City School system, and the Los Angeles City and County governments include as one criteria for employment in *all* jobs, that the individual be within a range of weight specified as normal for a given age, height, and sex group, usually according to Metropolitan Life Insurance Company tables. (See Metropolitan Life Insurance Co., New York: 1969.)

[5]The only counter-trend to the negative labeling of obesity is the development of a "fat power" movement to destigmatize the *category* "fat persons" rather than to destigmatize fat persons by making them thin. (See Allon, 1973.)

[6]"Stigma" encompasses the same phenomena as "deviant," except that (1) stigma focuses more clearly on the audience reaction than deviance (and more than the labeling theory of deviance, which includes the definitionally illegitimate concept "secret deviance"), and (2) stigma encompasses "bodily abominations" and "tribal stigma" whereas deviance is generally restricted to "defects of character."

ing, however, another member (who, to our knowledge, was not a researcher) was asked not to take down what the lecturer was saying, despite her claim that she was just practicing her shorthand. Note-taking therefore was covert. The themes, however, were frequently reiterated in the lectures, facilitating accurate field notes.

The focus of analysis was the organization's strategies for promoting behavior change, particularly the use of a stigmatized identity label as a way of promoting normalized behavior and a normal way of life. Using Glaser and Strauss' (1967) model for the generation of grounded theory, the analytic categories were generated during data collection and preliminary analysis.

Stigmatizing Identity as a Strategy for Behavior Change

The major strategy used by the organization to promote the desired behavior (adoption of a rigidly defined program of eating) is *intensive stigmatization of the members as fat persons and the continued application of the label "fat" as an essential identity*. Members are told that the world is dichotomized into two types of people with reference to food and weight: the fat, and the "civilians" (the slender). The stigmatized identity of the fat person is permanent. It cannot be erased by weight loss, although it can be shifted from a visible stigma to an invisible one—from discrediting to discreditable. For the fat person who has become thin, weight loss is always potentially reversible and is an ever-dangerous invisible stigma which threatens the individual:

Lecturer: I am a fat person who got thin.
Member (250 lb. loser): I still think of myself as really heavy.

At most, then, the fat person can expect a partial destigmatization: the destigmatization of behavior reflected in appearance, but not the destigmatization of identity.[7] According to the weight loss organization, a change of identity from fat to thin would remove one of the best safeguards the fat person has against future weight gains. The continual awareness of an essential fat identity, whether visible (in pounds and fat) or invisible, acts as a warning device against the type of eating behavior promoting the discredited fat state.

Lecturer: One doctor at UCLA says that he wishes that the word "obese" would appear on fat people's foreheads when they become 5% overweight, since that much body weight changes chemistry so you can't use the same drugs. Furthermore, fat can be concealed by clothes. It is those women with lovely faces and good dress sense who are worse off than anyone, because they can put it on and not even notice.

Although identity cannot and should not be changed, eating behavior is amenable to change. The behavior change promoted by the organization is a permanent change in the quality and quantity of the food consumed so that external slenderness can be maintained for life. The threat of compulsive eating, however, is always present. Therefore compulsive eating behavior must be changed, either toward more moderation in eating habits or toward less fattening objects:

Lecturer: You will learn moderation here, too— to have ½ cup of ice cream and feel satisfied with it. You will learn that 4 teaspoons of sour cream will be plenty on a baked potato and 1 teaspoon of cream cheese is enough on your bagel.
Lecturer: I am still a compulsive eater, but now I eat lettuce compulsively.

The fact that food must be consumed to live gives the weight loss organization a tactical problem in promoting the desired behavior change unlike the self-help organizations for smokers, drug addicts and alcoholics which forbid the undesirable behavior. Instead, an exactly opposite mechanism is substituted—continuously focusing on food and stressing to the members that they *must* eat. Members who do not eat breakfast or who have a skimpy lunch are lectured to about the dangers of not eating enough. For fat people, being hungry is a violation of their essential self. They must be sure both to eat regularly so that they do not become hungry, and to exercise constant vigilance over food.

---

[7] For a general discussion of the phenomenon of destigmatization, see Warren, 1975.

Lecturer to a member who complained about having to eat the weekly liver portion which is required: You must eat it. Everything you put in your mouth does not have to be a thrill of a lifetime.

Lecturer: Set up a barrier between you and food. A barrier that thin people have automatically, but for you it must be a conscious matter.

Being hungry is a violation of the essential self, and carries with it the danger to which fat people are always exposed: the "bad," uncontrolled eating which may occur if the member gets too hungry. The organization promotes the conception of food as a vital force in a person's life. Meetings are characterized by this focus on food, which also contributes to reinforcing the individual's identity as fat, since fat people are seen as preoccupied with eating.

The organization encourages a change in behavior where one set of foodstuffs (thinning, good, "treats") are substituted for another (fattening, bad, "monsters"). There is an emphasis on traditional recipes using "legal" ingredients, like lobster newberg made with blended cauliflower for sauce, rather than completely different foods. Members are forbidden to use dietetic foods except for sugar-free soda and substitute sweeteners. So while stressing the significance of a total change in eating habits, the organization attempts to charm the members by focusing on their favorite vice, food, as a central symbol and by promising slenderness through this "totally new way" of using old recipes. The sin of gluttony can be satisfied through the back door. One of the organization's slogans is "you will never be hungry on our program."

The preoccupation with food and eating, which comprises a large part of the program's rhetoric, of lecturers' materials, and informal interaction at the weekly meetings, relates to this common feature of fat people's essential identity. The weight loss organization's goal is to change the eating behavior of the obese. One of their strategies to achieve their end is to emphasize the identity of "being a fatty" and fat people's obsession with food and eating. Negative labels, then, which *reinforce the essential identity of the fat as fat,* are used as a means of *changing behavior from deviant to normal,* thereby presenting a challenge to the theory of secondary deviation, which would predict an escalation of deviant behavior to follow from the act of stigmatization.

Lifestyle Change

"Lifestyle" or "way of life" are ill-defined terms, used by both Lemert (1967) and the weight loss organization to describe the types of behavior change persons undergo that are related to but are not composed of the behavior under consideration. Persons losing weight are presented by the organization as undergoing not only behavior change related to eating but also to change in other personal attributes and the social life that accompanies both eating and a size that is stigmatized in our society.

Lecturer: When I was fat, I could never balance my check book. My husband had to do it for me. But now I am more independent and more able to take care of myself. You have to be more independent and you can do it.

The organization reinforces the image that the lifestyle of fat people is full of embarrassing and self-demeaning experiences. Lecturers tell of getting stuck in theatre seats and behind the wheel of a car, or requiring other people to push as one tries to pull oneself out of a pool. They tell stories of not going places they really wanted to go because of having to sit in the back seat of a small car and fearing they would not be able to get out of it, or not having clothes that fit. They also emphasize that fat people are self-deluding and make irrational excuses for themselves and their stigma:

Member: I have to have cookies in the house in case my grandchildren come to visit.
Lecturer: Where do your grandchildren live?
Member: In New York! (This study was done in California.)

While such stories are often told to amuse the membership, their serious meaning is clear: until fat people reduce their weight they will live with painfully reduced self-esteem in a restricted range of activities, and a correspondingly unsatisfactory lifestyle. Lecturers promote an imagery and provide examples of the "better" way of life automatically accruing to fat persons as they become slender. For instance, lecturers state that a variety of positive changes accompanied their weight loss—sparkling wit at parties, more energy, a greater ability to cope with life's vicissitudes. They suggest greater business and professional, as well as social, success are a consequence of eliminating the visible stigma of fat. Thus, there is no need to force members to exercise, quit smoking, or have better human relationships: these good things will automatically follow from the transformation in lifestyle accompanying weight loss.

The organization is concerned with lifestyle in the context of attributes and activities unconnected with eating behavior; it also claims that a life long commitment to its weight loss and loss-maintenance program must become part of the individual's way of life. Because the person's essential fat identity is always present, the threat of returning to "bad" eating behavior is always possible. This lifelong commitment is expressed linguistically in the organization's distinction between a "diet" and a "program."

A "diet" is what fat people go on and off; it involves a temporary behavior change followed by relapse. A "program" is a changed lifestyle and pattern of eating lasting a lifetime. A "diet" implies the illusory promise of the destigmatizing of the individual, the shedding of the fat self for a reborn thin one. A "program" establishes the alternative ideal of a lifelong struggle to divorce eating behavior and way of life from an inevitably fat identity.

Linked with the concept of "program" is a view of time encompassing a whole past, present and future of eating habits. The lifetime program is divided into three stages the initiate must pass through before the attainment of a stigma which is discreditable only: the basic weight loss program, the "leveling" program (beginning when the person is within 10 lbs. of goal weight) and the "maintenance" program theoretically continued for the remainder of the person's future. Free lifetime membership in the organization accrues to people who have achieved their goal weight, complete the "maintenance" program, weigh in monthly and do not gain more than 2 pounds above their goal weight. Initiates to the organization are given a master plan for their entire life, divided into four distinct time tracks: three as a member of the organization and one (always in the past) as a discredited fat person.

A tactical problem for the organization is posed, however, by the fact that members do not follow the master plan: they do not always lose weight (or worse still, sometimes gain) during the time they attend meetings. They return to the organization after losing forty pounds and regaining fifty. For such contingencies the organization has another perspective on time: it is

the present only, just the immediate day or even meal at hand, which counts—not the past, and not the future. The members are told, on the one hand, that the program is a master plan for their entire lives, and on the other hand that no past action constitutes failure. This paradox is illustrated by two quotes from an organizational pamphlet: "If you do the best and the most you can today, don't worry about tomorrow"; "Perfection is attained by slow degrees; she requires the hand of time." Since all acts will eventually become past, success is always possible and organizational membership is always available. No matter how often one joins or rejoins, lecturers tell new members "Today is the first day of the rest of your life."

The mixed perspective on time and an emphasis on the permanence of their fat identity enables the weight loss organization to place the responsibility for failure on the individual and not the organization. The membership, at any one time, includes many former members who failed to lose weight, or who lost weight and later regained it. They are welcomed back and reassured that behavior change is always possible. Through the use of stigma as a strategy for individual behavior change, the organization constructs a foolproof ideology: success comes from following the organization's program, while failure is the responsibility of the individual member reflecting his or her essential identity.

Lemert's theory of secondary deviation implies that a deviant identity, deviant behavior and a deviant way of life vary together. The weight loss organization's separation of identity, behavior and lifestyle—through its use of stigma both as a means of changing behavior and as a basis on which to attribute responsibility for failure to individual members—presents a further challenge to the theory as it has been formulated. Not only can a stigmatized identity lead to non-deviant behavior, but "normal" behavior can lead to a "normal" way of life despite the retention of an identity which bears a negative label. A lifestyle change is only possible, though, when the stigma becomes discreditable (i.e., when it is no longer visible).

Organizational Strategies for the Promotion of Behavior Change

The two major strategies of change employed by the organization to promote and reinforce a stigmatized fat identity, normalized eating behavior and a better lifestyle are (1) the fostering of an ingroup-outgroup sentiment and (2) the use of change agents who are themselves successful graduates of the program.

The ingroup-outgroup differentiation is dual: between fat members and fat nonmembers of the organization, and, more important, between fat "foodaholics" and thin "civilians." Civilians are regarded, much as Goffman defines them: as "normals." Fat non-members are unenlightened potential members; if they are not attempting to become thin they are slothful and immoral. At best they are to be pitied, and members may serve as models to help them to a future in which they may be discreditable rather than discredited persons. If they are following some other weight program, such as diet pills, they are doomed to failure. Whatever the case, they are potential converts through efforts of both members and organizational advertising.

Unlike some behavior changing institutions such as Synanon, the weight loss organization is not a total institution (Goffman, 1961), and cannot set up walls between the membership and the civilian world. Worse, housewives form a large proportion of the membership; they have the traditional female role tasks of making meals for their families—meals which include desserts, cookies, potatoes and creamy salad dressings. So the members are encouraged to *quarantine* themselves, either physically or mentally from the surrounding temptations of their everyday lives.

Quarantine involves both removal from the non-quarantined and association with other quarantined persons (the ingroup impulse). Unlike Alcoholics Anonymous, though, the organization can rarely suggest that the members socialize only with those who do not use the substance, both because everyone uses food, and because so much of the member's lives are involved with food preparation for and consumption with "civilians." But the members are exhorted mentally to disassociate themselves from civilians, who are pictured as dedicated to the members' failure.

Lecturer: Friends want us to fail because that is the only way they can succeed . . . you have to be prepared for them . . . or they may be a civilian, and then they do not understand.

Weekly organization meetings are presented as a kind of inoculation against external pressures which weaken will-power and resolve: waitresses in restaurants, children begging for homemade cookies, husbands asserting that they like cuddly women, are all threats:

Lecturer: We must have free will not to eat and resist others . . . fat people are afraid of asserting themselves in the face of pressures to eat by restaurants, hostesses, fat people and others. Besides, they don't want to resist pressure. When you say "no" and mean it there is a tone in your voice that says you mean it. But a fat person's "no" to a second helping may be accompanied by salivating and panting.

While the outgroup is the non-fat world, the in-group is the world of foodaholics, and most particularly the membership of the organization. In the early days of the organization, there was more stress on in-group participation (for example, members tempted to eat would telephone another member for moral support), but at the present time the organization has become so large that the notion of "interdependence of members' goals" is not used as a social control mechanism. Unlike other self-help groups such as Synanon and AA, group therapy and other group dynamics take at most a secondary place to the lecture as a primary focus of organizational meetings (see Crosbie et al., 1972). The difference may lie in the profit-making nature of the weight loss organization. Having more and smaller groups would reduce the money which the organization makes by increasing staff (lecturers, weighers and clerks) and hall rental costs.

In addition to quarantining and inoculation, which promote ingroup-outgroup differentiation, ingroup sentiment is fostered by organizational rituals. Among the most important of these are group rituals instituted by the organization to reward persons who lose weight; these include graduation ceremonies from the three phases of the program, special pins, and certificates of merit. Other rituals, which socialize and cement the group as an institution, are the semi-public weekly weighing of each member, shows of hands of persons who had gained, lost or remained at the same weight during the week, and rounds of hand clapping both for persons who had lost weight and others who were "trying."

Since goal interdependence and ingroup senti-ment is hard to manage in a nontotal institution of a large size which cannot forbid the addictive substance to members, the organization stresses the theme of self-discipline considerably more than that of discipline by peers: "it's up to you" is a phrase constantly used by the lecturers. Along with the theme of self-discipline, how-ever, there is the continuing suggestion that pressures from the out-group—the non-fat civil-ian society—is the source of external pressure on the individual:

Lecturer: We are victims of patterns taught us in childhood of obeying our mothers and eat-ing it all up because of the starving people in so-and-so country, but we must no longer be victims.

As with many other self-help behavior modifi-cation groups, however, the pursuit of "causes" such as this hypothetical one remains com-pletely secondary to the "major" goal of chang-ing behavior in the here and now.

Lecturer: I am not concerned with why you are fat because of past factors. You are rolling in mud because of your own choice. But if there are deep reasons for that, you should go to a doctor who can take care of you up here (points to his head).

As an enterprise, this weight loss organization has an additional reason to refrain from seeking the hidden psychological and medical causes of obesity: legal responsibility. Lecturers con-stantly stress that they are not psychiatrists and will not dispense psychiatric advice, nor will they dispense authoritative nutritional, medical or scientific knowledge about obesity. Members with special problems are always told to consult their doctors. A denial of scientific expertise is yet another way of establishing the organiza-tion's lack of responsibility for any member's failure, and of placing the blame on the individ-ual. Thus they cannot be held accountable for a failure of the program (the product) which they sell.

The Change Agent

We found the change agent to be one of the most important facilitators for the "escalation"

of behavior from deviant to normal (as defined by the organization). All the lecturers and other organizational personnel are fat persons turned thin-on-the-outside: they provide a vital symbol of identification for persons who believe that "no one ever loses weight and keeps it off." The major ways in which the lecturers accomplish such identification for the members are *stigma display* (linking the past of the lecturer with the soon-to-be-past of the member) and *deviance display* (linking the lecturer's present with the members').

Stigma display is the constant reiteration by the lecturers of their own identity as essentially fat persons, once discredited but now discredit-able. This is accomplished in various ways: dis-play of "before" and "after" pictures of the lec-turer, anecdotes of the past sins of eating, and sad tales of the lifelong misery of the discredited fat and the counterpoint happiness of the dis-creditable (leavened quite often with humor):

Lecturer F told a story about how her husband had given her (now that she is thin) a black lace night gown and black satin sheets for Xmas. "Before, when I was a fat lady, we had a king size bed. He stayed on his side and I stayed on mine and we didn't meet in the middle very often. Satin sheets are very slippery. You slide off them."

As Hurvitz (1968:4) notes, such identification of the change agents' past with the members' trials and tribulations is a fundamental aspect of most self-help type organizations.

But a sorry past does not always qualify one to win present peer identification, as studies of drug addicts who become "fat cat" bureaucrats have shown. Lecturers in this organization use a second tactic to promote members' identifica-tion with the change agent's *present* experience: *deviance display,* a tactic forbidden organiza-tions as AA which ban the use of the deviant substance. Change agents underline the fact of lifelong temptation by food by indicating that they, too, are sometimes tempted and fail (but that the organization gives them the ability to recoup failures quickly and effectively):

Lecturer: I ate three barrels of sauerkraut over the weekend and gained seven pounds, but now I know what to do and have taken almost all of it back off.

Deviance display serves to promote identifica-tion, underlines the *continued* necessity of organizational membership, and highlights the necessity for changed behavior and an ultimate commitment to "a new way of life," at the same time as it reinforces the stigmatized essential identity.

Summary and Conclusions

Our data lead us to the conclusion that an empirically grounded elaboration of Lemert's theory of secondary deviation is both possible and needs to be tested in various behavior change settings. Our elaboration of Lemert's theory of secondary deviation or, as would be more accurate in the situation described here, a *theory of secondary normalization,* adds the following propositions which delineate those features of the labeling situation which make secondary normalization more probable than secondary deviation.

1. The central change strategy in organizations which use "ex's" as change agents is the permanent acceptance of a stigmatized identity. This strategy is in opposition to the strategy of the promotion of a "cured" or "normal" identity, attempted by organizations which are staffed by professional agents, such as mental hospitals and jails. Successful behavior change under the conditions described above, however, may require lifetime organizational membership to enable the stigmatized identity to be reinforced as a "positive" feature of normal behavior and a normal way of life.
2. Individuals may change their behavior and way of life from deviant to normal on some relevant dimension, but may retain a stigmatized identity connected with that same dimension.

The ideal test of the theory of secondary normalization, would, like a test of the theory of secondary deviation, involve a long-term evaluative follow-up study of organizational graduates, something which has never been fully accomplished with any organization.[8] Since the weight loss organization does not give permission for social or medical research, it was not possible to obtain information permitting us to evaluate the success which they claim for their program.

This stance is typical of behavior-changing organizations, which generally resist independent evaluation of their success and failure rates. Some behavior changing organizations keep their own statistics of success and failure; this weight loss organization claims not to keep systematic records of any kind, and only occasionally gives any indication of the success or failure of the members. For example, the lecturers sometimes quoted gross total weight losses for the class (or for the city), but these were often misleading since gross weight gain was not subtracted. In one class where this *was* done, the gross class weight loss for the month was over a hundred pounds, but the gross weight gain was nearly a hundred—leaving a total weight loss of a few pounds to be distributed among sixty or so members!

Failing the ideal test of Lemert's theory of secondary deviation (independently measured rates of success and failure when negative labels are used as a strategy for changing deviant behavior) this analysis suggests that the self-help organization studied here does not accept the view that escalation to deviant behavior always follows negative social labels. Furthermore, under certain conditions, such labeling can be used as a means to normalize deviant behavior. It is also clear that, in conflict with the traditional formulation of the theory of secondary deviation, stigmatization or normalization of identity can be viewed as *independent* of and not coterminous with deviant or normal behavior and way of life.

In summary, negative social labeling, or stigmatization, may have fateful consequences for the individual, but these are not always in the expected direction. In an expanded study of many behavior change groups dealing with drug use and child abuse as well as obesity, we found that *groups who used ex's as change agents all used strategies of identity stigmatization in order to facilitate normalization of members' be-*

---

[8] A few empirical (but not organizational-evaluative) studies of the effects of stigma do, however exist. These studies illustrate that the process of stigmatization involves the exchange of meanings between participants and is not simply a matter of label-sticking and passive receiving. Furthermore, "mental labeling" or stereotyping is not the same thing as the behavior that is directed toward the person so labeled. (See for example, Fisher, 1972; Foster et al., 1972; Schwartz and Stryker, 1970.)

havior (Warren, 1974). Such data give further empirical thrust to the conclusion that normal or deviant identity, way of life and behavior are empirically separable phenomena, erroneously analyzed under the umbrella "secondary deviation."

REFERENCES

Allon, Natalie. 1973. "Group Dieting Rituals." *Society,* 10 (January-February): 36–42.

Becker, Howard S. 1963. *Outsiders: Studies in the Sociology of Deviance.* New York: Free Press.

Berger, Peter L. and Thomas Luckmann. 1967. *The Social Construction of Reality.* New York: Doubleday.

Dwyer, Johanna T., Jacob J. Feldman, and Jean Mayer. 1970. "The Social Psychology of Dieting." *Journal of Health and Social Behavior,* 11 (December): 269–287.

Fisher, Sethard. 1972. "Stigma and Deviant Careers in Schools." *Social Problems,* 20 (Summer): 78–83.

Foster, Jack D., Simon Dinitz, and Walter C. Reckless. 1972. "Perceptions of Stigma Following Public Intervention for Deviant Behavior." *Social Problems,* 20 (Fall): 202–209.

Goffman, Erving. 1961. *Asylums.* New York: Doubleday.

———. 1963. *Stigma.* Englewood Cliffs, N.J.: Prentice-Hall.

Hurvitz, Nathan. 1968. "The Characteristics of Peer Self-help Psychotherapy Groups and Their Implications for the Theory and Practice of Psychiatry." Paper presented at the San Francisco convention of The American Psychological Association.

Lemert, Edwin. 1967. *Human Deviance, Social Problems and Social Control.* Englewood Cliffs, N.J.: Prentice-Hall.

Metropolitan Life Insurance Co. 1969. "New Weight Standards for Men and Women." *Statistical Bulletin,* 20 (November-December).

Schur, Edwin. 1971. *Labeling Deviant Behavior: Its Sociological Implications.* New York: Harper & Row.

Schwartz, Michael and Sheldon Stryker. 1970. *Deviance, Selves and Others.* Washington, D.C.: American Sociological Association.

Stuart, Richard B. and Barbara Davis. 1972. *Slim Chance in a Fat World.* Champaign, Illinois: Research Press Co.

Warren, Carol A. B. 1974. "The Use of Stigmatizing Labels in Conventionalizing Deviant Behavior." *Sociology and Social Research,* 58 (April): 303–311.

———. 1975. "Destigmatization: Acts, Identities, and Categories." Unpublished paper.

Delabeling, Relabeling, and Alcoholics Anonymous

HARRISON M. TRICE and PAUL MICHAEL ROMAN

An increasing amount of research emphasis in social psychiatry in recent years has been placed upon the rehabilitation and return of former mental patients to "normal" community roles (Sussman, 1966). The concomitant rapid growth of community psychiatry as a psychiatric paradigm parallels this interest, with community psychiatry having as a primary concern the maintenance of the patient's statuses within the family and community throughout the treatment process so as to minimize problems of rehabilitation and "return" (Pasamanick *et al.,* 1967; Susser, 1968). Despite these emphases, successful "delabeling" or destigmatization of mental patients subsequent to treatment appears rare (Miller, 1965; Freeman and Simmons, 1963). It is the purpose of this paper to explore an apparent negative instance of this phenomenon, namely a type of social processing which results in *successful* delabeling, wherein the stigmatized label is replaced with one that is socially acceptable.

The so-called labeling paradigm which has assumed prominence within the sociology of deviant behavior offers a valuable conceptualization of the development of deviant careers, many of which are apparently permanent (Scheff, 1966). In essence, labeling theory focuses upon the processes whereby a "primary deviant" becomes a "secondary deviant" (Lemert, 1951:75–76). Primary deviance may arise from myriad sources. The extent and nature of the social reaction to this behavior is a function of the deviant's reaction to his own behavior (Roman and Trice, 1969), the behavior's visibility, the power vested in the statuses of the deviant actor, and the normative parameters of tolerance for deviance that exist within the community. Primary deviance that is visible and exceeds the tolerance level of the community may bring the actor to the attention of mandated labelers such as psychiatrists, clinical psychologists, and social workers.

If these labelers see fit "officially" to classify the actor as a type of deviant, a labeling process occurs which eventuates in (1) self concept changes on the part of the actor and (2) changes in the definitions of him held by his immediate significant others, as well as the larger community. Behavior which occurs as a consequence of these new definitions is called secondary deviance. This behavior is substantively similar to the original primary deviance but has as its source the actor's revised self concept, as well as the revised social definition of him held in the community.

Previous research and theoretical literature appear to indicate that this process is irreversible, particularly in the cases of mental illness or so-called residual deviance (Miller, 1965; Myers and Bean, 1968). No systematic effort has been made to specify the social mechanisms which might operate to "return" the stigmatized secondary deviant to a "normal" and acceptable role in the community. In other words, delabeling and relabeling have received little attention as a consequence of the assumption that deviant careers are typically permanent.

Conceptually, there appear to be at least three ways whereby delabeling could successfully occur. First, organizations of deviants may develop which have the primary goal of changing the norms of the community or society, such that their originally offending behavior becomes acceptable (Sagarin, 1967). For example, organized groups of homosexuals have strongly urged that children be educated in the dual existence of homosexuality and heterosexuality as equally acceptable forms of behavior.

Secondly, it is possible that the mandated professionals and organizations who initially label deviant behavior and process the deviant through "treatment" may create highly visible and explicit "delabeling" or "status-return" ceremonies which constitute legitimized public pronouncements that the offending deviance has ceased and the actor is eligible for re-entry into the community. Such ceremonies could presumably be the reverse of "status degradation" rituals (Garfinkel, 1956).

A third possible means is through the development of mutual aid organizations which encourage a return to strict conformity to the norms of

Reprinted from *Social Problems*, Vol. 17, No. 4 (Spring 1970), pp. 538–546, by permission of the Society for the Study of Social Problems and the authors.

the community as well as creating a stereotype which is socially acceptable. Exemplary of this strategy is Alcoholics Anonymous. Comprised of 14,150 local groups in the United States in 1967, this organization provides opportunities for alcoholics to join together in an effort to cease disruptive and deviant drinking behavior in order to set the stage for the resumption of normal occupational, marital, and community roles (Gellman, 1964).

The focus of this paper is the apparent success in delabeling that has occurred through the social processing of alcoholics through Alcoholics Anonymous and through alcoholics' participation in the A.A. subculture. The formulation is based chiefly on participant observation over the past 15 years in Alcoholics Anonymous and data from various of our studies of the social aspects of alcoholism and deviant drinking. These observations are supplemented by considerable contact with other "self-help" organizations. These experiences are recognized as inadequate substitutes for "hard" data; and the following points are best considered as exploratory hypotheses for further research.

The "Allergy" Concept

The chronic problem affecting the reacceptance into the community of former mental patients and other types of deviants is the attribution of such persons with taints of permanent "strangeness," "immorality," or "evil." A logical method for neutralizing such stigma is the promulgation of ideas or evidence that the undesirable behavior of these deviants stems from factors beyond their span of control and responsibility. In accord with Parsons' (1951) cogent analysis of the socially neutralizing effects of the "sick role," it appears that permanent stigmatization may be avoided if stereotypes of behavior disorders as forms of "illness" can be successfully diffused in the community.

Alcoholics Anonymous has since its inception attempted to serve as such a catalyst for the "delabeling" of its members through promulgating the "allergy concept" of alcohol addiction. Although not part of official A.A. literature, the allergy concept plays a prominent part in A.A. presentations to non-alcoholics as well as in the A.A. "line" that is used in "carrying the message" to non-member deviant drinkers. The substance of the allergy concept is that those who

become alcoholics possess a physiological allergy to alcohol such that their addiction is predetermined even before they take their first drink. Stemming from the allergy concept is the label of "arrested alcoholic" which A.A. members place on themselves.

The significance of this concept is that it serves to diminish, both in the perceptions of the A.A. members and their immediate significant others, the alcoholic's responsibility for developing the behavior disorder. Furthermore, it serves to diminish the impression that a form of mental illness underlies alcohol abuse. In this vein, A.A. members are noted for their explicit denial of any association between alcoholism and psychopathology. As a basis for a "sick role" for alcoholics, the allergy concept effectively reduces blame upon one's *self* for the development of alcoholism.

Associated with this is a very visible attempt on the part of A.A. to associate itself with the medical profession. Numerous publications of the organization have dealt with physicians and A.A. and with physicians who are members of A.A. (*Grapevine,* 1968). Part of this may be related to the fact that one of the co-founders was a physician; and a current long time leader is also a physician. In any event, the strong attempts to associate A.A. with the medical profession stand in contrast to the lack of such efforts to become associated with such professions as law, education, or the clergy.

Despite A.A.'s emphasis upon the allergy concept, it appears clear that a significant portion of the American public does not fully accept the notion that alcoholism and disruptive deviant drinking are the result of an "allergy" or other organic aberration. Many agencies associated with the treatment of alcohol-related problems have attempted to make "alcoholism is an illness" a major theme of mass educational efforts (Plaut, 1967). Yet in a study of 1,213 respondents, Mulford and Miller (1964) found that only 24 percent of the sample "accepted the illness concept without qualification." Sixty-five percent of the respondents regarded the alcoholic as "sick," but most qualified this judgment by adding that he was also "morally weak" or "weak-willed."

The motivation behind public agencies' efforts at promulgating the "illness" concept of behavior disorders to reduce the probability of temporary or permanent stigmatization was essentially upstaged by A.A. Nonetheless, the data indicate that acceptance of the "illness" notion by the general public is relatively low in the case of alcoholism and probably lower in the cases of other behavior disorders (cf. Nunnally, 1961). But the effort has not been totally without success. Thus it appears that A.A.'s allergy concept does set the stage for reacceptance of the alcoholic by part of the population. A more basic function may involve the operation of the A.A. program itself; acceptance of the allergy concept by A.A. members reduces the felt need for "personality change" and may serve to raise diminished self-esteem.

Other than outright acceptance of the allergy or illness notion, there appear to be several characteristics of deviant drinking behavior which reduce the ambiguity of the decision to re-accept the deviant into the community after his deviance has ceased.

Unlike the ambiguous public definitions of the causes of other behavior disorders (Nunnally, 1961), the behaviors associated with alcohol addiction are viewed by the community as a direct consequence of the inappropriate use of alcohol. With the cessation of drinking behavior, the accompanying deviance is assumed to disappear. Thus, what is basically wrong with an alcoholic is that he drinks. In the case of other psychiatric disorders the issue of "what is wrong" is much less clear. This lack of clarity underlies Scheff's (1966) notion of psychiatric disorders as comprising "residual" or relatively unclassifiable forms of deviance. Thus the mentally ill, once labeled, acquire such vague but threatening stereotypes as "strange," "different," and "dangerous" (Nunnally, 1961). Since the signs of the disorder are vague in terms of cultural stereotypes, it is most difficult for the "recovered" mental patient to convince others that he is "cured."

It appears that one of the popular stereotypes of former psychiatric patients is that their apparent normality is a "coverup" for their continuing underlying symptoms. Thus, where the alcoholic is able to remove the cause of his deviance by ceasing drinking, such a convincing removal may be impossible in the case of the other addictions and "mental" disorders. Narcotic addiction represents an interesting middle ground between these two extremes, for the cultural stereotype of a person under the influence of drugs is relatively unclear, such that it may be relatively difficult for the former addict to convince others that he has truly removed the cause

of his deviance. This points up the fact that deviant drinking and alcoholism are continuous with behavior engaged in by the majority of the adult population, namely "normal" drinking (Mulford, 1964). The fact that the deviant drinker and alcohol addict are simply carrying out a common and normative behavior to excess reduces the "mystery" of the alcoholic experience and creates relative confidence in the average citizen regarding his abilities to identify a truly "dry" alcoholic. Thus the relative clarity of the cultural stereotype regarding the causes of deviance accompanying alcohol abuse provides much better means for the alcoholic to claim he is no longer a deviant.

To summarize, A.A. promulgates the allergy concept both publicly and privately, but data clearly indicate that this factor alone does not account for the observed success at "re-entry" achieved by A.A. members. Despite ambiguity in public definitions of the etiology of alcoholism, its continuity with "normal" drinking behavior results in greater public confidence in the ability to judge the results of a therapeutic program. An understanding of A.A.'s success becomes clearer when this phenomenon is coupled with the availability of the "repentant" role.

The Repentant Role

A relatively well-structured status of the "repentant" is clearly extant in American cultural tradition. Upward mobility from poverty and the "log cabin" comprises a social type where the individual "makes good" for his background and the apparent lack of conformity to economic norms of his ancestors. Redemptive religion, emergent largely in American society, emphasizes that one can correct a moral lapse even of long duration by public admission of guilt and repentance (cf. Lang and Lang, 1960).

The A.A. member can assume this repentant role; and it may become a social vehicle whereby, through contrite and remorseful public expressions, substantiated by visibly reformed behavior in conformity to the norms of the community, a former deviant can enter a new role which is quite acceptable to society. The reacceptance may not be entirely complete, however, since the label of alcoholic is replaced with that of "arrested alcoholic"; as Gusfield (1967) has stated, the role comprises a social type of a "repentant deviant." The acceptance of the allergy concept by his significant others may well hasten his re-acceptance, but the more important factor seems to be the relative clarity by which significant others can judge the deviant's claim to "normality." Ideally the repentant role is also available to the former mental patient; but as mentioned above, his inability to indicate clearly the removal of the symptoms of his former deviance typically blocks such an entry.

If alcohol is viewed in its historical context in American society, the repentant role has not been uniquely available to A.A. members. As an object of deep moral concern no single category of behavior (with the possible exception of sexual behavior) has been laden with such emotional intensity in American society. Organized social movements previous to A.A. institutionalized means by which repentants could control their use of alcohol. These were the Washingtonians, Catch-My-Pal, and Father Matthews movements in the late 1800's and early 1900's, which failed to gain widespread social acceptance. Thus not only is the repentant role uniquely available to the alcoholic at the present time, but Alcoholics Anonymous has been built on a previous tradition.

Skid Row Image and Social Mobility

The major facet of Alcoholics Anonymous' construction of a repentant role is found in the "Skid Row image" and its basis for upward social mobility. A central theme in the "stories" of many A.A. members is that of downward mobility into Skid Row or near Skid Row situations. Research evidence suggests that members tend to come from the middle and lower middle classes (Trice, 1962; Straus and Bacon, 1951). Consequently a "story" of downward mobility illustrates the extent to which present members had drastically fallen from esteem on account of their drinking. A.A. stories about "hitting bottom" and the many degradation ceremonies that they experienced in entering this fallen state act to legitimize their claims to downward mobility. Observation and limited evidence suggests that many of these stories are exaggerated to some degree and that a large proportion of A.A. members maintained at least partially stable status-sets throughout the addiction process. However, by the emphasis on downward mobility due to drinking, the social mobility "distance" traveled by the A.A. member is maximized in

the stories. This clearly sets the stage for impressive "comeback accomplishments."

Moral values also play a role in this process. The stories latently emphasize the "hedonistic underworld" to which the A.A. member "traveled." His current status illustrates to others that he has rejected this hedonism and has clearly resubmitted himself to the normative controls and values of the dominant society, exemplified by his A.A. membership. The attempt to promulgate the "length of the mobility trip" is particularly marked in the numerous anonymous appearances that A.A. members make to tell their stories before school groups, college classes, church groups, and service clubs. The importance of these emphases may be indirectly supported by the finding that lower-class persons typically fail in their attempts to successfully affiliate with A.A., i.e., their social circumstances minimize the distance of the downward mobility trip (Trice and Roman, 1970; Trice, 1959).

A.A. and American Values

The "return" of the A.A. member to normal role performance through the culturally provided role of the repentant and through the implied social mobility which develops out of an emphasis upon the length of the mobility trip is given its meaning through tapping directly into certain major American value orientations.

Most importantly, members of Alcoholics Anonymous have regained self control and have employed that self control in bringing about their rehabilitation. Self control, particularly that which involves the avoidance of pleasure, is a valued mode of behavior deeply embedded in the American ethos (Williams, 1960). A.A. members have, in a sense, achieved success in their battle with alcohol and may be thought of in that way as being "self-made" in a society permeated by "a systematic moral orientation by which conduct is judged" (Williams, 1960:424). This illustration of self control lends itself to positive sanction by the community.

A.A. also exemplifies three other value orientations as they have been delineated by Williams: humanitarianism, emphases upon practicality, and suspicion of established authority (Williams, 1960:397–470). A definite tendency exists in this society to identify with the helpless, particularly those who are not responsible for their own afflictions.

A.A. taps into the value of efficiency and practicality through its pragmatism and forthright determination to "take action" about a problem. The organization pays little heed to theories about alcoholism and casts all of its literature in extremely practical language. Much emphasis is placed upon the simplicity of its tenets and the straightforward manner in which its processes proceed.

Its organizational pattern is highly congruous with the value, suspicion of vested authority. There is no national or international hierarchy of officers, and local groups maintain maximum autonomy. Within the local group, there are no established patterns of leadership, such that the organization proceeds on a basis which sometimes approaches anarchy. In any event, the informality and equalitarianism are marked features of the organization, which also tend to underline the self control possessed by individual members.

A.A.'s mode of delabeling and relabeling thus appears in a small degree to depend upon promulgation of an allergy concept of alcoholism which is accepted by some members of the general population. Of greater importance in this process is the effective contrivance of a repentant role. Emphasis upon the degradation and downward mobility experienced during the development of alcoholism provides for the ascription of considerable self control to middle-class members, which in turn may enhance their prestige and "shore up" their return to "normality." The repentance process is grounded in and reinforced by the manner in which the A.A. program taps into several basic American value orientations.

A.A.'s Limitations

As mentioned above, A.A. affiliation by members of the lower social classes is frequently unsuccessful. This seems to stem from the middle-class orientation of most of the A.A. programs, from the fact that it requires certain forms of public confessions and intense interpersonal interaction which may run contrary to the images of masculinity held in the lower classes, as well as interpersonal competence.

Perhaps an equally significant limitation is a psychological selectivity in the affiliation process. A recent followup study of 378 hospitalized alcoholics, all of whom had been intensely exposed to A.A. during their treatment, revealed that those who successfully affiliated with A.A. upon their re-entry into the community had personality features significantly different from those who did not affiliate (Trice and Roman, 1970). The successful affiliates were more guilt prone, sensitive to responsibility, more serious, and introspective. This appears to indicate a definite "readiness" for the adoption of the repentant role among successful affiliates. To a somewhat lesser extent, the affiliates possessed a greater degree of measured ego strength, affiliative needs, and group dependency, indicating a "fit" between the peculiar demands for intense interaction required for successful affiliation and the personalities of the successful affiliates. Earlier research also revealed a relatively high need for affiliation among A.A. affiliates as compared to those who were unsuccessful in the affiliation process (Trice, 1959).

These social class and personality factors definitely indicate the A.A. program is not effective for all alcoholics. Convincing entry into the repentant role, as well as successful interactional participation in the program, appear to require middle-class background and certain personality predispositions.

Summary

In summary, we shall contrast the success of A.A. in its delabeling with that experienced by other self help groups designed for former drug addicts and mental patients (Wechsler, 1960; Landy and Singer, 1961). As pointed out above, the statuses of mental patients and narcotic addicts lack the causal clarity accompanying the role of alcoholic. It is most difficult for narcotic addicts and former mental patients to remove the stigma since there is little social clarity about the cessation of the primary deviant behavior. Just as there is no parallel in this respect, there is no parallel in other self-help organizations with the Skid Row image and the status-enhancing "mobility trip" that is afforded by this image. The primary deviant behaviors which lead to the label of drug addict or which eventuate in mental hospitalization are too far removed from ordinary social experience for easy acceptance of the former deviant to occur. These behaviors are a part of an underworld from which return is most difficult. On the other hand, Alcoholics Anonymous possesses, as a consequence of the nature of the disorder of alcoholism, its uniqueness as an organization, and the existence of certain value orientations within American society, a pattern of social processing whereby a labeled deviant can become "delabeled" as a stigmatized deviant and relabeled as a former and repentant deviant.

REFERENCES

Anonymous. 1968. "Doctors, Alcohol and A.A." *Alcoholics Anonymous Grapevine* (October).

Freeman, H. and O. Simmons. 1963. *The Mental Patient Comes Home*. New York: Wiley.

Garfinkel, H. 1956. "Conditions of Successful Degradation Ceremonies." *American Journal of Sociology,* 61 (March): 420–424.

Gellman, I. 1964. *The Sober Alcoholic*. New Haven: College and University Press.

Gusfield, J. 1967. "Moral Passage: The Symbolic Process in Public Designations of Deviance." *Social Problems,* 15 (Winter): 175–188.

Landy, D. and S. Singer. 1961. "The Social Organization and Culture of a Club for Former Mental Patients." *Human Relations,* 14 (January): 31–40.

Lang, K. and G. Lang. 1960. "Decisions for Christ: Billy Graham in New York City." In M. Stein *et al.* (eds.), *Identity and Anxiety*. New York: The Free Press, pp. 415–427.

Lemert, E. 1951. *Social Pathology*. New York: McGraw-Hill.

Miller, D. 1965. *Worlds That Fail*. Sacramento, California: California Department of Mental Hygiene.

Mulford, H. 1964. "Drinking and Deviant Drinking, U.S.A, 1963." *Quarterly Journal of Studies on Alcohol,* 25 (December): 634–650.

Mulford, H. and D. Miller. 1964. "Measuring Public Acceptance of the Alcoholic as a Sick Person." *Quarterly Journal of Studies on Alcohol,* 25 (June): 314–323.

Myers, J. and L. Bean. 1968. *A Decade Later*. New York: Wiley.

Nunnally, J. 1961. *Popular Conceptions of Mental Health*. New York: Holt, Rinehart and Winston.

Parsons, T. 1951. *The Social System*. Glencoe, Ill.: The Free Press.

Pasamanick, B. *et al.* 1967. *Schizophrenics in the Community*. New York: Appleton, Century, Crofts.

Plaut, T. 1967. *Alcohol Problems: A Report to the Nation*. New York: Oxford University Press.

Roman, P. and H. Trice (1969). "The Self Reaction: A Neglected Dimension of Labeling Theory." Presented at American Sociological Association Meetings, San Francisco.

Sagarin, E. 1967. "Voluntary Associations among Social Deviants." *Criminologica* 5 (January): 8–22.

Scheff, T. 1966. *Being Mentally Ill*. Chicago: Aldine.

Susser, M. 1968. *Community Psychiatry*. New York: Random House.

Sussman, M. (ed.) 1966. *Sociology and Rehabilitation*. Washington: American Sociological Association.

Straus, R. and S. Bacon. 1951. "Alcoholism and Social Stability." *Quarterly Journal of Studies on Alcohol,* 12 (June): 231–260.

Trice, H. 1959. "The Affiliation Motive and Readiness to Join Alcoholics Anonymous." *Quarterly Journal of Studies on Alcohol,* 20 (September): 313–320.

———. 1962. "The Job Behavior of Problem Drinkers." In D. Pittman and C. Snyder (eds.), *Society, Culture and Drinking Patterns*. New York: Wiley, pp. 493–510.

Trice, H. and P. Roman. 1970. "Sociopsychological Predictors of Successful Affiliation with Alcoholics Anonymous." *Social Psychiatry,* 5 (Winter): 51–59.

Wechsler, H. 1960. "The Self-help Organization in the Mental Health Field: Recovery, Inc." *Journal of Nervous and Mental Disease,* 130 (April): 297–314.

Williams, R. 1960. *American Society*. New York: A. A. Knopf.

The Later Stages of Property Offender Careers
NEAL SHOVER

Most sociological research on deviant and criminal careers has focused on their initial stages. We know little about their later stages, and the pathways out of deviance (Frazier, 1976; Luckenbill and Best, 1981). This is unfortunate for scholars and policy makers alike, because evidence suggests that most serious youthful miscreants eventually alter or terminate their criminal behavior (Cline, 1980).

The concept of career refers to common experiences among individuals who have encountered, grappled with, and resolved similar problems. Careers have two related, though analytically distinct, sides—the objective and the subjective (Stebbins, 1970). The objective career is open to public view, and includes changes in life style and official position. The subjective career is less visible: it includes changes in identity, self-concept, and the framework employed to judge oneself and others. Changes in both the objective and the subjective careers often occur together. Thus, to understand careers adequately, not only must we examine each of the two sides, but also how they fit together.

Career contingencies are significant events, common to members of a social category, which produce movement along, or transformations of, career lines (Goffman, 1961:133). Just as we can speak of objective and subjective careers, so too can we distinguish between objective and subjective career contingencies. The former are "objective facts of social structure" while the latter designates "changes in the perspectives, motivations, and desires" of individuals (Becker, 1963:24).

This paper explores the later stages of the criminal careers of a group of ordinary property offenders. I begin with a review of previous research on the topic. . . . Then I discuss the major contingencies which led to a modification of the subjects' criminal behavior. I conclude with a discussion of the similarities between my findings and previous research, a theoretical interpretation of the findings, and some comments on the study's relevance for contemporary crime control programs.

Literature

For years, social scientists have known of the inverse relationship among adults between age and the probability of arrest (Glueck and Glueck, 1937; Hirschi and Gottfredson, in press; Moberg, 1953; Rowe and Tittle, 1977; Sellin, 1958). When referring to former offenders, this relationship has been known, albeit imprecisely, as the "maturation effect."

Bull (1972), Irwin (1970), and Meisenhelder (1975; 1977) have examined some aspects of the process of exiting from crime. Bull examined the merits of Kierkegaard's philosophy of the stages of personal and spiritual growth in the human life cycle. He found that as the 15 ex-convicts he interviewed aged, feelings of despair motivated them to modify their lives and so reduce their criminal behavior. The modifications represented a shift, in Kierkegaard's terms, from the aesthetic stage of life to an ethical one.

Irwin interviewed 15 ex-convicts who had remained out of prison for many years. Those who had modified or terminated their criminal involvement did so for several reasons: (1) fear of further imprisonment; (2) "exhaustion from years of a desperate criminal life and a deprived prison life" (1970:196); (3) a reduction in sexual and financial expectations; (4) "an adequate and satisfying relationship with a woman" (1970:203); and (5) involvement in "extravocational, extradomestic activities" such as sports or hobbies (1970:203).

Meisenhelder interviewed 20 incarcerated, nonprofessional property offenders about earlier periods of their lives when they temporarily had

Excerpt from "The Later Stages of Ordinary Property Offender Careers," *Social Problems,* Vol. 31, No. 2 (December 1983), pp. 208–218 by permission of the Society for the Study of Social Problems and the author.

This study was supported by a grant from the National Institute of Justice (80–IJ–CX–0047) during the author's tenure as a visiting fellow. Points of view or opinions expressed in this paper are the author's, and do not necessarily reflect the official position or policies of the Department of Justice. The author thanks Edward Bunker, Daniel Glaser, John Irwin, Patrick Langan, David Luckenbill, John Lynxwiler, Stephen Norland, and a *Social Problems* reviewer for their comments.

terminated their criminal behavior. Their motivation to discontinue crime was (1) "fear of 'doing more time' in prison" (1977:322); and (2) a "subjective wish to lead a more normal life" (1977:324). Successful exit from crime resulted from (1) establishment of a "meaningful bond to the conventional social order" (1977:325); and (2) symbolic certification by a noncriminal that the offender had changed and was "to be considered essentially noncriminal" (1977:329)[1] . . .

Temporal Contingencies

An Identity Shift

During their late 30s to early 40s, most of the men began to take stock of their lives and their accomplishments. In the process, most confronted for the first time the realization that (1) their criminality had been an unproductive enterprise; and (2) this situation was unlikely to change. In short, they realized that ordinary property crime was a dead end. They developed a critical, detached perspective toward an earlier portion of their lives and the personal identity which they believed it exemplified. Just as many aging non-offenders develop a wistful, detached perspective toward their youth, the aging men gradually viewed their youthful self as "foolish" or "dumb." They decided that their earlier identity and behavior were of limited value for constructing the future. This new perspective symbolized a watershed in their lives.

A 54-year-old man said he learned how to serve time when he was young.

> I can handle it, if I have to serve time. But now I know how stupid I have been. And for me now to do something as stupid as I have done, and go back to serving time, it would drive me crazy.
> *Q:* Why would it drive you crazy?
> *A:* Because now I, like I told you, I see these things. I see myself. And see how my path has been so wrong when I thought I was bein' smart, or thought that I was bein' hep, or thought that I was this or that. And it's a dream.

As this suggests, the aging process of most ordinary property offenders includes a redefinition of their youthful criminal identity as self-defeating, foolish, or even dangerous.

Incommodious Time

While taking stock of their lives, most of the men became acutely aware of time as a diminishing, exhaustible resource. They began constructing plans for how to use the remainder of their lives. As this new perspective developed, the future became increasingly valuable, and the possibility of spending additional time in prison especially threatening. Not only would another prison sentence subject them to the usual deprivations, but it would expropriate their few remaining, potentially productive years. They feared losing their last remaining opportunity to accomplish something and to prepare financially for old age. A 45-year-old parolee said he did not want to serve any more time in prison. Asked if he was "afraid of doing time now," he replied:

> No, I'm not really afraid of it. I don't know, I just don't want to do it. . . . It's just knocking time out of my life.
> *Q:* Are you trying to say that the years you have left are more precious to you?
> *A:* True. And they're a lot more precious to me than when I was 25 or 30. . . . I guess you get to the point where you think, well, . . . you're getting old, you're getting ready to die and you've never really lived, or something. You don't want to spend it in the joint, treading water.

The men dreaded receiving a long sentence, but believed that because of their previous convictions, any prison terms they received would be lengthy.

> Hey, I'm 47, you know. And if I get one of them big numbers [long sentences] now, hey, I'm through bookin', you know. I'm through bookin'. . . . One of them big numbers, man, would do me in, you know. And I could not stand it.

This growing awareness of time as a limited resource intensified subjects' fears of dying inside prison.

Aspirations and Goals

Many men no longer felt they wanted or needed to strive for the same level of material

---

[1] There is also a body of work on the process of "natural recovery" from heroin addiction (Brill, 1972; Jorquez, 1980; Waldorf, 1983; Waldorf and Biernacki, 1979; 1981; Winick, 1962).

fulfillment and recognition which they had sought when younger. As an ex-offender has written:

I've got to a point where things that were important to me twelve, fifteen years ago aren't important now. I used to have a lot of ambitions, like everybody else has—different business ventures, stuff like that. But today, why, with what I have to buck up against, why, I could be just as happy and just as satisfied with a job that I'm getting by on, where I knew I wasn't going to run into trouble or anything (Martin, 1952:277).

Just as important, the men revised their aspirations, assigning higher priority to goals which formerly were less important. Like the middle-aged non-offender, an interest in such things as "contentment" and "peace" became important to them. Referring to his earlier activities, a 56-year-old man said:

I don't want to live that kind of life no more. I want peace. I want joy and harmony. I want to be with my children and my grandchildren. I got a bunch of grand-kids, and I want to be with them. I want to be with my mother. And when she passes on—I was in prison when my daddy died, I got to come home for five hours in handcuffs to see him—and when my mother passes on, I want to be there with her.

This man's newly kindled interest in family members is not unique. Several other men revealed similar sentiments which, they acknowledged, developed only as they approached or attained middle age.

Many subjects realized that they could achieve their revised aspirations on a modest income, as long as it was consistent and predictable. Those who continued their criminal activities often were content with committing less hazardous offenses, even if this meant accepting smaller economic rewards. Those who turned to legitimate work began to appreciate the advantages of a job with secure benefits such as sick leave or a pension. A 56-year-old man said:

I'm satisfied now, you know. There ain't nobody can get me to do nothin' [commit a crime]. Not now. Not the way I'm goin' now. . . . Every year I go away on vacation. I got three weeks now. Next year I get four weeks. Yeah. So I'm happy, you know, right now.

Tiredness

The men began to see the entire criminal justice system as an apparatus which clumsily but relentlessly swallows offenders and wears them down. They began to experience the prison as an imposing accumulation of aggravations and deprivations. They grew tired of the problems and consequences of criminal involvement. Asked why he had abandoned crime, a 53-year-old man answered succinctly:

Being tired, you know. Just collapsing, that's all. I'd say age made me weak, made me tired, you know. That's all.

The men gave different reasons why they gradually tired of their former experiences. For example:

Q: Do the main problems of doing time change as you age?
A: They *intensify,* you know. The rhetoric, the environment itself, you know. I mean, who wants to walk around talkin' about fuckin' somebody all day long, or somebody gettin' fucked in the ass and shit? . . . I mean, this kind of shit, you, when you get older you can't relate to that kind of shit.

Still, for some ex-offenders the specific origins of this perspective are obscure and difficult to articulate. One has written:

I really don't know why I went straight. I just decided that after I got out. It wasn't fear of the law, it isn't fear of the penitentiary, 'cause I've sat down and thought it out very seriously, but I just had enough of it, that's all (King, 1972:158).

A 53-year-old man explained that he never committed and would never again attempt the "big score," the one highly lucrative crime which would permit him to retire in comfort. Asked why he had given up this dream of many thieves, he said: "Because I know how the system is. . . . The system is bigger than me."

Interpersonal Contingency

Of the 30 ordinary offenders not in prison, 27 reported experiencing one or more of the four temporal contingencies. Typically, for those men who altered their criminal behavior, these changes produced a disenchantment with the activities and lifestyles of their youth, and an interest in and a readiness for fundamental change in their lives. A 47-year-old man said that after two terms of imprisonment,

I had already been convinced that I couldn't beat the system anyway, you know. What I was doin' wasn't gettin' nowhere, you know. It was just a dream.

Disenchanted with themselves and their unsuccessful attempts at crime, the aging men wanted to "give something else a try." They frequently developed an interest in supportive and satisfying social relationships; actually building such a relationship represented an interpersonal contingency in their lives. More specifically, I use this concept to refer to the establishment of a personally meaningful tie to either another person, especially a woman, or an activity, especially a job. The social relationships resulting from this interpersonal contingency assumed a special importance for the men. It provided them with commitment or "side bets" which they realized would be jeopardized by involvement in crime—or at least high-risk crimes (Becker, 1962).

Ties to Another Person

The establishment of a mutually satisfying relationship with a woman was a common pattern. Of the 30 respondents not in prison, seven mentioned this, either alone or together with other contingencies, as an important factor in the transformation of their career line.[2] Although many subjects maintained involvements with women when younger, they said these were not important influences on their behavior. With age, the meaning of such relationships changed and they assumed more importance.

When I reached the age of 35 it just seemed like my life wanted to change. I needed a change in life, and I was tired of going to jail. And I wanted to change my life and stay out here. And by meeting the woman that I met, it just turned my life completely around. . . . When I met her it just seemed like something in my life had been fulfilled.

Another man, who still engaged occasionally in property crimes, said he had once stopped committing crimes entirely while living with a woman for several years.

I started living with this woman, you know, and my life suddenly changed. . . . I was contented, you know, bein' with her. . . . I cared about her, you know. I wanted to be with her, you know. That was it. . . . And, hey, I just found enjoyment there.

A 56-year-old man, separated from his wife at the time of the interview, talked about her influence on him during earlier periods of unemployment:

I loved my wife—I love her still—and she talked to me a lot. . . . And if it wouldn't been for her, no tellin' where I'd be at, 'cause I'd most likely had a gun in my hand and robbed a bank or something. Or took something from somebody to get some food, you know. . . . She helped me along.

Ties to a Job

Five of the 30 men indicated that having a satisfying job, either alone or combined with other experiences, was an important influence on their career. Several men acknowledged that they had held potentially satisfying jobs earlier in their lives but had not seen or appreciated them at the time. One man told of securing a job as a youth in the U.S. Government Printing Office, where an older employee wanted to teach him how to mix and use inks.

I said to myself I didn't even want to be there. As much as possible I went into the men's restroom and went to sleep. And I was glad to get out of there when it was time to get off, and I wound up resigning the job.

As the subjects' perspectives changed with age, legitimate employment assumed more importance. For example, a 56-year-old man remembered when, as a younger man, he was interviewed for a job with a beauty and barber supply company:

The guy liked me from the jump. And that's when I hooked up with him. And I went straight a long time *without the intentions* of going straight. . . . That was one turning point in the later part of my life.

A 48-year-old man recalled his experiences 17 years earlier:

When I got out [the second time] . . . I sold a suit for 10 dollars and I bought [some tools], just the bare necessities of what I needed, and I met a guy who carried me on the job. . . . So, at that time I could make $160 a week. . . . And so, with this earning power I didn't have—I didn't have to steal . . . so this was right down my alley.

[2] In one case, a long-term homosexual relationship produced similar effects.

Successful participation in either a personal relationship or a job provided personal rewards and reinforced a noncriminal identity. For many, development of commitment to someone or some line of action gradually generated a pattern of routine activities—a daily agenda—which conflicted with, and left little time for, the daily activities associated with crime.

In addition to ties to another person and a job, two men said that religious experiences and the close social relationships they were involved in influenced their criminal careers.

Contingencies: Temporal Order and Interdependence

The five contingencies discussed above did not occur in a fixed sequence. They varied in the age at which they occurred and their interdependence.

1. In some cases, the precise point of occurrence of the separate temporal contingencies could not be easily isolated. Rather, one or more occurred simultaneously. A 55-year-old man reported:

   > I think I had been up [at the state reformatory]. I just said to myself, "Well, shit, this isn't getting me nowhere." . . . So I come out and I did get a good job . . . and they treated me good, and they trusted me, you know. . . . And I figured, well, these people are good enough to trust me, I'm good enough to play it straight with them. . . . Then I got married and that more or less helped too.
   > Q: How so?
   > A: Well, I married a good woman, I guess.

2. While the temporal and interpersonal contingencies operated both independently and jointly, each produced modifications in the nature, or reductions in the frequency, of criminal behavior.[3] In several cases, the two types of contingencies interacted with or followed one another as part of a dynamic process, with one type preceding and increasing the probability of occurrence for the other(s). Imposition of a rigid temporal and causal order on this process would violate its dynamic

nature and, given our present state of knowledge, would be arbitrary and premature.

3. Although the temporal contingencies typically set the stage for the interpersonal one, occasionally the latter occurred independently. It then produced a set of subjective career contingencies which strengthened the man's sense of commitment and his resolve to avoid crime—or at least high-risk crime. Meisenhelder (1977) refers to these secondary subjective contingencies as the "pull of normality." They were of some importance in my subjects' retrospective accounts, especially the feeling of relief over no longer having to fear the police. Several men spontaneously mentioned this as one of the advantages of the "square" life.

   > I can go to bed, hey man, I don't have to worry about [the police] kickin' my door down, you know, comin' and gettin' me. Because I'm not doin' nothin'. And man, I can remember one time, every time I see the police, hey man, I know they was comin' to my house. And sometimes I wasn't wrong. . . . But I don't worry about that now.

4. While any combination of the five contingencies usually led to changes in criminal behavior, the nature of these changes varied. In general, the most abrupt and complete changes seemed to result when all five contingencies occurred.

Various combinations of the foregoing contingencies modified the subjects' attitude toward and willingness to engage in crime. First, men who experienced the interpersonal contingency were increasingly reluctant to risk losing their new-found social ties. They began to include factors which had previously been absent from their deliberations over potential criminal activities. A 45-year-old former addict said:

> If I go out there and commit a crime—now, I got to think about this: Hey, man, I ain't *got* to get away. See what I'm sayin'? I have—man, it would be just my luck that I would get busted. Now I done fucked up everything I done tried to work hard for, man, you know, to get my little family together.

Second, they began to see ordinary property crime as a poor risk. Not only was there little chance of reaping a large reward, but they be-

---

[3] In a sense, the latter provide negative incentives to change, while the former provide positive incentives.

lieved there was a good chance they would receive a long prison sentence if convicted. In sum, the perceived odds narrowed; the perceived risks became greater; and the offenders decided to avoid the high-visibility crimes they had engaged in when younger. One man said he could no longer imagine committing an armed robbery because "I would be so nervous, and my hand would be shakin' so bad."

When the men did commit crimes, they planned them more carefully than they had in their youth. And they often endeavored to minimize the frequency of their criminal acts. As one man said: "It's what they call 'exposure time,' you know. You don't want to get 'exposed' too much." This does not mean that they ceased entirely *thinking* about crime, only that they developed an extended and modified set of rationales for self restraint.

Negative Cases

Clearly, not all cases fit the pattern I have described. The most troubling and perplexing cases were men who, despite their failure at crime and the fact that they experienced one or more of the temporal contingencies, reacted alternately with resignation or desperation to the belief that it was "too late" for them to accomplish anything in life. The years they had spent in prison made it difficult for them to achieve some objectives. For example, a 50-year-old man said:

I wants to have a good life, you know, but certain things will always be out of my reach because it's been so long, you know. I've been incarcerated so long.

While most of the men revised their aspirations and grudgingly accepted this fact, others did not. Animated in part by a sense of "nothing to lose," some sustained a pattern of petty hustles or long-term drunkenness.[4] Searching for a magic solution of their problems, others resorted to desperate, high risk crimes, with apparent disregard for the potential consequences (Camp, 1968; Parker, 1963). For example, after several years of freedom, a divorced 56-year-old man

experienced severe strains in his family relationships. Making little effort to conceal his identity, he robbed a bank. Apprehended several hours later, he insisted on pleading guilty at arraignment. He told the judge that his only friends were police and correctional officials, and that prison was the only place in which he felt accepted and comfortable. He was pleased when he received a 20-year sentence.

Four men not in prison spontaneously mentioned the care older persons receive in nursing homes and similar establishments. Arguing that convicts are treated better than nursing home residents, they said they would opt to spend their final years in prison if they had a choice.

If I got to a point where it's either go to an old folks' home or an old soldier's home—[I'd] figure, hell, if I robbed a bank . . . if I got away I'd get enough money to last me the rest of my life, if I got caught I'd go to prison and they'd give me better treatment there. . . . They got the best doctors there, and they got the best medical care. . . . What would a fella have to lose, even if he went in and pretended to hold up . . . if he had nothing to lose on the outside? . . . You got somebody [in prison] checkin' on you *all* the time. And in an old soldier's home, if you call a nurse, you're lucky to get anybody.[5]

While viewing the prison as a tolerable residence in old age was rare among those I interviewed, an imprisoned 62-year-old said:

In a way, I'm looking forward to getting out, and another way it don't much matter to me. . . . I know everybody here. . . . I do almost like I want. I go to early chow. [Earlier today] I went down to the law library and used their copying machine. I can do fairly well what I want to do without anybody bugging me about it 'cause all the officials know me.

Conclusions

My findings support Glaser's (1980) theory of differential expectation. Focusing on the interpretive process which precedes decisions to forego or to engage in criminal acts, the theory asserts that a person refrains from or commits crime because of the expected consequences.

---

[4]Others commit suicide (King, 1972).
[5]Responding to a question, the man subsequently stipulated that his comments applied only to "federal joints." It had been 20 years since his last state confinement and, he acknowledged, "I don't know much about these state places."

Obviously, it assumes that individuals, based on personal experiences, may alter their expectations of potential outcomes of criminal behavior. I have shown that there are distinct, age-related changes in the expectations of likely criminal success held by ordinary property offenders. Insights and propositions based on this theory can be developed at both the individual and aggregate levels of analysis. In either case, empirical testing and theoretical reformulation would be enhanced substantially by an improved understanding of typical changes over the life cycle in the calculus of alternative types of criminal behaviors.

With two exceptions, my findings are compatible with those of both Irwin (1970) and Meisenhelder (1977). Contrary to Irwin, my analysis did not find "extravocational" and "extradomestic activities" especially important in the eventual termination of criminality. Similarly, unlike Meisenhelder I did not find that "certification" was a necessary or even an important component of the process of exiting from crime.

My study clearly shows age-related social psychological changes in the subjects' later criminal careers. On the one hand, some of these changes result from their unique experiences at the hands of the criminal justice apparatus. After one man described some age-related changes he experienced, I suggested these might be similar to those experienced by non-offenders as well. He replied: "Similar, yeah, yeah. Really. But I would say doing time has [affected me] too, because I didn't want to go back to the penitentiary." On the other hand, some other contingencies described here, such as changes in aspirations and goals, are not unique to men who have been involved in crime. Rather, they seem common to the broader, socially comparable segment of the non-criminal population (Kuhlen, 1968; Neugarten, 1968). Scholars and policy makers who sometimes are tempted to view offenders as a different species of human beings should take special note of this fact.

More importantly, my findings challenge the argument, used by proponents of the death penalty, mandatory and determinate sentences, and similar repressive crime-control measures that such "reforms" are justified by the existence of intractable offenders. The findings clearly show that even offenders who committed serious crimes while young are capable of, and do, change as they get older.

REFERENCES

Becker, Howard S. 1962. "Notes on the Concept of Commitment." *American Journal of Sociology,* 66 (July):32–40.

———. 1963. *Outsiders: Studies in the Sociology of Deviance.* New York: The Free Press.

Brill, Leon. 1972. *The De-Addiction Process.* Springfield, Ill.: Charles Thomas.

Bull, James L. 1972. "Coming Alive: The Dynamics of Personal Recovery." Unpublished Ph.D. dissertation, University of California, Santa Barbara.

Camp, George M. 1968. "Nothing to Lose: A Study of Bank Robbery in America." Unpublished Ph.D. dissertation, Yale University.

Cline, Hugh F. 1980. "Criminal Behavior over the Life Span." In Orville G. Brim Jr. and Jerome Kagan (eds.), *Constancy and Change in Human Development.* Cambridge, Mass.: Harvard University Press, pp. 641–674.

Frazier, Charles F. 1976. *Theoretical Approaches to Deviance.* Columbus, Ohio: Charles Merrill.

Glaser, Daniel. 1980. "The Interplay of Theory, Issues, Policy, and Data." In Malcolm W. Klein and Katherine S. Teilmann (eds.), *Handbook of Criminal Justice Evaluation.* Beverly Hills, Cal.: Sage Publications, pp. 123–142.

Glueck, Sheldon and Eleanor Glueck. 1937. *Later Criminal Careers.* New York: The Commonwealth Fund.

Goffman, Erving. 1961. *Asylums.* Garden City, N.Y.: Anchor Books.

Hirschi, Travis and Michael Gottfredson. In press. "Age and the Explanation of Crime." *American Journal of Sociology.*

Irwin, John. 1970. *The Felon.* Englewood Cliffs, N.J.: Prentice-Hall.

Jorquez, James S. 1980. "The Retirement Phase of Heroin-using Careers." Unpublished Ph.D. dissertation, University of California, Los Angeles.

King, Harry. 1972. *Box Man* (as told to and edited by Bill Chambliss). New York: Harper Torchbooks.

Kuhlen, Raymond G. 1968. "Developmental Changes in Motivation During the Adult Years." In Bernice L. Neugarten (ed.), *Middle Age and Aging: A Reader in Social Psychology.* Chicago: University of Chicago Press, pp. 115–136.

Luckenbill, David and Joel Best. 1981. "Careers in Deviance and Respectability: The Analogy's Limitations." *Social Problems,* 29 (December):197–206.

Martin, John Bartlow. 1952. *My Life in Crime.* New York: Harper & Row.

Meisenhelder, Thomas N. 1975. "The Nonprofessional Property Offender: A Study in Phenomenological Sociology." Unpublished Ph.D. dissertation, University of Florida.

———. 1977. "An Exploratory Study of Exiting from Criminal Careers." *Criminology,* 15 (November):319–334.

Moberg, David O. 1953. "Old Age and Crime." *Journal of Criminal Law, Criminology and Police Science,* 43 (March-April):764–776.

Neugarten, Bernice L. 1968. "Adult Personality: Toward a Psychology of the Life Cycle. In Bernice L.Neugarten (ed.), *Middle Age and Aging: A Reader in Social Psychology.* Chicago: University of Chicago Press, pp. 134–147.

Parker, Tony. 1963. *The Unknown Citizen.* London: Hutchinson.

Rowe, Alan R. and Charles R. Tittle. 1977. "Life Cycle Changes and Criminal Propensity." *The Sociological Quarterly,* 18 (Spring):223–236.

Sellin, Thorsten. 1958. "Recidivism and Maturation." *National Probation and Parole Association Journal,* 4 (July):241–250.

Stebbins, Robert A. 1970. "Career: The Subjective Approach." *The Sociological Quarterly,* 11 (Winter):32–50.

Waldorf, Dan. 1983. "Natural Recovery from Opiate Addiction: Some Social Psychological Processes of Untreated Recovery." *Journal of Drug Issues.* In press.

Waldorf, Dan and Patrick Biernacki. 1979. "Natural Recovery from Heroin Addiction: A Review of the Incidence Literature." *Journal of Drug Issues,* 9 (Spring):281–289.

———. 1981. "The Natural Recovery from Opiate Addiction: Some Preliminary Findings." *Journal of Drug Issues,* 11 (Winter):61–74.

Winick, Charles. 1962. "Maturing out of Narcotic Addiction." *Bulletin on Narcotics,* 14 (January-March):1–7.